"Feldman, combining laudable scholarship with delightful writing, does a brilliant job of showing how Madison's precise and reasoned mind, along with his personal friendships and rivalries, created our code as a nation."
—Walter Isaacson, *New York Times* bestselling author of
Leonardo da Vinci

"The most stimulating political book that I have read in as long as I can remember. Madison was a young genius obsessed with the idea of costitution-making and government structure and who, in his early twenties, started designing the American government. Almost every debate we're having now about politics comes back in some way or another to Madison's vision and the questions Madison was thinking about in the 1770s and 1780s . . . Madison was way more important to our country than Hamilton was."
—Jacob Weisberg, editor in chief of
the Slate Group and author of *The Bush Tragedy*

"Feldman skillfully explains the evolving genius of Madison with precision and clarity. The result is a narrative both epic in scope and intimate in detail."
—David S. Heidler and Jeanne T. Heidler, coauthors of
Washington's Circle: The Creation of the President

Deborah Feingold

NOAH FELDMAN is the Felix Frankfurter Professor of Law at Harvard University as well as a Senior Fellow of the Harvard Society of Fellows and a member of the American Academy of Arts and Sciences. He is a contributing writer for *Bloomberg Opinion*, host of the podcast *Deep Background*, and the author of *Scorpions: The Battles and Triumphs of FDR's Great Supreme Court Justices* as well as *Cool War: The Future of Global Competition*, among other books.

Twitter: @NoahRFeldman

BY NOAH FELDMAN

The Three Lives of James Madison: Genius, Partisan, President

Cool War: The Future of Global Competition

Scorpions: The Battles and Triumphs of FDR's Great Supreme Court Justices

The Fall and Rise of the Islamic State

Divided by God: America's Church-State Problem—and What We Should Do About It

What We Owe Iraq: War and the Ethics of Nation Building

After Jihad: America and the Struggle for Islamic Democracy

THE THREE LIVES OF
JAMES MADISON

...

THE
THREE LIVES
OF
JAMES MADISON

...

Genius, Partisan, President

...

NOAH FELDMAN

PICADOR

FARRAR, STRAUS AND GIROUX
New York

Picador
120 Broadway, New York 10271

THE LIBRARY OF CONGRESS HAS CATALOGED THE HARDCOVER EDITION AS FOLLOWS:
Names: Feldman, Noah, author.
Title: The three lives of James Madison : genius, partisan, president / Noah Feldman.
Description: New York : Random House, 2017. | Includes bibliographical references
and index.
Identifiers: LCCN 2017000125 | ISBN 9780812992755 | ISBN 9780679643845 (e-book)
Subjects: LCSH: Madison, James, 1751–1836. | Presidents—United States—Biography.
Classification: LCC E342 .F45 2017 | DDC 973.5/1092 [B]—dc23
LC record available at https://lccn.loc.gov/2017000125

Picador Paperback ISBN 978-1-250-26700-9

Designed by Simon M. Sullivan

To David Hackett Souter

I wish someone who was perfectly fitted for the task, would write a full and accurate biography of Madison. I fear that it can hardly be done now; for the men who best appreciated his excellences have nearly all passed away. What shadows we are!

...

—*Joseph Story to Ezekiel Bacon, April 30, 1842*[1]

Contents

...

Preface

...

I N ANY HISTORICAL ERA but his own, James Madison would not have been a successful politician, much less one of the greatest statesmen of the age. He hated public speaking and detested running for office. He loved reason, logic, and balance.

But Madison entered public life at a moment when revolution demanded that familiar institutions be reimagined and transformed. Time after time his close friends, the founders of the United States of America, struggled to find solutions as their hastily made arrangements failed. Each time, Madison retreated to the world of his ideas and books. There he thought, and worked, alone.

Within a few months, he would emerge with a solution that fit with the theory of a republic and was designed to work in practice. Deeply introverted and emotionally restrained, Madison directed his enormous inner energies into shaping ideas that could be expressed through precise, reasoned argument.

In this way, Madison devised the Constitution. He imagined its necessity. He designed its contours. He developed the theory that would justify it. He conceived the need for a national convention, brought his blueprint to Philadelphia, and after an intense struggle convinced the other delegates to adopt a version of it. If the Constitution was a new kind of governmental physics, Madison was its Newton or its Einstein.

Then Madison set out to convince the nation to ratify the constitution he had brought forth. With Alexander Hamilton, he wrote and published the *Federalist* papers, the most systematic arguments in its favor. He led the forces of ratification to victory over Patrick Henry in the pivotal Virginia convention. He proposed and drafted the Bill of Rights to head off a potentially disastrous second convention.

This extraordinary set of accomplishments—over the course of only about five years—earned Madison the nickname "father of the Constitution" and established his place in U.S. history and the global history of constitutions and democracy. But as it turned out, Madison had lived only the first of what would be three distinct, contrasting public lives.

Elected to Congress, where he began by setting the agenda and acting as George Washington's point man, Madison discovered his Constitution was not as secure as he had believed. Hamilton, now secretary of the treasury, set out to shape the national economy just as Madison had framed the republic's political system. To this end, Hamilton proposed a national debt and a national bank that together would permanently align the interests of the government with those of the financial markets. Madison denounced Hamilton's plans as a blatantly unconstitutional attempt to shift power from the people to the capitalists. Hamilton rejoined that Madison was wrong about the Constitution—and he had the support in Congress to back him up.

Having designed a Constitution intended to eliminate the need for political parties, Madison acknowledged the limits of his creation and adopted a tactic he thought he had rendered obsolete. With Jefferson, he formed the Republican Party to counter the Federalist Party. Once friends and allies, Madison and Hamilton became personal and political enemies. Their brutal struggle over the meaning of the Constitution and the future of the United States gave birth to American partisanship.

Agonizing partisan politics defined Madison's second public life. In the course of building alliances and writing the document that would become the platform for the first Republican Party, Madison became a different kind of politician. Chastened by the realities of deep division, he could no longer sustain the dream that his system would prevent faction through the genius of its own design. Now public opinion would have to be captured and deployed to protect the public interest. And that public opinion would, in turn, be used to target and destroy the enemies of the Constitution and of the republic—namely Hamilton's Federalists.

When the Republicans returned to power with Thomas Jefferson's election in 1800, Madison's third public life began. Previously he had always acted through collective bodies such as legislatures and conventions. Now for the first time he became a statesman, wielding executive power on an international scale. As secretary of state and then president, he undertook a sixteen-year odyssey to establish America's place in a world defined by the long war between Great Britain and France.

Madison's goal was to make the United States, with its new form of government, into a new kind of independent global actor. Convinced that a constitutional republic must operate differently from Europe's monarchies, Madison developed the idea that economic sanctions were the perfect republican lever of power. The goal was to force Britain and Napoleon's France to allow American shipping to the European continent—and to do so without an army or a navy that could potentially subvert the republic from within.

Alone, the economic sanctions did not work quickly enough. Slowly and painfully, Madison confronted the reality that the United States had to be willing to threaten force to make other states bend to its will. With his presidency on the line, Madison gambled on decisive action. Overcoming his republican aversion to military action, he asked Congress to declare the War of 1812.

Madison became the first wartime president, despite having designed the republic to avoid armed conflict. The limitations imposed by the Constitution made war fighting inefficient and invasion of other countries ineffectual. But when the British turned the tables and tried to invade the United States, the constitutional republic was strong enough to defend itself.

Madison emerged from the war as a hero. Unlike every subsequent wartime president, he avoided the temptation of using the circumstances of international conflict to curtail civil liberties. The republic survived. So did the Constitution that defined it.

Charting Madison's three public lives, this book follows Madison's character and his Constitution on the path from idealistic innocence to chastened, realist experience. Madison believed that creating a republican state free of faction was the greatest political problem the world had ever known. He also believed the U.S. Constitution would make this ideal an institutional reality.

Through his constitutional design, Madison initiated the distinctively American political ideal of nonpartisanship. The key component was to extend the sphere of government from many small states to one larger nation. Through expansion—conceived as a new technology of governance—Madison's federal republic was meant to minimize faction and eliminate the need for permanent political parties. Expansion would dilute the effects of particular, local interests. It would produce qualified, public-spirited national leaders who would govern in the public interest and (in Madison's original design) exercise a supervisory power over the states. Balanced, calm, and dispassionate by design, the Constitution was the blueprint for a structure that unconsciously resembled Madison's own character.

This character emerges most vividly through the cycles of Madison's extraordinarily close friendships. At almost every stage of his life, Madison had at least one contemporary friend with whom he was closer than any other, a closeness expressed in near-constant letters reflecting shared projects, hopes, and aspirations. Most of these friendship cycles eventually devolved into rivalry. Madison invariably tried to reconcile with his friends, believing that continued friendship should be possible even in the face of disagreement. Often, by exerting extraordinary emotional control, he succeeded in saving the friendship. His close friend and contemporary James Monroe twice tried to destroy Madison's political career by running for office against him, once for Congress and once for the presidency. Both times, Madison insisted that their differences were political rather than personal, and after winning, managed to make Monroe into an ally and colleague once again. But friends could also become enemies, as happened between Madison and Hamilton.

Overarching these cycles was Madison's long, intense relationship with Thomas Jefferson, who was old enough to be a mentor but young enough to be a friend. The two shared a common republican faith and were always politically allied. Yet they had drastically different personalities and minds, which alternately created tensions and revealed how much they needed each other.

This book, then, embodies an argument, one I track through its several stages at the beginning of each chapter: Madison's character and extremely close friendships helped him model his own political ideal of concord within a state. Political friendship allowed for reasoned disagreement among reasonable people who shared the same basic goals but differed on how to achieve them. Within such a state, there would be varied interests, but no permanent factions.

But once the Constitution was in place, the realities of political conduct—including Madison's own—revealed the fallibility of his creation. He came to see Hamilton as an enemy of the republic who wanted to subvert the public good for private interest and destroy the basic constitutional framework. In the course of an epic, decade-long battle for the soul of the republic, Madison developed the practice of using the Constitution as a tool to criticize the opposing party, a tactic that would become a recurring feature of American politics and is still much in use. Madison's friendships proved that in a republic, it is possible to create lasting institutions of political amity. But he also learned, despite himself, that there is no escape from partisan struggle.

Similarly, as secretary of state and then as president, Madison sought to accomplish another dream of republicanism: achieving genuine independence from more powerful countries without relying on military force and gradually turning into an empire, as Rome had done. His solution, economic sanctions, projected Madison's own calm rationality onto the great warring powers of Britain and France, expecting them to put aside ideology and listen to the voice of enlightened logic. Ultimately Madison learned that while sanctions worked, they were too slow in practice to be the sole tools of statecraft. He had to threaten force—and take the nation into its first declared war—to establish the constitutional republic as a respected global actor.

The consequences of Madison's trajectory can be felt today. Constitutions are born in the aspiration to political agreement, but they live out their lives (and sometimes die) in the world of partisan, political battle—and even in war. The ongoing tension between the ideal of concord and the reality of politics is what makes constitutional government unique.

Today, Americans frequently complain about partisanship. Yet at the same time we find ourselves unable to escape its lure. We regularly accuse our partisan opponents of trying to undermine the Constitution itself. We also imagine ourselves as having transformed international affairs into something more peaceful, even as we continue to deploy military force. The ongoing struggle between nonpartisan, friendly aspiration and partisan, even violent aggression is a legacy of Madison's ideal of constitutional friendship—as well as his own efforts as a party builder and war maker.

Madison's story is therefore entwined with that of the constitutional republic itself, its personalities, and its permanent struggle to reconcile unity with profound disagreement. Other books by excellent scholars and writers have told parts of this story, usually emphasizing the drafting of the Constitution. I have attempted to trace the entire trajectory of Madison's life and career, discovering Madison's ideas through the relationships in which he developed them.

Understanding Madison requires us to know Dolley, his politically skilled partner, who created a new republican social structure in the capital during her sixteen years as Washington's leading social figure. Dolley frequently expressed opinions and emotions that Madison hid from view. Often her observations and comments are the best evidence we have of Madison's own inner experience.

Comprehending Madison's whole life-world also demands that we understand his experiences with enslaved people, and his views and policies toward Native Americans. And it calls on us to comprehend the contemporaries who made the republic with him, from more familiar figures such as Jefferson, Washington, Adams, and Hamilton to less well-known personalities including Patrick Henry, Edmund Randolph, and Madison's friend, rival, and successor, James Monroe.

Above all, I hope to use Madison's creativity, commitment, and political flexibility to shed light on the birth, development, and survival of America's distinctive form of constitutional government. Madison's system survives today, albeit much altered and reshaped by events. And it has spread around the world, to places and circumstances utterly different from those Madison knew. To avoid disrupting the story from its proper frame, I mostly refrain from suggesting parallels or comparisons to contemporary debates or events. But they are there in plain sight. And for those who would like Madison's accomplishments and life to teach us lessons for our own, they are there aplenty.

Author's Note

...

To make the experience of reading easier, I have modernized capitalization, spelling, and punctuation in quotations. Emphasis in quotations is always original, but I have sometimes omitted emphasis that does not correspond to current norms. I capitalize Constitution and Bill of Rights only after ratification. In order to preserve the terminology of the era and distinguish people born into slavery in North America from those captured and enslaved in Africa, I generally refer to enslaved persons of African descent living in the United States as slaves. I occasionally use the word "enslaved" as a reminder of the social fact of enslavement and the self-conscious choice of masters not to emancipate.

BOOK I

CONSTITUTION

...

CHAPTER ONE

Friendships

...

THE ARGUMENT: *In college, Madison forms the pattern of intense friendship that will come to shape his political vision of the constitutional republic.*

As a southerner and an Anglican at mid-Atlantic, Presbyterian Princeton, Madison develops the interest that will bring him into public life and give him an almost accidental public career: religious liberty. As fervor for independence grows, Madison develops a distinction between religious dissent among Protestants who share common commitments, which should be protected as an absolute good, and Loyalist opposition to independence, which deserves to be suppressed because it threatens the political commitment to independence.

The Revolution gives Madison the chance to participate in writing the Virginia state constitution when he is just twenty-five. There Madison makes his first public mark, an improvement of the religious liberty provision. His career as a constitution designer and public official is launched.

HE CAME TO NEW JERSEY for the air. Arriving at Princeton in the autumn of 1769, James Madison, Jr., found something unique in the North America of the time: a college offering entrée into the European republic of letters and the ideas of the Enlightenment as well as a close-knit community of smart, ambitious young men intent on forming lasting friendships and getting ahead in the world. For the eldest son of a wealthy Virginia plantation owner, educated privately by tutors, this was the true start of his life.

Madison's eyes were a clear green, his hair was dark, and he was perhaps five feet five inches tall. Neat and tidy, he looked younger than his eighteen years. Like his peers, he thought of himself as a British subject.

Yet Madison was different. His classmates mostly came from the mid-Atlantic colonies of Pennsylvania, New Jersey, and New York. Madison was a Virginian from the Piedmont. The college was a Presbyterian institution teaching students from a range of dissenting Protestant denominations. Madison was a member of the Church of England. The students, who rarely had independent means, aspired to careers in law, medicine, and the ministry.[1] Madison, heir to four thousand acres and well over a hundred slaves, was a gentleman by birth. Indeed, he came up to Princeton accompanied by a slave named Sawney, whom his maternal grandmother had left to him in her will.[2]

What made Madison most unusual was his profound sense of intellectual purpose. For many students, friendship was the most important focus of college life. Educated young men in late eighteenth-century America often spoke and wrote to each other of their great mutual affection. Declarations of passionate friendship, even love, were not considered unmanly.[3] Madison had come to Princeton to learn, and his friendships reflected that priority. In his first year at the college, he formed a close bond with a Philadelphian named Joseph Ross, who had arrived the year before.[4] Attracted to the challenge of intense study together, they decided to try to accomplish the next two years of required coursework in just one year.

Together, Madison and Ross experimented with how little they could sleep—and got themselves down to five hours a night for weeks at a time. Constantly in each other's company, and constantly reading, the young men succeeded. Madison received his degree as bachelor of arts after just two years. This total commitment to a common project formed a paradigm for Madison's friendships that would persist throughout his life. Sixty years later, he would downplay the accomplishment. But he still remembered Ross. And he was proud enough of what they had done together to say they had learned more in one year than they would have in the more usual two or even three years' study.[5]

Madison also became seriously ill in the process—a result, he believed, of the exertion. At commencement in 1771, Ross gave an English oration entitled "The Power of Eloquence."[6] Madison was too sick to attend. He did not leave Princeton early, but ended up spending his third year there convalescing, reading, and studying according to his own interests, not for a degree.

Alongside his studies, Madison allowed himself to have a little fun. He belonged to the Whig Society, a debating-club-cum-fraternity of which Ross was a founding member. The Whigs engaged in "paper wars" with another club, the Cliosophic Society. Madison himself wrote three long, humorously insulting poems in one such war. The poems include sophomoric rhymes involving scatological humor ("Urania threw a chamber pot / Which from beneath her bed she brought / And struck my eyes and ears and nose / Repeating it with lusty blows") and sex ("[She] took me to her private room / And straight an Eunuch out I come").[7]

Yet despite humorous references to friends' whoring, pimping, drinking, and swearing,[8] Madison was well behaved and mainly serious. The president of the college, John Witherspoon, Presbyterian minister, philosopher, signer of the Declaration of Independence, and someone whose own seriousness was beyond question, told Thomas Jefferson a few years later that "in the whole career of Mr. Madison at Princeton, he had never known him to say or do an indiscreet thing." Jefferson considered the comment so funny that he liked to tease Madison about it.[9]

What Madison learned in college, much of it from Witherspoon himself, would influence the course of his thinking for the rest of his life. The students lived together in Nassau Hall, a massive structure that was the largest stone building in North America. Above the great hall, two stories high, used for prayer and lectures, were a library and forty rooms for students. The kitchen and dining room were just below ground. Although the hall would have been dwarfed by even the more modest university colleges of Oxford and Cambridge, by American standards, it was something special.[10]

Madison arrived with strong Latin and workable Greek, both of which he continued to study in college.* He had also been taught French by a Scottish tutor in Virginia. Except for Witherspoon, no one else at the college knew French, and it was not a subject of instruction. As Madison later recalled, one day a French visitor arrived at Princeton to see the

---

* Later in life Madison would say that he "availed himself of this opportunity of acquiring a slight knowledge of the Hebrew, which was not among the College Studies." Douglass Adair, "James Madison's Autobiography," *William and Mary Quarterly* 2 (1945): 197.

president. Witherspoon was not at home, and Madison, the only other French speaker, was called to the president's house to entertain the visitor. On meeting the Frenchman, Madison discovered, to his intense embarrassment, that he could neither understand spoken French nor make himself understood in it.[11]

Fortunately, instruction at Princeton went well beyond language. Witherspoon and the tutors he employed started with the classics and works of contemporary theology that dominated the curriculum elsewhere. But Witherspoon's lectures and assigned readings took the students into the heart of the most exciting intellectual event of the time: the Scottish Enlightenment.

Witherspoon came by this knowledge firsthand. A conservative, he made his academic reputation in his native Scotland by criticizing the philosopher Francis Hutcheson, who had himself taught Adam Smith and influenced David Hume. Remarkably, Witherspoon's critical attitude toward the Enlightenment, without which he would never have been made president of conservative Princeton, did not mean he neglected the importance of the movement. In his lectures on moral philosophy, which all Princeton students attended, Witherspoon quoted Hutcheson more than any other thinker. He never mentioned the towering philosopher and skeptic Hume without reproach, and Hume appeared not on the assigned reading list but on a list of outside readings. Yet Witherspoon did discuss Hume's views, and it would have been obvious to any student hearing the lectures that this was a figure whose work he had better read.[12] As a result of Witherspoon's leadership, Princeton far outstripped Harvard and Yale, at the time more parochial in their teaching.

It was Madison's good luck that he happened into Princeton and Witherspoon's intellectual orbit. Ordinarily, a young man of Madison's origin and wealth would have gone to the College of William and Mary in Williamsburg, Virginia, where Jefferson had studied a decade earlier. In a brief autobiographical sketch written many years later, Madison gave two explanations for why he had instead been sent to New Jersey. One was that his private tutor during his teens, the Reverend Thomas Martin, had studied at Princeton, as had his brother Alexander Martin. They recommended their alma mater for Madison.

The other was the climate. Madison's Virginia was not the Tidewater region in the eastern part of the state, already famous for its tobacco plantations, but the hills of the Piedmont farther west. In the era before germ theory or the recognition of mosquitoes as vectors of disease, explanations for illness depended heavily on geography. Hot, humid air was thought to be dangerous. Madison explained that the air of Tidewater Williamsburg "was unhealthy for persons going from a mountainous region" like the Piedmont, who were presumed more likely to become ill in an unaccustomed environment—and may conceivably have had less immunity to some diseases by virtue of less exposure.[13]

Throughout his life, Madison felt he had a propensity for getting sick.* As a result, he protected himself as much as possible from places and activities thought to produce disease. The care he took would sometimes have negative effects, chiefly in convincing Madison that he should not travel abroad. In the choice of Princeton, however, this concern had only fortunate consequences. It opened broader intellectual vistas than he would otherwise have encountered so early in his life. Perhaps most important, the fact that Madison, baptized an Anglican, received his education from Presbyterian ministers at a Presbyterian institution awakened in him an early and enduring interest in the protection of religious dissent.

An Obscure Corner

After commencement in March 1772, Madison was called home to Virginia to serve as a tutor for his younger siblings Nelly, William, and Sarah, ages twelve, ten, and eight, respectively. His brothers Francis and Ambrose, then nineteen and seventeen, had not gone to college, and were not suitable for the role.† Madison had tried to find a classmate who would be willing to assume the post of live-in tutor while he was at college, but no

---

* A year after Madison left Princeton, his friend and study partner Joseph Ross died in Philadelphia. On hearing the news, Madison wrote to a friend in a depressed mood that he was "too dull and infirm now to look out for any extraordinary things in this world" because his "sensations for many months past" had "intimated" that he should "not . . . expect a long or healthy life." Madison to William Bradford, November 9, 1772, *PJM*, 1:75.

† Francis and Madison were not close, although Francis lived nearby. Ambrose was closer to Madison and helped manage Montpelier until his death in 1793 at the age of thirty-eight; his daughter Nelly remained close to Madison thereafter, and was at his bedside when he died. Ketcham, *James Madison*, 370. Another surviving sister, Frances, was not born until 1774.

one would take it.[14] Without any definite professional plan, and with his family's educational needs unmet, Madison had no reason or excuse to remain at Princeton, or for his father to support him there.

Going back to Virginia meant leaving a world of intellectualism and camaraderie for what Madison called, in a letter to a close Princeton friend, William Bradford, "an obscure corner." The family farm in the Piedmont, not yet called Montpelier, featured a large, comfortable brick house with a fine view of the Blue Ridge Mountains. But Orange County, Virginia, was a backwater compared to Bradford's Philadelphia, which Madison rightly called "the fountain-head of political and literary intelligence" in North America.[15]

Life proceeded according to the regular rhythms of agriculture. The plantation, administered by James Madison, Sr., produced barley, wheat, and corn. Slaves did the field work, performed domestic duties around the house, and participated in the gradual expansion of the buildings on the property. The forms of slavery were well established from the standpoint of the slaveholders, and Madison did not then have much occasion to question them.

There were no active local newspapers in the county.[16] Religion consisted primarily of the established Church of England. The nearest parish church was some seven miles away. Madison's father was a vestryman, a wholly respectable, well-off member of the local society. Deference to such men was normal in the Virginia of the day. Madison himself, despite his youth, expected and received similar deference from the family's neighbors.

Apart from educating his brothers and sisters, Madison's primary responsibility once home was to figure out what to do with his life. Not that the task was pressing. It would have been perfectly acceptable for Madison to continue in his father's place, running the plantation, reading for pleasure, and eventually starting a family of his own: in short, following the quiet life favored by many Virginia gentlemen.

Madison missed college—and his letters from when he came home in 1772 until 1774 suggest a kind of post-graduation ennui. In a letter to Bradford, Madison spoke nostalgically of the days when they "were under the same roof" and Bradford "found it a recreation and release from business and books to come and chat an hour or two" with Madison.[17] By contrast, Bradford's letters to Madison are full of energetic, detailed analysis of whether Bradford should pursue law, medicine, or business. Bradford wanted his older friend's advice as he evaluated his own character, intelligence, strengths, and weaknesses.[18] He eventually chose law, which had been his preference from the start. In commercial Philadelphia with its culture of Quaker usefulness, there was no question of Bradford's simply doing nothing.[19]

On Madison's side, no such soul-searching appeared. He told Bradford that he himself intended "to read law occasionally," and that he would welcome any recommended readings on the topic because they would doubtless afford "entertainment and instruction." He explained that "the principles and modes of government are too important to be disregarded by an inquisitive mind" and, he thought, "are well worthy [of] a critical examination by all students that have health and leisure."[20] Madison, in other words, had a general intellectual interest in law and legal institutions, but little desire to become a lawyer.[21] He made no mention of medicine or business, each of which would have been an unusual choice for a Virginian of his class. He spoke highly of a career in the church, though without any indication that he thought of becoming a minister himself.

Madison did express a religious point of view in telling Bradford about his dissatisfaction with the London book reviews. He read them to keep up with the world of letters, but he found "them loose in their principles [and] encourage[r]s of free enquiry even such as destroys the most essential truths." The reviews were also "enemies to serious religion," he added.[22] This moralizing tone, conspicuously absent from Madison's later writings, provides an important clue to the single subject that actually seems to have excited Madison in the course of his readings. The young Madison took religion seriously. This interest would eventually blossom into a career that would shape the nation.

Religious Liberty

The subject that most animated James Madison was the freedom of religion and the question of its official establishment. On December 1, 1773, after numerous letters in which he had asked William Bradford for nothing except news of his friends and information about the latest interesting books, Madison finally requested something specific. Once Bradford had sufficiently studied "the constitution" of his "country"—meaning the organizing laws of Pennsylvania—Madison wanted him to send "a draft of its origin and fundamental principles of legislation; particularly the extent" of the colony's "religious toleration." Pointed questions followed: "Is an ecclesiastical establishment absolutely necessary to support civil society in a supreme government? And how far it is hurtful to a dependent state?" Although he insisted that he was not asking "for an immediate answer," Madison told Bradford that when he had "satisfied" himself "in these points," Madison "should listen with pleasure to the result of" his research.[23]

If this was intended as an assignment, Bradford ignored it. But Madison did not let it go. His next letter to Bradford, in late January 1774, commented on the Boston Tea Party, and on Philadelphia's own, more orderly refusal to permit a large tea cargo to be landed. Madison was impressed by Boston's "boldness" while hoping its residents might be more discreet, as the "heroic proceedings in Philadelphia" had been. He also commented encouragingly that political struggles were sometimes necessary "to afford exercise and practice and to instruct in the art of defending liberty and property."

Madison's striking (and original) analysis of why resistance had emerged in Massachusetts and Pennsylvania, not in Virginia, reflected his growing fascination with religious establishments and their connection to liberty:

> If the Church of England had been established and general religion
> in all the northern colonies as it has been among us here and
> uninterrupted tranquility had prevailed throughout the continent, it is
> clear to me that slavery and subjection might and would have been
> gradually insinuated among us.[24]

According to Madison, New England and Pennsylvania were protesting Britain's infringement on their liberties, while Virginia was not, because in Virginia, the Church of England was the officially established religion. In Pennsylvania, as Madison knew, there was no official established religion, and taxes did not go to support churches. A variety of religious sects coexisted without one of them dominating the others. The New England colonies had less religious diversity, but the Church of England was not formally established there either. Instead, local citizens voted to choose a minister of their liking, and their taxes in turn went to support that minister.[25]

Madison's point was that the establishment of the Church of England went hand in hand with unquestioned obedience to English laws: "Union of religious sentiments," he argued, "begets a surprising confidence."[26] When it came to religion, such agreement was a bad thing. In the case of Virginia, the established church created an attitude of collective, blind acceptance of political authority.

Madison's idea could be traced to the traditional argument in favor of an established church made by British writers such as Richard Hooker. To establishmentarians, obedience to religion taught obedience to the ruler, a lesson necessary for civil government. "No bishop, no king" had been the pithy observation of James I when his subjects challenged the principle that he should govern the church through an ecclesiastical hierarchy he appointed.[27]

Madison flipped that episcopal logic on its head. Accepting that a religious establishment did effectively teach subordination to authority, he redescribed obedience as slavery. Extending the argument, he concluded that if establishment produced obedience, then nonestablishment as in Pennsylvania or New England created an atmosphere for healthy resistance.[28]

Madison's argument suggested a harsh condemnation of Virginia. Later in the same letter, speaking of his plans to visit Bradford in Philadelphia, Madison made the point explicit. "I have indeed as good an atmosphere at home as the climate will allow," he wrote, showing his usual attention to geographical conditions, "but have nothing to brag of as to the state and liberty of my country."[29] There followed a catalogue of his home colony's sins: "Poverty and luxury prevail among all sorts: pride ignorance and knavery among the priesthood and vice and wickedness among the laity." If this jeremiad sounded a bit formulaic, Madison went on to describe what was really bothering him:

> This is bad enough but it is not the worst I have to tell you. That
> diabolical Hell conceived principle of persecution rages among some
> and to their eternal infamy the clergy can furnish their quota of imps
> for such business. This vexes me the most of anything whatever.[30]

Almost nowhere else in Madison's writing does such passionately inspired language appear. For Madison, the "principle of persecution" represented the worst that a society could do. Madison had a concrete example in mind. "There are at this time in the adjacent county not less than five or six well-meaning men in close [jail] for publishing their religious sentiments which in the main are very orthodox."[31]

By his own account, Madison had spent a great deal of time and energy talking to his neighbors about these religious dissenters facing persecution—to no avail. "I have squabbled and scolded abused and ridiculed so long about it, to so little purpose that I am without common patience." The contrast with the religious liberty of Bradford's environment seemed stark: "So I leave you to pity me and pray for liberty of conscience to revive among us."[32]

The preachers jailed in the adjoining Culpeper County were Baptists, which Madison was not. Madison's outrage at their confinement did not derive from any particular sympathy to their beliefs. Instead, Madison was incensed by the closed-mindedness of his Virginia neighbors and the willingness of the clergy to sanction it. He did not have any special hostility toward the clergy, a profession he had told Bradford to keep always in mind. Why, then, did this mild-mannered, bookish son of a respected Piedmont planter, poised to become a member of the Anglican establishment, find himself so powerfully moved by religious liberty?

The answer lies in Madison's experience at Princeton. The Presbyterian tradition that had founded Princeton was a dissenting one in its origins and in America. Presbyterians differed from the Church of England primarily with respect to church governance, favoring the election of leaders by the presbyteries that gave the denomination its name.[33] That posture of dissent made the denomination into a bulwark of support for the liberty of conscience.[34] Presbyterian Princeton's divinity graduates did not get posts at established churches, because their church was not the established faith of any colony. The college was unsympathetic to religious establishment and embracing of dissent.

Equally important, at Princeton Madison was a member of a religious minority. As an Anglican he suffered no discrimination. But by belonging to a different denomination from the one shared by his teachers and most of his fellow students, he experienced the reality of religious diversity, rather than the "union" of religious sentiments that he found so provincial in Virginia. That the teachers whom he respected were themselves dissenters, and that he was, in effect, a dissenter from their dissent, made the issue of religious liberty salient. The contrast between their free and tolerant discourse and what he saw in his corner of Virginia after his return home created a frustration akin to shame.

A couple of months later, in the spring of 1774, Madison was still totally focused on the religious dissenters. In a detailed letter he told Bradford that petitions would be filed with the colonial assembly on the part of the "persecuted Baptists," and that he hoped Virginia's Presbyterians would intercede on their behalf. Yet he was skeptical about the prospects of political relief in the form of formalized, legal toleration of dissent. In the previous session of the colony's assembly, Madison reported, efforts to help the Baptists had failed after supporters of the "ecclesiastical establishment" had told "incredible and extravagant stories" about the "monstrous effects" of religious "enthusiasm" among evangelicals.

The problem, Madison thought, was part cultural and part political. Respect for the rights of conscience was prevalent in Pennsylvania but was "little-known among the zealous adherents to our hierarchy" in Virginia.[35] As for politics, there were, he said, "some persons in the legislature of generous principles both in religion and politics." Yet there were not enough of them to make a difference: "Number not merit . . . is necessary to carry points there." The "numerous and powerful" clergy would unite to suppress the dissenters. After all, the clergy had the most to lose.[36]

Madison believed the consequences of these barriers to religious liberty were substantial. He suggested to Bradford that in Pennsylvania, immigration, motivated by religious liberty, had encouraged industry and virtue. Liberty had fueled a quest for "fame and knowledge" that, in turn, drove "continual exertions of genius" among the populace. Religious freedom was, in short, an engine of creativity. By contrast, "religious bondage shackles and debilitates the mind and unfits it for every noble enterprise, every expanded prospect."[37] That was the case in Virginia.

The young Madison, educating his sisters and brother while reading without any particular professional direction, had at last found a concern that truly stirred him. It lay, not by coincidence, at the intersection of religion, law, and politics—three topics in which Madison had been reading. And it was a matter of contemporary public concern.

Yet it was not clear where this engaged interest in religious liberty could take Madison. His efforts to convince others of the importance of religious liberty fell on deaf ears. Had the world continued to follow its usual courses, and "uninterrupted tranquility . . . prevailed throughout the continent," Madison's momentary excitement might have come to naught.[38] A passionate interest in liberty of conscience was not a career path.

Fortunately for Madison, all that was about to change.

Small Wars

By the summer of 1774, Massachusetts was simmering with anger and resistance toward the British Parliament. In May, Boston's Committee of Correspondence, an association of self-described "patriots," had sent letters to similar committees throughout the colonies proposing a voluntary ban on all trade to or from the mother country. New York's committee had replied by calling for a "congress of deputies from the colonies in general" to discuss the issue. What would soon be called the Continental Congress was planned for September in Philadelphia.

Revolutionary fervor came late to Virginia. Before July 1774, Madison had made only one comment about these events in his letters to Bradford. For Madison, as for others in Virginia, attention was focused not east to England but west to the colony's ill-defined frontier, south of the Ohio River. There war of another kind was brewing—and it engaged Madison's attention.

The colony of Virginia claimed much of the Ohio River Valley. France had ceded the Ohio territory to Britain at the end of the French and Indian War in 1763. Virginia's claim also derived from the Treaty of Fort Stanwix, signed in 1768, in which the Six Nations of the Iroquois Confederacy purported to grant the land south of the Ohio River to Britain.

The colony's interests in expansion overlapped with the personal interests of Virginians, including Madison's father and Thomas Jefferson, who had bought shares in land companies that promised to make acquisitions in the territory and then sell the land at a great profit.[39] The problem was that although the Six Nations has signed the treaty, they did not actually control the territory south of the Ohio. The people who lived there were Shawnees, an unrelated, Algonquian-speaking people. The Shawnees had signed nothing, had received nothing, and had no interest in giving up their hunting grounds. They resisted the white settlers who began to move south of the river after the 1768 treaty. Further opposition to settlement came from independent groups or tribes such as the "Mingo," a coalition of Iroquoian speakers who had migrated to the area in previous decades.

The unstable situation devolved into violence on April 30, 1774, when white settlers slaughtered the family of a Mingo leader known as James Logan.[40] Logan was a Cayuga Iroquois by origin, with close ties to white settlers. Despite this history of goodwill, the settlers killed his brother and two of his sisters. According to some reports, they took scalps and pulled a fetus from its mother's womb.

The settlers were not acting on their own. The royally appointed governor of Virginia, John Murray, the 4th Earl of Dunmore, had appointed Captain Michael Cresap to lead a war on the Shawnees, signaling that it was open season to kill Indians of whatever tribe or affiliation.[41] Logan had never previously resisted Europeans. After the massacre, however, he began a series of raids on white settlements and was eventually joined by Shawnees who had also lost family members to settlers' attacks. Settlers panicked, and as many as a thousand of them fled in just a few days.[42] From the Piedmont, 350 miles distant, Madison believed he was witnessing a war for survival. The Indians, he told Bradford (he called them "savages"), were "determined in the extirpation of the inhabitants, and no longer leave them the alternative of death or captivity."[43]

Governor Dunmore responded by raising an army of militia. "Lord Dunmore," Madison wrote to Bradford in August, intended "to march shortly with 2 or 3000 men to the Indian towns and to extirpate those perfidious people entirely."[44] In the end, Dunmore's numbers convinced the Shawnees to renounce their claims south of the Ohio River. The resulting treaty nominally established Virginia's title to what is now West Virginia and Kentucky. Dunmore considered the consolidation of the territory into Virginia a gain for British interests. Settlers, he believed, could not be allowed to set up "democratical governments" in newly settled land, but must be brought under the sovereignty of existing royal colonies.[45]

By the time the treaty was signed, Logan had withdrawn from the fight. But in a remarkable coda to what came to be called Lord Dunmore's War, Logan delivered a message to the royal governor.[46] Madison somehow obtained a translation of the message. He copied and sent it to Bradford with the comment that "it seems to be so just a specimen of

Indian eloquence and mistaken valor that I think you will be pleased with it."[47]

> I appeal to any white man to say if he ever entered Logan's cabin hungry and I gave him not meat, if ever he came cold or naked and I gave him not clothing. During the course of the last long and bloody war, Logan remained idle in his tent an advocate for peace; nay such was my love for the whites, that those of my own country pointed at me as they passed by and said Logan is a friend of white men: I even thought to live with you but for the injuries of one man: Col. Cresap, the last spring in cold blood and unprovoked cut off all the relations of Logan not sparing even my women and children. There runs not a drop of my blood in the veins of any human creature. This called on me for revenge: I have sought it. I have killed many. I have fully glutted my vengeance. For my country I rejoice at the beams of peace: but do not harbor a thought that mine is the joy of fear: Logan never felt fear: He will not turn his heel to save his life. Who is there to mourn for Logan? Not one.[48]

Bradford was also affected by the speech. "The last sentence," he wrote back to Madison, "is particularly pathetic and expressive; it raises a crowd of ideas and at one stroke sets in a strong light the barbarity of Cresap, the sufferings of Logan and his contempt for death." Sensing that others might be similarly moved, Bradford gave the text to his brother, who published it in the family's newspaper, *The Pennsylvania Journal*.[49] Other versions of Logan's Lament were also printed—the text appeared in Jefferson's 1782 *Notes on the State of Virginia*—and the speech became a classic.[50]

Madison's complicated fascination with Logan helps explain his views of Native Americans. Madison never for a moment hinted that the Indians had any right to land that was valuable to his native Virginia and to his own family's economic interests. He called the Shawnees a "perfidious people" and considered all Indians to be savages. Yet with Bradford, he could admire nobility and bravery in American Indians and even recognize the brutality of settler efforts to suppress them.

This ability to tolerate contradiction, or perhaps to imagine that no contradiction existed, would prove crucial for Madison's political career and thought. It would enable him to pursue policies of national expansion without worrying about the consequences for Native Americans, and to realize the injustice of slavery while crafting compromises that preserved the institution. Madison cared deeply about principles—but pragmatism governed his decisions.

Revolution and Dissent

Against the backdrop of Lord Dunmore's War, Virginia was slowly beginning to feel the effects of the northern colonies' resistance movement against England. Madison told Bradford that the people of Virginia felt "generally very warm" toward the Bostonians. He believed that Virginians would be "willing to fall in with the other colonies in any expedient measure, even if that should be the universal prohibition of trade" with England, as the Boston Committee of Correspondence had proposed.[51] For the first time, Americans were suggesting that despite costs to themselves, they might shape British policy by refusing to trade. Driving their efforts was the recognition that they had few other tools of influence available.

Still, neither Madison nor Bradford was speaking of all-out rebellion. Writing to Madison about the impending Continental Congress, Bradford said he hoped that the Congress would propose a "bill of rights" for the colonies that would require the repeal of oppressive legislation passed by Parliament. Should this bill of rights "be confirmed by his Majesty, or the Parliament, the liberties of America will be as firmly fixed and defined as those of England were at the revolution."[52] In this picture, the Continental Congress would act as the British Parliament had in the Glorious Revolution of 1688 when it required William of Orange and his wife, Mary, to approve a parliamentary Bill of Rights as a condition of making them joint sovereigns. That Bill of Rights had contained grievances against the deposed James II and asserted what were claimed as the ancient rights and liberties of Englishmen. Parliamentary and royal acceptance of a colonial bill of rights would allow for continued allegiance to Britain.

At the same time, Madison believed that Parliament had already exceeded its authority. He reported to Bradford that he had accidentally received some tracts by the English minister Josiah Tucker, and read them with "satisfaction and illumination." In the pamphlets, Tucker confusingly argued both for independent colonies and for Parliament's continuing authority over them. The arguments, said Madison, were so full of "defects and misrepresentations" that Tucker had inadvertently convinced him that Parliament did *not* have the authority to legislate for the colonies. His comparison came from religion, where, he said half-jokingly, the "specious arguments of infidels have established the faith of enquiring Christians."[53]

Madison was also beginning to entertain the possibility of armed conflict with England. Responding to Bradford's moderation, Madison wondered whether Bradford was presuming "too much on the generosity and justice of the Crown." Would it not be better, he asked, "as soon as possible to begin our defense" and to keep it up as needed depending on the response from London? Any delay would lessen the "ardor of the Americans inspired with recent injuries." Worse, delay "afford[ed] opportunity to our secret enemies to disseminate discord and disunion."[54]

Madison's concern here with the problem of disunion contrasted sharply with his belief that the "union" of religious sentiments led to slavish subjection. When it came to religion, Madison believed that diverse opinions deserved absolute protection. When it came to the politics of a potential revolution, however, he feared that discord would weaken collective resolve. When writing about the persecution of religious dissenters, Madison had nothing but contempt for clergy who considered disagreement a danger to authority. When writing about revolutionary politics, he did not hesitate to use the word "enemies" to describe those who would promote disagreement.

The difference marked the first sign of what would become a crucial aspect of Madison's political thinking. Calm, reasoned disagreement among people who shared common commitments—such as Protestant Christians of different denominations—was consistent with concord.[55] Such disagreement should be permitted and even nurtured because it bred independent thought. But when the disagreement extended to fundamental matters—like what political system should be in place—the rules changed. True enemies should be fought, and their opinions defeated and eliminated.

Friendship was at the heart of this vision—and Madison's political agreement with Bradford deepened their feelings of "affectionate" friendship.[56] Instead of discussing career plans and reading lists, the two friends now exchanged news and ideas about revolutionary politics. The Continental Congress was about to meet in Philadelphia, and Madison wished he were there to see it.[57] He asked Bradford to send him accounts of anything "singular and important" in the Congress that did not make it into the newspapers. He hoped, he said, that the congressional debates would be published. Not only would that "illuminate the minds of the thinking people among us," but the delegates to the Congress might show enough talent "to render us more respectable at home."[58] The "us" meant patriots: people like Bradford and Madison who shared a common cause.

Bradford's admiration for the Congress was similarly breathless. Its proceedings had been kept secret, but he reported that the librarian of the Library Company of Philadelphia, then located in the Carpenters' Hall where the Congress met, had told him that the delegates were referring regularly to the works of "Vattel, Burlamaqui, Locke and Montesquieu." From this intelligence, Bradford said, "We may conjecture that their measures will be wisely planned since they debate on them like philosophers."[59] The comment was made without irony.

When they did become public, the doings of Congress revealed a trend that would prove decisive for Madison's future. During his first several years back home, Madison had perceived that Virginia was slow to support any resistance against England. Now, however, Virginia emerged as a leader in the movement toward independence. The "scholars and orators" of Virginia, Bradford told Madison, "are highly celebrated for their zeal. Your province seems to take the lead at present; that silent spirit of courage which is said to reign there has brought you more credit than you can imagine."[60] Meanwhile, from Virginia, Madison reported that "a spirit of liberty and patriotism animates all degrees and denominations of men."[61]

The Continental Congress issued a declaration and resolves, dated October 14, 1774, not dissimilar from the bill of rights that Bradford had hoped to see. The document declared the rights of the colonies vis-à-vis Britain. It denounced the Intolerable Acts passed by Parliament in reaction to the Boston Tea Party. Then the Continental Congress proposed that the residents of the colonies "enter into a non-importation, non-consumption, and non-exportation agreement or association." The Continental Association, as it would be called, amounted to a voluntary form of economic warfare. It signaled that an actual war might not be far off.

In Virginia, where money was earned from agriculture, not direct commerce with the mother country, sentiment in favor of the association was strong. Virginians seemed confident that their produce would be purchased and consumed somewhere other than Britain even if war should break out. Behind this belief was the implicit economic theory that even if fancy British goods were not available to buy, Virginia would be fine so long as it could sell. Patriotism and economic self-interest were in harmony.

Virginia Quakers proved to be almost the only group in the colony whose members were systematically unwilling to join the Continental Association against Britain. Madison suspected them of being influenced by Quaker leaders in Pennsylvania, who he thought were motivated by business interests rather than religious sincerity.[62] The local Quakers, he said, unlike their Philadelphia counterparts, are "too honest and simple to have any sinister or secret views." More to the point, said Madison, "I do not observe any thing in the Association inconsistent with their religious principles."[63]

But of course a potentially violent revolution was inconsistent with Quaker principles. Drawn to the continental cause, Madison preferred to see Virginia Quakers as dupes. By placing the Quakers' dissent in the category of fundamental political choice and failing to acknowledge that it could be motivated by religious belief, Madison could sidestep his usual concern for liberty of conscience. In the process he demonstrated his two different categories of dissent. Sincere religious dissent deserved protection. But a threat to revolutionary unity fell into a separate category, because it undermined the foundations of coordinated political action.

The way that individual Virginia Quakers showed their dissent was by refusing to sign a document committing themselves to the Continental Association. In a political environment where most agreed on a course that constituted patriotism, the pressure to sign was enormous. Madison noted to Bradford that signatures were "the method used among us to distinguish friends from foes and to oblige the common people to a more strict observance" of the association.[64]

The language of friend and foe captured just how definitive the moment of signature was for Virginians. To sign was to put one's name formally on paper, joined by other patriots—friends of the Continental Congress and allies in the struggle against Parliament. To join this association publicly also meant becoming vulnerable to retaliation should the movement go awry. Not to sign meant becoming an enemy of the movement. To Madison, the structure of signatures would identify the camps which each individual had joined; and by doing so, it would also strengthen the rather uncertain authority of the association.

With the separation of the population into friends and foes came preparations for war. In the mounting enthusiasm, volunteer militias began to form and learn military discipline.[65] In the spring of 1775, Madison himself joined such a company and set out to train. "The strength of this colony," he told Bradford, "will lie chiefly in the riflemen of the upland counties."

Among these Madison counted himself. Even "inexpert hands," he claimed, reckoned it a poor shot "to miss the bigness of a man's face at the distance of 100 yards." As for Madison's own abilities, "I am far from being among the best," he said, "and should not often miss it on a fair trial at that distance."[66] This, the sole example of military boastfulness in Madison's entire life, reflected the enthusiasm of the moment—what Madison himself called "military ardor."[67] Madison's father became the lieutenant or titular leader of his county's militia. Madison himself, rewarded for his social position rather than any military knowledge, was named a colonel.

In later years, Madison explained that he did not see action in the Revolutionary War because of "the discouraging feebleness" of his constitution, confirmed by his "experience during the exercises and movements of a minute company" that he had joined.[68] In a document probably not intended for publication, he wrote that he was prevented from serving by "a constitutional liability, to sudden attacks, somewhat resembling epilepsy."[69] Madison did not suffer from seizures. The occasional attacks were very likely what today would be considered migraine headaches.[70]

Madison's contribution to the revolutionary cause would not come through arms.

The Committee

All successful wars of independence require organization, and organization requires procedures. But rarely has a revolutionary movement been so obsessed with procedures as the continental movement was in 1775 and 1776. Out of a handful of local militias and local governments under the thumb of colonial governors, the Americans had to forge a military structure and a government authority to replace that of the British.

The focus on procedures was more than practical. It grew naturally from the Americans' ideas about why their demand for independence was valid at all. Relying on the seventeenth-century British philosopher John Locke, the Americans claimed that they were dissolving a social contract that bound them to England—and remaking that social contract among themselves. Breaking and remaking contracts that included the entire population demanded a theory. Not every person could be present when such fundamental, momentous events occurred. Someone would have to represent those who were absent. And the representatives would have to organize themselves into some quasi-formal body—something more than an ad hoc mob and less than a sovereign government.

The answer, in Virginia as in the other colonies, was an important and ambiguous transitional institution, namely the committee. Madison had first joined such a committee in December 1774, when he became a founding member of the Orange County Committee of Safety—partly because he was educated, and partly because it was chaired by his father. The committee had no legal or formal authority. Its members were not elected, except perhaps by themselves. The committee's purpose was to provide an organized method for enforcing the economic sanctions adopted by the Continental Association.

As momentum built for independence, the isolated revolutionary committees of Virginia decided to join together. The form they adopted was the convention, a term used in England and the colonies alike to describe a body of people operating outside the ordinary legally constituted government.[71] An initial Virginia convention had been organized after Lord Dunmore dissolved the House of Burgesses in 1774, but its delegates had been chosen by the displaced burgesses themselves. On March 20, 1775, a second Virginia convention gathered in St. John's Church in Richmond, this one composed of delegates sent by committees around the colony.

The question of what the convention should do was put squarely before its members by the greatest speaker in Virginia: Patrick Henry. Jefferson would write that Henry's "talents as a popular orator" were such as he had "never heard from any other man."[72] In the midst of a revolution, the ability to use rhetoric to convince large groups of people to take collective decisions was absolutely essential—and it made Henry a powerful figure.

The son of a small merchant from the backcountry of Hanover County, Henry was self-made. Without the benefit of formal education, he had taught himself law. There was no written test for bar admission, and the examiners who interviewed him concluded that his intelligence and breadth compensated for the limits of his legal knowledge.[73] Henry used the earnings from his law practice to buy land and slaves to grow tobacco. At thirty-nine he was well-off, although not rich compared to the largest Virginia planters.

The members of the convention would have expected an important speech from Henry. A decade earlier, he had established a colony-wide reputation with a borderline treasonous attack on the Stamp Act delivered in the House of Burgesses. Henry did not disappoint, arguing in 1775 that the convention should direct and coordinate the arming of county militias. The surviving text of the speech dates from forty years after the event and cannot be treated as a verbatim record. Henry may not precisely have insisted "We must fight!" He may not have used the exact words "Give me liberty, or give me death!" But the speech certainly became famous as soon as it was given; and its effect was to convince the convention to issue commissions for officers in local militias.[74]

Following the increasing radicalization of the convention, Madison's Committee of Safety took a revolutionary step. Backed by militia, Henry had audaciously demanded that Lord Dunmore return gunpowder seized from local militia stores. Dunmore agreed to pay compensation, avoiding the bloodshed of Lexington and Concord. For Henry, the symbolic victory consolidated his growing reputation. A year later he, not Dunmore, would be the governor of Virginia.[75]

In a document signed by its members, including Madison and his father, the Orange County committee officially congratulated Henry on his "seasonable and spirited proceedings." As if to clarify its revolutionary intent, the committee then added a coda about Lexington and Concord. What had happened in Massachusetts, the committee said, "is a hostile attack on this and every other colony." That attack, in turn, justified a response. It was "a sufficient warrant to use violence and reprisal, in all cases where it may be expedient" for Virginia's "security and welfare."[76]

Patriotic Virginians did not take the step of rebellion lightly. They expected that they could resist British troops—but they feared their slaves, whom Dunmore encouraged to abandon their rebellious masters and fight for the British in exchange for freedom.* "To say the truth," Madison wrote to Bradford, "that is the only part in which this colony is vulnerable; and if we should be subdued, we shall fall like Achilles by the hand of one that knows that secret."[77]

The Madison family tradition included the possibility that enslaved Africans could resist their would-be owners. In 1732, Madison's grandfather Ambrose, who had purchased the land and moved to the site of Montpelier, died after a short illness. Three slaves—named Pompey, Dido, and Turk—were tried and convicted of poisoning the master. One, Pompey, was executed, and the other two were whipped and returned to the plantation.[78] The fear of slave uprising, never absent in the South, would recur frequently throughout Madison's life and career.

From Toleration to Liberty

Even after Dunmore fled the capital for a British warship anchored off Yorktown, the Virginia convention was still an irregular government. Its members had been chosen locally by committees, not elected by the public at large. So in July 1775, a third convention gathered, once more at Richmond, and announced plans to formalize itself. Styling itself the Committee of Safety for the Colony of Virginia, it called for elections nine months hence. In April 1776, the convention instructed, the white, male property holders of each county should choose two representatives to send to Williamsburg for a fresh convention to begin on the first Monday in May 1776.

When April 1776 came, the freeholders of Orange County chose James Madison, Jr., as one of their two delegates. He had just turned twenty-five years old, and it was his first elected office. In this brave new world, Madison's talents were about to find the ideal venue for their expression.

---

* Like Lincoln's Emancipation Proclamation ninety years later, Dunmore's proclamation freed only the slaves of those deemed rebels against the legitimate state. In the aftermath of the proclamation, as many as several thousand enslaved Africans deserted their Virginian masters. Some three hundred were organized under white officers into an "Ethiopian Regiment" that would see combat before many of its members succumbed to smallpox. On their uniforms they are reported to have stitched the words "Liberty to Slaves." See James Corbett David, *Dunmore's New World: The Extraordinary Life of a Royal Governor in Revolutionary America—with Jacobites, Counterfeiters, Land Schemes, Shipwrecks, Scalping, Indian Politics, Runaway Slaves, and Two Illegal Royal Weddings* (Charlottesville: University of Virginia Press, 2013), 107.

The elected Virginia convention of 1776 saw itself as engaged in the epochal act of founding a new polity based on the consent of the governed. Its first order of business was to propose a frame of government. Today such a step is expected for a new political entity, but then the notion of electing delegates to draft and propose their own constitutional document was an innovation.

The utopian impulse grew from the same political theory that the Virginians and other Americans relied on to justify dissolving their bonds of obligation to the throne. Human beings, according to this view, were naturally free and equal. They possessed, as Thomas Jefferson would write that same summer in homage to Locke, "unalienable rights" that government existed to protect.

A government that violated those rights lost the authority to govern. Logically, then, the government that had forfeited its authority must be replaced by one devoted to rights protection. Unlike any governments imagined before, the governments of the new states would rely for their justification on their capacity to protect individual rights—not their brute power to control territory and issue commands that would be obeyed.

Following this chain of reasoning, the Virginia convention drafted what it called a "Declaration of Rights and Form of Government." The principal draftsman of both was George Mason, a Fairfax County gentleman and plantation owner, then fifty. In intelligence and literary skill, Mason outranked all of his Virginia contemporaries except Jefferson, who was then in Philadelphia representing Virginia in the Continental Congress.

Madison, half Mason's age, at first watched the drafting and debating process from the sidelines. Yet there was one issue that motivated Madison to action, and on which he believed he had developed sufficient expertise to intervene. The issue was religious liberty, his central preoccupation even before the Revolution had really begun.

Religious liberty had received little attention in the Continental Congress. But as revolutionary sentiment mounted, religious liberty began to look like the refuge of Loyalist scoundrels. When in July 1775 the Continental Congress called for a day of fasting and prayer for divine help in the growing confrontation with Britain, a Church of England parson in a county near Madison's cited his liberty of conscience in refusing to comply. As Madison told Bradford, the local Committee on Safety "have their consciences too: they have ordered his church doors to be shut and his salary to be stopped."[79] In fact, Madison added with more than a little satisfaction, should the minister's "insolence not abate," he might well "get ducked in a coat of tar and a surplice of feathers." Madison was interpreting the dissent in revolutionary political terms—which put it on the side of impermissible disagreement by enemies, not liberty of conscience among friends.

Nevertheless, among those who sided with the Revolution, religious liberty was to be protected. Mason's proposed declaration of rights included a robust and far-reaching defense of the principle. The draft, slightly edited by committee, read as follows when presented to the whole convention:

> That religion, or the duty which we owe to our Creator, and the manner of discharging it, can be directed only by reason and conviction, not by force or violence; and therefore, that all men should enjoy the fullest toleration in the exercise of religion, according to the dictates of conscience, unpunished and unrestrained by the magistrate, unless, under colour of religion, any man disturb the peace, the happiness, or safety of society. And that it is the mutual duty of all to practice Christian forbearance, love and charity towards each other.[80]

The draft's reasoning followed the views of John Locke. Religion was a matter of individual conscience. Attempts to coerce individual religious beliefs would fail, either because they could not force inward conviction or because, even if they did, religious belief was meaningful only when freely chosen. It followed, for Mason as for Locke, that the government must afford toleration to religious dissenters so that they could practice their own religion without punishment or restraint.

As liberal as this provision was, it did not satisfy Madison. In his first public act as a member of an elected body, Madison proposed that the text be changed. It was his only recorded act at the Virginia constitutional drafting convention—but it made his reputation and set his course for the future.

Madison proposed changing the phrase "all men should enjoy the fullest toleration in the exercise of religion, according to the dictates of conscience," so that it would read, "all men are equally entitled to the full and free exercise of it [that is, religion] according to the dictates of conscience."[81] In place of toleration, he was proposing equal entitlement. Instead of saying toleration would be full, Madison made the exercise of religion itself "full and free."

At the level of principle, the proposed change was highly significant. Madison wanted religious liberty to be treated as an inherent right and an equal entitlement of all persons, not as a privilege conferred by a tolerant majority. Mason's draft never actually called religious liberty a right, much less an inalienable one. Madison's draft, by using the words "all men are equally entitled," firmly established religious liberty as an inalienable right alongside life, liberty, and property.

The convention accepted Madison's proposal. By its act, Madison earned the credit of becoming the author of the first official constitutional recognition of an inherent human right to religious liberty in the new colonies. It was also the first such recognition in any self-governing constitution in the world.[82]

What is most remarkable about the process whereby Madison changed the draft of the Virginia Declaration of Rights is the skill with which the twenty-five-year-old entered the process—and the enthusiasm of his engagement. Luck and timing came together for Madison. Three years earlier, a recent college graduate living at home, he had been unsure of his calling, reading without focus, unenthusiastic either about seeking a profession or maintaining the life of a gentleman farmer. Religious liberty was then an outgrowth of his interests in divinity and government, his experiences at Presbyterian Princeton, and the contrasting insularity of Orange County. But in 1772 or 1773, an intense interest in religious liberty could be little more than a hobby. In 1776, it was the entrée to a career.

CHAPTER TWO

Rise

THE ARGUMENT: *After losing his first real election because he refuses to ply the voters with drink, Madison enters state politics in Virginia. He forges what will be his longest lasting and most important friendship with Jefferson, eight years his elder. His closest contemporary friend is the fast-rising lawyer-politician Edmund Randolph.*

Elected to the chaotic and ineffectual Continental Congress, Madison develops his characteristic technique: delving into his books and writing short essays for himself on novel solutions to intractable national problems.

Horrified by the weakness of Congress, Madison advocates for amendments to the Articles of Confederation that would give it coercive military power. The effort is unsuccessful—as is his courtship of Kitty Floyd. Returning to Virginia doubly frustrated, Madison leads and ultimately wins a statewide struggle against Patrick Henry and writes the most important defense of religious liberty in American history. In the process, he learns the all-important lesson that the larger the number of political dissenters, the harder to adopt a uniform statewide policy favoring the majority.

LAUNCHED INTO A PROMISING PUBLIC CAREER by the extraordinary circumstances of revolution and constitution-making, the twenty-five-year-old Madison immediately sought a new challenge: to win a truly popular, contested election. The process by which he had been chosen to attend the Virginia convention had been an election of sorts. But because it occurred in April 1776, when the colonial government still nominally existed, it had not included all of the features of public elections as the colonists knew them. There had been no public hustings, and no elaborate attempt to win over ordinary voters. Most important of all for Madison, he had faced no opposition.

The elections for the Virginia assembly in April 1777 were the first republican elections in which Virginia's citizens had ever participated. Independence had been declared almost nine months before. Instead of roiling with dissatisfaction and the possibility of rebellion, Virginia was at war. A new political order was emerging. Virginians would be choosing the people who would actually govern them.

In eighteenth-century Virginia, county-based elections took place in a single public gathering or canvass. There was no secret ballot, no orderly lining up, no decorous air of predictable but dull public virtue. To the contrary, elections were a public holiday in the fullest sense of the term. The custom was for candidates to treat the assembled voters to copious amounts of alcohol, which in Virginia meant not just beer but whiskey.[1]

The festival atmosphere that resulted from all-day drinking at the candidates' expense no doubt encouraged turnout and contributed to the pleasures of the occasion. It also had a deeper symbolic meaning. Those running for office were hoping to represent the people, but they were not precisely *of* the people. In a culture that emphasized deference to authority, the candidates were presenting themselves as generous, gracious men of means, pleased to indulge the (slightly) lower orders. To provide voters with strong drink in prerevolutionary Virginia was to acknowledge the contradictions of electing representatives in a colonial mixed monarchy: The voters had some power, but that power was exercised at the sufferance of Parliament and the king.[2]

Inspired by the idealism of the new, revolutionary republic, Madison thought this election should be conducted differently, in the light of what he called "the purity of moral and of republican principles."[3] To Madison, buying liquor for the voters was tantamount to buying their votes. Later in his life Madison would provide his guests at table with the best wine he could afford, but he himself never took more than a glass at meals, and he never drank hard liquor. To a young man this abstemious, the "corrupting influence of spirituous liquors"—his rather prissy phrase—stood for the corruption of republican virtue. Feeling "anxious to promote . . . by his example, the proper reform," Madison decided not to provide alcohol for the voters gathered in front of the Orange County courthouse on April 24, 1777.[4]

Madison thought he was complimenting the electorate, treating them as equals who could not or should not be swayed by the effects of liquor on senses and morals. But customs do not change so quickly, nor does a new political philosophy immediately transform people's expectations— particularly when those expectations include a drink. The choice not to offer alcohol struck the Orange County voters as an expression of "pride or parsimony."[5] His opponent, Charles Porter, a tavern keeper, adopted a more traditional stance and provided plenty to imbibe. The voters elected Porter.

Later in life, Madison would tell the story of his first electoral defeat for a laugh. Yet it revealed patterns that would recur in Madison's political career. He would spend most of his adult life in public office, and devote himself to the idea of the republic as the rule of the people. But Madison was not a man of the people. He lacked the common touch. The ordinary person did not want to have a pint of ale with James Madison; and the feeling, Madison demonstrated, was mutual.

Equally important, Madison took political principles seriously—so seriously, in fact, that he tried to implement them. Virginia was now part of a republic, and for Madison it followed that he and the other Virginians should act as virtuous republicans. He approached politics from the perspective of ideas that seemed to him both logical and worthy. Few skillful politicians operate this way. The price of trying to carry out abstract ideas in real-world circumstances is often political defeat.

But Madison also knew how to learn from failure. He could accept being wrong and change his behavior, even at the expense of his original principle. Ideas-driven though he was, he had the makings of a successful politician. Never again would Madison fail to liquor up the voters when he ran for office.

Jefferson

The political setback did not last long. That fall, a spot opened on the Virginia Governor's Council, which was appointed by the House of Delegates. Madison was chosen for it.

Returning to Williamsburg to take up his post, Madison found that the heady days of constructing a new foundational document had given way to the realities of trying to run a government in wartime. The Governor's Council had been designed at a time when Virginians were eager to reverse the legacy of the powerful colonial governor, and it had to approve every significant decision that the elected governor took. This gave Madison the opportunity to learn about executive action firsthand.

At thirty-six, Thomas Jefferson was already among the most prominent men in America when he was elected governor. The Declaration of Independence, officially co-authored with Benjamin Franklin but understood to be primarily Jefferson's work, had made him world famous.[6] Jefferson was obviously brilliant, and obviously happy for people to know it.

A head taller than Madison, thin and blue-eyed, Jefferson was also physically striking. He did not carry himself regally like Washington, preferring dull, corduroy clothes to tailored uniforms, and often receiving guests in slippers rather than shoes. His dress was meant to convey that he was a gentleman farmer, oriented toward function not fashion. In body and in manner, he was a model of how a Virginia planter was supposed to look.

Jefferson liked to move quickly and make bold decisions. He favored radical statements of self-evident, revolutionary truths, and could move from subject to subject with head-spinning speed. Madison preferred to proceed carefully and cautiously, building structures that would last and focusing on the consequences of every move. This took intense, laser-like concentration and the willingness—indeed, the desire—to go over the same ground repeatedly, making subtle changes and improvements. Jefferson inspired Madison, and Madison moderated Jefferson. Eventually, the two complemented each other's strengths and compensated for each other's limitations.

The patterns of Governor Jefferson and Councilor Madison's collaboration quickly emerged. In one instance, Jefferson dreamt up a highly risky scheme to send a secret agent to Europe to borrow money and purchase uniforms and weapons for Virginia troops. For the task Jefferson picked his friend Philip Mazzei, a Tuscan physician and adventurer who had come to Virginia in 1773 in the hopes of growing grapes and olives.

It was proposed to Jefferson that Madison should accompany Mazzei on his secret trip.[7] This was a preposterous idea. Madison, who had no knowledge of Europe, would have been totally wasted in the role of assistant to a procurer of military supplies. Madison wisely declined, the first of several times he would turn down invitations to travel abroad, often at Jefferson's behest.[8]

Madison's self-restraint saved him from disaster and Jefferson from embarrassment. Mazzei was caught when a British privateer boarded his ship just off the Virginia coast. Just in time he jettisoned his private papers, which he had stored "with a 4 pounds ball in a bag to be thrown overboard, if prudence should require it."[9] Confined by the British in New York for several months, Mazzei was eventually sent to Ireland and reached Italy a full year after embarking from Virginia.[10] Over the next three years, he achieved some success in borrowing cash and spending it on military supplies for Virginia troops. Had Madison been caught, he could not have posed as a European traveler. His fate when captured by the British would have been much worse, and the connection of the whole plan to Jefferson would have become obvious.

Madison and Jefferson also cooperated in a less creditable enterprise: the lengthy, incommunicado detention of British general Henry Hamilton and two of his officers in the dungeon of the Williamsburg jail. Hamilton had been captured by Virginia militia after a series of battles at Fort Vincennes, on the Wabash River 155 miles east of St. Louis.[11] On the basis of frontier rumors and the testimony of a shadowy trader, Jefferson alleged that Hamilton bore the nickname of "hair-buyer" for offering to pay twenty dollars a scalp for men, women, and children alike. Hamilton had his own story to tell. Denying the accusations leveled at him, he accused the Virginia militia of massacring civilians with tomahawks in the streets of Vincennes.[12]

Jefferson directed his council to conduct an ad hoc tribunal. This time Madison did not moderate Jefferson. With his participation, the council held Hamilton responsible for encouraging Indian raids on settlements and offering a reward for scalps, but not prisoners.[13] It concluded that over "four years of unremitted war," British officers had savagely mistreated American prisoners, while British prisoners had been "treated with moderation and humanity." The time had come for "severe retaliation" according to the principle of "measure for measure." Hamilton and his colleagues were to be "put in irons, confined in the dungeon of the public jail, debarred the use of pen, ink, and paper, and excluded all converse except with their keeper."[14]

Manacles and solitary confinement for prisoners of war were highly unusual in eighteenth-century warfare—especially for high-ranking prisoners.* The incommunicado provision was especially troubling given

---

* After the Battle of Saratoga, for example, the British general William Phillips, who had served under John Burgoyne, had been captured and marched with his troops and officers

Hamilton's charges that Virginia militia had themselves engaged in atrocities. Jefferson demanded as a condition of release that Hamilton agree not to say anything offensive about the United States. Hamilton refused. It is tempting to infer that Jefferson and the council wanted to keep Hamilton from telling what he knew. The general remained in his dungeon for almost two years, even after George Washington advised Jefferson that he should be released.[15]

The episode foreshadowed another aspect of the dynamic between Jefferson and Madison. When Madison declined to restrain Jefferson, the two were capable of completely overcoming their scruples and going to war.

Money

Madison so enjoyed his position on the Governor's Council that when in 1778 he was elected to the House of Delegates by the same Orange County voters who had rejected him the previous year, he declined the seat.[16] Representing Virginia in the Continental Congress was, however, a better opportunity. In December 1779 he and three others were chosen by the Virginia legislature to go to Philadelphia and serve there. Madison planned to head directly for Philadelphia. But an exceptionally cold and snowy winter kept him home until March.

Stuck in Montpelier, Madison turned to his books. The most pressing issue facing Congress at the time was rapid inflation. The causes were various, but the most important was that the Revolutionary War was continuing with no end in sight. Individual states were issuing currency, and so was Congress. As the quantity of currency increased, its value declined—or at least that was the conventional wisdom.

Madison wanted to help put the country on a more stable financial footing, so he set out to read the most influential account of money supply that he knew, that of the Scottish thinker David Hume. Hume did not care for the credit economy or for paper money, both of which he would have been glad to abolish. He believed that money existed in what

---

to Virginia. Once in Virginia his officers were permitted to rent country houses. They formed friendly social contacts with local gentlemen, including Jefferson himself, who apparently discussed music with captured German-speaking Hessian officers. Phillips wrote Jefferson a letter protesting the treatment of Hamilton. See Burstein and Isenberg, *Madison and Jefferson*, 70–71.

he called a "natural proportion to labor and commodities." The ideal national bank would lock up its money, not lend it. This would keep the cost of labor low,[17] which was important since the natural level of the money supply was tied to a country's productive capacity.[18] Issuing paper money meant overshooting the balancing point, which caused the value of the money to go down.

With audacity that verged on cockiness, Madison disagreed with the giant Hume. There was no natural level of money in a given place, he reasoned. Rather, the *global* supply of money set its value. The difference was all-important. Hume thought it would be possible to eliminate inflation by eliminating credit. Madison realized that the value of paper currency "depends on the credit of the State issuing it."[19] As confidence in the government's ability to pay its debts declines, the value of paper money goes down with it. Confidence, not quantity, was the index of inflation.[20]

The lessons of Madison's analysis were clear. Each time Congress issued more money, it made it seem like the redemption of the entire supply was further in the future and less likely to occur. As a result, "it could not happen otherwise than that every additional emission would be followed by further depreciation." The United States, Madison said, was like "an individual engaged in an expensive undertaking"—with no cash. The poor fellow had to rely "on bonds and notes secured on an estate to which his title was disputed." On top of it, he faced "a combination of enemies" trying to undermine his ownership.[21]

This was a depressing picture of borrowing during the War of Independence, and existing policy proposals had no prospect of improving it. Congress had been trying to buy back some of the paper money by issuing loan certificates at high interest rates. Madison considered this policy "preposterous and unlucky." One form of debt was simply being exchanged for another. "In order to relieve public credit sinking under the weight of an enormous debt, we invent new expenditures" in the form of interest payments, when only "paying off the capital to the public creditors" would work.[22]

Madison organized his thoughts into a remarkably cogent essay that he kept to himself.[23] His process set a precedent that he would follow whenever he faced a challenging policy problem: He would retreat to his books, research the issue, attempt to improve on what the greatest authorities had to say, and put it together into a private essay. For a professional legislator, which Madison was about to become, the practice was as valuable as it was uncommon. It assured that Madison was always the best prepared participant in any public debate.

This cast of mind was unusual for a person entering public life. Most politicians prefer human contact to intellectual solitude. Jefferson loved to think and write, but not about politics, which he considered an obligation, not a subject of enduring interest. Most American intellectuals of the time had other preoccupations. When Madison's friend Samuel Stanhope Smith sent him a long, complex essay on the philosophical question of free will and determinism, Madison took the time to reply. But the contrast between Smith's preoccupations and his own could not have been more stark. Nothing practical turned on Smith's intellectual project. The future of the United States turned on finding the right solutions to the questions Madison considered worthy of focus. For Madison, politics was becoming a vocation, and he would address it with all the seriousness and force of character he could muster.

In Philadelphia

Rain and bad roads made Madison's journey of 230 miles from Montpelier to Philadelphia into a twelve-day ordeal. Arriving in Philadelphia on March 18, 1780, ready to participate in national government, Madison found the situation even worse than he had imagined. As he explained in a letter to his father, Congress had decided to gather $200 million of paper then in circulation in the states and exchange it for $5 million in newly issued debt. From then on, Congress would no longer issue money on its own authority. Rather, the states would have to guarantee any money issued by Congress.[24]

Giving up the capacity to print money based on the credit of future taxes deprived Congress of much of its power to finance the war. As Madison put it to Jefferson, so long as it could still issue money, Congress "had the whole wealth and resources of the continent within their command, and could go on with their affairs independently, and as they pleased." Now, he wrote, Congress "can neither enlist pay nor feed a single soldier, nor execute any other purpose but as the means are first put into their hands."[25] Madison had become a delegate in a body that was effectively putting itself out of business.

As Madison saw it, Congress's attempt to avoid hyperinflation by drastically limiting itself could not have come at a worse time. The army was in a near-disastrous state, he told Jefferson: "General Washington writes the failure of bread has already commenced in the army, and that for any thing he sees, it must unavoidably increase." Mutiny was likely. Everything depended on getting provisions immediately, and those must "be procured, without a shilling for the purpose, and without credit for a shilling."[26]

Madison's dire tone reflected the shock of seeing Congress up close for the first time. It was not the assemblage of philosophers he and Bradford had imagined five years before. At the most "truly critical" juncture of the war, Congress suffered "from a defect of adequate statesmen." Instead of taking decisive action, Congress was "complaining of the extortion of the people" even as the people complained "of the improvidence of Congress, and the army of both." The country needed "the most mature and systematic measures." What Congress instead provided was "temporizing expedients . . . generating new difficulties."[27]

Despite his sense of crisis, Madison, who turned twenty-nine on the road to Philadelphia, was in no position to make a transformative difference. As one of the youngest delegates, he certainly had energy, and he posted an impressive record of unbroken attendance at congressional sessions for the next three years. His committee assignment was to the Board of Admiralty, which afforded the inlander an opportunity to learn about naval affairs, which would become crucial to his later career. But the assignment was not very important in a country that, strictly speaking, had no navy of its own. The French ambassador reported to Paris with only a little exaggeration that Madison did not speak from the floor in his first two years in Philadelphia.[28]

Scholars have seen Madison's time in Congress as the moment when he came to have a national vision of the United States.[29] In many ways that was true. Madison supported the ratification of the Articles of Confederation, which had been drafted and sent to the states in 1777 but had not yet formally been adopted. The Articles were a kind of proto-constitution for what would otherwise have been a mere collection of thirteen independent states. They delegated to Congress, albeit imperfectly, the necessary authority to raise revenue under some conditions and field national armed forces. For Madison to encourage ratification meant embracing a degree of central authority. And where the Articles were proving inadequate, most importantly in their requirement of unanimity for many revenue-raising measures, Madison supported various amendments to strengthen Congress.

But it is equally true that Madison actively represented Virginia's particular interests, especially in preserving land claims—even when that meant holding up ratification of the Articles. In the ratification negotiations, Virginia proposed to cede to the United States its claims to all land northwest of the Ohio River while keeping Kentucky, south of the Ohio. A condition of Virginia's proposed cession was that Congress must not recognize existing private deals between land companies and Indians in the Northwest Territory. As Virginia's representative, Madison wanted to make the point that Virginia had total sovereignty there—which meant it also had complete sovereignty south of the Ohio.[30] Expansion into Kentucky was a core Virginia interest that brooked no compromise. Madison was giving priority to his state above the national vision of a more powerful Congress.

He was in Philadelphia when the British invaded Virginia at New Year's. The invasion was led by Benedict Arnold, who had dramatically switched sides to become a British brigadier. Arnold sailed from New York with a force of 1,600 troops, most of them Americans loyal to the British cause, and entered the Chesapeake River on December 30, 1780. Jefferson received word the next day. As governor, Jefferson had convinced the state legislature to move the capital from Williamsburg to Richmond, more central to the state and fifty miles closer to his house at Monticello. Arnold directed his force to Richmond, and by January 5 they had reached the new capital.

The Virginia Line, the state's main militia force, had been captured by the British at the siege of Charleston the previous spring, and Richmond was almost undefended. In advance of Arnold's arrival, Jefferson, never a military man, evacuated what gunpowder and ammunition were in the city and fled, leaving behind just two hundred men. After token resistance, the Virginia militia scattered, leaving Arnold in control. His troops took all the tobacco they could find—this was a saleable commodity—dismantled the foundry, dumped gunpowder into the river, cracked open Jefferson's casks of Madeira wine, and burned much of the city. Then they went back to their boats, followed by enslaved Africans who seized the opportunity to escape their Virginian masters.[31]

For Jefferson, the political cost of losing the capital was considerable. The perception that he was a weak leader deepened in April when he was nearly captured by a British raiding party.[32] Jefferson chose not to run for governor again, and announced his intention to retire from politics.

Jefferson's opponents, most notably Patrick Henry, would not let him walk away from public life untainted. Henry got his associates in the assembly to call an inquiry to determine what the former governor had known about the impending attack.[33] Although the legislature formally cleared Jefferson, Henry, who doubted that Jefferson's retirement would last, hoped to damage Jefferson's future forays into politics. And indeed, Jefferson's political future would come at the national level, not in Virginia, where his humiliation would never be wholly forgotten.

From Philadelphia, Madison watched the events with a sense of embarrassment.[34] When Jefferson told him of his decision, he gently suggested that it might not be the right time to leave office. "I cannot forbear lamenting that the state is in the present crisis" just when Jefferson was stepping down, he wrote.[35]

Madison was right. In August, Washington marched for Virginia from Rhode Island with three thousand continentals and four thousand Frenchmen under the Comte de Rochambeau. There was a hitch during this "celebrated march": Passing through Philadelphia, the American soldiers refused to continue without pay and bullied Congress into remunerating them. But on arrival in Virginia, joined with other forces, Washington and the French laid siege to Yorktown, defeated the British, and effectively won the war. Jefferson had stepped down too soon. With another term, he could have avoided the perception that he had abandoned his state at a time of great vulnerability.

Yet Madison stuck by Jefferson. Their friendship transcended the political alliance that had brought them together. In the letter in which he responded to Jefferson's plans to leave office, Madison spoke warmly of his anticipation of future correspondence between them. For the first time, he signed himself "Your sincere friend and servant."[36] Two weeks later, Madison wrote to Jefferson again, signing himself "Your sincere friend and obedient servant."[37]

After Jefferson's retirement, Madison for the first time took the lead in the relationship. He sought Jefferson's support for a radical amendment to the Articles of Confederation that would have authorized Congress to compel the states by "the force of the United States as well by sea as by land." This would have been a fundamental change in the consent-driven political structure created by the Articles. Madison must have known that

Jefferson might not approve, but that did not stop him from airing the idea to his friend.

This scheme for a national government that enforced its commands by a navy was ambitious—so ambitious that it had no chance of adoption. Yet Madison, who had become interested in naval coercion during his time on the admiralty committee, was prepared to embrace the scope of it. He told Jefferson that such a government would have to form a permanent navy, and that the navy in turn would have to be manned by citizens "taken in due proportions from every state."

The impetus for Madison's proposed amendment was the embargo on exports to Britain that Congress had adopted the year before. All of the states complied except Delaware, which took advantage of the reduced supply created by the embargo to raise prices and export produce. The result rendered the embargo ineffectual.

Madison saw his proposal as necessary to coordinate national policy and stop individual states from acting as free riders. It combined and foreshadowed what would become two of the great themes of his political life: constitutional reform transferring power to the national government, and a trade policy based on embargo.

Madison had no qualms about using force against the states to make them follow the dictates of Congress. For most states, he thought, "two or three vessels of force employed against their trade will make it their interest to yield prompt obedience." For states that lacked direct foreign trade, the solution to forcing compliance was to prohibit their trade with the states that sent them foreign goods. These states, in turn, could be forced to obey by blocking their foreign trade.[38]

A naval force under national control, Madison believed, would protect the United States as a whole "against aggression and insults from abroad." Equally important, it would guard the southern states "against the insults and aggressions of their Northern brethren." Arnold's invasion had shown how vulnerable southern states could be to seaborne invaders from the North. Madison anticipated that in the future, after the war, these attackers might not be British, but American.[39]

This highly nationalist proposal showed that Madison was committed to a future, unified United States with a Congress capable of enforcing its dictates and protecting the country against foreign threats. Simultaneously, however, Madison was considering the possibility of war between different sections of the country. His argument for the national naval force placed Virginia's interests at the center of his analysis, and assumed that Virginia would control the U.S. Navy. Madison was, then, both a nationalist and committed to Virginia's interests. The two impulses were not contradictory—because Madison expected that Virginia would dominate a more powerful and centralized national government.

After the British surrender at Yorktown, Madison became more skeptical about the future of the union. Again writing to Jefferson, he offered his opinion that Virginia should act on the presumption "that the present Union will but little survive the present war." The members of the Virginia legislature, he urged Jefferson, "ought to be as fully impressed with the necessity of the union during the war as of its probable dissolution after it."[40]

Madison, then, had a nuanced view of national power and union in the early part of his service in Congress. He foresaw difficulties under the Articles of Confederation because the structure did not allow Congress to make the states act in concert, which thwarted unified trade policy. He had creative ideas about how to address the problem, and embraced the idea of a national navy to force compliance. But he was also fully prepared for the possibility that the United States would not survive the structural challenges of union under the Articles. If that happened, Madison would preserve Virginia's interests.

Taxes

In the summer of 1781, Madison made a new friend in Philadelphia: Edmund Randolph, who had just been elected to Virginia's congressional delegation. Two years younger than Madison, Randolph was from a prominent Virginia family that counted Jefferson as a connection on his mother's side. Randolph had served as an aide-de-camp to Washington during the Revolutionary War, and was now a fast-rising figure in state politics.

Yet Randolph's life was not entirely charmed. His father, John Randolph, had remained loyal to Britain and fled Virginia in 1775, forfeiting his property. Edmund had associated himself with his uncle Peyton Randolph, a patriot who had served briefly as president of the Continental Congress before dying suddenly in 1775. That and his assignment to Washington's staff had enabled him to escape the taint of his father's Loyalism. Nevertheless, this brush with political misfortune left him with a sense of uncertainty—and an ambivalence so profound it bordered on weakness.

Madison and Randolph developed a close friendship, enhanced by their mutual respect for Jefferson, Randolph's distant cousin and a substitute father figure for both. They began to exchange letters almost weekly. The friendship, Madison's closest for much of the next decade, would last for twenty years, although it would eventually become fraught with many challenges and complexities.

As the war wound down, the most pressing issue Congress faced was still the problem of debt. Money was short, and raising it was an ongoing challenge as sources of capital dried up and interest rates soared. Madison experienced the difficulty personally: The Virginia assembly often failed to pay the salary due to him as a member of Congress. Madison wrote to Randolph that "I am almost ashamed to reiterate my wants so incessantly to you, but they begin to be so urgent that it is impossible to suppress them."[41]

To survive in Philadelphia, Madison borrowed money from the Jewish financier Haym Salomon, whom he referred to as "our little friend in Front Street near the Coffee House." He told Randolph that Salomon's "kindness . . . will preserve me from extremities." Madison was grateful, but also embarrassed by the loans from Salomon, who refused to take interest from Madison or other delegates to Congress. "I never resort to it without great mortification, as he obstinately rejects all recompense. The price of money is so usurious that he thinks it ought to be extorted from none but those who aim at profitable speculations," Madison told Randolph with a lightness that belied the gravity of the situation. "To a necessitous delegate he gratuitously spares a supply out of his private stock."[42]

But if an individual congressman could get a free loan, Congress was not so fortunate. Robert Morris, the Philadelphia merchant sometimes called the financier of the Revolution, had been appointed superintendent of finance of the United States. Morris urged Congress to adopt a comprehensive plan to manage the debt. The first step was to incorporate a national bank that would attract those with private capital to invest and, through loans, inject liquidity into the economy. Madison opposed Morris's proposal, which passed nonetheless.[43] Morris also wanted Congress to settle accounts between itself and the states. The states would be responsible for some private claims of debt while others would become the national debt of the United States itself. To pay that debt, Congress would need a regular source of revenue. Morris proposed various forms of taxes, including taxes on land, on individuals, and on trade.

As the congressional debate raged, it became clear to Madison that Congress would not be able to agree on land taxes or poll taxes. The divergences between the vast holdings of plantation owners in the southern states and the smaller, more value-added farms of the Northeast were simply too great. The unanimity requirement of the Articles reflected those different interests, but also blocked Congress from raising revenue.

On the evening of February 20, 1783, Madison spent the evening at the house of Thomas Fitzsimons, a Pennsylvania delegate to Congress. Four other delegates were there. All but one agreed with Madison that the only remaining realistic option was an "impost": in essence, a tax on imports.[44]

The exception was Alexander Hamilton of New York. Still in his twenties, Hamilton had risen to prominence as aide-de-camp to General Washington and was now serving in Congress, where he was already exerting influence through his sophisticated knowledge of finance. Morris's bank was at least partly his brainchild.[45] He argued unsuccessfully to his colleagues, including Madison, that a patchwork of different taxes might be negotiated to satisfy various constituencies. And he warned them that the army was becoming restive and might try to overthrow Washington and rebel if not paid soon.

The next day, Madison addressed Congress to propose a compromise that would allow revenue to be raised through an impost. He began his speech by acknowledging that there had been debate about whether the Articles of Confederation gave Congress the authority to establish a permanent source of revenue. Madison offered the argument that it could. The revenue would not be established on "the assumed authority of Congress," but would be an act "by the authority of the states at the recommendation of Congress." This, Madison said, "could not be deemed inconsistent with the spirit of the federal constitution, or subversive of the principles of liberty."[46]

Referring to the "constitution" was not an obvious use of terminology. In his notes, Madison wrote the word "constitution," then at some point crossed it out to write "compact," then again erased that to write "constitution."[47] In his comments he referred repeatedly to the British constitution, which was not a single document but a loose collection of laws, institutions, and customs taken to be the basis for legitimate government.[48]

Some of the congressmen present disagreed with Madison's interpretation of Congress's power. But at the end of the day, Congress appointed a committee to implement the impost compromise. Madison was on it—as were several of the others who had been there the night before, including Hamilton. On April 18, 1783, Congress adopted the committee's recommendation.

Along with Hamilton, Madison was named to a committee to compose a public letter to the states that would urge them to provide the funds. In a week the group produced a document of which Madison was the lead author. It made clear that the future of the republic—and of liberty itself—turned on the states' response. "The citizens of the United States," Madison wrote, "are responsible for the greatest trust ever confided to a political society." If the nation were to succeed, "the cause of liberty will acquire a dignity and luster, which it has never yet enjoyed; and an example will be set which can not but have the most favorable influence on the rights of mankind." If it should fail, however, "the last and fairest experiment in favor of the rights of human nature will be turned against them; and their patrons and friends exposed to be insulted and silenced by the votaries of tyranny and usurpation."[49]

The address would be described more than half a century later as "one of those incomparable state papers which more than all the deeds of arms, immortalized the rise, progress and termination of the North American revolution."[50] Yet at the time, it signaled a deep and growing uncertainty that the institutions devised to run the United States were capable of functioning successfully and durably. The Articles of Confederation made compromise difficult by allowing dissenting states to veto revenue-raising measures. Notwithstanding the momentary victory for those who wanted to fund the national government, the revenue the impost might raise would not be sufficient to resolve Congress's financial difficulties. The problem lay deeper than Congress. It lay in the Articles themselves—and in the states that had proposed them.

Pursuing the Affair

As a member of Congress, Madison had been thrown into broader social life in the cosmopolitan world of Philadelphia society. Congressmen generally lived in boardinghouses, and their social lives revolved around them. Madison boarded with Mrs. Mary House, a widow who lived at

Fifth and Market streets in a household that included her adult son and daughter, a son-in-law, and a grandchild. Congress met at the Pennsylvania State House, now Independence Hall, at the corner of Fifth and Chestnut streets, one block away. Between five and ten other congressmen boarded with Mrs. House at any given time. Mrs. House's residents referred to themselves as a "family."

More exciting social events took place in the rented houses of the few foreign ambassadors whose governments recognized the United States. In these last days of the ancien régime, the French presence brought a steady stream of minor aristocrats, many enlightened and liberal leaning. Martha Dangerfield Bland, the wife of Madison's fellow Virginia delegate Theodorick Bland, was overwhelmed by the difference from Virginia planter society. "I am taken up by the gay scenes of Philadelphia," she wrote to her sister-in-law back home. "Oh my dear! Such a swarm of French beaux . . . marquises, counts, viscounts, barons, and chevaliers."[51] Compared to these emissaries of European style, Madison lacked glamor. Martha Bland described him: "Mr. Madison, a gloomy, stiff creature, they say is clever in Congress, but out of it there is nothing engaging or even bearable in his manners—the most unsociable creature in existence."[52]

Given Madison's social limitations, it is perhaps unsurprising that, in his first several years in Philadelphia, he showed no greater inclination toward the company of women than he had in Virginia. A glimpse of his unfamiliarity with the emotions of romantic love and loss—and his idealization of Jefferson—can be seen in an exchange of letters with Randolph concerning the death of Jefferson's beloved wife, Martha Wayles Skelton, who died in September 1782, several months after giving birth to their sixth child.

Randolph wrote to Madison that Martha's death "has left our friend inconsolable." He passed along a "circulating report" that Jefferson's "grief [was] so violent" that he had been "swooning away, whenever he sees his children."[53] Madison was disbelieving. "I conceive very readily the affliction and anguish which our friend at Monticello must experience at his irreparable loss," he wrote back to Randolph. "But his philosophical temper renders the circulating rumor which you mention altogether incredible."[54] To Madison, a philosopher had to be a Stoic, and so he could not imagine Jefferson so much in the grips of his feelings.

Nevertheless, in the spring of 1783, Madison, for the first time, pursued the possibility of marriage. And Jefferson, living with Madison at the time, played a major role in the courtship. Catherine Floyd, called Kitty, was the daughter of New York congressman and fellow boarder William Floyd. Kitty would have been not quite thirteen when Madison first met her father. In 1783, when Madison made his intentions known, she was fifteen. He was thirty-two.

Jefferson's stay at Mrs. House's boarding establishment was unusual. While in political exile in Monticello, where he was writing *Notes on the State of Virginia,* Jefferson had hoped to be sent to Europe as a member of the commission that would negotiate a final peace treaty with Britain. In November, Congress appointed Jefferson as a commissioner, and in December 1782 he rose from mourning his wife and traveled to Philadelphia to feel out the political situation before departing for Europe. Winter weather stopped him from embarking, and Jefferson found himself spending three months with Madison at Mrs. House's—time that corresponded exactly to Madison's courtship of Kitty. In April, Congress withdrew Jefferson's appointment, and he went home to Virginia.

Writing from the road, Jefferson broached the topic of Kitty to Madison. He had asked Madison to give his regards to "the gentlemen and ladies" who lived at Mrs. House's. Then, introducing a delicate topic, he switched into cipher: "I desire them to Miss Kitty particularly. Do you know that the raillery you sometimes experienced from our family strengthened by my own observations gave me hopes there was some foundation for it"?[55] Jefferson was alluding to boardinghouse teasing of Madison for his attentions to Kitty. The strong implication of the letter was that Jefferson had never discussed the matter directly with Madison when they lived together. Now he wanted details.

"I wished it to be so," Jefferson continued in an encouraging vein, "as I know it will render you happier than you can possibly be in a single state."[56] Jefferson was blessing a union between Kitty and Madison. His emphasis on the value of marriage suggested that Madison might have some doubts on that score. Finally Jefferson put his cards on the table: He had been wooing Kitty on Madison's behalf. "I often made it the subject of conversation, more, exhortation with her," Jefferson wrote. As a result of his efforts, he had been "able to convince myself that she possessed every sentiment in your favor which you could wish." This was not quite a profession of love on Kitty's part, but it was certainly a start.

Having put the topic before Madison, Jefferson backed off: "But of this no more without your leave." He signed the letter, no longer in code, with the warmest written salutation he had ever given Madison: "I am with much affection[,] dear sir[,] your sincere friend, Thomas Jefferson."[57]

A week later, Madison replied to Jefferson. Even writing in cipher, Madison still used abstract terms and circumlocutions to describe his efforts. The dry style was intended to be arch, but its effect was nevertheless a bit distant from human emotion—and quite different from Jefferson's indirection, which aimed to preserve Madison's privacy.

In code, Madison explained the situation: "Your inference on that subject was not groundless. Before you left us I had sufficiently ascertained her sentiments. Since your departure the affair has been pursued." Then Madison delivered the denouement—if the ambiguity allows that term. "Most preliminary arrangements, although definitive, will be postponed until the end of the year in Congress. At some period of the interval I shall probably make a visit to Virginia."[58]

Did this sentence mean that Madison and Kitty were engaged to be married? Jefferson certainly took it as good news, writing back to Madison that "I rejoice at the information that Miss K. and yourself concur in sentiments. I rejoice as it will render you happier and will give to me a neighbor on whom I shall set high value."[59] Jefferson did not, however, expressly congratulate Madison on his engagement, which he would presumably have done had he interpreted the letters as a formal announcement.

"Preliminary arrangements" suggested a wedding. Postponement to a specific time—the end of the congressional term—also indicated that an agreement had been reached. Yet Madison also implied some uncertainty by his insistence that the arrangements would be postponed. If the arrangements were "definitive," as he said, why were they being put off?

Sometime around then, probably in early April, Madison and Kitty sat for the prominent Philadelphia artist Charles Willson Peale, who painted matching miniature portraits of each in watercolors on ivory.[60] The portraits were meant to be encased in gold lockets, exchanged, and worn as jewelry. Madison, in a green jacket and waistcoat that match his penetrating blue-green eyes, wears a white neck cloth with a bit of lace. His hair is powdered but not in a wig, brushed forward thinly and fuller over the ears, more or less as he wore it his whole life. His chin is prominent and his lips are full and almost pretty in repose. Encased behind Madison's portrait was a braided lock of his hair, a token of his affection and fidelity. Its chestnut color can still be seen on the reverse side of the locket.[61]

Kitty is wearing a purple dress with a plunging neckline and white lace edging. Her hair is styled up, dressed, and powdered, with a cascade of honey blond curls over her almost bare left shoulder. Her features are regular and her expression serious. There is no corresponding lock of hair on the back of her portrait.

Commissioning the portraits was intended to demonstrate that Madison and Kitty Floyd were a couple. But it was not a formal act of betrothal. Madison's proposed visit to Virginia hinted that he might wish to seek permission from his father, or get a sense of what property he might be able to settle on Kitty—another reason to doubt that the engagement was official.

Above all there was Madison's restraint, both in the use of code and in his language. If Madison and Kitty were engaged, why should that be a secret? Given the circumstances, the most likely interpretation is that Madison and Kitty did not understand themselves to be betrothed for marriage. They were, rather, engaged to be engaged.

On April 24, 1783, two days after Madison wrote to Jefferson, Kitty turned sixteen. Five days after that, Kitty and her family left Philadelphia for their estate on Long Island. Madison joined the family and traveled with them as far as New Brunswick, New Jersey. It was the first time he had left Philadelphia since arriving three years before.

Madison returned to Philadelphia several days later, fully intent on marriage. Asked to remain in Congress until March 1784, Madison told his friend Edmund Randolph that "the idea of protracting my service in Congress into a part of the ensuing year does not coincide with the plans which I have in view after November next. I had rather therefore not stand in the way of another gentleman whom it might suit better, and whose attendance would be more certain."[62] The clear implication is that Madison hoped the engagement would be announced in November, with the wedding and a return to Virginia to follow soon thereafter.

Over the summer, it all fell apart. On July 28, 1783, from Philadelphia, Madison wrote to Randolph: "Contrary to my intention, I shall be detained here several weeks yet by a disappointment."[63] He had apparently received a letter from Kitty expressing doubts. It must not have been a definitive rejection. If it had been, Madison would not have been de-

tained, but could either have made the trip or canceled it. That he believed he must wait several weeks suggests that he had written back to
Kitty and still awaited a reply.

During the next two weeks, that reply must have come. On August 11,
Madison wrote to Jefferson that the relationship was over. The letter is
barely legible. Many years later, after Jefferson's death, it came into Madison's hands, and in preparing his papers for eventual publication, Madison crossed out thirteen lines to the point where they are difficult to make
out. The letter begins: "At the date of my letter in April I expected to have
had the pleasure by this time of being with you in Virginia. My disappointment has proceeded from several dilatory circumstances on which I
had not calculated."[64]

The best reconstruction of the crossed-out lines reads:

> One of them was the uncertain state into which the object I was then
> pursuing had been brought by one of those incidents to which such
> affairs are liable. The result has rendered the time [of] my return to
> Virginia less material, as the necessity of my visiting the State of New
> Jersey no longer exists. It would be improper by this communication
> to send particular explanations, and perhaps needless to trouble you
> with them at any time.[65]

The necessity of meeting Kitty no longer existed—because she had told
Madison they would not be married.[66]

Why did Kitty change her mind? Kitty could have been in love with
someone else. Two years later, she married William Clarkson, a medical
student at the College of Philadelphia. Clarkson was nineteen in 1783,
which has led some Madison biographers to imagine Clarkson as the
dashing, attentive young suitor who edged out the unsociable, older
Madison. But there is no evidence that Kitty even knew Clarkson when
she rejected Madison.

Most likely, Kitty simply did not want to marry Madison. Her ambivalence may have been there from the start. Madison gave her a lock of
his hair, yet she did not reciprocate. That might have been because he
commissioned the portraits; but in romance, small gestures can take on
greater meaning.

In his letter to Jefferson, Madison added something more, though it is
impossible to decipher because of the cross-outs.[67] Jefferson responded

kindly, without implying that he thought Madison greatly affected. "I sincerely lament the misadventure which has happened, from whatever cause it may have happened," he wrote, acknowledging that Madison had not told him exactly why things had gone wrong. "Should it be final however," he went on, "the world still presents the same and many other resources of happiness, and you possess many within yourself."[68] Jefferson was still leaving room for the possibility that Kitty would change her mind. If not, there were other options.

Jefferson also had advice for bouncing back: "Firmness of mind and unintermitting occupations will not long leave you in pain," he wrote. And Jefferson could not end without referring back obliquely to his own role in the affair. "No event has been more contrary to my expectations," he wrote, "and these were founded on what I thought a good knowledge of the ground." His final word on the subject was expressly philosophical: "But of all machines ours is the most complicated and inexplicable."[69] There was no knowing exactly why humans do what they do.

Jefferson's mystification implies a third explanation for the break. During his three months in Philadelphia, Jefferson stirred up Madison's interest while encouraging Kitty. After his departure, the relationship lacked the independent energy to succeed. Madison's interests were triangulated through Kitty to Jefferson, as were Jefferson's warm feelings back to Madison.[70]

Certainly Madison's and Jefferson's parallel pursuit of Kitty on Madison's behalf deepened their friendship. Until the months of January, February, and March of 1783, Madison and Jefferson had been collegial, political friends, not personal ones. Now, after living under the same roof and failing to win Madison a wife, the two men were joined in a much more personal bond.

Heading Home

By the end of summer, 1783, Madison was ready to get out of Congress and go back to Virginia. In anticipation of marriage, he had already told his friends that he would not stay in Congress through the next spring. Term limits imposed by the Virginia legislature ensured that he could not serve beyond the following March. His mother had not been well.[71] It was time to go.

Rendering Madison's situation still more undesirable, Congress had moved to Princeton, New Jersey, after a group of frustrated, angry, and drunk soldiers surrounded the State House to demand the pay they were still owed. Uncertain whether Pennsylvania's officials would defend them, members of Congress thought it better to leave town. Princeton was smaller, more remote, and less likely to attract crowds of former fighting men.[72]

Far from feeling nostalgia for his old college town, Madison intensely disliked being there. If Princeton's advantage over Philadelphia was that it was small, the consequence was that there was no room at the inn for Congress or the congressmen. Madison and his colleague Joseph Jones found that "on our arrival [we] were extremely put to it to get any quarters at all." After some efforts, they were "at length put into one bed in a room not more than 10 feet square."[73] Worse from Madison's perspective than the shared bed was the fact that the room was "without a single accommodation for writing." With no desk or table, Madison was "obliged to write in a position that scarcely admits the use of any of my limbs."[74]

The uncertain location of the capital of the United States captured the tenuousness of the union in this delicate period.[75] Pennsylvania did not promise to protect Congress until the end of August, several months after the mutiny that had brought the members to Princeton.[76] Annapolis, the capital of Maryland, undertook to attract Congress permanently, "court[ing] their presence in the most flattering terms," Madison wrote.[77] Meanwhile, "during this contest among rival seats, we are kept in the most awkward situation that can be imagined." The Dutch ambassador was expected, yet on his arrival in the United States might not know where to go to meet the government—a state of affairs unlikely to create confidence in the durability of the union.[78]

Before leaving Congress, Madison took care of loose ends. One responsibility was to find accommodations for Jefferson, who had accepted an appointment to Congress and so planned to move wherever Congress would wind up. Madison's other important piece of business had to do with his most valuable personal property: Billey, a slave he had inherited from his maternal grandmother. Born in 1759, Billey had been transferred while an infant to James Madison, Sr., as a trustee for the younger Madison, then a boy of eight. Functioning as Madison's manservant, Billey had been in Philadelphia with Madison for the past three and a half years.

The quandary that Madison faced was legal, psychological, and financial. Slavery had been partially abolished in Pennsylvania in 1780 by freeing children born to slaves and by prohibiting the sale of slaves from one master to another.[79] This raised the question of whether Madison could legally compel Billey to return to Virginia, a slave state, with him. In 1772, in a famous judgment called *Somerset v. Stewart,* Lord Mansfield of the King's Bench in London had decided that a slave who had been brought to England from Jamaica could not be forced to return with his putative master.[80] The precise common-law implications of Somerset's case were not clear then or later. The Pennsylvania law specifically allowed members of Congress to keep their enslaved domestic servants, "provided such domestic slaves be not aliened or sold to any inhabitants"; but it did not say whether they could be brought home. Hence, it was at least possible that Madison lacked the legal authority to force Billey back to Virginia.

Madison was more concerned with the effect that Billey's experiences in antislavery Philadelphia would have on other slaves at Montpelier. He wrote to his father: "On a view of all circumstances I have judged it most prudent not to force Billey back to Virginia even if it could be done." The phrase "even if it could be done" probably alludes to the chance that Billey could legally have refused to go. Madison's reason, though, was psychological: "I am persuaded his mind is too thoroughly tainted to be a fit companion for fellow slaves in Virginia."[81]

The content of the "taint" was straightforward. Billey wanted to be free. He had lived in a place where some persons of African descent were free, and all would be in a generation. Madison assumed, and assumed that his father also assumed, that such a person would inevitably infect the mindset of other slaves. His concern was not for Billey, but for the preservation of the institution of slavery on the family plantation.

Money counted, too. Billey represented a significant financial asset for the cash-poor Madison. In Pennsylvania, Madison explained to his father, "the laws ... do not admit of his being sold for more than seven years." As a result, he did "not expect to get near the worth of him."[82] Madison could covenant with another master for Billey to serve a seven-year term of indentured servitude, as the laws of Pennsylvania allowed. This Madison apparently did, telling his father that he had "taken measures for his final separation" from Madison. Billey became free after seven years, married a seamstress in Philadelphia, had children, and took the name William Gardener.[83]

Yet Madison's understanding of Billey's situation had a further layer of complexity. If Madison could have gotten Billey to a slave state, he could have sold him to another southerner, or better yet to a slave dealer who would resell Billey in the West Indies. But, Madison wrote to his father, he could not "think of punishing him by transportation merely for coveting that liberty for which we have paid the price of so much blood, and have proclaimed so often to be the right, and worthy pursuit, of every human being."[84]

In a letter in which Madison frames Billey's exposure to liberty as an infectious taint, and bemoans that he will not get full value for him, this humanitarian sentiment comes as something of a shock. Madison was telling his father that Billey was *right* to covet liberty. But that was not all. Madison was also stating bluntly that "we"—those who fought the Revolutionary War and had been prepared to die for liberty—had "proclaimed" liberty to be a universal human right and a worthy pursuit. To Madison, there was no ambiguity about whether the "men" whom the Declaration of Independence had declared to be equal included persons of African descent. Liberty was for "every human being," including Billey.

If Billey was entitled to liberty as a human being, then why not just free him? How could Madison in the same letter write that slavery was wrong and worry that Billey's brush with freedom would "taint" other slaves?

The best answer is that Madison wanted to suggest that slavery violated revolutionary values, while simultaneously explaining why he was squandering an important financial asset. Madison depended heavily on money from his father, especially in those years of hyperinflation when his congressional salary was almost worthless. So he had to justify the financial losses associated with parting from Billey without selling him at full value.

Madison knew that the institution of slavery contradicted the humanitarian ideals of the Revolution. His livelihood, then and throughout his life, depended on slavery. He had no doubts about bringing Billey with him to Philadelphia in the first place. But he did feel it would be inhumane to sell Billey for wanting to be free. He was not trying to introduce abolition by subtleties. Madison was attempting the doubtful, self-contradictory goal of being a humane slaveholder, one actuated by revolutionary principles.

Back to the Beginning

Madison remained in Philadelphia long enough to catch Jefferson on his arrival there. Just as Jefferson reached Philadelphia, Congress decided to move to Annapolis. Madison and Jefferson therefore rode from Philadelphia to Annapolis in November 1783. Madison would continue from Annapolis home to Orange County, while Jefferson planned to remain. The trip took them four days in fine weather. They would not see each other again for six years.

No sooner had Madison begun riding alone than rainstorms hit. Jefferson wrote to Madison that he "pitied" his "probable situation in the tempestuous season which immediately succeeded" his departure.[85] Madison's journey was so delayed by rain and flooding that it took him nine days to travel the hundred miles to Orange County.[86]

His plans, too, were a bit vague. Madison wrote to Jefferson that he had "tasked" himself with a "course of law reading," for which Jefferson had agreed to let him use his extensive law library at Monticello.[87] Now that he had enforced free time, Madison was returning to a subject in which he had been interested a decade earlier, before the Revolution intervened. Then he had read law as part of his general education. Now he read law because he was actively involved in the epochal task of arranging legal and political institutions in novel ways.

Signs that this process of design was ongoing could be seen in the conversation that Madison had with George Mason, the eminent Virginia politician and primary draftsman of the Virginia Constitution, one evening on his muddy way home from Annapolis. When Madison first met Mason, he had been young and unknown, offering revisions to Mason's draft guarantee of religious liberty. Now they spoke as equals on the leading issues of the day. Madison, fresh from Congress, set the agenda.

Madison probed Mason on the question of calling "a convention for revising" the "form of government" in Virginia. Madison suspected that Mason was open to revising the constitution he had mostly written by himself in 1776.[88] Rewriting the Virginia Constitution had been a topic of serious discussion over the previous summer, and Jefferson had written extensive notes on proposed changes.[89] The live possibility of redrafting underscored how much state government was a work in progress.

When it came to his views on the future of the United States, however, Madison found Mason wanting. "His heterodoxy," he wrote to Jefferson, "lay chiefly in being too little impressed with either the necessity or the proper means of preserving the confederacy."[90] In other words, Mason was not truly committed to keeping the union in place now that the war was over.*

Like Jefferson, Madison thought that preserving the union was the only long-term solution. But Mason's lack of enthusiasm for keeping the confederacy alive neatly captured the challenge that their view faced. To survive, the states must act collectively. Yet their individual interests diverged, especially when it came to the difference between agricultural states such as Virginia and trading states such as Pennsylvania and those farther north. Why should Mason, focused on Virginia's interests, compromise to keep the union?

With the immediate threat of British conquest removed, it would be harder to motivate the states to act together. The Articles of Confederation made the problem much more difficult, requiring unanimity for amendments and a nine-state supermajority for appropriations. As a means of preserving consensus by protecting some states from being dominated by others, this arrangement had its virtues. As an enabler of collective action, it was seriously inadequate.

Madison, then, faced two challenges on his return to Virginia. First, in the aftermath of revolution and war, the state must be put on a firm footing. Second, Virginia's interests must be reconciled with those of the other states. This latter task would require a total rethinking of the terms on which the United States was organized.

Luckily for Madison, he had the time. Montpelier in the winter offered little else. The winter of 1783–84 in Orange County was the worst anyone could recall.[91] The county had no post office, and getting mail delivered to Montpelier was difficult under the best of circumstances. Snowed in, Madison spent his time reading. His "chief society during the winter," Madison told Edmund Randolph, was the legal tome *Coke Upon*

---

* The word "heterodoxy" reflected a lighthearted literary shorthand that Madison sometimes used in correspondence with close friends. Other people could be described as orthodox, heretical, or otherwise in reference to whether they shared Madison's political views.

Littleton "and a few others from the same shelf."[92] These were the key volumes that shaped the common law. Madison was doing the hard work necessary to teach himself to think like a lawyer.*

As winter retreated, Madison grumbled about the interruption to his legal reading, but his letters to Edmund Randolph suggest he was thrilled to hear that he would be elected to the Virginia House of Delegates. Part of his pleasure, he told his friend, was "the opportunity of being in" Richmond—Randolph's neighborhood.[93]

But Madison's legal reading had not been wasted—and it was influencing his ideas about the constitutional structure of the United States under the Articles. Randolph, who had trained as a lawyer under his father and uncle, had offered him a detailed opinion about whether one George Hancock of Virginia should be extradited to South Carolina on the charge of assaulting a public official there. Assuming that the states of Virginia and South Carolina were analogous to different European countries, Randolph had based his analysis on the Swiss writer Emmerich de Vattel's *Law of Nations,* the most influential treatise on international law in North America at the time.[94] Randolph asked Madison for his thoughts.

In reply, Madison started with the text of the Articles themselves.[95] With confidence drawn from his legal reading, Madison noted that original intent, even if it were known, would not solve the problem. "The truth perhaps in this as in many other instances, is, that if the compilers of the text had severally declared their meanings, these would have been as diverse as the comments which will be made upon it."[96] Put simply, a document composed by multiple authors did not have a single meaning.

Madison then turned to the underlying question of how to think about the relationship between the different states. Numbering his points, he first noted that citizens of every state were, under the Articles, "entitled to all privileges and immunities of free citizens in the several states." This meant, Madison argued, that citizens of any given state were in essence citizens of all the states, not just their own. The states were not separate

* In the couple of letters he managed to exchange with Jefferson before and after the snow, they wrote about the Comte de Buffon's theory of heat emanating from the center of the earth, the sort of scientific topic that Jefferson loved but that Madison almost never engaged in unless he was writing to Jefferson.

nations—and the United States was not an ordinary confederation of sovereign states.[97]

Second, Madison argued, the states had more or less the same laws as one another, including the right to trial by jury. When states were adjacent, transferring a defendant from one to the next might be easier than transferring a defendant to a distant location within the same state. This was very different from, say, Britain extraditing one of its own citizens to France.[98] Once again, Madison was arguing that the states were not different countries, because of both their common legal system and their geographical contiguity.

Madison also appealed to the states' common interest. If the citizens of one state could run to another and avoid trial and punishment, that would not serve the interests of any state. His conclusion was that the Articles of Confederation were inadequate: "The relative situation of the U.S. calls for a *droit public* much more minute than that comprised in the federal Articles."[99] *Droit public* meant "public law," or a constitutional law governing the relation between the state and the individual.

Such a new public law, Madison went on, must not treat the states as separate nations whose interests were mutually opposed. Describing the states as "societies" in order to stress their interdependence, Madison argued that a new public law must presuppose "much greater mutual confidence and amity among the societies which are to obey it, than the law which has grown out of the transactions and intercourse of jealous and hostile nations."[100] The United States was a new kind of political organization, and it required a new sort of law.

The technical question of extradition had brought Madison to the necessity of new forms of public law—and to the brink of imagining a new constitution. For Madison to get deeper into the topic would require further research. Jefferson had encouraged Madison to take advantage of Monticello in his absence. "I hope you have found access to my library," he had written in February. "I beg you to make free use of it."[101] Madison had not. Even without the snow, the trip was twenty-five miles. What was more, Jefferson did not have the right books.

Preparing to leave Montpelier for Richmond and the legislative session after what he called "the winter blockade," Madison wrote to Jefferson asking him to buy books about the constitutions and public law of other potentially analogous political organizations. He detailed his requests: He had noticed in a catalogue "several pieces on the Dutch, German, and the Helvetic," or Swiss, confederations. The Dutch Republic, sometimes called the Dutch Federation, had combined seven "united provinces" since it declared independence from Spain in 1581. Germany had not yet been organized into the confederation that would follow the Congress of Vienna in 1815, but its distinct *länder* entered and exited shifting alliances. Switzerland had been a confederacy of different cantons since the Middle Ages. "The operations of our own" confederation, Madison explained, "must render all such lights of consequence."[102]

Madison also wanted to learn more about international law. "Books on the law of nature and nations," he added, "fall within a similar remark." He specifically asked Jefferson to try to get the works of the important Dutch international lawyer Cornelius van Bynkershoek "in French if to be had rather than Latin."[103] Madison could handle the Latin if necessary, but French would make it easier for Madison to assimilate vast amounts of information about these newly crucial fields under the time pressure of contemporary political events.

There was one more personal matter that Madison needed to settle with Jefferson before setting out. Jefferson wanted Madison to come live near him.[104] He had found Madison "a little farm of 140 acres adjoining" Monticello "and within two miles, all of good land, though old."[105] Unconsciously imitating the rhythms of the most famous passage of the Declaration of Independence, Jefferson emphasized the importance of friendship: "Life is of no value but as it brings us gratifications. Among the most valuable of these is rational society. It informs the mind, sweetens the temper, cheers our spirits, and promotes health."[106]

Madison was moved by Jefferson's "affectionate invitation" but demurred, deferring the whole question to the indefinite future.[107] The decision reflected Madison's quiet sense of independence, even from Jefferson. He did not want to enter the familial circle in which Jefferson presided as patriarch.[108] Jefferson was an admired older friend, but not a substitute father. Madison would not shift his center of gravity from the home he would inherit in Montpelier to Monticello. He intended to become master of his own house.

Establishment

What would turn out to be the most significant issue of the 1784 legislative session took Madison by surprise: the question of government support for religion. Before 1776, the Church of England had been the established church of the colony. The Revolution had ended this official relationship. In the wake of the state's constitutional guarantee of religious liberty, the Virginia legislature had passed a law in October 1776 stating that no one would be compelled to attend or support "any religious worship, place, or ministry whatsoever."[109] With the church's tax base removed, ministers were no longer able to collect their salaries from the government, but had to rely on voluntary contributions from church members. Ownership of the church's extensive property holdings became uncertain.[110] Virginia's former Church of England, renamed the Episcopal Church for reasons of political correctness, was facing a crisis.

Two legislative proposals arose in response. One was to assure the church's statewide organization and centralized ownership of its property. Madison described it to Jefferson as driven by the clergy: "The Episcopal Clergy introduced a notable project for re-establishing their independence of the laity." To make the church established once again, the clergy proposed that the legislature grant a corporate charter to the whole body of the church. Thus incorporated, the church would own all "present property" held by the disparate churches. It would have the power to enact canons and bylaws "not contrary to the laws of the land." Priests would be appointed by committees of vestrymen, but once appointed could not be removed except by a convocation of the whole corporate body.[111]

To contemporary ears, the proposal may not sound especially shocking. Religious entities are often incorporated. The rights that the law would have conferred—owning church property, issuing internal bylaws, setting the conditions for selection and firing of clergy—all seem today to be legitimate functions of a self-governing religious body.

Madison thought otherwise. He wrote to Jefferson: "Extraordinary as such a project was, it was preserved from a dishonorable death by the talents of Mr. Henry. It lies over for another session."[112] What disturbed Madison was the combination of official recognition and the grant of property rights to a central organized church body. Assuming the land was sufficiently valuable, the church would then be to some degree self-sustaining. This would give the clergy independence from worshippers—and that independence would come at the behest of the state of Virginia. If provided for in this way, the Episcopal Church might not be the official established church of Virginia, but it would be empowered to function more or less as if it were the established church of the colony.

To Jefferson, whom Patrick Henry had humiliated by initiating an official inquiry after Benedict Arnold had burned Richmond, anything emanating from Henry must be tainted. Writing back to Madison when he finally got the letter in France, Jefferson left no doubt about his feelings for Henry. It was just as well that the program of constitutional reform had failed, he wrote. "While Mr. Henry lives another bad constitution would be formed, and saddled forever on us. What we have to do I think is devoutly to pray for his death."[113]

The animosity between Madison and Patrick Henry was not yet as definitive as that between Jefferson and Henry. Both Madison and Henry were supporters of the Italian adventurer Philip Mazzei, who had functioned as Virginia's agent in Europe during the war. Indeed, at Mazzei's suggestion, Henry had made an overture to Madison before the beginning of the session, writing him a flattering note encouraging him to come and serve. Madison deserved a "respite" after the "length and importance" of the services he had rendered to Virginia in Congress, Henry wrote. Yet "matters of the greatest moment forbid it," so that Madison must reenter public life. "Is not the federal government on a bad footing?" Henry asked Madison rhetorically. "If I am not mistaken you must have seen and felt that it is."[114]

What Henry wanted to do about the inadequacy of the government under the Articles of Confederation was unclear. In fact, he was vague about any aspect of his own agenda, writing that "this is not the only matter that wants correction and improvement," but not specifying what he had in mind.[115] Most likely, Henry simply hoped to establish warm relations with an important politician who was reentering the state legislature, which had always been Henry's political territory. Madison's comment to Jefferson about Henry's support for the reestablishment of the Episcopal Church suggests that Madison was more skeptical of any common ground.

A second proposal to save the Episcopal clergy from ruin was more creative. The proposal was for what was called a "general assessment" in favor of religious institutions. Taking its inspiration from the New England states, where the government had always mandated support for locally selected ministers, the assessment would require every citizen to pay a fee to the religious denomination of his choice. This approach sought to avoid the difficulty of coercing individuals to pay money to support religious teachings with which they disagreed, while simultaneously guaranteeing support of the church.

The assessment's supporters presumed that if forced to make a choice, enough Virginians would pick the Episcopal Church to put it on an economically viable footing. In principle, members of other religious denominations should not object, because their money would go to support their own churches and ministers. For the formerly established church, such an assessment would be a lifeline. Virginians were not accustomed to supporting the Church of England by voluntary contributions, since support had always come from the state, which in turn had raised the money for the church through taxes. The assessment would ensure quasi-mandatory contributions from people who belonged to the Episcopal Church but had never developed the habit of contributing to it directly.

Madison reported to Jefferson that the friends of the general assessment "did not choose to try their strength in the house" during the May 1784 legislative session.[116] His dismissive tone with regard to the bills for the Episcopal Church suggests that he did not take either proposal seriously, and he did nothing over the course of the summer and autumn to organize opposition.

Ignoring the proposed bills turned out to be a tactical mistake. In the October session that same year, Patrick Henry took up the cause of the general assessment, introduced a bill, and delivered a speech in its favor. Although the text of the speech does not survive, Henry's central argument was that the necessity of establishment could be inferred from the bad state of affairs in Virginia.[117] It was a commonplace among late eighteenth-century Americans that religion was necessary to ensure moral behavior. Henry's explanation for disintegrating moral standards was the failure of religion—and his solution to failing religion was renewed state support.

The previously revolutionary Henry was expressing a kind of conservatism. Peacetime required the reestablishment of binding social norms. Returning religion to its accustomed place in Virginia society was one way to re-create a sense of normality. Having entered the Virginia elite through his legal skill and business acumen, Henry wanted Virginia society to be stabilized. A sense of collapsing public morality fueled this aim.[118]

Henry's arguments found a receptive audience in the legislature. He introduced a resolution stating "that the people of this Commonwealth, according to their respective abilities, ought to pay a moderate tax or contribution annually, for the support of the Christian religion, or of some Christian church, denomination or communion of Christians, or of some form of Christian worship."

Madison thought that geography played a role in the initial public support for Henry's proposal. "Many petitions from below the Blue Ridge had prayed for such a law," Madison told Jefferson, most of them written by Episcopalians. Several petitions against such a bill came "from the Presbyterian laity beyond" the mountains, in what is now West Virginia. With no opposition organized, and the other denominations in the state "passive," the assembly adopted the resolution by a vote of 47 to 32.[119]

The bill proposed in fulfillment of the nonbinding resolution was described as one "establishing a provision for teachers of the Christian religion." It required county sheriffs to collect taxes that would be designated by the taxpayers for the religious "society" of their choice and used to pay for ministers or teachers of the Gospel. Quakers and Mennonites, who did not have clergy, could use their funds as they saw fit. Any money not earmarked by the taxpayer for a particular denomination would be put into a county fund to support local "seminaries of learning"—what Madison described as "the maintenance of a school in the county."[120]

The bill went out of its way to insist that it was consistent with the state constitution's guarantee of religious liberty. It recited its belief "that such provision may be made by the Legislature, without counteracting the liberal principle ... abolishing all distinctions of pre-eminence amongst the different societies or communities of Christians." The bill gave no special preference to any one denomination. It did not even require citizens to choose a denomination, since they could decline to specify, in which case their taxes would support schools, not churches. Couched in these avowedly liberal protections for dissenters, the bill stood a chance of being adopted.

Madison was worried anyway. The point of assuring religious liberty in the constitution had been to preclude coerced contributions in support of religion. Toleration might have allowed for the possibility of established religion, as it did in England, which had both official toleration and an official church. But in 1776, Madison had convinced the delegates to establish not tolerance, but the equal liberty of conscience. That principle of equality, he believed, did not allow the state to coerce its citizens to pay money in support of religion.

Having failed to anticipate support for the general assessment, Madison had to pick his battles. He abandoned his opposition to the bill that incorporated the Episcopal Church and instead undertook to block the passage of the general assessment bill.[121] Speaking against it on Christmas Eve, 1784, he argued that the law should not refer to "Christianity" because of the difficulty of defining what exactly counted as Christian. In the end, he warned, the government would have to decide "what is orthodoxy" and "what heresy."[122]

In response to Henry's argument about the decline in morals, Madison claimed the moral crisis resulted from the Revolutionary War itself. The New England states, he noted, were reporting the same problems—yet they had never ceased to provide financial support for religion. The remedy was "not establishment, but being out of war." Madison closed by offering what he described in his notes as a "panegyric" on religion—"on our side."[123] He would not give any ground in his support for the value of religion, but instead would maintain that voluntary contributions, not mandatory ones, best advanced the cause.

Madison's argument worked—barely. The day before Madison spoke, the bill was moved along by a vote of 44 to 42. After Madison spoke, on December 24, the legislature voted 45 to 38 to delay the third reading until the following November and in the meantime to print the bill and distribute it "for consideration of the people."[124]

The stage was set for a yearlong public debate. The topic, religious liberty, was the one that had brought Madison into politics in the first place. The fight would pit Madison against Henry, the state's most powerful politician—and the man who had tried to destroy Madison's friend and ally Jefferson.

Remonstrance

In order to win this debate, Madison would have to explain to the Virginia public what, exactly, was wrong with a bill that let citizens choose what denomination they wished to support. And he would have to do it against the advocacy of Virginia's most popular politician, Patrick Henry, who was elected governor for the second time in the middle of the session. Henry's election prevented him from making any more eloquent speeches in favor of the assessment bill in the legislature, Madison noted.[125] But it also meant that Henry would have a year in the governor's seat to gather support for the already popular provision.

By April 1785, Madison noted that the assessment bill was the only issue that "makes a noise through the country."[126] The politics broke down roughly on religious lines. "The Episcopal people are generally for it," Madison thought, "though I think the zeal of some of them has cooled." The other important denominations in Virginia were Presbyterians, Baptists, and Quakers. Members of these groups generally opposed the bill.

The quirk lay with the Presbyterian clergy, who had opposed the bill to incorporate the Episcopal Church because it put them at a relative disadvantage. They supported the bill for a general assessment, however, because it meant that the state would now collect taxes that would go to pay their salaries. Madison considered their two positions a "shameful contrast." He thought establishments were bad in principle, and had no sympathy for the institutional realities of trying to make a living as a minister.[127]

There was also a geographical component to the debate. Madison had previously told Jefferson that support for the bill came more from their side of the Blue Ridge Mountains than from the Appalachian Plateau on the other side. Now he reported that the bill "has produced some fermentation below the mountains and a violent one beyond them." The population on the other side of the mountains tended to be made up of Scots-Irish Presbyterians. And among them, opposition was apparently mounting. Madison predicted that "the contest at the next session on this question will be a warm and precarious one."[128] Victory was far from assured.

Aware of the growing debate, Madison decided to influence the statewide discussion before the fall legislative session. Back in Montpelier, he composed an essay against the assessment bill and in favor of religious liberty. He framed the essay as a petition to the General Assembly of the House of Delegates, one that could be circulated throughout the state and signed by people who agreed. Madison called it a "Memorial and Remonstrance" rather than a petition, because the document was a protest and because the words had religious overtones. The petition was to be distributed in the "upper counties" in the Piedmont and beyond the mountains, where he expected it would "be pretty extensively signed."[129]

Madison began by quoting the proposition enshrined in Article XVI of the Virginia Declaration of Rights: "That religion or the duty which we owe to our Creator and the manner of discharging it, can be directed only by reason and conviction, not by force or violence." The idea, first found in the writings of Baptist dissenters in early seventeenth-century England, was that religious belief and worship were of no value if they were coerced. "The religion then of every man," Madison wrote, "must be left to the conviction and conscience of every man; and it is the right of every man to exercise it as these may dictate."[130] This was the principle of liberty of conscience: The right to form beliefs and make religious decisions resided in the individual, not the government. No one could make up someone else's mind for him. This logically made the right to liberty of conscience as "unalienable" as the rights to life, liberty, and property. One could not give the government what it could never be logically possible to give.[131]

Madison also argued that God did not want forced faith. The essence of religion was for the believer "to render to the Creator such homage and such only as he believes to be acceptable to him." And worship of God came before government. "Before any man can be considered as a member of civil society, he must be considered as a subject of the Governor of the Universe."[132] From the principle of God before country it followed that the country could not tell you how to worship God.

The final logical step in the argument had to do with the different spheres belonging to faith and government. The purpose of entering civil society from the state of nature was to form a government that would protect life, liberty, and property. If making religious decisions had nothing to do with civil government, then all matters connected to religion must be treated as completely separate. Religion was "wholly exempt from [the] cognizance" of the state. The two existed in entirely separate spheres.[133]

Once religion had been taken out of the sphere of government, Madison's argument against the general assessment bill began to make sense. Religion had no place in a majoritarian system. On the surface, the general assessment bill, with its built-in exemptions, did not seem to impose a heavy burden on religious liberty. But the assessment bill would set a worrisome precedent.

To bring home the danger, Madison employed the extreme rhetoric of the Revolution, which had from the start insisted that even small incursions into liberty—like minor taxes on tea or paper—must be taken seriously because they created precedent for destructive taxation that was sure to follow. The general assessment, Madison claimed, would similarly set the precedent of religious tyranny. Designed to accommodate all Christian denominations, the general assessment could lead to the reestablishment of Episcopalianism. "The same authority which can force a citizen to contribute three pence only of his property for the support of any one establishment, may force him to conform to any other establishment in all cases whatsoever."[134] To a supporter of the general assessment, this claim would have sounded like paranoia. Yet it was paranoia of a familiar, revolutionary type, and it was designed to appeal to the feelings of Presbyterians, Baptists, and other dissenters in Virginia.

From principled arguments Madison moved on to practical ones. Religion did not need support from government to thrive. To the contrary, religious establishments had created "more or less in all places, pride and indolence in the clergy, ignorance and servility in the laity, in both, superstition, bigotry, and persecution."[135] Under conditions of establishment, Madison wrote, the clergy "have been seen upholding the thrones of political tyranny: in no instance have they been seen the guardians of the liberties of the people." This was a reference to the Church of England's loyalism during the Revolution. The alliance of an established church with tyrannical government was a warning against establishment, not religion itself.

Madison then chose the most extreme possible comparison. "Distant as it may be in its present form from the Inquisition," he said of the general assessment, "it differs from it only in degree. The one is the first step, the other the last in the career of intolerance."[136] If this comparison of the general assessment to the Inquisition were not so rhetorically effective, it would actually be funny.

Madison's final and most important argument was explicitly constitutional. The Virginia Declaration of Rights, he argued, ruled out the assessment because the bill violated "the equal right of every citizen to the free exercise of his religion according to the dictates of conscience." These talismanic words, he maintained, had greater authority than any act of the legislature, and demanded that it "leave this particular right untouched and sacred."[137] If the state constitution did not control the legislature's actions, then the Declaration of Rights would be a dead letter. The public might disobey an unconstitutional law, but there would be no other remedy.[138]

The Memorial and Remonstrance amounted to a document of historic significance—the most important systematic defense of equal religious liberty that had ever been written. It went far beyond Locke's argument for toleration. It went beyond religious appeals for the protection of conscience. Combining rational argument with stirring rhetoric, Madison's essay was the cornerstone of the theory that would become essential to the American conception of the separation of church and state.

Madison chose to publish anonymously.[139] It was one thing to be known as an opponent of the bill, but another to compare it to the Inquisition and describe it as an infringement on the fundamental liberties of Virginians. Passing the document to Washington, who was not unsympathetic to the proposed assessment,* Madison kept his authorship secret.[140]

The screen of anonymity seemed to free Madison of the need to appear calm and reasoned. For the first time in his career, Madison was willing to write passionately. The topic of religious liberty had brought him into politics and was near to his heart. No other issue had ever brought out so much enthusiasm in him. His sincerity and commitment to the cause could not be gainsaid. He did not accuse his opponents of being badly motivated, but he did assert that their proposal would lead to tyranny.

As an intervention into the political debate, Madison's petition had an effect. When the legislature reconvened in December 1785, it received thirteen copies of the petition bearing a total of 1,552 signatures. Another petition, more exclusively religious, was drafted and signed by Baptists, and it yielded twenty-nine copies and 4,899 signatures. A third, signed mostly by Presbyterians, accounted for more signatures than Madison's. In total, eighty petitions against the bill reached the legislature, signed by a total of 10,929 Virginians.[141]

Most important, the Presbyterian clergy, who had initially supported the assessment, eventually flipped to opposing it, "being moved either by fear of their laity or jealousy of the Episcopalians," Madison thought.[142] Presbyterians constituted a large portion of the population of the state, and organized opposition by a large and active group of religious dissent-

* Madison later said that Washington had not thought much about religion, but "took these things as he found them existing, and was constant in his observances of worship according to the received forms of the Episcopal Church in which he was brought up." Proctor, "After-Dinner Anecdotes of James Madison," 263.

ers made the bill unlikely to pass. Other dissenters—Baptists, Quakers, and Mennonites—also opposed it. The religious diversity of Virginia helped defeat the general assessment.

Madison had transformed the conflict from a struggle between religious minorities and the majority into a general debate over the nature of religious liberty. The arguments he made were clear, compelling—and universal. They applied to all Virginians, not just religious dissenters. As a result, Madison's contribution to the debate was definitive. The Memorial and Remonstrance has been read and analyzed far beyond its original context, precisely because it is based on principles that are presented as accessible to anyone, regardless of religious belief or affiliation.

Back in the legislature that winter, Madison pressed his advantage. He proposed that the assembly should not simply reject the general assessment, but should pass Jefferson's "Bill for Establishing Religious Freedom," which had been written years before but never adopted. The law, which passed, effectively put an end to compulsory support of religion, even of one's own denomination.[143]

Madison counted the passage of the bill as a personal victory. "I flatter myself," he wrote to Jefferson with more pride than he usually allowed, that its adoption "in this country extinguished forever the ambitious hope of making laws for the human mind."[144] Madison derived special pleasure from acting on behalf of beliefs that he and Jefferson shared. But he alone had formed the strategy, advocated for his position in the legislature and in his anonymous petition, and brought about the result, a near total reversal of Patrick Henry's proposals of the previous year.

Madison had won a major political victory. He had taken a brave and potentially unpopular stand against the denomination in which he was raised. He had directly opposed Patrick Henry, the most powerful politician in the state. Because of his efforts, a debate about funding became a paradigm case for the establishment of a universal and equal liberty of conscience. Relying on broad principles of rights, he had learned how to make local arrangements of government into a matter of universally applicable truths. At home in Virginia, Madison had learned how to win.

CHAPTER THREE

Crisis

...

THE ARGUMENT: *Madison convinces the Virginia legislature to call for a convention in Annapolis to revise the Articles of Confederation. The convention fails for lack of interest—but is saved by Alexander Hamilton, who persuades the delegates to call for another convention a year later in Philadelphia.*

In the crisis-driven year that follows, Madison experiences a period of extraordinary creativity. He works out his ideas in a series of essays, developing the view that factions, springing from economic interest, ruin republicanism. He invents a solution: enlargement of the republic. Madison's emerging vision dovetails with his ideal of friendship. He will create a government that can control and reduce the effects of faction, enabling friends to reason and deliberate without becoming enemies or creatures of self-interest.

WHEN HE PARTED FROM JEFFERSON in 1783, Madison had never traveled beyond New Jersey. He knew easterners, but not the eastern states. He had met Europeans, but never been to Europe. His years out of national politics gave him the opportunity to remedy these provincial limitations. In the autumns of 1784, 1785, and 1786, Madison undertook three trips north and east—what he called "ramble[s] into the Eastern States which I have long had a curiosity to see."[1]

The most significant of the trips was the first, in September and October 1784. Madison set off planning to travel alone. At Baltimore, however, he "fell in with the Marquis Lafayette," who, after returning to France a hero in 1781, was now making a triumphant postwar victory lap through the United States. Lafayette's trip had a personal purpose and a geopolitical one. He sought to maintain his association with the United

States, which, as Madison astutely noted, was "connected with his personal glory";[2] and to strengthen French-American ties.

Lafayette invited Madison to join him on a trip to Fort Stanwix (now renamed Fort Schuyler) for a major treaty negotiation between the six Iroquois nations and commissioners sent by Congress.[3] They took a barge from New York City directly up the Hudson to Albany.[4]

Traveling with Lafayette meant meeting pro-French Americans eager to provide what Madison called "marks of cordial esteem and affection" to the aristocrat who had made the cause of the United States his own. Like Jefferson, whom Lafayette had befriended in Paris, Madison favored a pro-French policy. Lafayette's trip enabled Madison to broaden his acquaintance among like-minded New Yorkers.[5]

The two discussed the U.S.-French alliance, and Madison told Lafayette of his concerns about Spain, which controlled both the Louisiana Territory that stretched west of the Mississippi River and included New Orleans and also the Florida Territory that included the Gulf Coast. It was clear to Madison that in the long run, "the ideas of America and Spain irreconcilably clash." The United States and Virginia in particular needed access to the port of New Orleans. Spain had no interest in granting Americans access. Lafayette agreed, telling Madison that he believed "Spain is bent on excluding [Americans] from the Mississippi."[6]

Madison drew several lessons from the trip. He believed he had gotten "a pretty thorough insight into" the character of Lafayette. The marquis, he told Jefferson, had "great natural frankness"; possessed "very considerable talents"; and topped it off with "a strong thirst of praise and popularity." Beyond the alliance between France and the United States, Lafayette cared most about the continued "union" of the United States—still very much in doubt—and "the manumission of the slaves."[7]

Madison was impressed by Lafayette's position on slavery, telling Jefferson that the view "does him real honor as it is a proof of his humanity."[8] That one slave-owning Virginia planter could comment to another that it was honorable for a non-slave-owning foreigner to care about manumission says much about how Madison and Jefferson thought about slavery.[9] The principle of abolition might be good, but the reality was not to be taken seriously. In the same vein, Madison could tell Edmund Randolph that he wished over the course of his career "to depend as little as possible on the labor of slaves," without ever changing his lifestyle.[10]

Madison's second lesson from his trip with Lafayette was that upstate New York was economically underdeveloped—and therefore a promising venue for land speculation. He conceived a plan to buy property there, and discussed the possibility the following autumn with the most experienced land speculator he knew: George Washington, who would eventually own fifty thousand acres of western land. Washington said he considered the Mohawk River valley a good investment, and had in fact just bought some land there himself.[11]

As a partner, Madison enlisted a new Virginian friend, James Monroe. Seven years younger than Madison, Monroe was an impressive figure, more than six feet tall with dark hair and gray eyes. He had been wounded leading his troops in the Revolutionary War, decorated for gallantry, and wintered with Washington at Valley Forge. Since then he had become a protégé of Jefferson and was now following closely in Madison's political footsteps. In short order he had been elected to the Virginia House of Delegates, served on the Governor's Council, and been chosen to replace Madison in Congress when Madison's term came to an end. As was the case with Randolph, the men's mutual relationship to the older Jefferson was significant. It created an immediate dynamic of common goals and aspirations—but it also hinted at the possibility of sibling rivalry, at least on the side of the younger Monroe.

As the son of a modestly endowed farmer at the lower end of the Virginia gentry, the ambitious Monroe needed money more than Madison did.[12] The two raised enough cash to buy one thousand acres on the Mohawk River for $1.50 per acre. In the postrevolutionary financial crunch, loans were hard to get. Madison's creative idea was to take advantage of Jefferson's presence in Paris to borrow money from French bankers, thereby allowing him and Monroe to buy a much bigger property. Madison was hoping that Jefferson could borrow "four or five thousand louis"— several hundred thousand dollars in today's money[13]—at a rate of 6 percent for a loan of eight or ten years. With the enthusiasm of a first-time investor, Madison told Jefferson that land prices would go up and that when the flow of currency to the United States restarted, the appreciation would save "at least" one year's worth of interest on the original loan.[14]

Jefferson had encouraged both his friends to buy property near him— property neither could afford—but he explained the money would not be forthcoming. French bankers had no interest in investing "on the other side of the Atlantic, where distance, want of punctuality, and habitual protection of the debtor would be against them." Jefferson promised to suggest the scheme to rich individual Frenchmen who might want to help.[15] But by then it was December 1786 in Paris. The crisis that led to the French Revolution would begin two months later, and such loans were out of the question.[16]

Jefferson thought Madison should visit him in Europe the next summer. He wrote to Madison that he had been "right" in finding it "worthwhile to pass the last summer in exploring the woods of America." Now, Jefferson suggested with just a hint of humor, "do you not think the men and arts in this country would be worth another summer"?[17] Knowing that Madison was short of cash, Jefferson offered to lend him money for the trip. Clothes, passage, and entertainments would cost two hundred guineas, Jefferson wrote. "You will for that have purchased the knowledge of another world."[18]

Madison declined the "very friendly invitation," offering three different excuses: A summer was too short; the timing was bad because "it would break in upon a course of reading which if I neglect now I shall probably never resume"; and "crossing the sea would be unfriendly to a singular disease of my constitution."[19] Madison was reading assiduously about constitutions and international law, and in the same letter he renewed his request for "treatises on the ancient or modern federal republics" and "the law of nations."[20] But his well-founded fear of the health dangers of an eighteenth-century sea crossing was likely the main reason. Indeed, Madison would never take an ocean voyage in his life.

Trade

Whatever the limits of his travels, Madison ranged very broadly in his intellectual life. In particular, he was thinking about trade between the United States and other countries. The immediate cause was the need to amend the Articles of Confederation so as to give Congress the capacity to raise revenue by taxing trade.

Influenced by his reading of Adam Smith's *Wealth of Nations,* Madison believed in "a perfect freedom" of trade, he wrote to Monroe in the summer of 1785.[21] In the real world, he knew, free trade was not practical. The government needed revenue to pay off its Revolutionary War debt—and the only plausible source of revenue was an impost on trade.

More fundamentally, independence had stripped the United States of access to the British colonial network and the advantages of British naval protection. Unlike the problem of debt, which was in principle temporary, the problem of getting access to foreign ports was potentially permanent.

"What is to be done?" Madison asked Monroe rhetorically. "Must we remain passive victims to foreign politics; or shall we exert the lawful means which our independence has put into our hands, of extorting redress?"[22] The answer was to force Britain and other nations to give American ships access. With no navy, "retaliating regulations of trade" were the "only" means by which the United States could trade on terms of equality with the other nations of the world.[23] Madison's belief in regulating trade as a creative weapon was fundamental to his thinking at the time, and would remain so for the next thirty years.

This analysis had an important consequence: The United States must be able to act as a single body. The states "can no more exercise this power separately," Madison wrote, "than they could separately carry on war, or separately form treaties of alliance or commerce."[24] Taxing trade was simply war and foreign relations by other means. The states could not possibly have won the war with Britain had they fought individually. They could not survive the peace without similar coordination.

In turn, coordination required constitutional reform. Under the Articles of Confederation, the states would have to agree unanimously on an amendment to give Congress power over trade. The eastern states had a shipping industry; the southern states did not. Madison acknowledged that retaliatory import taxes would cost the southern states money without offering them direct benefits. Yet he believed that the states' collective interests outweighed their particular ones.

The solution was to change the Articles. "I conceive it to be of great importance," he told Monroe, "that the defects of the federal system should be amended." Without amending the system, Madison warned, "I apprehend danger to its very existence from a continuance of defects which expose a part if not the whole of the empire to severe distress." States "cannot long respect a government which is too feeble to protect their interest."[25] The union was thus at stake.

Madison was offering a powerful argument for constitutional reform—within the Articles if at all possible, but if not, then by any means necessary. Coordination was critical for survival, and unanimity was, at least for the moment, incompatible with the change required to create coordination. The strong implication was that unanimity would have to go—and with it the fundamental principle of the Articles of Confederation.

In the fall 1785 session of the Virginia assembly, the Virginia legislature approved a proposal calling for commissioners to be appointed from all the states to discuss "the subject of general regulations" of trade. Madison thought the plan was "no doubt liable to objections and will probably miscarry." He would have preferred the legislature to take a stand. Yet on the whole, he told Monroe, "it is better than nothing." Such a gathering would be authorized to recommend "additional powers to Congress."[26] Madison was named as one of three Virginia commissioners, along with his friend Edmund Randolph. Then the legislature added five others. "It is not unlikely that this multitude of associates will stifle the thing in its birth," Madison wryly noted. "By some it was probably meant to do so."[27] No particular optimism accompanied the plan or the appointment. Yet a step had been taken to address Madison's concerns about national coordination—and it was the best step that Madison thought he could get.

In March 1786, a few months later, Randolph wrote to tell Madison that Annapolis, Maryland, had been selected as the site for what he proprietarily called "our convention." The Virginia legislature sent a circular letter to the other state legislatures issuing an invitation for the first Monday in September. Annapolis, where Congress had met in 1783–84, was chosen because it was "farther removed from the suspicion, which Philadelphia or New York might have excited, of congressional or mercantile influence."[28]

Madison wrote guardedly to Monroe: "I am far from entertaining sanguine expectations from it, and am sensible that it may be viewed in one objectionable light." The objectionable light was that the convention would take place outside the auspices of Congress, and so hinted in some way at the possibility of altering that institution. "Yet on the whole," Madison continued, "I cannot disapprove of the experiment." Something had to be done "towards the commerce at least of the United States."[29] "If anything can be done," he wrote, "it seems likely to result from the proposed convention, and more likely to result from the present crisis, than from any other mode or time."

Even if nothing could be done, Madison continued, learning that coordination was impossible would itself be valuable information: "Such a piece of knowledge will be worth the trouble and expense of obtaining it."[30] If the Annapolis convention failed, Madison thought, the union was unlikely to survive. Better to know that sooner than later, so that Virginia could plan accordingly.

Monroe fretted to Madison that the Annapolis convention would likely not be up to the task of correcting the problems of the confederation. It could propose gradual fixes. But if a convention specifically devoted to amending the Articles was required, then "the powers of the Virginia commissioners are inadequate."[31]

Madison acknowledged that Monroe was right in principle. But as a pragmatic matter they had to deal with those who did not understand the need for correcting the problems of the confederation as well as those who actively did not want to fix them. "As we have both ignorance and iniquity to control," he wrote, "we must defeat the designs of the latter by humoring the prejudices of the former." Opponents must be thwarted by catering to the ignorant and holding the convention on the one issue where they could be induced to permit the meeting to occur. If the Annapolis convention could fix the trade problem, "it can be repeated as other defects force themselves on the public attention, and as the public mind becomes prepared for further remedies." Meanwhile, given that the Virginia assembly refused to instruct their representatives in Congress, "the option therefore lay between doing what was done and doing nothing."[32]

Madison left no doubt that he considered circumstances dire. "I am not in general an advocate for temporizing or partial remedies," he wrote. "But a rigor in this respect, if pushed too far may hazard everything. If the present paroxysm of our affairs be totally neglected their case may become desperate."[33] Insisting on a broader convention would run the "hazard" of having no convention at all. The consequence of inaction might be dissolution of the union.

Confederations and Their Vices

Madison used the spring and summer before the September 1786 Annapolis meeting to study in anticipation of the fight. For two years he had been asking Jefferson to send him books about ancient and modern confederations. Two trunks of books on the subject finally reached Madison in January. Now, he wrote Jefferson, he "had leisure to review the literary cargo for which I am so much indebted to your friendship.[34] Working steadily through the spring, Madison drew on these works to produce a detailed analysis of the fundamental issues at stake.

It is difficult to overstate the creativity and intellectual precision that went into Madison's notes on "ancient and modern confederacies." Madison did not invent comparative constitutional study. Aristotle in his *Politics* had already engaged in comparisons between different sorts of constitutional arrangements, and Montesquieu had tried to offer a general theory of the relationship between the "spirits" of different polities and the way they were organized. But as a systematic effort to identify the core working elements of all the confederacies known to have existed, Madison's document was unprecedented.

His method was to describe first the origin of each confederacy, then its form of "federal authority," and finally what he labeled the "vices" of each one. As he went, he cited the sources for each element. Once in a while, in an unconscious show of his scholarship in documents intended for no one but himself, Madison would quote a paragraph or two in Latin without bothering to translate. He was now thirty-five, and the scholarly skills attained in his youth were still sharp. Acquired out of intellectual curiosity, they now had enormous practical value.

Each set of vices carried a trenchant lesson. The Amphictyonic League of ancient Greece, for example, suffered from the unequal strengths of its members—in parallel to the wide variations in size, wealth, and population of the United States.[35] The Achaean Confederacy suffered from too much power asserted by the center, leading Rome to "seduce" its members away through individual negotiations. This was a warning against subjecting the states to unpopular authority and thus driving them into the arms of Britain.

The Dutch confederacy had articles of union that specified that "everything done contrary to them [is] to be null and void"—Madison's first reference to the principle of constitutional supremacy. But because the Dutch articles, like the Articles of Confederation, required unanimity of all member states for important decisions, they were ignored. Special assemblies of the Estates General over 130 years—in essence, constitutional conventions—had all failed to remedy the defect.

The Dutch confederacy should not have worked. And yet it did, through the agency of a powerful stadtholder and the shared hatred of the House of Austria.[36] The idea was that external threat provided an incentive for maintaining unity despite poorly made constitutional arrangements. Madison's counterintuitive lesson was that strong central authority could emerge even among states that feared being dominated by other members of the confederacy—provided fear and hatred of Great Britain persisted to create national unity.

In the case of Germany, Madison was fascinated by the "Imperial Chamber" that had been established in 1495 as a kind of "supreme court" to resolve controversies between different states. The court could not itself stop civil wars, Madison noted, and it relied on the emperor to effectuate its decrees. At the same time, he speculated that "jealousy of the imperial authority seems to have been a great cement of the confederacy."[37] Madison was slowly deriving a theory of constitutional balancing. Central authority made the court's decrees relevant. Simultaneous fear of that necessary authority kept the federation from pulling apart.

To Annapolis

Surveying conditions in the weeks before the planned Annapolis convention, Madison saw crisis mounting. Virginia, unlike most states, had never issued paper money, and there was now a serious shortage of hard currency. Madison thought it probable that there would not be enough gold or silver in the state to cover the cost of the 1786 taxes. The inevitable result would be the introduction of the "evil" of paper money in Virginia.[38]

At the national level, things looked grimmer still. Madison was horrified to hear from Monroe that Congress was discussing a treaty with Spain that would acknowledge Spanish sovereignty over the mouth of the Mississippi River at New Orleans. The eastern proponents of the treaty, Monroe told Madison, would stop at nothing. If they could not prevail, "they will labor to break the union." On the eve of the Annapolis convention, then, Monroe was seriously gaming the possibilities of civil war.[39]

In a spirit of pessimism, Madison set off in July for the East Coast, riding through Virginia, Maryland, and Pennsylvania "in the midst of harvest." Crossing the Potomac at Harpers Ferry, he had "an opportunity of viewing the magnificent scene which nature" there presented, he wrote to Jefferson, who in his *Notes on the State of Virginia* described the same view as "perhaps one of the most stupendous scenes in nature" and "worth a voyage across the Atlantic."[40] But the crossing, in a fog, went badly:

"The air was so thick that distant objects were not visible at all, and near ones not distinctly so." Madison's party missed the path in the mist, "ascended the mountain . . . at a wrong place," and "fatigued ourselves much in traversing it before we gained the right position."[41]

In Philadelphia, Madison got the bad news that only seven states, and only one of those southern, had named commissioners to the Annapolis convention.[42] When he reached Annapolis, Madison quickly recognized that collective action would be impossible. On Monday, September 11, 1786, the appointed day, five states' representatives had arrived. Just three states (Virginia, Delaware, and New Jersey) had enough delegates present to act. The twelve delegates in attendance halfheartedly asked Edmund Randolph to draft a resolution. Randolph prepared a draft that simply acknowledged that those present had "no authority" to act, and encouraged the appointment of a committee "urging the necessity of a meeting to be held in Philadelphia on the 10th day of May next." Edited, the draft resolution limply suggested that the states appoint commissioners for that future meeting whose power would extend "to every other matter respecting the Confederation."[43]

Then Alexander Hamilton swept into action. Red haired, well dressed, and flamboyant, Hamilton cut a figure in the all-but-empty statehouse. Madison had met him when they both served in Congress in 1783, but the two were not yet friends.[44] In background and personality they were almost opposites. Madison was the eldest son of a respectable Piedmont planter. Hamilton was the illegitimate fourth son of a Scottish laird, born on the Caribbean island of Nevis to a mother married to another man. His early circumstances were so unfortunate that even the year of his birth is not known with certainty.

Madison was emotionally reticent and a bachelor with a single failed courtship to his credit. Hamilton regularly spoke and wrote of his passionate love for his wife and his comparably passionate feelings of affection for his closest male friend.[45] From Annapolis he wrote home to his wife, Elizabeth:

> Happy . . . I cannot be, absent from you and my darling little ones. I
> feel that nothing can ever compensate for the loss of the enjoyments I
> leave at home or can ever put my heart at tolerable ease. . . . The
> prospect of detention here for eight or 10 days, perhaps a fortnight,
> fills me with an anxiety which will best be conceived by my Betsey's

own impatience, . . . Think of me with as much tenderness as I do of
you and we cannot fail to be always happy.[46]

If Madison had written these words, they would have been the most pro-
fuse expression of emotion of his entire life. To Hamilton, they were a
perfectly ordinary statement of his feelings on taking a trip of two weeks'
duration.

On the surface, Hamilton's interests and those of the Virginians should
have diverged. Hamilton was a personal friend and political associate of
John Jay, the New Yorker who had been negotiating the treaty with Spain
that Madison so feared.[47] Madison disliked Jay, commenting years later
that "he had two strong traits of character, suspicion and religious bigotry."[48] Yet Hamilton had bothered to come, and at his own expense.[49] He
believed the United States needed a central government, and for years
had floated the idea of a convention to reform the Articles.[50] At Annapolis, the convention to which almost no one had shown up, Madison's goals
overlapped closely with those of Hamilton.

As Madison later recalled it, Hamilton took the lead in drafting an
"address to the states" that would be the definitive statement of the non-
convention.[51] According to a possibly apocryphal story, Hamilton's first
redraft was too assertive in describing the flaws of the existing government and the need to replace it with something more powerful. Edmund
Randolph objected, and when Hamilton refused to budge, Madison told
him, "You had better yield to this man, for otherwise all Virginia will be
against you."[52] The statement does not sound much like Madison. But
the story nevertheless hints at something true about the document eventually adopted: It seemed to reflect a compromise between Hamilton's
characteristic boldness and Madison's customary restraint.

Unlike Randolph's draft, Hamilton's address no longer admitted that
the delegates had no authority. If another convention was to be called, it
was crucial not to suggest that it, too, would be invalid without full representation from all states. Instead it simply said that, faced with "so partial and defective a representation"—a polite way of describing the
washout—the commissioners present "did not conceive it advisable to
proceed on the business of their mission."[53]

If it was inadvisable for the Annapolis delegates to take action, then
why take the action of calling for a national convention? The sleight of
hand required was considerable, but Hamilton was up to the job. The

commissioners were, Hamilton wrote, "deeply impressed . . . with the magnitude and importance of the object confided to them on this occasion." Thus impressed, they could not help themselves: "Your Commissioners cannot forbear to indulge an expression of their earnest and unanimous wish that speedy measures may be taken, to effect a general meeting, of the States, in a future Convention." If the commissioners were going too far, they were prepared to apologize in advance: "If in expressing this wish, or in intimating any other sentiment, your Commissioners should seem to exceed the strict bounds of their appointment, they entertain a full confidence, that a conduct, dictated by an anxiety for the welfare of the United States, will not fail to receive an indulgent construction."[54]

The language of emotions—indulgence, anxiety, sentiment, intimation—bespoke Hamilton's distinctive style. The cumulative effect was of an eighteenth-century rake overstepping his bounds in pursuit of a potential conquest, insisting without much sincerity that she must forgive his trespass because he was acting out of love.

Then Hamilton put the proposition. When choosing delegates for the next convention, the states should charge them to deal not just with commerce and trade but with all of the faults of the Articles of Confederation. "There are important defects in the system of the federal government," Hamilton asserted, which had been implicitly "acknowledged by the acts of all those states, which have concurred in the present meeting." The commissioners would decorously "decline an enumeration of those national circumstances" that made a convention necessary. In any case everyone knew that "the situation of the United States" was "delicate and critical."[55]

Hamilton's claim was presumptuous—and cleverly subversive. In naming commissioners, the states had at most been saying that the Articles should be amended to enable coordinated trade policy. As Hamilton reframed it, the states had already shown they knew the Articles needed a total overhaul. The future convention would therefore hold "a deliberate and candid discussion" of the Articles and would "digest a plan for supplying such defects as may be discovered to exist." The goal would be to propose provisions "necessary to render the constitution of the federal government adequate to the exigencies of the Union."

Hamilton had changed the terms of the discussion. The new convention would address itself to Congress, which would approve its proposal and then send it to the states—a logical procedure, since the Articles of Confederation specified that amendments must be adopted first in Congress and then unanimously by the states. The convention would meet on the second Monday in May 1787—six months later almost to the day.

Ultimate Happiness

When Madison returned to Virginia, he learned the most pressing issue before the state legislature was still whether to issue paper money. Madison considered paper money unjust and a violation of the Virginia Constitution. By losing value, paper money effectively took property from creditors and gave it to their debtors. The state's reputation and honor would suffer.[56]

In thinking about paper money, Madison was beginning to develop a theory of minority protection. The legislature that adopted paper money was serving the interests of the majority. This was a fundamental principle of republican government—the idea that, as Madison put it in a letter to Monroe, "the interest of the majority is the political standard of right and wrong."[57]

Increasingly, Madison found himself unhappy with the consequences of the majoritarian principle. If the majority's "interest" meant its "ultimate happiness," he conceded, "the proposition is no doubt true." But most people understood "interest" to mean the "immediate augmentation of property and wealth." If interest were interpreted this way, Madison believed, "nothing can be more false" than the idea that the majority's interest ought to be followed. If this were true, "it would be the interest of the majority in every community to despoil and enslave the minority of individuals."[58] Similarly, "in a federal community," he wrote, it would often be in the immediate interest of the majority to "make a similar sacrifice of the minority of the component states."[59] For a country that had made a revolution in the name of republicanism, the danger that the majority might oppress the minority to serve its immediate interests was the single most significant political problem. Madison was grappling with a challenge that seemed to doom republicanism itself.

In the autumn of 1786, Madison did not yet have a robust answer to the problem of minority oppression. In arguing against the general assessment for religion and against paper money, he had invoked the Virginia Declaration of Rights and insisted that the proposed measure was "unconstitutional." Yet in neither instance had the argument been decisive.

In Congress, the difficulty appeared still worse. The nine-state supermajority necessary for important decisions and the unanimity for amendment safeguarded individual states. Yet the nine-vote rule hamstrung Congress's ability to get anything done, and no one could agree exactly when a decision was important enough to require unanimity. In Madison's fantasy, the federal government would be able to coerce the states to act by economic sanctions enforced by a federal navy. Yet this was hardly a recipe for protecting states' rights.

The experience of being in the minority within his state on the question of paper money, and federally with respect to the Spanish treaty, was therefore a major test for Madison's constitutional thinking. He believed in the ideal of a republic. He was certain the national government must have power over trade. He understood that unanimity and the requirement for supermajorities made collective action impossible. Now he also recognized that the majority might govern in its immediate interest rather than the "true" interest of the people. Whether these concerns might be reconciled—and if so, how—was the question on which the future of the United States rested.

Crisis and Response

The national situation in the fall of 1786 was profoundly worrisome to Madison and most other national observers. The Revolutionary War had been financed by debt. The shortage of hard currency was driving states to issue more debt, rather than dealing with what they owed. Trade, a key source of revenue, was curtailed to the east by Britain and the west by Spain. The makeshift governmental structures produced in the midst of revolution were beginning to fall apart.

Massachusetts began to crumble first. The immediate impetus for the troubles came when the merchant elite in Salem and Boston decided to exercise fiscal responsibility and retire the considerable war debt by enforcing tax collection. The farmers of western Massachusetts had fought in the Revolutionary War—and left the Continental army or the militia with their salaries unpaid. They simply did not have the currency to pay taxes. In economic terms, the Massachusetts merchants were trying to get the Revolution for free, making the farmers pay off the debts that the state government owed them for their military service.

State institutions, especially the courts, were the mechanism used to collect taxes. So when state courts began to declare forfeitures and tax collectors began to seize property, impoverished farmers turned against the courts. On August 29, 1786, a group of protesters blocked the court in Northampton, Massachusetts, from convening. They did it again in Worcester on September 5.

Worried that the movement would spread further, the governor got the Supreme Judicial Court to issue indictments against eleven alleged leaders. The move backfired. When court was next scheduled to meet in Springfield on September 29, a group of some 1,200 angry and armed men gathered in protest. The commander of the local militia raised a force of 800 to oppose them, and violence was averted—but the judges of the court got the message and withdrew without taking any action.

Word of this dramatic confrontation spread rapidly through the states. Madison got details from Henry Lee III, a former war hero and Princeton acquaintance who was now representing Virginia in Congress. Lee reported that "the eastern commotions are becoming very serious." The total population of men in Massachusetts between the ages of sixteen and sixty was 75,000, and "the five seditious counties possess 40,000 of this number." Lee was anticipating civil war. "Upon a fair calculation," he suggested, "I believe we may reckon that state divided for and against government." The federal government would not be able to help—it was "scarcely able to maintain" itself.[60]

Lee's account of the demands of the "insurgents" was especially telling. "Their ostensible object is the revision of the constitution," he wrote. "But they certainly mean the abolition of debts public and private, and division of property and a new government founded on principles of fraud and inequity, or reconnection with Great Britain."[61] The abolition of debts and division of property were ancient fears in republican governments.[62] In Lee's panicked telling, what had begun as a protest movement against the collection of unpayable taxes had become a revolution.

Lee's worries reflected the concern that the union could plausibly dissolve. Lee put it bluntly to Madison: "The present appearances portend extensive national calamity. The contagion will spread and may reach Virginia."[63] Paranoia gripped landowners, who worried that the protesters wanted to redistribute their property.[64]

To George Washington, the lesson of what was coming to be called Shays's Rebellion was clear: Constitutional reform was imperative. "Without some alteration in our political creed," he wrote to Madison, "the superstructure we have been seven years raising at the expense of much blood and treasure, must fall. We are fast verging to anarchy and confusion!"[65] The core of the problem was the weakness of the governments of the United States, both local and national: "Thirteen sovereignties pulling against each other, and all tugging at the federal hand, will soon bring ruin on the whole." What the United States needed was "a liberal and energetic constitution, well-guarded, and closely watched, to prevent encroachments."

The alternative was disaster. The country was beset by "designing disaffected and desperate characters," Washington wrote in reference to the protesters. "If there exists not a power to check them, what security has a man of life, liberty, or property?"[66] Washington, whose confidence had rarely faltered through the darkest days of the Revolutionary War, was not given to alarmism. Now he saw immediate ruin.

Receiving Washington's letter on November 8, 1786, Madison immediately sought to enlist its strong tone for his cause. He wrote back that he intended to introduce Washington's name "at the head" of nominees to represent Virginia at the Philadelphia convention.[67]

But Washington's private outrage at Shays's Rebellion did not translate into a willingness to sign on immediately for the Philadelphia convention. He took ten days to write back, offering the doubtful excuse that he had not checked the post office "with my usual regularity." He began by saying that he had, at the end of the war, "bid a public adieu to the public walks of life, and had resolved never more to tread that theater." The reputation he had earned as a modern Cincinnatus—the illustrious Roman general called from behind his plow to lead the armies of the republic—indeed rested on Washington's decision to return to his farm after the war like his ancient model. By reentering public life, Washington implied, he might lose this honor.*

---

* Washington had another concern. He had been president of the Society of the Cincinnati—a national organization of officer-veterans of the Revolutionary War that was holding a national meeting in Philadelphia on the first Monday in May, a week before the Philadelphia convention was slated to begin. Washington had told the membership that he wished not to be reelected as president and would not be at their meeting because he was ill and finished with public life. His real reason, he told Madison in confidence, was that the society was being accused of trying to create a new aristocracy by making membership hereditary. Washington thought he could not go to the convention in Philadelphia without giving offense to the Cincinnati, whom he called "a very respectable and deserving part of the community—the late officers of the American Army." Washington to Madison, November 18, 1786, *PJM,* 9:171.

Madison chose to read Washington's letter as an expression of ambivalence rather than an outright refusal, and introduced his name as the first delegate to the convention anyway. He then offered Washington a way to say yes. Perhaps, he suggested, "the acknowledged preeminence" of the Philadelphia convention "over every other public object" might "reconcile" him to attendance.[68]

Washington left himself some room for maneuver. "The present era is pregnant of great, and strange events," he told Madison in almost Shakespearean terms. Circumstances might change. "What may be brought forth between this and the first of May to remove the difficulties which at present labor in my mind . . . it is not for me to predict."[69]

Madison kept a steady pressure on Washington to attend the convention. On Christmas Eve, 1786, he expressed to Washington the "wish that at least a door could be kept open for your acceptance hereafter, in case the gathering clouds should become so dark and menacing as to supersede every consideration, but that of our national existence or safety."[70] Madison was arguing that by the time the convention met, conditions could be so dire Washington would be able to say that paramount concerns—the very existence of the nation—mandated his attendance.

On the Anvil

As 1786 came to a close, Shays's Rebellion showed no signs of abating. The Massachusetts legislature had taken a hard line, banning speech critical of the government and suspending habeas corpus. At the end of November, the state had arrested movement leaders, and one, Job Shattuck, was wounded by a sword blow in the process. The blood was the first of the confrontation. The protesters had not initially planned the sort of takeover that the nervous state leadership imagined. Now, however, with tensions rising, they began to organize and to talk as though revolutionary change was in fact their goal.[71]

In Virginia, Madison received the news with concern. He believed it "not improbable that civil blood may be shed"—and in case of war, he considered it "somewhat uncertain whether the government or its adversaries will be victorious."[72] Madison also credited continuing rumors that the protesters were "secretly stimulated by British influence."[73] The challenge was very real, he wrote: "These events are distressing beyond measure to the zealous friends of the Revolution."

To Madison, the rebellion gave further reason for constitutional re-form. Relying on the ancient metaphor of the body politic as a physical person, he argued that the government must have sufficient "vigor" so as "to be able to restore health to any diseased part of the federal body." The solution lay in Philadelphia. "An attempt to bring about such an amend-ment of the federal constitution is on the anvil," he wrote to a correspon-dent in Kentucky.[74]

From Paris, Jefferson offered a different and more benign view. The protests, he wrote to Madison, "do not appear to threaten serious conse-quences." Blocked commerce had made "money scarce" in Massachusetts, and this would inevitably "make the people uneasy."[75] But protest by the people against their government was actually healthy. "I hold it that a little rebellion now and then is a good thing," he told Madison serenely.[76]

Jefferson's view rested on his more general view of government. He allowed that he tended to think that anarchy was best, but "inconsistent with any great degree of population," and so impractical. The next best arrangement was a government in which the will of the people exercised real influence: "The mass of mankind under that enjoys a precious degree of liberty and happiness." The corresponding danger was "the turbulence to which it is subject." But this concern "becomes nothing" when "weigh[ed] against the oppressions of monarchy." Government by force was "a government of wolves over sheep."[77]

This rather casually stated theory had all the hallmarks of Jefferson's thought. It was memorably expressed, speculatively framed, and wholly unsystematic. Jefferson assumed that rebellions would turn out to be un-successful without offering any account of how or why that should be so.[78] For Madison, who respected Jefferson so deeply, such casually bril-liant formulations were a spur to the deeper, more measured analysis that characterized his own thinking.

The merchant class of Massachusetts thought as Madison and Wash-ington did, not like Jefferson. A resolution to raise federal troops for in-tervention had been introduced in Congress, but nothing had been done about it.[79] With even their own state government unable or unwilling to mobilize against the protest movement, the merchants took action on their own. Some 140 of them pooled resources and raised a private army, which marched to Worcester, Massachusetts, with a strength of 3,000 men.

In late January 1787, a rebel force attacked the armory at Springfield,

Massachusetts. It was repelled by local militia, who used two cannons to fire loose shot into the advancing rebels, killing four. The rebels retreated, and the hired army marched the fifty miles from Worcester to Springfield, scattering the suddenly ineffectual rebels before it. As it turned out, the protest movement lacked the character of an organized revolution. The whiff of grapeshot had put it down.

This outcome fit Madison's views and Jefferson's equally well. To Madison, the reversion to private force showed that state government on its own could not manage internal crisis—and that Congress under the Articles of Confederation lacked the express authority to interfere "in the internal controversies of a state."[80] Madison reported to Washington "that a calm has been restored" by the show of force. But "precautions" proposed by the state legislature—particularly a plan for a quasi-permanent militia force of 1,000 to 1,500 men—indicated that the Massachusetts leadership feared the rebellion could recur. A general amnesty had been offered, and yet "at least half of the insurgents decline accepting the terms." This amounted to "defiance of the law against treason." Former rebels were even being elected to local office.[81] The dangers posed by the rebellion had not disappeared.

To Jefferson, the mildness of Shays's Rebellion was proof that it had never been serious in the first place. "Calculate," he urged Madison, "that one rebellion in 13 states in the course of 11 years, is but one for each state in a century and a half." The rarity of uprisings in the United States was a function of their weak governments, in which the will of the people could be expressed. The stronger the government, the more the rebellion, Jefferson argued. The Ottoman Empire was "despotic," he claimed, yet "insurrections are the events of every day." France, for the moment still an absolute monarchy, had experienced "three insurrections in the three years I have been here." England was a bit more moderate, and as a result rebellions "happen every half dozen years" there.[82]

In contrast to these uprisings, Shays's Rebellion was evidence of the benefits of self-government. "Compare again the ferocious depredations of their insurgents with the order, the moderation and the almost self extinguishment of ours." Shays's Rebellion had indeed almost self-extinguished. But Jefferson ultimately would have accepted a different outcome if the public had supported the rebels. "After all," he wrote Madison, "it is my principle that the will of the majority should always prevail."

Madison disagreed. If the majority looked only to its immediate interests, it should not prevail. And for Madison, the public's pressing desire for inflationary policy to abrogate its debts was a perfect example of the false, temporary majority. Government must be strong enough to check this kind of majority rule, not give in to it.

Deadly Blow

Madison had now been out of Congress for three years, allowing him to be reelected under Virginia's rules. He slogged his way to New York in early February, the last part of the journey "with a northeastern snowstorm incessantly in our teeth."[83] On arrival, he observed that "a great disagreement of opinion exists as to the expediency of the recommendation from Congress" for a Philadelphia convention.[84] Some states disliked the idea of the convention "because it is an extraconstitutional measure," never contemplated in the Articles of Confederation and not within the powers of Congress to call.[85] Others disagreed. Political confusion was the order of the day.

Yet Congress reached enough consensus to pass a resolution formally calling for a convention. This event was momentous—and the congressmen knew it.[86] "It appeared from the debates and still more from the conversation among the members that many of them consider this resolution as a deadly blow to the existing Confederation," Madison wrote in his private notes. Others saw it "as the harbinger of a better confederation." But "all agreed and owned," Madison insisted to himself, "that the federal government in its existing shape was inefficient and could not last long."[87]

Virginia had named delegates, including Madison, to the convention the preceding fall. North Carolina, Delaware, Pennsylvania, and New Jersey had chosen delegations by February. Gradually, over the course of the spring, other states appointed delegates, too. Madison watched the process intently. He had hopes for South Carolina, Maryland, and Georgia. "New York has not yet decided on the point," he noted, but might still make appointments. Connecticut "has a great aversion to conventions," yet Madison insisted that "her concurrence nevertheless is not despaired of." Massachusetts had not been "well inclined" before, but now, in the aftermath of the rebellion, was expected to send a delegation. Finally, "Rhode Island can be relied on for nothing that is good." Madison's contempt for Rhode Island was tempered by his belief that "on all great points [Rhode Island] must sooner or later bend to Massachusetts and Connecticut."[88]

While in Congress until April, Madison sought to "gather the general sentiments of leading characters touching our affairs and prospects"—to form, as he told Washington, a plan for the convention. He was, he wrote, "inclined to hope" that the national leaders "will gradually be concentered in the plan of a thorough reform of the existing system."[89]

Madison's attitude about the content of such a reform plan was modestly optimistic. There were, he told George Washington, "those who may lean towards a monarchical government." But, he added, such people "I suspect are swayed by very indigested ideas."[90] The ideas were undigested because they were a product of recent events, namely the panic caused by Shays's Rebellion.[91] Madison believed—or at least wanted Washington to believe—that even someone with a preference for a strong executive would agree to a strengthened republican government, because consensus in favor of a quasi-monarchic one could not be achieved.

As for "those who remain attached" to republicanism—primarily those "from the southern and middle states"[92]—they "must soon perceive that it cannot be preserved at all under any modification which does not redress the ills experienced from our present establishments." Republicans would support thorough constitutional reform, Madison believed, because they had nowhere else to go.

Madison's certainty of imminent collapse had a strong basis in fact. Congress was broke. It had issued a call for revenue to pay the expenses and debts of the United States, and in response only one state, Virginia, had "made any provision at all" for taxes in support of Congress. Even that provision, urged by Madison while still in the state legislature, was a partial one.[93] "No money comes into the federal treasury," Madison wrote to his friend Edmund Randolph. "No respect is paid to the federal authority; and people of reflection unanimously agree that the existing confederacy is tottering to its foundation." If the existing confederation could not be amended, he told Randolph, the result would be the restoration of a monarchy or the "partition of the states into two or more confederacies."[94] Either way, the new American republic was on the brink of dissolution.

Randolph took these concerns seriously. Chosen as a Virginia delegate, he was committed to attending the convention in Philadelphia, notwithstanding what he called "the terror on" his "spirits" raised in his mind by the prospect of being away from home while his wife was expecting a child. (In the end, the baby was born in April.)[95] Now that Madison was in New York, Randolph also took the lead in trying to convince Washington to attend as well. He wrote to Madison of his plan to "press in warmest terms our friend at Mount Vernon to assent to join us."[96] He would, he said, pressure Washington "again and again; but I fear ineffectually."[97] To Washington, Randolph consistently made the argument of necessity. "Every day brings forth some new crisis," he wrote, "and the confederation is, I fear, the last anchor of our hope." Congress, he told Washington, might well not exist by the end of the year.[98]

By the end of March, Washington was showing signs of relenting. In response to Randolph's letter, he replied that "as my friends, with a degree of solicitude which is unusual, seem to wish my attendance on this occasion, I have come to a resolution to go if my health will permit." The proviso about his health still left him a way out. He had been, Washington added, "so much afflicted with a rheumatic complaint in my shoulder that at times I am hardly able to raise my hand to my head, or turn myself in bed."[99] Randolph acknowledged Washington's health concerns, yet would not let them serve as an excuse. "Indeed, my dear sir," he wrote to Washington, "every thing travels so fast to confusion, that I trust one grand effort will be made by the friends of the United States." A grand effort would not be grand unless it included Washington. Come May 14, Randolph wrote, "it is my purpose to take you by the hand" into the convention.[100]

Washington's slow, stepwise movement toward possible attendance was a good sign. But another prominent Virginian was heading the opposite way. Randolph wrote to Madison that Patrick Henry was hostile to "the objects of the convention." Although Henry had not been one of the original delegates named by the assembly, Randolph had still hoped to add him. Randolph told Madison that he had "assayed every means to prevail on him to go" to Philadelphia, without luck. Madison thought Henry's refusal to go to Philadelphia was "ominous," he wrote back to Randolph.[101] If Henry attended the convention, he would be more likely to approve whatever it did—which is exactly why Randolph and Madison wanted him there in the first place. By staying out, he could become the key figure in ratifying or rejecting whatever proposals the convention made.

Henry had substantive objections to amending the Articles and achieving a closer and more effective union. Chief among them was his opposition to the potential treaty with Spain conceding control of the Mississippi. Simply blocking the treaty in Congress, as Virginia thus far had done, would not be enough to win Henry over, Randolph told Madison. There would have to be "a negative with some emphasis" to remove Henry's suspicion of closer union with the eastern states.[102] Nor was Henry alone in his disgust. "The tendency of this project," Madison wrote, was "to foment distrust among the Atlantic states at a crisis when harmony and confidence ought to have been studiously cherished."[103]

In the hopes of blocking the treaty and thus encouraging support for constitutional reform, Madison took an unusual step on his own. On March 13, 1787, in the company of Pennsylvania congressman William Bingham, who also opposed the treaty, Madison went to meet with Don Diego de Gardoqui, the Spanish ambassador to the United States—the man with whom secretary of foreign affairs John Jay had been negotiating the terms of the treaty. Jay, not Madison, was empowered by Congress to conduct foreign affairs and negotiate treaties. By meeting with Gardoqui, Madison was trying to counter the diplomacy being pursued by the national government.

Madison kept careful, almost verbatim notes of the meeting—and they are important for what they reveal about his foreign policy learning process.[104] In his first diplomatic exchange, Madison held nothing back. He told Gardoqui that even if Congress agreed to a treaty ceding the right to navigate the Mississippi, "it would be out of their power to enforce" it. He predicted that the reaction would increase the population west of the Alleghenies. The westerners would then unite with Britain, secede from the United States, and turn against Spain's possessions in America, now with the leverage of the British fleet behind them. Meanwhile, Madison complained, the so-called concessions that Spain was offering to the United States in exchange for giving up any claims to navigate the Mississippi were nothing special. All Spain was offering was commercial access that it already granted "to all other nations from motives of interest."[105]

As a diplomatic approach, this was (to be kind) amateurish. Madison was combining two arguments, each flawed in its own way. He was purporting to tell the Spanish ambassador that the treaty was not in Spain's interests—an implausible, ludicrous argument. And he was petulantly insisting that Spain was not offering enough in exchange for a deal that was not supposed to be in its interests in the first place. In fact, a U.S. concession regarding the Mississippi might or might not be enforceable in the long run. But the treaty cost Spain nothing at all, since it could just as easily have allowed U.S. access to Spanish ports without getting anything in return.

Gardoqui responded with a lesson in diplomacy. He began with the fundamental basis for the Spanish position: The United States could not have any right to navigate the Mississippi, because Spain owned both sides of the river where it reached the sea in New Orleans. "Spain never would give up this point," he explained. Then Gardoqui "lamented" that he had been in the United States so long "without effecting anything," foreseeing "that the consequences would be very disagreeable." Madison and Bingham rather crudely asked him what consequences he had in mind. Gardoqui diplomatically "evaded an answer by repeating general expressions." He added pointedly that "Spain would act according to her own ideas. She would not be governed by other people's ideas of her interest."[106]

Things had gone badly for Madison and Bingham to this point. Madison made them worse by offering a series of legal arguments for an American right of access to the Mississippi, claiming among other things that in 1608 Spain had demanded that the Dutch give its ships navigational access to the Scheldt River. Gardoqui made it clear that he did not understand these legal arguments, knew nothing of Spanish claims 150 years previously, and could not have cared less about them if he had. The meeting had a central purpose to Gardoqui, and he had the last word to make sure Madison knew it. "When we rose to take leave," Madison wrote in his notes, "he begged us to remember what he had said as to the inflexibility of Spain on the point of the Mississippi and the consequences to America of adherence to her present pretensions."[107] Madison's first foray into diplomacy ended as it began: with Gardoqui in full control of the field.[108]

Madison did salvage something from the meeting. It revealed to him that the negotiations between Gardoqui and Jay were at a standstill, or, as he put it dramatically to Jefferson, "the Spanish project sleeps." It might seem strange, he wrote to Jefferson, that he learned this information directly from the Spanish ambassador rather than from his own foreign secretary. "Yet such is the footing on which the intemperance of party has put the matter that it rests wholly with Mr. Jay how far he will communicate with Congress as well as how far he will negotiate with Gardoqui." Blaming Jay for hiding the state of negotiations from Congress was rather backhanded considering that Madison had met with Gardoqui without informing Jay. But Madison clearly believed that "the intemperance of party"—namely, the distrust between supporters of Jay's proposed treaty and its opponents—justified his efforts.[109]

Indeed, the whole question of who was supposed to conduct foreign policy, Congress or the states, was not perfectly clear under the Articles. As Madison also reported to Jefferson, Virginia had unilaterally voted in its legislative session to reduce import duties on French wine imported on French ships. Jay objected in Congress that "the states have no right to form tacit compacts with foreign nations." As far as he was concerned, Virginia was pursuing its own pro-French foreign policy, thereby jeopardizing the relationship between Britain and the United States.[110] Congress adopted resolutions declaring that the peace treaty between Britain and the United States must have the force of law and must not be contradicted by any state. But this only proved that Congress wanted the peace treaty to be superior to state law—not that it actually was.[111]

To Madison, there was little doubt that a congressional pronouncement could invalidate existing state laws. Yet to determine whether Congress could preemptively invalidate future state laws, "it would be necessary to examine the foundation of the federal authority, and to determine whether it had the validity of a constitution, paramount to the legislative authority in each state."[112] Madison was saying that Congress could only preempt future state laws if its authority was higher than that of the state legislatures.

The Articles of Confederation were not, in themselves, a constitution: Some states had sanctioned the Articles in their state constitutions, while others had merely agreed to the Articles in an ordinary legislative enactment.[113] But if the Articles were incorporated into all the state constitutions, Congress could be treated as having authority over future state laws via the states' own commitments to it. A constitution was, on this logic, a form of higher law, able to trump whatever laws states might enact.

This enormously complicated analysis, which Madison reported in detail in his own notes, provides a window into Madison's mind in the months before the Philadelphia convention. He was trying very hard to figure out the relationship between federal authority and the constitutional authority of the states. Under the Articles, this relationship was so unclear as to be impossible to ascertain. Reform was needed not only to coordinate national trade policy and put down local rebellions, but to arrange the legal affairs of the United States sensibly. The states would have to take definitive action to enshrine whatever proposal the Philadelphia convention devised. If they did not, the new constitution would rest on foundations as shaky as the Articles of Confederation, and independence would have been achieved in vain.

Monarchical Government

By the end of March, Madison and the others in the Virginia congressional delegation could report to Governor Edmund Randolph that "the appointments for the convention go on auspiciously." Nine states had appointed delegates. Of those that remained, they believed, Maryland was certain to send delegates, and Connecticut and Rhode Island were expected "to follow the example of their neighbors."[114]

The time had now come to start planning the Philadelphia convention concretely. Randolph wrote to Madison suggesting that new proposals be "grafted on the old confederation." By supplementing the Articles of Confederation, the delegates in Philadelphia could propose "what is best in itself, not merely what can be obtained from the assemblies" in the states. Then, by framing the proposals so "as to permit a state to reject one part, without mutilating the whole," the delegates could send their proposals to the states, accepting as the outcome whatever provisions all the states agreed to adopt.[115]

Although his approach was cautious, Randolph nonetheless favored taking the initiative. "Ought not some general propositions to be prepared for feeling the pulse of the convention on the subject at large?" he asked Madison. "Ought not an address to accompany the new constitution?"[116] This was an open invitation to Madison to get to work on a plan. Randolph was, he said, "hourly interrupted" by his duties as governor. Madison had more time to himself and could take on the task.

Washington, too, was thinking seriously about the convention. He wrote to Madison that "those who lean to a monarchical government, have . . . not considered the public mind." Washington noted with some surprise that southerners did not favor a strong executive. "One would have expected" the birth and "rapid growth" of such hierarchical ideas in the southern states, where "habitual distinctions . . . have always existed among the people," he wrote. Instead, the tendency to monarchical ideas was coming from eastern states traditionally possessed of "leveling principles." The former New England impulse to less hierarchical government had been "entirely eradicated" by Shays's Rebellion.[117]

Washington's own view on "monarchical government" he expressed cautiously. "I am also clear," he wrote to Madison, "that even admitting the utility—nay the necessity of the form—yet that the period is not arrived for adopting the change without shaking the peace of this country to its foundation."[118] Saying that the time was not right for a return to monarchical government hinted that Washington was open to such a development at some future time. If Congress "fritter[ed]" its powers, "then, and not till then, in my opinion" could monarchy "be attempted without involving all the evils of civil discord."[119]

The explanation for Washington's sympathy to the possibility of monarchy lay in his reduced confidence in the public. "I confess . . . that my opinion of public virtue is so far changed," he wrote to Madison in his unencoded letter, "that I have my doubts whether any system without the means of coercion in the sovereign, will enforce obedience to the ordinances of the general government." In the light of national experience under the Articles, the sovereign—by which Washington clearly meant a king, not the people—must have the power to enforce the laws. Without obedience, he concluded, "everything else fails."[120] Madison had written to Jefferson a couple of weeks earlier that the national crisis had "tainted the faith of the most orthodox Republicans."[121] Washington was a case in point.

Madison took note. For the first time, he expressed some concern about whether Washington should actually attend the whole convention. On April 15, 1787, Madison wrote to Randolph proposing that Washington should be advised "to postpone his actual attendance until some judgment can be formed of the result of the meeting."[122]

Madison and Randolph had been laboring for five months to convince Washington to come. Yet Madison offered only a weak explanation for this proposal that would almost reverse what they had accomplished, telling Randolph that Washington's friends would not wish "that he should participate in any abortive undertaking." Madison added that, by appointing Benjamin Franklin to its delegation, Pennsylvania had created the opportunity for "putting sufficient dignity into the chair" by having

Franklin, not Washington, preside.[123] Franklin was known to believe in a weak executive made up of several members. Washington, lauded globally for not seeking a crown after the Revolution, had been so affected by Shays's Rebellion and the states' unwillingness to help the federal government that he was flirting with monarchism. Far from wanting to preserve Washington's dignity, Madison now preferred to have the inveterate republican Franklin chair the convention.

Vices

As for his own preparation, Madison as usual proceeded systematically. In April, serving in Congress, he had written an essay on what he called the "vices" of the political system of the United States. It turned the same exacting lens on the United States that he had focused a year earlier on the vices of other ancient and modern republics.

What he found was devastating. In twelve numbered points, Madison painted a picture of a confederacy too weak to accomplish anything. First and most significant, he noted that the states did not comply with perfectly "constitutional" requisitions for funds set by Congress. This problem had been "so fully experienced both during the war and since the peace" that it could not be doubted by anyone. The same problem of member noncompliance could be seen "in every similar confederacy"— and it was "fatal" to its object.[124] Indeed, Madison wrote, because Congress under the articles had no ability to sanction violation of its laws or coerce states, the system lacked "the great vital principles of a political constitution." The United States under the Articles was "in fact nothing more than a treaty of amity of commerce and of alliance, between so many independent and sovereign states."[125]

How had the drafters of the Articles failed to anticipate that the states would ignore Congress? Madison offered a simple answer. The drafters had suffered from "a mistaken confidence" in the "justice, the good faith, the honor, [and] the sound policy" of the state legislatures, imagining they would put aside self-interest. Such confidence, he wrote, "does honor to the enthusiastic virtue of the compilers."[126]

But reality had shown that virtue had nothing to do with it. All laws adopted at the national level would affect different member states differently. Individual states would think of "their own interests and rights," not those of the United States as a whole. Each state would imagine the others likely to defect from a general agreement, and the result was a complete breakdown.[127]

The rest of the problems were no less serious. The Articles of Confederation had a different legal status from place to place, so that when state laws contradicted congressional pronouncements, it was not clear which controlled.[128] The country had no unified foreign policy. States were violating international treaties as well as the "rights" of other states, for example by favoring trade from some states over others and treating imports from other states the same way they did foreign imports.[129] There was no national trade policy and no realistic possibility of collective action to create one.[130]

And the confederacy did not protect the states, as Shays's Rebellion demonstrated. According to "republican theory," Madison wrote, the majority was supposed to exercise both the right to rule and the actual power to do it. But in reality, a minority with military organization could conquer a majority. One-third of the population could defeat the other two-thirds. Madison added a distinctive southern concern to the lesson he was drawing from Massachusetts: "Where slavery exists the republican theory becomes still more fallacious." In slave states, the rulers might not even be a majority. The federal government should be empowered to protect the majority of citizens in a free state—and if necessary, the white minority in a slave state.[131]

By the spring of 1787, Madison also had a dim view of state legislatures. They had passed too many laws, "a nuisance of the most pestilent kind." The laws, he believed, should be one-tenth as long, in which case they would be ten times more useful.[132] They were unjust, favoring the temporary interests of the majority over the long-term interests of the whole. This was a challenge to "the fundamental principle of republican government, that the majority who rule in such governments, are the safest guardians of the public good and private rights." Nothing could be more basic to the future of the United States as a republic. If justice could not be assured under conditions of majority rule, then Washington's instincts were correct, and the country would have to revert to monarchy.

Madison divided the challenges to majority rule into the threat from the elected legislature and from the people themselves. There were, he said, three reasons to serve in a legislature: ambition, personal interest, and public good. Election was supposed to weed out those motivated by self-interest, but self-interested legislators could mask "base and selfish measures . . . by pretexts of public good and apparent expediency." And they could do it again and again. Similarly, the "honest but unenlightened representative" could easily become "the dupe of a favorite leader, veiling his selfish views under the professions of public good."[133]

This was a devastating criticism of the elected legislature, but it was nothing compared to Madison's profound critique of republican government derived from "the people themselves." He formalized the concerns he had first raised in his letter to Monroe. "All civilized societies," he wrote, "are divided into different interests and factions." The divisions included "creditors or debtors—rich or poor—husbandmen, merchants and manufacturers—members of different religious sects—followers of different political leaders—inhabitants of different districts—owners of different kinds of property etc. etc." According to republican principles, the majority, "however composed" at a particular moment of legislation, would make the law. This led to a basic problem: "Whenever therefore an apparent interest or common passion unites the majority what is to restrain them from unjust violations of the rights and interests of the minority, or of individuals?"[134]

Madison was suggesting—in the form of a novel, general rule about politics[135]—that republicanism itself might have a fatal flaw. Given that there were multiple interests in society, there would be a constant pressure for those temporarily in the majority to violate the rights of those in the minority. If that was true, republicanism would inevitably produce injustice. Its premise—that majority rule was a good system that would preserve rights—was simply naïve. And if that was true, nothing could save the United States except abandoning the republican form of government.

Enlargement

There were three motives that might restrain the majority from oppressing the minority, Madison suggested. All were sadly inadequate. The majority might know "their own good"; but it was "found by experience to be too often unheeded."[136] The majority might be concerned about their reputations; but this would not work at the level of the majority taken as a whole. Reputation depended on "public opinion"—and within a particular society, public opinion was simply the opinion of the majority. Thus, "the standard is fixed by those whose conduct is to be measured by it."[137] Religion might in theory motivate self-restraint, but "when indeed religion is kindled into enthusiasm, its force like that of other passions, is increased by the sympathy of the multitude." Even when there was no religious fervor in the community, "religion in its coolest state, is not infallible, [and] it may become a motive to oppression as well as a restraint from injustice."[138] Republicanism seemed condemned by experience, if not by logic.

Here, in the most important passage of his essay on vices, Madison took the first steps toward the solution that would become the cornerstone of his constitutional thought. He imagined three people who formed a little society in which any two of them could make a decision affecting the third. "Will the latter be secure?" he asked rhetorically. The answer was no: "The prudence of every man would shun the danger." Two thousand people would be just as likely "to encroach on the rights of one thousand."

But, Madison now for the first time[139] suggested, "an enlargement of the sphere" might be "found to lessen the insecurity of private rights." Bigger was better—or at least might be. It had been a commonplace of the theory of republics that they could exist only on a small scale, in which every citizen could vote for himself or alternatively elect officials who would be close to the people he represented. Building on a conjecture made by the Scottish enlightenment thinker David Hume, Madison was turning the received view on its head.[140]

Why would a larger republic be any less susceptible to the problem of majority violation of minority rights than in the small republic? The answer was that "a common interest or passion is less apt to be felt and the requisite combinations less easy to be formed by a great than by a small number." In the larger community, he wrote, "the society becomes broken into a greater variety of interests, of pursuits, of passions, which check each other, whilst those who may feel a common sentiment have less opportunity of communication and concert."[141]

Here in its essence was the radical, original claim about expansion that Madison would develop and expand over the next several years. It had at least three elements.

First, Madison was arguing that the bigger the political society, the more different political, economic, and religious interests would exist within it. This was not self-evidently true: The creditor-debtor relationship, for example, might have just two basic components no matter how many creditors or debtors were aggregated. It might possibly be true of religious sects, at least in the United States and especially among Protestants; but in other places, whole nations might be Catholic, or all belong to a single Protestant denomination.

Second, Madison was suggesting that divergent interests would "check each other," that is, that different minority interests would actively block one another from controlling policy. He did not explain precisely how this checking process would work. But the implication was that none would want the others to be in control. So long as none of the interests could command an actual majority, the proposition could potentially be valid.

Third, Madison was arguing that common interests would have more difficulty organizing in a larger republic. In the United States of 1787, more space meant slower communication. But this was also a counterintuitive argument in favor of expanding the republican structure from the state level to the federal. It would ordinarily have been counted as a significant disadvantage in a republic that people could not easily communicate or organize within it. And it was far from clear that the difficulties posed by distance would serve the interests of minorities, rather than of the majority. Members of a potentially oppressive majority might well be more effective at organizing nationally than members of minority groups.

Madison's claim, then, was not obviously correct—far from it. But it led him to a highly original conclusion about what should be done to make republican government work. "The great desideratum in government," he wrote, "is such a modification of the sovereignty as will render it sufficiently neutral between the different interests and factions, to control one part of the society from invading the rights of another."[142]

This was a "desideratum" that had not yet been accomplished by politics or those who studied it, including Hume—and Madison was self-consciously breaking new ground by proposing a way to achieve it. The idea was to modify the very seat of power so that the sovereign government would not be controlled by any interest in particular and the majority would not violate the rights of the minority. The goal was protection. The mechanism was government neutrality as between interests, factions, and parties.

"At the same time," Madison added, there was one further precaution that must be taken. The government must also be "sufficiently controlled itself, from setting up an interest adverse to that of the whole society."[143] A government that was neutral between different interests could easily become self-interested. "In absolute monarchies," Madison observed, "the prince is sufficiently neutral towards his subjects, but frequently sacrifices their happiness to his ambition or his avarice." Monarchy solved the problem of majority oppression by denying the majority ultimate power. Yet at the same time it made the king into a potential oppressor, because he himself was not checked or balanced.[144]

Here Madison offered a wisp of precedent for his idea of the extended republic: "As a limited monarchy tempers the evils of an absolute one; so an extensive republic meliorates the administration of a small republic." Monarchy had been tweaked and improved in Britain by limiting the powers of the king through a parliament and guarantees of rights. Republicanism, he was proposing, could now be tweaked and improved by limiting the powers of the majority. The comparison was intriguing. But it also raised a deeper question, one that Madison chose to ignore: If a limited monarchy offered neutrality as between factions while controlling the monarch's tendency to absolutism, why not adopt limited monarchy instead of extended republicanism?

Madison closed his private reflections with a final objective. By modifying "the process of elections" that presently existed, Madison hoped to "extract from the mass of the society the purest and noblest characters which it contains." These leaders would "feel most strongly the proper motives" of good government, and would also be "the most capable to devise the proper means of attaining it."[145]

Writing for himself, Madison made no effort to hide his belief that there was a natural elite who would govern not out of self-interest but on behalf of the general good. The democratic process did not automatically choose the members of that elite, however. They had to be "extract[ed] from the mass of the society" by some more precise and effective means than the ordinary elections that took place in the states.[146] Madison did not argue that it was possible to change the motives of already elected representatives. Rather, the solution, if any existed, must lie in choosing those of character and relying on them to govern.

Madison's two desiderata had in common the aspiration to neutrality, self-restraint, and virtue. When it came to the problem of majority interests, his goal was to make the sovereign neutral, and he conjectured that expansion might make it harder to oppress minorities. When it came to selecting representatives, his goal again was a neutral, publicly interested government, and he hoped to find a method of election that would choose pure and noble men to bring it about. Madison's desired ends were wholly idealistic. The means he proposed to use were guardedly more realistic—and still undeveloped. Having stated his goals, Madison now needed a plan to achieve them.

The Plan

Madison's essay on the vices of the United States was designed to clarify the problems of republicanism and describe what fixes were needed. In a series of letters to Jefferson, Edmund Randolph, and Washington, Madison laid out what was becoming his plan of action for Philadelphia—and the practical challenges of getting it adopted.

The letter to Jefferson was the most general and systematic, and also the least detailed. Jefferson could be expected to be sympathetic to the effort to save republicanism, but skeptical of any efforts to compromise along the way. Still in Paris as ambassador, Jefferson would not attend the convention; his support was personally important to Madison, but not politically so. It is therefore noteworthy that Madison stressed his core idea of a national "negative," or veto power, that would allow Congress to reverse any state law, thus blocking the tyranny of local majorities. Madison had to suspect that Jefferson would not like the idea of a new national body with the capacity to control the people's representatives in the states. Yet his respect for Jefferson—and his confidence in the originality and power of his new idea—led him to present his views frankly.

"Over and above the positive power of regulating trade and sundry other matters in which uniformity is proper," he wrote, he intended "to arm the federal head with a negative *in all cases whatsoever* on the local legislatures."[147] This "negative" would make Congress truly supreme, but Madison believed the "defensive" power to negate state laws was utterly necessary. "Experience and reflection have satisfied me," he wrote, that without it, "however ample the federal powers may be made, or however clearly their boundaries may be delineated on paper, they will be easily and continually baffled by the legislative sovereignties of the states." Congress must either dominate the states or be dominated by them.[148]

A federal veto that could be effectuated by delegates of Congress located in the states, and ratified by the whole Congress later, amounted to a massive transformation of the system of government as it existed under the Articles. Madison was reaching for the stars. His goal was, he said, "not only to guard the national rights and interests against invasion, but also to restrain states from thwarting and molesting each other."[149] And he told Jefferson that a national veto would stop state majorities "from oppressing the minority within themselves by paper money and other unrighteous measures which favor the interest of the majority." For Madison, the protection of "minority" creditors and property holders was now as strong a motive for the federal negative as uniformity—perhaps stronger.

Madison offered a further structural innovation. He proposed "to change the principle of representation in the federal system" so that different states would not all have the same number of votes in Congress. It was one thing for a weak Congress, dependent on the state legislatures, to rest on a system where large and small states had the same say. But since Madison's proposal was meant to give Congress the ability to be "efficient without the intervention of the legislatures," it would make no sense if a vote "from Delaware would be of equal value with one from Massachusetts or Virginia." A Congress with real power would have to reflect the actual distribution of population and power among the states. "This change," he wrote to Jefferson, "is therefore just."[150]

As Madison knew, however, when it came to constitutional reform, justice had little to do with it. Madison predicted to Jefferson that the proposal would also "be practicable." He expected that the eastern states would like the idea of proportional representation in Congress because they were at present more populous, and that the southern states would like it because they expected to be more populous in the future. As for the small states, Madison was dismissive: "If a majority of the larger states concur, the fewer and smaller states must finally bend to them."[151]

Madison closed his description of his plan to Jefferson with a general idea "to organize the federal powers in . . . separate departments." Congress already exercised powers that were "frequently mismanaged from the want of such a distribution of them." A federal government with real authority needed separation of powers even more.

Writing to Randolph three weeks later, Madison revealed his strategy. Where Randolph had proposed grafting new proposals onto the Articles, Madison proposed starting from scratch. "I am not sure that it will be practicable to present the several parts of the reform in so detached a manner to the states," he gently explained. Some states might ratify all the proposed amendments as a package, while others would ratify only a subset. His real reason for rejecting piecemeal ratification was that "in truth" his "ideas of reform strike so deeply at the old confederation, and lead to such a systematic change, that they scarcely admit of the expedient."[152]

Madison then described exactly what his deep reform ought to accomplish. "I hold it for a fundamental point," he wrote, "that an individual independence of the states, is utterly irreconcilable with the idea of an aggregate sovereignty." Madison had not said so to Jefferson in as many words, probably to avoid upsetting him. But Madison wanted nothing less than to abolish the states as individually independent sovereigns; and he did not think Randolph would balk as Jefferson might have done. It was not, he clarified, that he wanted to consolidate the states "into one simple republic," a goal that would be "unattainable" as well as "inexpedient." Instead what he wanted was a "middle ground" that would "support a due supremacy of the national authority" while also "leav[ing] in force the local authorities so far as they can be subordinately useful."[153]

Under the Articles, the states were sovereign and supreme, while Congress was subordinate. Under Madison's allegedly "middle" way, the federal government would be sovereign and supreme, and the states would become subordinate. Their existence would be tolerated only insofar as they would be "useful."

To Randolph, Madison admitted, as he had not to Jefferson, where he got the idea of a federal negative: from the British king, who had given charters to the colonies and retained the right to veto any legislation they might pass.[154] He proposed extending "national supremacy . . . to the judiciary department," and creating "some national tribunals"—he used the plural—to hear cases involving foreigners or inhabitants of other states.[155]

He was also much more explicit than he had been to Jefferson about the distribution of powers. The legislature should be divided into two houses, one elected by either the state legislatures "or the people at large," the other "consist[ing] of a more select number, holding their appointments for longer terms and going out in rotation." The federal negative would belong to the second, more select chamber. It might be worth adding a "council of revision," a kind of supervisory body that would review the laws and include "the great ministerial officers."[156]

Madison stated expressly that "a national executive will also be necessary." He insisted that he had "scarcely ventured to form my own opinion yet of the manner in which it ought to be constituted or of the authorities with which it ought [to be] clothed."[157] If this was true, it was because Madison did not have a sweeping view of what the executive should be able to do on its own. The possible council of revision, coupled with the fact that the national veto would lie with the legislature, suggest that Madison had a rather modest executive in mind.

Having laid out his plan, Madison found himself confronted by its vast ambition. "I am afraid," he wrote to Randolph, "you will think this project, if not extravagant, absolutely unattainable and unworthy of being attempted."[158] Trying to reassure Randolph, and probably also himself, Madison repeated what he had rather hopefully told Jefferson: The changes would be welcomed by populous northern states as well as potentially populous southern states; and the small states must "ultimately yield to the predominant will." The only alternatives to republican reform were disastrous: "A much more objectionable form may be obtruded"—he meant monarchy—or the American "empire" would be partitioned "into rival and hostile confederacies."[159]

To Washington, Madison sent a nearly verbatim copy of what he had proposed to Randolph, a sign that his thinking was coalescing into a concrete plan. In the middle of it, in direct response to Washington's hinted preference for monarchy, Madison inserted a justification for the national negative that was drawn from his essay on the vices of the Articles. "The greatest desideratum which has not yet been found for republican governments," he wrote, "seems to be some disinterested and dispassionate umpire in disputes between different passions and interests in the state." A king might be "neutral to the interests and views of different parties," as Washington had suggested. "But unfortunately he too often forms interests of his own repugnant to those of the whole."[160]

The solution was the federal negative, which Madison named the "national prerogative," after the royal "prerogative" familiar from British constitutional terminology. The veto might "be sufficiently disinterested for the decision of local questions of policy, whilst it would itself be sufficiently restrained from the pursuit of interests adverse to those of the whole society."[161] The negative was the centerpiece of Madison's constitutional plan because it represented, he believed, his original answer to the as-yet-unsolved core problem of republicanism. A central legislature, or at least the upper house of such a legislature, would not oppress minorities the way local majorities would.

There was a final component in Madison's letter to Washington that had not appeared in his letter to Randolph. It related to Washington's expertise: the use of military force. "The right of coercion should be expressly declared," he wrote. Coercion could be accomplished by blockade: "With the resources of commerce in hand, the national administration might always find a means of exerting it either by sea or land."[162] This was the same idea Madison had considered years earlier of compelling the states to obey Congress by blocking their trade routes.

Now, however, Madison accepted that this model might be hard to achieve: "The difficulty and awkwardness of operating by force on the collective will of the states, render it particularly desirable that the necessity of it might be precluded." He offered his new idea of the federal negative as a possible peaceful solution: "Perhaps the negative on the laws might create such a mutuality of dependence between the general and particular authorities, as to answer the purpose."[163] Madison, however, seemed to realize that this was putting the cart before the horse. A state unwilling to listen to the federal government would not be likely to obey a federal veto of one of its laws. He added another possibility: "or perhaps some defined object of taxation might be submitted along with commerce, to the general authority." But again, a federal taxing power would likely be ignored by a state already committed to ignoring its obligations under federal law.

In the end, Madison acknowledged, federal coercion might well have to take the form of military force. His bold, ambitious plan would move sovereign power from the state governments to a new national government that could force the states to obey. The result, if adopted as he intended, would utterly transform the structure of the United States.

CHAPTER FOUR

Philadelphia

...

THE ARGUMENT: *With the future of the republic in the balance, the convention opens with Madison's blueprint for national government introduced by his close friend Randolph. Enlargement is supposed to create a government free of faction, with the authority to protect against the tyranny of the majority by negating state laws. The plan is Madison's grand theory, running parallel to his vision of political friendship.*

But the plan runs into trouble. First the national veto, the payoff of enlargement for Madison, gets watered down. Then, more dramatically, the small states balk at proportional representation in both houses of the legislature. They refuse to continue, and introduce the New Jersey plan as a stalking horse for negotiation. The convention is not proceeding as Madison intended.

JAMES MADISON ARRIVED IN PHILADELPHIA on May 3, 1787. Untroubled by any memory he may have had of his romance with Kitty Floyd, he immediately took up residence in Mrs. House's boarding establishment.[1]

Madison encouraged the other members of the Virginia delegation, including Washington, to join him at Mrs. House's, and several did.[2] Edmund Randolph started there but soon moved to more spacious rooms in a house nearby so that his wife and their new baby could join him. Washington preferred Robert Morris's elegant brick mansion. Conscious as ever of his dignity, the general entered town with an escort of Philadelphia Light Horse cavalry.[3]

The ceremony of Washington's arrival did not mean the convention was ready to start as scheduled. There was no quorum when the Virginia delegation met the Pennsylvania delegation on Monday, May 14, in the

Pennsylvania State House. For the next eleven days, no official business was transacted.

Madison and the other Virginians made excellent use of the time. Meeting daily at three o'clock for several hours, the delegation settled on what would come to be called the Virginia plan, which corresponded almost exactly to the ideas Madison had suggested in his letters to Randolph, Washington, and Jefferson. It transformed Congress into a body with two houses, each elected in proportion either to free population or taxes. This measure alone would transform the confederation created by the Articles into a nationally representative government.

In keeping with Madison's key theory, the plan gave the legislature a negative over state laws—and the authority to use force to make the states comply. It also created three independent branches of government with checks over one another. To be introduced by Edmund Randolph, whose position as governor made him an appropriate initial spokesman, the plan would set the agenda for the convention from the very start.

On Friday, May 25, 1787, a quorum was reached and the convention officially came to order. From the outset, Madison placed himself front and center. He recalled many years later that he "chose a seat in front of the presiding member, with the other members on my right and left hand." From this position he kept copious notes of the proceedings. Madison wrote out his notes during each session or within a few days, according to his own account.[4] He was not producing a perfect verbatim shorthand record. In paraphrasing, he smoothed out others' remarks. He would add material from written versions of the speeches, including his own, and he sometimes omitted or combined speeches, again including his own. In subsequent years, he edited the notes more than once, occasionally replacing whole pages.[5] Still, the notes, juxtaposed with more fragmentary notes taken by other delegates, remain the best record of the convention. They reveal how the convention looked through Madison's eyes, and how he came to understand its significance over time.

His goal, Madison later said, was nothing less than to produce a historical document. In researching other confederacies, particularly ancient ones, he had found it difficult to understand "the process, principles, the reasons, and the anticipations, which prevailed in the formation of them." His "exact account" would be, he hoped, a "gratification promised to future curiosity." He would reveal "an authentic exhibition of the objects, the opinions, and the reasonings from which the new system of government was to receive its peculiar structure of organization." He wanted his notes to make a "contribution" to the eventual "history of a constitution on which would be staked the happiness of a people great even in its infancy, and possibly the cause of liberty throughout the world."[6]

This startling historical ambition was consistent with Madison's strong sense of the importance of the convention's undertaking.[7] The stakes were enormous, he believed. Madison told the convention that the plan they would produce "would decide for ever the fate of republican government."[8]

Madison was not alone in seeing the convention as a decisive moment in the global history of self-government. Hamilton, echoing Madison, made it explicit. If the delegates failed to implement republicanism with "due stability and wisdom," he said, "it would be disgraced and lost among ourselves, disgraced and lost to mankind for ever."[9]

The convention's first order of business was to elect Washington as presiding officer. Though he continued to act and vote as a member of the Virginia delegation, Washington did not express his opinions in the convention's proceedings thereafter. He was known to be generally quiet in public unless he had a prepared speech to deliver. A popular story claimed that he had never laughed. Madison later told friends that this was "wholly untrue; no man seemed more to enjoy gay conversation, though he took little part in it himself."[10] The observation confirmed both that Washington was human, and that he was not well suited to the cut and thrust of spontaneous debate in the convention.

After choosing a secretary to record official votes, the convention read aloud the states' commissions to their delegates. Apparently everyone expected that, as in Congress, each state would get a single vote at the convention. Everyone also assumed that, again as in Congress, not all the delegates would be in attendance at any one time. Seventy-five men in total were named by the twelve states that eventually participated. Of these, only fifty-five appeared at the convention—not all at the same time. At any given moment, the average attendance hovered around thirty.[11]

Two small states were absent: New Hampshire, which had decided to name delegates but would not pay for them to come until July, and Rhode Island, which had not appointed representatives at all.[12] Delaware had told its delegates that they could not vote to alter the provision of the

Articles of Confederation specifying that all states were entitled to a single, equal vote in Congress.

Madison had predicted that the small states would have no choice but to go along with whatever the big states decided—and the discussion for the next two weeks seemed to confirm it. On May 30, 1787, the convention organized itself into what it called "a committee of the whole," a procedural form designed to create a looser conversation than when it constituted itself as "the convention." Randolph, pressing his initiative, then proposed three resolutions that undergirded the Virginia plan:

1. That a union of the states merely federal will not accomplish the objects proposed by the Articles of Confederation, namely common defense, security of liberty, and general welfare.
2. That no treaty or treaties among the whole or part of the states, as individual sovereignties, would be sufficient.
3. That a national government ought to be established consisting of a supreme legislative, executive and judiciary.[13]

Following the logic of Madison's letters, Randolph was setting the terminology that would dominate the first half of the convention. A "merely federal" union meant a government based on a treaty-like agreement among separate, sovereign states. Such a government, resolutions one and two made clear, could not successfully achieve the collective action necessary for common defense, liberty within states, or even "general welfare." The alternative to a federal union was "national government." In this context, "national" meant a government that bypassed the states and exercised sovereignty itself.

Clarifying what was meant by "national," Pennsylvania delegate Gouverneur Morris explained "that in all communities there must be one supreme power, and one only."[14] The ultimate sovereign must be either the individual states or the federal government. The necessity of a single sovereign was a commonplace of political theory that dated back at least a century, to the philosopher Benedict Spinoza:[15] There could be no "imperium in imperio"—no kingdom within a kingdom. Logically speaking, there could be no true sovereign who was subordinate to another sovereign. The choice between a federal government, in which states were sovereign, and a national one, in which sovereignty lay with the central authority, was therefore binary. The United States could be federal or it could be national. It could not be both.

Morris was easily the most colorful of the delegates present; he may have been the most colorful man in North America. A New Yorker by birth, he entered King's College (later Columbia) at twelve and was graduated at the age of sixteen. His unusual first name was that of his mother's French Huguenot family.[16]

During his college years, Morris had been seriously injured when a pot of scalding water spilled on his right arm. The permanent crippling exempted him from military service during the Revolutionary War. Morris was elected to Congress, and after observing conditions in Valley Forge, he became an advocate for providing greater resources to the army. When he failed to be reelected in 1779, Morris moved to Pennsylvania, where in 1780 he suffered another accident, losing his left leg below the knee after it was caught in a carriage wheel. Rumor had it that Morris was fleeing a jealous husband who had almost caught him in bed with his wife. In another version of the story, Morris shattered the leg by leaping from a window to escape the lady's chamber as her husband arrived.[17]

A kind of revolutionary Casanova, Morris kept diaries that record his sexual exploits in detail. He was regarded both as a brilliant conversationalist and as thoroughly lacking in conventional American sexual morality.[18] (These traits would later make him a successful ambassador to France when he replaced Jefferson in 1792.) Morris spoke more times at the convention than any other delegate, and his comments tended to be pithy and memorable. His attitudes were aristocratic as befitting the descendant of an old New York family, and his distrust of the people was deep and consistent.

By describing the choice between federal and national government as either-or, Morris was being undiplomatic. In his wake, George Mason put the point more delicately. The central government could never hope to coerce the states collectively. As a result, what was needed was a government that "could directly operate on individuals."[19]

The upshot of what Madison called Mason's "cogent" argument was that a federal government composed of sovereign states could act directly on the states alone. A sovereign or supreme national government could operate directly on citizens, without the intermediation of a sovereign state. This did not necessarily mean that the Virginia plan required the abolition of the states. But it did imply the elimination of their sovereignty.

The delegates grasped the implication. Charles Pinckney, a twenty-nine-year-old South Carolinian who alone among the delegates had prepared and submitted his own personal draft constitution, asked Randolph whether he "meant to abolish the state governments altogether." Young Pinckney's older cousin, General Charles Cotesworth Pinckney, also of South Carolina, said that Randolph's ideas amounted to "a system founded on different principles from the federal constitution," namely the Articles of Confederation. The elder Pinckney expressed doubt about whether the act of Congress that had led to the convention, or the commissions the several states had given their delegates, could "authorize" discussion of such a fundamentally different system.

This concern went to the very essence of the convention. Could the delegates replace the federal system of the Articles with a national system? They had been charged with fixing the existing union, not replacing it. Their authority came from a Congress composed of states, and from the states themselves that had appointed them. Could they propose undercutting the foundations of the very system that had directed them to act?

The solution that the convention adopted was to skip resolutions one and two and vote only on Randolph's third. By embracing a resolution that had the word "national" in it, they would be endorsing the overall vision of the Virginia plan without expressly condemning a federal union. Dividing powers into three parts within the national government also signaled that this government would look essentially different from Congress under the Articles.

The resolution passed easily. Only one state, Connecticut, which had dragged its feet in sending delegates to the convention, voted no. New York was unable to cast a vote. It had two delegates in attendance. Alexander Hamilton, who had done so much at Annapolis to facilitate the Philadelphia convention, voted yes. The other delegate, who was rumored to be against a stronger national government, voted no.[20]

The easy victory of Randolph's resolution gave Madison reason to push what he considered the most basic element of his plan: making representation in Congress proportionate either to tax contributions or to the free population. He explained to the convention, as he had in his earlier letters to his friends, that in a federation among sovereign states, it might make sense for all states to have the same vote. But in a "national" government, equality among states made no sense. "The acts of the general government would take effect without the intervention of the state legislatures," and it would be illogical if "a vote from a small state would have the same efficacy and importance as a vote from a large one."[21]

The topic of proportional representation was the Delaware delegates' cue to warn the convention that they might have to "retire from the convention" if there was a move to change the equality of states' voting rights.[22] The statement was dangerous. Gouverneur Morris quickly replied that if Delaware withdrew, "so early a proof of discord in the convention" would be regrettable. The delegates had agreed on the first day to maintain secrecy as to the proceedings. But if one delegation went home, the fact would become public, threatening the convention's success.[23]

Madison proposed various possibilities to address Delaware's worries. The convention could take the sense of the members without formally voting, thus helping the Delaware delegates avoid "embarrassment," he suggested. Or it could refer the issue to a committee. Several delegates commented that even if other states voted for the resolution, it did not follow that Delaware's delegates would have to leave. Nothing seemed to satisfy the Delaware contingent, and the convention adjourned for the day.

Thus, notwithstanding the easy success of the resolution for a national government, there were signs of trouble ahead. Several states had voted for a national government. But four small states—Georgia, Maryland, New Jersey, and New Hampshire—did not have enough delegates present to cast their votes. And tiny Delaware had already blocked the convention from voting on what Madison considered the most basic and necessary change for a true national government.

Filtration

The next day Madison urged that the larger house be directly elected by the people. The decision was not automatic. Elbridge Gerry of Massachusetts proclaimed that the people, although virtuous, were "the dupes of pretended patriots . . . daily misled into the most painful measures and opinions by false reports circulated by designing men."[24] Gerry was a well-off merchant who had been an active patriot before the Revolution and served in the Continental and Confederation congresses. In principle, he feared a strong central government. Yet like others of his class, he had been deeply affected by the experience of Shays's Rebellion, and he now feared popular elections more.

Siding with Madison, James Wilson of Pennsylvania used an architectural metaphor to explain why the legislature should be elected directly: "He was for raising the federal pyramid to a considerable altitude, and for that reason wished to give it as broad a basis as possible," Madison noted.[25] A powerful national government, Wilson argued, would have to rest upon "the confidence of the people." He wanted a strong national government—and believed that a popularly elected legislature would serve that interest.

The best-educated person at the convention, Wilson had been born in Scotland and studied at St. Andrews, Glasgow, and Edinburgh. The thinkers of the Scottish Enlightenment whom Madison knew indirectly through Witherspoon's lectures at Princeton had been Wilson's actual teachers. He had arrived in Philadelphia in 1766 and set up shop as a lawyer, teaching on the side at the Academy and College of Philadelphia, which later became the University of Pennsylvania. Wilson wore his erudition on his sleeve. The Georgian William Pierce, who recorded character sketches of nearly all the delegates, noted that "government seems to have been his peculiar study, all the political institutions of the world he knows in detail, and can trace the causes and effects of every revolution from the earliest stages of the Grecian commonwealth down to the present time."[26]

Wilson's politics were thought to be mildly aristocratic, not republican. During the Revolution, after the British had left Philadelphia, he had successfully represented twenty-three Philadelphia Loyalists who were charged with aiding the enemy. A crowd gathered outside the house where he was living on Third and Walnut streets with the aim of tarring and feathering Wilson, or worse. In what came to be called the "Fort Wilson Riot," Wilson and his friends defended themselves from inside the barricaded house. They were eventually saved by militia and Continental troops, but lives were lost. These events, taking place just a few blocks from where the convention now sat, had confirmed in Wilson a preference for strong government.[27]

Madison, for his part, expressed a moderate, centrist view: One branch of the legislature should be popularly elected; the other should be chosen indirectly. He was, he said, "an advocate for the policy of refining the popular appointments by successive filtrations, but thought it might be pushed too far."[28]

Complications arose when the delegates turned to the second house. Randolph had proposed that the members of the second house should be elected by the first on the basis of nominations made by the state legislatures. This, it was objected, took too much power away from the states.

Randolph answered that the point of the Senate was to check the popular will: "to provide a cure for . . . the turbulence and follies of democracy."[29] The delegates would not have been surprised to hear "democracy" disparaged. To them it meant direct rule by the people, as opposed to republicanism, which mediated the people's will through what Madison had called "filtrations," multiple layers of elected officials.

But the delegates could not agree on a system for electing the upper house, because they could not imagine a proportionate upper house big enough to accommodate representatives from small states like Delaware. They voted down Randolph's proposal, leaving what Madison in his notes called "a chasm" in the Virginia plan.[30] The word was apt.

The convention then turned to the powers of the partly imagined legislature. The Virginia plan proposed giving the new Congress "legislative power in all cases to which the state legislatures were individually incompetent." A few delegates worried that the vague term "incompetent" gave too much power to Congress and took it away from the states; they preferred a specific list enumerating Congress's powers. Madison weighed in to say that he had come to the convention strongly preferring that Congress's powers be listed and limited, and was still unsure of his final position. But, he added, he "would shrink from nothing which should be found essential to such a form of government as would provide for the safety, liberty, and happiness of the community." All "necessary means for attaining" this end "must, however reluctantly, be submitted to."[31]

If Madison meant what he said, the principle would have been far-reaching. He was telling the other delegates that they ought to "submit" to extensions of the national power in order to get an effective government—to achieve constitutional reform no matter what it took. The delegates appeared to agree. All the states present except for Connecticut voted in favor of a significant grant of power to Congress.

As if to demonstrate how thoroughly Madison was now in command, the convention then approved with no debate and no dissent a version of his original idea to grant the new Congress the power to negate any state laws that violated the new constitution.[32] This was not the same as an absolute power to negate all state laws for any reason; but it did put Congress in a supervisory role of constitutional review. Franklin proposed adding a power to negate state laws contradicting treaties made under the authority of the union. This, too, was readily adopted.

Madison then announced that he no longer believed it necessary to grant Congress the power to use force against states that were ignoring its dictates. The way things were going in the convention, there would be no need to make the states do anything, because the most important powers were being transferred to a national government that could act directly on citizens. If the Virginia plan was adopted, states would become increasingly irrelevant. As Madison put it, he "hoped that such a system would be framed as might render this recourse [to force] unnecessary."[33] The design of such a system seemed to be well under way.

A Considerable Pause

The next day, Friday, June 1, 1787, the convention took up the question of the executive. Madison had told Randolph before the convention that he had given the question of the executive little thought. As a result, the Virginia plan left the matter almost entirely open. The resolution proposed "that a national executive be instituted, to be chosen by the national legislature." It left the length of term blank, specified a single term only, and concluded that the executive would "possess the executive powers of Congress."[34]

The first person to speak was young Charles Pinckney. Diving into the subject with more enthusiasm than tact, Pinckney said he was "for a vigorous executive" but was afraid that pursuant to the Virginia plan "the executive powers" would include making peace and war. This, he said, "would render the executive a monarchy of the worst kind, to wit an elective one."[35]

James Wilson, who had spent many years thinking about executive power, then took the lead. In the run-up to the Revolution he had argued that the colonies were not rebelling against the king but against Parliament.[36] Now Wilson moved "that the executive consist of a single person."

After his motion was seconded, "a considerable pause ensu[ed]." The silence was pregnant with meaning. All the delegates knew that they had reached a crucial and delicate juncture. Unlike Wilson, many Americans thought precisely that the Revolution had been against the idea of monarchy itself. To others, including some in the room, the absence of a monarch lay at the heart of the troubles that the United States faced under the Articles of Confederation. To both, a single executive suggested monarchy—the word Pinckney had been uncouth enough to mention moments before.

To make matters more complicated, all the delegates knew that the man overwhelmingly likely to fill the role of a single executive was before them in the convention's chair. To speak on the topic would be by implication to speak about the national hero himself, and to do so directly to his face. The hush in this room of eloquent and active debaters reflected a respect for the topic—and for the general—that verged on a kind of awe.

Perhaps sensing that he was a source of discomfort, Washington broke the silence by asking if he should put the question for a vote. Franklin, the elder statesman, intervened. With careful understatement he "observed that it was a point of great importance and wished that gentlemen would deliver their sentiments on it before the question was put."[37] The delegates may have believed that Franklin himself, influenced by his European celebrity as a radical republican, harbored doubts about a single executive. More likely, though, they needed Franklin, the second most distinguished person in the convention, to give them permission to speak obliquely about the first.

It worked. John Rutledge, the former governor of South Carolina and one of the leading orators of the day,[38] criticized "the shyness of gentlemen." He said that the silence "looked as if" the delegates believed that once they expressed their opinions they could not change them afterward. This he "did not take to be at all the case." By giving an innocent explanation for the strange pause, Rutledge normalized the debate.[39]

Roger Sherman of Connecticut then made the first statement on behalf of those who opposed the unitary executive. Unusual among the delegates, Sherman was a self-made man who had begun his career as a shoemaker. William Pierce described Sherman's rise: "Despising the lowness of his condition, he turned almanac maker, and so progressed upwards to a judge." The southern Pierce found the New Englander an unfamiliar type: "Mr. Sherman," he wrote, "exhibits the oddest shaped character I ever remember to have met with. He is awkward, un-meaning, and unaccountably strange in his manner." What was more, Pierce noted Sherman's use of northeastern slang: "that strange New England cant which runs through his public as well as his private speaking make[s] everything that is connected with him grotesque and laughable." Yet at the same time, Pierce believed that "in his train of thinking there is something regular, deep, and comprehensive.... He deserves infinite praise—no man has a better heart or a clearer head."[40]

The former shoemaker believed the executive was "nothing more than an institution for carrying the will of the legislature into effect." The legislature was "the depository of the supreme will of the society," and so it should appoint "the person or persons" who would execute its will. Since the executive would be working for the legislature, the Constitution should not fix a specific number of executives. Rather, "the legislature should be at liberty to appoint one or more as experience might dictate."[41]

Wilson, the advocate of executive power, answered that he "preferred a single magistrate, as giving most energy, dispatch, and responsibility to the office." Voicing the concern that was on everybody's mind, Wilson explained that "he did not consider the prerogatives of the British monarch as a proper guide in defining the executive powers."[42]

This was too much for Randolph. He "strenuously opposed a unity in the executive magistrate," he announced. Randolph, who had gone to such great lengths to bring Washington to the convention, now asserted bluntly that he regarded executive unity "as the fetus of monarchy." The United States had "no motive to be governed by the British government as our prototype."[43]

This was a dig at Wilson, who could not let the point pass. "Unity in the executive" was not a path to monarchy but rather "the best safeguard against tyranny"—like the mob that had attacked his house. Wilson denied being "governed by the British model." Yet his explanation was wobbly: The United States was so big, he said, and its "manners so republican, that nothing but a great confederated republic would do for it." Wilson was equivocating, admitting that he was not committed to the British model because the republican political culture of the United States would not allow him to admit that he was.[44]

Madison favored a single executive.[45] But, perhaps sensing rising tension, he changed the subject away from the unitary or plural executive to the executive's powers. He successfully pushed through a motion giving the executive authority "to carry into effect the national laws," appoint officers, and execute powers delegated by the legislature. The topic then turned to electing the executive and his term of office.[46]

Again Wilson took the initiative. In an apologetic preamble, he said he "was almost unwilling to declare the mode which he wished to take place, being apprehensive that it might appear chimerical." The radical idea that Wilson had, "at least . . . in theory," was direct "election by the people." The governor was directly elected in New York and Massachusetts, he noted, and the experiment was both "convenient and successful." The winners would be "persons whose merits have general notoriety."[47]

Sherman took the opposite position: The executive should be appointed by the legislature and be "absolutely dependent on that body." An independent executive "was in his opinion the very essence of tyranny."[48] Direct election of the executive would make him independent of Congress and the will of the people. Wilson, Sherman implied, was trying to create an elected king who would be superior to the legislature.

Through the exchange, Madison remained silent. For the next week, as the convention considered various topics, the theme of the unitary executive came up repeatedly. Randolph now became the primary opponent of a single executive. He felt, he said, "an opposition to it which he believed he should continue to feel as long as he lived."[49] Randolph's intransigence was a worrying sign. He had introduced the Virginia plan, and that plan was proceeding as well as or better than could have been hoped—yet Randolph was taking an irreversible stand on an issue that was not in the plan and that he might not be able to win. For a body that hoped to create consensus, such inflexibility posed a serious threat.

The Farmer

John Dickinson of Delaware took on the opposing views of Randolph and Wilson. Dickinson was a particularly quirky member of the convention. Born to significant wealth on a Maryland tobacco plantation, he was famous across the country for his "Letters from a Farmer," a series of essays written in 1767–68 against Parliament's Townshend Acts. Notwithstanding the literary guise of the farmer, Dickinson had spent all his adult life as a practicing lawyer in Philadelphia, and his forensic skill was considerable. In the letters, which were widely read across the colonies, Dickinson had argued that Parliament violated the British constitution by levying taxes on the colonies. The argument had established Dickinson as a leading patriot.

Yet on July 1, 1776, Dickinson spoke in the Continental Congress against independence. On July 4, when the time came to sign the Declaration, he refused. This triggered his automatic resignation from Congress. A subsequent brief stint in the Pennsylvania militia also ended in his resignation. His house in Philadelphia confiscated as a war hospital, Dickinson retreated to his ample Delaware estate, and spent the war there in relative quiet. As if to prove he was not a Loyalist, he served as a private in the local militia. Brought up as a Quaker, he took the opportunity of the war to free the thirty-seven slaves on his large Delaware plantation. These were honorable acts, and he was subsequently elected president of Delaware and then president of Pennsylvania—yet his national reputation never fully recovered from his failure to sign the Declaration.

In the convention, Dickinson openly praised the British constitution. "A limited monarchy," he said, was "one of the best governments in the world. It was not certain that the same blessings were derivable from any other form. It was certain that equal blessings had never yet been derived from any of the republican form."[50] On the basis of experience, then, the British constitution was superior to any form of republicanism. As a practical matter, in the United States, "a limited monarchy however was out of the question. The spirit of the times—the state of our affairs, forbade the experiment, if it were desirable."

Faced with the reality that monarchy was not now possible, Dickinson introduced an alternative. The United States, he said, should take advantage of "the accidental lucky division of this country into distinct states." Some delegates, he said, "seemed desirous to abolish altogether" those divisions. But this was a mistake. The states should be used to limit the central government more or less in the way that the House of Lords limited the British monarchy.[51]

Dickinson then boldly predicted that the debate over representation in the national legislature "must probably end in mutual concession." He foresaw a compromise in which "each state would retain an equal voice at least in one branch of the national legislature." He also speculated that states' tax revenue, not their population, should determine representation in the popular house.[52]

Madison made no immediate reply to Dickinson's idea of electing the two houses of the legislature by different means and preserving in one the equal representation of the states. He had already expressed his views against equal state representation; indeed, he was one of the people Dickinson had in mind when he warned against those who would "abolish" the states altogether. As for compromise, at this early stage of the convention, none was needed. Events seemed to be proceeding as Madison had planned: The big states continued to win important votes, and the small states, he believed, would ultimately have little choice but to go along.

Factions

On Monday, June 4, and Wednesday, June 6, Madison gave two important speeches, together intended to put his imprint directly on the convention. In his notes, he combined the speeches into a single text, which he edited and dated June 6.[53]

In the speeches, Madison introduced the argument for a national veto and the enlargement of the republic.[54] The keystone of his position was that the delegates should provide "more effectually for the security of private rights, and the steady dispensation of justice. Interferences with these were evils which had more perhaps than any thing else produced the convention."[55]

It was astonishing for Madison to claim that the protection of property rights had been a greater cause than any other for the convention. The original purpose of the convention as conceived by Madison and others had been the coordination of national policy and the imminent collapse of Congress, given its inability to collect taxes from the recalcitrant states. Shays's Rebellion had motivated more states to send delegations to Philadelphia than to Annapolis. The delegates had *not* come believing that a new constitution could protect property rights within the states.

According to the speech that appears in his notes, Madison proceeded to enlighten them. Drawing on his research, he laid out what he considered the greatest problem with democracy. "All civilized societies," he explained, would inevitably "be divided into different sects, factions, and interests." Those would "consist of rich and poor, debtors and creditors, the landed, the manufacturing, and commercial interests, inhabitants of this district, or that district, followers of this political leader or that political leader, the disciples of this religious sect or that religious sect."[56] Those different factions would have a tendency to organize: "In all cases where a majority are united by a common interest or passion, the rights of the minority are in danger."[57]

No political system had ever solved the problem of majority tyranny. Madison told the delegates that his claims could be "verified by the histories of every country ancient and modern. In Greece and Rome the rich and poor, the creditors and debtors, as well as the patricians and plebeians alternately oppressed each other with equal unmercifulness." Imperial Rome, imperial Athens, and imperial Carthage each dominated and exploited their respective provinces. In more recent memory, America had been "justly apprehensive of parliamentary injustice" because Great Britain had oppressed its own colonies.

In a stunning twist, Madison pointed to slavery as the ultimate example of a majority oppressing a minority: "We have seen the mere distinction of color made in the most enlightened period of time, the ground of the most oppressive dominion ever exercised by man over man."[58] A lifelong slaveholder whose entire material existence depended on slave labor was using the example of slavery to demonstrate the evil of majority government. In the process, he implicitly denied that people of African descent were inferior, and affirmed that slavery was obviously unjust. Ignoring the paternalistic claim that race slavery served the interests of slaves, Madison frankly called it "the most oppressive dominion" that had ever existed.[59]

As he had done when writing to his father about Billey's human right to liberty, Madison was capable of speaking clearly about the immorality of slavery without for a moment acting to end it. Nor did Madison think his audience—which included both slaveholders and opponents of slavery—would find his reference to slavery jarring. He was trying to illustrate the oppressiveness of the majority, and like a good theorist, he was prepared to draw on any powerful example.[60]

Madison's audience would not have easily imagined themselves in the position of slaves, so Madison also gave some contemporary economic examples. "Debtors have defrauded their creditors," he explained. "The landed interest has borne hard on the mercantile interest. The holders of one species of property have thrown a disproportion of taxes on the holders of another species." In every case, the bad result derived from a majority that was "united by a common sentiment" and had "an opportunity" to infringe on "the rights of the minor party." In republican government, Madison concluded, "the majority if united have always an opportunity."[61]

The answer to this structural problem could not come from individuals' honesty, character, or conscience, or from religion.[62] Madison's solution, which he considered his major contribution to the history of republican theory, was expansion:

The only remedy is to enlarge the sphere, and thereby divide the community into so great a number of interests and parties, that in the first place a majority will not be likely at the same moment to have a common interest separate from that of the whole or of the minority; and in the second place, that in case they should have such an interest, they may not be apt to unite in the pursuit of it.[63]

Enlarging the republic from individual states to the entire United States would multiply the number of different interest groups or parties, thereby protecting each group. Madison offered two reasons why expansion would have this effect. First, having more parties and interests would, he claimed, actually reduce the likelihood of overlap among them. Second, even if those interests overlapped, it would be harder for them to organize themselves, presumably because of the difficulties of organizing any coordinated action over an expanded distance.

Writing for himself, Madison had reasoned that it would be harder to communicate across large distances. He did not say so at the convention, however—because the difficulty of coordination was a reason for preserving important government decisions in the states. It would be harder for anyone to create collective action of *any* kind in a large and disparate republic, not only for oppressive majorities. But Madison's whole argument in favor of enlarging the republic required shifting government away from the states to the national level.

In his own notes, Alexander Hamilton identified counterarguments. "There is truth" in Madison's claims, he wrote, "but they do not conclude so strongly as he supposes." For example, he jotted down, "paper money is capable of giving a general impulse" that would transcend national differences. Creditors were creditors and debtors were debtors wherever they might be. Furthermore, large republics could be influenced by demagogues in the same way as small ones: "An influential demagogue will give an impulse to the whole." Such demagogues, Hamilton wrote, drawing on his own historical knowledge, "are not always inconsiderable persons— Patricians were frequently demagogues."[64] Aristocratic demagogues of national reputation could unite factions into a majority at the national scale.

Madison's argument for the greater difficulty of coordination at the national scale was not definitive, either. Hamilton noted privately to himself that "the assembly when chosen will meet in one room [even] if they are drawn from half the globe—and will be liable to all the passions of popular assemblies."[65]

Madison did not specifically identify the mechanism by which the national negative would operate. Other delegates noted that he was suggesting that the judiciary and the executive should be involved in the negative.[66] The details of where the negative power would lie mattered less to Madison than establishing a structural check: The enlarged national government, where local interests would be diffused or eliminated, must be able to block state legislation that oppressed minority property holders.

Gravity

The national veto over the action of state legislatures was central to Madison's project of enlarging the scope of government and transferring authority to the center.[67] On Friday, June 8, 1787, Madison seconded a motion transforming the power to negate laws that violated the Articles into a congressional authority "to negative all laws which to them shall appear improper."[68] With his usual lack of tact, Pinckney opened the debate by stating what Madison had mentioned only in private communication: The "universal negative" was based on the veto that the British Crown had possessed over the colonial legislatures, a prerogative that "had been found beneficial" during the colonial period.[69]

Madison was more circumspect but also more insistent. The general negative was, he said, "absolutely necessary to a perfect system." The states had regularly encroached on federal authority, one another, and national treaties. The only alternative to the negative was forcible coercion.

The day before, John Dickinson, criticizing Madison and trying to protect states from national power, had introduced the metaphor of the new constitution as the solar system, with the national government as the sun in the center and the states orbiting as planets.[70] Madison now transformed the metaphor, in the process turning it against Dickinson. The national veto "is the great pervading principle that must control the centrifugal tendency of the states; which, without it, would continually fly out of their proper orbits and destroy the order and harmony of the political system."[71]

In Madison's brilliantly transformed account, the congressional negative was gravity itself. In Newton's scheme, the gravitational pull of the sun at the very center of the solar system kept the planets from flying off into space. The power to negate state legislatures combined Madison's original impetus—effective coordinated action among the states—with what he considered his discovery—that states left alone were too small to function as effective republics because the majority would oppress the minority. A congressional negative was the elemental force that would solve both problems.

Madison received an unexpected endorsement from Dickinson, who said it would be "impossible to draw a line" between "proper and improper . . . exercise of the negative." It was impractical to restrict the negative to cases where states had violated the constitution. The choice was between putting states in danger of being injured by the national government or the national government in danger of being injured by the states. Between the two, Dickinson "thought the danger greater from the states."[72]

Dickinson's support should have been a good sign for Madison's proposal. It was not. Elbridge Gerry of Massachusetts, still obsessing over Shays's Rebellion, said the national negative might stop states from organizing their own militias. "The national legislature with such a power may enslave the states," he concluded bleakly. "Such an idea as this will never be acceded to. It has never been suggested or conceived among the people. No speculative projector, and there are enough of that character among us . . . has in any pamphlet or newspaper thrown out the idea."[73]

Gerry was touching on a serious flaw in Madison's approach: The idea of the federal negative, nurtured in Madison's bosom and now revealed for the first time, was so original that it was unknown. An idea that no one had ever proposed in public would have trouble being accepted precisely because of its novelty. It would appear that the delegates had sprung it on an unsuspecting public.

Why had Madison kept the idea of the federal negative private prior to the convention, expressing it only to his closest associates? The answer, no doubt, lay precisely in its radical nature. Madison's proposal subordinated the states to the national power. Madison opposed a role for the state legislatures in electing either house of Congress, and supported Wilson's plan to elect the president without the involvement of the state legislatures. His imagined states were planets whose revolutions depended utterly on the national government at the center: the sun would hold their orbits in check, but they would exercise no reciprocal influence on the sun.

A further attack came from a younger Delaware delegate who contradicted Dickinson, his senior colleague. The federal negative, he argued, was "meant . . . to strip the small states of their equal right of suffrage." Delaware would have about one-ninetieth of the vote in Congress, "whilst Pennsylvania and Virginia would possess ⅓ of the whole." The large states would "crush the small ones whenever they stand in the way of their ambitions or interested views." Pennsylvania and Virginia, he said, "wished to provide a system in which they would have an enormous and monstrous influence."[74] This was the harshest statement yet made in the convention.

In the vote that followed, Madison's proposed congressional negative was decisively defeated. Only Virginia, Pennsylvania, and Massachusetts—the three largest states—voted yes. The Delaware delegation split, and the seven other states with enough delegates to count all voted no. The small states had realized that they would be especially vulnerable to dominance by a popularly elected national legislature.

In a worrisome development, both Randolph and Mason voted against the negative—suggesting that even some large-state republicans were concerned that a national veto would abolish the states. Until now, the convention had mostly endorsed the Virginia plan, leaning toward a stronger federal government. Friday, June 8, 1787—the day Madison's federal negative went down 7 to 3 to 1—marked the end of this momentum toward strong nationalism.[75]

The centerpiece of Madison's plan, the manifestation of his grand theory that an enlarged republic could protect local minorities, had not come close to passing. The three most intellectually significant participants in the convention up to that point had all spoken in its favor. And then the vote had gone against them—despite the fact that those who spoke in opposition had none of their sophistication or prestige. For the first time, the states had voted purely by size. Interest, it seemed, was trumping reason. The convention was about to get ugly.

Never Give Up

Sensing weakness, the small states pressed their advantage. On June 9 the committee of the whole once more discussed the idea of equal representation in the Senate. William Paterson of New Jersey opened with a long speech insisting on equal representation. Paterson, the former attorney general of New Jersey and a Princeton graduate, had thus far spoken little at the convention. William Pierce thought Paterson was a dark horse. "A man of great modesty, with looks that bespeak talents of no great extent," Paterson was nevertheless "one of those kind of men whose powers break in upon you, and create wonder and astonishment." Despite initial appearances, Paterson was "a classic, a lawyer, and an orator" so capable that "every one seemed ready to exalt him with their praises."[76]

Paterson reminded the delegates that Congress had charged them with amending the Articles of Confederation, which upheld equal representation of the states. "We ought to keep within its limits," he asserted, "or we should be charged by our constituents with usurpation."[77] Behind his principle lay the self-preservation of small states. "New Jersey will never confederate on the plan before the committee," he concluded. "She would be swallowed up." He would "rather submit to a monarch, to a despot, than to such a fate." Furthermore, he "would not only oppose the plan here but on his return home do everything in his power to defeat it there."[78] Paterson was drawing a line. Equal representation of the states would not be compromised—even if it meant there would be no constitution.

The next Monday, June 11, 1787, the convention shifted to the closely related topic of representation in the lower house: Should it be by the numbers of free inhabitants, according to tax contributions, or some other principle? Benjamin Franklin had written a speech on the topic, which he asked James Wilson to deliver because of his age and frailty. With his characteristic eye for the mood of the convention, Franklin began by noticing that until the topic of proportional representation had come before the convention, "our debates were carried on with great coolness and temper." Now things were beginning to feel otherwise; and Franklin hoped that such sentiment would "not be repeated; for we are sent here to *consult*, not to *contend*, with each other."[79]

Reasoning calmly, Franklin went on to make the case for proportionality. After the speech had been read, the delegates voted on a general resolution that representation in the lower house would be "according to some equitable ratio of representation" to be decided later. The compromise resolution passed.

Then Wilson and Charles Pinckney of South Carolina introduced an amendment to this resolution. They proposed that the ratio be specified as proportional to "the whole number of white and other free citizens and inhabitants of every age, sex, and condition including those bound to servitude for a term of years and three-fifths of all other persons not comprehended in the foregoing description, except Indians not paying taxes, in each state."

The origins of the three-fifths rule lay in congressional negotiations in 1783. Desperately attempting to raise revenue, Congress had recommended that the states together give the federal government $1.5 million annually, distributed among the states proportionally based on population. A debate had ensued over how and whether to count slaves in the population. Southerners sought to count slaves as little as possible to reduce their proportionate share of taxation. Northerners wanted to count slaves fully so the South would pay more.

Madison, then in Congress, had proposed three-fifths as a compromise. As he recalled it later, the proposal derived "from accident" rather than "accurate calculation." But Madison persisted his whole life in believing that his compromise had been "very near the true ratio" with respect to the taxable wealth produced by slaves.[80] The principle of representing slaves partially had been introduced into American political discourse, and had not been repudiated since.

Now that the issue was representation, not taxes, the tables were turned. The small slave states, particularly South Carolina and Georgia, wanted slaves to count equally in population totals to maximize their representation. Only Elbridge Gerry objected to the proposed three-fifths rule for counting slaves of African descent. Why, he asked, "should the blacks, who were property in the South, be in the rule of representation more than the cattle and horses of the North?" No one responded, and the delegates then voted 9 to 2 to adopt the amendment, with only New Jersey and Delaware voting against. No one commented on the immorality or symbolism of counting slaves differently from free persons.

With consensus on representation in the lower house apparently achieved, the small states thought the moment was right to press for equal representation in the Senate. Roger Sherman of Connecticut called for a vote. "Everything he said depended on this," Madison noted. "The smaller states would never agree to the plan on any other principle."[81]

The small states lost—barely. The three biggest states by population—Virginia, Massachusetts, and Pennsylvania—voted no. The small southern states—North Carolina, South Carolina, and Georgia—joined the big states in voting no, apparently because their numbers would be markedly enhanced by the three-fifths rule. In favor were Connecticut, New York, New Jersey, Delaware, and Maryland, all comparatively smaller states.* The result was a vote of 6 to 5 against equality in the Senate. James Wilson, seconded by Alexander Hamilton, then immediately moved that the role of suffrage in the Senate be the same as the one in the lower house. The delegates replicated their votes, and the motion passed, 6 to 5.

On June 13, 1787, the delegates paused to take stock. They had before them the structure of a basic draft constitution that came relatively close to the Virginia plan. It called for two houses of Congress, one directly elected, the other chosen by state legislatures, with both apportioned by population as supplemented by the three-fifths rule. Congress would have the power to pass laws whenever the states lacked the power to do so and to negate or block all state laws that contradicted the constitution. The executive would be chosen by the national legislature for a single seven-year term. The plan called for a "supreme tribunal" of judges serving life tenure, and lower courts to be created at the discretion of the legislature. The United States would guarantee that each state had a "republican constitution," thus promising to protect the states from rebellion or uprising. Amendment would be possible by some as yet unspecified process. Ratification would take place after the "approbation" of Congress—a deliberately vague term—in some sort of "assembly or assemblies" that would be "recommended" by the state legislatures and "expressly chosen by the people."[82]

The only major missing element, from Madison's perspective, was a robust mechanism to stop state majorities from oppressing minorities. Yet the absence of a national veto was not the greatest problem facing Madison or his allies. The biggest potential roadblock was proportional representation in the Senate, which had passed by a single vote.

The intense disagreement over representation reflected a much deeper division in the convention. Madison wanted a totally new, truly national constitution, and by taking the initiative, he had managed to get one

---

* At the convention, the delegates thought Virginia had more than 400,000 white inhabitants and just under 300,000 slaves, while Massachusetts and Pennsylvania were thought to have roughly 350,000 whites each. In contrast, New York, the biggest of the smaller states, was thought to have fewer than 240,000 white inhabitants.

provisionally approved. But delegates from the smaller states had not come to replace a federal union with a national government. Rallied by Dickinson of Delaware, they had so far focused upon the issue of equal representation in the Senate. Their concern about the potential abolition of the states ran deeper. Now they knew that Madison, supported by Wilson, wanted to make states almost wholly subordinate to a national government.

Looking back at the document the convention had tentatively approved, these more cautious delegates panicked. Without quite realizing it, they had in two weeks allowed Virginia to drive the convention in the direction of a radically national government. The time had come to make a response. It fell to William Paterson of New Jersey to make it.

Authorized

Paterson was a master of timing.[83] On Thursday, June 14, 1787, the day after the review of the Virginia plan, he dropped a bombshell. The New Jersey delegation, Paterson said, intended to introduce its own alternative plan—one that would be "purely federal, and contradistinguished from the reported plan." He asked the convention to adjourn without doing any business and promised to deliver his plan the next day.

On June 15, Paterson was as good as his word. From his seat he read out an entirely new draft plan, one he had orchestrated with delegates from Connecticut, New York, Delaware, and his own state of New Jersey. The New Jersey plan thus represented the vision of the smaller mid-Atlantic states that had formed a core in voting for equal representation in the Senate.

The essence of the plan was to preserve the existing Congress while augmenting its powers so that it could effectively raise revenue and coordinate trade policy. Congress would still be a single body in a single house in which all the states enjoyed equal representation. It would be given the power to tax imports and make requisitions of revenue, to be apportioned among the states on the basis of population, computed according to the number of free persons plus three-fifths of slaves. If a state failed to comply with Congress's demands, Congress could set up its own system to collect the revenues directly, provided some unspecified number of states agreed.[84] If any state or group of people in a state tried to prevent the execution of federal law or treaties, the executive was authorized "to call forth the power of the confederated states" as necessary "to enforce and compel an obedience."[85]

The plan also provided for an executive of multiple "persons"—the number was not given—to be directly elected by Congress for a single, nonrenewable term, and removable by Congress on application by a majority of the governors of the states. These executives would appoint all federal officers and direct all military operations, but without taking command of any troops.[86]

In essence, Paterson's New Jersey plan combined various proposed reforms of the Articles with a few well-chosen ideas from the first two weeks of the convention, such as the supremacy of federal law and treaties. Had such a reform of the existing Articles been made two years before, Madison would have supported it.

Now, however, Madison understood that the proposal was meant to defeat his Virginia plan. Outside the convention hall, John Dickinson of Delaware, who had predicted trouble early on, reportedly told Madison:

> You see the consequence of pushing things too far. Some of the members from the small states wish for two branches in the general legislature, and are friends to a good national government; but we would sooner submit to foreign power than submit to be deprived, in both branches of the legislature, of an equality of suffrage, and thereby be thrown under the domination of the larger states.[87]

The next day, John Lansing, the mayor of Albany, New York, asserted that Paterson's plan "sustains the sovereignty of the respective states, that of Mr. Randolph destroys it."[88] He claimed that the convention lacked even the power to discuss the Virginia plan that had been under consideration for two weeks. New York, he said, "would never have concurred in sending deputies to the convention, if she had supposed the deliberations were to turn on a consolidation of the states, and a national government."[89] Given that the states had never authorized proposal of such a plan, Lansing concluded, there was no chance that the states would ratify it.

Madison had an answer. "The opinions of the people," he opined, could not be "our guide." No delegate knew, he insisted, "what the opinions of his constituents were at this time." Instead of worrying about public opinion, "we ought to consider what was right and necessary itself for the attainment of a proper government."[90]

Madison then gave his vision of how ratification would proceed. After the secret deliberations of the convention, the plan would be revealed, and the delegates' "respectability" would give weight to their recommendations. "All the most enlightened and respectable citizens," he predicted, would become the "advocates" of the constitution—provided its contents were good.[91] If, however, the proposed plan fell short of what was "necessary and proper," then "this influential class of citizens will be turned against the plan." Should the influential political class not approve of the proposed constitution, he added, "little support in opposition to them can be gained . . . from the unreflecting multitude."[92]

Madison saw nothing wrong with asserting that the people would follow the elite, and that the delegates could therefore safely ignore the "unreflecting multitude." Madison understood that the constitution was being negotiated as an agreement among political elites. Although some of the members of the convention were self-made men, none was of the multitude. If they had been, they would not have been chosen by their state legislatures to go to Philadelphia. He expected that they—or people very much like them—would govern the country under the new constitution.

To Madison, the looming danger was not public disapproval but instability. As he put it later in the day, it was "of great importance that a stable and firm government organized in a republican form should be held out to the people." Otherwise the unstable republicanism that existed under the Articles would produce "universal disgust" and lead the people to "be ready for any change that may be proposed to them," including monarchy.[93]

Lansing took a view squarely opposed to Madison's. "The states," he asserted, "will never feel a sufficient confidence in a general government to give it a negative on their laws. The scheme is itself totally novel. There is no parallel to it to be found."[94] Madison's general national negative had already been rejected, but that was no reason for Lansing to stop criticizing it. As Dickinson had warned Madison, in proposing the negative Madison had gone too far.

Lansing had weakened the prey, and Paterson went in for the kill. His powers of oratory on full view, he declared, "I came here not to speak my own sentiments, but the sentiments of those who sent me. Our object is not such a government as may be best in itself, but such a one as our constituents have authorized us to prepare, and as they will approve." This was a direct attack on Madison's statement that the delegates should get it right and not worry about their constituents' views.

Paterson then argued that the Virginia plan was fundamentally illegitimate because it would destroy the sovereignty of the states. "If proportional representation be right," he asked devastatingly, "why do we not vote so here?" The fact that the states had equal votes in the convention was evidence for the basic nature of the union. The Articles of Confederation, he explained, were a treaty. All treaties required unanimous consent: "What is unanimously done, must be unanimously undone."[95]

From this analysis it followed that the New Jersey plan was the only legitimate solution to preserving the union. "If the sovereignty of the states is to be maintained, the representatives must be drawn immediately from the states, not from the people: and we have no power to vary the idea of equal sovereignty." Above all, the New Jersey plan was what the people wanted, Paterson argued. "Do the people at large complain of Congress? No: What they wish is that Congress may have more power."[96]

James Wilson offered a lengthy reply, contrasting the Virginia plan and the New Jersey plan point by point. The convention itself, he maintained, was "authorized to *conclude nothing*" but "at liberty *to propose anything.*" If the people did not like the convention's recommendations, they could decline to ratify them. Drawing on his comparative knowledge, Wilson argued that a single legislative body could easily be corrupted; two houses were needed. A plural executive, however, was equally disastrous, as the examples of the Roman triumvirates, the kings of Sparta, and the consuls of Rome showed.

The speeches given by Paterson and Wilson gave the impression of high-flown, principled debate. But Charles Pinckney, with his usual lack of finesse, reduced them to mere posturing with the damning observation that "the whole comes to this . . . Give New Jersey an equal vote, and she will dismiss her scruples, and concur in the national system."[97] In his artless, youthful way, Pinckney was saying what was on everyone's mind. Paterson and New Jersey were taking a stand in the hopes of driving the convention toward the compromise that Dickinson had foreseen weeks before.

There was a catch, however. A Senate representing state legislatures would no longer be a pure instance of a national system. It would be part national, and part federal. When Randolph rose to defend the plan he had introduced, he reminded his fellow delegates that "the true question is whether we shall adhere to the federal plan, or introduce a national plan." A federal plan like Paterson's could only force the states to act by coercion. But such coercion, Randolph argued, would be "impracticable, expensive, [and] cruel to individuals." A national plan, by contrast, provided for legislation over individuals and therefore did not require any collective coercion. And a national government with this capacity would have to be elected directly by the people. "He begged it to be considered that the present is the last moment for establishing one," Randolph concluded. Otherwise, "after this select experiment" of the convention, "the people will yield to despair."[98] Randolph was insisting on a national system, Paterson on a federal. No one had yet articulated the logic of something in between.

Pork Still

On Monday, June 18, 1787, Alexander Hamilton attempted to break the stalemate. Although the attempt was idiosyncratic, Hamilton was an unusual delegate. The New York delegation was unsympathetic to the national plan or a strong executive. Hamilton, however, had been a key actor in Annapolis pressing for major constitutional reform.

Hamilton explained that he "had been hitherto silent on the business before the convention" partly because he was younger than his New York colleagues and partly because he disagreed with them. But the time had come. "The crisis however which now marked our affairs, was too serious to permit any scruples whatever to prevail over the duty imposed on every man to contribute his efforts to the public safety and happiness."[99]

With this dramatic introduction, Hamilton cursed both houses, announcing that he was "obliged therefore to declare himself unfriendly to both plans." A national plan was necessary. But there were "essential defects" in the Virginia plan as well as the New Jersey plan.

Hamilton began by listing the "great and essential principles necessary for the support of government." The people must have "an active and constant interest in supporting" a government, yet the states had no such interest in the federal government. Next came power: "Men love power," Hamilton stated simply.* States were the same, and sovereign states would try to wrest power away from the national government.

The New Jersey plan, Hamilton said, conferred insufficient authority on Congress while at the same time poorly preserving state sovereignties. "Two sovereignties cannot coexist within the same limits," he argued, drawing on the principle that imperium in imperio must fail. "Giving power to Congress must eventuate in a bad government or in no government."[100]

The point forcefully made, Hamilton asked the inevitable question: "What then is to be done?" The country was big, and government was expensive. The logical answer was to eliminate the state governments. This would "shock the public opinion," Hamilton admitted. But there was no other reason not to do it. The state governments were "not necessary for any of the great purposes of commerce, revenue, or agriculture." Local authorities would always be needed and could be subordinated to the national government.

The only tricky part of his proposal, Hamilton said, was how to draw representatives into Congress from throughout the country. The wages of elected office would draw moneygrubbing mediocrities. "This view of the subject," he explained, almost led him to "despair that republican government could be established over so great an extent." Personally he had "no scruple in declaring," that "the British government was the best in the world." He "doubted much whether anything short of it would do in America."[101]

Other delegates had spoken positively of limited monarchy. But only Hamilton had the bravado to assert that a constitutional monarchy alone could govern the United States. Nor was Hamilton provoking his colleagues thoughtlessly. Congress had once been seen as an adequate institution. Now everyone knew that Congress had failed. Today, even the staunchest republicans were busy "declaiming against the vices of democ-

---

* Here, as at other times, Hamilton demonstrated the difference between his view of politics and Madison's. For Hamilton, deeply influenced by Hobbes, politics must be seen in the first instance through the lens of power and glory. For Madison, influenced by Aristotle and Francis Hutcheson, politics ideally reflected the human impulse to sociability, which in turn produced friendship and concord. Cf. Hont, *Politics in Commercial Society*, 7–13.

racy." This was "progress," he announced. He looked forward to a time when others would join him in the belief that the British constitution was the only one in the world that, as the French politician Jacques Necker had put it, "unites public strength with individual security."[102]

The British, according to Hamilton, had solved this problem by balancing the House of Lords against the House of Commons. The Virginia plan came nowhere close to empowering its "temporary" Senate sufficiently to protect property holders.[103] The answer was to let the senators hold their places for life or at least during good behavior, like judges—or British peers.

Hamilton next turned to the executive branch. A hereditary king's interests were "interwoven with that of the nation." A king was so rich "that he was placed above the danger of being corrupted from abroad—but at the same time was both sufficiently independent and sufficiently controlled, to answer the purpose of the institution at home." The solution was to give the executive life tenure, too.[104] "It will be objected probably," he went on, "that such an executive will be an elective monarch." To that he replied that "monarch is an indefinite term. It marks not either the degree or duration of power." The executive under the Virginia plan, he claimed, would be a monarch elected for seven years—and that was worse than a life monarch, because "the object of his ambition would be to prolong his power," through war and the state of emergency.[105] Elected for life, Hamilton's monarch would have no need of such stratagems.

Hamilton had a central theme: The government could succeed only if it could channel "all the passions of individuals," as he wrote in his own notes for the speech.[106] Passionate himself, Hamilton believed that theories of politics and constitutional design could be reduced to competing theories of passion. "Gentlemen," he explained to the other delegates, "differ in their opinions concerning the necessary checks" in the Senate based on "the different estimates they form of human passions." The correct view was to see these impulses as wildly risky: "When the great object of government is pursued, which seizes the popular passions, they spread like wildfire, and become irresistible."[107]

Madison, calmer and more dispassionate by temperament, thought the danger to republicanism came from the competing interests of different groups of citizens. Given this diagnosis, he proposed tools such as the enlargement of the republic and the national veto to cure the problem.

For Hamilton, "interests" was too weak a term. A worldview that began with the proposition that "men love power" could not be put into practice by tweaking republicanism.

By now Hamilton had spoken for "between five and six hours," filling the entirety of the day's session.[108] Hamilton "confess[ed]" that his own plan and that of Virginia were "very remote from the idea of the people." The New Jersey plan might be "nearest their expectation." But things were on the move. The people were "gradually ripening in their opinions of government—they begin to be tired of an excess of democracy." Then Hamilton delivered his most stinging verdict: "And what even is the Virginia plan," he asked rhetorically, "but *pork still, with a little change of the sauce?*"[109]

Hamilton's conclusion, delivered with the same verve that characterized all of his doings, reflected the logic that had animated his entire astonishing speech. The Virginia plan was still republicanism. Madison's theories of enlargement and the federal negative amounted to a bit of sauce spread upon the same pork dish already served in the form of the Articles of Confederation. The note of contempt implicit in Hamilton's metaphor was not accidental. The same dish, probably smelly and a bit old, was being served up with ornamentation.

Disobedience of the Members

Hamilton's daylong speech in praise of monarchy and life peerage did not shock the delegates out of their deadlock. The next day Madison gave a long speech of his own, aimed at demolishing the New Jersey plan once and for all.

Madison briefly dismissed the idea that the states had entered the union the way that individuals entered the social contract from the state of nature. If they had, Madison explained, a majority could bind the rest. And if the Articles must be understood as a treaty, well then, according to international law, "a breach of any one article, by any one party, leaves all the other parties at liberty, to consider the whole convention as dissolved."[110] Madison went on to claim that there had been "numerous and notorious" breaches of the Articles, including by New Jersey, which had openly refused to pay money lawfully demanded by Congress.[111]

After addressing the failings of the New Jersey plan, Madison tried to offer a compromise: allowing states to merge with their neighbors. The mid-Atlantic states could then, if they chose, join together into a single larger state. It is doubtful whether Madison believed his proposal had any chance of being adopted. He was simply trying to find some way out of the thicket.

Over the next several days, there was no progress on the most important question of the convention, and the delegates settled into squabbling over details such as salaries and lengths of terms. On Monday, June 25, 1787, they returned to the main subject. First they voted to change the description of the houses of Congress as "national" bodies to the more neutral legislature "of the United States." Then, after extensive discussion, the convention voted 9 to 2 that the members of the Senate should be chosen by the state legislatures. Only Virginia and Pennsylvania voted for direct election.

Definitively voting to have the state legislatures elect the Senate was not itself a breakthrough, but it was movement toward resolution on the question of proportionality—because it treated the senators as representatives of the states, not the people directly. On June 26, the convention debated the length of Senate terms. Madison argued that the Senate would both "protect the people against their rulers," and also protect the same people "against the transient impressions into which they themselves might be led."[112] The two houses of Congress would "watch and check each other." This was the first clear reference to internal checks and balances made at the convention.

Madison repeated his argument that "in all civilized countries" there would be conflict between different economic interests, and that a majority "might under some impulses be tempted to commit injustice on the minority." He left no doubt that the majority would be those without money, which could lead to the redistribution of property. "Symptoms of the leveling spirit"—he meant Shays's Rebellion—"have sufficiently appeared . . . to give notice of the future danger."[113]

The stakes were historic, Madison concluded. It was "more than probable" that the convention was "digesting a plan which in its operation would decide forever the fate of republican government." It therefore behooved the convention "not only to provide every guard to liberty that its preservation could require, but be equally careful to supply the defects which our own experience had particularly pointed out."[114]

On June 28, 1787, Madison introduced a new argument: The big states were so different in economic interests, "in manners, religion, and the other circumstances" that they would never combine to oppress the small states. The main industry of Massachusetts was fish, of Pennsylvania flour, and of Virginia tobacco. There was no reason to expect a convergence of interests.[115] Turning back again to history, Madison argued that large states tended to compete with each other in rivalry, not combine "to devour the weaker nations of the earth." Carthage and Rome, he said, "tore each other to pieces."

But the record of large countries was not as benign as Madison claimed. When Madison asked rhetorically, "Have we seen the great powers of Europe combining to oppress the small?" Paterson jotted in his notes, "Yes—the division of Poland."[116] And despite divergent economic interests, the delegates from the large states, especially Madison and Wilson, were already cooperating in the convention to the detriment of the small states.

Babel

After Madison had spoken, Benjamin Franklin took the floor. In the past, Franklin had written down his remarks and given them to someone else to deliver. This time he read the speech himself, a sign that something important was happening.

Franklin began on a depressive note. "The small progress we have made after four or five weeks close attendance and continual reasonings with each other—our different sentiments on almost every question . . . is methinks a melancholy proof of the imperfection of the human understanding." The delegates, Franklin said, were searching for answers without success. "We indeed seem to *feel* our own want of political wisdom, since we have been running about in search of it." Arguments increasingly were coming from ancient history. "We have viewed modern states all round Europe," he commented, "but find none of their constitutions suitable to our circumstances."[117]

Then came Franklin's surprising recommendation. If the delegates were "groping as it were in the dark," perhaps they should turn to "the Father of lights to illuminate our understandings." Franklin, the libertine darling of the French Enlightenment, was recommending public prayer.

During the Revolution, Franklin remembered, the Continental Congress meeting "in this room" had offered daily prayer "for the divine protection"—and its prayers "were heard, and they were graciously answered." Franklin now delivered something that sounded very much like a profession of faith: "I have lived, sir, a long time, and the longer I live, the more convincing proofs I see of this truth—*that God governs in the affairs of men*. And if a sparrow cannot fall to the ground without his notice, is it probable that an empire can rise without his aid?" Without God's help, Franklin concluded, "we shall succeed in this political building no better than the builders of Babel. We shall be divided by our little partial local interests; our projects will be confounded, and we ourselves shall become a reproach and bye word down to future ages."[118]

As an adult Franklin had barely set foot in church, and it was surprising that he now recommended that each session of the convention begin with a prayer to be performed by "one or more of the clergy of this city." Yet his New England childhood stood Franklin in good stead as he admonished his colleagues. Like a Puritan preacher comparing current events to biblical archetypes, Franklin was drawing an analogy. The lesson for the delegates was to put aside "partial local interests" and act as a single body—or face destruction.

Hamilton, himself no churchgoer, objected to Franklin's proposal to initiate daily prayer. It would have been fine had it been proposed at the outset of the convention, Hamilton maintained. But starting to pray "at this late day" might "lead the public to believe that the embarrassments and dissensions within the convention, had suggested this measure."[119] Edmund Randolph came to Franklin's rescue by proposing that the convention request a sermon on July 4, and then naturally continue the prayers thereafter. The convention agreed, although not without "several unsuccessful attempts for silently postponing the matter by adjourning."[120]

The whole episode was strange to the point of being surreal. It momentarily injected religion into the midst of a convention in which all participants had spoken on the basis of logic, reason, history, and comparative politics. The notorious Deist Benjamin Franklin had declared his belief in specific divine providence rather than the watchmaker God who wound up the works and let them run on their own.

The possibility that Franklin was having a late-in-life Christian conversion can be discounted.[121] What, then, was happening? Why did Franklin want to introduce daily prayer at the midstream point, when crisis loomed?

Perhaps Franklin thought that some change—any change—could

break the delegates out of their current frame of mind. He himself had not spoken to the convention in several weeks. The simple fact of his personal intervention might have some effect. Prayer could do no harm, and might even help remind the delegates of their central purpose.

But a more plausible explanation is that Franklin intended to lay the groundwork for a compromise between the New Jersey plan and the Virginia plan. While overtly praying for national unity, Franklin was pressuring both sides to fold. By framing the criticism in religious terms, Franklin could to some degree mask its specificity. Who, after all, could dissent from a prayer urging the entire body to act as one to reach agreement and avoid the ignominy of failure?

Middle Ground

The next day, June 29, 1787, the possibility of compromise between a truly national government and a truly federal one was put on the table. William Samuel Johnson of Connecticut opened the session by asserting that "the controversy must be endless" so long as one side thought of the states as "districts of people" who collectively composed a single political society, while the other considered the states to be distinct political societies. Johnson took a middle position. "On the whole," he argued, "in some respects the states are to be considered in their political capacity, and in others as districts of individual citizens." Therefore, the ideas of the different sides, "instead of being opposed to each other, ought to be combined." The combination was a compromise envisioned nearly a month earlier by John Dickinson. "In one branch the *people*, ought to be represented; in the other, the *states*."[122]

Johnson, a lawyer and judge, was almost sixty years old, a generation older than most active delegates. He had lived in England as the agent for the colony of Connecticut during the late 1760s, and had received an honorary doctor of laws degree from Oxford University while there. His reputation for scholarship was strong—Pierce reported that Johnson was "said to be one of the first classics in America." His colleagues in the convention always called him "Dr. Johnson," and he had just been appointed president of Columbia College in New York, where his father had been the founding president nearly twenty-five years before. Pierce thought that "there is nothing in him that warrants the high reputation which he has for public speaking. There is something in the tone of his voice not pleasing to the ear."[123] Yet Johnson's reputation for knowledge made his proposal serious. Where others so far had maintained that the government must be either national or federal, Johnson was suggesting that it could be both.

Oliver Ellsworth, also of Connecticut, agreed. The United States was "partly national; partly federal." Proportional representation in the lower house "was conformable to the national principle and would secure the large states against small. And the equality of voices was conformable to the federal principle and was necessary to secure the small states against the large. He trusted on this middle ground a compromise would take place." Ellsworth insisted that "he was not in general a halfway man, yet he preferred doing half the good we could, rather than do nothing at all."[124]

Madison responded to Johnson that the "mixed nature of the government ought to be kept in view"—but ought not be accepted. It made no sense to give "an *equal* voice" to "*unequal* portions of the people."[125] Grasping at straws, he added that if the United States were to break up, the states would go to war with one another. Each would strengthen itself, and all the states "would soon be transformed into vigorous and high toned governments," aristocratic cabals that would build standing armies to defend themselves. In Madison's telling, these garrison states would become tyrannies. "A standing military force, with an overgrown executive will not long be safe companions to liberty."[126] The prospect was so far from the reality of the weak state governments that no one bothered to respond.

Alexander Hamilton had had enough. He rose to debunk the theory that the small states were fighting to preserve their liberty. "The truth is it is a contest for power, not for liberty," he said boldly. Those in small states would be no less free than those in large states. But "the state of Delaware having 40,000 souls will lose power, if she has 1/10 only of the votes allowed to Pennsylvania having 400,000."

Hamilton echoed Madison's argument that the large states had no common interests that would hold them together going forward. "The only considerable distinction of interests" among states, he argued, "lay between the carrying and non-carrying states"—between those that relied on seaborne trade, such as Pennsylvania and Massachusetts, and those such as Virginia that did not.[127] Hamilton's astute economic analysis might have been valuable if anyone had listened.

Building to a conclusion, Hamilton said he wished to point out a problem "of a most serious nature" that would happen if the union broke down. Different states would then align themselves with different European powers, "who will foment disturbances among ourselves, and make us parties to all their own quarrels." Countries with "American dominions"—Britain, France, and Spain—were already "jealous" of the United States. The ambassadors of these foreign nations were ready to pounce if the convention should fail.

The United States needed a strong national government in order to stand up to these European states. "No government could give us tranquility and happiness at home, which did not possess sufficient stability and strength to make us respectable abroad." Republican isolationism was naïve and idealistic. If other countries did not consider the government of the United States sufficiently powerful, they would take steps that would disrupt its functioning.[128]

The time for reform was now or never. "This was the critical moment for forming . . . a government" worthy of respect, he asserted. "It is a miracle that we [are] now here exercising our tranquil and free deliberations on the subject" of the constitution. "It would be madness to trust to future miracles," he concluded.[129] Hamilton was reminding the delegates just how difficult the road to Philadelphia had been. Having helped save the failed Annapolis convention, he now saw the Philadelphia convention on the verge of collapse.

Hamilton had run out of patience. Where Madison continued to reach for new ideas and Franklin proposed prayer, Hamilton left the convention and went back to New York for six weeks. He would not return to active participation until the middle of August, after which he would disappear again until early September. Others could do the work of trying to resolve the conflict between large and small states.

With Hamilton gone, Madison tried to expand on the suggestion that the large states did not have common interests—and he once again added a new element to his case. The states had different interests not because of their size, "but by other circumstances; the most material of which resulted partly from climate, but principally from the effects of their having or not having slaves." As a consequence, "the great division of interests" was not "between the large and small states: It lay between the northern and southern."[130]

The prophetic nature of Madison's analysis should not obscure the reason he was making it. He was once again looking for a way out of the deadlock. Reframing the problem might be a way to change the patterns of voting in the convention. He had been, he said, "casting about in his mind" for some mechanism to deal with the problem of representation. The idea he had come up with was that, instead of representing slaves as three-fifths of free persons in apportioning both houses of the legislature, one house should be apportioned only according to free inhabitants, while the other should be apportioned on the basis of "counting the slaves as if free." The former would favor the northern states, and the latter the southern.

Franklin, for his part, had read the tea leaves, and decided the small mid-Atlantic states could not be accommodated except by compromise. Franklin now introduced a proposal that matched the Connecticut delegates' suggested middle ground. The states would have equal representation in the Senate, and would be guaranteed equal representation "in all cases or questions wherein the sovereignty of individual states may be affected." In all decisions about appropriation, however, the states would have suffrage in proportion to their actual contribution to the treasury.[131]

With these various proposals on the table, the convention adjourned for its Sunday recess. On Monday, July 2, 1787, the delegates began with a vote on whether to give each state equal representation in the Senate, as proposed by Oliver Ellsworth. The convention split, with five states for, five against, and one divided. The three big states were joined by the southern states of North Carolina and South Carolina, with Georgia unable to cast its vote because of internal disagreement. The small mid-Atlantic states voted as a bloc in favor.

The equally divided vote represented the culmination of the crisis that had been building since the New Jersey plan was introduced two weeks earlier. Charles Cotesworth Pinckney expressed the sense of the convention. "The states being exactly divided," he observed, "some compromise seemed to be necessary." He proposed creating a committee of one member from each state to devise it.[132]

The writing was on the wall. The delegates who had voted for equal representation in the Senate spoke in favor of referral to a committee. So did several of the more moderate delegates from states that had voted against, such as Gerry of Massachusetts. Edmund Randolph said that he supported a committee "though he did not expect much benefit from the expedient."

Madison and Wilson were squarely against. Madison insisted that the committee would do nothing but cause delay. Wilson complained that the committee would vote according to the rule of state equality, which was itself "the very rule of voting which was opposed on one side."[133]

These arguments were specious. The committee would have a significant advantage over the convention because its sole purpose would be to make a compromise. The real reason Madison and Wilson did not want a committee is that they knew precisely what it would do: recommend that one house of the legislature be elected proportionally and the other on the basis of equality between the states. They were about to lose their fight for a truly national government.

The committee met the next day, Tuesday, July 3. Robert Yates of New York, following the lead of Dr. Johnson and Oliver Ellsworth of Connecticut, made a speech arguing for a "national government on federal principles"—a hybrid of the Virginia and New Jersey plans. Then Franklin introduced a compromise motion that grew from the proposal he had made the previous Saturday. As he put it this time, the first branch of the legislature would have one member for every forty thousand inhabitants. All bills for raising and apportioning money would have to originate in the first branch, "and shall not be altered or amended by the second branch." In the second branch, "each state shall have an equal vote."[134]

The Work of the Sword

On July 4, 1787, the convention did not officially meet, but many of its members convened in the Old First Reformed Church to hear a sermon by the Reverend William Rogers of Philadelphia.[135] Rogers, a Baptist, was a logical choice. He had served as a brigade chaplain in the Continental army and was the first student enrolled at Rhode Island College, which later became Brown University. He had lived in Philadelphia for years and had honorary degrees from Yale, Princeton, and the University of Pennsylvania.[136] He was, in short, a mid-Atlantic man.

In the sermon, Rogers prayed that delegates would "prove happy instruments in healing all divisions and prove the good of the great whole."[137] There is no reason to think he had any specific knowledge of the proceedings of the convention, which had been successfully kept secret until that point. At the same time, a better framing for the committee's proposed compromise could not have been imagined. The wily Franklin had managed to get God on the side of the compromise he now espoused.

On July 5, the compromise was presented to the convention—and Madison denounced it. Originating money bills in the popular house would have no impact, he predicted, nor would the nominal denial to the Senate of the power to amend them, which could easily be circumvented. In essence, the small states had made no concessions at all. Faced with a choice of "either departing from justice in order to conciliate the smaller states" or else "gratifying the larger states and the majority of the people," Madison said he could not "hesitate as to the option he ought to make."

Madison's preferred course was drastic. The convention should ignore the small states, impose proportional representation, and "with justice and the majority of the people on their side, have nothing to fear."[138] Once the large states had agreed on a constitution, the small states would have no choice but to adopt it. Delaware would ratify the constitution even if not to its liking rather than "brave the consequences of seeking her fortunes apart from the other states." It would be desirable, Madison said, if the states could achieve "harmony in the convention." But if they could not, "the principal states, comprehending a majority of the people of the United States, should concur in a just and judicious plan." After they did, "he had the firmest hopes that all the other states would by degrees accede to it."[139]

Madison got support from Gouverneur Morris, who after an extended absence had returned to the convention just as Hamilton was leaving. Morris spoke in grand, cosmopolitan tones. "He came here as a representative of America," Madison noted in paraphrase. "He flattered himself he came here in some degree as a representative of the whole human race; for the whole human race will be affected by the proceedings of this convention." As a citizen of the world, Morris "wished gentlemen to extend their views beyond the present moment of time; beyond the narrow limits of place from which they derive their political origin." It sometimes seemed, he said, as though "we were assembled to truck and bargain for our particular states."[140]

Morris was trying to flatter the other delegates into transcending local political interests. If Madison's urging of a national perspective had not convinced the small states to give up their equal suffrage, maybe a global perspective would. Morris had been born a New Yorker and become a

Pennsylvanian. Now he asked the delegates, "Who can say whether he himself, much less whether his children, will the next year be an inhabitant of this or that state?"[141]

That was not all Morris had to say. Shifting suddenly from uplifting universalism to power politics, he delivered a brutal message to the small states. "This country must be united," he intoned. "If persuasion does not unite it, the sword will." There would be a civil war, very possibly involving foreign intervention—and the large states would win. "The stronger party will then make traitors of the weaker; and the gallows and halter will finish the work of the sword."[142]

The prospect was horrible, but the fault lay with the states. "State attachments, and state importance have been the bane of this country; we cannot annihilate; but we may perhaps take out the teeth of the serpents." To Morris, the states were serpents, dangers to the possibility of a truly united country. They must concede political authority or be forced to do so.[143]

Morris's provocative invocation of the sword guaranteed that no one would remember the appeal to cosmopolitanism he had made just moments before. One Delaware delegate responded with outrage. "To hear such language without emotion," he declared, "would be to renounce the feelings of a man and the duty of a citizen."[144] Paterson added that he "thought the sword and the gallows" were "little calculated to produce conviction."[145] For the first time since the delegates had discussed executive power weeks before, tempers were running high.

Elbridge Gerry, who had chaired the compromise committee, tried to reconcile the sides. He had voted for the report in committee, he said, despite having "very material objections to it." The reason was that the United States was "in a peculiar situation. We were neither the same nation nor different nations. We ought not therefore to pursue the one or the other of these ideas too closely."[146] A Massachusetts man was now echoing Johnson's idea that a compromise between the national and the federal was not simply an expedient, but actually made logical sense. The tactic of appointing a committee was beginning to bear fruit.

A Species of Property

On Tuesday, July 10, 1787, the convention considered a report from a committee that had been asked to provide hard numbers for what the composition of the lower house would look like if it had a total of sixty-five members. The numbers led to a detailed—and dysfunctional—debate over whether, for example, New Hampshire should have three representatives or two. Once again, the three-fifths rule came to the surface, and now it became the center of the debate. South Carolinian delegates argued that blacks should be represented equally with whites. Slaves, one "insisted," produced as much labor as free men and were just as valuable as "means of defense."[147] Northerners insisted on keeping three-fifths as the ratio.[148] As Madison had predicted, the division between South and North over slavery was becoming crucial to the work of the convention.

Compromise did not come easily. On July 11, the delegates rejected the three-fifths compromise by a vote of 6 to 4. On July 12, Gouverneur Morris insisted that "the people of Pennsylvania will never agree to a representation of Negroes."[149] Oliver Ellsworth then proposed an amendment to the three-fifths rule that would allow Congress in the future to enact some new rule "that shall more accurately ascertain the wealth of the several states."[150] This combination was enough to worry Edmund Randolph. He "perceived that the design was entertained by some of excluding slaves altogether; the legislature therefore ought not to be left at liberty" to make such a change in the future. With the politeness of a Virginia gentleman, Randolph "lamented that such a species of property existed. But as it did exist the holders of it would require this security."[151] The South Carolinian Charles Pinckney, with his usual willful blindness to the delegates' positions, proposed to drop the three-fifths compromise and count blacks as equal to whites. The convention rejected the suggestion 8 to 2, with only South Carolina and Georgia voting for it.[152]

The debate was becoming hopelessly confused. On July 13, 1787, Gouverneur Morris summed up the trouble. He had, he said, previously considered the idea of a distinction "between the northern and southern states" as "heretical." But now, by insisting on the representation of slaves, the southerners had set up such a distinction and persisted in it. The result would be "a transfer of power from the maritime to the interior and landed interest."[153]

Now Morris turned prophet. His analysis combined Madison's theory of a difference between northern and southern interests with Hamilton's view that the true difference lay between states whose economy depended on the seagoing trade and those that did not. If there were to be a struggle "between the two ends of the union," he proposed, the mid-Atlantic states would join the northeastern states, while the future western states (whose existence all anticipated) would join the South. The southerners and westerners united would "inevitably bring on a war with Spain for the Mississippi." That war, in turn, would affect the northern and mid-Atlantic states that relied on trade—but would not affect the southern and western states that wanted it, because those states had "no property or interest exposed on the sea." The result would be a nation split in two. If his assessment was accurate, Morris thought, "instead of blending incompatible things, let us at once take a friendly leave of each other."[154]

The chilling picture of a nation divided spurred the delegates toward compromise. Wilson argued that the solution was to eliminate any reference to regional wealth from the measure of representation and rely on population alone, always tempered by the three-fifths rule.[155] The convention was in favor, and the three-fifths compromise was alive. Wilson still opposed equal representation in the Senate, and on July 13, Wilson repeated his argument that this compromise—unlike the three-fifths rule—was fundamentally unjust. "What hopes will our constituents entertain," he asked, "when they find that the essential principles of justice have been violated in the outset of the government?"[156]

Madison agreed. In the light of what had transpired over the previous several days, he added a new conclusion: Equal representation would give the northern states a permanent advantage over the southern ones.[157] Madison did not mince words in explaining the split: "The institution of slavery and its consequences formed the line of discrimination. There were five states on the south, eight on the northern side of this line." More nonslave states than slave states meant more power for the nonslave states in the Senate. Proportional representation might still give the northern states a slight advantage, but the advantage would fade over time as the population "tend[ed] towards an equilibrium."[158] In contrast, a Senate with fixed equal representation would give a perpetual advantage to the nonslave states—and by implication, would turn the total number of states into a battleground for the issue of slavery.

On Monday, July 16, what would come to be called the "great compromise" passed—barely. The small mid-Atlantic states—Connecticut, New Jersey, Delaware, and Maryland—voted in favor of equal representation in the Senate, their goal from the start. They were joined by just a single state that had voted against them three weeks before: North Carolina, which was also small but slaveholding. New York did not have enough delegates present to vote, Hamilton being long gone.

The five votes in favor were thus met by four against. Pennsylvania and Virginia did not budge from their preference for proportional representation. Georgia and South Carolina, which had been in Virginia's camp from the start, joined them. Had Massachusetts, the other large state, voted as it had in the past, the convention would have been deadlocked 5 to 5, just as it was before Benjamin Franklin's pious intervention in the first week of July. But Massachusetts split its vote, with Elbridge Gerry voting for the compromise and Rufus King against, each joined by one of the other, less consequential delegates from the state.[159] With Massachusetts out of the voting, the proposal passed with a bare majority.

The vote hit the Virginians hard. It was one thing for the convention to deadlock on the Senate. It was quite another for the coalition that had pushed the Virginia plan so close to adoption to find that its progress toward a truly national government had been reversed. The vote, Edmund Randolph said frankly, "had embarrassed the business extremely." He had hoped to propose further compromise possibilities. But now he could not help but think the small states "were unprepared to discuss this subject further." He proposed that the convention adjourn, "that the large states might consider the steps proper to be taken in the present solemn crisis of the business, and that the small states might also deliberate on the means of conciliation."[160]

Randolph's proposal to adjourn was presented in such a dire spirit that General Pinckney asked whether he meant to adjourn the convention altogether or just to stop for the day. Randolph replied darkly that he was sorry that his "meaning had been so readily and strangely misinterpreted." He intended only to adjourn for the day, he explained. But "in case the smaller states should continue to hold back, the larger might then take such measures . . . as might be necessary."

Randolph's promise for the large states to take whatever measures "might be necessary" sounded like a threat. But in reality, Virginia had little leverage. John Rutledge of South Carolina, who had been a member of the compromise committee, expressed the predicament. He "could see no need of an adjournment" because he "could see no chance of a compromise. The little states were fixed. They had repeatedly and solemnly declared themselves to be so. All that the large states then had to do was to decide whether they would yield or not."[161]

Rutledge was right: The small states had the large states where they wanted them. The compromise—if such it was—had been produced by

pure intransigence. Madison had believed that the small states would follow the large states because they would have no choice: The strong would
do what they could and the weak would have to bear it. Yet in his hopes
of achieving a national government where power would be deployed from
the center and act directly on the citizens, he had failed to consider the
dynamics of a convention.

It was not a coincidence that a convention voting according to state
equality had blocked constitutional reform aimed at making representation proportional to population. To Madison, the vagaries of British colonial organization that had produced state boundaries seemed irrelevant
to the question of how to run a new country in America. The reality was
otherwise. When it came to agreeing on a constitution, the accidental
divisions of history mattered enormously.

The convention adjourned, and the delegates of the larger states, along
with a few from the smaller, remained where they were to meet and discuss what to do. Madison noted that "the time was wasted in vague conversation on the subject, without any specific proposition or agreement."
Yet even by his own frustrated account that was not quite right. Some of
the delegates, probably including Madison, argued to the group that "the
side comprising the principal states, and a majority of the people of
America, should propose a scheme of government to the states" regardless of what the smaller states wanted. If that meant two separate recommendations from the convention, so be it. "Others," Madison noted,
"seemed inclined to yield to the smaller states, and to concur in such an
act however imperfect and exceptionable," even though it had been "decided by a bare majority of states and by a minority of the people of the
United States." The result of this disagreement, Madison concluded,
probably "satisfied the smaller states that they had nothing to apprehend
from a union of the larger." The small states did not need to fear Randolph's threat of any "necessary" measures because the large states could
not even agree among themselves.

Madison had lost, and the compromise was a fait accompli. The post-
adjournment meeting had not been a waste of time. It had been a confirmation of defeat.

CHAPTER FIVE

Compromise

...

THE ARGUMENT: *As a result of the great compromise, Madison loses the national negative. He struggles through the rest of the convention, repeatedly trying and failing to get it back. Ultimately, he leaves the convention disappointed despite the adoption of a document mostly based on his blueprint—because he knows he has lost the centerpiece of his theory. Writing to Jefferson, he develops and deepens the argument for the negative again, trying to exorcise the defeat.*

Hamilton enlists Madison to write essays for what will become the Federalist *papers. Madison's first is also his most famous. In* Federalist No. 10, *he introduces his enlargement theory for the first time to the public—without the negative that was its essential feature from its birth.*

Jefferson writes back to Madison from France, skeptical of the constitution for its lack of a bill of rights. Jefferson's worries prefigure those of many Virginians. Patrick Henry is poised to lead the fight against ratification. By January 1788, Madison foresees that the constitution may be in danger.

THE NATIONAL NEGATIVE OVER STATE LAWS had already been watered down. Now the compromise that was necessary for the convention to succeed promised to kill Madison's brainchild. On July 17, 1787, the convention took up the negative, and Luther Martin of Maryland, deeply skeptical of national authority, "considered the power as improper and inadmissible." He asked, reasonably enough, "shall all the laws of the states be sent up to the general legislature before they shall be permitted to operate?"[1]

Madison responded, but restricted himself to arguing that the state courts could not be trusted to rule against their own laws and that national coordination required a central authority. His only example was the British Empire, in which "nothing could maintain the harmony and subordination of the various parts" other than the Crown's prerogative to stifle "in the birth" any local laws "tending to discord or encroachment."[2]

When Madison finished his brief speech, Gouverneur Morris, whose aristocratic tendencies and love of the British constitution should have made him a supporter, got up to say that he was "more and more opposed to the negative. The proposal of it would disgust all the states."[3] Not a single delegate spoke in support of Madison. In the vote that followed, Virginia voted Madison's way and was joined by Massachusetts and North Carolina. But every other state voted to abandon even the mild form of Madison's national negative—including Gouverneur Morris's Pennsylvania, which had not previously voted against any aspect of the Virginia plan.

Madison gamely tried to bounce back. After the topic moved to whether the executive should serve "during good behavior"—that is, for life—Madison spoke twice to insist that above all, the executive should not be dependent on the legislature for reappointment. The great risk, he believed, was not a monarchy but an all-powerful legislative branch. "Experience," he said, "had proved a tendency in our governments to throw all power into the legislative vortex. The executives of the states are in general little more than cyphers; the legislatures omnipotent."[4]

The next day Madison made small but useful suggestions, including the proposal that the judiciary be appointed by the executive subject to the agreement of the Senate. The day after that he again beat the drum of separation of powers, urging appointment of the executive by electors chosen directly by the people to avoid making the executive depend upon the legislature.[5]

Several days after the defeat of the national negative, on July 21, 1787, Madison roused himself for another try at a substantive proposal for a veto power. James Wilson had recommended that the national judiciary— the Supreme Court—work alongside the executive in vetoing legislation that might be dangerous without being definitively unconstitutional.[6] Luther Martin objected that joining the judiciary to the executive for purposes of the veto violated the separation of powers. Madison responded that judicial participation in the veto would give the judiciary the ability to maintain its independence. The goal was not to rely on "discrimination of the departments on paper," which might prove inadequate to ensure the separation of powers. Instead it was "necessary to in-troduce such a balance of powers and interests, as will guarantee the provisions on paper."[7] Only concrete powers could assure that the theo-retical separation would be respected in the real world.

This was the first time at the convention that Madison had expressly told the delegates that he did not consider paper guarantees sufficient to achieve constitutional goals. The distinction between theory and practice had been implicit in his constitutional thinking before. Now, with the structure of the new constitution taking shape, he made it explicit.

Madison had an example to prove his point: the British constitution, which was the modern origin of the balance of powers among legislative, executive, and judicial branches. It was, Madison explained, "the most regular example of this theory." Yet the British constitution did not sepa-rate those powers in a formalistic way. British judges sat in parliament and on "executive councils." What was more, Madison added, "It was a part of their constitution that the executive might negative any law what-ever." This veto, he added, "had been universally regarded as calculated for the preservation of the whole" of the British system.[8]

Madison's arguments were intellectually formidable, but the example of the British constitution was once again poorly chosen. Wilson's pro-posal was defeated, with even the Pennsylvania delegation divided. Un-daunted, Madison immediately offered another option: The judges should be selected by the executive, and take office unless two-thirds of the Senate voted against them.

Earlier proposals had included the possibility that the Senate would select the judges. Now that the Senate would be selected by the states, however, Madison thought that "the people" should have the most im-portant say in choosing the judiciary. The executive, he said, should "be considered as a national officer, acting for and equally sympathizing with every part of the United States." Relying on the Senate for judicial ap-pointments would put the judiciary entirely into the hands of the north-ern states, who would control the Senate by virtue of their numbers. Madison recognized he had lost the battle over the Senate, but he was still trying to mitigate its effects and keep the government as national as possible.

Everyone understood what was happening. The delegates voted, but only the large states—Virginia, Massachusetts, and Pennsylvania—supported Madison's proposal. For good measure, the other states all voted expressly to keep judicial appointments in the Senate. Madison, it appeared, had lost yet again.[9]

Entirely at a Loss

Sensing momentum, Oliver Ellsworth of Connecticut went a step further and proposed that ratification be undertaken by state legislatures, not specially chosen conventions. Madison replied that since the constitution would change the powers of the state legislatures, it must be consented to not by the legislatures, but by the people who authorized them. The convention voted affirmatively to send the constitution to specially selected state conventions "after the approbation of Congress," with only Delaware dissenting.

As a result of Ellsworth's overreach, Madison had regained some authority—all was not lost. On July 25, Madison spoke against electing the national legislature. The fight over choosing an executive, he argued, would polarize the legislature. Furthermore, Madison continued, the executive who emerged "would derive his appointment from the predominant faction, and be apt to render his administration subservient to its views."[10] Electing the executive in Congress would drive partisanship, and should therefore be rejected.

Madison then attacked the option of state legislatures selecting the executive. Congress, he said, was meant to check the state legislatures. The executive was meant to check Congress. If the state legislatures could choose the executive, it would defeat the whole structure of control. The inmates would be running the asylum.[11] Having eliminated the national legislature and the state legislatures as credible electors of the executive, Madison concluded that the people were the only choice that remained; they could choose the executive either through a body of electors or directly. Madison's speech did not immediately convince the other delegates. Elbridge Gerry fretted that any form of popular election of the executive would give an enormous advantage to any national organization with the capacity to exert influence locally across the country.[12]

The next day, July 26, George Mason called for the executive to be elected by the national legislature for a single, nonrenewable seven-year term. The motion passed. There followed a brief but intense debate about whether elected representatives should be subjected to qualifications such as owning land or not being indebted to the general government. Madison, Morris, and Wilson all argued against including any such qualification for Congress.

In the process, Madison shared his views on the political economy of the country. There were three classes in the United States, he said: landed, commercial, and manufacturing. Although at present more people owned land than traded or manufactured, "the proportion however will daily increase," he predicted. "We see in the populous countries in Europe now, what we shall be hereafter."[13]

For republican government to work, all of these classes would have to be represented. Madison thus disagreed with the traditional republican impulse to restrict government to landowners like himself. He understood that the economy of the United States was changing, and did not want to fix the system of government so that it would not be responsive to altered circumstances.[14]

Madison's pithy account captured the imagination of some of the delegates. Speaking a few minutes later, Nathaniel Gorham referred to "the commercial and manufacturing part of the people," echoing Madison's taxonomy. All the proposals for qualifications on membership in Congress were voted down. With the matter of the executive apparently settled at a single seven-year nonrenewable term, the convention referred the last of its resolutions to the committee that would prepare a constitutional draft. For the first time since May, the convention took a substantial break. It adjourned until Monday, August 6, 1787, nearly two weeks later. A constitution was within view.

The Curse of Heaven

Randolph, not Madison, was appointed to the Committee of Detail that produced the first draft of what would become the U.S. Constitution. Many delegates left Philadelphia, where the temperature was getting hotter. Madison remained, glad to be free from what he told Jefferson was "the drudgery" of taking "lengthy notes of everything that has yet passed."[15] His correspondents, including his father[16] and Jefferson, wanted to know what was going on in the convention; but Madison apologetically told them he must keep faith with the promise of confidentiality that all the delegates had given. "As soon as I am at liberty I will endeavor to make amends for my silence, and if I ever have the pleasure of seeing you shall be able to give you pretty full gratification," he explained to Jefferson.[17]

We do not know whether and to what extent Madison may have advised Randolph, James Wilson, or other allies who sat on the Committee of Detail. We do know that during the adjournment, Madison got in touch with his former slave, Billey, whom he had sold into indentured servitude before leaving Philadelphia in 1783. Their encounter forms a striking backdrop for the work performed by the Committee of Detail.

Sometime in 1786, an enslaved seventeen-year-old named Anthony had run away from Montpelier.[18] Subsequently, Anthony returned or was returned home—and Madison and his father wanted to know how he had run away and what had happened to him while he was gone. Madison wrote to his father that "the inquiries which I have at different times made of Billy [*sic*] concerning Anthony satisfy me that he either knows, or will tell nothing of the matter."[19]

Madison had a suspect in mind who he believed might have assisted Anthony: another slave named John, who had replaced Billey as Madison's servant and accompanied him to Philadelphia for the convention. Yet Madison told his father, "I have not communicated to John the suspicions entertained of him." The reason was instrumental. "Whilst he remains in my service it will be well for him to suppose that he has my confidence, and that he has a character staked on his good behavior." The plan seemed to be working, he told his father: "He has been very attentive and faithful to me as yet, particularly since I left Virginia." John had engaged in some "misbehavior" while in Fredericksburg. But Madison had dealt with this misbehavior "by some serious reprehensions, and threats from me, which have never lost their effect."[20] Madison was, essentially, bragging to his father that he had cowed his own slave into at least temporary obedience.

Anthony had told his masters a story about his escape; Madison doubted that it was completely accurate. "It does not appear to me probable that all the circumstances mentioned by Anthony with regard to his rambles can be true. Besides other objections which occur, there seems to have been scarcely time for all the trips which he pretends to have made."[21]

This uncertainty about the trajectory of the fugitive slave Anthony, coupled with Madison's suspicion of John and Billey, reflect the pervasive anxieties of southern slaveholders. Masters could not trust their slaves not to flee to freedom. Government could not guarantee the return of slaves who had run off.

Small wonder, then, that among the handful of additions that the Committee of Detail proposed to the convention when it met again on August 6 was one relating to slavery. General Pinckney had charged the committee to make some guarantee against the emancipation of slaves. The committee's draft specified that Congress lacked the power to tax or prohibit the "importation of such persons as the several states shall think proper to admit."[22] In almost the same sentence, the draft constitution prohibited the taxation of exports, another boon to the southern agricultural states. Over the rest of the convention, slavery would become a central preoccupation.

On August 6, the draft was presented. On August 8, Rufus King of Massachusetts announced that the draft constitution had made him rethink the three-fifths compromise. He considered "the admission of slaves" into the population totals "a most grating circumstance to his mind," and believed it "would be so to a great part of the people of America." He had not, he explained, "made a strenuous opposition to it heretofore" because he "had hoped that this concession" would be traded for strengthening the national government. But now King observed that under the draft, the central government was actually weakened by slavery. It could not prohibit the slave trade, and it could not tax exports— including those created by slave labor.

The result, King argued, was to bind the North to protect the South without getting anything in return. "There was so much inequality and unreasonableness in all this, that the people of the northern states could never be reconciled to it," he maintained. "No candid man could undertake to justify it to them." King had hoped that the Committee of Detail would at least propose a time limit for the importation of slaves. Frustrated that no "accommodation" had been made, King asserted that he "never could agree to let them be imported without limitation and then be represented in the national legislature. Indeed," Madison wrote, "he could so little persuade himself of the rectitude of such a practice, that he was not sure he could assent to it under any circumstances. At all events, either slaves should not be represented, or exports should be taxable."

King's moral outrage was mitigated by his admission that, in fact, he could accept the slave trade for some period of time. And his conclusion that either slaves should not be counted, or else exports should be subject to taxation, suggested horse trading rather than principle. But slavery was now on the table, and the possibility of moral objection had at least been raised.

Gouverneur Morris needed no further invitation. In 1777, participating in the drafting of the first New York State constitution, the young Morris had unsuccessfully proposed the eventual abolition of slavery "so that in future ages, every human being who breathes the air of the state, shall enjoy the privileges of a freeman."[23] New York took several decades more to begin the partial abolition of slavery, and Morris himself came from a slaveholding family. Nevertheless, he delivered the closest thing to an abolitionist sermon to be heard at the convention.

Slavery "was the curse of heaven on the states where it prevailed," Morris began.[24] He took the delegates on a geographical tour of the United States with special reference to the effects of slavery[25] and condemned the three-fifths compromise. "Upon what principle is it that the slaves shall be computed in the representation? Are they men? Then make them citizens and let them vote. Are they property? Why then is no other property included?"[26] Morris knew that white southerners had no intention of making African slaves into citizens or allowing them to vote. In adopting the three-fifths compromise, the convention had acted without a defensible rationale. Morris provided a devastating description of the consequences:

> The admission of slaves into the representation, when fairly explained, comes to this: that the inhabitant of Georgia and South Carolina who goes to the coast of Africa, and in defiance of the most sacred laws of humanity tears away his fellow creatures from their dearest connections and damns them to the most cruel bondages, shall have more votes in a government instituted for protection of the rights of mankind, than the citizen of Pennsylvania or New Jersey who views with a laudable horror, so nefarious a practice.[27]

At the time, the slave trade was considered worse than slaveholding. By depicting his slaveholding colleagues as slave traders, Morris was drawing attention to the cruelties of the entire institution. Technically, however, Morris was not calling for the abolition of the slave trade, much less slavery. He was arguing that it was absurd for slave states to "have more votes in a government instituted for the protection of mankind" than would states that had abolished the practice.

Morris had one more argument to make against the three-fifths rule. "He would add," Madison wrote, "that domestic slavery is the most prominent feature in the aristocratic countenance of the proposed constitution. The vassalage of the poor has ever been the favorite offspring of aristocracy."[28] For the aristocratically minded Morris to condemn the constitution-in-progress as aristocratic sounds strange. But Morris was pointing out that the draft constitution now empowered white southerners from small states more than any other group. He preferred an aristocracy of wealthy eastern commercial traders to one of southern gentlemen, whom he considered backward.

Slavery was not the very heart of this concern, but Morris used it effectively. "The bohea tea used by a northern freeman," Morris declaimed, "will pay more tax than the whole consumption of the miserable slave, which consists of nothing more than his physical subsistence and the rag that covers his nakedness." Invoking the injustice of a tax on tea was meant to have revolutionary resonance. Morris was connecting the injustice of slavery to the injustice of unfair taxation, and asserting that the South was responsible for both.[29]

For a King

The delegates chose to ignore the issue Morris had raised.[30] In the meantime, they hammered out details connected to Congress. Madison fought hard to keep decision-making power over elections out of the hands of the state legislatures, which he continued to distrust.[31] (He lost.) The delegates squabbled about where Congress should meet and where the capital should be established.[32] They argued about how long immigrants from foreign lands should have to live in the United States before they could be elected to Congress.[33] They revisited the question of whether money bills should originate in the lower house, which they had begun to refer to as the House of Representatives.[34] They deliberated at length about whether the states or the national treasury should pay Congress. And they marched through the Committee of Detail's proposal for Congress's power to legislate.

Madison sought to check Congress's power. On August 15, he moved that "all acts before they become laws should be submitted both to the executive and supreme judiciary departments." If either the executive or the court objected, it would take two-thirds of each of the houses to override the veto. If both the executive and the Supreme Court objected, it would take three-quarters of each house "to overrule the objections and give to the acts the force of law."[35] The delegates had already agreed to a presidential veto. Madison was proposing a further check on Congress, this time from the Supreme Court.

Madison got support from John Francis Mercer of Maryland. Mercer believed that by giving the judges the power of review *before* a law took effect, they would not have the power of judicial review *after* the law was enacted. Mercer thought "laws ought to be well and cautiously made, and then to be uncontrollable" by the judiciary.[36] But Madison's proposal was rejected, with only Delaware, Maryland, and Virginia voting in favor.[37]

Madison's major role in the debates over Congress was to keep the delegates focused on the need for effective national power. When the delegates argued about whether Congress would lack the power to tax exports—the point that Gouverneur Morris had attacked in his speech on slavery—Madison intervened. He was the only delegate from an agricultural state to argue that Congress should be able to tax exports. Logically, he explained, such taxes would be passed on to the end purchasers of exported products. Virginia's taxes on tobacco were in effect "paid by the European consumer."[38]

For Madison, the power to tax exports was a necessary tool of a unified foreign policy. Exports would have to be regulated as part of the goal of "procuring equitable regulations from other nations." In particular, Madison predicted, "an embargo may be of absolute necessity, and can alone be effectuated by the general authority."[39] An embargo was the distinctive tool of a nation whose economy was based on export and trade. By refusing to sell goods at all, he believed, the United States could coerce other nations to agree to reasonable trade terms. Such an embargo might be an "absolute necessity" for the simple reason that the United States had no other means of coercion.

Madison did not carry the day. He did not even carry his own delegation. George Mason pointedly used Madison's own arguments against him. He relied, he said, "on a principle often advanced and in which he concurred, 'that a majority when interested will oppress the minority.'" Madison and no one else had repeatedly advanced this principle. "The eight northern states," Mason concluded, "have an interest different from the five southern states" and would tax exports, including Virginian tobacco.[40] In the Virginia delegation, only Madison and George Washington voted to allow Congress to tax exports. New Jersey, Pennsylvania, and Delaware, all mid-Atlantic trading states, agreed, as did New Hampshire. But every other state voted that no tax should be allowed on exports, either because their state interests dictated the result or because they were sticking with the recommendation made by the Committee of Detail.[41]

Infernal Traffic

The question of Congress's power over exports led to the related matter of Congress's power over the slave trade. Luther Martin of Maryland was not an abolitionist, and indeed owned several slaves himself. But he rose to say that it was "inconsistent with the principles of the Revolution and dishonorable to the American character" for the constitution to guarantee the slave trade.[42] His remarks were opposed by Rutledge and Charles Pinckney of South Carolina—but also by Oliver Ellsworth of Connecticut.[43] The next day, August 22, Ellsworth was joined by his fellow Connecticut delegate, Roger Sherman, who urged compromise. Sherman insisted that he "disapproved of the slave trade." But "as it was expedient to have as few objections as possible to the proposed scheme of government," he "thought it best to leave the matter as we find it."[44]

The Connecticut delegation's eagerness to change the subject notwithstanding, the issue of slavery was once again before the convention. George Mason, who possessed some three hundred slaves on his plantation in Fairfax County, mounted a powerful argument for stopping the slave trade, an "infernal traffic," which, he insisted, "originated in the avarice of British merchants."[45] Mason warned of the danger of slave revolt and the perverse economic effects of slavery on white productivity. He concluded that slaves "bring the judgment of heaven on a country. As nations cannot be rewarded or punished in the next world they must be in this. By an inevitable chain of causes and effects providence punishes national sins by national calamities."[46] Mason was not arguing that a personal God would directly wreak vengeance on slaveholders. Rather, he was proposing that states built on slavery would find themselves overcome by the "calamities" of civil strife and war.

Oliver Ellsworth, defender of the status quo, attacked Mason for hypocrisy. As he had never owned a slave, Ellsworth began his remarks, he "could not judge of the effects of slavery on character." This was a solid blow to Mason, and Ellsworth followed it with more. "If it was to be considered in a moral light," he continued, "we ought to go farther and free those already in the country."[47] Mason had condemned slavery without so much as a nod toward the abolition that would have made him a poor man.

Having made Mason look bad, however, Ellsworth concluded rather lamely that it would be "unjust" to South Carolina and Georgia to block the slave trade. Unlike the situation in Virginia and Maryland, he suggested, "in the sickly rice swamps" of the deeper South "foreign supplies are necessary." Ellsworth ended his performance with the truly laughable proposition that "the danger of insurrections" that Mason had raised "will become a motive to kind treatment of the slaves."[48] Ellsworth, like Sherman, wanted to keep South Carolina and Georgia in the fold and perhaps continue to create profits for Connecticut slave traders.

The impetuous Charles Pinckney now offered a full-throated defense of slavery. "If slavery be wrong," he stated bluntly, "it is justified by the example of all the world." From antiquity Pinckney cited Greece and Rome. Then he invoked "the sanction given by France, England, Holland and other modern states." Slavery was ubiquitous—and always had been. "In all ages," Pinckney concluded, "one-half of mankind have been slaves."[49] It is easy to imagine the reaction of those delegates who did not want the proposed constitution expressly to sanction slavery and the slave trade. Pinckney was speaking no less than the truth—but did he have to be so crude about it?

Dishonorable to National Character

By now the convention knew that committees were an effective tool for producing compromise. Gouverneur Morris put it clearly. He recommended that "the whole subject" be sent to a committee that would consider the importation of slaves and taxes on exports. "These things," Morris put it, "may form a bargain among the northern and southern states."[50]

Edmund Randolph raised the temperature by condemning the clause protecting the slave trade. "He would never agree to the clause as it stands," Madison recorded. "He would sooner risk the constitution." These were unusually strong words in a convention that was moving in the direction of a consensus draft. The convention, Randolph said, faced a "dilemma." On the one hand, "by agreeing to the clause, it would revolt the Quakers, the Methodists, and many others in the states having no slaves. On the other hand, two states might be lost to the union." Therefore, Randolph concluded, they should "try the chance" of submitting the matter to a committee that would seek compromise. The convention agreed.[51]

Two days later, on Friday, August 24, 1787, the committee proposed that Congress be required to allow the importation of slaves until the year 1800, thirteen years in the future. Until then, imported slaves could be taxed "at a rate not exceeding the average of the duties laid on imports." And the committee proposed language that would studiously avoid use of the word "slave." Instead slaves would be referred to as "such persons of the several states now existing shall think proper to admit."[52]

The next day, August 25, the delegates took up the committee's report. General Pinckney immediately proposed extending the safe harbor for the slave trade to 1808. Only Madison bothered to speak against him. "Twenty years," he protested, "will produce all the mischief that can be apprehended from the liberty to import slaves." There would be no practical difference between a twenty-year safe harbor and an absolute protection, Madison believed. Worse, the pro-slavery provision would now go down in the history books. "So long a term will be more dishonorable to the national character than to say nothing about it in the constitution."[53] Madison's concern was justified—and irrelevant. Pinckney's proposal passed 7 to 4.

As part of the compromise, the committee had recommended that Congress be able to tax slave imports at the same average rate used to tax other imports. Roger Sherman objected to the provision "as acknowledging men to be property, by taxing them as such under the character of slaves."[54] As he had a few moments before, Sherman seemed to be concerned with the semantics of whether the constitution would mention slavery and hence seem to endorse it.

Rufus King quickly objected that this tax was "the price of the first part" of the proposed compromise. George Mason pointed out that "not to tax . . . will be equivalent to a bounty on the importation of slaves." The statement was consistent with both Mason's moral stand against the slave trade and his economic interest in maintaining the value of the numerous slaves he already held.

As a slaveholder, Madison shared Mason's economic interest. He now focused on the moral question. Madison explained that he "thought it wrong to admit in the constitution the idea that there could be property in men." It was no excuse that slaves could be treated as articles to be subjected to taxation: "The reason of duties did not hold, as slaves are not like merchandise, consumed."[55] Madison's argument carried the day. The delegates agreed simply to say that "a tax or duty may be imposed on such importation not exceeding $10 for each person."

Madison's position reflected the contorted moral logic of slaveholders enacting a slavery-protecting constitution while claiming to oppose that very institution. Mason, with his three hundred slaves, had argued that slavery was harmful. Madison, who owned slaves throughout his life, thought that the constitution should not "admit" the very "idea that there could be property in men."

This contradiction can be explained in part by the notion that Mason and Madison aspired to a world in which slavery would be abolished. They knew that, in various more civilized corners of the world, the journey to abolition had already begun, and they felt ashamed of their association with slavery. It was, as Madison had said of the twenty-year protection of the slave trade, "dishonorable," not simply to the national character, but to the character of men such as Mason and Madison. They just did not feel sufficiently ashamed to do anything about it, at least not while their livelihoods and those of their families depended on the labor of enslaved persons. They could compromise on slavery in the constitution—because they had always compromised on slavery in their own lives.

Dangerous Power

Something strange was happening to Edmund Randolph. He had introduced the Virginia plan and contributed meaningfully to the debates. But sometime in mid-August, his occasional objections had started to get stronger. On August 13, he mused about what would happen "when people behold in the Senate, the countenance of an aristocracy; and in the president, the form at least of a little monarch."[56] He had also sounded overheated on August 22 when he said he would rather have no constitution than guarantee the slave trade.

On August 29, before the document could be submitted to a Committee of Style for final tweaking, Randolph made a breathtaking statement. There were "features so odious in the constitution as it now stands," he told the delegates, that he "doubted whether he should be able to agree to it." Then on August 31, Randolph suggested that the state conventions should "be at liberty to propose amendments to be submitted to another general convention which may reject or incorporate them, as shall be judged proper."[57] As Randolph must have understood, this proposal was preposterous. All the work of the past three and a half months could be undone if a new convention were to be called. Randolph was essentially suggesting that the convention self-destruct.[58]

On September 10, Randolph listed his objections—which were self-contradictory and random to the point of being incoherent. Some of them favored a stronger executive; others aimed to make the president weaker. Randolph criticized Congress's authority to make all "necessary and proper" laws as making the national government too powerful. But he also defended the original Virginia plan, conceived by Madison, which had envisioned a more powerful national government than had been produced by the process of compromise.[59] Having stated his objections, Randolph announced that he must keep himself "free . . . to act according to the dictates of his judgment" at the Virginia ratifying convention.[60]

Why had Randolph turned against the convention he helped create? Possibly he could not accept a compromise that, he believed, would rob him of the distinction of having introduced the plan that became the constitution. But Randolph mostly seems to have been worried that the public would not ratify the constitution, and he did not want his political career to be destroyed by supporting it.[61]

George Mason was also having second thoughts. On September 12, after the Committee of Style had reported back, Mason said he wished that the proposed constitution "had been prefaced with a bill of rights," which "would be a great quiet to the people; and with the aid of the state declarations, a bill might be prepared in a few hours."[62] As the principal author of the Virginia Declaration of Rights, Mason had an obvious model in mind. He should have proposed the idea earlier. It occasioned almost no discussion, with Roger Sherman of Connecticut answering in a perfunctory way that the states' bills of rights "are not repealed by this constitution; and being in force are sufficient."[63] The delegates voted down the proposal 10 to 0.*

The delegates tried hard to keep Mason on board. The next day they accepted his proposal about state taxes.[64] Indulged, Mason now suggested that the constitution should provide for sumptuary regulations—laws of the kind that, since the Middle Ages, had been used to prohibit the sale of especially fancy and expensive goods.[65] The convention respectfully agreed to create a committee to consider Mason's sumptuary laws, although it never reported back.

Notwithstanding the courtesy to Mason, the delegates were ready to be done. Madison discovered this after he proposed a tiny bit of constitutional housekeeping on September 13. Article I, Section 7, provided that if the president failed to sign a bill, it would become law ten days later. It read, in part, "If any bill shall not be returned by the president within ten days (Sundays excepted) after it shall have been presented to him." Madison moved to "insert between 'after' and 'it' . . . the words 'the day on which,'" in order to prevent a question whether the day on which the bill be presented . . . ought to be counted or not as one of the ten days."

The eminently reasonable suggestion, which could have been approved in seconds, reflected Madison's precise thinking and sense of ownership over even the minutest details of the document. But Gouverneur Morris disagreed. "The amendment is unnecessary," he insisted. "The law knows no fractions of days."[66] The delegates were in no mood for a hairsplitting debate about the word "day." As Madison drily put it in his notes, "A number of members being very impatient and calling for the question," a vote was immediately taken. It was 8 to 3 against Madison.[67] Mason could get away with obscure or irritating requests because his vote was in doubt. Madison, however, had pushed his colleagues' patience to the breaking point.

On Sunday, September 15, with the constitution finally ready to be approved, the delegates convened. Mason objected that there was no way for the people to initiate an amendment outside Congress.[68] Gouverneur Morris and Elbridge Gerry suggested that two-thirds of the states could

* On September 14, 1787, Elbridge Gerry and Charles Pinckney moved to insert a declaration "that the liberty of the press should be inviolably observed." Sherman responded dismissively that it was "unnecessary," because "the power of Congress does not extend to the press." The proposal was defeated 7 to 4 with no further discussion.

call for a convention. Madison said that the proposal was unnecessary, because Congress already had to send out for ratification any amendments proposed by two-thirds of the states. The truth was that Madison never wanted another convention.[69] But he could not state the inconvenient truth that the Philadelphia convention was itself a runaway convention that should never be repeated. The convention adopted the proposal that Morris and Gerry had made without further debate.

Despite the notable solicitude that had been shown Mason in the final days—and even the final minutes—of the convention, he ultimately declined to sign. Randolph repeated that he would not sign and might vote against the proposed constitution in Virginia.[70] Mason predicted the constitution "would end either in monarchy, or tyrannical aristocracy," Madison noted. "Which, he was in doubt. But one or [the] other, he was sure." The draft "had been formed without the knowledge or idea of the people," giving reason for a second convention. Going further than Randolph, Mason stated that "as the constitution now stands, he could neither give it his support or vote in Virginia."[71] Mason's concerns were, unlike Randolph's, at least consistent with the republican positions he had maintained throughout his political life.

Conventions Are Serious Things

The irrepressible Charles Pinckney wanted the last word. He began with an awkward observation. "These declarations from members so respectable at the close of this important scene," he said, "give a peculiar solemnity to the present moment." Pinckney then told the delegates another thing they already knew: that a new convention to consider proposed amendments was a recipe for disaster. "Nothing but confusion and contrariety could spring from the experiment," Pinckney reasoned. As was his wont, Pinckney then said to the convention what Madison and the other delegates were too circumspect to assert directly: "Conventions are serious things, and ought not to be repeated."[72] It was, in its way, a stunning admission in a speech intended to be the final historic word of a historic convention.

Pinckney was robbed of the chance to speak last by Elbridge Gerry, who had also decided not to sign. Influenced by Shays's Rebellion to fear popularly elected bodies, Gerry thought Congress was too powerful and could create a legislative dictatorship.[73] His final warning met with no reply, and Randolph's motion for a new convention was rejected unanimously.

The proposed constitutional draft was then adopted by a vote of all the state delegations. Madison's notes had an almost poetic simplicity:

> On the question on the proposition of Mr. Randolph. All the states answered—no.
> On the question to agree to the Constitution, as amended. All the states ay.
> The Constitution was then ordered to be engrossed.
> And the House adjourned.[74]

Yet the convention was not quite over. Worried that the headline would be the dissents of Randolph, Mason, and Gerry, not the unanimity of the states, the constitution's supporters decided to convene one final time—Tuesday, September 17, 1787—for a last-ditch effort to produce the appearance of complete agreement.

Gouverneur Morris thought the convention could submit to Congress a statement that the proposed constitution had been adopted unanimously by the state delegations, and all the members present could sign as witnesses to that fact. Technically, they would not be endorsing the document. Franklin agreed to introduce the idea as his own.

Franklin's intimate connection to the Declaration of Independence, signed in the same room, made him the right person to advance the suggestion. The shadow of that heroic act loomed over the signing of the draft constitution. Franklin began by suggesting that the dissenters should reconsider. "The older I grow," he said, "the more apt I am to doubt my own judgment, and to pay more respect to the judgment of others."[75]

He went on to defend the proposed constitution "with all its faults, if they are such." Some "general government" was needed—and he had faith that despotism could take root only "when the people shall become so corrupted as to need despotic government, being incapable of any other." This was a trenchant critique of Mason's worries. As a republican, Mason should have had faith in the people's virtue as a guard against the tyranny he purported to fear.

Franklin then offered an encomium on the convention's efforts. "I doubt too," he continued, "whether any other convention we can obtain, may be able to make a better constitution. For when you assemble a number of men to have the advantage of their joint wisdom, you inevitably assemble with those men, all their prejudices, their passions, their errors of opinion, their local interests, and their selfish views. From such an assembly can a perfect production be expected? It therefore astonishes me, sir, to find this system approaching so near to perfection as it does."[76]

Their success, Franklin explained, was that they had *agreed*. "I think it will astonish our enemies, who are waiting with confidence to hear that our councils are confounded like those of the builders of Babel; and that our states are on the point of separation, only to meet hereafter for the purpose of cutting one another's throats." Franklin could therefore reach the conclusion that "I consent, sir, to this constitution because I expect no better, and because I am not sure, that it is not the best" that the delegates could possibly have produced.[77]

The constitution had been voted on, endorsed, and engrossed. But Nathaniel Gorham of Massachusetts rose to ask for a change. Instead of the House of Representatives containing one congressman for each forty thousand people, he proposed increasing the number by making the ratio one per thirty thousand, a marked increase in the size of the House. The proposal "could not be thought unreasonable,"[78] Gorham said.

What could have been thought unreasonable was reopening an important and heavily debated issue after the deliberations were long completed. But before anyone could say so, Washington put the question before the convention—and for the first time weighed in on the substance of a proposal. "As late as the present moment was for admitting amendments," Madison wrote, Washington "could not forbear expressing his wish that the alteration proposed might take place." Possibly he wanted the convention over; or perhaps he simply wanted to be on the record as having participated. In any case, Washington had spoken, and the amendment passed unanimously.

The delegates then voted to "enroll the constitution"—physically to unroll the document and lay it on the table—in order for it to be signed. Randolph, still unwilling to compromise, got up and "apologized" that despite Franklin's urgings, he still would not sign "notwithstanding the vast majority and venerable names that would give sanction to its wisdom and its worth."[79] He now added a fresh justification: "Nine states will fail to ratify the plan and confusion must ensue." In light of this anticipated failure, Randolph "ought not, he could not, by pledging himself to support the plan, restrain himself from taking such steps as might appear to him most consistent with the public good."

Gouverneur Morris responded that "the moment this plan goes forth" there would be only two possibilities: Either the constitution would be ratified or "a general anarchy will be the alternative."[80] Morris then reminded the delegates of the solution he had given Franklin: "that the signing in the form proposed related only to the fact that the states present were unanimous."[81]

Alexander Hamilton wanted a final say, as well. Uniquely among the delegates, Hamilton was going to sign the constitution without his state having voted for it. As usual, Hamilton expressed himself in emotional terms, declaring "his anxiety that every member should sign."[82] Hamilton then explained his fears: "A few characters of consequence, by opposing or even refusing to sign the constitution, might do infinite mischief by kindling the latent sparks which lurk under an enthusiasm in favor of the convention which may soon subside." Hamilton told the delegates that, despite his signature, he did not much like the constitution. "No man's ideas were more remote from the plan than his were known to be," Madison recorded Hamilton saying, an allusion to Hamilton's June speech in favor of British-style monarchy. Nevertheless, the choice was "between anarchy and convulsion on one side, and the chance of good to be expected from the plan on the other."[83] Only Hamilton could have considered this brief but remarkable performance a useful statement on behalf of signing.

Randolph replied rather cleverly that he had himself suggested a middle way between acceptance and rejection: The state conventions should be able to propose amendments. It was not his refusal to sign that might cause trouble, but rather the up-or-down nature of ratification. This was in a sense true. Morris and Hamilton wanted anarchy to be the only alternative to ratification, because it would give the public no choice but to ratify.

Elbridge Gerry took up Randolph's theme. Gerry imagined a civil war that would grow not from failure to ratify, but from the battle over ratification itself.[84] In Massachusetts, Gerry explained, "there are two parties, one devoted to democracy, the worst he thought of all political evils, the other as violent in the opposite extreme."[85]

Morris's proposal as introduced by Franklin had failed to sway the nonsigners, but it was adopted anyway. The delegates had watered down their endorsement in the name of compromise.

A Rising Sun

A final matter had to be addressed before the signing could occur. What should be done with the official journals of the convention, which recorded motions and votes but not the content of the debates? Should the secrecy of the convention, so successfully preserved, extend to the written record? The delegates voted 10 to 1 to hand the journals over to Washington for safekeeping, asking him to "retain the journal and other papers, subject to the order of the Congress, if ever formed under the constitution."[86]

The delegates then ceremoniously signed the proposed constitution. Franklin, more alert than any of the other delegates to the creation of shaping anecdotes, managed the very last word. Madison told the story in the final lines of his notes:

> Whilst the last members were signing, Franklin looking towards the president's chair, at the back of which a rising sun happened to be painted, observed to a few members near him, that painters had found it difficult to distinguish in their art a rising from a setting sun. I have said he, often and often in the course of the session, and the vicissitudes of my hopes and fears as to its issue, looked at that behind the president without being able to tell whether it was rising or setting: But now at length I have the happiness to know that it is a rising and not a setting sun.[87]

Franklin's poetic observation was, like all his comments at the convention, intended to make a practical point. The chair, magnificently carved and gilded at the top,[88] had been before the delegates for three months, and Franklin had had plenty of time to think up his closing bon mot. By alluding to the sun as rising, Franklin ended the convention on a note of optimism. But by mentioning the possibility that the sun might have been setting, he reminded the other delegates of the stakes of the enterprise—and how easily it could have failed.

Franklin had another quick-witted reply on leaving the convention. According to the journal kept by a Maryland delegate, one Mrs. Powel asked Franklin the next day,

> Well, Doctor, what have we got? A republic or a monarchy?
> A republic, replied the Doctor, if you can keep it.[89]

Yet the constitution never called the government it was forming "republican."[90] It never called the new government "national." Perhaps most remarkably, it never called the government it was forming "federal." On the question of what sort of government was being created, the proposed constitution was assiduously silent.

That silence, as the delegates knew, resulted from the indefinite nature of the compromise the convention had wrought. The Virginia plan was national, the New Jersey plan federal. A hybrid plan had emerged that was not exactly either. The proposed government would be able to act directly on individual citizens. But not all the members of the government would be chosen directly by those they governed. The House would be chosen by the people, the Senate by the state legislatures, and the president by electors who would themselves be chosen by processes to be specified by the states. This compromise formation did not yet have a name.

The Degree of Concord

Madison laid out his contemporaneous thinking about the constitution that had emerged in a letter to Jefferson on October 24, 1787. He had obeyed the code of silence throughout the summer in Philadelphia. Now it was time to describe what had occurred to the person whose opinion mattered most to him. Madison believed the convention had achieved something historic. It was thus a serious understatement when he told Jefferson that his "observations . . . will help to make up a letter, if they should answer no other purpose."[91]

The challenges faced by the convention, Madison wrote, "formed a task more difficult than can be well conceived by those who were not concerned in the execution of it." If one added that people naturally disagreed on "all new and complicated subjects," Madison concluded, "it is impossible to consider the degree of concord which ultimately prevailed as less than a miracle."[92] Neither Madison nor Jefferson believed in direct divine intervention in human affairs. The miracle of concord was manmade.

Madison had mentioned his pet idea of the national negative to Jefferson before. Now, taking "this occasion of explaining" himself, he offered his friend an essay embedded within the letter.[93] Going beyond what he had written or said before, Madison asserted that "without such a check in the whole over the parts, our system involves the evil of imperia in imperio." A successful government needed "a controlling power" in order to defend the general authority "against encroachments of the subordinate authorities."[94]

Madison was predicting the struggle between the states and the federal government that would not be resolved fully for more than 150 years. The old system was "a confederacy of independent states," he said. The new government was more like "a feudal system of republics, if such a phrase may be used."[95] In Madison's view, the constitution created a permanent state of conflict between the national government, likened to a medieval king, and states, compared to fractious feudal barons. This was a further argument in favor of a national negative: The states were in no serious danger from the general government; the "danger of encroachments" came from the state governments.

Apart from the negative, Madison mentioned a different possibility for resolving the conflict between the general government and the states. Perhaps, he suggested, "the judicial authority under our new system will keep the states within their proper limits, and supply the place of a negative on their laws."[96] This—reviewing state laws for constitutionality—would ultimately become the role of the modern Supreme Court. Madison thought it "more convenient to prevent the passage of the law, than to declare it void after it is passed." He added "that a state which would violate the legislative rights of the union, would not be very ready to obey a judicial decree in support of them." If the states refused to listen to the courts, that would call for "a recurrence to force"—which was, he concluded, "an evil which the new constitution meant to exclude as far as possible."[97] Here Madison unknowingly anticipated southern resistance to judicially mandated integration.

Closing his essay, Madison took on the problem of why he believed that Congress would be more likely than the state legislatures to "secure individuals against encroachments on their rights."[98] This involved the reiteration of his grand theory of the enlargement of the republic. He told Jefferson, not without some pride,

A full discussion of this question would, if I mistake not, unfold the true principles of republican government, and prove in contradiction to the concurrent opinions of theoretical writers, that this form of government, in order to effect its purposes, must operate not within a small but an extensive sphere.

Madison was taking on Rousseau and Montesquieu, and he wanted Jefferson to know it. More thoroughly than anywhere else in his writings, Madison explained the flaw with "simple democracy, or a pure republic": It assumed a situation "which is altogether fictitious." Its advocates imagined "that the people composing the society . . . have all precisely the same interests, and the same feelings in every respect." If this were true, then "the interest of the majority would be that of the minority also," and "within a small sphere," majority rule would work. The problem was that "no society ever did or can consist of so homogeneous a mass of citizens."[99]

Madison now launched into his account of divergent interests, which brought him to his theory of enlargement as the answer.[100] He added a new twist, one clearly reserved for private communication: "Divide et impera, the reprobated axiom of tyranny, is under certain qualifications, the only policy, by which a republic can be administered on just principles."[101] This use of the maxim "divide and rule" turned its meaning upside down. Instead of the imperial master dividing his subject peoples, the ruling people themselves were being divided so that their rule would not become oppressive.

Finally Madison offered another new and important caveat to his theory of enlargement. "This doctrine," he wrote, "can only hold within the sphere of the mean extent." By "mean," Madison meant the golden mean, or middle ground. "As in too small a sphere oppressive combinations may be too easily formed against the weaker party; so in too extensive a one, a defensive concert may be rendered too difficult against the oppression of those entrusted with the administration."[102] Madison was arguing for the first time that too large a republic would make it difficult for a minority seeking to defend itself in an organized way. More important, he was recognizing a flaw in his own theory.

Madison concluded his analysis by returning to the "great desideratum of government": making it "sufficiently neutral between different parts of the society to control one part from invading the rights of another, and at the same time sufficiently controlled itself."[103] The United States, he said, satisfied this aim, because "the general government would hold a pretty even balance between the parties of particular states, and be at the same time sufficiently restrained by its dependence on the community, from betraying its general interests."[104]

Madison was not just repeating language that he had previously used. He was hinting at something new: that his extended republic theory could succeed *even without the national negative.* In making the argument for the national negative in sophisticated detail one final time, Madison was exorcising it from his system. As a practical politician, he knew the idea was dead. Writing to Jefferson, however, he could be an intellectual giving his great idea a final airing before consigning it to history.

In the process, Madison was developing the claim that the extended republic would display less faction at the level of "the general government" than did the state legislatures. He had originally developed the idea of extension and enlargement in the context of proposing a national negative. He would now retain the core of the idea to justify a constitution that lacked this feature.

Madison finished his account of the convention much more briefly. He told Jefferson that the "different interests of different parts of the continent" had been addressed by the preservation of the slave trade, because "South Carolina and Georgia were inflexible on the point of the slaves." Then he described the struggle between small and large states that had plagued the convention. This conflict, he said, "created more embarrassment, and greater alarm for . . . the convention than all the rest put together."[105] The struggle "ended in the compromise which you will see," Madison explained to Jefferson, "but very much to the dissatisfaction of several members from the large states."[106] Madison obviously referred to himself.

It seems remarkable that Madison could spend many pages discoursing on his theory of the national negative—which the convention rejected—while spending just a paragraph on the great compromise between the large and small states, the subject that dominated the convention and that, in his account, had created the greatest danger that the convention might fail. That he did so explains something important about how Madison perceived the proposed constitution.

To Madison, the structure of the new government was all-important. He had imagined a constitution that extended the republic from individual states to a general government—and that constitution had been achieved. True, he had considered a national negative crucial to his design, and had not gotten it. But the overall structure that then emerged from Philadelphia matched his theory of the "great desideratum." The national government would be unlikely to join the factions within the states, but it would also be "sufficiently controlled" by its internal structure and by the states that it would not turn against the people.

The compromise that had created a Senate featuring equal representation was unfortunate and objectionable, but it did not destroy the whole plan. It made the government something less than national—the word "general" was a temporary placeholder until something better could be found—but it did not turn the government into a confederation. Although Madison had some serious concerns about the proposed constitution, he was taking ownership of the Philadelphia draft. Preparing to argue for its ratification, Madison closed the letter by reviewing the constitution's prospects in all the states. He concluded optimistically that upon the whole, although "the public mind will not be fully known, nor finally settled for a considerable time, appearances at present augur of a more prompt, and general adoption of the plan than could have been well expected."[107]

Calumniations

Madison had spoken too soon. His prediction was based on the attitudes of serving legislatures in the states he surveyed. Representatives to state assemblies tended to be more educated than their average constituents and met in capital cities, where they were influenced by local politics. Farther into the rural backcountry of republican farmers, opposition to the proposed constitution was much greater.

In New York, meaningful opposition could be found even in the big city. Congress, based there, had officially received the proposed constitution on September 20, 1787, three days after the word had gone out from Philadelphia. In the debate that ensued, supporters of the constitution argued that Congress should pass the document to the states with a general endorsement. The other side thought that Congress could not endorse a plan that so obviously violated the Articles of Confederation.[108] Some opponents suggested that Congress engage in a paragraph-by-paragraph analysis of the draft and propose amendments. Madison, who hurried to New York after being warned that he would be needed to cast the decisive vote for the divided Virginia congressional delegation, insisted that Congress lacked the authority to do so. Madison badly wanted to avoid the possibility that there would be "two plans" of government circulating before the states at the same time. As he had at the convention, Madison wanted an up or down vote on the constitution—because he wanted the alternatives to be ratification or potential collapse.

After two days of debate, in which Richard Henry Lee of Virginia advanced many of George Mason's arguments against the proposed constitution, Congress agreed to pass the draft along without comment to the state legislatures, who would, in turn, place it before state conventions. The official resolution said that the delegates "resolved unanimously" to do so. Opponents of ratification insisted the word "unanimously" applied only to the decision to transmit the draft, while supporters hoped it would be taken as a unanimous endorsement of the constitution.

Congress had debated in secret, but the New York newspapers quickly began to publish criticism of the constitution. In September, Thomas Greenleaf's *New-York Journal* carried the first of seven essays by an anonymous writer calling himself "Cato," suspected by many to be New York governor George Clinton.[109] Another series, under the authorship of "Brutus," began in October in the same newspaper. The use of symbolic noms de plume taken from antiquity was common in the eighteenth century.[110] By choosing archetypal Roman republicans who had in one case struggled with Julius Caesar and in the other actually stabbed him, the authors of these essays were framing the constitution as a dangerous threat to republican principles.

By mid-October, Madison reported to Washington from New York that "the newspapers here begin to teem with vehement and virulent calumniations of the proposed government."[111] Madison observed, "Judging from the newspapers one would suppose that the adversaries were the most numerous and the most in earnest."[112] He noted that one "combatant" in particular—probably Brutus—"with considerable address and plausibility, strikes at the foundation." This writer, Madison said, argued that "the situation of the United States" was such that any government "which forms the states into one nation and is to operate directly on the people" would be "improper and impracticable."[113]

Some reply was necessary—and Alexander Hamilton decided to make it. In conjunction with John Jay, who had not attended the convention, Hamilton initiated his own series of essays in favor of ratification. The first one appeared in the New York *Independent Journal* on October 27, 1787. As a pen name, Hamilton chose "Publius," a reference to Publius

Valerius Publicola, one of the men who overthrew Rome's monarchy and founded the Roman republic.

According to the Roman historian Livy, Publius had been accused of aspiring to become the new king of Rome. Responding to the accusation, Publius showed deference to the public, lowering the fasces—the insignia of office—before the crowd. He then voluntarily moved the house he was building at the summit of Mount Velian down to the valley. Finally he proposed laws "which not only cleared the consul from the suspicion of seeking kingly power, but took such an opposite turn that they even made him popular and caused him to be styled Publicola, the People's Friend."[114] Hamilton was choosing the name of a well-known republican—but a republican who was an aristocrat and had been falsely accused of monarchism. To those who knew the story in detail, the implication was that those who had written the constitution were themselves mistakenly charged with anti-republicanism.

From the start, the essays were entitled *The Federalist*—a name that would end up having a deep resonance. At the convention, the delegates had expressly told one another that a *federal* constitution was one in which the states were confederated as they had been under the Articles. A *national* constitution was one in which the government would act directly on the citizens.

When Hamilton chose the term "Federalist" to represent the pro-constitution position, he was making a brilliant rhetorical ploy. In essence, Hamilton was co-opting the term from the small-state opponents of a national government and using it to refer to the government proposed by the constitution itself, a hybrid between a truly national government and a truly federal one. By calling the national-federal constitution simply "federal," Hamilton was taking what could have been his opponents' preferred name and appropriating it for his own side of the debate.

Hamilton kicked off the series in his distinctive mood of passionate overstatement, predicting that in the debate over ratification of the constitution, "a torrent of angry and malignant passions will be let loose."[115] The two sides would, he expected, try to "increase the number of their converts by the loudness of their declamations and by the bitterness of their invectives." Supporters' "enlightened zeal for the energy and efficiency of government will be stigmatized as the offspring of a temper fond of despotic power and hostile to the principles of liberty."

For their part, the pro-constitution forces, Hamilton said, would present their opponents' call for a bill of rights as "mere pretense and artifice." Supporters of ratification would forget, in Hamilton's inimitable phrase, "that jealousy is the usual concomitant of violent love." The truth, he insisted, was that the greatest danger to "the liberties of republics" came from the demagogues who "have begun their career by paying an obsequious court to the people."[116] Hamilton announced in the first essay that the purpose of the series would be to provide calm, rational argument to counteract the "intolerant spirit" that he expected to pervade the debate. But it was far from clear that Hamilton was the man to provide such dispassionate analysis.

Jay, who had been secretary of foreign affairs under the Articles, was enlisted by Hamilton to write the next four essays. He began by arguing that the union was necessary for purposes of war and peace.[117] He went on to make the case for what he called "an efficient national government"[118] that could coordinate national defense and make treaties that would be respected. Foreign nations active on the North American continent, particularly Spain from the west and Britain from the north, would be more inclined to respect a unified United States than thirteen splinter colonies in several confederacies.

Jay then abandoned the project. He seems to have told Hamilton that his rheumatism would not allow him to continue.[119] But in fact Jay was simply not well placed to write much more. Although he was a skilled lawyer who had helped draft the New York Constitution, Jay did not attend the Philadelphia convention nor had he thought through the many relevant issues that would have to be addressed at high speed. He would write just one more paper, *Federalist* No. 64, on the treaty power.

Hamilton wrote Nos. 6 through 8, arguing that, if separated, the states would end up making war on one another. But Hamilton knew that he needed help. He asked Gouverneur Morris, who shared many of his views. Morris turned him down.[120]

Hamilton then asked Madison, who was in New York serving in Congress. Madison agreed. Until this request, the two were not close. They had met in Congress and collaborated at the failed Annapolis convention, but there is no evidence that they spent time together outside the convention in Philadelphia. Hamilton must have asked Madison for the simple reason that, as he well knew, no other person had a comparable understanding of the proposed constitution. Madison was not a New Yorker like Hamilton, Jay, and Morris. But he was present in New York, where the *Federalist* essays would be published first.

Hamilton knew that Madison did not share his vision of a British-style monarchic executive that he had advocated at the convention. Yet the extended project of co-authorship turned the two into friends and allies. For Hamilton, who correctly considered himself a master of polemic, this was a rare opportunity to exchange ideas with an equal. For Madison, who always wrote alone but whose closest friendships had grown from commitment to common political and intellectual projects, it was a unique experience of joint literary undertaking.

The unlikely pair influenced each other—to their mutual benefit and to the good of their combined effort. Madison's cautious, dry analysis of political actors' rational self-interests expanded to include human passions, which were Hamilton's personal specialty. And Hamilton's insistence on the primacy of the will to power was tempered by a more fine-grained, interest-oriented account of how government institutions would and should work. Madison's idealized picture of politics driven by friendship and mutual interest affected Hamilton's vision of politics shaped by the human impulses to power and pride—and vice versa.[121] For the length of their collaboration, Madison became more Hamiltonian, and Hamilton more Madisonian.

Federalist *No. 10: A Republican Remedy*

In *Federalist* No. 9, Hamilton set the stage for Madison by arguing that the proposed constitution "corresponds, in every rational import of the term, with the idea of a federal government."[122] Hamilton was doing what no one in the convention could have done with a straight face: declaring the hybrid national-federal government to be federal.

Federalist No. 10, published on November 23, 1787, was Madison's first contribution. He made the most of it, producing what eventually became the single most influential account of the constitution and its basic structure. So much has been written about the essay, and so often has it been invoked for widely different purposes, that it can be challenging to make sense of what Madison actually intended to say.

The essays by Hamilton and Jay had argued for the constitution on the ground of national coordination to achieve international respect. Madison advanced his argument from the other direction. He claimed that "a well-constructed union" would be more effective domestically. Such a union, he contended ambitiously, would have "the tendency to break and control the violence of faction."[123]

The enemy of republican constitutional design was faction, defined as a group organized around "some common impulse of passion, or of interest, adverse to the rights of other citizens, or to the permanent and aggregate interests of the community."[124] This definition of "faction" as *party* echoed what Madison had written privately and said at the convention. Now he clarified that "faction" could comprise a majority or a minority, so long as it was acting against the true public interest.

Madison introduced the public to his theory of how "the circumstances of civil society" led to differences of opinion and of interest—but he did so in a new way. Madison had been reading Hamilton, and the latter's fascination with emotion had influenced him. In addition to economic interest, Madison now spoke of "a zeal for different opinions," and of "attachment to different leaders ambitiously contending for preeminence and power." He even imagined the public following leaders "whose fortunes have been interesting to the human passions"—what today would be called celebrities.

This recognition of nonrational motivations was new for Madison, who in the past had written as though other people shared his dispassionate character. Under Hamilton's influence, he now ventured to speculate that there existed a "propensity of mankind to fall into mutual animosities." Even "frivolous and fanciful distinctions" could unleash "unfriendly passions" and "violent conflicts." Madison was arguing, for the first time, for a natural instinct to political difference. Yet it is far from clear that he recognized the implication of this position: If people were inevitably prone to enmity, a constitution structured to produce friendship would face enormous and perhaps insurmountable challenges from human nature.

Only then did Madison give the explanation for the cause of faction that he had preferred in the past: economic motives. Creditors and debtors, landholders, manufacturers, merchants, and financiers all had different interests. The purpose of government—"the principal task of modern legislation"—was to regulate and manage "these various and interfering interests." It would be "vain" to rely on "enlightened statesmen" to resolve these "clashing interests" in the public good. "Enlightened statesmen will not always be at the helm."[125]

The essay was building to Madison's grand theory. The real "object" of government was "to secure the public good and private rights against the danger of such a faction, and at the same time to preserve the spirit and the form of popular government." Avoiding oppression by the majority while preserving republicanism was, he said, "the great desideratum," the only way to rescue republicanism "from the opprobrium under which it has so long labored."[126]

Madison explained to his readers that a republic, unlike a pure democracy, could be subverted by bad representatives. In a large republic, the representatives would be chosen from a larger population, which would increase the odds that they would be "fit characters." There was, Madison insisted, a happy "mean." If the constituency got too big, "you render the representative too little acquainted with all the local circumstances and lesser interests." If it got too small, "you render him unduly attached" to local interests, and "too little fit to comprehend and pursue great and national objects." Magically, "the federal constitution" formed a "happy combination." Congress could focus on national interests, while state legislatures could focus on local affairs.[127]

Having proposed that a bigger republic would produce better representation, Madison now introduced what would become the canonical statement of his enlargement theory: "Extend the sphere and you take in a greater variety of parties and interests; you make it less probable that a majority of the whole will have a common motive to invade the rights of other citizens; or if such a common motive exists, it will be more difficult for all who feel it to discover their own strength and to act in unison with each other."[128]

Madison still had a conclusion to draw from this theory: Just as a republic was better than a democracy, so the same advantage was "enjoyed by the union over the states composing it." Congress, unlike the state legislatures, would likely be made up of "representatives whose enlightened views and virtuous sentiments render them superior to local prejudices and to schemes of injustice." It would have a greater number of parties, reducing the likelihood of "any one party being able to outnumber and oppress the rest." The extended sphere would create "greater obstacles opposed to the concert and accomplishment of the secret wishes of an unjust and interested majority."[129]

Madison concluded with a flourish: "In the extent and proper structure of the union, therefore, we behold a republican remedy for the diseases most incident to republican government." At least since Aristotle, framers and theorists of government had compared themselves to physicians. Madison was putting himself in that tradition by offering a "remedy" for republicanism's most serious "disease." The word "constitution," after all, could mean both a frame of government and also an individual's state of health and temperament.

Madison the theorist had conceived the enlargement of the republic as a solution to the problem of majority oppression. Madison the framer had, at the convention, gotten the theory adopted. Now Madison the political actor was advocating for ratification using the same theory.

Yet between the convention and *Federalist* No. 10, Madison's theory had undergone a crucial, all-important, change. When he first committed the idea to paper in 1786,[130] Madison had believed that the extension of the republic demanded a specific tool to make it useful: a national negative that Congress could exercise over state legislatures. Madison had convinced himself, and argued to others, that majority oppression in state legislatures was the most serious problem facing the United States under the Articles of Confederation. According to this theory, Congress needed the power to supervise and reverse the actions of the state legislatures in order to curtail this oppression.

Now, in *Federalist* No. 10, Madison abandoned the negative entirely. Instead, Madison was using the theory of enlargement to argue that Congress would be better than the state legislatures. He could not claim, however, that Congress would *fix* the problem of majority oppression in the state legislatures—because Congress had no express power to do so under the proposed Constitution.

Deprived of the purpose for which his enlargement theory had been developed, Madison was unwilling to give up the theory. When compared with the ambition of the national negative, it must have seemed second best to Madison to use the theory simply to argue for the advantages of a federal government. But a combination of political practicality and attachment to his big idea allowed Madison to do so. He lost the fight for the national negative. He would use the enlargement theory anyway.

Suspicious and Jealous

Madison's alliance with Hamilton was the most intense of the new relationships he forged during the battle for ratification. Another was with
Tench Coxe, a Philadelphia merchant who had attended the conventions
in Annapolis and Philadelphia. In August, during the dog days of the
convention, Coxe had asked Madison for a letter of introduction to Jefferson, which Madison had promptly provided.[131]

As soon as the convention ended, Coxe, writing as "An American
Citizen," produced a series of four essays in favor of ratification that were
published in the Philadelphia papers—and he sent them to Madison for
his approval. Madison replied, congratulating Coxe and promising to
send the essays to Virginia through some intermediary more objective
than a convention delegate such as himself.[132] Coxe built on the assistance, asking Madison to get them printed in the New York and Virginia
newspapers, and requesting "the favor" of Madison's "perusing them
with Colonel Hamilton."[133] Coxe, drawing himself closer to Madison,
both reflected and encouraged the closeness between Madison and
Hamilton.

Throughout the ratification process, Madison also drew much closer
to George Washington. On September 30, 1787, Madison sent Washington a detailed account of the debate in Congress over the transmission of
the constitution to the states.[134] On October 10, Washington wrote back.
Discussing their mutual Virginia acquaintances and their positions on the
constitution, he took a much freer tone with Madison than he had the
previous spring.[135]

Madison sensed it. In a letter to Washington on October 14, he signed,
"With the most perfect esteem and most affectionate regard, I remain[,]
dear sir, your obedient friend and servant."[136] Madison was still being respectful. But the term "affectionate regard" was for Madison a mark of
intimacy. And to call himself Washington's "friend" signified a high degree of confidence that the feeling was mutual. Neither man was given to
expression of emotions, but each was precise in his writing, and such
small touches were full of meaning.

Friendship, however, was no guarantee of support for ratification, as
the case of Edmund Randolph showed. Madison kept writing to Randolph, and continued to address Randolph as "my dear friend." He ended
one letter in October by saying, "Present me respectfully to Mrs. R. and

accept the most fervent wishes for your happiness from your affectionate friend." Randolph had brought his wife with him to Philadelphia and was known to be especially close to her.

In his letter, Madison reviewed the prospects for ratification from different states, and discussed various essays against ratification—all without urging Randolph to change his attitude or, in fact, mentioning Randolph's skepticism at all. This reticence could be interpreted as strategic: By Madison's treating Randolph as an ally, Randolph might become one. But equally, it showed that Madison did not consider Randolph's breach of unanimity a breach of their personal relationship. He believed that gentlemen could remain affectionate friends even while disagreeing about the future of the union. The proposed constitution was modeled on this vision. It would minimize the effects of parties so that representatives of the people could reasonably debate the public good without losing the capacity to be political friends.

Tench Coxe, who may have assumed otherwise, trod lightly in discussing Randolph's position with Madison. Randolph's conduct, he wrote, "is viewed with pain and regret." In his opinion, Coxe wrote, Randolph would "suffer from the circumstance" of his opposition to ratification.[137] Coxe added a subtle dig at Randolph: "If his views were pure, it is to be regretted that he should suffer—if otherwise we must rejoice that it produces, or tends to produce, public benefits."[138] Another correspondent, writing from closer to the action in Virginia, agreed with this assessment, telling Madison that Randolph "on his return here was coolly received, upon which it is said he discovered much anxiety."[139]

Randolph wrote to Madison from Virginia at the end of October addressing him as "my dear friend" and signing "Be assured of my most affectionate friendship." He wrote Madison that the Virginia legislature had reached unanimous agreement on language that called for a convention "freely to discuss and deliberate on the constitution." This language, reached as a compromise, did not imply any disapproval of the proposed constitution—but it did imply that the ratifying convention could propose amendments, as Randolph had wanted at the Philadelphia convention. Randolph told Madison, "This is a happy and politic resolution; for I am thoroughly persuaded, that if it had been propounded by the legislature to the people, as *we* propounded it, the constitution would have been rejected and the spirit of union extinguished."[140] The letter was an attempt to justify his refusal to sign the constitution.

Clinging to the friendship in the face of disagreement, Randolph mustered a joke about their differences. In a separate letter telling Madison that he had been reelected to Congress, Randolph quipped, "So that you see, circumcision and uncircumcision avail nothing."[141] Even such stark differences (the reference was to the biblical distinction between Israelites and others) had no effect on Madison's popularity. The humor both minimized and emphasized that in Virginia, people were beginning to take sides over the ratification of the constitution.

Even within his own family, Madison could not be sure of complete support. Madison's namesake cousin, the Reverend James Madison, wrote Madison an uninhibited letter offering his "observations" on the proposed constitution. He began by praising the new government.[142] But he was worried that the legislative and executive departments were not "entirely distinct and independent." The president "who may be for life" could veto legislation, while the Senate, "which may also be for life" functioned as part of the executive in cases of appointments and treaties. The draft, the Reverend Madison went on, "presents to my mind so strong a stamp of monarchy or aristocracy" that within a few generations, "one or other would spring from the new constitution provided it were to continue in its present form."[143] James Madison's own cousin was telling him that the proposed constitution was severely flawed.

Dr. James McClurg, who had been part of the Virginia delegation in Philadelphia before leaving in August, explained his perception of what was happening in Virginia to Madison. The proposed constitution "was first received with a pre-possession in its favor almost enthusiastic, in our towns especially." But circumstances had "caused this disposition to subside sooner than it might otherwise have done." Writing on the last day of October 1787, McClurg said the draft was already beginning to generate political opposition driven by "suspicion and jealousy" of what a powerful federal government might do. Now, he said, "every man's mind is turned to a subtle investigation of the plan."[144]

Washington wrote to Madison, "No subject is more interesting, and seems so much to engross the attention of everyone, as the proposed constitution."[145] And arguments for and against ratification were spreading quickly, despite the vagaries of communication and reprinting.[146] Thus, for example, on November 9, 1787, a Virginia correspondent of Madison's sent him a copy of one of the first *Federalist* essays that had appeared in the Virginia newspapers within two weeks of its initial publication in New York.*

Madison would have to leave New York to attend Virginia's ratifying convention—that much was clear. One friend wrote him, "For God's sake do not disappoint the anxious expectations of your friends and let me add of your country."[147] When Madison's brother Ambrose wrote him asking whether he would be a candidate to represent Orange County, Madison replied affirmatively. He insisted that initially he had not wanted to serve in the ratifying convention, "supposing that it would be as well that the final decision thereon should proceed from men who had no hand in preparing and proposing" the constitution. But as it turned out, "in all the states the members of the general convention are becoming members of the state conventions." His friends were asking him to do it. Most important, he wrote, "I have reason to believe that many objections in Virginia proceed from a misconception of the plan, or of the causes which produced the objectionable parts of it." Madison's experience in Philadelphia would allow him "to contribute some explanations and information which may be of use." Madison left it to his brother to explain all this to his constituents: "You may let this be known in such way as my father and yourself may judge best."[148]

Supporters of ratification in Virginia, worried about the rising tide of sentiment against the proposed constitution within the state, were relieved that Virginia decided to hold its convention later than many other states. One wrote to Madison that "opponents to [ratification] are many, able, and busy. Converts are daily made."[149] Supporters also hoped that Edmund Randolph's idea that the state legislature should propose amendments and send them to other states had been abandoned. "The other states are adopting the constitution with avidity," one of them wrote with hopeful optimism, "and would pay little attention to any proposed amendment."[150]

In the meantime, in New York, Madison was increasingly focused on the project of the *Federalist* essays. He sent the first seven numbers to

---

* Apparently in all innocence, Madison's associate wrote that he was "extremely pleased" with the essay, and said of the anonymous author that "from his introduction I have the highest expectations from him." He asked Madison to send the rest of the essays "if it would not impose too great a task upon you." Archibald Stuart to Madison, November 9, 1787, *PJM*, 10:245.

George Washington, explaining that the whole series was intended to be comprehensive. "If the whole plan" of the essays "should be executed, it will present to the public a full discussion of the merits of the proposed constitution in all its relations." Madison disclosed to Washington that he was one of the anonymous authors: "I will not conceal *from you,*" he wrote, "that I am likely to have such *a degree* of connection with the publication here." He also hinted that Hamilton was one of the others, telling Washington that "you will recognize one of the pens concerned in the task." Washington knew Hamilton's writing well, since Hamilton had been his aide-de-camp during the war.[151]

Size

As a Virginia delegate to Congress, Madison could not yet leave New York, but Congress had no quorum, and would not have one until February. Madison used the time in his usual way: by study and research intended to prepare him for political controversy. It is a mark of Madison's dedication that he was not satisfied with what he had already done, and sought to supplement a base of constitutional knowledge already more extensive than that of any other person in America.

In the weeks that followed, the size of the republic and its place in human history was on his mind. *Federalist* No. 14 began with a warning that opponents of the constitution were confusing pure democracy with a republic. The natural limit to the size of a republic was that "which will barely allow the representatives of the people to meet as often as may be necessary for the administration of public affairs."[152]

Seen in these geographic terms, the United States was not too big. Congress had been "almost continually assembled" since the Revolution. Madison estimated the length of the United States on average as "eight hundred, sixty-eight miles and three fourths," and its width as no more than 750 miles. This was, he said, "not a great deal larger than Germany, where a diet representing the whole empire is continually assembled." Although Great Britain was smaller, "the representatives of the northern extremity of the island," namely northern Scotland, "have as far to travel to the national Council, as will be required of those of the most remote parts of the union."[153]

Madison reminded his readers that the states were not being abolished, and local government would still take place within them. Better roads and canals would make travel easier. Far-flung states would be especially sure to send representatives to Congress, because they would be most vulnerable to invasion.

Having advanced these characteristically rational arguments, Madison did something very rare in his writing: He admonished the citizens of the United States directly:

> Hearken not the unnatural voice which tells you that the people of America, stitched together as they are by so many cords of affection, can no longer live together as members of the same family. . . . Hearken not to the voice which passionately tells you that the form of government recommended for your adoption is a novelty in the political world; that it has never yet had a place in the theories of the wildest projectors; that it rashly attempts what it is impossible to accomplish. No my countrymen, shut your ears against this unhallowed language.[154]

Unable to deny that a republican federal union was a novelty, Madison depicted its novelty as a virtue—the result of a distinctly American discovery:

> Why is the experiment of an extended republic to be rejected merely because it may comprise what is new? Is it not the glory of the people of America, that . . . they have not suffered a blind veneration for antiquity, for custom, or for names, to overrule the suggestions of their own good sense? . . . Happily for America, happily we trust for the whole human race, they pursued a new and more noble course. They accomplished a revolution which has no parallel in the annals of human society: They created the fabrics of governments which have no model on the face of the globe.[155]

The world, Madison prophesied, would be indebted to America. What made the Revolution great, infusing it with world-historical significance, was not independence but the invention of functioning republics.

The act of creation, however, remained incomplete. The revolutionary generation had "erred most in the structure of the union." It was now "incumbent on their successors to improve and perpetuate" the confederacy. Madison and his colleagues in Philadelphia had continued the work of the Revolution. Now responsibility had shifted to the citizens: "It is that act on which you are now to deliberate and to decide."[156]

At no other time in his life would Madison state so clearly—or in such inspiring terms—his understanding of the purposes and ideals of the American Revolution and republic. Independence from England was not an end in itself. Madison defined the Revolution in terms of the invention of new forms of government. His own innovation would, he hoped, save the essence of the Revolution by perfecting republicanism for posterity. This solution in turn would benefit "the whole human race." In *Federalist* No. 14, Madison was seeking to define his own contribution to global history.

The Phenomenon

The Pennsylvania ratifying convention convened in Philadelphia on November 21, 1787. From New York, Madison followed with intense interest. He wrote to Edmund Randolph that on "preparatory questions," the newspapers suggested that "the party in favor of the Constitution" had a significant advantage. He also sent Randolph two *Federalist* essays, commenting that he did not have copies of all the essays that had appeared in the newspapers, but was not worried about it because they would be published as a pamphlet. Madison revealed to Randolph in code that he had authored a few of the essays, and that "one besides myself" of the other authors "was a member of the convention."[157]

In Virginia, George Washington was swept up in the excitement of the ratification process. On December 7, he wrote to Madison saying that he "anxiously expected" to hear results of the Pennsylvania and Delaware conventions soon. Concerned for the prospect of ratification in Virginia, Washington was already anticipating the possibility that "the states eastward and northward" of Virginia might ratify, while Virginia might not. If that happened, he said, "The citizens of this state will have no cause to bless the opponents of it here." It was difficult to see how the constitution could take effect unless ratified by Virginia, the largest state.

Washington also wrote to Madison that he had seen a report in a Baltimore newspaper to the effect that John Jay had flipped on the constitution and, "from being an admirer of it, he has become a bitter enemy." On its face, Washington said, he would "discredit" the report. Yet he professed that he was "anxious however to know, on what ground this report originates, especially the indelicacy of the expression."

The report was "an arrant forgery," Madison informed Washington as soon as he got the letter. He did not tell Washington that Jay had authored several of the *Federalist* essays, but he did say to Washington that "tricks of this sort are not uncommon with the enemies of the new constitution."[158] Such was indeed the case. One correspondent from Virginia reported to Madison, "I daresay you will be greatly surprised to hear that it is reported that you are opposed to the system and I was told the other day that you were actually writing a piece against it."[159] Madison's language reflected his mounting frustration. Washington had used the word "enemy" only in paraphrasing the report about Jay. Madison was using the word "enemies" to describe his political opponents.

By the second week of December, Madison had begun to discern a pattern. He anticipated that Pennsylvania would likely ratify and that Connecticut could, too. He was also optimistic about New Hampshire, New Jersey, and Delaware. Given that these small states had been at the forefront of demanding equal representation in the Senate, the anticipated embrace of ratification reflected the fact that their delegates had gotten what they wanted at the convention, and would have significant influence over the ratification decision.

Then there were the trouble spots. The outcome in Massachusetts was uncertain. New York, Madison wrote to Jefferson, "is much divided." In Maryland, "a more formidable opposition is likely to be made . . . than was at first conjectured."[160]

Worse was Virginia, for which Madison now had more detailed information. The state, he suggested, could be divided into three parties. One, which included George Washington and Madison himself, was for "adopting without attempting amendments." A second party, led by Edmund Randolph and George Mason, wanted ratification with amendments. Then there was a third party, "at the head of which is Mr. Henry." Patrick Henry's cohort "concurs at present with the patrons of amendments," but would probably aim for "such a strike at the essence of the system" as would either lead to keeping the Articles or alternatively "a partition of the union and several confederacies."[161]

Madison also wrote to Jefferson that it was "worthy of remark" that in Virginia, "the men of intelligence, patriotism, property, and independent circumstances" were divided on ratification. Judges and lawyers were generally opposed.[162] "The mass of the people," however, who were usually "accustomed to be guided by their rulers on all new and intricate questions," seemed supportive. In all this Virginia was an outlier. In the eastern and middle states, Madison said, elites were "zealously attached to the proposed constitution." In New England, "the men of letters, the principal officers of government, the judges and lawyers, clergy, and men of property" were overwhelmingly in support of ratification as well.[163]

Madison did not underestimate Patrick Henry, telling Jefferson that "Mr. Henry is the great adversary who will render the event precarious." Henry was "working up every possible interest, into a spirit of opposition." Given his expectation that Henry would exploit the proposal of new amendments to block or break the constitution, Madison was totally unwilling to concede any ground to the proponents of the amendment scheme. If the Virginia ratifying convention were to adopt amendments, it would "either dismember the union, or reduce her to a dilemma, as mortifying to her pride, as it will be injurious to her foresight."[164]

Procuring the Good, Getting Rid of the Bad

Madison's December letter to Jefferson crossed a letter from Jefferson commenting on the proposed constitution. Jefferson understood Madison's pride of authorship, and he echoed Madison's caution in his earlier letter to Jefferson by saying that he had little news "to fill a letter" and would "therefore make up the deficiency by adding a few words on the constitution proposed by our convention."

He began with the positive. Jefferson liked the idea of a self-sustaining government that would not depend constantly on the state legislatures for funding, and he liked the separation of powers. He noted approvingly that a directly elected House of Representatives with the power to tax would preserve the principle of no taxation without representation.[165] And he told Madison that he was "captivated by the compromise of the opposite claims of the great and little states, of the latter to equal, and the former to proportional influence." Having missed the convention, Jefferson was among the first thinkers to consider the accidental compromise as desirable in itself, not as an unfortunate consequence that could be depicted as positive for rhetorical reasons. For him, the compromise produced balance. He also liked the presidential veto, "though I should have liked it better had the judiciary been associated for that purpose, or invested with a similar and separate power."[166]

Having offered some praise, Jefferson turned to what, he said, "I do not like." The most serious problem was "the omission of a bill of rights."[167] Jefferson firmly believed "that a bill of rights is what the people are entitled to against every government on earth, general or particular, and what no just government should refuse or rest on inference."[168] Put so directly, and in stirring Jeffersonian language, this was a rebuke of Madison by the man whose friendship he valued most in the world. Madison's proposed constitution had fallen short when it came to liberty.

Jefferson had one further serious objection, a feature that, he said, "I dislike, and greatly dislike": the possibility of reelection, especially for the president. According to Jefferson, "Experience concurs with reason in concluding that the first magistrate will always be reelected if the Constitution permits it. He is an officer for life." The danger of a president with de facto life tenure was that foreign nations would therefore find it desirable to interfere in the election process "with money and with arms." This, in turn, would push American politicians to choose European sides: "A Galloman or an Angloman will be supported by the nation he befriends."[169] Considering that Jefferson, ambassador to France and admiring contemporary of enlightened French intellectuals, was considered a Francophile, it was noteworthy that he was expressing fear of a political system divided between supporters of the French and English.

Jefferson must have guessed that his views might depress Madison. He finished his assessment by writing, "At all events I hope you will not be discouraged from other trials, if the present one should fail of its full effect." This was meant as encouragement, but it, too, could have been read as discouraging, because it implied that the constitution Madison had designed might well fail. Given the multiyear effort and intense negotiation that had gone into producing the proposed constitution, trying again was not a realistic option.

Jefferson closed with the prediction that, "Our governments will remain virtuous for many centuries; as long as they are chiefly agricultural; and this will be as long as there shall be vacant lands in any part of America." If Americans were to "get piled upon one another in large cities, as in Europe, they will become corrupt as in Europe."[170]

Madison did not see the United States as "chiefly agricultural." He had designed a constitution that was intended to deal with the inevitable faction that would arise as the result of differing interests—interests derived from the fact that Americans were farmers and merchants, creditors and debtors. He did not believe that the future success of the federal republic depended on the expansion of land and the avoidance of cities. Perhaps Jefferson did not wholly believe it, either; but then it was his preference to express himself in absolute terms, and Madison's to speak precisely.

The two men's mutual appreciation of their character differences helps explain the depth of their friendship. Jefferson signed with "assurances of those sentiments of esteem and attachment with which I am, dear sir, your affectionate friend and servant." Their disagreements about the proposed constitution would not affect their closeness. And Madison would not receive Jefferson's letter until late the following spring, by which time he would be deeply enmeshed in the Virginia ratification convention, and would have to explain away Jefferson's worries to the other delegates.

A Strange Change of Opinion

The authorship of the *Federalist* essays was a secret, but not a closely guarded one. On December 18, 1787, a Richmond acquaintance wrote to Madison that "Publius is variously ascribed to M——d——n, H——lt——n, J——y."[171] Meanwhile, Madison's commitment to the project was deepening. Madison and Hamilton collaborated on *Federalist* Nos. 18, 19, and 20.

These essays were history lessons—with a point. The erudition was Madison's, a product of his recent research. The arguments, too, had a Madisonian bent. But the brevity and directness sounded more like Hamilton. The first lesson they offered, drawing on ancient Greece, was that too weak a confederacy could not avoid oppression. Had the Amphictyonic League "been united by a stricter confederation," then they might "never have worn the chains" of Alexander the Great, "and might have proved a barrier to the vast projects of Rome." In contrast, the Achaean Confederacy, a league of smaller and less important Greek states, worked better because its members were compelled to adopt common laws. Projected onto a (doubtful) interpretation of ancient history, this was a version of Madison's theory of enlargement.

Federalist No. 19 moved to modern Germany. The only thing that held the German confederation together, it argued, was the weakness of the individual members and the vestigial pride of the emperor at being an important European monarch. Madison and Hamilton ignored the trend toward absolutism exemplified by the rule of Frederick the Great of Prussia, who had died just the year before. They did not mention the telling example of France, where feudalism had given way to absolutist monarchy.

Federalist No. 20 visited the Netherlands with the purpose of "confirm[ing] all the lessons" of the earlier essays. The idea was that the United States under the Articles resembled the weak Dutch confederacy. The essay maintained that a weak constitution was more likely to produce tyranny than a strong one. Fears of too much power in the new proposed Congress and executive were therefore misplaced.

This lesson concluded the subsection of the *Federalist* essays that focused on other federal experiments. Hamilton would write Nos. 21 through 36 alone, describing the effects of the existing system and the powers that the new federal constitution needed to provide. Madison would take over again with Nos. 37 through 58 and 62 and 63, in which he defended the structure of the proposed constitution that had been produced in Philadelphia.

In the meantime, reports of the Pennsylvania ratifying convention reached Madison. The news was good: Ratification by a vote of 46 to 23, achieved on December 12. It also turned out that, when no one was looking, Delaware had ratified the constitution on December 7—unanimously, after just four days' deliberation.[172] New Jersey ratified unanimously on December 18; Georgia did the same on December 30.[173] Four states had ratified in just three months.

Yet by the middle of January, Madison foresaw disaster. He expected Connecticut to have ratified already, as indeed it had done on January 9, 1788, by a vote of 128 to 40.[174] He was still uncertain about Massachusetts, where he had heard that there might be "a considerable party" against ratification. But what really worried Madison was North Carolina, which had "postponed for convention till July, in order to have the previous example of Virginia."[175] Making North Carolina depend on Virginia opened the door to the possibility that if Patrick Henry could block ratification in Virginia, the constitution would not be ratified.

Henry Lee had written to Madison of "the strange change of opinion on the worth of the federal government" that had been taking place in Virginia.[176] "My apprehensions of this danger increase every day," Madison wrote to Edmund Randolph. It was "impossible . . . that the example of Virginia and North Carolina should not have an influence" on the politics of South Carolina and Georgia.* "I consider everything therefore as problematical from Maryland southward."[177]

Henry was thus a threat not only to ratification in Virginia, but to ratification nationally. Madison had been thinking about his motivations, and arrived at a theory. "You are better acquainted with Mr. Henry's politics than I can be," Madison wrote to Randolph, "but I have for some time considered him as driving at a southern confederacy and as not farther concurring in the plan of amendments than as he hopes to render it subservient to his real designs."[178] Madison was insinuating that Henry wanted to be at the head of a confederated country of his own.

Madison wanted to blame someone for the parlous situation—and that person was his close friend Randolph. In a show of frankness, Madison told Randolph so. His letter began "My dear friend," and then argued that Randolph's arguments in favor of a second convention had produced disastrous results. To begin with, Madison explained, "It is to me apparent that had your duty led you to throw your influence into the opposite scale, that it would have given it a decided and unalterable preponderancy." The authority and prestige of the members of the Philadelphia convention mattered. The constitution "would have commanded little attention" if it had been drafted "by an obscure individual."[179] Had Randolph supported ratification, Madison speculated, "Mr. Henry would either have suppressed his enmity, or been baffled in the policy which it has dictated."[180]

Madison told Randolph bluntly that he had contributed to the divided opinion in Virginia.[181] Mason started advocating for a second convention only after Randolph proposed the idea. Responsibility, therefore, rested primarily with Randolph. Holding a second convention would "strike" at the "confidence in the first" convention, undermining the very condition necessary for new government. A second convention would release a plethora of "human opinions; which must be as various and irreconcilable concerning theories of government, as doctrines of religion." It would "give opportunities to designing men which it might be impossible to counteract."[182] Madison ended by writing, "I wish you every happiness, and am with the sincerest affection yours." Yet Madison's letter made it clear that he believed the two men were deeply at odds.

---

* Madison had not yet heard that Georgia had already ratified on December 30, 1787.

Notwithstanding Madison's belief that political disagreement should not make a personal difference, the friendship was in jeopardy. Madison was struggling with the problem of what to do when political disagreement could not be comfortably cabined in the framework of mutually shared beliefs and ideals. He wanted to keep Randolph close, both to preserve the friendship and to convince his friend to abandon his call for a second convention. Yet he believed that Randolph was genuinely threatening the constitution that was necessary to save the republic. Potentially, then, Randolph might not be an ally to republican government but an opponent, witting or otherwise. And if Randolph became a hindrance to the possibility of republicanism itself, he and Madison would no longer be friends. They would be something altogether darker.

CHAPTER SIX

Ratification

...

THE ARGUMENT: *With the outcome of ratification uncertain, Madison produces* Federalist *Nos. 37 through 58 in an astonishing six-week surge. He calls the overall unanimity of the Philadelphia convention a miracle, produced by the absence of party animosities. In retrospect, the convention comes to embody Madison's ideal of political friendship, in which reasonable disagreement was managed by rational deliberation and compromise.*

Madison develops the idea that the constitution embodies a newly invented technology of checks and balances. Ambition will counteract ambition, thus blocking parties and solving the "great desideratum" of republican government. This marks a new stage in Madison's constitutional thinking. At the convention, he wanted a strong national government to overrule the states. He now repurposes the Senate compromise that he originally opposed into a key example of how the states would balance the federal government.

As the fight for ratification in Virginia begins, Madison keeps Randolph close, determined to maintain their friendship. His enemy is Patrick Henry, who Madison believes is committed to the destruction of the republic.

IN JANUARY 1788, nervous about the prospects of ratification in Virginia, Madison turned to the writing of twenty-two more *Federalist* essays, Nos. 37 through 58. They appeared between January 11 and February 20, marking an extraordinary burst of creativity on Madison's part, and the most sustained and systematic writing project he had ever undertaken.

In these essays, Madison aimed for a spirit of moderation. The essays did not address people with "predetermined" sentiments for or against the proposed constitution, but rather reasonable and undecided readers.[1]

His goal was to put the reader into the minds of the drafters of the constitution.

The immediate purpose was persuasion. Yet the essays also revealed Madison in a philosophical frame of mind. Again and again his arguments transcended the particularity of the circumstances facing the United States and appealed to fundamental human nature and the science of governing. Whether he knew it or not, Madison found himself writing for a different audience from the one that actually existed in the moment.

Consider his argument in defense of the difficulty of clearly delineating federal from state power. A more polemical writer would have insisted that the line could be drawn clearly. Madison offered a disquisition on the challenges of line drawing by scientists who had "never yet succeeded, in tracing with certainty," the boundary between vegetable and animal.[2] In politics, Madison continued, the difficulty similarly stemmed from the blurry, imprecise nature of human institutions.

Madison did not rest on theory alone. "To the difficulties already mentioned," he wrote, "may be added the interfering pretensions of the larger and smaller states." Now Madison was almost winking at the reader, hinting that the essay was being written by someone privy to the deliberations at Philadelphia. "We may well suppose that neither side would entirely yield to the other, and consequently that the struggle could be terminated only by compromise."[3] The imprecision of the constitutional text resulted from the differing opinions of the large and small states.

Madison went further by revealing the process by which the compromise had been developed. "It is extremely probable also," he wrote coyly,

> that after the ratio of representation had been adjusted, this very compromise must have produced a fresh struggle between the same parties, to give such a turn to the organization of the government, and to the distribution of its powers, as would increase the importance of the branches, in forming which they had respectively obtained the greater share of influence.[4]

Here was a master explanation for the politics of the Philadelphia convention. There had been a compromise between large and small states over "the ratio of representation." The large states had gotten a proportional House; the small states had gotten equal representation in the Senate. There had then followed "a fresh struggle," in which the large states tried to give more power to the House and the small states favored the Senate and the state legislatures. There were, Madison explained, "features in the constitution which warrant each of these suppositions."

As a result of these practical, real-world differences, Madison explained, the convention had "been compelled to sacrifice theoretical propriety to the force of extraneous considerations." The resulting constitution therefore included "some deviations from that artificial structure and regular symmetry" that an "ingenious theorist" might have devised for "a constitution planned in his closet or in his imagination."[5]

This autobiographical explanation for the imperfections of the constitution was close to self-revelation. Madison's original planned constitution, dreamt up in his closeted "imagination," had been beautifully symmetrical. Protected by a veneer of anonymity, Madison told the general reader what he had previously told only Jefferson. He, Madison, was the "ingenious theorist" of the idealized constitution. Its limitations derived from the unpleasant but inevitable necessity of compromise.

Yet the overall product was still extraordinary, Madison believed. He had told Jefferson that given the constraints, the consensus that had produced the constitution was nothing short of a miracle. Now he wrote it would be "impossible for any man of candor" not to be astonished by the unanimity that had been achieved. The convention had "enjoyed in a very singular degree, an exemption from the pestilential influence of party animosities."*

Indeed, Madison concluded, "it is impossible for the man of pious reflection not to perceive in it a finger of that Almighty Hand which has been so frequently and signally extended to our relief in the critical stages of the revolution." Madison did not insist that his reader see divine providence at work. He did not even invoke God's whole hand as the shaper of the convention. But Madison was not ashamed to invoke the finger of God that the Egyptian magicians had seen in action.

---

* In retrospect, the convention's consensus over economic interests was because backcountry farmers, now increasingly vocal against the constitution in the state ratification conventions, had not been represented in Philadelphia. Men who saw no need for reform had no reason to attend. Those who sought seats in Philadelphia, were selected, and chose to come were mostly well-off, educated men who lived on the coast and favored stronger national government.

The Lycurgus Cure

In *Federalist* No. 38, Madison went on the attack. His first target was a second convention. He began by reviewing the extremely difficult process of constitution formation in the ancient world. The most extreme example was Lycurgus, who, according to legend, convinced the Spartans to adopt his constitutional reforms by making them swear to follow his laws until he returned—then leaving the city and starving himself to death.[6]

America had improved on this method, Madison noted wryly. If there were to be a "second convention, with full powers and for the express purpose of revising and remolding the work of the first," he predicted, it would be marked by "discord and ferment." It would "not stand as fair a chance for immortality, as Lycurgus gave to that of Sparta." Madison was proposing that the Philadelphia convention should be understood as a modern-day collective Lycurgus: Having drafted the constitution, it disbanded itself—and should never be reassembled. A second convention would render the sacrifice pointless.

Madison next targeted the critics of ratification. Reverting to the classical metaphor of the state as a sick patient, he compared the constitution to a medical cure. The critics were busybodies telling "the patient that the prescription will be poison"—but who could not agree on a substitute despite the dire situation. Madison went on to list more than a dozen different arguments that had been raised by opponents of ratification. The proposed constitution, he concluded, did not have to be perfect. It just had to be better than the Articles of Confederation.

Federalist No. 39 appeared on January 16, 1788, as the Massachusetts convention was beginning its deliberations. Supporters of the proposed constitution were wary. Elbridge Gerry, who had refused to sign at the end of the Philadelphia convention, had not been elected to the Massachusetts ratifying convention. Yet, as Rufus King wrote to Madison, "the opponents of the constitution" wanted Gerry to be seated anyway "to answer such inquiries as the convention should make concerning facts which happened in the passing of the constitution." The suggestion was "very irregular," King noted. But supporters of the constitution were so nervous about exciting "the jealousies" of the opponents that they deemed it wiser to agree to let Gerry sit.[7]

New York was still in doubt, and Madison thought the outcome in Massachusetts would determine the result in that convention. At the same time, "the minority of Pennsylvania," who had lost their own battle against ratification, "are extremely restless under their defeat" and would try "to undermine what has been done there."[8] He wrote back to Rufus King that "it is impossible to express how much depends on the results of the deliberations of your body." He told King that he had received a letter from Washington opining that if nine states had ratified by the time of the Virginia convention, the state would go along with it. If Massachusetts said no and New York followed, there would not be nine ratifications before the Virginia convention.[9]

Forms Ought to Give Way to Substance

Madison kept his *Federalist* essays coming, and his friends maintained a steady stream of praise and encouragement. Archibald Stuart wrote from Virginia that "Publius is in general estimation, his greatness is acknowledged universally."[10] From Philadelphia, Tench Coxe asked to be added to the subscription to buy a copy of the complete letters of Publius when they were printed. He called the essays "most valuable disquisitions of government in its peculiar relations and connections with this country."[11]

In *Federalist* No. 39, Madison denied that the proposed constitution created a national government. This was a partial admission of defeat. In Philadelphia, he had consistently advocated for a national government and never fully embraced the idea that the new constitution should be a hybrid, neither truly national nor truly federal. The violation of symmetry had troubled him as a constitutional designer. Now Madison was turning the necessity of compromise at Philadelphia into a virtue of the document that had emerged.

His primary motivation was to refute the criticism that the Philadelphia convention had overstepped its bounds by transforming a confederated republic into a national one. In *Federalist* No. 40, he tackled the argument that the convention had violated the charge given to it by Congress, which said its "sole and express purpose" was revision.

Madison did his best. He pointed out that in the preamble to its resolution, Congress had stated that the convention would be "the most probable mean of establishing in these states, a firm national government." He argued rather questionably that the proposed constitution was nothing more than a revision of the Articles. He came closer to a good answer when he said the delegates had been "deeply and unanimously impressed

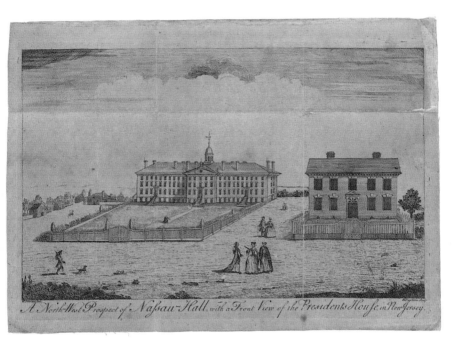

Nassau Hall, Princeton, by Henry Dawkins, 1764. The College of New Jersey at Princeton as it would have looked when Madison arrived in 1769.

Catherine (Kitty) Floyd by Charles Willson
Peale, 1783. Madison commissioned the
miniature portraits of himself and Kitty
when they were engaged to be engaged.
She was fifteen going on sixteen.

James Madison by Charles Willson Peale,
1783. Madison's miniature for Kitty.
He was thirty-two.

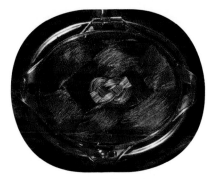

A lock of James Madison's hair, 1783.
Madison attached a lock of his hair to
the miniature he gave Kitty as a love
token. Some day perhaps this could
be used as a source of the childless
Madison's DNA.

Thomas Jefferson by Mather Brown, 1786.
The young Jefferson as a would-be philosophe.

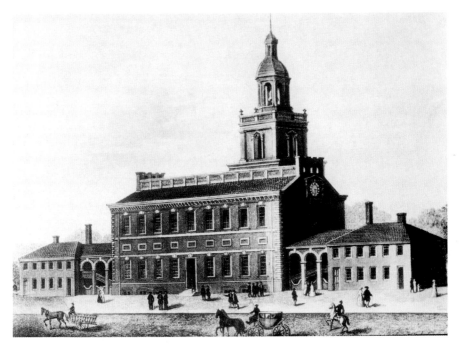

Independence Hall, circa 1770s. The scene of the constitutional convention.

UNITED STATES COMMISSION OF FINE ARTS

Notes on the Federal Convention by James Madison, May 29, 1787.
Note the excellent handwriting and the editing.

Patrick Henry by Lawrence Sully, 1795. Madison's
great adversary in the ratification debate. The only
known image from his lifetime.

Montpelier circa nineteenth century.

with the crisis" facing the country and believed the reform they proposed "was absolutely necessary." The delegates had concluded "that in all great changes of established governments, forms ought to give way to substance."

He then hauled out the biggest gun he had: the American Revolution. In the run-up to independence, Madison reminded his readers, "committees and congresses were formed for concentrating their efforts, and defending their rights. . . . Conventions were elected in the several states, for establishing the constitutions under which they are now governed." All those conventions depended on a single theory, namely the people's inherent capacity for self-government.

This was the saving grace of Madison's near-acknowledgment that the Philadelphia convention had gone beyond its lawful authority. The proposed constitution, he pointed out, was worth no more "than the paper on which it is written, unless it be stamped with the approbation of those to whom it is addressed." Only the people had the inherent power to create and destroy a government.

Madison was revealing the depths of his historical confidence in the proposed constitution. Its creation had been, in its way, a revolutionary act. Ratification would complete the Revolution. The failure of ratification would reverse it.

Having justified the necessity of the constitution and the (revolutionary) authority of the Philadelphia convention, in *Federalist* No. 41 Madison turned to the specific powers conferred on Congress. In particular, his account of the power to tax is important because it is the very first instance in which Madison engaged in constitutional interpretation, offering his own method for reading a document that had not yet even been ratified.

Madison explained that, logically, Congress must have the power to tax exports as well as imports, because eventually the economy, now driven by the export of raw materials, might become more of a manufacturing economy that needed to import raw materials cheaply. "A system of government, meant for duration, ought to contemplate these revolutions, and be able to accommodate itself to them," Madison wrote. The idea that the economy might fundamentally change went hand in hand with the idea that the constitution ought to be capable of enduring such developments.

Madison then focused on criticism of the clause giving Congress

204 THE THREE LIVES OF JAMES MADISON

power to "lay and collect taxes, duties, imposts and excises, to pay the debts, and provide for the common defense and general welfare of the United States." Opponents of ratification argued that the language gave Congress potentially limitless powers. This was a prescient and altogether reasonable objection given the open-endedness that "general welfare" and "defense" implied.

To answer, Madison needed a theory of interpretation. He began by acknowledging that if Congress's powers had been described in the constitution only by that clause, then "the authors of the objection might have had some color for it." But that was not the case. Congress's powers were "immediately" enumerated after this clause, and that enumeration was "not even separated by a longer pause than a semicolon."

Bringing some flair to the game of interpretation, Madison asked:

Shall one part of the same sentence be excluded altogether from sharing the meaning; and shall the more doubtful and indefinite terms be retained in their full extent and the clear and precise expressions, be denied any signification whatsoever?

This was the embryo—still undeveloped, to be sure—of a theory of narrow construction of Congress's enumerated powers. Madison was relying on a standard principle of legal interpretation that gives meaning to all parts of a law. But he was pressing that familiar idea by insisting that the "doubtful and indefinite terms" of Congress's power should not be given their broadest meaning. Instead the "clear and precise expressions" of enumeration should control.

Federalist Nos. 42, 43, and 44 marched through the proposed constitution provision by provision. Generally, Madison devoted just a sentence or two to each clause. A few topics got extra attention, however. Madison devoted a long paragraph to the protection of the slave trade.[12] He had opposed it at the Philadelphia convention. The best he could do as a polemicist was to mention there were only "a few states which continue this unnatural practice," hinting to the reader that there had been no choice but to placate them.

He made another reference to slavery while explaining the necessity of the laws guaranteeing each of the states a republican form of government. The purpose of the clause was to enable Congress to intervene against insurrections, he said.[13] This brought him to the topic of slave rebellions.

"I take no notice of a species of population abounding in some of the states," he wrote. Ordinarily, in peacetime, such people were "sunk below the level of men." But during "tempestuous scenes of civil violence," he went on, the slaves "may emerge into human character." Having become men by virtue of taking up arms in civil war, slaves would be able to "give a superiority of strength to any party with which they may associate themselves."[14]

Madison was referring to the British effort during the Revolutionary War to offer freedom to Virginia's slaves in order to induce them to join the British side. Yet even as Madison appealed to his fellow slaveholders to endorse a constitutional provision that would give federal protection from slave rebellion, he chose language that ennobled the slaves who might rebel. In Madison's telling, slaves were kept below the level of humanity by the institution of peacetime slavery. When civil strife broke out, slaves could seize the opportunity to humanize themselves by the consummate act of self-determination. The combination of commitment to slavery as an institution with brutal honesty about its moral wrongfulness was not unusual for Madison. In his public writings as in his private letters, Madison made no attempt to mask the contradiction.

Powers

Madison was approaching his most important contribution to the *Federalist* papers and the insight that would become the linchpin of all subsequent thinking about the genius of the U.S. Constitution: the idea that power would check and balance power. His originality was sparked by his need to defend the most controversial component of the proposed constitution: Congress's authority to enact laws "necessary and proper" to execute the other powers enumerated.

Madison declared that without the substance conveyed by this clause, "the whole constitution would be a dead letter."[15] If the Congress acted beyond the constitution, the people could vote them out of office.[16] Alternatively, the states could "sound the alarm to the people."[17] He made the same point again in *Federalist* No. 46, insisting that any overreach by Congress would generate "signals of general alarm . . . Plans of resistance would be concerted. One spirit would animate and conduct the whole."[18] Using terms drawn from the American Revolution, Madison was claiming that federal overreach would lead to quasi-revolutionary resistance.

Once again, Madison was making a constitutional virtue out of an aspect of the proposed constitution that he had opposed in Philadelphia. He had never wanted the state legislatures to be able to compete with Congress for authority. Given half a chance, he believed, state legislatures would destroy the powers of Congress. But with ratification on the line, Madison was claiming that the state legislatures could be the bulwarks of defense against an overreaching Congress and an insufficiently protective executive and judiciary.

In *Federalist* Nos. 47, 48, and 49, Madison shifted gears. With a brilliant exposition of checks and balances, he refuted the criticism that the proposed constitution violated the ideal separation of powers. These essays, too, turned the arguments against the proposed constitution upside down. Unless the different departments were "so far connected and blended as to give each a constitutional control over the others," separation of powers could "never in practice be duly maintained."[19] The overlap between the powers of the distinct departments did not derogate from the separation of powers but fulfilled it.

Madison disparaged the "parchment barriers" on which the state constitutions had relied to assure the separation of powers. The idea that explicit constitutional provisions limiting government's exercise of power were mere "parchment," susceptible to being ignored, might seem surprising coming from the principal architect of a new written constitution. But, in fact, the attack on written guarantees lay near the heart of Madison's constitutional vision. For Madison, a constitution could not limit government power by simple declaration. Instead, the *structure* of the constitution must be designed so that participants in the government would enforce those limits. Madison was not rejecting written constitutions per se. He was dismissing the notion that pronouncements without structural support could work in the real world.

Power was the key to creating structures that would actually enforce limitations. The "encroaching spirit of power" was to be feared, and it could only be opposed by countervailing power. The greatest despotic threat came from the "legislative department," which was "everywhere extending the field of its activity, and drawing all power into its impetuous vortex."[20] This was another reference to the theory of gravity, this time with the sun as a dangerous source of power.

In *Federalist* No. 49, Madison paused to consider and reject a potential solution to legislative overreach first proposed to him by Jefferson: that two branches of the government should have the power to call a new constitutional convention if two-thirds of their members agreed that the third branch had breached the constitution.

Madison thought this was a terrible idea:

> Frequent appeals [to a convention] would in great measure deprive the government of that veneration which time bestows on everything, and without which perhaps the wisest and freest governments would not possess the requisite stability.[21]

At the Philadelphia convention, Madison had not gone so far as to argue that the proposed constitution should itself become a quasi-permanent monument. Now Madison was arguing that the constitution would succeed better if it grew old and respected.

Madison acknowledged that venerating the ancient was not, strictly speaking, rational. "In a nation of philosophers," he wrote, "this consideration ought to be disregarded." If all the world were Jeffersons, there would be no reason to rely on the age of the constitution to judge its quality. But not everyone was a Jefferson, and "a nation of philosophers is as little to be expected as the philosophical race of kings wished for by Plato."

In the real world, Madison reminded his readers, governments rested "on opinion." Individuals' opinions, in turn, rested on two other things. One source was safety in numbers: "The reason of man, like man himself, is timid and cautious, when left alone." But if the individual imagined many other people "to have entertained the same opinion," that would fortify his own. The other source was antiquity. "When the examples . . . are *ancient* as well as *numerous,* they are known to have a double effect."[22]

Enmeshed in the politics of ratification, Madison was working on a theory of public opinion. As he had explained to Edmund Randolph in the course of blaming him for opposing ratification in Virginia, most uneducated people were not capable of reaching their own opinions about a matter so complicated as ratification. The two ideas that the individual would follow the crowd and that a constitution would take on veneration by virtue of its antiquity were additions to Madison's emerging view.

Now Madison reached the immediate purpose for which he had invoked and opposed Jefferson's proposal: Conventions might unleash faction. The state constitutions had been drafted during the Revolution, "in the midst of a danger which repressed the passions most unfriendly to order and concord." As a result, "No spirit of party . . . could mingle its leaven in the operation."[23] But such luck would not recur. Conventions were "experiments . . . of too ticklish a nature to be unnecessarily multiplied," he wrote. Madison's miracle of consensus at Philadelphia would not happen again.* Constitutional experiments were by their nature unrepeatable. Future conventions would likely destroy "the constitutional equilibrium of the government" because "the *passions* . . . not the *reason*, of the public, would sit in judgment."[24]

Madison believed that the Philadelphia convention had been an exception to the usual control by passionate interests. That was why the constitution deserved veneration: It had been produced as an exercise in reason.

Personal Motives

Federalist No. 51 presented the apex of Madison's new theory of how the constitution worked. The essay began with the all-important declaration that, since "exterior provisions" were "inadequate" to preserve the separation of powers, the answer must come from "the interior structure of the government." The written provisions of a written constitution lacked the capacity to create balance.

The solution was to align the incentives of the people in government with the balance of powers. The constitution must give "those who administer each department, the necessary constitutional means, and personal motives, to resist encroachments of the others."[25] If the danger to the separation of powers came from the human will to maximize power, then it should be opposed by the very same will.

"Ambition must be made to counteract ambition," Madison wrote in what would become the single most famous sentence of the *Federalist* essays. "The interest of the man must be connected with the constitutional rights of the place." The result would be a structural balance, crafted from the juxtaposition of human nature onto man-made constitutional powers.

---

* In *Federalist* No. 50, Madison took the point a step further. Not only must constitutional conventions be avoided, even periodic reviews of constitutional practice were problematic. Considering the example of Pennsylvania's reviewing censors, Madison argued that political faction had predominated: "Unfortunately passion, not reason, must have presided over their decisions," he concluded.

Madison sensed that some readers might find this power-driven, Hamilton-esque view of human nature too pessimistic. "It may be a reflection on human nature," he wrote, "that such devices should be necessary to control the abuses of government." Madison embraced the charge: "But what is government itself but the greatest of all reflections on human nature?" The human will to power was the very reason that government was necessary. "If men were angels, no government would be necessary"— because men would not try to oppress one another. "If angels were to govern men, neither external nor internal controls on government would be necessary"—because the government would operate altruistically. In the real world, however, the challenge was to create "a government which is to be administered by men over men."[26]

Real-world government faced a basic difficulty, Madison wrote: "You must first enable the government to control the governed; and the next place, oblige it to control itself." This goal was closely connected to what Madison had been calling the "great desideratum" of republicanism. His answer lay in a "policy of supplying by opposite and rival interests, the defect of better motives."[27]

The details were a bit difficult to work out, Madison admitted. The different departments could not be fully equal because "in republican government the legislative authority necessarily predominates." The solution to the problem was to "divide the legislature into different branches." In Philadelphia, Madison had wanted the House and Senate both to be elected based on population, in which case they would not have had very different compositions or interests. Now he was using "the different modes of election" of the two houses of Congress to his advantage.

Madison then trumpeted the other accidental feature of the constitution: federalism. "In a single republic," Madison wrote, the only defense against "usurpations" was the internal separation of powers. But "in the compound republic of America," the people gave their power to "two distinct governments," state and federal, which, in turn, "subdivided" their own powers into separate departments. This produced "a double security," according to Madison: "The different governments will control each other; at the same time that each will be controlled by itself."[28] In Philadelphia and before, Madison had wanted state governments weak so they would not overwhelm the federal government. He had given in to the smaller mid-Atlantic states out of necessity, not choice. Now, he was turning what he had considered a flaw into a key benefit.

210 THE THREE LIVES OF JAMES MADISON

Finally, Madison shifted to protection of the property-holding minority against the majority. A hereditary monarch could protect minority rights but might side with the majority or turn against all the citizens. As in *Federalist* No. 10, enlargement was the answer. "The society itself will be broken into so many parts, interests and classes of citizens, that the rights of individuals, or of the minority, will be in little danger from interested combinations of the majority."[29]

Madison added a new twist to the enlargement argument, one drawn from the issue that first brought him into politics: religious liberty. He proposed that "in a free government, the security for civil rights must be the same as that for religious rights." For civil rights, security lay "in the multiplicity of interests." For religious rights, it consisted "in the multiplicity of sects." The more "interests and sects," the harder to coordinate oppression, and the more liberty there would be. Increasing the number "may be presumed to depend on the extent of country and number of people comprehended under the same government."*

Madison then concluded his refinement of the theory of enlargement by going back to first principles. "Justice is the end of government," he wrote. "It is the end of civil society." The whole point of government was not to facilitate the will of the majority but to protect individual rights. "If the stronger faction can readily unite and oppress the weaker," then "anarchy may truly be said to reign, as in a state of nature where the weaker individual is not secured against the violence of the stronger."[30] From the familiar premise that government aimed to provide justice, Madison had moved seamlessly to the rather extreme claim that if a majority could oppress the minority, a republic was no better than anarchy.

Madison went on to predict confidently—too confidently—that in

---

* David Hume had made an analogous argument about the multiplicity of religious sects increasing the likelihood of religious liberty, and Madison had observed in the fight for religious liberty in Virginia that the presence of Presbyterians and Baptists had made it harder for the Anglican Church to reestablish itself. It would be appealing to conclude, as some scholars have done, that Madison's whole theory of enlargement came from the context of religious liberty. Yet this was the first time Madison had juxtaposed the two, including in his private writing. Possibly the reason Madison thought to make the comparison had to do with his desire to convince religious dissenters in Virginia to support the proposed constitution. In a letter written January 30, 1788, Madison's father had reported from Virginia that "the Baptists" were "now generally opposed" to ratification. James Madison, Sr., to Madison, January 30, 1788, *PJM*, 10:446. It was too soon for Madison to have received the letter when he wrote *Federalist* No. 51, which was published on February 6. But Madison might have heard the same rumor from other sources.

such a republic, even the more powerful would come to embrace the idea of a government that would protect majorities and minorities alike. That was what happened, according to the political philosophies of Hobbes and Locke, in anarchy or the state of nature: The strong would agree to government under law in order to protect their own rights. Madison was proposing that the same thing would take place in a majoritarian republic.

Madison closed with a still more optimistic prediction about "the extended republic of the United States" under the proposed constitution. In it, "a coalition of the majority of the whole society could seldom take place upon any other principles than those of justice and the general good." The key claim was that "the larger the society . . . the more duly capable it will be of self-government." Of course the size would also have to enable practical government. But "happily for the republican cause, the practical sphere may be carried to a very great extent, by judicious modification and mixture of the federal principle."[31]

Madison never got more Panglossian than this. He had begun the essay with the limits of human nature and the need to make ambition counter ambition. Yet despite the brilliance of the analysis, he had not been willing or able to focus on the details of how individual ambition would maintain the separation of powers. Instead, he had found his way back to the theoretical ground of his grand theory of enlargement. In the comfort of this by now well-developed idea, Madison could conclude that the extended federal republic provided the best of all solutions to the problem of protecting individual liberty from the majority. The United States as a constitutional federal republic was not too small or too large, but "happily"—that is, accidentally—just right.

Two Orders in the Society

As Madison reached the heights of his post-constitution creativity, the Massachusetts ratifying convention was in full, controversial swing. On January 23, 1788, Rufus King wrote to Madison, "Our prospects are gloomy, but hope is not entirely extinguished." The supporters of ratification were developing a new strategy: ratify the constitution and simultaneously propose some amendments that could be addressed by Congress at its discretion.[32] By relying "upon this plan" of "recommendatory" amendments, another supporter told Madison, "we may possibly get a majority of 12 or 15."[33]

The trouble, King told Madison, came down to social class. "The opposition complain that the lawyers, judges, clergymen, merchants and men of education are all in favor of the constitution," he reported. Opponents were convinced that "some injury is plotted against them, that the system is the production of the rich and ambitious." They believed that "the consequence will be . . . the establishment of two orders in the society, one comprehending the opulent and great, the other the poor and illiterate."[34]

King was not just being a snob. He was describing the dynamics of social class that had fomented Shays's Rebellion. Less educated members of the ratifying convention, mostly from the rural, agricultural western part of the state, were the main bloc opposed to ratification. Madison shared King's trepidation. In nearly identical letters to Edmund Randolph and George Washington, he reported that "the antifederal party" in Massachusetts was being supported by "the insurgents" who had participated in Shays's Rebellion, as well as by delegates from Maine, which was seeking to become its own state.[35] "The probability is that the voice of [Massachusetts] will be in the negative," Madison wrote.[36]

Word of Massachusetts's recalcitrance was spreading quickly. Tench Coxe wrote to Madison from Philadelphia that Pennsylvania opponents of the constitution—who had continued to make political noise even after ratification—"were possessed of the temper of the western and eastern members of the Massachusetts convention very minutely." Just as Madison kept up a steady stream of letters with fellow supporters of the constitution, opponents, Coxe speculated, "keep up a minute and regular correspondence" across the states.[37]

It was crucial for the entire ratification process that supporters in Massachusetts find a solution. King and Gorham approached the legendarily egocentric John Hancock, governor of the state, and offered him the chance to become the decisive factor in the convention. They presented him with a list of amendments and suggested that he propose them as his own, resolving the disputed convention in favor of the constitution—and of his own prestige.[38]

King was not fully confident that Hancock, whose "character is not entirely free from a portion of caprice," would accept the proposal.[39] But he did. In a dramatic gesture, Hancock entered the ratifying convention wrapped in flannel blankets to show that he had been ill.[40] Over the next several days he proposed the recommendatory amendments, which were then endorsed by Samuel Adams, who had "been hitherto silent in the convention."[41] The amendments were debated and mildly edited, but in the end they carried the day—barely. On February 6, 1788, King wrote to Madison, "I have the satisfaction to inform you that on the final question of assenting and ratifying the constitution our convention divided, and 187 were in the affirmative and 168 in the negative."[42] Massachusetts had ratified the constitution by just 19 votes.

The Massachusetts supporters believed that New Hampshire would certainly follow,[43] and Madison thought so, too. On February 15, he wrote to George Washington with the news, noting that "the amendments are a blemish, but are in the least offensive form." The vote against had been "very disagreeably large," Madison admitted. New Hampshire's convention was sitting, he said, and "there seems to be no question" that it would ratify.[44]

Madison was mistaken. He reported to Edmund Pendleton on March 3, "The convention of New Hampshire have disappointed much the general expectation. Instead of adopting the constitution they have adjourned without any final decision until June." The adjournment had been strategic: Supporters of the proposed constitution thought that they were about to lose the vote by three or four votes, and preferred the "expedient" of adjournment "to prevent a rejection."[45]

New Hampshire's decision reversed the momentum briefly created by ratification in Massachusetts. Madison thought that the effect of New Hampshire's adjournment "will be very considerable in this state (New York) and in several others."[46] The time was coming for Madison to turn his full attention to Virginia.

A Degree of Depravity

Before he could go home, Madison had to finish his contribution to *The Federalist*. Its publication as a single volume had already been advertised. George Washington, from Virginia, asked Madison to put aside three or four copies for him, one of them to be bound, and offered to pay.[47] After the climactic No. 51, Madison wrote eight more essays. Seven of them, Nos. 52 through 58, dealt with the House of Representatives. In Nos. 52 and 53, Madison defended the choice of biennial elections, as opposed to the annual elections traditional within most states. In No. 54 he discussed apportionment. This required him to defend the three-fifths rule for counting slaves.

The chief objection to the rule, raised already in Philadelphia, was that slaves were either property or persons, not both.[48] Madison rejected the binary choice, arguing that slaves were "considered by our laws, in some respects, as persons, and in other respects, as property." A slave was property in that he must labor for his master; could be sold; and was "at all times . . . restrained in liberty, and chastised in his body, by the capricious will of another." In these respects, Madison observed, "The slave may appear to be degraded from the human race, and classed with those irrational animals, which fall under the legal denomination of property."[49]

Yet at the same time, a slave could not be killed or maimed without legal consequence. The slave was also "punishable himself for all violence committed against others." From these features it followed that the slave was "evidently regarded by the law as a member of the society" and "as a moral person, not as a mere article of property."[50] Madison argued that "the laws have transformed the negroes into subjects of property." Yet if the laws creating slavery were revoked, "The negroes could no longer be refused an equal share of representation with the other inhabitants."

As always Madison eschewed overt racism in describing slavery. Instead he adopted an objective tone, neither sanctioning slavery nor opposing it—and certainly never acknowledging that his economic welfare depended on the labor of slaves. He then expressed "some surprise" that northerners who condemned "the barbarous policy" of "considering as property, a part of their human brethren," were saying that "this unfortunate race" should be considered "more completely in the unnatural light of property, than the very laws of which they complain."[51]

Madison's argument can only be described as perverse. Of course there was a contradiction in the northern position that slavery was wrong and that slaves should nevertheless not be counted. But it was nothing to the hypocrisy of southern whites who both held slaves and also maintained that, for purposes of representation, slaves should be counted as persons.

This analysis left a further problem with the three-fifths compromise: Why should slaves be counted for representation if they were not allowed to vote? Madison's weak answer was that different states already had different voting rules defined by property qualifications. "In some of the states the difference is very material," Madison wrote. Yet all white inhabitants, regardless of whether they could vote, were "included in the census by which the federal constitution apportions the representatives."[52]

The argument proved too much. If taken seriously, Madison acknowledged, it meant that slaves should be counted fully in the census, not as three-fifths of a person. All he could say was that the southerners had waived the principle in favor of compromise: The "compromising expedient of the Constitution regards the *slave* as divested of two fifths of the *man.*"[53] The conclusion was morally repulsive but an accurate description of the compromise. His reasoning "may appear to be a little strained in some points," Madison concluded with understatement. "Yet on the whole, I must confess," he wrote, "that it fully reconciles me to the scale of representation, which the convention have established." The use of the first-person singular in *The Federalist* was rare, as was the admission of strained reasoning.

In *Federalist* No. 55, Madison defended the House of Representatives against the charges that it would be too small, too elitist, and too ignorant of local circumstances. With regard to size, Madison admitted that there was no exact solution. A certain size was always necessary "to secure the benefits of free consultation and discussion, and to guard against too easy a combination for improper purposes." Madison's fear of collusive majority action was never far from his mind. Yet it was also true that too big a legislature would fall prey to enthusiasm. "In all very numerous assemblies, of whatever characters composed," he wrote, "passion never fails to wrest the scepter from reason." Madison was expressing a classic—and classical—fear of democracy. "Had every Athenian citizen been a Socrates," he wrote memorably, "every Athenian assembly would still have been a mob."[54] No matter how virtuous the individual members of a legislature, putting too many of them together, as the Athenian assemblies had done, would unleash the irrationality of the group.

Madison was caught between two different conceptions of the passions. Sometimes he wrote as though electoral majorities would be engaged by "passions" in the sense of economic interests that deviated from the true self-interest of the people as a whole. Enlargement of the republic—and of the legislature—was supposed to solve this problem. But sometimes, as here, Madison used the more Hamiltonian definition of passions to mean emotional irrationality. Either way, such impulses must be avoided or repressed. In Madison's conception, the federal constitution was a machine for keeping the passions out and reason in.

Nevertheless, Madison still could not avoid insisting that human virtue must play its part in republican government. Some critics were saying that Congress would be subverted by the desire of its members to fill executive offices. To even imagine this possibility, he argued, "is to renounce every rule by which events are to be calculated, and to substitute an indiscriminate and unbounded jealousy, with which all reasoning must be vain." Yes, there was "a degree of depravity of mankind which requires a certain degree of circumspection and distrust." But at the same time, "there are other qualities in human nature, which justify a certain portion of esteem and confidence."[55]

Human nature comprised both vice and virtue; but republicanism did not treat them both equally. "Republican government presupposes the existence" of virtue "in a higher degree than any other form." Without some assumption of goodness, republicanism would not be possible. If the critics were right, "the inference would be that there is not sufficient virtue among men for self-government; and that nothing less than the chains of despotism can restrain them from destroying and devouring one another."[56] The constitution could and would solve the problems of passion. Self-restraint could be achieved, Madison believed—he had only to look at himself to see how much was possible.

Friends of the Constitution

For months, Madison's friends and family had been urging him to return to Virginia in time to run for a place in the state ratifying convention. Attitudes toward the proposed constitution in Virginia had been oscillating dangerously. There had been an initial period of enthusiasm, followed by strong backlash. Then, in January or February 1788, support for the constitution began to return.

Madison left New York on March 4, 1788, in a worried state. The trip, delayed by bad roads and by stops in Philadelphia to see the Houses and in Mount Vernon to see Washington, took Madison more than two weeks. On arrival in Orange County on March 23, he found that matters were worse than he had feared. The county was "filled with the most absurd and groundless prejudices against the federal constitution."

There was no time to waste. On March 24, the day after Madison's arrival, the people of the county were electing delegates to the ratification convention. "I was therefore obliged," Madison wrote, "to mount for the first time in my life, the rostrum before a large body of the people, and to launch into a harangue of some length in the open air and on a very windy day."[57] In a political career of twelve years, Madison had represented his county in a state constitutional convention and the Virginia House of Delegates; he had represented the state of Virginia in Congress and at the Philadelphia convention. He had even lost a congressional election after failing to buy drinks for the voters. But such had been the gentility of Virginia politics that Madison had never had to give a public speech.

Whether as a result of his "experiment" in addressing the voters directly "or the exertion of the Federalists or perhaps both," Madison wrote, "the misconceptions of the [proposed] government were so far corrected that two federalists, one of them myself, were elected by a majority of nearly 4 to one."[58] Madison had cut it very close. Had he not been there, he believed, he probably would not have been elected.

The overall results of the elections were favorable. George Nicholas, a prominent Virginia judge and lawyer who would later become the principal drafter of the Kentucky Constitution, told Madison, "I think a majority of [delegates] are federal. . . . But that majority if it exists, will be but small . . . unless the conduct of the other states will justify it." The trouble with relying on the other states was that New Hampshire's decision to adjourn had put an end to "the hope that nine will adopt before the meeting of our convention." Six states had ratified. Nicholas wrote that Maryland and South Carolina might still ratify before the Virginia convention met in June, which would at least give Virginia the opportunity to become the decisive ninth state.[59]

Nicholas told Madison that George Mason had returned from the Philadelphia convention saying that "notwithstanding his objections to particular parts of the plan he would take it as it was rather than lose it altogether." Now, however, "Mason's sentiments are much changed," and he had become an implacable opponent. Nicholas attributed the change "to two causes: first the irritation he feels from the hard things that have been said of him, and secondly to a vain opinion he entertains (which has industriously been supported by some particular characters) that he has influence enough to dictate the constitution to Virginia, and through her to the rest of the union."[60]

Nicholas's view of Patrick Henry was more cynical still. "Mr. Henry is now almost avowedly an enemy to the union, and therefore will oppose every plan that would cement it," Nicholas wrote. He thought Henry was hiding his desire to break the union in order to win votes for his side: "His real sentiments will be industriously concealed, for so long as he talks only of amendments, such of the friends to the union, as object to particular parts of the Constitution will adhere to him." These dupes, Nicholas thought, would not stick with Henry for "a moment, if they could be convinced of his real design."[61] Nicholas hoped to gather "sufficient information by the meeting of the convention to make that matter clear."

When it came to Edmund Randolph, Nicholas was more careful. "Our friend E.R. talks of a compromise between the friends to the union," he wrote, "but I know of but one that can safely take place, and that is on the plan of the Massachusetts convention." It seemed "impossible," he continued, "that another continental convention . . . should ever agree on any general plan."[62]

Nicholas concluded with two requests. Supporters of the constitution needed a single "address to the people at large" in support of ratification, and, Nicholas told Madison, "No person in the convention can so well prepare this address as yourself."[63] Nicholas also noted that "the greater part of the members of the convention will go to the meeting without information" on the constitution. "Publius of the *Federalist* if it is published in a pamphlet, would do it better than any other work." He asked for thirty or forty copies to distribute. The goal would be to get the *Federalist* essays to the delegates "as early as may be, and if possible before they go from home" to attend. If collected into a single volume, the *Federalist* could be used as a road map for the debate.

Madison responded vigorously. He would, he said, write to supporters in Maryland and South Carolina to urge them not to follow the example of New Hampshire, and he urged Nicholas to do the same. In Maryland, Madison reported, the opposition "despairing of success in a direct attack on the constitution, mean to contend for a postponement of the question."[64] Madison agreed with Nicholas on the importance of the outcome in Maryland and South Carolina—as well as the potentially decisive importance in the Virginia convention of delegates elected from Kentucky.[65]

Madison declined to prepare an address to the people in defense of ratification. It would be better to wait, he suggested, until "the views of the adverse party are brought forward in the convention."[66] He agreed with Nicholas that "conditional amendments or a second general convention" would be "fatal." He then shared with Nicholas the confidential fact that "in one stage of the business" the Philadelphia convention had feared "an abortive issue to their deliberations." So strong was the fear of failure that "there were moments during this period in which despair seemed to many to predominate." What had made the convention succeed was "nothing but the temper with which the members assembled, and their ignorance of the opinions and confidence in the liberality of their respective constituents."[67] Madison was saying that had the delegates known what the public really thought, the Philadelphia convention would have failed.

Friends and Enemies

As Madison entered the political fray of the Virginia convention, he began to identify the "friends to the constitution" and its "enemies." Madison wrote to Jefferson that Mason "is growing every day more bitter and outrageous in his efforts to carry his point." Mason, he predicted, "will probably in the end be thrown by the violence of his passions into the politics of Mr. Henry." Henry, for his part, "is supposed to aim at disunion." To Madison, these men were real enemies, driven in Mason's case by violent passion and in Henry's by the secret aim to destroy the union and lead a new confederacy of his own. This view of Patrick Henry, in particular, rested on supposition and rumor, not fact. It transformed Henry's professed opposition to the proposed constitution from a defensible populism into a conspiracy to end the United States.

Randolph, who was still calling for a second convention, was a more complicated case. Madison remained frustrated with Randolph's unwillingness to endorse ratification. Yet he still felt personally close to Randolph. He told Jefferson that Randolph "is so temperate in his opposition and goes so far with the friends of the constitution that he cannot properly be classed with its enemies." To maintain the personal friendship, Madison had to insist that Randolph was not really an enemy of the constitution.

Meanwhile, Madison received news from friends of the constitution elsewhere. On May 5, 1788, one informed him that Maryland "has acceded to the proposed constitution by a great majority." The writer predicted a similar positive result in South Carolina. He "lamented" opposition in Virginia and New York, yet reflected optimistically, "I am rather inclined to believe that in the course of 12 months we shall have the government in operation." The writer was not, he said, "so sanguine as Hamilton" on the matter, however.[68]

Hamilton had stayed in close touch with Madison throughout this period, the closest ever in their friendship. In letters they discussed details of their arguments in favor of ratification, and Hamilton continued to send Madison copies of *Federalist* papers he was still writing.[69] They had decided to bring out the collected essays in two separate volumes, the first of which appeared on March 22, the second in the middle of May. Each time, Hamilton sent copies to Madison.[70]

The two men shared a recurring, cyclical nervousness about the outcome of ratification. George Clinton, governor of New York since the Revolution, was "inflexibly obstinate," Hamilton told Madison. In a characteristic Hamiltonian touch, he wrote, "I count little on overcoming opposition by reason." According to Hamilton, "Our only chance will be the previous ratification by nine states, which may shake the firmness of his followers; and a change in the sentiments of the people which have been for some time traveling towards the constitution." Feeling, not logic, would decide the outcome. "We shall leave nothing undone," he promised, "to cultivate a favorable disposition in the citizens at large."[71]

To Hamilton, Virginia's convention was all-important. "We think here that the situation of your state is critical," he wrote. The timing of the two conventions, which would meet more or less simultaneously, made Virginia especially influential. "It will be of vast importance that an exact communication should be kept up between us at that period," Hamilton wrote. "The moment *any decisive* question is taken, if favorable, I request you to dispatch an express to me with pointed orders to make all possible diligence, by changing horses etc. All expenses shall be thankfully and liberally paid."[72]

The fantasy of a fast-riding express messenger, exhausting multiple horses and arriving breathless with the news of Virginia's ratification as the clinching ninth state, reflected Hamilton's excited state of mind. As close allies, co-authors, and friends of the constitution, Madison and Hamilton were acting in tandem in their respective states. Hamilton signed his letters with "Your affectionate and obedient servant,"[73] "Believe me with great attachment yours,"[74] and "With great sincerity and attachment."[75]

Into the Federal Scale

When the Virginia ratifying convention came to order on Monday, June 2, 1788, eight states had ratified. Virginia, the most populous state, would either provide the ninth vote or derail the entire process. Mason, who opened the substantive part of the convention on June 3, hoped to prevent a quick up or down vote, and recommended that "no question general or particular should be propounded till the whole plan should be considered and debated clause by clause."[76] Madison and the other supporters surprised Mason by agreeing to a detailed analysis.[77] Madison understood that his strength in the convention lay in his capacity to offer detailed responses to any criticism. He was, after all, the single best informed person in the United States on the subject.

On June 4, Patrick Henry asked that Congress's charge to the Philadelphia convention be read. Henry wanted to argue that the Philadelphia convention had gone rogue, replacing the Articles of Confederation instead of amending them as Congress had intended. Henry also described his own role: "I consider myself as the servant of the people of this commonwealth, as a sentinel over their rights, liberty, and happiness," he announced. The people, he declared, were "exceedingly uneasy" about the proposed constitution.[78] "A year ago," he insisted, "the minds of our citizens were at perfect repose." He "conceived the republic to be in extreme danger," not from the Articles but from the "proposal to change our government."[79]

Henry was working his way to a conspiracy theory. The Philadelphia convention had overreached by producing a proposal for "a great consolidated government, instead of a confederation." Why, he demanded to know, had the convention sought to destroy the states? "I have the highest veneration for those gentlemen; but, sir, give me leave to demand, What right had they to say, We, the people? . . . Who authorized them to speak the language of, We, the people, instead of, We, the states?"[80] Washington himself was not exempt. "Even from that illustrious man who saved us by his valor, I would have a reason for his conduct."[81]

Washington had chosen not to appear at the ratifying convention. But Edmund Randolph took Henry's challenge as a personal affront, and tried to explain his own convoluted course to and from Philadelphia. Randolph started by saying that, contrary to Henry's assertion, the situation on the eve of the Philadelphia convention had indeed been dire. The

Articles of Confederation were "a political farce" and had "proved totally inadequate." Some "alteration" was necessary—and "this necessity was obvious to all America."[82]

This was music to Madison's ears. For the previous nine months, he had been assiduous in his efforts to cultivate Randolph, insisting on their continued friendship and mutual respect even as he prodded him toward supporting unconditional ratification. Henry had now done the rest of Madison's work for him, forcing Randolph to defend the constitution.

Randolph still had to explain why he had refused to sign the proposed document. He claimed that he trusted in the wisdom of the people, who had not yet been consulted when the draft constitution was signed in Philadelphia. "I therefore would not bind myself to uphold the new constitution, before I had tried it by the true touchstone; especially, too, when I foresaw that even the members of the general convention might be instructed by the comments of those who were without doors." Randolph was saying, as he had all along, that he believed that people needed an opportunity to introduce amendments before ratification.[83]

Randolph had come full circle. He now explained that amendments could still be proposed, but only *after* ratification—not, as he had previously argued, as a condition of it. After all, eight states had already ratified without conditions. If Virginia did not do the same, the consequences would be dire: "inevitable ruin to the union." Randolph would not be a party to Patrick Henry's attack: "The union is the anchor of our political salvation; and I will assent to the lopping of this limb [he pointed to his arm], before I assent to the dissolution of the union."[84]

Randolph's switch in time reflected his character as much as his prevarication had before. He always wanted desperately to be on the winning side of any question, as his father had failed to do in the Revolution. Unsure of how or whether ratification would occur, Randolph had spent the last year trying to hedge his bets. Now that eight states had ratified without conditions, he was prepared to recommend that Virginia do the same.

Randolph's motives aside, his public announcement for unconditional ratification was a major victory for Madison. Randolph had, as Madison put it, "declared the day of previous amendments passed, and thrown himself fully into the federal scale."[85] By arguing that refusal to ratify would destroy the union, Randolph was all but saying that Henry was motivated by the desire to break it. The convention had barely begun, and opposition to ratification was being put on the defensive.

George Mason now had to insist that he was not calling for dissolution. "I solemnly declare that no man is a greater friend to a firm union of the American states than I am," he insisted. But the union could not be maintained by a single central government.[86] History showed "that there never was a government over a very extensive country without destroying the liberties of the people." The reason could also be demonstrated historically: Republicanism was impossible at scale. "Monarchy may suit a large territory, and despotic governments ever so extensive a country." In contrast, "popular governments can only exist in small territories. Is there a single example, on the face of the earth, to support a contrary opinion?"

If Henry presented himself as the people's tribune unmasking conspiracy, Mason posed as the last classical republican revealing the historical impossibility of Madison's bold, theory-driven design. Montesquieu had taught that republics could only function if they were small. He had recommended federating those small republics to achieve scale; and that was precisely the scheme that Mason favored. The central power of taxation assured, according to Mason, that the proposed constitution would violate Montesquieu's teaching.

Mason's argument demanded a response. Instead of defending his enlargement theory on the convention's first full day, Madison parried tactically, objecting that Mason's concerns were out of order. The convention would debate the constitution clause by clause, as Mason had insisted—and now Mason was jumping to the question of the power to tax.

At the end of the day on June 4, 1788, Madison was feeling optimistic. He believed that "Henry and Mason made a lame figure and appeared to take different and awkward ground" in their respective forms of opposition. He wrote to Washington that the Kentucky delegates were thought to be "generally adverse," and so all efforts were being made "to work on the local interests and prejudices" of the Kentuckians. Nevertheless "the federalists," Madison said of his fellow pro-ratification colleagues, "are a good deal elated by the existing prospect."[87]

Suspicion Is a Virtue

It was much too soon to discount Henry. On June 5, Richard Henry Lee, who also opposed ratification, criticized Henry for his "appeal to the fears of this house."[88] Henry responded with a show of rhetorical brilliance, cutting to the very heart of the case for the constitution:

Here is a revolution as radical as that which separated us from Great Britain. . . . Our rights and privileges are endangered, and the sovereignty of the states will be relinquished: and cannot we plainly see that this is actually the case? The rights of conscience, trial by jury, liberty of the press, all your immunities and franchises, all pretensions to human rights and privileges, are rendered insecure, if not lost, by this change.[89]

Madison himself had compared the constitution to the Revolution of 1776. Henry was turning the point against him. State governments exercising sovereignty over their citizens had been restrained by state bills of rights. The federal government created by the proposed constitution had none. Revolutionary freemen were therefore relinquishing rights they had earned with blood.

Henry attacked Madison's pragmatic arguments. "You are not to inquire how your trade may be increased, nor how you are to become a great and powerful people," he instructed the delegates. They should be asking "how your liberties can be secured; for liberty ought to be the direct end of your government."[90]

Knowing he could be dismissed as paranoid, Henry defended vigilance in the cause of liberty: "I may be thought suspicious when I say our privileges and rights are in danger," he intoned. "But, sir, suspicion is a virtue as long as its object is the preservation of the public good."[91] As for the argument that the republic was in danger, Henry simply denied it. "Has there been a single tumult in Virginia?" he asked. "Is there any revolution in Virginia?"[92] The supposed dangers to the union were, he said, "out of the sight of the common people."

And it was the common people on whom the burden of the new government would fall. "I dread the operation of [the proposed constitution] on the middling and lower classes of people," Henry thundered. In biblical terms, he advised his listeners to "go to the poor man, and ask him what he does. He will inform you that he enjoys the fruits of his labor, under his own fig-tree, with his wife and children around him, in peace and security."[93] Poor, rural farmers were Henry's constituents and ultimately his intended audience. This class had not been represented in Philadelphia.

Henry kept talking for days—one time as long as seven hours straight. With only a bit of overstatement, one newspaper later reported that

Henry spoke not only on Thursday, June 5, 1788, but "all Friday, Saturday, Monday, Tuesday, and Wednesday, and he was still speaking on [the following] Thursday."[94] Yet he still claimed he had "not said the one hundred thousandth part of what I have on my mind, and wish to impart."[95] The greatest rhetorician of the Revolutionary era was giving his last great performance.

In exasperation, Edmund Randolph commented, "If we go on in this irregular manner . . . instead of three or six weeks, it will take us six months to decide this question."[96] That clearly would not have bothered Henry, for whom delay would count as victory. It was time for a substantive reply. No one in the hall doubted that the right person to make it was Madison.

A Calm and Rational Investigation

Madison did not deal in grand pronouncements, nor did he have Henry's gift for oratory. When he addressed the convention, "he spoke so low that his exordium could not be heard distinctly," the convention's reporter noted. Fortunately for Madison, however, his ability to convince lay elsewhere. We do not know exactly what he said, but according to the best text we have, he made a virtue of his limitations.[97]

The standard orator's technique, used effectively by Henry, was to begin by skillful self-promotion. Madison did the opposite. "I shall not," he told the audience, "attempt to make impressions by any ardent professions of zeal for the public welfare." A man should be judged, Madison said, "not by his professions and declarations, but by his conduct." Others had made "comparisons . . . between friends of this constitution, and those who oppose it." Madison said he "disapprove[d] of such comparisons." He would say nothing against Henry's reputation or in support of his own.[98]

Madison then explained how the convention should decide whether to ratify. "We ought, sir, to examine the constitution on its own merits solely," he asserted. The delegates should "inquire whether it will promote the public happiness: its aptitude to produce this desirable object ought to be the exclusive subject of our present researches." Madison was inviting his fellow delegates to focus on the practical outcome, and to consider every important question a matter of research, as he did.

Madison continued with what could have been a description of his entire worldview:

We ought not to address our arguments to the feelings and passions, but to those understandings and judgments which were selected by the people of this country, to decide this great question by a calm and rational investigation.[99]

By deploying rhetoric to condemn rhetoric, Madison was establishing himself as the anti-Henry, the advocate of calm rationality against Henry's passionate feeling. He then criticized Henry's suspicious attitude toward the new constitution. "Let the dangers which this system is supposed to be replete with be clearly pointed out. . . . Let us not rest satisfied with general assertions of danger, without examination."[100] Henry had offered generalities. Madison demanded specifics.

Henry, Madison continued, had argued that the "loss of liberty" would likely come from "the tyranny of rulers." Yet Henry was wrong, Madison claimed. In republics, the danger lay not with rulers, but with the majority. "Turbulence, violence, and abuse of power, by the majority trampling on the rights of the minority, have produced factions and commotions, which, in republics, have, more frequently than any other cause, produced despotism."[101]

Distilled for public consumption, this was the essence of Madison's new political philosophy. The proposed constitution would not destroy republicanism, but save it from the tyranny of the majority.[102] Those listening were delegates elected directly by the people, and many served in the very state legislature that Madison implicitly condemned as prone to faction. To tell these delegates that the purpose of the proposed constitution was to thwart the majority was an act of great candor—and great risk.[103]

Henry had made too many arguments for Madison to respond to all of them point by point, but he tried. Among the most interesting of Madison's responses related to Congress's power to raise and support standing armies. "I wish there were no necessity of vesting this power in the general government," Madison said. But there was no alternative. If Congress lacked the power, "any powerful nation, prompted by ambition or avarice, will be invited, by our weakness, to attack us." Disciplined regular forces from abroad would inevitably defeat "irregular, undisciplined militia."[104] This justification of the need for a military would not be popular in Virginia.

Madison also addressed the charge that a national religion could be introduced under the proposed constitution. The federal government would have no such authority, he insisted. "The government has no jurisdiction over" religion. An attempt to introduce "uniformity of religion" would thus be "ineligible." Practically, there was "no reason to conclude . . . that uniformity of government, will produce that of religion."[105]

Finally, Madison turned to the core argument that the proposed constitution would, in effect, abolish the states. "This government is not completely consolidated, nor is it entirely federal," he countered. The proposed constitution was a bit of both. "Who are parties to it?" he asked. "The people," he answered, "but not the people as composing one great body—but the people as composing thirteen sovereignties." If all thirteen states ratified, it would become "a government established by the thirteen states of America, not through the intervention of the legislatures, but by the people at large." The resulting structure was "of a complicated nature, and this complication, I trust, will be found to exclude the evils of absolute consolidation, as well as of mere confederacy."[106]

Only Madison could have thought it was a good idea to advocate for the proposed constitution on the grounds of its complication, which was itself the result of accidental compromise, not design. Madison ended with the "hope" that "the patriotism of the people will continue, and be a sufficient guard to their liberties." This was not a rousing conclusion of the kind favored by Patrick Henry. But then, Madison had not started like Henry, either.

The Philosopher's Stone

At the Virginia ratifying convention, Madison's ideas about the tyranny of the majority began to be adopted by others. On June 7, 1788, Francis Corbin, a supporter of the proposed constitution, defined the government under the document rather ably as "a representative federal republic." He then proceeded to describe the challenges to republicanism in wholly Madisonian terms.

"The evils that are most complained of in such governments (and with justice)," Corbin explained, "are faction, dissension, and consequent subjection of the minority to the caprice and arbitrary decisions of the majority, who, instead of consulting the interest of the whole community collectively, attend sometimes to partial and local advantages." Corbin presented this analysis of the tyranny of the majority as though it were conventional wisdom. In fact, he was echoing Madison's novel view, reflected by the signature phrase that Corbin used: "To avoid this evil is perhaps the great *desideratum* of republican wisdom; it may be termed the philosopher's stone."[107]

Corbin was followed by Randolph, and then Madison rose again. Displaying the expertise that he had developed during his months of preparation for the Philadelphia convention, Madison gave the delegates an overview of the failures of confederacies past and present.[108] He emphasized that the "feebleness" of government must lead to violation of individual rights. During the Revolution, precisely such violations had occurred as militias and states directly requisitioned supplies from individual citizens. The revolutionary "scene of injustice, partiality and oppression" had brought "heavenly vengeance," he said poetically. "We are now by our sufferings, expiating the crimes of the otherwise glorious revolution."[109] Madison intended his comments as an observation on political reality, not direct divine intervention. The bad situation under the Articles was the price that Americans were paying for having failed to create an effective government during the Revolution.

Madison then invoked an authority higher even than a metaphorical divinity: George Washington. He reminded the delegates that in 1783, at the end of the war, Washington had published a circular essay calling for fundamental government reform. Then Madison apologized for invoking Washington's authority: "I did not introduce that name to bias any gentleman here. Much as I admire and revere the man, I consider these members as not to be actuated by the influence of any man."[110] As a politician, Madison was citing the authority of the greatest Virginian to great effect. Yet he still felt the need to insist that only logic, not personal authority, must decide the question of ratification.

Madison concluded his speech with a little sermon on foreign policy. Henry was right, he said, "that national splendor and glory are not our objects." But Henry had failed to recognize that domestic security and foreign reputation were two sides of the same coin. "If we be free and happy at home," Madison explained, "we shall be respectable abroad." At present, "the confederation is so notoriously feeble, that foreign nations are unwilling to form any treaties with us." The results for trade were disastrous: "The imbecility of our government enables [foreign nations] to derive many advantages from our trade, without granting us any return." Madison's concern about trade, which had driven him to imagine the need for a new constitution in the first place, would remain fatefully with him for the rest of his career.

By now Madison was fading. He told the delegates that he would "no longer fatigue the committee at this time, but will resume the subject as early as I can."[111]

Madison went home and immediately fell ill with what he called a "bilious attack"—probably a migraine—that lasted several days.[112] In a brief note to Hamilton, Madison blamed it on "the heat of the weather etc."[113] In an equally short note to Rufus King, Madison explained that given how he was feeling, "writing is scarcely practicable and very injurious to me."[114] In both notes he reported that he believed proponents of ratification were holding their majority but that things could change: "The other party are ingenious and indefatigable," he told King.[115]

A Neutral Nation

On June 11, 1788, Madison resumed his seat in the convention, though he still felt "extremely feeble." He wrote to Tench Coxe in Philadelphia that "the enemies of the Constitution" were trying "to procrastinate the debates, till the weariness of the members will yield to a postponement of the final decision to a future day; and to an intermediate adjournment." Meanwhile, "the extreme heat of the weather, the approach of the harvest, the meeting of the assembly at the latter end of the month, and a nice division of parties will favor such a project."[116]

Notwithstanding his illness and the heat, Madison spoke at length again to the convention. Addressing the topic of foreign affairs, Madison made an observation of vast future importance. The United States, he said, was committed to "the principle that free ships shall make free goods, and that vessels and goods shall be both free from condemnation." This meant that in the case of war, ships not belonging to either side should be treated as neutral and should be allowed to carry their goods without being seized in the legal form of war at sea.

But there was a problem. "Great Britain did not recognize" the principle of neutrality. As the greatest naval power in the world, Britain treated neutral ships as lawful targets of capture if they were carrying goods to a belligerent nation. What would this mean for the United States if France and England should go to war, which Madison said "is judged probable"?

Ideally the United States, "remote from Europe . . . ought not to engage in her politics or wars," Madison suggested. American ships would want to "carry on the commerce of the contending nations," trading with both sides. This would be a splendid business opportunity—"a source of wealth which we ought not to deny our citizens."[117]

Madison was proposing that the optimal strategy for the United States in case of a war between Britain and France would be to remain neutral and trade with both sides. Yet Britain would not want that to happen, Madison predicted. "If American vessels have French property on board, Great Britain will seize them." The United States would then be faced with a stark choice: "We shall be obliged to relinquish the advantage of a neutral nation, or be engaged in a war." Either the United States would have to stop trading with France, giving in to British pressure, or it would have to go to war with Britain.

The United States must be capable of commanding respect and potentially defending itself. "A neutral nation ought to be respectable, or else it will be insulted and attacked." Disunited, and with no capacity to coordinate policy or raise a navy, "America in her present impotent situation would run the risk of being drawn in as a party in the war, and lose the advantage of being neutral." The way to achieve international respect was for it to "be known that our government can command the whole resources of the union." If so, Madison concluded, "we shall be suffered to enjoy the great advantages of carrying on the commerce of the nations at war."

Thus, at the Virginia ratifying convention in 1788, Madison first addressed the question of how exactly to combat British violations of neutrality. The question would become by far the most important one in Madison's years as secretary of state and president—and would lead Madison into the War of 1812.

Dangerous Powers

As the convention proceeded, Madison engaged with other Virginians who were taking the opportunity to establish their own reputations. One was John Marshall, a rising lawyer four years younger than Madison who had served for several years in the House of Delegates and on the council that advised the governor. Marshall, a cousin of Thomas Jefferson, strongly supported the proposed constitution. Madison complimented him, noting that Marshall had "entered into the subject" of political representation and taxation "with a great deal of ability."[118]

Another up and coming Virginia politician was Madison's friend and sometime investment partner James Monroe. Remarkably, Monroe opposed ratification. On June 10, 1788, Monroe gave a lengthy speech dismissing Madison's analysis. The United States, Monroe argued, had an ocean between it and any potential enemies—and its members showed no inclination to fight one another.[119]

Monroe went on to argue that, since the United States was not under any threat of external war, only modest reforms to the Articles were necessary. Congress should have a general power over commerce, but no power of direct taxation. There must be either a bill of rights or an explicit statement that Congress's powers were limited to those enumerated in the constitution.[120] Beyond this, Monroe denied that the proposed constitution included a meaningful set of checks and balances.[121] Unlike the British constitution, the different branches did not represent different class interests. The result was "a dangerous government, and calculated to secure neither the interests nor the rights of our countrymen."[122]

If Madison was personally troubled by Monroe's opposition, he did not show it. Nevertheless, the next day, June 11, Madison responded. He called Monroe his "honorable friend over the way," and maintained a tone of cordiality and respect. He had no knockdown answer to Monroe's concerns about the danger of the different parts of the national government together suppressing the states. The best Madison could do was to explain: "I have my fears as well as the honorable gentleman—but my fears were on the other side." The danger was, according to Madison, the "powerful and prevailing influence of the states," which would likely trump "the interests of the union." Madison was reduced to criticizing Monroe for his pessimism. "I choose rather to indulge my hopes than fears,"[123] he insisted. If the proposed constitution did not seem to be working out, amendments were always possible.

Madison was losing his focus. The personal attacks on the framers of the constitution were getting to him. And his fixation on Patrick Henry was growing. He wrote to his Princeton friend John Blair Smith on June 12 that Henry "has descended to lower artifice and management . . . than I thought him capable of. His gross . . . and scandalous misrepresentations of the new constitution . . . and design of its enlightened authors awaken contempt and indignation."[124] Madison had tried, he told his friend, "to suppress such feelings" of contempt for Henry—and had failed. From now on Madison would see Henry only in completely paranoid terms. "It grieves me to see such great natural talents abused to guilty purposes," he told Smith.[125]

Henry, for his part, was hitting his stride. Speaking to the convention again he invoked the authority of Thomas Jefferson, whom he hated and who hated him in return. On the basis of a letter from Jefferson that was circulating in Virginia, Henry asserted that the author of the Declaration hoped to see ratification by nine states and rejection by four, an eventuality that would produce compromise: "He wishes to secure amendments and a bill of rights, if I am not mistaken," Henry advised.[126] Jefferson's proposed "amendments go to that despised thing, called a *bill of rights,* and all the rights which are dear to human nature—trial by jury, the liberty of religion and the press, etc." Henry assured the delegates, "I speak from the best information, and if wrong, I beg to be put right."[127] Henry was right at least in part. Jefferson objected to the absence of a bill of rights, and had told Madison so.

Warming to the subject, Henry denounced Madison's argument that no bill of rights was necessary because "all powers not given are reserved." The rights of Englishmen, he pointed out, were "undefined" and frequently violated until the Glorious Revolution of 1688 brought about the English Bill of Rights. The states all had bills of rights or the equivalent, Henry noted. Why should not Congress be bound by the same? "Why is the trial by jury taken away? . . . Wherefore is religious liberty not secured? . . . This sacred right ought not to depend on constructive, logical reasoning."[128] Henry was attacking Madison using Jefferson, Madison's closest friend, and religious liberty, Madison's favorite cause.

Provoked, Madison now had no alternative but to invoke his closer relationship with Jefferson: "I believe that, were that gentleman now on this floor, he would be for the adoption of this Constitution," Madison insisted. "I am, in some measure, acquainted with his sentiments on this subject: It is not right for me to unfold what he has informed me; but I will venture to assert that the clause now discussed is not objected to by Mr. Jefferson." Finally, he concluded lamely, "Whatever be the opinion of that illustrious citizen, considerations of personal delicacy should dissuade us from introducing it here."[129]

To the convention, Madison staunchly defended the absence of a guarantee of religious liberty like the one he himself helped frame for Virginia. On its own, a constitutional guarantee of liberty meant nothing: "Is a bill of rights a security for religion? Would the bill of rights, in this state, exempt the people from paying for the support of one particular sect, if such sect were exclusively established by law? If there were a majority of one sect, a bill of rights would be a poor protection for liberty."[130]

Madison was talking about his fight with Patrick Henry over the religious assessment bill four years before. He was also subtly misrepresenting Henry's proposed assessment bill, which did not require the people to pay "for the support of one particular sect," but rather allowed each individual to designate the recipient of his religious assessment.

Madison went on to offer a second argument as to why a guarantee of religious liberty was unnecessary at the federal level. "Happily for the states," he said, "they enjoy the utmost freedom of religion." The source of religious liberty was not a constitutional guarantee, but a political reality:

> This freedom arises from that multiplicity of sects which pervades America, and which is the best and only security for religious liberty in any society; for where there is such a variety of sects, there cannot be a majority of any one sect to oppress and persecute the rest. . . . A particular state might concur in one religious project. But the United States abound in such a variety of sects, that it is a strong security against religious persecution; and it is sufficient to authorize a conclusion, that no one sect will ever be able to outnumber or depress the rest.[131]

Madison was applying his grand theory of the expansion of the polity. There would be no national establishment of religion, even without a constitutional guarantee: There were too many sects across the country for them to join together to form a majority in favor of a national establishment.

This was more convincing than Madison's initial claim that majority factions would be unlikely to form in the national legislature. Yet as an argument against the value of a guarantee of religious liberty, it was poor stuff. Madison had at most shown that a guarantee was not strictly necessary. But he had certainly not refuted Henry's claim, backed by Jefferson, that such a guarantee would be highly desirable.

Madison was left to remind the delegates of his own lifelong commitment to religious liberty: "I can appeal to my uniform conduct on this subject, that I have warmly supported religious freedom."[132] Yet an appeal to personal authority was not an argument from principle, as Madison had been telling the delegates throughout the ratifying convention.

Henry, Madison's old foe on religious liberty, had managed to turn the issue against him. Privately, Madison fretted that Henry "has found a means to make some of the best people here believe, that a religious establishment was in contemplation under the new government." Henry was forgetting that "the northern states are more decided friends to the voluntary support of Christian ministers" than was Henry himself, "the author or at least, the warm abettor of the assessment bill in this state."[133] All of this was true—and irrelevant. Omitting a bill of rights from the proposed constitution had been a mistake. Madison was now dealing with the consequences.

The Most Ticklish State

The Virginia ratification convention was going badly—and the problem was not just the missing bill of rights. Madison wrote to Washington on June 13, 1788, "The business is in the most ticklish state that can be imagined. The majority will certainly be very small on whatever side it may finally lie; and I dare not encourage much expectation that it will be on the favorable side."[134]

Meanwhile, in New York, Hamilton faced his own worries about ratification. He believed that what he called "the Anti-Federal party" had won two-thirds of the seats in the ratifying convention, and "according to the best estimate I can form" enjoyed a majority "of about four sevenths in the community." Their goal, Hamilton believed, was to delay a decision, and "resolve upon a long adjournment as the safest and most artful course to effect their final purpose." True to form, Hamilton did not suppress his anxieties. The more he knew about the Anti-Federalists, he wrote to Madison, "the more I dread the consequences of the nonadoption of the constitution by any of the other states, [and] the more I fear an eventual disunion and civil war. God grant that Virginia may accede. The example will have a vast influence on our politics."[135]

When Madison got the letter, he responded to Hamilton that it confirmed his suspicion that "a negotiation for delay is on foot between the opposition here and with you" in New York. "We have conjectured for some days that the policy is to spin out the session in order to receive overtures from your convention; or if that cannot be, to weary members into adjournment without taking any decision." Madison told Hamilton of his exhaustion: "I have been partially recovered" of his bilious attack, he wrote, "but today have a bit of relapse. My health is not good, and the business is wearisome beyond expression."[136]

Madison's speeches in the convention were becoming shorter and more reactive. On June 16, after Patrick Henry attacked the possibility of a standing army and the clause empowering Congress to call out the militia to enforce the law or put down insurrections, Madison's response sounded almost desperate. He asked rhetorically, "Would it be wise to say . . . that we should have no defense?"[137] Henry, of course, was saying no such thing; he was saying that a standing army would threaten republicanism, and that a militia would protect it.

As for Henry's worry that Congress's power over the militia could be abused, Madison asked, "How is it possible to answer objections against the possibility of abuses?" Every government had to have the capacity to execute its laws, by force "if necessary." Under the proposed constitution, the militia, not the army, was the force of last resort. Southerners in particular, Madison added, should want to give the government "as extensive means as possible to protect us"—against slave revolts.[138] None of this answered Henry's objection to giving Congress, rather than states, the power to call out the militia.

The next day, June 17, Madison once again addressed the topic of slavery. The occasion was George Mason's astonishing double attack on the proposed constitution's treatment of the slave trade and slavery itself. Mason first denounced the clause protecting the trade for twenty years. The slave trade was "diabolical in itself, and disgraceful to mankind," Mason charged. Its abolition, he claimed, "was one of the great causes of our separation from Great Britain."[139] Mason went on: "And, though this infamous traffic be continued, we have no security for the property of that kind which we have already," namely slaves. The draft should have banned the slave trade *and* guaranteed the permanence of slaves born in the United States.

Madison responded pragmatically to Mason—and, more important, to those Virginia delegates who were also deeply invested in slavery. The clause extending the slave trade was "impolitic," he said, but necessary to get Georgia and South Carolina to stay in the union. Madison said the slave trade was an "evil," but the loss of the slave-importing states to the union would be "worse."[140]

Madison then argued that the proposed constitution did secure slavery through the fugitive slave clause: "At present, if any slave elopes to any of those states where slaves are free, he becomes emancipated by their laws; for the laws of the states are uncharitable to one another in this respect."[141]

At the Philadelphia convention, there had been no public discussion of the fugitive slave clause, probably out of a desire to avoid an argument over it. But the delegates to the Virginia ratifying convention could not know that. Madison explained to them that "this clause was expressly inserted . . . to enable owners of slaves to reclaim them. This is a better security than any that now exists."[142] In order to get the constitution ratified, Madison—whatever his private beliefs on slavery—was willing to argue that the proposed constitution left slaveholders better off than they had been before.

Is There No Virtue Among Us?

Madison was feeling "not yet restored and extremely feeble," he wrote to Washington.[143] The outcome of the ratifying convention was in the balance: "A few days will probably decide the matter."[144] Madison spoke little during the brief debate about the executive branch.[145] The convention then turned to the judiciary. Madison cautiously reported to Hamilton: "It is calculated that we still retain a majority of three or four; and if we can weather the storm against the part under consideration I shall hold the danger to be pretty well over."[146]

Cognizant of the risk, Madison gave his longest speech in weeks. First he went through the jurisdiction of the federal courts in some detail, explaining and justifying their necessity.[147] He tried to address the objection that there was no constitutional jury guarantee. "The trial by jury is held as sacred in England as in America," he noted, and in England was protected only by legislation, not by a written constitution. It was a "misfortune" if trial by jury "should be departed from, yet in some cases it is necessary. It must therefore be left to the discretion of the legislature." He concluded that "this is a complete and satisfactory answer"—but to the constitution's critics, it certainly was neither.[148]

It was typical of Madison as a speech maker that the most eloquent part of his address was buried in the middle and, in fact, barely connected to the judiciary at all. "I have observed that gentlemen suppose that the general legislature will do everything mischievous they possibly can, and that they will omit to do every thing good which they are authorized to do," Madison commented. This was a fair description of the concerns of the opponents to the proposed constitution, who consistently assumed the worst about human nature.

It was not "reasonable"—Madison used his favorite word—to assume that people were always bad. "I consider it reasonable to conclude that they will as readily do their duty as deviate from it." People sometimes did act with the interests of the public in mind.

Madison hastened to add that he was not a starry-eyed optimist: "Nor do I go on the grounds mentioned by gentlemen on the other side—that we are to place unlimited confidence in them, and expect nothing but the most exalted integrity and sublime virtue." Men were not angels, as Madison had said in the *Federalist* essays. "But I go on this great republican principle, that the people will have virtue and intelligence to select men of virtue and wisdom. Is there no virtue among us? If there be not, we are in a wretched situation. No theoretical checks, no form of government, can render us secure."

The entire edifice of constitution building rested on a republican article of faith: in the people. Ultimately, the people would have to choose the government—and would have to vote it out of power if it oppressed them: "To suppose that any form of government will secure liberty or happiness without any virtue in the people, is a chimerical idea. If there be sufficient virtue and intelligence in the community, it will be exercised in the selection of these men; so that we do not depend on their virtue, or put confidence in our rulers, but in the people who are to choose them."[149]

The point reflected the modesty that accompanied Madison's brilliance. He was justifiably proud of his original constitutional design. But Madison knew the design mattered little if the people lacked the capacity to make it work.

One of the Most Fortunate Events That Ever Happened

On the morning of June 24, 1788, poised to make his last speech in favor of the proposed constitution, Madison wrote to his brother Ambrose, "The vital question is likely to be decided by a very small majority. I do not know that either party despairs absolutely." Although his side—"the friends of the government"—seemed to be "in the best spirits," he wrote, "at the same time it is not impossible they may miscalculate their number." The outcome of the convention was still in doubt.

Patrick Henry had focused his arguments on the absence of a bill of rights.[150] To the familiar dangers he now added a new, last-minute argument calculated to appeal to white Virginians: The proposed constitution, he argued, would allow Congress to abolish slavery. Suppose the United States found itself at war. Congress had the power to provide for national defense, Henry reminded the audience. "May Congress not say, that every black man must fight? Did we not see a little of this last war? We were not so hard pushed as to make emancipation general; but acts of assembly passed that every slave who would go to the army should be free."[151] In fact the British, not the Americans, had pioneered the idea of offering slaves their freedom in exchange for their service in arms. That did not matter. Henry was invoking a very real fear that many Virginians shared.

Nor was war the only situation where slavery might be abolished. "Another thing will contribute to bring this event about," Henry predicted: "Slavery is detested. We feel its fatal effects—we deplore it with all the pity of humanity. Let all these considerations, at some future period, press with full force on the minds of Congress. . . . They will search that paper, and see if they have power of manumission. And have they not, sir? . . . May they not pronounce all slaves free, and will they not be warranted by that power?"[152]

Henry then returned to class politics. He pointed out that ratification would take place against the wishes of many Virginians, especially ordinary farmers. "I believe it to be a fact that the great body of yeomanry are in decided opposition to [the proposed constitution]," he asserted. There would be no national breakdown if Virginia ratified with conditional amendments, Henry further insisted. If anything, ratification without conditions would be followed by disunion.[153]

Henry appropriated Virginia's leadership in proposing the constitution—which had been Madison's—in order to argue that Virginia should take the lead in proposing amendments: "We proposed that convention which met at Annapolis. . . . We proposed that at Philadelphia. . . . But Virginia is now to lose her preeminence. Those rights of equality to which the meanest individual in the community is entitled, are to bring us down infinitely below the Delaware people. Have we not a right to say, Hear our propositions!"[154]

Everyone at the convention knew that Madison would have to reply. Now, like Henry, he had to compress his many responses into a single, final address.

Madison opened by reminding the delegates of the stakes:

> Mr. Chairman, nothing has excited more admiration in the world than the manner in which free governments have been established in America; for it was the first instance, from the creation of the world to the American Revolution, that free inhabitants have been seen deliberating on a form of government, and selecting such of their citizens as possessed their confidence . . . to determine upon and give effect to it.[155]

Once more, as he had done in the *Federalist* essays, Madison compared the creation of the constitution to the creation of the American republic. If it was so impressive to the world that Americans had created free governments "in the middle of war and confusion," he asked,

> how much more astonishment . . . and admiration will be excited, should they be able, peaceably, freely, and satisfactorily, to establish one general government, when there is such a diversity of opinions and interests—when not cemented or stimulated by any common danger?[156]

The creation of a new peacetime constitution would be, Madison was saying, a world historical event. He could not help but describe the constitutional process in the terms that he himself had innovated in imagining its outcome: "How vast must be the difficulty of concentrating, in one government, the interests, and conciliating the opinions, of so many different, heterogeneous bodies!" The phrase may have lacked the eloquence of Patrick Henry, but it contained the genius of James Madison.

Ratification conditioned on amendments would throw the entire process into doubt. Every state that had already ratified would need to start over, Madison insisted. Henry and his allies had brought forth "no less than forty amendments, a bill of rights which contains twenty amendments, and twenty other alterations, some of which are improper and inadmissible."[157] If these were adopted, the other states would do the same, and the result would be the collapse of the constitution. Madison was willing to allow those of Henry's proposed amendments that were "not objectionable, or unsafe"—as long as they were "subsequently recommended," not conditional. "But I can never consent to his previous amendments" as conditions, Madison explained, "because they are pregnant with dreadful dangers."[158]

Madison also presented the positive consequences of unconditional ratification. "If Virginia will agree to ratify this system," he told the delegates, "I shall look upon it as one of the most fortunate events that ever happened for human nature."[159]

The debate should have ended with Madison's final speech. But Patrick Henry was not a man to allow the other side the last word. He rose to make a small point—that the other states might disagree with the amendments, thus preventing their adoption—before moving rapidly to an accurate account of the fundamental difference between his worldview and Madison's: "[Madison] tells you of the important blessings which he imagines will result to us and mankind in general from the adoption of this system. I see the awful immensity of the dangers with which it is pregnant. I see it. I feel it."[160]

Madison had indeed emphasized the benefits of ratification and minimized the possible costs. Henry, who had participated in the Revolution but not the drafting of the new constitution, focused exclusively on what could go wrong.

Henry had a last run of eloquence in him. Madison had invoked the sweep of human history. Henry invoked the angels themselves:

> I see beings of a higher order anxious concerning our decision. When I see beyond the horizon that binds human eyes, and look at the final consummation of all human things, and see those intelligent beings which inhabit the ethereal mansions reviewing the political decisions and revolutions which, in the progress of time, will happen in America, and the consequent happiness or misery of mankind, I am led to believe that much of the account, on one side or the other, will depend on what we now decide.[161]

On cue, the heavens responded to Henry. As the convention's notetaker put it, "Here a violent storm arose, which put the house in such disorder, that Mr. Henry was obliged to conclude."[162]

The next day, June 25, 1788, the delegates voted. Virginia ratified the constitution 89 to 79. Believing that Virginia's ratification brought the total to nine, Madison sent out a fast rider to Hamilton in New York to tell him the good news. A few days later Madison would discover that New Hampshire had voted to ratify on June 21, becoming the decisive ninth state.[163]

Madison had won. He still did not trust Henry, and told Hamilton that he felt "so uncharitable as to suspect that the ill will to the Constitution will produce every peaceable effort to disgrace and destroy it."[164] But Madison was wrong. Henry would indeed remain a political opponent—but he would not actively seek to undermine the newly ratified Constitution. Instead he would continue to advocate in favor of a bill of rights. And Madison, to his own surprise as much as anyone's, would join him.

PARTY

...

CHAPTER SEVEN

The Bill of Rights

...

THE ARGUMENT: *Madison's second political life begins as the Constitution goes into effect—and the government devolves into factional division. Madison first tries to deny the signs. But ultimately and painfully he comes to believe that his erstwhile friends and allies are trying to subvert the very structure of the republican government he designed. In opposition to his character and his beliefs, Madison becomes a partisan.*

This process of personal and professional transformation begins when Madison seeks his first elected office. Patrick Henry initially blocks Madison from the Senate, then convinces Madison's close friend James Monroe to run against him for the House in a gerrymandered district. To win election to Congress, Madison promises his constituents a bill of rights, which he had previously opposed.

In an attempt to preserve his ideals, Madison maintains the race has not affected his friendship for Monroe. Reasonable people who share a common goal may disagree and remain friends. This notion, the epitome of Madison's constitutional design, is already under enormous pressure—and the constitutional government has not yet even been seated. He then drafts the bill of rights to avoid a second convention that might be used to weaken or destroy the government created under the Constitution.

THE CONSTITUTION RATIFIED, Madison might have felt triumphant. Patrick Henry made that impossible. Henry had lost the battle over ratification, but he still controlled the Virginia House of Delegates. He now proposed a second national constitutional convention to amend the Constitution and add a bill of rights to protect "all the great unalienable and essential rights of freemen—many of which if not canceled are rendered insecure" by the new Constitution.[1]

To Madison and his allies, a second convention was a ruse to destroy the new federal government by eliminating its power to tax. "The cloven hoof begins to appear," Madison's friend George Lee Turberville wrote him from Richmond.[2] Henry's proposal for a convention was "his fire-brand," one that Turberville feared "we can scarcely withstand." Its introduction marked "a fearful day" for "the cause of federalism."[3]

Madison could do nothing to block Henry directly. Still a member of the old Congress, Madison had traveled from Virginia to New York almost as soon as ratification was accomplished. George Washington, now expected to become president, invited him to stop at Mount Vernon. He had heard of Madison's "indisposition" during the ratifying convention, and urged that "relaxation" was "indispensably necessary for your health."[4]

Madison, however, felt he had no time to spare. He proceeded to New York via Philadelphia, pausing there only long enough to see other supporters of the Constitution. He traveled with his manservant, a slave called John who had been ill in Richmond and became much sicker in Philadelphia.[5] So brief was Madison's stop in Philadelphia that he was unable to fulfill his father's request that he inquire after the family's slave Anthony, who had run away for a second time and might have been staying with Madison's former slave Billey in Philadelphia.[6]

Madison found Congress gridlocked on the question of where the new government should meet. The Constitution had provided for a federally controlled capital ten miles square. But until such a capital was carved out of the existing states, the government would need to find a temporary home. New York and Philadelphia were both candidates, with Madison favoring the latter because New York was too far from the South.[7]

Congress also had to figure out when it would next convene. This debate, too, kept Madison in New York. Ultimately, the old Congress decided that the new Congress would meet in March 1789. There was little time to lose in selecting senators and congressmen for that body.

Madison was an obvious candidate for the Senate. With Washington slated for the presidency and Jefferson still in France, Madison's friends put his name before the state legislature. The two other candidates were Richard Henry Lee and William Grayson. Both had opposed ratification. On November 5, 1788, Edmund Randolph wrote to Madison, "We are well assured of success."[8]

Randolph had not given Patrick Henry enough credit. On November 8, the day of the vote, Henry rose in the legislature and "expatiate[ed] largely in favor of Mr. Lee and Mr. Grayson."[9] Although Madison possessed "talents and integrity," Henry allowed, his election would be "unseasonable" because his "federal politics were so adverse to the opinions of many members."[10]

When the ballots were cast, Lee received 98 votes, Grayson 86, and Madison 77. The man who had just convinced Virginia to ratify the Constitution had been beaten by not one but two Anti-Federalists.

From Richmond, Madison's friends urged him not to take the defeat personally. "I am confident that two thirds of the Assembly are Antis who meditate mischief against the government," one wrote to him. Given that, Madison should have been happy to get as much support as he did: "Many [Anti-Federalists] must have voted from personal regard [for Madison] against their own principles, or you could not have received so great a ballot."[11] Randolph, embarrassed at having predicted success, assured Madison of "the anxiety, and affection which were discovered by your friends indoors, and your favorers without."[12]

For Madison, however, personal feelings were almost beside the point. The more serious problem was the victory for the opponents of the Constitution. "The triumph of Anti-Federalism is complete," his friend George Lee Turberville told him. Madison should run for the House of Representatives now, Turberville suggested. He could expect to be elected "in any of the lower districts in the state."[13]

This was very different from saying Madison could be elected anywhere in Virginia. Turberville told Madison he would be happy to give him the property necessary to qualify him to run "in the lower end of the Northern neck," where he would be likely to win. But Turberville also urged Madison "to come onwards to your native country" of Virginia before elections would be held in February 1789. "It would glad my very soul to see you in this city before the session rises," he continued. The Anti-Federalists were "aspiring assassins . . . triumphing in their calumnies of absent characters."[14]

Henry was not finished with Madison. On November 13, Henry's supporters proposed the new congressional districts—which were specially designed to keep Madison out of office. Orange County, Madison's home, was grouped together with heavily Anti-Federalist counties. Virginia's very first act of setting congressional districts was thus also its very first partisan gerrymander. "The object of the majority of today has been to prevent your election to the House of Representatives as demonstratively as if they had affirmed it," Turberville wrote to Madison.[15]

Before the vote on the district, Henry "without argument—or answering a single reason urged against it—launched into a field of declamation" that "brought all the imaginary horrors of the new government upon us—and carried a decided and large majority with him."[16] The gerrymander aimed at Madison also seemed to aim at the Constitution. Madison was facing a resourceful and effective adversary who had not given up the fight just because he had failed to block ratification.

As far as Madison was concerned, Henry's object was not simply to limit taxation or create a bill of rights. "His enmity was leveled," Madison insisted, "against the *whole system;* and the destruction of a whole system, I take to be still the secret wish of his heart, and the real object of his pursuit."[17] Against this onslaught, Madison needed a strategy. At all costs, he must block a second convention. But in order to do so, he had to get elected to something.

An Electioneering Appearance

Patrick Henry was not the devil. But his scheme to keep Madison out of the federal government was fiendishly clever. Like Turberville, the Reverend James Madison encouraged his cousin to abandon his home district and instead run from "this lower part of the country" farther south, where "your election appears certain."[18]

Madison had represented Orange County in the state legislature. He had served, albeit briefly, in the local militia during the Revolutionary War, when his father had been the titular leader. Running from another district was possible in principle, but unpleasant in practice. A local candidate would be able to say that Madison could not get elected at home. If Madison was lucky, the race might be about the Constitution and not his own political character. If he ran and lost in a pro-Constitution district, however, his career in statewide politics might well be over.

Madison's friends were divided on strategy. One, Edward Carrington, wrote from Richmond that there was no need for him to return from New York. He would be represented in "each county" by several "active characters in your behalf," local gentlemen who would urge his election.[19] Another friend, Alexander White, wrote to Madison "to express my anxious wish ... that you may be chosen in your own district." To this end, White added, Madison had better come home. "To render it more certain your presence among the people would have great effect."[20]

On learning of his Senate defeat, Madison wrote to Edmund Randolph that he was "extremely disinclined" to return to Virginia for the House race. "It will have an electioneering appearance which I always despised and wish to shun," he explained frankly. Even if he did come back, he would show himself "in Orange only," rather than appearing in the surrounding counties. Since Madison believed he would win the vote in his home county anyway, his presence "could have no very favorable effect." If he went to Virginia instead of serving the final term of the old Congress, this "might by a dexterous misinterpretation" be used against him.[21]

As late as November 23, 1788, Madison leaned strongly toward remaining in New York and choosing to "leave things to their own course in Virginia." He did not yet know of the gerrymander against him. After two contemplative weeks, however, Madison decided to travel to Virginia and contest the election in his home district. On December 8, from Philadelphia, he wrote to Jefferson that "my friends who wish to cooperate in putting our political machine into activity ... press me to attend." He informed Jefferson that his Senate bid had been "defeated by Mr. Henry who is omnipotent in the present legislature," and he also told him about Henry's gerrymander.[22]

What Madison did not tell Jefferson—probably because he did not yet know it—was that his opponent was going to be his friend James Monroe, Jefferson's other protégé. Notwithstanding Monroe's opposition to ratification at the state convention, the men had remained friends. As recently as October 26, Monroe had written a warm letter to Madison explaining that he had just bought a farm near Jefferson's house and signing it "Very respectfully your friend and servant." On November 5, Madison had written a pleasant response, wishing him well with the purchase. He sent regards to Mrs. Monroe and offered Monroe "the sincere esteem and affection with which I am, dear sir, your obedient friend and servant."[23]

The bad news reached Madison in a letter sent December 8. Culpeper County had been added to Orange County as part of Henry's machinations. The vote in that county was "much at the disposal of *one man*," an ally wrote to Madison, referring to French Strother, a Culpeper planter and politician who was closely allied with Henry and had opposed ratification. "It is pretty certain that he means to exert himself in favor of your opponent, Col. Monroe, who has declared himself for the district."[24] Although the ally did not say so directly, his letter implied coordination between Henry, French, and Monroe. The majority of the assembly was "under the control" of Henry, and was "disposed to do everything they can to disappoint and hurt your feelings."[25]

Recruiting Monroe to run against Madison was a stroke of political genius. Like Madison, Monroe had served in Congress and the state assembly. In general, Monroe's views and Madison's were closely aligned. The only salient difference between them was that Monroe had opposed ratification. He had done so temperately and moderately, not in the way Henry had—and that made him a particularly good choice to run against Madison. No one, least of all Madison, could say that Monroe was a radical.

According to reports that reached Madison later, Monroe had misgivings, but "the party as it is called had too much influence with him." The "party" meant Henry's Anti-Federalists. According to the source, Monroe "resisted for a time" but "they at length prevailed on him to come forward."[26] Monroe's decision to run also marked his desire to eclipse Madison, who had once been roughly his equal and now, with ratification, had surpassed him. This, too, was evidence of Henry's political brilliance. By pitting Monroe against Madison, he was breaking an alliance that might have threatened him.

Madison's friends told him that he must visit Culpeper "and attend their public meetings." There was no substitute for showing up and electioneering: "For the interest of our country *you must* take some trouble however disagreeable it may be to you," one wrote. Baptists were a key constituency, he was told, and Madison would have to address them.[27]

Turberville wrote to Madison on December 12 to inform him that "great exertions" were being "made in Mr. Monroe's favor," which "will most probably be greatly assistant towards his election."[28] Another supporter wrote two days later that "the sooner your personal appearance could be in those counties the better."[29] The election would be February 2, 1789, and Madison would not reach the state until December 18.[30]

Madison's opponents depicted him as an opponent of any change to the Constitution. "Great endeavors are making," one supporter wrote to

Madison, "to propagate an idea that you are wholly opposed to any alteration in the government having declared that you did not think that a single letter in it would admit of a change."[31] Another explained that "every art has been used to prejudice the minds of the people against you." The people were being told that

> you tricked this country [that is, Virginia] into the business by the
> manner in which you first proposed a general convention to our
> legislature; that you had a chief hand in sending forth the
> Constitution from the convention without the amendments generally
> wished; and you are now opposed to all amendments.[32]

The most devastating form of the criticism was the claim that, at the Virginia ratifying convention, Madison had said that "the Constitution had no defects, and it was the nearest to perfection of anything that could be obtained." There was no written record of the statement, but opponents said the quote

> could be proved on you, if the second volume of the debates of the
> convention could be had; and intimated that it was by the printer
> withheld from the public, until the election be over, for the purpose of
> secreting some of its contents, and preventing them from operating
> against the authors who might be candidates.[33]

The allegation that he had declared the Constitution close to perfection put Madison in a bind. He had not used precisely those words, but the sentiment was accurate.[34] Madison's opponents were using his authorship of the Constitution against him. He would either have to admit flaws in the document he had helped design and ratify, or succumb to the charge that he opposed amendments.

Circumstances Are Now Changed

If he lost to Monroe, Madison might have no role in the new government. He had designed the Constitution, but he lacked the specialized knowledge or experience for a cabinet position. Winning a seat in the House was the only way to avoid a massive setback in his political career.

The consequences of a possible defeat were not merely personal. Madison knew that his absence from national office could weaken or even block the Constitution as it was going into effect. He would not be on hand to guide it, and a second convention could be called to reverse its basic form. That was, he believed, Henry's goal in trying to keep Madison out of office.

With the personal and constitutional consequences of defeat looming, Madison had to save himself. His solution was to advocate a bill of rights to be drafted by the first Congress. This represented a major shift in Madison's public views. Until now, Madison had publicly insisted that no bill of rights was necessary. In private, he had essentially maintained the same view.

Endorsing a bill of rights would show that Madison did not consider the Constitution perfect. Proposing that it be drafted by Congress would avert a new constitutional convention. If Madison himself could draft the bill of rights in Congress, he could try to restrict the amendments to individual liberties without limiting the federal government's power vis-à-vis the states.

Madison had barely a month to make his views known, and no reliable mass medium to do it. One supporter wrote to him that he had only two courses available: to "visit the different counties on their court days, or to publish an address to the people."[35] The supporter thought that visiting each county would be "the most disagreeable and the least likely to have a good effect," because in the middle of winter relatively few people would attend. If Madison were to print copies of an address to the people, however, it would "convey your sentiments to every freeholder's fireside."[36]

Following a more traditional approach, Madison rolled out his proposal in a series of open letters to supporters in his district. The first, dated January 2, 1789, went to George Eve, an Orange County Baptist minister. Madison began by acknowledging frankly that he did not think the Constitution needed changing: "I freely own," he wrote, "that I have never seen in the Constitution as it now stands the serious dangers which have alarmed many respectable citizens." That was why, Madison explained, he had "opposed all previous alterations as calculated to throw the states into dangerous contentions, and to furnish the secret enemies of the union with an opportunity of promoting its dissolution."[37]

Having begun with a defense of his record, Madison pivoted: "Circumstances are now changed," he wrote. After ratification, "amendments, if pursued with a proper moderation and in a proper mode, will be not only safe, but may serve the double purpose of satisfying the minds of well-meaning opponents, and of providing additional guards in favor of liberty."[38]

This was hardly a strong argument for a bill of rights. In essence, Madison was saying that a bill of rights would have been dangerous to advocate during the ratification process, and was in fact still not necessary. But now that the Constitution had been ratified, a bill of rights could do no harm.

Madison went on to announce that it was his "sincere opinion that the Constitution ought to be revised, and that the first Congress meeting under it, ought to prepare and recommend" a bill of rights. These would include, he proposed, "particularly the rights of conscience in the fullest latitude, the freedom of the press, trials by jury, security against general warrants etc."[39]

After this uncertain start, Madison realized that more and better efforts would be needed. On January 12, 1789, an Orange County supporter, Benjamin Johnson, wrote that Monroe had left for Louisa County in order to address "a political meeting of the Baptist ministers of the district" as well as the public on the local court day. Johnson wanted Madison to attend both. He wrote a note to the prominent Baptist minister and religious liberty activist John Leland asking him to tell Madison the time and place of the Louisa meeting "by special messenger at my expense" if necessary. [40]

On January 13, with the election just three weeks away, Madison was in Louisa. From here he wrote a new open letter. He began by acknowledging the charge that he was "an inflexible opponent to the change of a single letter" of the Constitution. This time, however, Madison no longer insisted that the Constitution would be fine unamended. Rather, he claimed, "The truth, on the contrary, is . . . that I have ever thought it might be improved in several points, although I never could see the dangers which alarmed many."[41]

The stakes were high, and Madison was evolving. Having adopted a better formulation, Madison one-upped himself: "What is more, [I] was an unsuccessful advocate in the general convention, which framed the instrument, for several of the very amendments, since recommended by this . . . and other states."[42]

Madison was now claiming to have argued for at least some of the newly proposed rights in Philadelphia. The records of the Philadelphia convention were sealed by agreement of the participants, and the only really complete record of deliberations was Madison's. His claim was therefore unverifiable. It was also, strictly speaking, untrue. In Philadelphia, Madison had not advocated for express protection of the rights of conscience, trial by jury, protection against general warrants, or any of the other core rights since proposed by the state ratifying conventions.

Madison went on to explain that he had opposed conditional amendments during the ratification process in order to avoid "a dangerous road to political confusion." Now he was free to recommend amendments that would either make the Constitution better or at least "appear better to those, who now dislike it" without making it worse.[43] Madison was asserting both that things had changed and that his support of amendments was "consistent" with his prior position. This was electoral politicking at its finest. Madison was learning to play the game in a way he never had before.

The letter was reprinted in *The Virginia Independent Chronicle* on January 28. The election was just a few days away. From Louisa, Madison undertook a series of last-minute trips around the district, addressing public meetings wherever he went, generally in conjunction with Monroe. The two appeared in Culpeper on January 19 and at the Orange County courthouse on January 26.

Many years later, Madison told the story of a meeting at a German church in Culpeper County:

> Service was performed and then they had music with two fiddles. They are remarkably fond of music. When it was all over we addressed these people and kept them standing in the snow listening to the discussion of constitutional subjects. They stood it out very patiently—seemed to consider it a sort of fight of which they were required to be spectators. I then had to ride in the night *12* miles to quarters; and got my nose frostbitten, of which I bear the mark now.[44]

According to the source of the story, Madison then touched the end of his nose on the left side, indicating his "scar of battle."

Saved Our Friendship

Election day, February 2, 1789, would determine Madison's political future. The weather was bitterly cold, with temperatures falling below o°F.[45] Monroe was at the Culpeper County courthouse in the hopes of exerting some final influence.

Yet remarkably, despite predictions that Monroe would win easily in Culpeper, Madison carried the county, 256 to 103. Madison won Albemarle and Louisa counties comfortably, and he won his home county of Orange 216 to 9.

Monroe won Spotsylvania County, where he practiced law, by a vote of 189 to 115. He also won Amherst County 246 to 145; Goochland County by a single vote, 133 to 132; and tiny Fluvanna County. Each man won four counties, signaling how close the race had been. But the total vote was 1,308 for Madison to 972 for Monroe.[46] Madison had survived Patrick Henry's revenge.

The margin of victory was not large. (George Washington generously called it "a respectable majority."[47]) Madison's assiduous efforts in the home stretch had paid off, and the Baptist vote had helped immensely.[48] Edward Carrington, who had originally told Madison to stay in New York, was "exceedingly glad" Madison had ignored his advice. The victory was "an event which I am convinced would not have taken place a fortnight sooner, had it then been tried, and I am equally well convinced, that had you stayed away, it would not have happened at all."[49]

Madison agreed that it had been a close call. Writing to Edmund Randolph after the election, he observed dryly, "My presence in the district was more necessary to my election than you then calculated. . . . My absence would have left room for the calumnies of Anti-Federal partisans." He believed that the election had turned on "Culpeper, which was the critical county"—and there "a continued attention was necessary to repel the multiplied falsehoods which circulated."[50]

Madison had avoided disaster and defeated the gerrymander by advocating for the bill of rights he had so long opposed. He had averted a humiliating defeat that would have repudiated his constitutional efforts. And he had headed off a direct challenge to his political future brought by his close friend Monroe.

If Madison felt recrimination or anger toward Monroe, he did not show it. Nor did Madison ever suggest that Monroe should have stepped aside. Reporting to Jefferson on the results of the election, Madison produced a paragraph that was a masterpiece of understatement:

> It was my misfortune to be thrown into a contest with our friend, Col. Monroe. The occasion produced considerable efforts among our respective friends. Between ourselves, I have no reason to doubt that the distinction was duly kept in mind between political and personal views, and that it has saved our friendship from the smallest diminution. On one side I am sure it is the case.[51]

Each line of this extraordinary passage was full of meaning. Madison depicted Monroe's run against him as a "misfortune," not the outcome of Monroe's willingness to serve Patrick Henry's interests. Jefferson detested Henry, and would have been extremely unhappy to think of his protégé, Monroe, helping him—so Madison spared Jefferson the knowledge. In the same sentence Madison referred to Monroe as "our friend," acknowledging Jefferson's bonds to both of them. If Monroe had run against Madison because of an implicit sibling rivalry, Madison was offering their shared father figure a picture of brotherly reconciliation.

The final sentence, which affirmed Madison's still-cordial feelings, revealed the purpose of the whole paragraph. Madison was demonstrating to Jefferson that he could separate the personal from the political—and he was quietly asking Jefferson to make sure that Monroe felt the same. Madison was trying to maintain a friendship in the face of what would seem to most people an insurmountable challenge.[52]

Here in a nutshell was Madison's vision of friendship within a constitutional republic. He and Monroe were friends who disagreed about ratification and ran against each other for office. But because they both sought the public good, they could (he insisted) still remain friends.

Madison believed that the new government would operate on the same principle. Respectful divergence of opinion would continue in the name of the public interest. Party and faction would be avoided as all pursued the common good. Yet the evidence of the gerrymander and the election suggested that the situation would be far more complicated—and that it would be difficult to curtail partisanship simply by insisting that friendship still remained.

I Foresee Contentions

Madison left Orange for New York on February 18, 1789, stopping along the way in Mount Vernon.[53] The week Madison spent there with Washington, whose election as president was now under way, inaugurated a new period of political and personal closeness between them. Madison had relied on Washington to make the Philadelphia convention a reality. Now he would be Washington's chief ally in Congress. In letters following the meeting, Madison began to give political advice to Washington with a directness that previously would have been unthinkable.[54]

Madison arrived in New York on March 19 to find that a quorum had not yet been reached in Congress.[55] He had reason for enthusiasm at the prospect of participating in the new government he had done so much to help shape. His cousin, the Reverend James Madison, predicted that "the prosperity of the federal government will depend in a great measure upon the wisdom of the laws and arrangements first proposed." Within a century, he anticipated, America would be home to "at least 60 millions of free men." And "the only chain by which such a multitude will be bound together is that of wise and just law."[56]

Yet Madison felt not excitement but foreboding. "I foresee contentions first between federal and antifederal parties," he told Edmund Randolph, and subsequently "between northern and southern parties."[57] The word "parties" was telling. The Virginia election had shown Madison that there were now two increasingly well-organized political forces. Originally forged through the debate over ratification, they could be called Federal and Anti-Federal.[58]

It took until April 6 for both houses of Congress to convene. Their first order of business was to count the presidential electors' votes. Washington was elected unanimously. The vice-presidential candidate with the most votes was John Adams, who got 34 out of the 69 cast, fewer than many people had expected.

Madison did not have a high opinion of Adams. He had been dismissive of Adams's *Defence of the Constitutions of the United States*, copies of which had reached Philadelphia just as the constitutional convention had begun. In a coded letter to Jefferson in October 1788, Madison had reiterated the criticism, asserting that "John Adams has made himself obnoxious to many particularly in the southern states by the political principles avowed in his book."[59] To Madison, Adams's emphasis on a powerful executive and an aristocratic senate to check popularly elected legislatures was out of step with republican values and the superiority of a federal Congress. Then he added a further, more biting criticism:

> Others recollecting [Adams's] cabal during the war against General Washington, knowing his extravagant self-importance and considering his preference of an unprofitable dignity to some place of emolument better adapted to private fortune as a proof of his having an eye to the presidency, concluded he would not be a very cordial second to the general and that an impatient ambition might even intrigue for a premature advancement.[60]

Madison almost never spoke so negatively even about people who were his avowed enemies. He was impugning Adams's character, asserting that Adams wanted the otherwise pointless vice presidency only so he would be next in line. Madison was even going so far as to insinuate that Adams might not wait until Washington stepped down to try to replace him.

This attack on Adams was a rare instance of Madison's jealousy. Adams was the one American with pretensions to be a serious constitutional philosopher. He had a book to his name on the topic.* Madison, for his part, could boast authorship of an actual constitution and a good chunk of the *Federalist* papers; but, unlike Adams's work, these were both anonymous. The tenor of Madison's statement is all the more notable because it was made to Jefferson, who respected and liked Adams.[61]

His distaste for Adams aside, Madison wasted no time in setting Congress's agenda. On April 8, he introduced a scheme of imposts—taxes on imported goods—that roughly followed the proposals the old Congress had never been able to enact. Introducing the measures, he said the subject was "of the greatest magnitude," and therefore "requires our first attention, and our united exertions."[62]

Beginning Congress's new deliberations with trade was no accident.

---

* Madison's cousin, the Reverend James Madison, wrote to him humorously that Adams might want to entitle himself "Ambassador Extraordinary, Author of His Luminous Book, Member of the Boston Academy, LL.D. etc. etc." Rev. James Madison to James Madison, August 15, 1789, *PJM*, 12:338. The jest revealed that the book was not the least of Adams's distinctions. He had, among other things, founded the American Academy of Arts and Sciences, of which Madison was not a member.

Madison had first conceived the need for a Constitution because of the old government's inability to raise revenue from trade or use trade policy to force the British to open their ports to American shipping. Accordingly, Madison's draft bill had two parts. One of them listed goods that would be subject to duties when imported. (He left the amounts blank in order for Congress to negotiate them.) This component, he explained, was meant to raise revenue.

The other part specified that additional duties would be charged to all vessels docking in the United States. These duties would vary depending on whether the vessels came from the United States or other countries with which it had trade treaties, or came from countries with whom no such treaties existed. The point was to create an incentive for Britain to open its closed ports. Taxing British vessels more highly than American vessels or treaty partners would lead British traders to pressure their own government to reach a treaty with the United States. If Congress were to enact such a provision, it would be fulfilling Madison's first constitutional dream.

Madison hoped that the law could be passed in time for the arrival of the spring vessels. This would bring the new government much-needed revenue—and send an early signal of consensus and resolve to Britain. Yet almost as soon as Madison had introduced the measure, a Pennsylvania congressman proposed further duties that were intended not to raise revenue but to protect domestic manufacturing from foreign competition.[63]

In response, Madison gave a speech on April 9, delivered from hastily prepared notes, that set the tone for his contributions to the first Congress. Concisely and logically, Madison offered a theory of trade duties. Many of his listeners in Congress knew something of trade; but few, if any, had thought systematically about the issue. As he would do repeatedly in the Congress—and as he had done in the constitutional debates—Madison went beyond policy, setting the terms of the debate and educating his colleagues into the bargain.

This combination was Madison's unique skill, and it accounted for his outsize influence in Congress. One colleague, Fisher Ames of Massachusetts, who often disagreed with Madison, nevertheless stated unequivocally, "He is our first man."[64] Madison would speak more than 150 times in the first session of Congress alone.

To most politicians in most historic periods, erudition of the kind Madison possessed would be a handicap. Even the admiring Ames

thought he was "a little too much of a book politician."⁶⁵ Yet in a body
trying to figure out how to run itself and make national policies, the ability to construct political systems from the ground up was an enormous
advantage. Madison's deep and broad knowledge allowed him to understand and explain the political world to people who, like him, were operating in zones where they had little or no past experience.

The Respect of Nations

For the speech on import duties, Madison relied on what had clearly been
a careful reading of Adam Smith's *Wealth of Nations.* He began by explaining that he was a "friend to a very free system of commerce," and
believed "that commercial shackles are generally unjust, oppressive and
impolitic." Madison was confident that the efficiency of the free market
would lead to productivity "in a more certain and direct manner than the
wisdom of the most enlightened legislature could point out." Madison
illustrated the point by referring to the division of labor: "It would be of
no advantage to the shoemaker to make his own clothes to save the expense of the tailor, nor of the tailor to make his own shoes to save the
expense of procuring them from the shoemaker." Rather, "all are benefited
by exchange, and the less this exchange is cramped by government, the
greater are the proportions of benefits to each." In a distinctly Smithian
conclusion, Madison observed that "the same argument holds good between nation and nation, and between parts of the same nation."⁶⁶

Having stated what he called his "general principle" that "commerce
ought to be free, and labor and industry left at large to find its proper
object," Madison moved on to "exceptions." The first and most important
was that if the United States opened her ports to all without differentia-
tion, "while other nations make this discrimination," the result would be
"to exclude American shipping altogether from foreign ports."⁶⁷ In a
world of reciprocity, American ships would only get equal access through
the threat of unequal treatment at U.S. ports. The necessity of retaliation
justified deviating from free trade.

The core of Madison's argument was that the Constitution had been
adopted to enable the United States to make foreign nations "pay us that
respect which they have neglected on account of our former imbecility."
This insistence on respect, he said, represented the "sentiments of our

constituents." And "the organization of the new government"—namely the new Constitution—"has its foundation in these sentiments."

States had tried and failed on their own to combat England's "selfish policy." Finding that they could not, "with an united voice they called for a new arrangement . . . to obtain that reciprocity which justice demands."[68] The people had not actually demanded a new constitution so they could stand up to Great Britain on trade. But this had been Madison's goal when he first imagined a new constitution.

The argument for retaliatory trade policy led Madison into his first and most important foreign policy idea—one that would follow him to the presidency and the brink of war. As Madison told the story, Britain after the Revolution had initially "showed a disposition" to sign a trade treaty, because Britain feared "that the United States possessed both the power and inclination to do themselves justice." All this changed "the moment she discovered we had not the power to perform our contracts." Now that the Constitution allowed the United States to make coherent trade policy, failure to do so would give Britain "no motive . . . to alter its conduct." Without a threat, Britain would "persevere in her selfish interests and narrow policy, excluded from a reciprocal share of trade."[69]

New York congressman John Laurance expressed the fear that if the United States began a trade war, it would suffer reprisals. Madison answered defiantly: "For my part, I am not afraid of suffering in the contest; her interests can be wounded almost mortally, while ours are invulnerable." Madison meant that the British West Indies depended on American trade. If the United States should decide that "no article should be exported from America to the West Indies" except on American ships, Britain would fold, he predicted.

Madison's theory, in other words, was that Britain's colonial interests made Britain vulnerable to trade sanctions. The colonies of the West Indies produced sugarcane and needed slave labor to do it. They did not produce grain, sheep, beef, salted fish, or manufactures. Feeding and clothing the slaves—and the rest of the colonial population—required North America.

Madison believed that if shipping to the West Indies were closed, Britain would be at America's mercy. Unless it gave in, the colonies would starve. They could never, he argued, draw sufficiently reliable "supplies from the mother country" across the Atlantic. As he put it, "We must make the other nation feel our power to induce her to grant us reciprocal advantages."[70]

Madison argued articulately and at length—but on the key issue of discriminatory duties, commerce and caution defeated bold assertions of national power. New Yorkers such as Laurance saw U.S. interests through the lens of merchants, who favored the freest trade possible, cared little about what ships did the carrying, and feared a trade war with England. Madison's national-power arguments held little force for those motivated by commerce. If Great Britain retaliated against American sanctions by closing its home ports to American ships and American goods, trade would come to a standstill.

Ultimately, Congress declined to treat British shipping differently from the shipping of countries that had trade treaties with the United States. Convincing the merchant class to stand up for broader U.S. interests against Britain would be a recurring challenge—one that would last for decades and which would shape Madison's career.

Republican Dignity

Although Madison did not prevail in the trade debate, he was given an opportunity to influence the relationship between the president and Congress. George Washington was approaching the presidency with the same caution he had brought to every undertaking of his life, major or minor. He believed that he ought to make an opening address to Congress in recognition of his election—and he entrusted the responsibility of composing it to Madison.

Madison wrote Washington's address, which was presented to Congress on April 30, 1789. He then wrote the address that the House of Representatives made in response to Washington on May 5. That was not all. Washington asked Madison to write a presidential reply to Madison's congressional reply to the presidential address that Madison himself had written. Since the authorship of these presidential documents was confidential, the nation did not know that, through these state documents, Madison was holding a discourse with himself.

When writing as George Washington, Madison did a good job of capturing the general's distinctive voice. The opening presidential address began with insistence on the president's "anxieties" at being elected, his "veneration and love" for the country, and his reluctance at leaving private retirement to enter public life. All three were vintage Washington themes—and the love of country, at least, was sincere. Madison added "fervent supplications to the Almighty Being who rules over the universe, who presides in the Councils of Nations." This sort of high-flown yet generic religious rhetoric never came to Madison's pen when he was writing as himself. Attributed to Washington, the sentiments seemed altogether natural.*

Madison gave voice to his own views when he had Washington urge Congress that "no local prejudices, or attachment; no separate views, nor party animosities" should affect their deliberations. Paraphrasing his own statements at the Philadelphia convention and in *The Federalist*, Madison declared through Washington that "The destiny of the republican model of government [is] justly considered as *deeply*, perhaps as *finally* staked, on the experiment entrusted to the hands of the American people." Madison advanced his own agenda by referring to the drafting of a bill of rights as "expedient at the present juncture by the nature of objections that have been urged against the system, or by the degree of light which has given birth to them."[71] He apparently could not resist the temptation still to justify the bill of rights as instrumental to satisfy critics, not necessary in itself.[72]

An important aspect of the House's reply was the form of address that Congress would use. This would be the first official communication to the president from another branch of government, and would therefore set a precedent. Madison rather proudly told Jefferson in forwarding him the document, "It will not have escaped you" that it "was addressed with truly republican simplicity to George Washington, president of the United States."[73]

The Senate, however, would make its own reply to Washington—and in that body, a different opinion existed. Under the influence of John Adams, who as vice president presided over the Senate, a committee recommended addressing Washington as "His Highness the President of the United States of America and Protector of the Rights of the Same."[74] Adams's preference, according to Madison, was for "His Highness the President of the United States of America and Protector of Their Liber-

---

* Madison surely intended no irony when he had Washington say, "No people can be bound to acknowledge and adore the invisible hand, which conducts the affairs of men, more than the people of the United States." It is just possible that the metaphor of the divine "invisible hand" came to Madison's mind because he had been reading Adam Smith for his speeches on trade.

ties." Madison told Jefferson that Adams "espoused the cause of titles with great earnestness."[75]

Jefferson agreed with Madison. "The president's title as proposed by the Senate was the most superlatively ridiculous thing I ever heard of," he wrote. Nevertheless, he expressed his affection for Adams. He quoted Benjamin Franklin's assessment of his "friend," Adams: "always an honest man, often a great one, but sometimes absolutely mad."[76]

A legislative debate over titles ensued, which Madison considered "serious." In his view, Adams's proposal "would have subjected the president to a severe dilemma and given a deep wound to our infant government."[77] Addressing the House, Madison said that although titles were less important than constitutional powers, they were not "reconcilable with the nature of our government, or the genius of the people." Titles would "diminish the true dignity and importance of the republic," and indeed would "diminish the true dignity of the first magistrate himself." Inventing titles by "fantasy" would make the government "phantom, ridiculous, and absurd." Borrowing them from other countries would be "servile imitation" and "odious, not to say ridiculous also."[78]

This conclusion revealed much about the connection between Madison's aesthetics and his political and intellectual values. "The more simple, the more republican we are in our manners, the more rational dignity we acquire," he said.[79] The short phrase summed up Madison's personal ethic. Simple and republican manners produced the distinctive sort of dignity that was based in reason. Aristocratic titles, conversely, were irrational and undignified. Man's highest status was the exercise of reason, and the republican Constitution was meant to be its embodiment.

The Permanent Exposition of the Constitution

Madison knew that he had to propose a bill of rights, both in order to fulfill his campaign pledge and to head off the possibility of a constitutional convention. Before he could get to it, however, another constitutional question loomed. In late May, Congress began the process of establishing the departments of State, Treasury, and War—the first cabinet offices. The Constitution made it clear that such high executive officers would be appointed by the president with the advice and consent of the Senate. But the Constitution was silent as to how cabinet secretaries might be removed except by impeachment.

Taken on its own, the question of whether the president could fire cabinet members at will would not determine the future of the republic. But the debate nonetheless mattered enormously—because it posed the problem of how (and whether) the new republic would be governed under the Constitution. Madison, the author of the motion to establish the departments, sought to clarify the constitutional ambiguity. His motion included the statement that the secretaries could be removed from office by the president alone, without seeking the advice and consent of the Senate.

This was an attempt at constitutional interpretation, the first made in the first Congress. Crucially, Madison was arguing for a pragmatic reading of the Constitution, not a literal one. The debate that followed presaged what would become a perennial struggle over how to determine the meaning of the document, one that has not abated since.

Some congressmen objected to Madison's interpretation by focusing on the text of the Constitution. They maintained that because impeachment was the only mechanism mentioned, it must be the only way to remove cabinet secretaries. Others, relying on the document's structure, thought that since the Senate must give its advice and consent to an appointment, the Senate must have the identical role in removal.[80]

Madison spoke in Congress against both views, focusing on functionality. If impeachment were the only option for removal, this "would in fact establish every officer of the government on the firm tenure of good behavior." Such a design, he said, would amount to "a fatal error interwove in the system and one that would ultimately prove its destruction."[81]

As for giving the Senate a decisive say on removal, Madison urged his colleagues "to consider the inconvenience." The Senate, Madison said, would have to be constantly in session in case it needed to exercise this power—which would be expensive. To modern ears, this is a slightly odd argument. Surely the president could fire an officer temporarily during the recess. Yet this argument demonstrated Madison's determination to interpret the Constitution based on its function.

On June 16, 1789, the issue was still alive, and Madison put forth two different kinds of arguments. First he inaugurated what would eventually become an important political argument in favor of presidential power. He did not wish to presume, he said, that every president would possess "the splendor of the character of the present chief magistrate," Washington. Nonetheless, the president was the first chief executive in modern history to be elected by the people—and his virtue would therefore reflect theirs: "When we consider the first magistrate is to be appointed at present by the suffrages of three millions of people ... it is not to be presumed that a vicious or bad character will be selected."[82] The president enjoyed distinct and unique legitimacy under the Constitution. He was therefore worthy of more confidence than the Senate.

Then Madison abandoned pragmatism and politics to argue that Congress was "absolutely tied down to the construction" of the Constitution that he proposed. Madison's argument ran as follows: The Constitution had assigned all legislative powers to Congress, the executive power to the president, and the judicial power of the United States to the Supreme Court. The Constitution then made certain exceptions, for example by giving the president a veto over legislation. Congress therefore could not add any further limitations on the executive power. Madison insisted, not unreasonably, that "the power of appointing, overseeing, and controlling those who execute the laws" must be executive. From this analysis it followed that his proposed legislative provision was nothing more than "the true construction."[83]

Madison was trying to establish norms for how the Constitution would be interpreted in the future, and he wanted to stress the gravity of the precedent. "I feel the importance of the question," he said in Congress the next day, June 17, "and know that our decision will involve the decision of all similar cases. The decision ... will become the permanent exposition of the Constitution; and on a permanent exposition of the Constitution will depend the genius and character of the whole government."[84]

Finally Madison articulated a much broader theory of Congress's obligation to interpret the Constitution. When it came to the separation of powers, Congress was as important as the courts:

> The Constitution is the charter of the people to the government; it specifies certain great powers as absolutely granted, and marks out the departments to exercise them. ... I do not see that any one of these independent departments has more right than another to declare their sentiments on that point.[85]

Madison's overarching goal was to model for all time the seriousness of constitutional reasoning, seeking "the true meaning of the Constitution," to be guided by "the true spirit of liberty."[86] The act of interpreting according to liberty—and getting the meaning right—was intended to enshrine the norm of obedience to constitutional authority. In retrospect, for Madison, the constitutional debate over the removal power would turn out to have been a halcyon moment, suspended in time before passion and faction would make themselves felt.

Rights

Throughout May 1789, Madison spent his few spare moments drafting his proposed bill of rights, drawing on, refining, and adding to the amendments proposed by the state ratifying conventions—while ignoring the ones he did not like. With his task of privately advising Washington, his repeated speeches on the impost, and the debate over the president's removal power, Madison "never had less time that I could truly call my own than at present," he told Randolph.[87] But the introduction of proposed amendments was a pressing issue. Correspondents were telling Madison that amendments would encourage North Carolina and Rhode Island to ratify, which they still had not done.[88] Madison had promised amendments to his constituents, and feared a second constitutional convention if Congress did not act.

On June 8, 1789, Madison introduced his bill of rights to Congress, urging the House to consider the amendments in detail. Any further delay, he warned, "might make the public suspect that we are not sincere in our desire to incorporate such amendments in the Constitution as will secure those rights, which they consider as not sufficiently guarded." Madison knew whereof he spoke: His own sincerity on the topic was very much open to question.[89]

The issue seemed less pressing to Madison's colleagues. Realizing that he was losing steam, Madison launched into the very long speech he had planned, in which he laid out his new theory of the desirability of a bill of rights. At least he could tell his constituents that he had broached the topic on the floor of the House.

Madison openly acknowledged to his colleagues that the main reason for the bill of rights was to convince Anti-Federalists that the Federalists were not closet aristocrats.[90] He would not be proposing any amendments that would limit the taxing power or otherwise "injure the Constitution." He calculated that "we have in this way something to gain, and, if we proceed with caution, nothing to lose." Caution was important because of the danger of amendments that would go too far. "We must feel for the

Constitution itself," Madison proposed, "and make that revisal a moderate one."[91] His creation required protection.

Madison then laid out his proposed amendments. First came a declaration that power was derived from the people, that government was instituted for their benefit, and that the people retained an inalienable right "to reform or change their government."[92] These were general principles drawn from the philosophy of John Locke and the Declaration of Independence. Doubtless Madison believed they could do no harm.

Second, Madison wanted to amend the upper limit of the ratio of congressmen to population so that it could be flexible as the population grew. Strictly speaking, this change had no place in a bill of rights. Yet Madison had left Philadelphia thinking the ratio needed revision, and this was the best opportunity. As he put it in the speech, "I confess I always thought this part of the Constitution defective, though not dangerous."[93]

Madison's third proposed amendment also had nothing to do with rights. It said that Congress could not raise its own pay during a given congressional term. Madison explained in the speech that he did not actually expect that "in the ordinary course of government," the power was likely to be abused.[94] This amendment was designed simply for public consumption.

The fourth proposed amendment finally got to the substance of basic inalienable rights:

> The civil rights of none shall be abridged on account of religious belief or worship, nor shall any national religion be established, nor shall the full and equal rights of conscience be in any manner, or on any pretext, infringed.[95]

Here was a bold, clear, and definitive statement of the issue that had brought Madison into politics. Its three components each protected different aspects of religious liberty. The "civil rights" provision guaranteed equal treatment of all regardless of religious commitment—a kind of foreshadowing of the equal protection clause for adherents of different religions. No "national religion" would be established, a provision sparing Congress from any debate over an official church. Finally, the right of conscience—the right not to be coerced to act against one's beliefs— would be protected absolutely. This echoed Madison's wording in the

Virginia Bill of Rights, where the rights of conscience were expressly stated to be equal among all.

Next came the freedom of speech, also expressed very fully:

> The people shall not be deprived or abridged of their right to speak, to write, or to publish their sentiments; and the freedom of the press, as one of the great bulwarks of liberty, shall be inviolable.[96]

This formulation distinguished the people's speech from freedom of the press. Madison said nothing, positive or negative, about laws that might punish false or seditious speech after it was made public.

Madison next guaranteed the right to peaceful assembly and petitioning the legislature. The right to bear arms was described this way:

> The right of the people to keep and bear arms shall not be infringed; a well armed, and well-regulated militia being the best security of a free country: but no person religiously scrupulous of bearing arms, shall be compelled to render military service in person.[97]

The language left little doubt that the right to bear arms meant neither more nor less than the right to serve in a well-regulated militia. The protection afforded to conscientious objectors at the end of the sentence further underscored the purpose of the amendment: It authorized the right to serve in a militia while simultaneously guaranteeing that pacifists such as Quakers could not be made to serve.

Madison then protected against the quartering of soldiers in any house without the consent of the owner; against double jeopardy; against being compelled to be a witness against oneself; against any deprivation "of life, liberty, or property without due process of law"; and against anyone being "obliged to relinquish his property, where it may be necessary for public use, without a just compensation." There would be no excessive bail, excessive fines, "nor cruel and unusual punishments inflicted."

All these provisions, drawn from ratifying-convention proposals, would ultimately become part of the Constitution with almost no changes. The same was true of "the right of the people to be secure in their persons, their houses, their papers, and their other property from all unreasonable searches and seizures"; and of the right to a "speedy and

public trial" in criminal cases and to confrontation of accusers and witnesses.[98]

Madison then paused to introduce a general provision to guide future
interpretation:

> The exceptions here or elsewhere in the Constitution, made in favor
> of particular rights, shall not be so construed as to diminish the just
> importance of other rights retained by the people; or as to enlarge the
> powers delegated by the Constitution; but either as actual limitations
> of such powers, or as inserted merely for greater caution.[99]

This provision was intended to satisfy Madison's goal of introducing new
rights without doing any harm to the Constitution as it existed.

Having laid out these rights—and having added the trial by jury, which
he explained was not "a natural right, but a right resulting from the social
compact," Madison proposed a further amendment that had not been
proposed in the various state ratifying conventions: "No state shall violate
the equal rights of conscience, or the freedom of the press, or the trial by
jury in criminal cases." This provision applied not to Congress but to the
states.

The reason no one had thought to have the Constitution limit the
powers of state legislatures was twofold. First, the states had bills of rights
themselves. Second, and more important, the Constitution existed to
confer power on the newly created federal government. Skeptics were
worried about the federal government violating basic rights. The topic of
state legislatures' rights violations was far from the public mind.

Madison, however, had not given up his own worry that state legislatures often violated rights. Unlike Madison's proposed national veto,
which would have belonged to Congress, this provision would likely have
been enforceable primarily by the courts. Thus, Madison was not repli-
cating his rejected proposal. He was trying to devise a new way to block
state legislatures from tyrannizing the minority and violating fundamental rights.

In doing so, Madison anticipated what would become a central element of the American constitutional order: federal judicial review of state
legislation. The Supreme Court would not start overturning state laws as
unconstitutional until after the enactment of the Fourteenth Amend-

ment; but when it did, judicial review would permanently change the power balance between the federal government and the states.

This was not a coincidence. Madison understood, as he had told Jefferson, that without some national authority to make the states follow the Constitution, the structure of the document created a contradiction, opposing federal sovereignty to state sovereignty. For the structure to work coherently, he knew, ultimate power must lie somewhere. The theory of central control had been at the heart of his invention, and its absence left a gap that would cause serious trouble until it was repaired.

Defending his proposal, Madison praised the fact that the existing Constitution prohibited states from passing bills of attainder or ex post facto laws. He implied that this constitutional provision, the only one that expressly limited what state legislatures could do, created the precedent for the Constitution to regulate the states, not just the federal government. Madison acknowledged that "in some of the state constitutions the power of the government is controlled by such a declaration" already. But, he explained, "I cannot see any reason against obtaining even a double security on those points."

Madison's last two proposed amendments related to constitutional structure. One, redolent of the debate in Philadelphia over the president's removal power, expressly asserted the separation of powers. "The powers delegated by this Constitution," it read, "are appropriated to the departments to which they are respectively distributed" so that no department could ever exercise the powers that belonged to the other two.

The final amendment stated that "the powers not delegated by this Constitution, nor prohibited by it to the states, are reserved to the states respectively."[100] Madison preempted objections by saying that these words "may be considered as superfluous. I admit they may be deemed unnecessary; but there can be no harm in making such a declaration."[101] This provision was intended as a concession to critics of the Constitution.

A Defense

Most statesmen would have stopped there. Madison had made an argument for proposing amendments and had specified the content of a bill of rights. But Madison possessed a unique pride of authorship and confidence in his own capacity for good design. He now undertook to defend the whole exercise of the bill of rights against unnamed critics who considered the undertaking "not only unnecessary, but even improper."

It was true that, among others, James Wilson of Pennsylvania had argued that a bill of rights might actually restrict rights rather than protect them. But there was no public movement against the bill of rights, and precious little public discourse opposing the idea. At every turn in the remainder of the speech, Madison set out to address the objections that he himself had made privately to Jefferson. With an eye toward history, Madison wanted to defend the bill of rights against himself.

The first step was to compare the proposed American bill of rights to the English Bill of Rights of 1689 adopted by Parliament as part of the Glorious Revolution that brought William and Mary to the throne. To Jefferson, Madison had offered the brilliant insight that the English Bill of Rights worked because it served as a public measure of the laws and called the people to action against royal usurpation. Consequently, a bill of rights was much less necessary in a republic.

Now Madison took the opposite tack. He acknowledged "the ingenuity of those arguments which were drawn against the Constitution, by a comparison with the policy of Great Britain." But he claimed that the differences were too great to make the comparison useful. In the British declaration of rights, Madison said, "the truth is, they have gone no farther, than to raise a barrier against the power of the crown; the power of the legislature is left altogether indefinite."[102] Nine months before, Madison had claimed that a bill of rights was useful only if it could inspire the majority. Now he was claiming that a bill of rights was useful only if it could *limit* the majority. "The greatest danger," he said, "is not found in either the executive or legislative departments of government, but in the body of the people, operating by the majority against the minority."[103]

This left the problem Madison had raised to Jefferson, namely that "paper barriers" might not limit the majority in practice. He now answered that a bill of rights might "establish the public opinion" in favor of rights, leading to greater respect by drawing "the attention of the whole community."[104] He went on to acknowledge the arguments that specifying particular rights might suggest that unmentioned ones belonged to the federal government and not the people. "This is one of the most plausible arguments I have ever heard against the admission of a bill of rights into this system," Madison confirmed.[105] But he had, he said, "guarded against" it with the statement that the enumerated rights "shall not be so construed as to diminish the just importance of other rights retained by the people." Such provisions, Madison further admitted, had sometimes been violated despite appearing in state constitutions. "But . . . they may have, to a certain degree, a salutary effect against the abuse of power."[106]

Here again Madison was working his way to a new argument. If the rights were "incorporated into the Constitution," the courts would enforce them:

> Independent tribunals of justice will consider themselves in a peculiar manner the guardians of those rights; they will be an impenetrable bulwark against every assumption of power in the legislative or executive; they will be naturally led to resist every encroachment upon rights expressly stipulated for in the Constitution by the declaration of rights.[107]

This was the first time Madison—or possibly anyone—had ever made the argument that a written bill of rights would transform judges into protectors of fundamental liberties. Far from being a commonplace, this view would not become part of constitutional orthodoxy for many years. State judges had no serious track record of enforcing fundamental rights against the will of majorities. Today, the idea that judges are the guardians of constitutional rights is the foundation stone of liberal constitutional thought around the world.

In the ratification debates, Madison had downplayed the power of the federal judiciary, and in the *Federalist* papers, Hamilton had described the federal judiciary as "the least dangerous branch," emphasizing the severe limits on its capacity to act. Here, to the contrary, Madison was asserting that the courts would "resist every encroachment upon rights expressly stipulated in the Constitution."[108]

He next explained why the bill of rights had "a great probability" of being enforced in a federal system. "The state legislatures," he predicted, "will jealously and closely watch the operations of this government, and be able to resist with more effect every assumption of power than any other power on earth can do." Even "the greatest opponents to a federal government," he pointed out, "admit the state legislatures to be sure guardians of the people's liberty."[109] Until this moment, Madison had always depicted the state legislatures' jealousy toward Congress as a bad thing. His research had taught him that confederations came apart because the component parts had too much authority.

Making a virtue of necessity, Madison was now arguing that the state legislatures had the incentive and the power to check the federal government—and that this power could solve what might be called the "parchment barriers" problem. It would be difficult for any one republican institution to limit the majority. The state legislatures, on the other hand, answered to their particular constituencies, not to the republic as a whole. That was precisely what made them jealous, and gave them the capacity to act.

Madison was using the Anti-Federalists' preference for state legislatures as a tool in favor of the Constitution. He still thought state legislatures were laboratories in which the tyranny of the majority might daily be observed. That was why his proposed bill of rights included new provisions that would control state legislatures.[110] His paean to the state legislatures as protection against federal usurpation was an argument of convenience. But it was also his best argument in favor of the bill of rights.

Kill the Opposition

As the summer progressed, Madison received messages of support for his proposed bill of rights from Federalist allies. Tench Coxe, author of a public essay supporting the amendments, wrote, "The most ardent and irritable among our friends are well pleased with them." The truth was, Coxe said, opponents had been "stripped of every rational, and most of the popular arguments they have heretofore used."[111]

An anonymous public letter addressed to Madison appeared in the New York *Daily Advertiser* denouncing all "paper declarations of rights" as "trifling things and no real security to liberty." Indeed, the author ("Pacificus") wrote, "In general they are subject of ridicule." A bill of rights, Pacificus mockingly observed, amounted to the statement that "We are all born free, and have a few particular rights which are dear to us and which we will not deprive ourselves, although we leave ourselves in full liberty to abridge any of our other rights." This, Pacificus concluded, "is a farce in government as novel as it is ludicrous."[112] Madison probably did not entirely disagree—but he had written the bill of rights to achieve a practical political goal, not a theoretical one. Through the negotiations at the Philadelphia convention, the ratification process, and now the efforts to pass the bill of rights, he had become steadily more and more pragmatic.

In the relatively brief formal congressional debates over the bill of rights, Madison stuck with this pragmatism. Thus, for example, he suggested interweaving the new proposed amendments into the text of the existing Constitution rather than keeping them separate as a bill of rights. He believed that interpretation would be easier if the provisions were integrated. Yet Madison was not insistent. "Form, sir, is always of less importance than the substance."[113] The main thing was to get the bill of rights passed in the current congressional session.

On the same theory of practical dispatch, Madison resisted the introduction of amendments he had not drafted. "I venture to say that if we confine ourselves to an enumeration of simple acknowledged principles," he told his colleagues, "the ratification will proceed with but little difficulty."[114] When other congressmen complained that the debate was moving too quickly, Madison replied that speed was not a problem because the people had spoken in favor of these rights already and would quickly consent to them. Introducing any other amendments would delay the process.[115]

In private correspondence, Madison demonstrated the same pragmatism. "If amendments had not been proposed from the federal side of the house," he told a friend, "the proposition would have come *within three days,* from the adverse side." Better for the amendments to "appear to be the free gift of the friends of the Constitution rather than to be extorted by the address and weight of its enemies." What was more, Madison added, a bill of rights "will kill the opposition everywhere." Failure to enact it would "revive the Anti-Federal cause, and . . . blow the trumpet for a second convention."[116]

There was one partial exception to Madison's repression of his theoretical impulses. When his amendment limiting the states was challenged in the House, Madison rose briefly to say that he "conceived this to be the most valuable amendment on the whole list." If it was necessary to restrain the federal government "from infringing upon these essential rights," he asserted, then it should be equally necessary to restrain the states.[117]

The argument was notably weak. The bill of rights was an attempt to assuage fears about the power of the federal government, not of the states. Only Madison thought the state legislatures more dangerous than Congress, because only he had theorized that a nationally elected Congress would be less oppressive than a local legislative body.

The House listened, and rejected the motion to drop the amendment. But in the Senate, Madison had no voice, and his unique amendment aimed to limit state legislation was dropped. This marked the final failure of the idea that had occupied Madison's mind since he was preparing for the Philadelphia convention—the idea that under the Constitution, the federal government should, in some way, be able to protect minorities against state legislatures. Although the idea would eventually become central to American constitutional thought, Madison could never convince his contemporaries of its value.

Madison complained to Edmund Pendleton that "the work" of addressing the amendments in Congress "has been extremely difficult and fatiguing," partly because of Anti-Federalists' "dilatory artifices" and partly because of "the diversity of opinions and fancies" in a body like Congress.[118] Yet in fact the "8 or 10 days" that the process took was remarkably short, especially compared with the Philadelphia convention. By the end of August, Madison could tell an ally that only a formal vote remained. The amendments would appear "by way of an appendix" to the Constitution rather than be incorporated. But this was "necessary, to the despatch if not the success of the business."[119] Congress would adjourn, he expected, by the end of September—and it would adjourn having adopted the bill of rights.

Without Madison, the bill of rights would not have been enacted.[120] He had delivered on his promise to his constituents. He had eliminated the remaining argument for the proposed second constitutional convention that he feared. And in the process, he had created what would eventually come to be the most influential list of basic rights and liberties in world history.

The entire episode showcased Madison's unique combination of theoretical brilliance and flexibility. Although theory had told him a bill of rights was not necessary, political controversy and the need to get elected had shown that it was. Once committed, Madison worked relentlessly to achieve the goal. He did not abandon his original theory; instead he amended it in the light of real-world consequences. The ten amendments to the original Constitution were also amendments to Madison's vision of

a design that would protect minorities through nothing but its own ingenious structure.

The Capital

Before Congress recessed, it had to address the location of the capital of
the United States, both its permanent home and the temporary home it
would occupy until the new one was built. These questions were politically linked—and intensely controversial. It was common consensus that
the permanent capital should be located on the banks of a major river
somewhere in the middle of the country. The leading candidates were the
Delaware River, the Susquehanna River, and the Potomac.

It was assumed by all that Pennsylvania had the upper hand in negotiations. It could ally itself with New York and do a deal in which the
temporary capital would remain in New York and the permanent capital
would be somewhere along the Susquehanna, perhaps even in Philadelphia. Alternatively, Pennsylvania could reach agreement with the southern states to put the permanent capital on the Potomac in exchange for
moving the temporary capital to Philadelphia. Then Pennsylvania could
gamble that Congress would never actually get around to building a permanent capital on the Potomac and that the capital would remain in
Philadelphia by default.[121]

Madison wanted the capital on the Potomac. Political and personal
motives converged for him. His Virginia constituents, many of whom
owned land to the west, strongly preferred the capital be close to Virginia
to orient the nation toward the growing regions of Ohio, Kentucky, and
the Mississippi. Madison had also invested in land on the Potomac River
near Great Falls, Virginia. This land would increase in value as canals
made the falls navigable—but it would increase far more if the capital was
situated along the Potomac.[122]

By September, Pennsylvania's congressional delegation had decided to
make common cause with New York to put the permanent capital in
Pennsylvania and leave the temporary capital in New York. Madison was
outraged. On September 3, 1789, he made four separate speeches against
the plan. He criticized the fact that the negotiation had taken place not
on the floor of Congress but "preconcerted out of doors." He demanded
to be shown that the permanent seat of government would be "at, or near
the center of wealth, population, and extensive territory."[123]

Madison also insisted that, contrary to the claims of others, the Potomac was better than the Susquehanna as a route to access "the western territory." For once, he had not prepared properly for the debate, and now, belatedly, he realized it: "I did not suppose," he said,

> it would have been necessary to bring forward charts and maps, as has been done by others, to show the committee the comparative situation of those rivers. I flattered myself it was sufficiently understood, to enable us to decide the question of superiority; but I am now inclined to believe, that gentlemen have embraced an error.

Madison pledged himself to prove "that the communication with the western territory, by the Potomac, is more certain and convenient than the other."[124] But with a vote impending, Madison needed more rhetorical tools. He told the Congress that while he had earlier praised the "moderation and liberality" that prevailed in Congress, he was now prepared to take it back. Had a "prophet" in the Virginia ratifying convention predicted "the declarations and proceedings of this day," Madison said, Virginia might not have ratified the Constitution.

The next day, September 4, 1789, Madison begged for more time. He made two speeches, one extremely long, urging his colleagues to consider principled arguments rather than rely on political compromise. He emphasized the old worry "that no free government can exist" in a country "within so great a space." The solution to the problem, he said, was "to place the government in that spot which will be least removed from every part of the empire."[125] On its own terms, this was a reasonable argument for a centralized location relative to western expansion. But the debate over the location of the capital was not really a matter of principle. It was a matter of who would get a valuable good.

On September 21, with the end of the session rapidly approaching, the House of Representatives stood poised to vote for the Susquehanna site. Madison now tried to convince his colleagues that there was a constitutional reason not to pass the bill as drafted. He insisted that it was solely up to the two houses of Congress to choose where they might wish to convene at any given moment. This power belonged exclusively to Congress, he insisted, and so it was inappropriate for a law signed by the president to specify where Congress would meet. Thus the bill was "irreconcilable with the spirit of the Constitution" and should be opposed.[126] No one cared, and the bill in favor of the Susquehanna passed the House.

All was not yet lost, and Madison turned to the Senate for a last-ditch effort to block the deal between Pennsylvania and New York. He told Edmund Pendleton that if the bill could not be voted down, it might be possible to substitute a different location for the proposed Susquehanna location in the Senate bill.[127] This was in fact what happened. The Senate amended the House's bill to specify that the capital would be in German-town, an area adjoining Philadelphia. When the bill came back to the House, Madison insisted that the amendment "deserves the name of a new bill" and must "proceed on principles different from those which serve the basis of the bills sent up to them from this House." He de-manded that there be an opportunity for public attention to the new pro-posal and moved for adjournment.[128] This final parliamentary maneuver worked. The House adjourned without approving the Senate bill. Madi-son had averted, for the moment, a permanent capital in Pennsylvania.[129]

Cabinets

Before Congress adjourned, Washington hoped to choose the members of his first cabinet. Madison's alliance with the president ensured that his friends took prominent positions. Edmund Randolph had written to Madison in July asking for an appointment in the new government. In the letter, Randolph hoped that his friends would recognize the "consis-tency" and "above all things" the "purity" of his conduct in regard to the drafting and ratification of the Constitution. Others, he fretted, "insinu-ated (and in defiance of truth)" that his behavior had "alienated" even al-lies of the Constitution from him.[130]

Madison remained loyal to Randolph, as he had despite Randolph's insistence on calling for a second constitutional convention. Randolph needed money to pay for medical treatment that he believed his wife needed—they feared briefly that she might have cancer—and to pay per-sonal debts. He told Madison that renewing his private legal career could not earn enough money to cover these requirements.[131] Madison appar-ently went to Washington and advocated for Randolph.

On September 28, 1789, Washington wrote to Randolph offering him the position of attorney general. Washington specifically told him that the salary would be such as to "confer preeminence on its possessor," evidence that Madison had told Washington that Randolph needed money.[132] Randolph was qualified for the job. But he got it because of Madison's friendship and support.

Alexander Hamilton was confirmed as the first secretary of the treasury in September. He had his own close relationship with Washington going back to the Revolutionary War and a substantial knowledge of the New York financial world. Hamilton did not need Madison's recommendation to get the position. Yet he too was Madison's friend and ally.

Almost as soon as Hamilton took office, he wrote to Madison about the best way to increase revenue and the possibility of some "modifications to the public debt" that might be possible "consistent with good faith, the interest of the public and of its creditors." Hamilton acknowledged that with regard to revenue, "the question is very much what further taxes will be *least* unpopular." With respect to what could be done about the federal debt, Hamilton did not elaborate. Both men knew that the questions of debt and credit would be among the most important that the republic would face under the new Constitution.

The collegial tone of the letter reflected the closeness that had developed between the two during the writing of the *Federalist* essays and deepened during the final push for ratification. Hamilton wrote familiarly to Madison, speaking of "your friendship" and signing, "Adieu, my dear sir. Your affectionate and obedient Alexander Hamilton."[133] They had yet to disagree on any major question of policy. But Hamilton realized that they might not see eye to eye about a possible "modification" of debts.

Madison wrote back to Hamilton proposing taxes on home distilleries and an increase in the duty on imported "spirituous liquors." He also recommended that the federal government institute "a land tax" before the states started to do so themselves, and proposed to tax all "proceedings in the federal courts." On the debt, Madison said cautiously it was "a subject on which I ought perhaps to be silent, having not enough revolved it to form any precise ideas." But he ventured to suggest that America's foreign debt should be refinanced at a lower interest rate, and that western lands should be used in part to redeem the domestic debt.[134]

Then Madison turned to the more delicate matter of whether the United States should try to retire its domestic debt altogether. He told Hamilton that he considered it "very desirable" to "put the debt in a manifest course of extinguishment." He understood, Madison continued, that there were "respectable opinions in favor of prolonging if not perpetuating it." This, in fact, was Hamilton's view, and Madison surely knew it. He was gently explaining to Hamilton that, in the United States at least, there were special reasons to make the debt go away altogether.

One was public opinion against debt. Dislike of debt meant, Madison predicted, that the public would prefer higher tax burdens that eliminated the debt over lower tax burdens that perpetuated it. Madison's second reason was that he expected any federal debt to "slide into the hands of foreigners." Foreigners "have more money than the Americans, and less productive ways of laying it out." As a result, "they can and will generally buy out the Americans." Madison did not want the majority of U.S. debt to be held by foreign hands.[135] He signed the letter "With affectionate regards I am, my dear sir, your friend and servant, James Madison, Jr."

Henry Knox, Washington's secretary of war, was the only member of the first cabinet who was not a good friend of Madison's. Knox, a Bostonian by birth, had served with Washington and Hamilton in the early days of the war. He had consolidated his position as one of Washington's closest advisers by planning the famous operation in which Ethan Allen and his Green Mountain Boys dragged British cannon two hundred miles from Fort Ticonderoga to the outskirts of Boston, ending the British siege of the city. Knox and Madison had corresponded about Shays's Rebellion in the run-up to the Philadelphia convention, and he had been a strong supporter of ratification.

Madison was closest to the new secretary of state: Thomas Jefferson, recalled from France for the job. For the past several years, Jefferson had observed firsthand the building tensions between the king, the nobles, and the French populace. In the summer of 1789, he had been present in Paris when the French Revolution broke out. On July 22, Jefferson had written to Madison describing the storming of the Bastille, the first beheadings, the appointment of the Marquis de Lafayette by a committee as commander-in-chief, and other "such events as will forever be memorable in history."

Jefferson was enthusiastic about the course the French Revolution seemed to be taking. The similarities to the American Revolution— including the popular committees of safety—struck him as meaningful. The participation of Lafayette further brought home the parallel. Jefferson told Madison that he wished Adams, with his love of governing elites, could have been there to see it. "If he could then have had one fiber of aristocracy left in his frame he would have been a proper subject for bed-lam," Jefferson wrote.[136] No sane person, Jefferson believed, could have favored aristocracy in the face of such misjudgment by the nobles and manly revolutionary behavior by the public.

Jefferson expected the National Assembly that had called itself into existence to draft its own constitution, and conveyed the details to Madison with respectful interest. He told Madison that "the leading members (with some small differences of opinion)" intended the executive power to rest with a hereditary monarch "with a negative on laws and power to dissolve the legislature." There would be a house of representatives as well as a senate "chosen on the plan of our federal senate by provincial assemblies."[137]

As Jefferson explained it to Madison, the imitation of the United States was no accident. "It is impossible to desire better dispositions towards us, than prevail in this assembly," he wrote. "Our proceedings have been viewed as a model for them on every occasion." The authority of the American example "has been treated like that of the Bible, open to explanation but not to question."[138]

Jefferson then derived a political conclusion, one congenial to Madison: The United States should not adopt trade policies that put friendly France and contemptuous Britain on the same "footing." The man who was about to become secretary of state explained his attitude toward France and England:

Of two nations, one has engaged herself in a ruinous war for us, has spent her blood and money to save us, has opened her bosom to us in peace, and received us almost on the footing of her own citizens, while the other has moved heaven, earth and hell to exterminate us in war, has insulted us in all her councils and peace, shuttered doors to us in every part where her interests would admit it, libeled us in foreign nations, [and] endeavored to poison them against the reception of our most precious commodities.[139]

In the light of these differences, it would be immoral to treat England and France the same. Jefferson rejected as old-fashioned and unenlight-ened the view "that gratitude is never to enter into the motives of national conduct." Such an idea was kindred to "the lawfulness of assassination, poison, perjury etc." Those ideas were "legitimate principles in the dark ages . . . but exploded and held in just horror in the 18th century." Jefferson insisted, "I know but one code of morality for men whether acting singly or collectively." The same gratitude that would be appropriate for an individual must apply to the conduct of the nation taken as a whole.[140] With this embrace of France on the grounds of gratitude, and outright dismissal of realpolitik, Jefferson intended to shape the foreign policy of the United States.

An Experiment

The Bill of Rights drafted, it was time for Madison to go home. He hoped to meet Jefferson in New York or Philadelphia on his arrival. Madison therefore went to Philadelphia and waited for several weeks in the hopes of seeing him.[141]

While Madison was in Philadelphia, his attention was drawn to the most important national problem that the Constitution had not resolved: slavery. Staying as usual with Mrs. House, Madison met William Thornton, a British physician of Quaker origin who had moved to the United States a couple of years before. Thornton was connected with a London organization called the Committee for Relief of the Black Poor, founded in 1786 by a group of antislavery activists and supported by donations from fashionable aristocrats. The organization distributed charity to poor people of East Indian and African origin in London. At least some had been enslaved in America and had come to Britain as Loyalists during and after the Revolutionary War.[142]

The Committee for the Relief of the Black Poor had, however, a more ambitious goal than charity. Its members aimed to create a colony in Sierra Leone where London Africans could settle in exchange for a grant of British citizenship and protection by the Royal Navy. In 1787, a group of almost four hundred had traveled to Sierra Leone in three ships. Thornton discussed the affair with Philadelphia Quaker supporters of the abolition of slavery, who were in general sympathetic—and he discussed the matter with Madison as well.

To Madison, the idea of creating "a settlement of freed blacks on the coast of Africa" seemed inspired. Presumably at Thornton's behest, Madison wrote a memorandum of his thoughts on the subject for Thornton to send to other abolitionists. Madison did not address the "practicability or the most proper means" of resettlement. But he made the point that "if such an asylum was provided, it might prove a great encouragement to manumission in the southern parts of the United States." What is more, such an asylum might "even afford the best hope yet presented of putting an end to the slavery in which not less than 600,000 unhappy Negroes are now involved."[143]

Madison went on to explain that laws in the southern states presently allowed masters to free their slaves. But he feared those laws might be changed because of "the effects suffered from freedmen who retain the vices and habits of slaves." Indeed, Madison asserted, "the same consideration" affected "many humane masters" who might otherwise free their slaves: "It is found in fact," he claimed, "that neither the good of the society, nor the happiness of the individuals restored to freedom is promoted by such a change in their condition."[144]

For manumission to benefit both society and former slaves, Madison argued, "it would be necessary" to achieve "a complete incorporation" of former slaves into society. But such integration was "rendered impossible by the prejudices of the whites." Such biases, "proceeding principally from the difference of color . . . must be considered as permanent and insuperable."[145] Madison was careful to say that the barrier to integration was white race prejudice, not African inferiority. Yet he apparently gave no thought to the possibility of changing the "permanent and insuperable" prejudice. Instead some other solution was necessary.

Madison dismissed the option of resettling freed slaves in the American interior. If settlements were created "at a considerable distance from the white frontier," they would be destroyed by "the savages who have a peculiar antipathy to the blacks." If, however, freed slaves were to live near white settlements, "peace would not long be expected to remain." The societies would be "distinguished" by racial difference, and both sides would retain "the feelings inspired by their former relation of oppressors and oppressed."[146]

That left Africa or "some other foreign situation." Madison concluded by favoring "an experiment" of creating a settlement that "might induce the humanity of masters" to manumission, "and by degrees both the humanity and policy of the governments, to forward the abolition of slavery in America."[147] Manumission was the short-term goal. Abolition was a goal for the longer term, to be encouraged "by degrees."

Neither Madison nor Thornton made the letter public, although Thornton did send it to the president of a French organization devoted to abolition. It is unlikely that Madison was concerned about being thought hypocritical for favoring abolition. Hypocrisy was normalized, at least with respect to slaveholding. Thornton himself had been born to a slaveholding family in Tortola, and still owned some seventy slaves on a sugar plantation there. But as a representative of Virginia, Madison could not have expressed abolitionist views in public without political consequences. He would not do so until he was an old man, many years retired from public life.

Having written the Bill of Rights that he had initially deemed unnecessary, Madison was emerging as an increasingly adept, realistic politician. He possessed strong convictions, including those he held on the value of eventual abolition. But he was beginning to understand which views had to be kept private and which could be put in the service of the greater public good. And he was learning how to shape and respond to public opinion. The skill would be increasingly necessary in the difficult years that lay ahead.

CHAPTER EIGHT

Debts

...

THE ARGUMENT: *Jefferson's return from revolutionary France occasions a debate with Madison over whether a society may justly bind future generations to debt or a constitution. Madison's forceful "Yes" to both reflects not only the difference between the two friends, but also the closely related difference between their characters: Jefferson favors quick action and radical principles; Madison values slowness and caution.*

Back in Congress in 1790, Madison confronts Hamilton's three-part plan to shape the U.S. economy and financial system. The men, friends since the Federalist, *begin to diverge. Hamilton considers debt a "national blessing"; Madison considers it a "public evil."*

As differences grow, Madison's friends begin to distrust Hamilton's power. Fatefully, Madison argues that the bank is not merely wrong but unconstitutional. He thus initiates what will become a repeated practice of claiming that political enemies are bent on subverting the basic principles of the Constitution.

MADISON SPENT NOVEMBER AND DECEMBER of 1789 at home at Montpelier taking a well-deserved break from work. Over the course of the past three years, he had, in essence, invented the Constitution. He had been the first person to theorize the vices of the confederation and the need for something new. He had brought delegates to Annapolis and then to Philadelphia, drafted the Virginia plan, and accepted compromise. He had justified the Constitution in the *Federalist* and led the fight for ratification. Finally, reversing his earlier position, he had drafted the bill of rights, which Congress had now sent to the states. In terms of creativity and impact, these accomplishments were and remain unmatched in the history of constitutions. In the history of ideas and of statesmanship, they have few equals, either.

Yet despite Madison's achievements, the debate in the Virginia House of Delegates over the bill of rights did not go as smoothly as he would have liked. After the assembly ratified the first ten proposed amendments,* Edmund Randolph, astonishingly, led the charge against the last two amendments that Madison had proposed and Congress had sent to the states for ratification. These amendments specified that the enumeration of rights in the Constitution "shall not be construed to deny or disparage others retained by the people," and added that powers not delegated to the federal government nor prohibited to the states "are reserved to the states respectively, or to the people."

Randolph objected to the word "retained." He argued that the provisions should prohibit Congress from extending its own powers rather than protecting unspecified rights retained by the people. As Madison told George Washington, he could not see "the force of the distinction," which appeared "altogether fanciful." Protecting retained rights was in practical terms no different from restricting Congress from acting.[1]

Once again, Randolph was demonstrating his incredible capacity to waffle for political advantage. On the one hand, he wanted to support the bill of rights. On the other, he wanted to assert that the bill of rights did not go far enough. To occupy the middle political ground, Randolph was opposing Madison based on a very small, almost arbitrary point of difference. It was as if he wanted to create distance between himself and his friend—regardless of the political costs to Madison.

With an exercise of self-restraint that must have taken real effort, Madison wrote to Washington, "The difficulty started against the amendments is really unlucky, and more to be regretted as it springs from a friend to the Constitution." On Madison's recommendation, Washington had just offered Randolph the job of attorney general. As he had during the initial Virginia ratification struggle, Madison was trying to preserve his friendship with Randolph despite the latter's efforts to drive a wedge between them.

Randolph's opposition could have had serious consequences had it encouraged the Virginia assembly to call for further amendments. This would have reopened the possibility of a second constitutional conven-

---

* These were what would become today's First through Eighth amendments, plus the change in the ratio of representation and the limitation on Congress's ability to raise its salary until elections have taken place, today the Twenty-Seventh Amendment.

tion, precisely the result that Madison had drafted the Bill of Rights to avoid.

The real source of opposition to the Constitution, Madison argued to Washington, was still Congress's power of direct taxation. Opponents who wanted the power taken away believed that Congress itself would never propose an amendment to reduce its authority. So long as Madison had influence in Congress, they were entirely correct. Thus, Madison concluded, even if Randolph's technical distinction were plausible, "it does not seem to be of sufficient importance to justify the risk of losing the amendments, of furnishing a handle to the disaffected, and of arming North Carolina with a pretext, if it should be disposed, to prolong her exile from the union."[2]

Fortunately, the House of Delegates ultimately rejected Randolph's position and agreed to ratify the whole slate of amendments. But the Virginia Senate refused, relying in part on Randolph's arguments. The session closed with the Bill of Rights unratified in Virginia.[3] Madison, delayed at Montpelier for "8 or 10 days" when his mother became seriously ill, left Virginia in late December with his own state having refused to ratify the bill of rights he had drafted to satisfy his own constituents.[4]

Before he left Virginia, Madison rode the thirty miles to Monticello to see Jefferson. He discovered that Jefferson was unenthusiastic about becoming secretary of state. The trouble was not the prospect of engaging with foreign affairs, which Jefferson enjoyed. It was that Jefferson had no appetite for the domestic, administrative aspects of the job, which included promulgating laws and distributing commissions to executive appointees. Madison assured him that "the domestic part will be very trifling." He wrote to Washington that "if the whole business can be executed by any one man, Mr. Jefferson must be equal to it." And he predicted that Jefferson would ultimately accept, which, in fact, he did, even after Washington gave him the choice to remain ambassador to France.[5]

Madison set off for New York and the new term of Congress. His journey was delayed in Georgetown, Maryland, with an attack of "pretty severe dysentery," a malady that occasioned no embarrassment and which Madison reported to Washington, to his father, and to Thomas Jefferson.[6] He was treated by Dr. David Stuart, a former colleague in the Virginia assembly and ally at the Virginia ratifying convention, who saw him daily for a week until he was well enough to travel. At length he reached New York and took his seat in Congress on January 20, 1790.

The first person Madison saw on arrival was Alexander Hamilton, who came to meet him at his boardinghouse.[7] The secretary of the treasury already had well-developed private views on how to address the debt situation. He was emphasizing his friendship with Madison and asking for advice in the hope of winning Madison over before he introduced his plan in Congress.

Usufruct

Soon after arriving in New York, Madison received a letter from Jefferson that was radical even by Jefferson's standards. It had been written the previous September in Paris, and Jefferson had brought it home with him rather than sending it. He mentioned it to Madison when they were together in Monticello, but "forgot" to give it to him and so sent it on to New York. The double delay suggested that Jefferson had some trepidation about the ideas in the letter. But he wrote to Madison that after the letter "lying so long by me, and further turning the subject in my mind, I find no occasion to alter my mind." With that resolve he mailed it on January 9, 1790, and it reached Madison at the beginning of February.[8]

The letter went back to the opening days of the French Revolution, which had put Jefferson in mind of the question "whether one generation of men has a right to bind another." His answer was no. In his uniquely confident prose, Jefferson asserted that it was "self-evident, *'that the earth belongs in usufruct to the living':* that the dead have neither powers nor rights over it."[9]

The argument depended on the distinction between natural rights and those created by the laws of society. As a matter of natural right, Jefferson claimed, no child could be obligated to pay his father's debts—only the laws of society could require that. Otherwise, the father might amass more debt than could be paid off in his lifetime, thus "in effect" controlling the use of the lands "for several generations to come." If this were allowed, "then the lands would belong to the dead, and not to the living, which would be the reverse of our principle."[10]

There were serious difficulties with Jefferson's reasoning, most particularly his claim to know what was naturally right. If the premise was self-evident, however, Jefferson did not need to defend it—a lesson he had learned in composing the Declaration of Independence. From the premise, Jefferson went on to argue that "no generation can contract debts greater than may be paid during the course of its own existence."[11]

Of course, existing laws of actual countries allowed debts to be passed down by individuals and governments, the same as wealth. Still, Jefferson was expressing the hope that, "in the constitution they are forming," the revolutionary French would specify that "neither the legislature, nor the nation itself, can validly contract more debt than they may pay within their own age, or within the term of nineteen years"—the length of a generation.[12]

Jefferson went on to insist that "on similar ground it may be proved that no society can make a perpetual constitution, or even a perpetual law. The earth belongs always to the living generation." This logic brought him to a startling view: "Every constitution then, and every law, naturally expires at the end of 19 years. If it be enforced longer, it is an act of force, and not of right."[13]

Jefferson loved to state political principles in the most extreme way possible—especially to Madison—so he may actually have believed what he was writing. This was, after all, the same Jefferson who had a couple of years earlier told Madison that occasional rebellions were good for the spirit of liberty. And in France, with the revolution still young, Jefferson was seeing his ideals brought to fruition.

Jefferson urged Madison to take his excursus on obligation and run with it. "Turn this subject in your mind, my dear sir," he wrote, "and particularly as to the power of contracting debts; and develop it with that perspicuity and cogent logic so peculiarly yours." In Jefferson's presentation, which was at once complimentary and very slightly insulting, he would provide the grand principles—which would transform society, property, and government—and Madison would figure out the details. The relationship between the Declaration and the Constitution was not far in the background.

In Jefferson's fantasy, Madison would provide practical political implementation, by introducing Jefferson's ideas into the congressional debate about the future of the national debt.[14] The United States was well placed to carry out the plan because "we do not owe a shilling which may not be paid with ease, principal and interest, within the time of our own lives."[15]

On receiving the letter Madison at once recognized the importance of the ideas—and set out to refute them. He cared enough to produce two drafts of his response, the second of which he sent to Jefferson on February 4, 1790. Having just designed a constitution that he hoped would last forever, Madison could not possibly have agreed that no legal undertaking could last more than a generation.

Madison began by telling Jefferson that the "idea" of his letter "is a great one, and suggests many interesting reflections to legislators; particularly when contracting and providing for public debts."[16] Having praised his friend, Madison rebuffed him. "However applicable in theory the doctrine may be to a constitution, it seems liable in practice to some weighty objections." A constitution that dissolved every nineteen years would create an "interregnum" during which "all the rights depending on positive laws, that is most of the rights of property would become absolutely defunct."[17] If property rights were to be radically readjusted on a periodic basis, "the most violent struggles [would] ensue" between those who wanted to change the property regime and those who wanted to keep it. Jefferson's plan would create "pernicious factions" and lead to "anarchy."[18] A government that changed so frequently would lose the legitimacy acquired through familiarity and use and would never gain public "prejudice in its favor."[19]

Not content to dismiss Jefferson's suggestions as impractical, Madison rejected Jefferson's theory in principle. Echoing the preamble to the Constitution, Madison continued: "Debts may . . . be incurred principally for the benefit of posterity," like the debts accumulated by the United States in fighting the Revolutionary War.[20] These debts had been taken on for the good of future generations—and should be repaid by those who benefited.[21]

Madison then offered his account of how a constitution could bind generations unborn when it was ratified. He endorsed "the received doctrine that a *tacit* assent may be given to established governments and laws, and that this assent is to be inferred from the omission of an express revocation."[22] Following the reasoning of David Hume, Madison understood that the later generations' implied consent to the Constitution was a kind of fiction.[23] But he could see no way to "exclude wholly the idea of implied or tacit assent, without subverting the very foundation of civil society."[24]

These were deep waters, but Madison did not hesitate to wade into them. Majority rule was a convenience, not an immutable law of nature.

To justify majority rule, one had to accept that everyone embraced the principle of majoritarianism. The only way to get to such a conclusion was by a heroic, fictional assumption of implied consent. Jefferson's letter unsettled the assumption of consent—and thereby upset the apple cart of republicanism.

A half a century before, Hume had argued that the doctrine of tacit consent was unnecessary because, as a practical matter, society could not exist if people did not keep their promises and follow the law.[25] But unlike Hume, Madison had just participated in the most notable episode of self-conscious collective contract-making known to the modern world. The Revolution had been one kind of exercise of the dissolution and re-creation of an original political contract. The drafting and ratification of the Constitution had been more deliberative, more inclusive, and much more formalized. In writing and ratifying the Constitution, Americans had acted as though they actually did have the choice of consenting to the form of the new government. Having to an important degree dreamt up the entire process and participated centrally in it, Madison could not drop the idea of consent altogether.

Madison ended his response to Jefferson by reassuring him as to "the utility of the principle as applied to the cases you have particularly in view," namely the national debt, and as to "the general importance of [Jefferson's principle] in the eye of the philosophical legislator." Madison said that he would derive "singular pleasure to see it first announced to the world in a law of the United States," as Jefferson had proposed.[26]

But having politely acknowledged Jefferson's idea so far as he could, Madison could not resist saying it would have no takers: "This is a pleasure however of which I have no hope of enjoying," he told Jefferson. Congress was not a body of philosophers. "The spirit of philosophical legislation has not prevailed at all in some parts of America, and is by no means the fashion of this part, or of the present representative body."

The problem America had faced thus far was "weakness in government and licentiousness in the people." Consequently, the people's efforts were focused on "strengthening the powers" of government, not "narrowing their extent."[27] Pointedly, Madison was telling Jefferson that this was no time for philosophy. The country needed more and more effective government, not less. With the passage of the Constitution, the era of the ordinary politician had begun.

A National Blessing, a Public Evil

The most pressing issue facing Congress was debt. Alexander Hamilton had produced an ambitious report on public credit, intended as a blueprint for the financial architecture for the United States. In it, the new secretary of the treasury argued for paying off the debts contracted during the Revolutionary War and since.

Hamilton's argument was altogether different from the speculation about natural right that had passed between Jefferson and Madison. Hamilton reasoned that paying off the debt would increase the standing and credit of the United States. Good credit would allow the government to borrow more money at reasonable interest rates. In short, Hamilton argued that the United States should pay existing debts in order to borrow more.[28]

The benefits of a stable, ongoing public debt, Hamilton believed, would be enormous. "It is a well known fact," he wrote in his report, "that in countries in which the national debt is properly funded, and an object of established confidence, it answers most of the purposes of money."[29] The American economy was starved for cash. If bonds issued by the United States were likely to be paid, they would become stable in value. They would then circulate like cash, injecting liquidity into the economy. There would be, Hamilton explained, more capital available for trade, agriculture, and manufacturing. Interest rates would go down, because there would be more money to be had. Property values, which had fallen between 25 and 50 percent since the Revolution, would rebound.[30]

Hamilton wanted to align the interests of the financial markets with the interests of the United States. The best way to do that was to encourage potential investors to become holders of U.S. debt. "This," Hamilton concluded, was "the true secret for rendering public credit immortal."[31] Ultimately, Hamilton concluded, "the proper funding of the present debt . . . will render it a national blessing," provided that it "always be accompanied with the means of extinguishment," namely the collection of revenue to pay the debt.

Hamilton's idea of "the good effects of a public debt"[32] contrasted markedly with the beliefs of Madison's circle of friends. As Benjamin Rush, a Philadelphia ally of Madison's, put it to him, "It is amusing to hear gentlemen talk of the 'public blessing' of a debt contracted to foreigners and a few American speculators of four or five millions of dollars a year."[33] Rush believed that such a debt would be "fundamentally *unjust*," and would "lay the foundation of an aristocracy in our country" through the creation of a capitalist class. By rewarding the investment of capital instead of labor, a national debt would be "a lasting monument of the efficacy of idleness, speculation, and fraud above industry, economy, and integrity in obtaining wealth and independence."[34] To republican critics, Hamilton's idea amounted to a transfer of power from hardworking people to the speculators who invested in markets in the first place.

Henry Lee warned Madison that "national debt will be encouraged by wanton expeditions, wars and useless expenses." Worse, he argued, "Funding systems belong to arbitrary governments; they are not congenial to the true spirit of general, common freedom—they are an excellent means to change the latter into the former." Great Britain was a perfect example. Britain's debt, contracted to fund foreign wars, drove it to a system of "unbounded commerce" that ultimately "must terminate in national bankruptcy."[35]

These worries derived from a republican tradition that closely associated national debt with war making. Rush summed it up in a simple catechism about Hamilton's plan:

After all the encomiums upon it—what is it? An ability to borrow money. But for what? Only for the purpose of carrying on unjust offensive wars—for where wars are just and necessary, supplies may always be obtained by annual taxes from free people.[36]

Any war that was really necessary would also be popular, and could therefore be supported by popular taxes. Congress, Rush said, "appear as if they were legislating for British subjects, and for a nation whose whole business was to be, *War*."[37] It would not have mollified Rush or Lee to know that Hamilton considered Great Britain the ideal financial model for the United States.

In Congress, the first debate about Hamilton's plan focused on how the United States should pay off its existing domestic debt holders. After the Revolution, the government had not paid back its debts in gold or silver at 6 percent interest, as it had initially promised to do. Instead, the government had forced debt holders to accept paper obligations— essentially IOUs. The paper, never worth anything close to face value, had plummeted since, selling for as little as fifteen cents on the dollar. Naturally, many debt holders had sold their paper, because they either needed money immediately or did not trust that the debts would eventually be paid in full. As a result, a good part of the $54 million in national debt and $25 million of state debt—no one knew exactly how much—lay in the hands of speculators.

To pay off the debts at one hundred cents to the dollar would give these speculators a huge windfall—profits on the order of 700 or 800 percent. Inevitably, the public objected strongly to this outcome, which smacked of unjust enrichment. In newspapers and elsewhere, it was argued that the original debt holders should be paid back the full value of the loans plus interest. But there should be "discrimination," or distinction, made between original bondholders and those who had bought the bonds in the secondary market. The speculators, it was suggested, should be paid only what they had actually paid for the instruments plus interest.

In his report, Hamilton rejected this idea outright. Distinguishing between original holders and subsequent purchasers would be "unjust and impolitic . . . highly injurious, even to the original holders of public securities; [and] ruinous to public credit." The bond was a contract between the government and whoever held the bond. It would violate the government's contractual obligations not to pay them off at full value. Discrimination would cast doubt on the transferability of future bond issues and hence decrease their worth.

Hamilton went further, arguing that discrimination would actually be unconstitutional. The Constitution provided that "all debts contracted and engagements entered into, before the adoption of this Constitution, shall be as valid against the United States under this Constitution, as under the confederation." That provision, Hamilton argued, required the new government to honor the federal debt at full value.[38]

Madison disagreed. In a series of speeches before Congress in February, he introduced a compromise. Original debt holders should be paid what they were owed when they sold off their debt. Subsequent purchasers of the bonds should all be paid at the highest price for which the bonds had ever sold in the secondary market. The money saved by not paying the current debt holders the full face value of the bonds should be used to compensate the original debt holders who had sold off their paper.[39]

Madison acknowledged that his proposal might be perceived as impractical. But the identity of the original purchasers of the debt should appear on the public books, he reasoned, and so could be ascertained. More important, although his approach "will not do perfect justice . . . it will do more real justice, and perform more of the public faith, than any other expedient proposed." The current bondholders would make "a profit that cannot reasonably be complained of."[40]

Madison's compromise was meant to be practical as well as moral. He insisted that public credit would not suffer, "especially abroad," because the country would continue to make its interest payments. He further argued that future debt issues would not be affected by the precedent, because "all future loans will be founded on a previous establishment of adequate funds." It would be "impossible," therefore, for the situation to recur. Thus, Madison concluded, "I cannot but regard the present case as so extraordinary, in many respects, that the ordinary maxims are not strictly applicable to it."[41]

Madison held out for the better part of a month, and his proposal was, he was later to learn, popular in at least some parts of Virginia.[42] But ultimately, he was defeated by a large majority in Congress. As Hamilton had planned, the bond market would get what it wanted—full payment of one hundred cents on the dollar, and windfall profits for speculators.

The Class Who Takes Their Places

Madison was unusually troubled by the fight he had lost. This did not feel like an ordinary policy disagreement, but something more profound, more connected to fundamental questions of justice. "It seems indeed scarcely possible for me ever to be persuaded," he wrote to Benjamin Rush, "that there is not something radically immoral, and consequently impolitic," in the wealth transfer to the speculators. The "rewards due for . . . the defense of liberty" had passed from "the gallant earners" to "that class of people who now take their places."[43] Republican bravery was being replaced by financial speculation. The political system was allocating wealth to capitalists, in accordance with their wishes and lobbying efforts.

A basic difference between Madison's worldview and Hamilton's was emerging. For the secretary of the treasury, finance was solely a tool to achieve utilitarian economic ends, and respecting the market's outcome was the best way to get results. Madison cared about practical consequences. But his view of the market was tinged with moral judgment that he could not and did not want to escape.

Congress now moved on to a further recommendation of Hamilton's report: that the federal government should assume and pay off all remaining *state* debts. Hamilton offered various justifications for the provision, but the essence was that it made no economic sense for individual states to develop new tax systems to pay off what they individually owed. Congress should do the job, because the Constitution required that duties and excises be "uniform throughout the United States," Hamilton emphasized.[44]

Hamilton's approach was meant to strengthen the central government. Assuming responsibility for state debt would both require and enable the federal government to raise taxes and generate revenue. This, in turn, would give the federal government the funds to undertake important projects—and strip that ability from the states.

Hamilton offered another rationale: He wanted all the holders of government bonds to be allied in a common interest.[45] If some bondholders held state bonds and others federal ones, their interests might diverge, he explained: "There will be distinct interests, drawing different ways." The goal was to produce "that union and concert of views among the creditors, which in every government is of great importance to their security and to that of public credit."[46]

Over the previous three years, Madison and Hamilton had made thoughtful and sophisticated arguments about the structure of government and its relation to the interests of different parts of society. Hamilton was going further, openly acknowledging a close link between the structure of government and the structure of public finance. Once state and federal debts were paid, new debt would be issued, and its holders would form a powerful interest group to assure that the government raised enough revenue to pay them. The assumption of state debt was therefore a crucial part of Hamilton's overall plan, comparable in importance to paying off federal creditors in full.

Once again, Madison proposed a variation on Hamilton's plan. He supported the federal assumption of state debts on the condition that the federal government reimburse states that had already paid off their war debts. It was widely believed that Virginia had done so. Madison wrote, "My idea is, that instead of considering the debts as they are found at this moment, we contemplate them as in the state they existed at the close of the late war." This would give the plan the "appearance of equality and liberality" and reconcile Virginia.[47]

Hamilton's supporters objected to Madison's proposal. Acting defensively, Madison suggested that Congress task Hamilton with examining in detail the affordability of assuming state debts before voting unconditionally for assumption.[48] The maneuver succeeded. Hamilton reported back to the House on March 4, and on March 9, the House adopted Madison's amendment to the plan for federal assumption of state debts, according to which states would be credited for their efforts to pay off their war debts.[49]

Madison believed that he had "succeeded in part" but that the result remained "very doubtful."[50] A week later, on March 21, Madison wrote to Edmund Randolph, "The assumption will, I think, ultimately be defeated." As he explained it, "Besides the host of objections against the propriety of the measure in its present form, its practicability becomes less and less evident."[51] Sure enough, on April 12, Congress rejected the assumption of state debts by the narrow vote of 31 to 29.[52]

In theory, Madison still believed that assumption of state debts would be desirable if it could be done fairly. In practice, however, Madison was becoming an opponent of assumption, the position that Hamilton's supporters had attributed to him all along. On April 22, Madison gave a lengthy speech on the topic in the House, praising assumption faintly as "under certain aspects, a measure not unworthy of favorable attention." If it were not so, he said respectfully, "I am sure it would not have originated in the quarter which proposed it," namely Hamilton. But, Madison said, "the arguments used in favor of the measure" were "unsupported."[53] Specifically, Madison asserted that the state debts were "the debts of the particular states," not the debts of the United States. He argued that the northern states, which had paid off the least of their debts, would in effect gain a windfall if assumption were to occur.

This much Madison had said before, but now he went further. "If the public debt is a public evil," he argued, "an assumption of the state debts will enormously increase, and, perhaps, perpetuate it."[54] The words "public evil" directly denied Hamilton's description of a funded public debt as "a national blessing." Madison's statement that assumption might "perpetuate" the debt was equally intended to counter Hamilton's boast that a properly funded debt would be "immortal."

Madison ended by rejecting Hamilton's argument that assuming state debts "would add strength to the national government"[55]:

> There is no man more anxious for the success of the government than I am, and no one who will join more heartily in curing its defects; but I wish the defects to be remedied by additional constitutional powers, should they become necessary. This is the only proper, effectual, and permanent remedy.[56]

The comment revealed a divergence between Madison and Hamilton that went deeper even than their disagreement about whether a national debt was a curse or a blessing. Madison believed that constitutional design was the single legitimate way to strengthen the national government. That was why he had devoted himself to the design, drafting, ratification, and amendment of the Constitution between 1786 and 1789.

Hamilton, however, did not believe that the Constitution alone could make a government strong. For that, a system of finance was needed—and that would be created not by the written Constitution but by the real-world interactions of money and power. This was why, after expressing his radical view in favor of a British-style constitutional monarchy at the Philadelphia convention, Hamilton had not bothered to stay for the rest of the painful summer of negotiations. The details of constitutional design could be left to Madison and others. Hamilton's talent and genius would be devoted to creating the financial infrastructure of the new government.

In this realm, Hamilton's talents were as great as Madison's were in the sphere of constitutional design. Adam Stephen, a Virginian who had emigrated from Scotland and respected Hamilton,[57] did not exaggerate when he told Madison that Hamilton was the Newton of finance:

> Resources and revenue laws lay hid in night
> 'Twas said Let Hamilton be! and all was right.[58]

But Madison could not accept that a government's financial infrastructure was as important for its survival and prosperity as its constitutional structure. Relying on finance to strengthen the government, he believed, was not "proper, effectual," or "permanent."

This divergence helped explain why Madison came to resist the federal assumption of state debt so strongly. It was not only that he believed it unfair to Virginia. He did not believe the financial class should be used as a tool of governmental design.

A Deep-Rooted Abuse

Apart from the crucial question of debt, one other important matter troubled Congress—and Madison—in the spring of 1790: the status of the slave trade. The previous autumn, a large meeting of the Society of Friends from the mid-Atlantic states had drafted a petition to Congress demanding the abolition of the trade. New York Quakers had added another.

As a formal matter, Congress had to vote to refer these petitions to a committee. Madison believed this should have happened quickly and quietly. The Constitution guaranteed that slaves could be imported for another eighteen years. It was therefore impossible for Congress to ban the trade outright. There were a few things Congress could possibly do, including banning the importation of slaves into any new states that would be "formed out of the western territory." These possibilities, Madison thought, could be considered by the committee.[59]

The representatives from Georgia and South Carolina, the states that had insisted on the constitutional provision in the first place, were worried about giving any recognition to petitions expressing disapproval of the slave trade. They preferred for Congress to refuse to accept the petitions at all. The result was an extended, weeklong congressional debate about the trade itself.

Speaking like a skilled politician, Madison privately criticized Georgia and South Carolina for their lack of strategy. "The true policy of the southern members," he told Edmund Randolph, should have been to "let the affair proceed with as little noise as possible, and to make use of the occasion to obtain . . . a recognition of the restraints imposed by the Constitution."[60]

Instead, his southern colleagues acted in a manner that was "intemperate beyond all example and even all decorum," Madison told Benjamin Rush. "They are not content with palliating slavery as a deep-rooted abuse, but plead for the lawfulness of the African trade itself." This was "folly," Madison told the antislavery Rush, but it was actually a good

thing for "the patrons of humanity and freedom." The southerners' protestations in favor of the slave trade would "hasten . . . the progress of
those reflections and sentiments which are secretly undermining the institution" of slavery.[61]

There was a subtle difference between Madison's discussion of the
slavery issue in his letters to Randolph and Rush. In both he commented
that the Georgia and South Carolina congressmen were acting in a self-
defeating way. But only in the letter to Rush did he express some pleasure
in their miscalculation. To Randolph, Madison sounded like a concerned
friend and fellow Virginian slaveholder.

Yet a third attitude emerged in an exchange of letters between Madison and his Philadelphia ally Tench Coxe. Madison told Coxe that the
debate on Hamilton's report had "been long interrupted" by the slavery
petitions. "Whether the time of presenting these was proper, will admit
of doubt," Madison said.[62] He was implying that the leading Philadelphia
Quakers, whom Coxe knew, had misjudged. They should not have sent
the petitions demanding the abolition of the slave trade to the first Congress. This criticism of the strategy adopted by the Society of Friends was
not one that Madison expressed to Rush and certainly not to Randolph.

Coxe got the hint. In reply, he told Madison that he had tried to dissuade the Quakers from pressing the issue.[63] "The address of the Friends
is impolitic and unhandsome," Coxe wrote. Yet the southerners had also
been unwise, Coxe charged, in how they responded to the Quakers.[64] As
was often the case with respect to the question of slavery and the slave
trade, Madison wished the whole public debate had never occurred. His
internally held moral views could not realistically be adopted, and so as a
politician he favored silence over the Quakers' irrepressible exercise of
public conscience.

By the end of May, Madison hoped he had found a resolution. He
urged a delegation of Pennsylvania Quakers who visited him to give up
their petitions during the current session of Congress. They should rein-
troduce them, he urged, only when they could prove that some states were
actively helping foreign slave traders circumvent their own countries' bans
on the trade.[65] Indirectly, Madison was telling the Society of Friends to
go away.

They would not. John Parrish, Jr., a Quaker abolitionist, called Madison's bluff by sending him a list of ten foreign vessels outfitted for the
slave trade in Rhode Island. As Parrish acknowledged, because Rhode

Island had still not ratified the Constitution, "it does not come within the jurisdiction of Congress and therefore no remedy can be applied to them at present." Parrish reported, however, "The skipper of the boat when we left New York, who appeared to be a man of veracity," had told the Friends that "he knew of fourteen that had been latterly fitted out of New York."[66]

Parrish urged Madison to introduce a bill prohibiting the outfitting for the slave trade of foreign vessels from countries that did not allow the practice. He was writing, Parrish said, "from a persuasion that thy* influence is such that the matter may be accomplished before the House rises." His moral tone was definitive. It would be sad if

> even one vessel load of this unhappy race of people should be torn
> from their native shore, from all that is near and dear, to linger out
> their lives in the state of unconditional slavery when perhaps a little
> exertion in the present critical juncture might prevent [it].[67]

Parrish ended his exhortation with an indication of his doggedness. If Madison would introduce a bill in the current session, he explained, it would "save the people called Quakers the trouble of interfering at the next session on this very disagreeable though necessary business."[68]

But Madison's mind was made up. He wrote back to Parrish kindly yet firmly that "should the evil still go on," the federal government would then take some action "as far as may be constitutional." He intended to wait and see if the practice of outfitting foreign ships disappeared on its own in Rhode Island. Surely, Madison wrote to Parrish, he must believe "that such a remedy ought in prudence to be forborne in case it be not absolutely necessary." After all, Madison explained, it was likely that "a revival of the subject in Congress would be equally unseasonable and unsuccessful." It would, therefore, be better to wait for "future opportunities."[69]

In fact, there was no reason to think that Parrish "must" share Madison's assessment. Parrish the believer was speaking the language of conviction and faith. Madison the politician was speaking the language of prudence and calculation.

---

* Using "thee" and "thou" was a distinct linguistic marker adopted by the Quakers, which was originally intended to be simple, "plain speech" but ended up making them sound biblical after the rest of English speakers dropped the distinction between the less formal "thou" and the formal "you."

The Gentleman at the Head of That Department

As the debate over Hamilton's report on the debt continued, Madison's circle of allies and political correspondents began to feel a strong foreboding about the direction of the republic—and a deep skepticism of Hamilton. Edward Carrington, writing from Virginia, opposed the federal assumption of state debt. "All descriptions of men who think at all," he asserted, believed the plan was unfair to Virginia. Carrington warned that faith in the new Constitution was at issue. "Whether the Constitution is yet so firmly on its legs that it cannot be shocked I will not undertake to decide," he wrote. "However I am certain . . . the adoption of this measure will have considerable effect in abridging the confidence of the people in it."[70]

George Lee Turberville, another Virginian who opposed a national debt, was more worried about having Alexander Hamilton in charge of the Treasury:

> I am not unacquainted personally with that *Gentleman* at the head of that department of the revenue and still less so with the powers of his mind—his acquirements, disposition and character. I tremble at the thoughts of his being at the head of such an immense sum as *86* millions of dollars—and the annual revenue of the union.[71]

Turberville's comment on Hamilton's intelligence was not meant as a compliment. Republicans feared not only Hamilton's views, but Hamilton himself. Everyone "interested in the funds (in opposition too to the landed interest of the United States)" would "in some measure be dependent" on Hamilton, Turberville predicted.[72] Hamilton would become the head of a class of financial traders and speculators whose interests opposed the landed class to which Madison and the other leading Virginians belonged.

From Philadelphia, Benjamin Rush attacked the methods Hamilton was using to get his recommendations passed. "I question whether more dishonorable influence has ever been used by a British minister (bribery excepted) to carry a measure tha[n] has [been] used to carry the report of the secretary," Rush charged. He had in mind "visits—promises—compromises—sacrifices—and threats."[73] The comparison to British ministers was apposite. Hamilton, the first member of the executive

branch to take an active role in Congress, was indeed trying to set a precedent for effective cabinet governance. What made Hamilton's political
pressure tactics "dishonorable" seems to have been Hamilton's involvement. Rush's ideology condemned Hamilton's report, and so it seemed
natural for Rush to condemn Hamilton himself.*

Henry Lee went further still, writing to Madison in April 1790 that
Patrick Henry's warnings that the North would dominate the South
under the Constitution were coming true. "Henry already is considered as
a prophet, his predictions are daily verifying," Lee insisted. The result,
Lee himself predicted, would be disunion. "I had rather myself submit to
all the hazards of war and risk the loss of everything dear to me in life,
than to live under the rule of a fixed insolent northern majority."[74] This
was a noteworthy sentiment from Light Horse Harry Lee, whose son,
not yet born, would be Robert E. Lee.[75]

Madison did not fully share his correspondents' worries. "I cannot feel
all the despondency which you seem to give way to," he wrote back to Lee
in the middle of April, on the verge of opposing assumption in Congress.
"I think with you that the report of the secretary of the treasury is faulty
in many respects," he allowed. But the main thing wrong with it was that
it "departs particularly from that simplicity which ought to be preserved
in finance." This was not a profound criticism. Madison went on to say
that "the novelty and difficulty of the task" that Hamilton "had to execute
form no small apology for his errors." He hoped that the errors would be
"diminished, if not remedied" by legislative action.[76]

Madison's protective tone extended even to Adams, whom he otherwise disliked. Lee had repeated the rumor that Adams had said that "the
southern people were formed by nature to . . . be slaves to the North."[77] "I
have never heard of the report you mention of the vice president," Madison told Lee. "It is but justice to say that I cannot believe it originated in
fact."[78] For now, Madison remained committed to the idea that reason-

---

* Opponents loved to question Hamilton's character. In the midst of the assumption debate, South Carolina congressman Aedanus Burke attacked Hamilton for a line in a
speech he had given the previous July in which he referred to militia dismissively as "the
mimicry of soldiership"—not as good as regular troops. Burke, claiming indignation on
behalf of brave Revolutionary War militia veterans, announced dramatically from the floor
of the House, "I give the lie to Col. Hamilton." Hamilton tried to explain that in context,
he had been referring not to all militias but simply to "small fugitive bodies of the volunteer militia." But a duel was only narrowly averted. Chernow, *Alexander Hamilton*, 308–9.

able men could disagree about policy while remaining friends. Hamilton had been his associate and ally, and deserved credit for trying to design a system of national finance. Even Adams deserved the benefit of the doubt.

A Friendly Discussion

By June 1790, Congress had still not voted definitively on federal assumption of state debts—and as a result, it had not passed a comprehensive bill implementing Hamilton's *Report on Public Credit.* The lobbying on both sides had been intense. Divided on geographical lines, Congress had reached gridlock.

The other gridlocked issue was the location of the temporary and permanent capital, which now returned to public conversation. No deal had been reached, and Congress had continued to meet in New York by default. With travel slow through the United States, the location of the federal government was expected to reflect and shape the destiny of the country. Each region wanted the capital for itself. The stakes were high—at least as high as in the assumption debate.

In a letter to his father in which he sent along "a few grains of upland rice, brought from Timor by Captain Bligh" (the unfortunate commander of the *Bounty*), Madison described the state of play. A bill had narrowly passed the House to move the temporary seat of government to Baltimore instead of Philadelphia.[79] Informal negotiations continued to take place, but it seemed that the northern states and New York would reach a deal with Pennsylvania to put the final location in or near Philadelphia. Madison told his father that he feared "the final event will not square with the pretensions of the Potomac." Yet there was a glimmer of hope. "In the chances to which this question is liable, it may possibly turn out otherwise."[80]

With Congress stuck on the two most pressing and important issues facing the country, the possibility of linking them in order to resolve both became suddenly attractive. The idea was inspired, but its originator is unknown. An unsigned note in Madison's papers indicates that someone offered the Pennsylvania delegation "carte blanche" to choose "the permanent and tempore seat of Congress if they consent to the assumption of the state debts as reported by the secretary of the treasury." The same note indicates that several prominent Pennsylvanians "would not consent."[81] The person with the greatest motive and opportunity to make such an offer would certainly have been Hamilton, who was deeply concerned, not to say obsessed, with getting his bill passed.[82]

According to an account he wrote for himself a year later, Thomas Jefferson swung into action. It began with a chance meeting. Visiting George Washington's house on Cherry Street in New York, Jefferson encountered Hamilton. "His look was somber, haggard, and dejected beyond description. Even his dress uncouth and neglected," Jefferson recalled. He surmised that Hamilton was profoundly upset that he could not get assumption through the House. Hamilton asked to speak with Jefferson, and the two "stood in the street near the door" and conferred.[83]

Hamilton began by repeating to Jefferson his belief in the "absolute necessity" of assumption. The northern states, Hamilton insisted, believed that the whole country was responsible for the debts they had incurred individually during the Revolutionary War—so much so "that they would make it a sine qua non of a continuance of the Union." Hamilton then told Jefferson dramatically that unless he could get the assumption passed, he was prepared to resign from Treasury. As Jefferson recalled it, Hamilton said that "if he had not credit enough to carry such a measure as that, he could be of no use, and was determined to resign."[84] The tone of desperation and the financial metaphor were both consistent with Hamilton's style of expression. Hamilton then asked Jefferson to lobby the southern states on his behalf. He clearly meant Madison, whose friendship with Jefferson was well known to him.

In the street in front of Washington's house, Jefferson was noncommittal. He had been in France for a long time, he explained, and had "lost familiarity" with American affairs. What he knew of the assumption made him skeptical of it. Yet he promised to "revolve what he had urged in my mind." Certainly, Jefferson acknowledged in his memorandum to himself, he was concerned that northern and southern members of Congress "had gotten into the most extreme ill-humor with one other." The tension "broke out on every question with the most alarming heat, the bitterest animosities seemed to be engendered, and though they met every day, little or nothing could be done from mutual distrust and antipathy."[85]

Having told Hamilton he would consider the matter, Jefferson made a decision. "I thought the first step toward some conciliation of views would be to bring Mr. Madison and Col. Hamilton to a friendly discussion of the subject." The key word in the sentence was "friendly." Madison and Hamilton had been collaborators on the *Federalist* essays and colleagues in urging ratification of the Constitution. Jefferson was posing the idea of their friendship against the animosity of the debate over assumption, which had divided them.

Jefferson invited Madison and Hamilton to join him for dinner the next day, probably June 20, 1790. He told them they would be alone, and that the point of the dinner was "to find some temperament for the present fever"—a cure for the disease of gridlock. Both came. According to Jefferson, he himself raised the topic of assumption, asserted his neutrality by insisting "that my situation had not permitted me to understand it sufficiently," and left the rest of the conversation to Madison and Hamilton.[86]

Jefferson's story decorously omitted the details of the negotiation that ensued. But by the end of the evening, he indicated, Madison and Hamilton had made a historic trade. Madison would agree to the assumption of state debts. Hamilton's comprehensive finance bill would pass. In return, Madison would get what he and his fellow Virginians wanted but had considered unattainable: Hamilton would guarantee that New York's delegation would allow the permanent home of government to be built along the Potomac. As a consolation to Pennsylvania, the temporary seat of government would be moved to Philadelphia for a decade. (Philadelphia could still hope that, before the decade was out, Congress would change its mind and stay put.)[87]

The political details were important. Hamilton agreed to modify the state assumption of debts to satisfy Madison's concern that Virginia be treated more fairly. Madison's original position had been to support assumption under the right conditions; he would now be getting most of what he had originally sought. So that he did not appear to be flip-flopping, however, Madison would not actually support the assumption. Instead he would allow it to be reintroduced in the House and though he "would not vote for it, nor entirely withdraw" his opposition, he "should not be strenuous, but leave it to its fate."[88] This, Madison believed, would provide sufficient political cover for him despite the unpopularity of assumption in Virginia.

As Jefferson told it in his memorandum, he facilitated the deal between Madison and Hamilton but did not specifically broker it. Indeed, with respect to the crucial element of the location of the capital, Jefferson claimed somewhat implausibly not to remember whether it had come from Madison or Hamilton:

> It was observed, I forget by which of them, that as the pill [of assumption] would be a bitter one to the southern states, something should be done to soothe them; that the removal of the seat of government to the Potomac was a just measure, and would probably be a popular one with them, and would be a proper one to follow the assumption.[89]

None of the three men present took public credit for the compromise, then or later. Madison never acknowledged having negotiated the trade at all. He himself had previously condemned secret, "out of doors," bargaining about the capital—and now he had achieved the ultimate backroom deal. Madison's part in what became known as the Compromise of 1790 was that of a practical politician coming into his own. The compromises made at the Philadelphia convention had to be defended on grounds of principle, convincingly or otherwise. The deal over the capital came with no principles attached. It was not especially republican—and it could only be justified by the fact of agreement.

In a note to James Monroe sent on July 4, 1790, three days after the Senate had voted to fix "the permanent seat of government on the Potomac," Madison told Monroe that passage through the House was "probable, but attended with great difficulties." He then gave his friend the closest thing to a hint he would ever venture: "If the Potomac succeeds, even on these terms," he wrote, "it will have resulted from a fortuitous coincidence of circumstances which might never happen again."[90]

In the very next sentence Madison explained that the public debt question "has been suspended for some time . . . by the question relating to the seat of government," which now would be taken up again and resolved. The assumption would pass, he predicted. He offered an oblique account of Hamilton's strategy: "It seems, indeed, as if the friends of the measure were determined to risk everything rather than suffer that finally to fail."[91] Madison was implying to Monroe that Hamilton had been willing to pay an enormous price to get the assumption of state debts passed: giving up the location of the capital.[92]

Despite his reticence about acknowledging his role, it is just possible to sense a note of quiet satisfaction in Madison's otherwise dry, impersonal letter. By holding out on the assumption of state debts, he had moved the capital to the Virginia-Maryland border, close to the population center of the country. The modifications to which Hamilton had agreed assured that the assumption would not even seriously disadvantage Virginia. Jefferson, for his part, must have felt the same.

Whether Madison and Jefferson actually got the better of Hamilton is doubtful. What is most telling about the compromise is how both sides won with respect to the elements of the deal that they considered most important. Madison, who believed in constitutional structure, had created a federal republic that would be governed from the center. The location of the capital determined where republican politics would take place. Therefore, the seat of government needed to be near Virginia and the West, as far away as possible from the financial centers of New York and, to a lesser degree, Philadelphia. A capital near Virginia would also consolidate support for the union in his home state.

For his part, Hamilton thought the constitutional structures of political government were less crucial than the financial structures. By convincing Madison—and through him, the southern states—to have the federal government assume the state debts, Hamilton was achieving the goal of financial centralization. The federal government would have to raise much more revenue than the individual states to pay off the vastly expanded debt load it would now hold. That would establish the precedent for Congress to raise larger amounts of revenue than the states. At the same time, the assumption of state debts would help create a permanent and deep relationship between the government of the United States and its debt holders.

As Hamilton had said in his *Report on Public Credit*, his goal was to align the interests of the bond markets with the interests of the federal government. This would create a powerful, effective lobbying constituency to make sure that the government both issued debt and remained fiscally solvent enough to pay it. Madison wanted to design a constitutional "machine" that could be put "into operation" and run indefinitely.[93] Hamilton sought to do the same thing for the financial system—to set it up once and for all, push the debt button, and watch as perpetual motion ensued.

When Madison agreed to assumption, Hamilton got nearly all of this. From Hamilton's perspective, it might have been desirable for the political capital to be in New York, which could then have been, like London, the hub for both politics and finance. But Hamilton realized that, to align the interests of the markets and the government, it was not necessary for them to be co-located. Bondholders could exercise the necessary influence from afar. Indeed, the appearance of separation between political and financial structures might even be an advantage, obscuring the appearance of undue influence and allowing republicans to continue to believe in the independence of political government from finance.

The Mask of Hypocrisy

In the fall of 1790, Madison would have to be reelected to Congress, but this time his seat was far safer than it had been when Monroe had challenged him at Patrick Henry's behest. Instead of traveling back to Virginia for the September election, Madison wrote to his father that he planned to wait several weeks in New York and travel home with Jefferson, thus avoiding electioneering altogether. The excuse he gave the public was that his health was "not at present very firm, and would be particularly exposed on a long and rapid journey at this critical season of the year," namely late summer. To his father he wrote similarly, "The weather being extremely hot, I have thought it necessary in order to avoid the danger of the bilious attack to which I have become very subject, to stay here a few weeks which will render the journey more safe."[94]

In fact, Madison hated running for office, and was confident of reelection in the absence of a serious competitor. He wrote to his constituents that there had been two important issues in Congress: the assumption of state debts and the seat of government. The location "has been decided in a manner more favorable to Virginia than was hoped," he reported with satisfaction. The assumption might "be less acceptable," but "has however been purged of some of its objections and particularly of its gross injustice to Virginia," Madison wrote. "In a pecuniary view," the state was "now little affected one way or the other."[95] This was a fitting conclusion to Madison's deal with Hamilton. He had delivered the capital to Virginia while assuring that his state would not pay more than its fair share of the assumed debts. These accomplishments should have been more than sufficient to get Madison reelected—as indeed they were.

The most eventful aspects of Madison's visit to Virginia were his travel from New York back to Montpelier and from Montpelier to the new temporary capital in Philadelphia. He made both trips with Jefferson, and their already close friendship grew closer still. They stopped to see Washington at Mount Vernon, and George Mason at his fine home, Gunston Hall, which was just down the Potomac. The topic of conversation with Mason was exactly where along the Potomac the new capital should be sited. Mason favored the vicinity of Georgetown, where he owned property.[96]

Jefferson's affection for Madison extended to the gentlemanly quirk whereby Madison insisted on paying more than his fair share of mutual expenses. In buying Madison's horse after the trip was over, Jefferson refused to allow Madison to set the price, because he believed Madison would set it too low. "I know nobody with whom it is so difficult to settle a price, and with whom I should be so likely to differ," Jefferson wrote fondly. "Witness the money disputes on our journey."[97] Jefferson, though master of Monticello in his own right, was even more strapped for cash than Madison. The expense of serving as ambassador in Paris had been considerable. He told Madison he would pay for the horse "not till our return to Philadelphia, perhaps not til the receipt of our December quarter."[98]

While he was home, Madison did not, as on many previous visits, bury himself in his books. Instead for the first time he took an active role in arranging the affairs of the plantation at Montpelier, leaving detailed instructions for his overseer Mordecai Collins regarding the administration of the estate. These ranged from constructing a shelter for the cattle and building dams on the meadows, to the instruction "to treat the Negroes with all the humanity and kindness consistent with their necessary subordination and work."[99]

Madison also left instructions for Sawney, the slave who had once accompanied Madison to Princeton and now functioned as supervisor of other slaves and of a significant portion of the plantation. The Madisons divided not only tasks but also control of the property between Collins and Sawney. Madison referred to "Sawney's" ground and to "Sawney's" store of pork. Sawney was instructed "to stem and get down as soon as may be convenient his crop of tobacco," and "to have all his wheat *well* cleaned and got down as soon as possible."

Madison's role at Montpelier was growing as his father was aging. He instructed Collins "to apply to my father on all occasions where application would be made to me if present."[100] The comment reflected the shift of authority. At the age of thirty-nine, the son was gradually assuming the father's position as head of the family.

Madison and Jefferson traveled together back to the seat of government in November. This time their destination was Philadelphia, where Madison as usual took up residence at Mrs. House's establishment. On his arrival, the first person to call on him was Hamilton, who sent him a report, probably his follow-up report on public credit, to read in preparation for the meeting.

Hamilton signed "I remain with great esteem and regard, dear sir, your obedient servant." This was more formal and less effusive than Hamilton had been in the past. But the request for the meeting as well as the cordiality suggested that, at least in Hamilton's mind, he and Madison still had a good working relationship. They had resolved the difficulties of the previous Congress through their mutual compromise, and were poised to work together in the future. Madison, Hamilton, and Jefferson all participated in drafting Washington's address to Congress, delivered in writing on December 8, 1790, and setting forth his agenda for the new congressional term.[101] Madison alone wrote the friendly reply from the House.[102] Once again, as he had done in the first year of Washington's presidency, Madison wrote brief replies from Washington to the House and Senate.[103]

Washington's address to Congress raised the topic of war. He told Congress that Wabash "Indians from the northwest side of the Ohio" had been making "incursions" into the territory of frontier settlers. Washington, with the goal of expansion, had already called out the militia and authorized an expedition that would combine regular troops with "such drafts of militia as were deemed sufficient." He had done all this in the absence of Congress, and was informing Congress of the campaign before he knew what its result would be.

The address put the question of militia squarely before Congress. Over the rest of the month, Congress debated a bill to standardize the raising and training of militias throughout the United States. Madison took part several times. First, he tried to convince his colleagues not to exempt themselves from service. It was "an important principle," he said, "that all laws should be made to operate as much on the lawmakers as upon the people." This was "the greatest security for the preservation of liberty."

The government must "have a sympathy with those on whom the laws act, and a real participation and communication of all their burdens and grievances."[104] The idea was noble and certainly correct. It was also naïve. Congress ultimately exempted its own members from militia service.

Madison returned to the floor to propose a new exemption from the bill, this one for "persons conscientiously scrupulous of bearing arms." The intended beneficiaries were the Quakers, who, he said, had shown their merit "by a uniform conduct of moderation." Madison mounted a general defense of the rights to religious conscience, which he called "the boast of the Revolution, and the pride of the present Constitution."[105] Now that the Bill of Rights was in place, he could claim that the Constitution had broken new ground in assuring liberty of conscience.

There was also no danger that nonbelievers would falsely claim the exemption, he maintained. "Would any man consent to put on the mask of hypocrisy in order to avoid a duty which is honorable?" Aware of the limits of this idealistic notion, he concluded with a more pragmatic argument for exempting conscientious objectors: It would be "in vain to force them into the field," because they would not fight.[106]

The rest of Congress was considerably less sympathetic to conscientious objectors than was Madison. After his motion was defeated, he reintroduced it, this time with the proviso that Quakers "should pay an equivalent in money . . . appropriated to the purposes, to which the revenue, arising from the post office, was appropriated." He preferred the exemption to be free, Madison said, but he was willing to be realistic.[107] The proposal was carefully crafted so that Quakers' payments would not go directly for military purposes but rather into the general Treasury.

More details still needed to be specified. Madison suggested that the individual's declaration of pacifism should suffice. The other possibility was to get a certificate "or other voucher" from the "religious society of which he is a member" to prove the need for an exception. But Madison did not want to "confine our attention to this or that particular sect." What was more, the Quakers were accustomed to excluding members from their "meetings," as their congregations were known, for various infractions. Madison pointed out to his colleagues in Congress that it would not make sense to deny an exemption to a believing Quaker just because the person had been separated from his meeting. It followed that "our criterion must apply to individuals, and not to societies."[108]

It was noteworthy that Madison gave so much attention to religious liberty, the topic that had brought him into public life in the first place. He had good relations with Quakers, to be sure. But in the lengthy debate over the bill to regulate the militia, Madison's greatest interests lay not in military preparedness or strategic concerns, but in justly exempting those who deserved protection and drafting those who did not.[109] Emerging as a politician, Madison was exploring the dark arts of compromise. But he had not abandoned principle. He remained firmly committed to his ideals. He was, rather, learning to use the tools of politics to achieve them.

The Bank

Meanwhile, Hamilton continued to press his financial agenda. Hamilton proposed and Madison supported a bill to impose an excise tax on distilled spirits. In defending the bill, Madison told Congress that "he conceived taxes of all kinds to be evils in themselves," and that taxes were never "admissible" except "in order to avoid still greater evils." Yet after this formulaic pronouncement Madison argued that a tax on "ardent spirit" was a proper one, and was "least inconsistent with the spirit and disposition of the people of America." (The pun seems to have been unintentional.)[110]

Far more controversial was Hamilton's proposal for the creation of a new national bank, which Hamilton introduced in a report just as remarkable and just as contentious as his *Report on Public Credit*. Hamilton sent it to Congress on December 14, 1790. As he had in his first report, Hamilton laid out the purposes of his proposed institutional innovation in detail.

The first advantage of the bank, he explained, was that it transformed inactive capital—gold or silver sitting in a vault—into active capital. By depositing anything of value in a bank, the depositor enabled the bank to lend out the assets in the form of banknotes that would circulate through the economy and function as cash. A bank, Hamilton argued, could safely circulate somewhere between two and three times its assets in notes.[111]

This much was not controversial. But Hamilton added another "obvious" and "undisputed advantage of public banks." By combining capital belonging to many different individuals and placing it "under one direction," the national bank created a financial force that could be directed to the interests of the government. "There is in the nature of things," Hamilton wrote, "an intimate connection of interest between the government, and the bank, of a nation."[112]

Hamilton was saying that the creation of a national bank would help align the interests of capital—and capitalists—with the interests of the government. The influence would naturally run in both directions. To Hamilton, this was common sense. A national government should be responsive to the economic interests of the country, which he identified with the interests of those citizens who made important deposits in the national bank. This proposition, however, was not self-evident to Madison or his allies, who would soon object that the interests of landholders, likely to be in debt to a national bank, would probably oppose the interests of capitalist depositors who would be the bank's creditors.

Hamilton offered a third major benefit of a national bank: Circulating banknotes of uniform value would greatly improve the nation's capacities for commerce and trade, and would be useful "to business of every kind." More than any other institutional mechanism, a national bank could introduce liquidity into the national economy.

Hamilton sought to reassure Madison and other readers who feared that paper money would drive gold and silver hard currency into the hands of foreign investors. He argued that the amount of currency in the country was actually determined by its "balance of trade," defined simply as "the proportion between its abilities to supply foreigners, and its wants of them; between the amount of its exportations, and that of its importations." The more productive a country was, the more hard currency would flow into it. It followed that a bank issuing paper money would improve the balance of trade by improving the country's productivity. This, in turn, would bring hard currency into the economy.

As for the worry that circulating currency would encourage free spending and the creation of household debt, Hamilton dismissed it. "There is good reason to believe . . . that where the laws are wise and well executed and the inviolability of property and contract maintained, the economy of the people will, in the general course of things, correspond with its means." Here Hamilton was assuming the conclusion. To critics of paper money, the problem was precisely that debtors—through their representatives in the legislature—might dilute the currency so they could pay their debts more easily. Hamilton may have believed that the power of the depositors would counteract the tendency, but if he did, he was too discreet to say so. Rather, he argued that the Constitution gave "additional security to property," which would help attract foreign investment.

Madison had reservations about the bank based on the intuition that a bank could do permanent damage to a constitutional republic. But initially he avoided public comment. At the beginning of January 1791, he wrote drily to Edmund Pendleton in Virginia about the report and said, "I augur that you will not be in love with some of its features."[113] Later in the month, Madison wrote to his father that the Senate had approved Hamilton's bank bill, but in the House it "will not go through if at all, without opposition."[114]

In late January and early February, Madison went back to the practice that had served him so well in the past: He dived into his books, undertaking serious research on the history and origin of banks going all the way back to Italian city-states in the Middle Ages and Renaissance. When it came to the Constitution, Madison's deep and wide reading had led him to develop path-breaking new political ideas that had set the agenda in Philadelphia. During the ratification fight, his superior historical and comparative knowledge had conferred a huge advantage. This time, Hamilton had already set the financial agenda by proposing the bank. Madison was turning to research when he was already in a defensive posture.

The notes show him trying to support his instinctively negative reaction. Discussing the bank of the Italian republic of Genoa, Madison noted that it had been "produced by public debt." The holders of the bank's debt—that is, its depositors—had a council of their own to manage their affairs. "They became by good management very rich and granted aids to the state." Through this process, the depositors increasingly gained power relative to the state itself. Madison cited the judgment of Niccolò Machiavelli, the greatest republican theorist since ancient times: "Machiavel of opinion that by degrees the bank would get possession of the whole city and republic."[115]

Hamilton argued that the national bank would align the interests of the bank's depositors with the interests of the government. To a true republican like Madison, this alliance was not beneficial but deeply pernicious. In a republic, government should be controlled by the people, not the creditors of the bank. The alliance of interests between capital and government would take power away from the people and transfer it to the capitalists. As he had in analyzing the vices of the Articles of Confederation, Madison was standing on the shoulders of giants—and trying to see farther.

Madison's notes then turned to the Bank of England, which he considered comparable to Hamilton's proposed bank. Such banks, like the banks of Genoa, Naples, and Bologna, "advanced money to the state, have a perpetual fund of interest, and are banks of loan and deposit."[116] Following his main source, Adam Anderson's *Origin of Commerce* (1762),[117] Madison noted that the Bank of England had been established by the Puritan, Cromwellian side in the English Civil War, the very model of a legislative dictatorship. He wondered to himself how much of Great Britain's national debt had been lent by the bank—because he wanted to know just how obligated the British government was to the bank's depositors.

Madison also noted that the Bank of England was "not [the] only nor greatest lender" to the government. Both the East India Company and the South Sea Company lent money to the Crown. The logical implication was that the government of Britain was less dependent on the Bank of England than the government of the United States would be on its own bank. Yet Madison added that the "rivalship" between the different lenders may have been the "cause of [the] South Sea bubble," the famous episode in which the stock of the South Sea Company rose, then crashed.[118]

The most important note that Madison made on the Bank of England was also the most worrying. "In time of war," he wrote, "government at mercy of bank—vice versa in peace."[119] In peace, he thought, the British government could dictate terms to the bank because it could support itself from ordinary tax revenues. In war, however, the government suddenly needed much more money than it brought in, and so the bank could set whatever terms it wanted, essentially exercising a financial veto over conduct of the war. This was in danger of being an overgeneralization, but in a separate set of notes Madison attempted to substantiate it, listing every important financial transaction from 1697 through 1781.[120]

On February 2, 1791, Madison delivered a systematic speech in Congress arguing that a national bank would be a disaster. He admitted that banks were helpful to merchants and made it easier for the government to pay its debts "when deficiencies or delays happen in the revenue." A bank might also help reduce extortionate interest rates. Using banknotes while keeping gold and silver locked up would "sav[e] the wear of the gold and silver kept in the vaults."[121]

As an account of the value of a national bank, this was minimalist to the point of being laughable. In general, Madison's practice had always been to begin his public political arguments by acknowledging strong arguments on the other side. This time, however, he was taking no chances—or could not see the merit in Hamilton's arguments. To say in 1791 that a major benefit of a national bank would be to save wear and tear on precious metal reserves was a way of saying that the national bank was almost useless.

Madison then turned to what he considered "the principal disadvantages" of the bank from the standpoint of policy. The use of banknotes would send gold and silver abroad. "This effect was inevitable," Madison maintained. "It was admitted by the most enlightened patrons of banks, particularly by Smith on the *Wealth of Nations*." Madison could cite no higher economic authority.

In his report on a national bank, Hamilton had addressed this issue by saying that the supply of hard currency was actually determined by the balance of trade, and that greater productivity would bring in hard money. Madison reframed this defense. He admitted that hard currency sent abroad would bring "something equally valuable" to be "imported in return." But he expected that, "in the present habits of the country," the goods imported would be "articles of no permanent use to it"—consumer goods rather than precious metals. Madison was suggesting that Americans, flush with banknotes, would use the easy money to buy foreign-made consumer goods and thus shift the balance of trade against the United States and lower the supply of hard currency in America.[122]

A further disadvantage of a bank, according to Madison, was introducing the danger of "all the evils of a run on the bank, which would be particularly calamitous in so great a country as this." A bank run could be caused by "false rumors, bad management of the institution, an unfavorable balance of trade," or other unspecified events.[123] Madison added that it would be better to have "several banks properly distributed" rather than a single one, spreading the risk of bank failure. In England, "the genius of the monarchy favored the concentration of wealth and influence at the metropolis." Focusing financial power in a single location made sense if the goal was consolidating royal authority. It did not make sense in a republic.[124]

Constructive Authority

Madison's policy arguments against the national bank, however, were a prelude to the main event. He now turned to the argument he was uniquely placed to advance: that the incorporation of the bank would violate the Constitution. In particular, Madison argued, the incorporation of a national bank did not fall within the limited powers that the Constitution granted to Congress.

Madison began by introducing what he called "rules" for interpreting the Constitution. The first was the most striking: "An interpretation that destroys the very characteristic of the government cannot be just." This was a far-reaching principle. It required identifying the most distinctive characteristics of government under the Constitution. Once they were known, they could not be contradicted.

Madison was setting the table for the argument that a national bank was inconsistent with the republican form of government. And he was asserting that the correct interpretation of the Constitution could be ascertained by looking at how a proposed interpretation would affect republicanism itself.

Madison's next principle was still more goal oriented. Clear meaning would have to be accepted regardless of consequences, he admitted. Yet where the meaning of the Constitution was "doubtful," it should be "fairly triable by its consequences."[125] The true test of constitutionality lay in the practical effects of legislation. This was another way of saying that if a proposed law would destroy the core of republican government, it could not be constitutional.

Madison then offered a different, backward-looking guide to interpretation. "In controverted cases," he proposed, "the meaning of the parties to the instrument, if to be collected by reasonable evidence, is a proper guide." Evidence of the parties' meaning consisted of "contemporary and concurrent expositions."[126] Madison was saying that interpretation could be guided by historical evidence of what the parties to the Constitution intended. He did not say who exactly the parties to the Constitution were—whether he meant the Philadelphia delegates, the delegates to the state ratifying conventions, or the general public. Nor did he speak of

320 THE THREE LIVES OF JAMES MADISON

"intention," preferring the term "meaning." Yet Madison was certainly trying to introduce the idea that the debates around the adoption of the Constitution mattered for subsequent interpretation.

Finally, Madison turned to the validity of what he called "a constructive authority," namely a governmental power that was not expressly stated in the Constitution. If a power was very important, it was unlikely that it had been "left to construction" rather than being granted outright.[127] A power as important as the creation of a national bank would not have been left to implication.

With these principles for interpreting the Constitution in mind, Madison said, "it was not possible to discover in it the power to incorporate a bank." There were just three relevant clauses. Congress had the power to tax in order to pay debt and provide for the common defense and "general welfare"; it had the power to borrow money; and it had the power "to pass all laws necessary and proper to carry" its other powers "into execution." The bank laid no taxes, and so the first clause was irrelevant. The reference to the "general welfare" was limited to granting Congress power to impose taxes to achieve such general aims, so the second clause also offered no authority for the bank.[128]

Madison had to acknowledge a problem with his argument: Congress under the Articles of Confederation had actually established a national bank. The old Congress generally had fewer powers than the new one. How, then, could it be outside the powers of the new Congress to do what its predecessor had already done? The answer was that the earlier bank "was known . . . to have been the child of necessity. It could never be justified by the regular powers of the Articles of Confederation." This was a fairly weak argument, and Madison did not belabor it.

A stronger argument on behalf of the bank was that the Constitution authorized it by empowering Congress to borrow money. To this Madison replied bluntly that the bank bill was not a bill to borrow money. "It does not borrow a shilling," he asserted literally. "The obvious meaning of the power to borrow money, is that of accepting it from, and stipulating payment to those who are able and willing to lend." The bank, on the other hand, was "creating the ability, where there may be the will." In actuality this was an excellent explanation of what the bank would be doing: enabling the government to achieve the end of borrowing money more easily.

But Madison insisted that it would be "a dangerous principle" to treat the facilitation of borrowing the same as borrowing itself. With more rhetorical force than logic, he asserted that making it easy to lend money to the government would be just as bad as requiring people to lend it. Madison was fear-mongering—a technique he had always avoided before.

Finally, Madison turned to the necessary and proper clause. In Philadelphia as well as at the state ratifying conventions, skeptics of the Constitution had charged that this clause opened the door to Congress's usurpation of state functions. Madison had reassured them that nothing could be further from the truth.

Now Madison found himself confronting the very danger of which the critics had warned. The meaning of the clause must "be limited to means necessary to the end, and incident to the nature of the specified powers," he maintained. The necessary and proper clause should be read narrowly, not broadly.

This was the climax of Madison's constitutional argument. If the necessary and proper clause allowed Congress to choose any convenient means to achieve its permissible ends, then "the essential characteristic of the government, as composed of limited and enumerated powers, would be destroyed." A parade of horribles followed. If Congress could incorporate a national bank, it could incorporate companies like the East India Company and the South Sea Company in order to borrow money from them. It could "give monopolies in every branch of domestic industry," and regulate "agriculture, manufactures and commerce."[129] Ultimately "a chain may be formed that will reach every object of legislation, every object within the whole compass of political economy."[130]

Madison concluded by evincing concern about the Constitution and its future. "With all this evidence of the sense in which the Constitution was understood and adopted," he worried, "will it not be said, if the bill should pass, that its adoption was brought about by one set of the arguments, and that it is now administered under the influence of another set?" The problem would be worse, he added, because "so many individuals"—most prominently himself and Hamilton—had been involved "in both the adoption and administration" of the Constitution.[131]

This stated the problem clearly. Madison had been the prime mover in getting the Constitution drafted and ratified. In the course of ratification, he had reassured the Anti-Federalists that the Constitution was not a tool to expand government and ultimately oppress the people. From Madison's perspective, this charge had been not only wrong but paranoid. He had publicly committed himself to insisting that the government under the Constitution would not overreach.

Madison had been closely allied with Hamilton on ratification despite knowing that Hamilton favored the British model. Now circumstances were changing. The northern states were prepared to back Hamilton on the national bank. Madison's identification with the Constitution and its "true" meaning was nearly absolute—and he was confident that the Constitution did not authorize the creation of a national bank. Yet in fact, the Constitution was silent on the question. If Congress authorized the creation of a national bank, Madison would lose control of the interpretation of the Constitution. He would be made a liar retroactively. The ravings of Patrick Henry and the other Anti-Federalists would turn out to have had substance.

Madison's arguments for the unconstitutionality of the bank did not prevail. A few days after his final speech, the House passed the bill, 39 to 20.[132] The vote overwhelmingly followed geographical lines. Almost all northern congressmen voted in favor of the bank. Almost all southerners voted against it.

A veto by Washington was Madison's last hope. As Madison later recalled it, the president "held several free conversations with me on the subject, in which he listened favorably as I thought to my views of it, but certainly without committing himself in any manner whatever."[133] Jefferson and Edmund Randolph both advised Washington to veto the bill as unconstitutional.

Washington then asked Madison to draft a message that he could use to explain his position should he decide to veto the bill.[134] On February 21, 1791, Madison sent Washington two paragraphs that would have asserted that the power to incorporate a national bank was not expressly delegated by the Constitution. The draft veto message also objected to the bill on policy grounds, expressing the worry that people who lived close to the bank would be able to buy all the available stock offered on the first day, disadvantaging those living at a greater distance.

Hamilton advised Washington to the contrary in a trenchant fifteen-thousand-word document that he finished in a manic all-night effort on February 22 and brought to Washington himself the next morning. There was, he maintained, a *general principle . . . inherent* in the very *definition of government.*" The principle was that "every power vested" in a sovereign government "includes by the *force* of the *term* a right to employ all the *means* requisite and fairly *applicable* to the attainment of the ends of such power."[135] The very Hamiltonian emphasis conveyed his enthusiasm for the key argument, one that justified his whole picture of the function of government.

Washington waited until "the last moment allowed him" by law.[136] On February 25, 1791, a supporter of the bank told Madison that ten days had elapsed and that the bill was therefore law even without the president's signature. While he was speaking, the president's secretary, Tobias Lear, arrived to inform Madison that the president had signed the bank bill. Years later, Madison told dinner companions that even if Washington had vetoed the bill that day, supporters of the bank would have argued it was too late.

Madison's defeat was total. Not only had he failed to convince Congress that the Bank of the United States was unwise and unconstitutional. Washington had chosen Hamilton's counsel. Madison had failed to convince his fellow Virginian.

Never More Happy

The shared loss brought Madison and Jefferson closer. After Congress rose in early March, Jefferson invited Madison to leave Mrs. House's boarding establishment and "come and take a bed and plate" with him, moving into the four-bedroom house Jefferson had rented on High Street, now Market Street, Philadelphia.[137] Madison declined, giving the excuse that he was working on a self-appointed task—probably editing his notes on the Philadelphia convention—and would not like to move while his "papers and books are all assorted," around him.[138] But, he told Jefferson, "as the weather grows better" he would like to dine frequently with Jefferson, and he was "never more happy than partaking that hour of unbent conversation" with his friend. He was, he concluded, "never more sincere than in assuring you of the affection with which I am yours."[139]

The exchange was reminiscent of the occasion several years before in which Jefferson had proposed that Madison buy property close to Monticello. Both times Jefferson intended seriously to bring Madison into his household. Both times Madison declined, taking the opportunity to express his affection for Jefferson in what for him were extremely strong terms. When Madison said his greatest happiness was in sharing an uninterrupted hour of conversation with Jefferson, he was not exaggerating. In 1791, there was no one on earth to whom Madison was closer.

Before leaving Philadelphia for Virginia, Madison hoped to make a trip to New England. He had never been north of New York, and as he told his brother Ambrose, "I have often projected this ratification to my curiosity and do not foresee a more convenient opportunity."[140] Rather than traveling alone, he "hoped to form a party for the purpose." Without much difficulty, he convinced Jefferson to travel with him.

Madison began planning the trip at the end of April, producing a rough and ready list of good and bad country taverns to be found "over the bridge" on the way to Lake George at the foot of the Adirondack Mountains.[141] The route would allow him to inspect and perhaps complete a purchase of land in Mohawk with Monroe, who had been trying to back out of the deal.[142] Madison still hoped Monroe would go in fully on the purchase.[143]

Stopping in Princeton on his way to New York, Madison missed Witherspoon, his former teacher. But he did encounter another old Princeton acquaintance—one who would become important to the plans he was forming with Jefferson. Philip Freneau, the son of a French Protestant immigrant, had achieved early success as a poet, and was sometimes even called "the poet of the American Revolution." Since then, however, his career had stagnated. He had worked in the post office and captained a brig that sailed to the West Indies. More recently he had worked briefly as an editor for a New York newspaper and had resolved to settle in New Jersey after getting married in 1790.[144]

Madison had other ideas for Freneau. He had prevailed on Jefferson to offer Freneau a position as a translator of French in the State Department. The job was a cover. Freneau could translate French into English, Madison wrote to Jefferson, but was not "able to translate with equal propriety into French." Freneau told Madison that he assumed this disqualified him for the translator's job. Madison "set [him] right as to this particular."[145]

In reality, Madison and Jefferson wanted Freneau for his writing skill and newspaper experience. For two years, since the spring of 1789, associates of Hamilton had been publishing a newspaper called the *Gazette of the United States*. It often included anonymous essays by John Adams, and had served as a useful mouthpiece for promoting Hamilton's *Report on Public Credit* as well as the national bank. Madison and Jefferson hoped to create an alternative paper to advance their political agenda, and they wanted Freneau to edit it.

Madison had not been in touch with Freneau since the 1770s, but the old connection explained his enthusiasm for the choice. "The more I learn of his character, talents, and principles," Madison wrote to Jefferson, "the more I should regret his burying himself in the obscurity he had chosen in New Jersey." Madison was trying to convince himself. "It is certain," he wrote Jefferson with a typical overstatement, "that there is not to be found in the whole catalogue of American printers, a single name that can approach towards a rivalship."[146] Certainly there was no other newspaperman in America who had also been at college with Madison and was at present unemployed.

Freneau resisted, so Jefferson and Madison had to make the offer as explicit and attractive as possible. In a letter meant to be shared with Freneau in the hopes of enticing him to Philadelphia, Jefferson wrote to Madison that Freneau

> would have set out on such advantageous ground as to have been
> assured of success. His own genius in the first place is so superior
> to that of his competitors. I should have given him the perusal of all
> my letters of foreign intelligence and all foreign newspapers; the
> publication of all proclamations and other public notices within my
> department, and the printing of the laws, which added to his salary
> would have been a considerable aid.[147]

This was a plan not only to give Freneau unparalleled access to foreign news—including State Department documents—but also to give him official government contracts in order to keep his newspaper afloat. The only competition, Jefferson continued, was the *Gazette of the United States*. This was "the only weekly or half weekly paper, and under general condemnation for its Toryism and its incessant efforts to overturn the government." As a result, "Freneau would have found that ground as good as unoccupied."[148] Jefferson was borrowing the British political term "Toryism" to describe Adams and Hamilton, pro-monarchists who in his view wanted to overturn the republican form of government.[149]

The seduction worked, and Freneau at length set out for Philadelphia. He needed money to start the newspaper, so Madison took it upon himself to try and raise it, sending identical notes to several of his Philadelphia friends and associates asking them to become subscribers and provide financial backing for the paper. Madison wrote that he had "been long and thoroughly acquainted" with Freneau. "He is a man of genius, of literature, of experience in the business . . . and of great integrity," Madison promised. The newspaper would be "a vehicle of intelligence and entertainment to the public."[150]

The impetus for the planned newspaper was Madison and Jefferson's increasing belief that Hamilton and his associates were acting as a party, understood by them as a faction organized against the true public interests of the United States. This party was, in turn, attempting to control George Washington. From New York, Madison told Jefferson that during the period when Washington was deciding whether to veto the bank bill, the law's "partisans here indulged themselves in reflections not very decent." Madison explained that "the meanest motives were charged on [Washington], and the most insolent menaces held over him." All this had happened "if not in the open streets, under circumstances not less marking the character of the party."[151] Madison apparently accepted the rumors that Hamilton's "partisans" had been privately threatening Washington.

Jefferson was already enmeshed in a political controversy that involved Hamilton's newspaper. Thomas Paine, author of the famous 1776 pamphlet *Common Sense,* had written another global bestseller condemning monarchy, *The Rights of Man,* this time in praise of the French Revolution. Jefferson had sent a copy of the pamphlet to a Philadelphia printer with a cover note telling the printer that it was about time something was said "against the political heresies which had of late sprung up among us." The printer happily printed the cover note with the pamphlet—creating Jefferson's first major national scandal.

The heresies Jefferson referred to came from the pen of John Adams and had been published anonymously in the *Gazette of the United States.* Jefferson later told Madison that he had "certainly never meant to step into a public newspaper with that in my mouth." He expected that Adams "will be displeased." To make matters worse, "Col. Hamilton and Col. Beckwith are open mouthed against me, taking it . . . as likely to give offense to the court of London."[152] Paine was persona non grata in England, while Beckwith was an emissary from the royal governor of Canada, functioning as a kind of unofficial British ambassador.[153] Hamilton could credibly argue that the secretary of state should not be endorsing a pamphlet that condemned monarchy. Jefferson, for his part, was suggesting that Hamilton was just as close to Britain as an actual servant of the Crown.

Madison reassured Jefferson by return mail. He had seen the preface to Paine's pamphlet and it had "immediately occurred" to him that Jefferson had been quoted without his permission. "But I had not foreseen the particular use made of it by the British partisans," Madison wrote. "The sensibility of H&B to the indignity to the British court is truly ridiculous," Madison continued.

As for John Adams, he could "least of all complain" about being impugned by Jefferson, Madison wrote:

> Under a mock defense of the republican constitutions of this country, he attacked them with all the force he possessed, and this in a book with his name to it while he was representative of his country at a foreign court.[154]

Madison had slighted Adams's *Defence* before, but he had never expressed his resentment of the work so directly. In his telling, Adams's book was not a defense of the state governments' republicanism but an attack from the standpoint of monarchy, written while Adams was ambassador to the Court of St. James's. Madison's claim was overstated to say the least. To call Adams's writing a betrayal reflected the politics of 1791, not 1787, when the book had been published.

Madison went on to say that since Adams had become vice president, "his pen has constantly been at work." Adams's writings had been published without his name attached, but "the author has been as well known as if that formality had been observed." To Madison, Adams's "anti-republican discourses" excused Jefferson's indiscretion.[155]

Madison's arguments revealed how strongly he could condemn Hamilton and Adams when Jefferson's reputation was on the line. It also showed that the dispute over the Bank of the United States had deepened the rift between him and Hamilton. Notwithstanding Madison's loyalty, however, Jefferson had made a serious political blunder in regard to the Paine pamphlet.

The United States was not France. Its revolutionary age was past. In a new political era that belonged to the new Constitution, national executive power was being built and consolidated, not pulled down. To question authority was to challenge the new constitutional institutions and the personal, charismatic authority of George Washington. Jefferson could no longer play the radical philosophe without political consequences. To criticize and try to restrain the new government would require an entirely different and new kind of strategy.

The Trip

In the last week of May 1791, Madison and Jefferson set off, planning to "cross over through Vermont to [the] Connecticut River and down that to New Haven, then through Long Island to New York and so to Philadelphia."[156] The trip came at a pivotal juncture in their linked political lives. Over the course of the previous year, Alexander Hamilton had outmaneuvered them twice—once with their acquiescence, the second time against their best efforts. In retrospect, it was clear, the assumption of state debts had given Hamilton momentum to pass the bank bill. Through a permanent national debt and the bank, Hamilton had invented a national financial infrastructure every bit as important as Madison's Constitution. In the process, he had shown that George Washington was prepared to side with him rather than his fellow Virginia planters.

Just as vexing as Hamilton's success was the ascent of John Adams. Madison and Jefferson had expected him to be largely irrelevant in the vice presidency, and he had begun his term badly by calling for quasi-aristocratic titles. Yet Adams had subsequently found his footing, using his considerable literary talents to write the "Discourses on Davila," a sustained defense of mixed monarchy and precedent-based tradition.[157] To Madison and Jefferson, sympathetic to the Revolution, Adams's writings were anti-republican and even pro-monarchic.

Before the trip, Madison and Jefferson had begun to plot a course for a response, as the recruitment of Freneau indicated. But they had not, it seems, gone much further. The three weeks they spent entirely in each other's company gave them the opportunity to plan under relaxed and enjoyable circumstances.

Although Madison and Jefferson were attuned to politics on the trip, they acted like landowning late eighteenth-century travelers. They took constant notice of the quality and price of property. They considered what crops were being planted and the prices they fetched. Jefferson especially, but also Madison, reported on flora and occasionally fauna. Together with

Jefferson's slave James Hemings and Madison's slave Matthew,[158] they traveled from New York City up the Hudson Valley to Lake Champlain, and on May 31, 1791, went from Champlain to Fort Ticonderoga. On June 1 they reached Lake George.

In Lake George, Madison observed a 250-acre farm "owned and inhabited by a free Negro" named Prince Taylor.[159] Taylor piqued Madison's interest. He wrote that the African American cultivated the land "with six white hirelings . . . and by industry and good management turns to good account." The farmer "is intelligent; reads, writes, and understands accounts, and is dexterous in his affairs. During the late war he was employed in the commissary department."

Madison carefully noted Taylor's preference for bachelorhood: "He has no wife, and is said to be disinclined to marriage: nor any woman on his farm."[160] Still himself unmarried at forty, Madison seemed almost as intrigued by Taylor's reported disinclination to marriage as he was by the fact of a free, independent African American farmer who hired white laborers.

On June 2 the travelers reached Fort Edward. On June 3 and 4 they traveled thirty-one miles from Saratoga to Bennington, Vermont. Entering Vermont, Madison noted that the settlers were "chiefly emigrants from New England. Their living is extremely plain and economical particularly in the table and ordinary dress." The settlers' wooden houses "make a good figure without; but are very scantily furnished within."

By June 6 they had made it to western Massachusetts—the only time Madison would ever set foot in the state. They traveled south thirty-four miles to Northampton on the Connecticut River. From there they traveled by boat downriver to the Long Island Sound, making the crossing to Long Island. Eventually, closing the loop of their journey, they made their way back to Manhattan on the Brooklyn ferry.

From New York, Jefferson returned to Philadelphia. Madison remained, considering a further trip to Boston. "I am still resting on my oars," Madison wrote to Jefferson on June 27.[161] He gave various excuses: His horse was sick; the stagecoach "travels too rapidly for my purpose." But ultimately the real reason was that Madison did not want to go without Jefferson. "A journey without a companion . . . makes me consider whether the next fall may not present a better prospect."[162] In July, Madison abandoned the plan altogether.[163]

The Thomas Paine affair continued to rankle. Madison wrote to Jefferson that "an attack on Paine has appeared in a Boston paper under the name of Publicola." He assumed it was by John Adams, since it "has an affinity in the style as well as sentiments" to the essays that Adams had written anonymously for the *Gazette of the United States*. (In fact, the Publicola essay was by Adams's son John Quincy Adams, all of twenty-three years old.)[164]

Madison followed up to Jefferson that "Mr. Adams seems to be getting faster and faster into difficulties." He predicted "the attack on Paine . . . will draw the public attention to his obnoxious principles, more than everything he has published." This was wishful thinking. Adams's position was perfectly acceptable to Hamilton and his supporters.

Jefferson wrote back to Madison that in Philadelphia, "nobody doubts who is the author of Publicola." He added neutrally, even a bit sympathetically, that Adams "is very indecently attacked" in the Philadelphia newspapers.[165] The most important point was that, even after Jefferson and Madison's trip out of town, the Paine issue created by Jefferson's indiscretion had not yet gone away.[166] The subject was being kept alive to gain political advantage. This was an ominous sign: Partisan politics was emerging.

Speculation

Madison watched the progress of funding the national bank with a gimlet eye. He had criticized Hamilton's plan because it would make the initial purchasers instantly rich and was therefore unfair insofar as it was limited to people who lived near Philadelphia. But before shares were sold in the eighteenth-century version of an initial public offering, the original plan was modified so that not all of the stock would be sold at a single location and not all of it would be of a single type.

As the offering was actually implemented, stock was sold in Philadelphia, Boston, and New York. Purchasers bought subscriptions— abbreviated as "scrip"—for $25 in gold or silver. Each scrip entitled the bearer to buy one share of bank stock for $400, payable in June 1793, some two years later.[167]

The day of the offering, would-be buyers flocked to the purchase centers carrying the gold and silver they would need to buy the scrip. Some 24,600 subscribers sought to buy stock, "4600 more than could be received," Jefferson told Madison from Philadelphia. As a result, "many persons [were] left in the lurch." Those who had tried and failed to get stock "accused the directors of a misdeal," and were divided on whether it would be better to sue the directors of the bank or "haul them up before Congress."

The value of the scrip went up immediately. Jefferson reported to Madison that "every $25 actually deposited, sold yesterday [after the initial subscription] for from $40–$50 with the future rights and burdens annexed to the deposit."[168] The stock's immediate appreciation gave the purchasers profits of between 60 and 100 percent.

Madison wrote to Jefferson from New York that "the bank shares have risen as much in the market" as in Philadelphia. Instead of feeling pleased that the bank was popular with the markets, Madison interpreted the event as an inside deal designed to make the rich richer:

> It seems admitted on all hands now that the plan of the institution
> gives a moral certainty of gain to the subscribers with scarce a physical
> possibility of loss. The subscriptions are consequently a mere scramble
> for so much public plunder which will be engrossed by those already
> loaded with the spoils of individuals.[169]

The concentration of wealth worried Madison specifically because he believed the bank would give political power to the capitalists who owned its shares. "It pretty clearly appears also in what proportions the public debt lies in the country," he wrote to Jefferson, "what sort of hands hold it, and by whom the people of the U.S. are to be governed."[170] He also reported to Jefferson the rumor that "the cards were packed, for the purpose of securing the game to Philadelphia."[171]

The concentration was the more worrisome because, as Jefferson reported back to Madison, "the subscriptions to the bank from Virginia were almost none." Even Hamilton, Jefferson added, was experiencing "uneasiness" at the asymmetry, and wanted to "propose to the president to sell some of the public shares to subscribers from Virginia and North Carolina, if any more should offer." Jefferson thought that Virginians would not buy the shares even if offered to them directly. "Sober thinkers," he said, could not "prefer a paper medium at 13 percent interest to gold and silver for nothing."[172] What Jefferson considered sobriety reflected an instinctual rejection of financial instruments in favor of hard currency. The evidence suggests that most well-off Virginians thought similarly. Yet seen in national terms, their view was anachronistic.

Madison, partaking in Jefferson's distrust of financial speculation, found the entire spectacle distasteful. "Of all the shameful circumstances of this business," he wrote to Jefferson, among the worst was "to see members of the legislature who were most actively pushing this job, openly grasping its emoluments." A "job" meant a stockjob, a deceitful financial maneuver designed to push a stock up or down to make profits. To Madison, the bank was a stockjob by self-dealing members of Congress.

He feared that the pattern would recur. On August 8, 1791, Madison reported to Jefferson the rumor that in the next term, Congress would make a provision for "deferred debt," a portion of government bonds the payment of which had been delayed until after 1800. The rumor had led to speculation in these bonds. Furthermore, the rumor suggested that speculators were trying to buy up such debt in the southern states. Madison wrote to Jefferson that "I have had a hint that something is intended and has dropped from —— —— which has led to this speculation." The blanks hinted at Alexander Hamilton, the sole person whose power was great enough to make the rumor mill turn. "I am unwilling to credit the fact, until I have further evidence, which I am in a train of getting, if it exists," Madison told Jefferson.[173]

Madison feared that the new system, in which the federal government paid its debts to the benefit of financial speculators, might be just as bad as the old system in which the state governments failed to pay their debts and issued paper currency to the benefit of debtors. It was unclear which system was "chargeable with the greater substantial injustice," Madison wrote to Jefferson. "The true difference seems to be that in the former the few were the victims to the many; by the latter the many to the few."

In the years before the Constitution, Madison had feared paper money as a threat to private property. Now the greatest threat was that private capital would come to run the entire system. If the deferred debt was funded, he intoned, "my imagination will not attempt to set bounds to the daring depravity of the times." He predicted "the stockjobbers will become the praetorian band of the government—at once its tool and its tyrants; bribed by its largesses, and overawing it . . . by its clamors and combinations."[174]

Madison was depicting the dark side of Hamilton's idealized picture of financial markets. In Madison's bleak vision, the capital markets were like the Roman Praetorian Guard, used by the government to achieve its goals, but simultaneously dominating the government to accomplish their own ends. This was the very opposite of republicanism. It was not government by the people. It was government by capital.

Madison's principled republican concerns were mixed with a cultural concern about the effects of financial speculation on public attention. "Nothing new is talked of here," he told Jefferson. "In fact, stockjobbing drowns every other subject. The coffeehouse is in an eternal buzz for the gamblers."[175] New York had ceased to be the political capital. Its conversation had turned to finance, a topic it would never give up again.

Henry Lee, as usual ready to offer Madison the most extreme form of republican fear, went one better. Having traveled from Philadelphia back to Virginia, Lee wrote, "My whole route presented to me one continued scene of stock gambling." It was not only in the coffeehouses that financial speculation was being discussed. "Agriculture, commerce, and even the fair sex relinquished . . . to make way for unremitted exertion in this favorite pursuit." He quoted in Latin the old Greek adage, "Whom the gods would destroy they first make mad."[176] To Lee, the neglect of farming and trading were bad enough; but ignoring the pursuit of women was evidence of insanity.

The public, Lee observed, did not seem upset by this turn of events. To the contrary, it considered the success of the stock to be evidence that Hamilton's bank had been a good idea. "What is astonishing in this business," Lee wrote, "is, that all orders of people seem to reckon this appreciation of the public paper a positive proof of wisdom and integrity in government." He concluded that the rise of public finance was now a fait accompli: "I cannot devise any plan of correcting this evil without risking a greater. Government has so connected the thing with itself that the destruction of the one will convulse the other."[177]

By August 11, 1791, the price of scrip originally bought for $25 had risen to $300 in the orgy of speculation. The success of the public offering had created a bubble. The bubble then did what all bubbles do: It burst. The price of scrip began to plummet.

Hamilton responded in two ways. First, he let it be known that he believed the value of the scrip had been too high at $300. In a private letter to a friend of his, William Duer, who had briefly been assistant secretary of the treasury and had now invested heavily in scrip, Hamilton said he thought the value of the scrip should be $190. Rumors abounded that Duer was manipulating the market. Hamilton warned his friend that the rumors would harm "your *purse* and . . . your *reputation.*" But in effect Hamilton was instructing Duer to try and maintain the price at $190.[178]

Second, in consultation with other members of a special committee,[179] Hamilton ordered the Treasury itself to buy $150,000 in government securities in the open market. The idea was to communicate confidence and thereby calm the market.[180]

Together these efforts paused the decline in the value of the scrip. Still, Madison and his friends saw the whole cycle as absurd and dangerous. They felt, with Jefferson, that anyone of "sober" judgment would act rationally and stay out of the market. If that was true, however, it meant that such sobriety was not to be the norm in the United States.

Misrepresentations

Madison and Jefferson were now significantly at odds with Hamilton on matters of policy, yet Madison, at least, still hoped to keep personal relations civil. In July 1791, Madison went to see Hamilton in the hopes of quashing a rumor that had disturbed Hamilton. The job of comptroller of the treasury had recently come open. Madison's ally Tench Coxe of Philadelphia wanted it. Madison and Jefferson supported Coxe, and may have communicated this to Hamilton. But Hamilton wanted Oliver Wolcott, Jr., of Connecticut, who was already auditor of the treasury. As Madison told it to Jefferson, "This circumstance has got into circulation in the shape of an attempt in you and myself to intermeddle with the Treasury Department, to frustrate the known wishes of the head of it, and to keep back the lineal successor, from southern antipathy to his eastern descent!"[181]

Madison told Hamilton face-to-face that he and Jefferson had no desire to interfere in the decision. Indeed "it was impossible from the very nature of the case," because Jefferson and Madison could not possibly have entertained "the idea of working against his purposes in his own department." Hamilton made it clear to Madison that he had been ruffled: He "has certainly viewed it through a very wrong medium," Madison reported to Jefferson. But after the conversation, Hamilton "seemed disposed to admit the right one." The rumor mill was reflecting genuine political tensions. This was not, Madison said, "the only instance I find in which the most uncandid and unfounded things of like tendency have been thrown into circulation."[182]

Jefferson thought Madison was being naïve. He believed Hamilton himself had spread the rumor. "Nobody could know of T.C.'s application but himself, H., you and myself," Jefferson wrote to Madison. Among those who knew, "Which of the four would feel an inclination to excite an opinion that you and myself were hostile to everything not southern?"[183] The whole episode was preposterous in Jefferson's view. The only explanation was that Hamilton was trying to make Madison and Jefferson look bad.

In response, Madison told Jefferson that he admitted it was "a little singular, no doubt, that so serious a face should have been put on it by [Hamilton,] who ought to have known the circumstances." Apparently Hamilton had said that he got "his wrong impressions" from another, unnamed candidate for the office.[184] This suggested that Madison was open to Jefferson's interpretation—but also that he was not quite ready to accept Jefferson's frank condemnation of Hamilton's character.

Despite Hamilton's obvious and growing influence over Washington, Jefferson and Madison still remained close with the president. Urging Madison to come to Philadelphia from New York so that they could travel together back to Virginia, Jefferson wrote that Washington had been asking if Madison had arrived. "It has been the first question from the president every time I have seen him for this fortnight." Washington very much wanted to see Madison, Jefferson told him. "If you had arrived before dinner today, I had a strong charge to carry you there."[185]

To all appearances, Madison retained his traditional role as Washington's congressional ally. Although he did not draft Washington's opening address to Congress, he was on the committee that wrote the House's response, and Washington asked him to draft the presidential answer to the congressional address.[186]

Yet something important had changed as a result of Madison's unsuccessful opposition to Hamilton's finance legislation. Within the presidential administration, power lay with Hamilton. In Congress, power had shifted to Hamilton's allies.

The initiative in the creation of the new form of government had turned from Madison to Hamilton. Having played a central role in the creation of the constitutional structure, Madison now wanted the government to step back. Hamilton, however, had established a new financial structure, and intended the government to promote economic growth.

Hamilton had supported Madison when he was shaping the country's constitutional structure. But now that Hamilton was leading the charge, Madison found himself unable to support him in return. To Madison, Hamilton was gradually revealing his intention to subvert republican government.

These disagreements were not the sort about which reasonable republican gentlemen could disagree. They were fundamental; they were cultural; and, ultimately, they were existential for republicanism. Having created a Constitution designed to avoid the emergence of parties, Madison was moving inexorably into opposition.

CHAPTER NINE

Enemies

...

THE ARGUMENT: *Having designed the Constitution to centralize power and eliminate the need for political parties, Madison—aiming to defeat Hamilton—joins Jefferson to create a party designed to preserve states' influence. His onetime friendship with Hamilton, reflecting his ideal of concord, is transformed into a relationship of personal and political enmity. Hamilton and the Federalists become, to Madison, enemies of the constitutional republic, bent on its subversion to monarchy and control by financial markets.*

Madison's earlier emphasis on the constitutional technologies of checks and enlargement is now supplanted by the new idea of "public opinion" as the ultimate check—and public opinion can be reflected only through party organization. The need to build a party drives Madison to polemics in favor of farmers and against merchants. He tries to pressure Washington to reject Hamilton's Federalism in favor of democratic Republicanism. He fails. In the first national partisan electoral battle—for Washington's vice president in his second term—Madison's Republicans lose.

WITH NOTHING TO DO in Congress except oppose Hamilton, Madison turned to writing. On November 21, 1791, he published the first in a series of eighteen anonymous essays in Freneau's newly created *National Gazette*. Together they represented a major new direction in Madison's thought. Until now, he had spent the bulk of his intellectual efforts designing a republican constitutional government on a national scale. Now, belatedly, Madison turned to the question of how to run that government—a question Hamilton had already begun to answer.

Madison began with first principles. His initial essay, "Population and Emigration," opened with a deceptively simple question. What, Madison asked, was to become of "the surplus of human life"? Malthus's answers were infanticide, starvation, and death by war and disease. But another option was emigration, which invariably went "from places where living is more difficult to places where it is less difficult." Freedom of emigration was therefore always "in the general interests of humanity" and "favorable to morals." This included not only emigration from the Old World to the New but from the East Coast of the United States to the newly emerging West.[1]

Targeting Hamilton's efforts to centralize power, Madison was trying to establish a theoretical justification for spreading political authority across the states. If nature dictated that people must move west, and republicanism required self-government, then there was no choice but to extend power with the expanding people. The consequences to Native Americans were obvious and, to Madison, unremarkable: They would have to accommodate expansion across the continent or be destroyed.

Madison's next essay, published December 5, 1791, attacked the consolidation of the states into one government. If the states were eliminated, then either the executive must be multiplied to avoid giving the president too much power, or else the president would become a king. What was more, if the state governments were abolished, Congress could not effectively represent "the voice nor the sense of 10 or 20 millions of people, spread through so many latitudes as are comprehended within the United States." Deprived of "expressions of the public mind," the government would act in its own self-interest—"which, it must be owned, is a natural propensity of every government."[2]

This about-face was stunning. Since 1786, Madison had been arguing for stronger central government. Every time opponents warned of the danger of concentrated power, Madison responded that the lesson of history was that federal governments were destroyed by the autonomy of their constituent members, not by the central government. Now Madison himself was warning against the dangers of consolidation.

To be sure, there was no inherent contradiction between Madison's earlier views and those he expressed here. It was logically possible to believe both that the federal republic would be unable to function if the state legislatures had too much power and also to believe that the republic would fail if the states had no power at all. What had changed so drastically was the point of emphasis. Madison was transforming himself from an advocate of strengthening centralized government into an advocate for maintaining state prerogatives.

The Old Gentleman

One observer who noticed the shift in Madison's political thinking was his old adversary Patrick Henry. By the end of 1791, Henry had begun to withdraw from politics—but he remained the preeminent lawyer in Virginia. In a highly visible lawsuit in the Virginia Supreme Court over the validity of British debts, Henry argued the defendant's case with notable skill. Edmund Pendleton, who shared Madison's low opinion of Henry, wrote to Madison that "Mr. Henry was truly great, and for the first time I ever heard him, methodical and connected for two days and a half."[3]

Henry instructed an intermediary to tell Madison's youngest brother, William Madison, then serving his first term in the Virginia House of Delegates, that he wished to be in touch with Madison. Henry wanted a "renewal of a correspondence," William wrote to his brother from Richmond. Henry had authorized him to say "that such an intercourse will not only be extremely acceptable but its decline is a subject of regret to Col. Henry and his lady."

William wanted his brother to accept Henry's overture, which would certainly have benefited William in his fledgling political career. He told Madison that he did not "see any impropriety" in correspondence with Henry, "but on the other hand great advantage probably resulting from the communication as it is in his power to give you more information of the disposition of the different parts of the state than perhaps any other man in it."[4]

The most probable explanation for why the wily Henry reached out to Madison's impressionable younger brother is that Henry, observing Madison's opposition to Hamilton develop, now saw in him a potential ally. William ended his letter to Madison optimistically: "I wish to know your sentiments on the subject and if you do not see any greater obstacle than I do, I hope you will gratify the old gentleman."[5] William had been at least partially seduced.

In his response to William, Madison made no concession to family feeling or to helping William's career. William and James Madison were far apart in age, and had never been close. Indeed, when he first heard that William wanted to become a politician, Madison wrote to Ambrose Madison skeptically that he was "at a loss what to say as to brother William's adventuring into public life."[6] And Madison did not need Henry's political contacts, which had always been used to try to destroy him politically.

On the other side of William's letter, Madison copied out for posterity his pointed, carefully crafted, answer. With gentlemanly reserve he began by saying that he had "never, in the midst of political contests indulged any personal ill-will to that gentleman, and at all times admired his eminent talents." It was not true that Madison's sense of competition with Henry had been business, not personal. Madison had privately believed that Henry sought nothing but individual aggrandizement, even if it came to dismembering the United States. Madison was presenting himself as the gentleman who could differ from his political opponents without "ill will."

In the driest possible terms, Madison told his brother that because he had never harbored a grudge against Henry, he could not be "supposed insensible to any friendly sentiments he may have expressed towards me." The double hypothetical in the double negative distanced Madison as much as human language would allow: If Henry had actually said anything nice about him, then it should not be assumed that he would not care. If "occasion might prompt," he might find himself prepared to give proof that he had nothing against Henry.[7]

"On the other hand"—and here came Madison's thrust—"having never been in the habit of a correspondence with him, an abrupt commencement of one . . . is not perhaps so proper a proof as you seem to have conceived."[8] Madison was explaining to his brother, the political neophyte, that he and Henry were not friends but bitter opponents who had never written to each other except on a single occasion in 1784 when Madison was just starting out in the state legislature and the battle between them had not yet begun.[9] "I do not well understand," Madison wrote to his brother, "what is meant by the words in your letter" referring to the "decline" of correspondence: "It cannot refer to any pre-existing intercourse," because there had not been any. If Henry had written to him and not received an answer—"a construction extremely improbable"— then William should tell Henry that "no such letter has been received and for that reason only, not answered."[10]

This was Madison at his most acerbic. His intention was to rebuff

Henry's subtle advances directly, and to chide William for allowing himself to be drawn into Henry's orbit. Madison's views were shifting in a direction that would make him an advocate of states' rights. But whatever Henry hoped, Madison utterly rejected the thought of any connection to him, much less the alliance that might have been suggested by a political correspondence. Madison's sense of his enemies was becoming keener than it had ever been before—and he had no desire to have any contact with them, much less keep them close in the guise of friends.

Public Opinion

On December 19, 1791, the *National Gazette* published Madison's "Public Opinion," a short essay that represented an important evolution in his thought. From theories of constitutional structure and ratification, Madison was moving toward applied knowledge of how government actually worked. That knowledge would then form the basis for a concrete plan to change the balance of political power.

His first insight was that "public opinion sets bounds to every government, and is the real sovereign in every free one."[11] Madison explained to his readers that sometimes, public opinion was fixed, and so "must be obeyed by the government." Other times, however, public opinion was flexible, and so could be "influenced by the government." Where public opinion influenced government, government would then be influenced by the impulse that formed public opinion. As an example, Madison gave the Bill of Rights. Public opinion had demanded the drafting of the Bill of Rights—and, in turn, the Bill of Rights would therefore exert an influence on government.

In notes he took while preparing to draft his *National Gazette* essays, Madison had jotted down that "the best provision for stable and free government is not a balance of the powers of the government, though that is not to be neglected, but an equilibrium in the interests and passions of the society itself."[12] Madison's constitutional design had sought a balance of powers within government. This balance was not working according to plan, as the adoption of the national bank demonstrated. Public opinion was something different: the manifestation of the people's interests and passions. This would be Madison's new focus.

Reflecting on public opinion led Madison back to his interest in the size of the country.[13] "The larger the country," he wrote, the harder it would be to ascertain "real opinion" and the easier for nefarious actors to "counterfeit" opinion. Yet in a large country, the importance of public opinion when actually fixed or imagined to be fixed would be all the greater. As a consequence, a large country would be "favorable to the authority of government" as well as "unfavorable to liberty." The United States was, therefore, vulnerable to the danger that the government would become too powerful and violate liberty as it became more removed from ordinary citizens.

This concern about the dangers of size was very nearly the opposite of the view Madison had repeatedly expressed while drafting and ratifying the Constitution. Then he had insisted that a larger country was not a threat but a guard of liberty, because it would be more difficult to form unified factions. Now, faced with the rise of Hamilton and his policies, Madison was worried that by creating the perception that public opinion favored debt and a bank, Hamilton's party would enable the government to dominate the public.

Madison closed this brief but penetrating essay with a counterpoint. How could a large territory be, in effect, contracted to reduce the threat to liberty? His solution lay in the flow of information. "Good roads, domestic commerce, a free press, and particularly a circulation of newspapers to the entire body of the people, and representatives going from, and returning among every part of them," were "equivalent to a contraction of territorial limits, and . . . favorable to liberty."[14]

This was more than just a plug for the *National Gazette*. Madison was trying to figure out how to counterbalance centralized authority. The strategy he was proposing depended on bringing people from all over the country—he particularly meant Virginia and the West—into political debate. Newspapers would bring information to and from the "entire body of the people," not just the centers of government and finance. And elected representatives must themselves circulate as well. The *Gazette* was a "national" newspaper because it was supposed to transcend Philadelphia and indeed transcend the government.

In his next essay, which appeared on January 2, 1792, Madison continued the argument. Monarchy, he claimed, "contrary to the received opinion," was actually a bad form of government for a large state, because even "the eyes of a good prince cannot see all that he ought to know" while a bad king could not be restrained "by the fear of combinations against him." His point was that a confederated republic such as the United

States avoided both of these dangers. "Every good citizen will be at once a sentinel over the rights of the people; over the authorities of the federal government; and over the rights and the authorities of the intermediate government."[15] The people collectively would see everything, and thus have better knowledge than a monarch.[16] The division between central and state governments would protect against usurpation.

Madison was implying that Hamilton wanted to create a centralized monarchy—the view he had espoused at the Philadelphia convention. Nervous that others might consider this a good idea in such a large country as the United States, Madison was trying to find some logic to contest it. It was a sign of the times that, less than five years after Hamilton's speech, Madison could think that he needed to mount a convincing public argument against a king. Under Washington, the executive branch was achieving prestige and authority. To some worried observers, the emerging excesses of the French Revolution seemed to underscore the value of monarchy. In Madison's mind, republicanism could no longer be taken for granted.

The Parchment in the Fire

On December 5, 1791, Hamilton had sent Congress his *Report on Manufactures*, the third and final in a series of reports designed to lay out a financial and economic infrastructure for the United States—and the document that would catalyze the most radical of Madison's *National Gazette* essays. Hamilton's first argument was that the United States should, in his phrase, "diversify" its economic base so that industry would become as important as agriculture. Hamilton then argued that the best way to promote manufactures was through "bounties," direct government subsidies to favored industries. He also embraced protective tariffs on imported goods that would give an advantage to domestic manufactures. Bounties were better than tariffs because they gave domestic producers an instant advantage over foreign competitors even in foreign markets.

As a veteran of the national bank controversy, Hamilton could anticipate the objection that Congress lacked the authority to pay subsidies because there was no specific constitutional provision allowing for them. He therefore pointed to the term "general welfare" in the Constitution, which, he said, was "doubtless intended to signify more than was expressed." As a matter of "necessity" it must be up to Congress "to pronounce upon the objects which concern the general welfare." Money could be appropriated for anything "requisite and proper" to satisfy the general welfare.[17]

Madison sent a copy of the report to Henry Lee, asking, "What think you of the commentary on the terms 'general welfare'?" Then he preemptively answered his own question: "The federal government has been hitherto limited to specified powers, [even] by the greatest champions for latitude extolling those powers." Hamilton's followers had in the past simply argued that Congress's enumerated powers, combined with the necessary and proper clause, implied that Congress had all the powers needed to fulfill its explicitly enumerated ones. Now, however, "if not only the *means,* but the *objects* are unlimited, the parchment had better be thrown into the fire at once."[18] The constitutional structure of enumerated powers would be utterly destroyed.

As prompted, Lee responded to Madison with the most extreme possible interpretation of Hamilton: He contemplated the "debasement of the species," the creation of *Homo economicus.* Instead of agricultural man, "a stout, muscular ploughman full of health . . . with his eight or ten blooming children," Hamilton favored "squat, bloated fellows all belly and no legs who can walk two miles in the hour and manufacture a little."[19]

Madison was inclined to agree. He wrote back to Lee that if the "usurpation of power recommended in the report on manufactures" should be enacted, he would "consider the fundamental and characteristic principle of the government as subverted." The principle at stake was the notion of a government of limited powers. If bounties were adopted, "It will no longer be a government possessing special powers taken from the general mass, but one possessing the general mass with special powers reserved out of it." The Constitution would thereby be subverted as well: "This change will take place in defiance of the true and universal construction, and of the sense in which the instrument is known to have been proposed, advocated and ratified."[20] The constitutional visions of the two lead authors of the *Federalist* essays were now irrevocably at odds.

Drawing on his new argument about public opinion, Madison told Lee that the test of how things would go lay with the public: "Whether the people of this country will submit to a Constitution not established by themselves, but imposed on them by their rulers, is a problem to be solved by the event alone." The job of "all those who are friendly to their rights" was to spread the word so that "their situation should be understood by them, and that they should have as fair an opportunity as possible of judging for themselves."[21]

Madison asked Lee to keep his sentiments "for yourself alone at present." But in letters to other friends, he reiterated that Hamilton's approach contained in the *Report on Manufactures* would, if adopted, subvert "the fundamental and characteristic principle of the government, as contrary to the true and fair, as well as the received construction . . . in which the Constitution is known to have been proposed, advocated and adopted."[22]

Madison was not yet making his argument in a precise way, but its drift was that Congress had no general authority to enact subsidies as part of its trade policy. Within a few weeks, he would explain in the speech to Congress that there was no enumerated power in Congress to award bounties.[23] Given that Madison had first conceived of the need for the new national, unified Constitution precisely in order to create a unified national trade policy, this was a remarkable position. His emphasis on limited powers, developed during the debate over the national bank, did not fit the question of trade policy anywhere near as well.

Yet Madison had chosen the Constitution as the ground of his opposition to Hamilton, and he could not now abandon it in favor of mere policy disagreement. His constitutional argument was designed to appeal directly to the people. Madison believed that the people had enacted the Constitution and knew what it meant. Only collective opinion could rein in Hamilton's runaway undertaking.

The die was now cast. Mobilizing public opinion would require something that had previously been anathema to Madison's entire constitutional vision. It would require the creation of a political party to protect the Constitution from the government itself.

Parties

The public must be warned. On January 23, 1792, Madison, the scourge of faction, published an anonymous *National Gazette* essay exploring the creation of a political party. The shift in Madison's political thought could hardly have been more momentous. His underlying republican commitments had not changed. But the reality of government under the Constitution was driving him in a direction he could not have anticipated and into the arms of a political strategy he had long rejected as counter to the very spirit of constitutional government.

Called simply "Parties," the essay began with the assertion that "in every political society, parties are unavoidable." Madison had explained at length in the *Federalist* that factions arose from differences of material and economic interests. He repeated that argument now in compressed form.[24]

As he had in the past, Madison continued to assert that "the great object should be to combat the evil" of party. But now he offered a new set of arguments. The way to avoid the evil of party was first to establish "political equality among all." Then politicians ought to maintain some measure of economic equality to go alongside political equality. They should avoid giving "unnecessary opportunities ... to increase the inequality of property, by an immoderate, and especially an unmerited, accumulation of riches." This was a direct jab at the stockjobbing operations by which the initial public offering for the Bank of the United States had made a few men rich.

What was more, politicians should "by the silent operation of laws ... reduce extreme wealth towards a state of mediocrity, and raise extreme indigents towards a state of comfort." Such laws should not "violat[e] the rights of property," but they should be designed to produce as much economic equality within society as possible.

This vision of promoting economic equality by law was surprising from Madison. Classical republicans had long believed that some measure of economic equality was necessary to maintain political equality.[25] But Madison, son of a rich man, had never before argued against wealth either publicly or privately. His great worry in the run-up to the Constitution had been the danger that state legislatures would dilute property rights by easing the conditions for the collection of debt and issuing paper money—a worry about government equalizing rich and poor.

Something truly unsettling was happening to Madison. The government should, he went on, abstain from "measures which operate differently on different interests and particularly such as favor one interest at the expense of another." This was a none-too-veiled criticism of Hamilton's latest report, which favored manufacturing over agriculture. In two consecutive sentences, Madison urged the government to equalize wealth and then said that it should not adopt measures that affected different interest groups differently.

The most stunning recommendation was still to come. Politicians could minimize party, Madison said, "by making one party a check on the other, so far as the existence of parties cannot be prevented, nor their views accommodated." On the surface this sentence seemed innocuous. After all, according to *Federalist* No. 51, the Constitution itself was designed to balance factions against one another.

On closer examination, however, Madison was not speaking about a general feature of constitutional design that set parties against each other to the detriment of both. Madison was proposing the self-conscious creation of a political party designed to block the operation of another party. If parties could not be "prevented" or "accommodated," Madison was saying, the right response was to make more. Unable to defeat the partisans, Madison proposed to join them.

Madison understood that the intentional creation of a political party ran against every theoretical principle he had ever expressed or endorsed. His next sentence offered an apologetic justification. "If this is not the language of reason," he wrote, "it is that of republicanism." Again, the sentence sounded superficially ordinary—yet again, its meaning was actually extraordinary.

Taken literally, Madison was saying that creating a party might not follow the pure dictates of reason, but was necessary to preserve republicanism against countervailing forces. Underneath this simple suggestion lay a total reversal of Madison's longtime commitment to the idea that reason and republicanism were two sides of the same coin. If Madison had one fundamental commitment in his entire political life—a commitment mirrored in personal affairs—it was to the exercise of reason. Reason alone was the ideal guide to political judgments and to the common good. The Constitution had been designed so that reason, not passion, would guide the nation's political judgment. It had been worthy of ratification, he had believed and argued, precisely because it enabled reason to prevail. Republicanism, for its part, was the form of government best suited to the use of reason, because it relied on rational deliberation by the people's representatives. Factions or parties were the opposite of reason.

Now, for the first time, Madison was asserting that the preservation of republicanism might require the abandonment of reason. Indeed, Madison defined a faction as a group of people organized against the reasoned and correct policy that represented the true interests of the people. To create a new political party in order to counterbalance other parties was to create a new instrument of unreason to combat those already in existence. If this was the "language" of "republicanism," it was a language Madison had until now wholly neglected.

Cynics might have expected parties to emerge under the Constitution. But Madison's idealistic constitutional design had been intended to eliminate or at least dampen the effects of party. Now he was not merely accepting partisanship as inevitable—he was advocating for it.

Opinion and Circumstances of the Times

In an essay published January 30, 1792, Madison paused his argument for political parties to argue that "the force of public opinion" kept the government of Great Britain stable—not, as Hamilton and Adams believed, its constitutional design. Madison's proof was that the British constitution had changed radically between the Middle Ages and 1688, when it had assumed something like its modern form after the Glorious Revolution. The old system had persisted for centuries—because it was "supported by the opinion and circumstances of the times," just like "the intermediate variations, through which the government has passed."[26] In other words, the British government worked because the British people liked it.

This excursus on Britain might have seemed irrelevant to Madison's audience in the *National Gazette*, but it was not. In shaping the Constitution and arguing for its ratification, Madison had himself subscribed to the idea that the constitutional design of government determined whether a government would succeed or fail. The separation of powers between the branches, alongside the federal structure dividing state governments from the central government, were the keys to constitutional success.

But now Madison was claiming that public opinion ensured the government's stability and protected fundamental liberties. The written constitution would be of use in so far as the people treated it as a reference point and demanded that the existing government comply with it. Beyond that, no written document was necessary—and indeed Great Britain lacked a single formal, written constitution.

Madison was rethinking his original view of the power and importance of constitutional structure because he had seen Hamilton's supporters run roughshod over what he had considered the obvious meaning of the Constitution. In thinking about the Bill of Rights, Madison had told

Jefferson that its value came not from the parchment promises it made but, rather, from fixing the idea of basic rights in the public mind. Now he was extending that insight to cover the building blocks of the Constitution as well. Astoundingly, Madison was questioning the very premises on which he had built the government of the United States.

At least some of his correspondents shared his doubts. Henry Lee wrote to Madison that the constitutional design, though excellent in itself, was under threat of fundamental change. "I admire the Constitution," Lee wrote. "I reverence the principles on which it is founded and love affectionately the objects which are contemplated." The problem lay with how the Constitution was being implemented. "All that grieves me," Lee went on, "is the perverseness of its administration." Hamilton's approach had produced results that were false to the spirit of the Constitution. "But [they] have been so successful as to render in my judgment a change of constitution in operation certain although there will be no change for a long time in names."[27]

Lee was telling Madison directly what Madison was too cautious to say himself: that Hamilton's measures amounted to a silent constitutional revolution. The United States was in danger of turning into Great Britain, abandoning agricultural republicanism for monarchic manufacture. Lee was acting as one of Madison's sentinels, warning from outside the government of the dangers of government usurpation—and of Hamilton's role in it.

Lee was also urging Madison into a position of overt opposition. "The longer is procrastinated the attempt of men like yourself to force the administration to do obedience to the constitution," he warned, "the more difficult and doubtful will the work be."[28]

The Life of the Husbandman

On February 6, 1792, the *National Gazette* published yet another essay by Madison, this one entitled "Government of the United States" and devoted to a restatement of the importance of the separation of powers.[29] On the one hand, consolidation of the states was "the high road to monarchy." On the other, schism would guarantee "anarchy." He then reached the main political thrust of the essay, which turned out to be a gentle invitation toward party: "Those who love their country, its repose, and its republicanism, will therefore study to avoid the alternative." They must do so "by inculcating moderation in the exercise of the powers of both" state and federal governments, and they must abstain from exercising powers that "might nurse present jealousies, or engender greater."[30]

The tone was moderate, but the content was pointed. Madison was addressing people "who love their country." By implication, there existed others who did not. Since the lovers of the United States would not propose any exercise of powers calculated to create disagreements, it followed that Hamilton and his allies, who were proposing controversial legislation, did not love their country. Instead of damping down "present jealousies," they were increasing them.

Madison closed the essay by insisting that, notwithstanding his emphasis on constitutional "checks of power," such structural checks were "neither the soul nor the chief palladium of constitutional liberty." According to Madison's new emphasis, liberty lay with "the people who are the authors of this blessing . . . [and] also its guardians."[31] The steady drumbeat of his *National Gazette* essays was getting louder as Madison's plan of action was slowly being revealed. The Constitution as written would not matter unless the lovers of the country would rally to his standard and demand its enforcement. Republicanism could only be preserved, and liberty maintained, by the organization of popular opinion.

As Madison increasingly began to think of his own republican allies as a self-organizing party seeking to oppose the partisans of Hamilton, his political language began to change. On February 6, the same day his essay on the government appeared, he argued to Congress that the Constitution did not authorize subsidies or bounties. He called the Hamiltonians' interpretation of the general welfare clause a "novel idea . . . never before entertained by friends or enemies of the government."[32]

The idea of an expansive congressional power under the general welfare clause was not actually completely novel. Supporters of the national bank had been claiming it for more than a year, over Madison's objections. But Madison's suggestion that opponents of the government were its "enemies" was new.

Madison's picture of politics had been one in which close friends—like he and Monroe—could run against each other for office without threatening their friendship. In this idealized world of political friendship, an underlying republican concord would protect individuals as well as the country against outright breakdown. Yet now Madison was speaking publicly of the "enemies" of constitutional government who adopted a broad interpretation of Congress's powers to establish the general welfare.[33]

Forming a political party would require a political constituency—and by the beginning of March, Madison was trying to identify who that would be. His transformation into a partisan politician could not be complete until he could win actual voters to his standard. In a *National Gazette* essay published March 5, 1792, he chose his first target—and launched an uncharacteristic, Jeffersonian defense of farmers over city dwellers.

Before now, Madison, unlike Jefferson, had never favored a purely agricultural republic. At the Philadelphia convention, he had confidently predicted that the economy of the United States would increasingly include manufacturing and trade on a par with agriculture—and he treated that likelihood in the most positive terms. But then he was trying to design a single Constitution to unify the nation and take advantage of its disparate interests. Now Madison was going to war against the promotion of manufacturing.

"The life of the husbandman is preeminently suited to the comfort and happiness of the individual," he wrote. As for intelligence, a mind "in retirement" on a farm might have less "polish," but it would be "more capable of profound and comprehensive efforts."[34]

Madison took a further crack at city life with its "extremes both of want and of waste." Using a borrowed phrase, Madison commented that "'Tis not the country that peoples either the Bridewells or the Bedlams," the prisons or the madhouses.[35] The gratuitous and doubtful condemnation of cities as producers of crime and madness sounded unconvincing from Madison. But Madison was doing politics, and pandering to rural prejudices came with the territory.

In describing his cultural ideal, Madison spoke of "the class of citizens who provide at once their own food and their own raiment"—Americans who both worked the land and also produced "much of the ordinary and most essential consumption." Nothing could be better, Madison claimed, than combining agricultural work with basic production, especially clothing. This group of people "may be viewed as the most truly independent and happy," he claimed. Indeed, "they are more: They are the best basis of public liberty, and the strongest bulwark of public safety." The more people like this there were in society, "the more free, the more independent, the more happy must be the society itself."[36]

Madison was idealizing the small farmer because he hoped to represent small farmers. This political calculus gave him reason to oppose any manufacturing subsidies. He concluded that manufacturing and industry must be evaluated on the grounds of what they did to "the vigor of body, to the faculties of the mind, or to the virtues or utilities of life."[37] Subsidies were bad because they did not serve the true republican agricultural class, the "bulwark of public safety."

In his next *National Gazette* essay, published March 22, Madison turned to Britain and the nascent industrial revolution. Entitled "Fashion," the essay opened with a crisis that had occurred as the result of an epochal change in the footwear industry. In 1786, buckled shoes had fallen out of fashion, and some twenty thousand buckle workers found themselves "without employ, almost destitute of bread, and exposed to the horrors of want of the most inclement season." Madison told his readers that a group of buckle manufacturers had gone so far as to submit a petition to the Prince of Wales "imploring" him to start wearing buckle shoes in the hopes of reversing the fashion trend. The buckle industry was trying to get a celebrity endorsement in the hopes of saving itself from "the *mutability of fashion*."[38]

From this anecdote, Madison derived a series of lessons. The central one was that "the least desirable" jobs "in a free state" were those that "produce the most servile dependence of one class of citizens on another class." The buckle workers needed their jobs for the "absolute necessaries" of life. Yet their livelihoods rested upon "the mere caprices" of shoe purchasers. This was "the evil in its extreme"—and, in fact, was still worse, because, at least according to the hopes of the buckle manufacturers, "the caprice of a single fancy directs the faction of the community." Everything turned on the Prince of Wales: "*Twenty thousand* persons are to get or go without their bread, as a wanton youth . . . may fancy to wear his shoes with or without straps, or to fasten the straps with strings or with buckles." This was "the lowest point of servility."[39]

Madison was proposing that concentrated industry put an economy at risk—and therefore undermined republicanism itself. "What a contrast is here to the independent situation and manly sentiments of American citizens," he wrote. Americans "live on their own soil. They are occupied in supplying wants, which [are] founded in a solid utility," not in fashion. Instead of being dependent on the fashion choices of the rich, Madison's Americans enjoyed "reciprocity of dependence, at once ensuring subsistence, and inspiring a dignified sense of social rights."[40]

The essay was a highly effective piece of political rhetoric, using a suggestive incident to draw far-reaching conclusions that were not necessarily justifiable on grounds of pure logic. It was, in short, an exercise in partisan politicking, tainting manufacturing by association with both servility and monarchy. Madison had never written this way before.

From the specificity of buckles, Madison turned in his next essay to the more abstract topic of property rights. His argument was powerful and important. A just government must protect property—and property must be extended beyond the ownership of "land, merchandise, or money." Property included religious opinion, the safety and liberty of the person— and "an equal property in the free use of his faculties and free choice of the objects on which to employ them."[41]

By associating fundamental rights such as the right to free speech and freedom of religion with the people's right to "free use of their faculties, and free choice of their occupations," Madison was making a case for economic liberty. In particular, he wanted to argue that a government that used "unequal taxes [to] oppress one species of property and reward another species" was unjust and oppressive. Where a government self-consciously used taxes to encourage certain kinds of labor, it violated "that sacred property, which Heaven, in decreeing man to earn his bread by the sweat of his brow, kindly reserved to him."[42]

This was the first time that Madison had expanded his lifelong concern for fundamental rights to include work. He acknowledged the difference between the direct violation of individual rights and what he called legislation "which indirectly violates [the people's] property" by shaping the nature of their labor.[43] Not content to say that Hamilton's plans for manufacturing subsidies exceeded Congress's power, Madison wanted to claim that the entire subsidy approach violated fundamental rights. He would never make the argument again—but then, never again would he be engaged in creating a political party of his own.

The Enemies of the Union

By the end of March 1792, considering the political situation around him, Madison could not help but feel that everything that could be going wrong, was. Congress had passed a bill distributing 120 members of the House of Representatives among the states according to a formula that, Madison believed, was "absolutely irreconcilable with the Constitution."

It was about to consider Hamilton's proposed duties on trade, as well as "a further assumption of the remaining state debts." Madison believed he was likely to lose on all three.

Meanwhile, news arrived of a slave rebellion on an unprecedented scale in Saint-Domingue, modern Haiti. Led by Toussaint Louverture, the uprising seemed to Madison not a harbinger of revolutionary liberty comparable to the French Revolution, but a dangerous threat to the institution of slavery. Information from Saint-Domingue, he told fellow Virginian Edmund Pendleton, "paints the distress of the island in the most gloomy colors."[44]

The only slightly positive political development was another piece of bad news. Hamilton's friend and former Treasury colleague William Duer, the single largest speculator in scrip, had gone spectacularly bankrupt. Duer owed millions of dollars—a huge sum at the time—and his bankruptcy affected many others. "Every description and gradation of persons from the church to the stews are among the dupes of his dexterity and the partners of his distress," Madison wrote to Pendleton.[45] Perhaps, Madison thought, financial collapse would cure the mania for speculation. Even if it did, the human cost would be considerable.

Meanwhile, Madison considered Hamilton and his allies to be ever more openly supporting the idea of monarchy. Madison wrote to Henry Lee of what he called "a small circumstance . . . worthy of notice, as an index of political biases." The federal government was going to issue a coin for the first time, and the Senate voted to put George Washington's head on it. In the House, "this was attacked . . . as a feature of monarchy, and an amendment agreed to substituting an emblematic figure of liberty." The Senate refused the amendment and sent the bill back to the House, which now confirmed its original vote "by a larger majority"—and the Senate this time agreed.[46] The symbolic threat had been staved off; but the danger of monarchy still remained.

It was in this environment that Madison wrote and published what would be his single strongest statement of his break from Hamilton—and from his former vision of republican government. The essay, published April 2, 1792, in the *National Gazette*, was entitled "The Union: Who Are Its Real Friends?" Its goal was nothing less than to divide the political universe into "friends" and "enemies" of republican government.

The essay made the division between friends and enemies explicit. The real friends of the union were "not those who charge others with not being its friends, whilst their own conduct is wantonly multiplying its enemies."[47] Madison was saying that the Hamiltonians were the true enemies of the United States, "multiplying" their own numbers while simultaneously charging Madison and his followers with not being friends of the government. (Madison made no effort to address the embarrassing fact that he, too, was accusing the other side of being the enemy.)

This was a new kind of political thinking. Gone was the Madison who insisted that he could remain on amicable terms with political adversaries. In its place was a Madison who had no compunction about identifying the enemy.

From there Madison's rhetoric began to build. The enemies of the union included "those who favor measures, which by pampering the spirit of speculation within and without the government, disgust the best friends of the union."[48] This was a direct reference to William Duer's speculation. Madison was saying that Hamilton had pampered Duer, which was akin to accusing him of aiding and abetting speculation. And by describing his own reaction as one of "disgust," Madison was expressing himself with more emotion than he had ever deployed in writing before.

If the reference to Hamilton was not clear enough, Madison went on to say that the true friends of the union were

> not those who promote unnecessary accumulations of the debt of the union, instead of the best means of discharging it as fast as possible; thereby increasing the causes of corruption in the government, and the pretexts for new taxes under its authority.[49]

Madison was restating the essence of Hamilton's report on the debt—and attributing it to the enemies of the union. The allegation that the purpose of debt was to facilitate corruption was also a direct reference to the British system of government that Hamilton favored. At the Philadelphia convention, Hamilton had favorably cited the British government's ability to affect decisions in Parliament by money and patronage. He was putting into effect publicly what he had advocated privately five years before. To Madison, this was corruption.

Madison now shifted to the political realm. The enemies of the union were trying "by arbitrary interpretations and insidious precedents, to pervert the limited government of the union, into a government of unlimited discretion, contrary to the will and subversive of the authority of the people."[50] This was Madison's condemnation of Hamilton's argument that Congress had the power to define the objects of the general welfare. Again, the identity of the enemy could not possibly be in doubt.

Not content with the claim that Hamilton was against a government of limited powers, Madison went further still. The enemies of the union "avow or betray principles of monarchy and aristocracy in opposition to the republican principles of the union, and the republican spirit of the people."[51]

Here was Madison's whole attack reduced to its simplest form. Hamilton was a monarchist who wanted to turn the United States into Britain. He had revealed this goal by espousing "a system . . . more accommodated to the depraved examples of those hereditary forms, than to the true genius of our own" republican form of government. As a result, the Hamiltonians "would force on the people the melancholy duty of choosing between the loss of the union, and the loss of what the union was meant to secure."[52] If Hamilton's policy succeeded, the people would have to choose between fighting for liberty and thus ending the union, or acceding to monarchy.

Madison believed that Hamilton's private monarchism was becoming public policy. This made Hamilton into something other than an ordinary political adversary with whom one could maintain friendship. It made him into an enemy. Edmund Randolph had refused to endorse the Constitution in Philadelphia and had endangered ratification in Virginia, yet Madison had remained his friend and ally. James Monroe had opposed ratification and run for Congress against Madison, yet Madison had insisted on remaining friends with Monroe.

Hamilton was different—because the nature of his opposition was different. Randolph and Monroe were fellow republicans with variant views of how the republic should be designed. To Madison, both existed within the sphere of republican concord and friendship. Each, Madison insisted on believing, was sincerely promoting the public good as he saw it.

Hamilton, however, was in Madison's view trying to destroy republicanism itself and replace it with British-style constitutional monarchy. He would turn Congress into an all-powerful Parliament and the president into a king. He would transform the United States into an industrial and trading power on the model of Great Britain. He was, therefore, an enemy of the union that had been created to secure the blessings of republican liberty. And he would have to be defeated.

The people who would defeat Hamilton were "the real friends of the union," Madison explained—and he went on to identify them. They were "friends to the authority of the people, the sole foundation on which the union rests." They were "friends to liberty, the great end, for which the union was formed." They were "friends to the limited and republican system of government."[53]

That was not all. The real friends of the union were enemies of public debt, which was "injurious to the interests of the people, and baneful to the virtue of the government." They were therefore also "enemies to every contrivance for *unnecessarily* increasing its amount, or protracting its duration, or extending its influence."[54] According to this formulation, the debate over the public debt was not simply a disagreement among reasonable people. For Madison, it had come to define who was a true republican and who an enemy of the union. It was as though Madison had forgotten the deal he and Hamilton had reached a year and a half before, trading the location of the capital for Madison's practical acquiescence in the assumption of state debts. Madison was also silent about his view, previously expressed in public, that a moderate national debt was a perfectly acceptable policy.

This was more evidence that Madison had now fully embraced the idea of a distinct political party. His objections to Hamilton's positions were supposed to be so fundamental that they justified treating him as an enemy and therefore becoming an enemy to him in return. In practice, however, politics could not be so neatly divided between fundamental issues and issues allowing for reasonable disagreement. If Hamilton was a monarchist, then the public debt was a tool for making the United States into a monarchy, and must be opposed.

Madison concluded that "the real friends to the union" were those "who are friends to that republican policy throughout." The word "throughout" captured the reality of politics defined by friends and enemies. To be a republican, one must be a republican entirely and wholly. Only republicanism could "cement . . . the union of a republican people." The alternative was "a spirit of usurpation and monarchy" that would not unify the republic, but would be "capable of dissolving it."[55] If Hamilton's plan was monarchy, Madison would be its enemy.

A Spirit of Party

The partisan political division between Madison and Hamilton put George Washington in a difficult situation. That the two of them were increasingly in outright conflict made it look as though Washington was now presiding over the fissuring of republican concord. Within the cabinet, Jefferson and Edmund Randolph sided with Madison. Henry Knox, the secretary of war, sided with Hamilton. Washington's cabinet was evenly split on most of the essential questions of government.

In early April, Washington had to decide whether to sign or veto reapportionment legislation that had been passed by large majorities in the House and Senate and yet ignored the Constitution's formula for assigning representatives. Some republicans were skeptical that the president would do what they considered the right thing. To such skeptics, the written Constitution was failing to limit the government: "Our system on paper either is or is construed to be so amphibious, it is fish or flesh as it happens to suit the market."[56]

Yet Washington, perhaps realizing that the apportionment bill was not of great consequence to Hamilton, gave the republicans a victory by vetoing it before Congress could adjourn. Madison was pleased by the decision,[57] as were other republicans, especially in Virginia.[58] Increasingly, it looked as though the presidential veto was the only credible check against a Congress that set its mind on ignoring the Constitution.*

Having exercised the veto, temporarily placating Madison, Washington had to consider the delicate question of whether he should run for office a second time. It had not escaped his attention that Madison was accusing Hamilton of monarchism—and if the de facto monarch of the United States was anybody, it was Washington. After all, the Senate had proposed to put Washington's face on the coin. The grand title for the president proposed by John Adams had been intended for Washington. If Washington announced that he did not wish to run for another term, that

---

* The courts did not yet seem to be an effective check on unconstitutional laws. The first time any federal court had declared an act of Congress to be unconstitutional was in *Hayburn's Case*, 40 Dallas 409 (1792). Madison commented that the decision "gives inquietude to those who do not wish Congress to be controlled or doubted whilst its proceedings correspond with their views." But at the same time he also commented that the judges "perhaps . . . may be wrong in the exertion of their power." James Madison to Henry Lee, April 15, 1792, *PJM*, 14:288 and n.2.

would certainly put an end to the speculation that he was on the way to becoming a constitutional monarch.

It had always been Washington's preferred political technique to disclaim any interest in seeking office; and now he insisted he had no desire to continue for another term. He informed his cabinet that he intended to return to Mount Vernon and resume life as a farmer. On cue, Hamilton, Knox, and Jefferson told the president that he should remain in office. On May 5, 1792, shortly before Congress was to adjourn, Washington asked Madison to call on him. In the conversation that ensued, Washington explained that he wanted Madison's advice on the question of how and when he should tell Congress and the country that he was leaving public life.[59]

Madison did Washington the courtesy of formally saying that he understood how much Washington wanted to retire. But Madison told Washington that "his retiring at the present juncture, might have effects that ought not to be hazarded."[60] The way to avoid being accused of remaining too long in office was "a voluntary return to private life as soon as the state of the government would permit."[61] The present situation, however, gave an overwhelming reason for Washington to remain.

According to Madison's detailed notes, Washington now took the initiative in the conversation, giving the reasons that he wanted to retire immediately. Some, such as health and fatigue, were conventional. But in the main, Washington chose to give Madison reasons that were extremely pointed, clearly intended to let Madison know how displeased he was with the political disagreement between Madison and Hamilton. Washington could express his concerns to Madison because he was accustomed to treating him as his confidant and his leading congressional ally and operative. It is unlikely that he would have been prepared to speak the same way to Jefferson.

Washington emphasized "his unfitness to judge of legal questions, and questions arising out of the Constitution." This was his way of saying that he disliked having to determine the fate of the Constitution by vetoing or signing legislation. Then Washington addressed the conflict more directly. "It was evident moreover," he said, "that a spirit of party in the government was becoming a fresh source of difficulty, and he was afraid was dividing some ... more particularly connected with him in the administration." Madison noted that this was an allusion to "the secretary of state and secretary of the treasury."[62]

Washington then spoke about the emergence of party division. "Although the various attacks against public men and measures had not in general been pointed at him," he observed, "yet in some instances it has been visible that he was the indirect object."[63] Washington had a lifelong fixation on maintaining his honor and reputation. The attacks on Hamilton, including those penned by Madison, were coming too close to Washington for his own comfort.

At an earlier stage of his life, Madison might have taken Washington's account of his concerns as a reproach, and reassured Washington that reconciliation was his only goal. Yet at this moment, Madison was engaged in a full-on effort to become a party man and a party leader. He told Washington that "with respect to the spirit of party," he "was sensible of its existence but considered that as an argument for his remaining, rather than retiring." Washington must stay in office, he urged, "until the public opinion, the character of the government and the course of its administration should be better decided."[64]

This was a bold statement given that Washington had just said he was worried about the spirit of partisanship. In essence, Madison's answer was that the fate of Washington's administration depended on which party would win, his or Hamilton's. One of the parties—clearly Hamilton's— might include "a few who retained their original disaffection to the government [and] might still wish to destroy it." That party's associates "were in general unfriendly to republican government and probably aimed at a gradual approximation of ours to a mixed monarchy."[65]

Madison was pulling no punches. He was telling Washington that his own secretary of the treasury, one of his closest associates, wanted to destroy constitutional republicanism and replace it with a British-style monarchy. At the same time, Madison was telling Washington that he intended to defeat and destroy Hamilton's party by relying on public opinion—and that he planned to do so as soon as possible.

Madison's candor made sense only if he believed that Washington was ultimately more on his side than Hamilton's. He then told Washington bluntly that none of his possible successors was satisfactory. Madison explained that Jefferson might very well refuse to run for office given "his extreme repugnance to public life and anxiety to exchange it for his farm and his philosophy."[66] Even if Jefferson were to run, "local prejudices in the northern states, with the views of Pennsylvania in relation to the seat of government," might very well "be a bar to his appointment."[67] Jefferson was hated in the North not only for his politics, but also for his religious skepticism, expressed most recently in his endorsement of Thomas Paine. If his role in bringing the capital to the Potomac also cost him the votes of Pennsylvania, Jefferson could not be elected.

That left John Adams and John Jay. Madison said that Adams was "out of the question" because of his "monarchical principles."[68] There might be some who were "friendly to his private character, and willing to trust him in a public one, notwithstanding his political principles," Madison added, referring to Jefferson and perhaps Washington himself, both of whom respected Adams. But those people would not be able "to make head against the torrent" of opposition against Adams among republicans, especially in the South.[69]

If Jefferson and Adams were both unelectable, Jay would become president. Madison told Washington that he believed Jay's election would be "extremely dissatisfactory." According to Madison, many people believed Jay had "the same obnoxious principles with Mr. Adams," except that Jay would be "more successful in propagating them" because he kept his monarchist views secret. "By others (a pretty numerous class)," Madison went on, Jay "was disliked and distrusted." He was perceived as having favored the claims of British creditors in treaty negotiations over Revolutionary War debts. And "among the western people," Jay "was considered as their most dangerous enemy and held in peculiar distrust and disesteem"[70] because of his extended pre-Constitution discussions with Spain over the possibility of ceding the Mississippi.

Madison noted that Washington appeared "not to be in any wise satisfied with what I had urged."[71] Two weeks later, as Madison was traveling to Virginia after the end of the legislative session, he ran into Washington on the road. Washington handed him a letter dated May 20, 1792, that had been written specially to take up the issue again. In it, he stated that he still planned to retire. He asked Madison once more for advice on timing the announcement, and asked Madison to "turn your thoughts to a valedictory address for me to the public."[72]

Washington gave Madison some notes for what he should include in a possible farewell address. He wanted to announce "that we are *all* children of the same country.... That our interest, however diversified in local and smaller matters, is the same in all the great and the central concerns of the nation." Besides pressing the idea of national unity, Washington wanted to say that "the established government ... with the seeds of amendments engrafted in the Constitution" was "as near to perfection as any human institution ever approximated."[73] Washington was complimenting Madison by heaping praise on the Constitution. Nonetheless, he warned Madison that he did not plan to "touch, specifically, any of the exceptionable parts of the Constitution."[74] Washington did not want his speech to refer to Congress's enumerated powers, one of the key topics on which his lieutenants had gone to war with each other.

Washington nevertheless left himself room to maneuver. He explained that he would remain in office only if he became convinced "that my dereliction of the chair of government . . . would involve the country in serious disputes respecting the chief magistrate."[75] That was precisely what Madison had told him when they met earlier in May: that the country needed him, and that the only alternative to a second term was deeper partisan division over who would become the next president. Washington's letter was thus closer to a statement that he would run than a declaration that he would not.

A month later, June 20, Madison wrote back to Washington urging him to make "one more sacrifice" and run again.[76] Yet he also enclosed in the letter what the president had asked him for: a draft of a farewell speech. For the most part, Madison obediently avoided partisan rhetoric. The closest he came to implicit criticism of Hamilton was a prayer that the "free Constitution" be protected "by that watchfulness over public servants and public measures, which . . . will be necessary to prevent or correct a degeneracy."[77] The word "degeneracy" referred to the national debt, the bank, and the extension of Congress's powers. Had Washington actually given the speech, he would surely have dropped it.

Personal and Political Enemy

Over the summer of 1792, the partisan debate between Madison and Jefferson on one side and Hamilton on the other burst into the newspapers. The *Gazette of the United States,* edited by Hamilton's friend John Fenno, attacked Jefferson in particular and republicans generally. Jefferson responded with outrage. From Philadelphia he sent a note to Madison in Virginia pointing to an article that he believed was by Hamilton defending the bank "and daring to call the republican party *a faction.*"[78] Considering that Jefferson was prepared to call the republicans a party, it may seem surprising that he could be upset to have them described as a faction. The two words "party" and "faction" had been, after all, very close to synonyms in prior usage, with each designating a group of people devoted to promoting its own particular interest ahead of the public good.

Jefferson's note indicated that these meanings were changing. "Faction" was still a dirty word and indicated deviation from the public interest. But "party" was not. Republicans could organize themselves into a party intended to promote the good of the whole nation—specifically, by destroying Hamiltonian monarchism.[79] In this emerging conception of politics, a party such as the Republicans could stand for the true values of an entire people, even as it found itself in pitched battle with its political opponents.

In August, Madison received a letter referring to the party's "ticket" and of a corresponding "Federal ticket" proposed by "anti-Republican men."[80] Parties were taking on a national character. Hamilton was trying to build support in the West, casually remarking to a general that the United States should consider seizing the Mississippi "with a strong hand" if negotiations for free navigation should stretch on too long.[81] He even sought a foothold in Virginia, encouraging John Marshall to run for Congress. "I conclude that Hamilton has plied him well with flattery and solicitation," Jefferson told Madison. "I think nothing better could be done than to make him a judge."[82]

On August 11, the *Gazette of the United States* published two anonymous articles by Hamilton attacking Jefferson and Madison for having encouraged Philip Freneau to create the *National Gazette*. "It may be very true, in a literal sense," Hamilton wrote, "that no negotiation was ever opened with Mr. Freneau by Thomas Jefferson, secretary of state." But that was because Madison, referred to indirectly as "a *particular friend* of that officer," had been the middle man.[83]

From Philadelphia, Edmund Randolph sent Madison the bad news. "Fenno's paper of yesterday has made a virulent assault on Mr. Jefferson; and you are involved in having concerted within the establishment of the paper for party-views." Randolph told Madison that he had not known how to respond, not knowing "what was the state of the facts." The facts would not have helped Randolph much: The newspaper story was accurate.

Hamilton's main target was Jefferson. But his view of Madison was if anything more negative. A republican correspondent, John Beckley of Philadelphia, wrote to Madison: "Mr. H. unequivocally declares, that you are his *personal* and *political* enemy."[84] By now Madison in his *National Gazette* essays had already declared Hamilton an enemy in the political sense. Hamilton, as passionate and intense as ever, added the personal element.

The moment was significant. Four years before, Hamilton and Madison had been not only allies and co-authors of the *Federalist* essays but also friends, communicating constantly and working closely together to promote ratification. The battle over shaping the country in the aftermath of the Constitution had turned them into political opponents and personal enemies. Madison had delayed the process as long as he could, giving Hamilton the benefit of the doubt well after Jefferson and others had condemned his character. And unlike the stormy Hamilton, Madison did not have it in him to make quasi-public declarations of personal enemy status, any more than he made passionate protestations of friendship. But the transformation of their relationship was now complete.

With his anonymous newspaper articles, Hamilton had put Madison and Jefferson on the defensive. Madison tried rather ineffectually to respond. In a letter to Edmund Randolph meant to be made public and intended as a primer for a defense, Madison admitted "recommend[ing]" Freneau for his government job and added that another "gentleman"— apparently Henry Lee—had actually proposed the job to Freneau.[85] Madison further admitted encouraging Freneau to start "a free paper meant for a general circulation and edited by a man of genius, of republican principles, and a friend to the Constitution." He acknowledged he had hoped the paper would be "some antidote to the doctrines and discourses circulated in favor of monarchy and aristocracy."[86]

So far Madison had admitted everything charged. He denied that the paper's goal was "to sap the Constitution." He also denied that he had been in any way involved in "an implicit or improper connection between the functions of a translating clerk in public office, and those of an editor of a gazette."[87] It strained credulity to think that Madison had both recommended Freneau as a translator and encouraged the creation of his paper but that those two things were unconnected. All Madison could do was tell Randolph that such a charge was "not to be credited, until an unequivocal proof shall be substituted for anonymous and virulent assertions."[88]

In politics, circumstantial proof was more than enough. Perhaps when Madison originally lured Freneau to Philadelphia he did not think about how it would look. Or perhaps in the heated partisan atmosphere he simply did not care if others knew that he had helped Freneau get the translation job. In any case, Madison told Randolph, he would not be making any public response.

To help him defend Jefferson, Madison enlisted James Monroe. Together, drafting and editing through the mail, they produced an anonymous newspaper article, published in *Dunlap's American Daily Advertiser* on September 22, 1792.[89] It defended Jefferson against two charges: that "he was always inimical to the present government," meaning the Constitution; and that he had "abused the trust reposed in him" by hiring Freneau at the salary of $250 a year.

To the first claim, Madison and Monroe said simply that anyone was entitled to have criticized the proposed constitution, to which Jefferson had been "an interested, but distant spectator" from France.[90] They then quoted, selectively and at length, from Jefferson's private letters to Madison about the proposed constitution. This would sufficiently refute the charge that Jefferson had opposed the Constitution from the start.

On October 20, they published their reply to the charge regarding Freneau. This job was much trickier, since the allegations were completely true. They said derisively of the anonymous author that "the full force of his genius appears to have been collected, his passions roused, and his imagination to have displayed an unusual degree of brilliancy" in attacking Jefferson. Readers in the know would easily have recognized Hamilton, who was famous for his genius, brilliance—and above all, his passions. For good measure, Madison and Monroe added that the author was among the "idolaters of monarchy, friends of the imperial cause." They further charged that the "malign and unfriendly passions, which prey on the mind of the writer, are entirely personal."[91] The word "personal" recalled Hamilton's statement that he considered Madison a personal as well as a political enemy. To the extent it was in his character, Madison was fighting back.

Yet this was all distraction. The minimal defense offered to the charge of hiring Freneau was that he was qualified as a translator because he understood French; that "he had been liberally educated at Princeton"; that he had been a prisoner of war during the Revolution; and that the job was anyway poorly paid. Naturally so ill-paid a figure would start a newspaper! To attack Freneau, they hinted, was almost to threaten the freedom of speech.[92] The march to partisanship was continuing along its increas-

366 THE THREE LIVES OF JAMES MADISON

ingly extreme course. Freneau had been hired to do the work of party. The hiring itself had become subject to Hamilton's powerful partisan attack. And the defense, with its accusations of monarchism, imperialism, and personal politics, took partisan rhetoric further still.

Enemies and Friends to Republican Government

Given the weak responses that Madison made to Hamilton's attacks, the best defense was certainly a good offense. Having laid the groundwork for the creation of a new political party, Madison now set about expressly defining its program and goals. His essay of September 26 in the *National Gazette*, entitled "A Candid State of Parties," was the first step. He opened by telling his readers that it was important to "understand the actual state of" parties so as to take away from "designing men" the opportunity to manipulate politics. He then reviewed the history of parties in the United States.[93]

Three "periods" mattered in the history of American parties, Madison wrote. The first was the Revolution, in which the two parties were those who sought independence and those "who adhered to the British claims"—if there were even enough Loyalists "to deserve the name of a party." The treaty of 1783 had put an end to this division, he explained. Between 1783 and 1787, there had been "parties in abundance." But these had been "rather local than general," so Madison proposed to ignore them.[94]

The introduction of the Constitution to the public in 1787 created the second era of political parties, Madison argued: "Everyone remembers it, because everyone was involved in it." The two parties were those who "embraced the Constitution" and those who opposed it. Of the first group—his own—Madison said that "the great body were unquestionably friends to republican liberty." Yet there had also been, "no doubt, some who were openly or secretly attached to monarchy and aristocracy." This was a reference to Hamilton. At the time, Madison must not have fully believed that Hamilton was a monarchist. Now retrospectively he was suggesting that this had been the case all along.[95]

Of those on the other side of the party divide, Madison said, "the great body were certainly well affected to the union and to good government." He admitted that "there might be a few who had a leaning unfavorable to both"; his paranoid view of Patrick Henry had not been abandoned. But Madison's intent was now to define the Anti-Federalists as well-meaning in order to welcome them into the newly forming Republican Party. To that purpose, Madison also described Anti-Federalism as irrelevant. Just as the close of the Revolutionary War had ended the relevance of the first division of parties, "the regular and effectual establishment of the federal government in 1788" had put an end to the division between supporters of the Constitution and its opponents.[96]

As a historical account of what had actually happened, this was far too simple. The Anti-Federalists had not simply melted away with ratification. The political and economic conditions that had created their opposition to the Constitution had not disappeared, either. Already in western Pennsylvania, resistance was building to the collection of the excise tax on whiskey that had been passed—with Madison's support—to raise revenue for the federal government. This backcountry opposition to central government had more than a little in common with the Shaysite resistance that had preceded the drafting of the Constitution. Both were connected to Anti-Federalism, one as its precursor and the other as its aftershock.[97] Yet Madison's oversimplification could be overlooked in the light of his political objective, which was to explain the emergence of a new division, one that had arisen "out of the administration" of the constitutional government.

Madison now got to the main business of his essay, which was to define the two parties. He started with the enemy: "Those, who from particular interest, from natural temper, or from the habits of life, are more partial to the opulent than to the other classes of society." Madison was saying that Hamilton was fundamentally biased toward the rich—and that he believed "mankind are incapable of governing themselves." To such people, "government can be carried on only by the pageantry of rank, the influence of money and emoluments, and the terror of military force."[98] By creating financial instruments that encouraged speculation, the government would be gradually "narrowed into fewer hands, and approximated to an hereditary form."[99]

This depiction of monarchic absolutism was a distortion of Hamilton's views, which favored a mixed constitutional government with a strong financial and industrial base. In reality, Washington was childless, and no dynastic candidate was on the horizon. Madison was painting Hamilton as a hereditary monarchist because it was the worst thing he could say—and because it nicely contrasted with his depiction of the political party he was forming.

Madison's party was "the Republican party, as it may be termed."[100] It consisted of those who believed "in the doctrine that mankind are capable of governing themselves, and hating hereditary power as an insult to the reason and an outrage to the rights of man." It opposed any law that did not "appeal to the understanding and to the general interest of the community." It opposed any policy "not strictly conformable to the principles, and conducive to the preservation of republican government."[101]

Madison was naming his party. During ratification, he never especially embraced the party name "Federalist." This time Madison was choosing a banner to which he could repair with pride. A republican was what he had always been. His constitutional design had been intended to save the very idea of republican government from the collapse of the United States under the Articles of Confederation. Now his political party would be devoted to saving republican government from the subversive efforts of Hamilton.

As for Hamilton's party, it was "the Anti-Republican party, as it may be called." It was the party of the rich, "the men of influence, particularly of money, which is the most active and insinuating influence." The Anti-Republicans would try to "weaken their opponents by reviving exploded parties," in other words by trying to drive a wedge between Madison's Republicans and the old Anti-Federalists. The Anti-Republican party would try to exploit past divisions to prevent "a general coalition of sentiments" behind Republicanism.[102]

Madison insisted that his Republicans sought to banish "every other distinction" except one: "that between enemies and friends to republican government." Here was the essence of Madison's political vision of partisanship and his definition of the Republican Party. The friends of republican government must all come together in "a general harmony"—and destroy the enemy.[103]

Who would win? The Republicans had the numbers, but the Anti-Republicans had "stratagem" which "is often overmatch for numbers." Madison acknowledged that there were some unspecified "peculiarities, some temporary, others more durable, which may favor" Hamilton's Anti-Republicans. Nevertheless, he concluded that the Republicans' great advantage lay in their practice of "making a common cause, where there is a common sentiment and common interest." He predicted that "no temperate observer of human affairs will be surprised" if Republicanism should prevail and "the government be administered in the spirit and form approved by the great body of the people."[104]

Madison did not acknowledge that there was anything strange about insisting on the Republican preference for "making a common cause" in the course of an essay devoted to hardening the partisan divisions between himself and Hamilton. Republicans were unifiers; Anti-Republicans were dividers. The unified Republicans could therefore treat the Anti-Republicans as the enemy. And, as if by magic, they would still be unifiers while they did so.

A Disagreeable Dilemma

Madison spent the autumn of 1792 intriguing over the upcoming election. Whether he had always intended to do so or not, Washington had decided to stand for the presidency again. His stature guaranteed him the votes of all 132 presidential electors. As a result, any political drama would center on the choice of a vice president. John Adams, an avowed Federalist, would stand for reelection, with the presumption that if reelected he would become the leading Federalist presidential candidate after Washington's eventual retirement. The Republicans needed a candidate of their own. By October, Madison and Jefferson expected it would be Governor George Clinton of New York.

The natural Republican candidate for vice president would have been Jefferson. But a state was not allowed to vote for its own citizens for both president and vice president. Virginia, crucial for Republican victory, could not vote for Jefferson since it would cast its presidential votes for Washington. Beyond this impediment lay the sense that the Republican Party should not be the party of Virginia alone.

George Clinton was, nevertheless, an awkward choice. He had lobbied against ratification of the Constitution and strategized with Patrick Henry to achieve that goal; and he was unpopular in his own New York. Sensing his weakness, New York senator Aaron Burr mounted an effort to replace Clinton on the Republican ticket. Thirty-six years old, known for his piercing, dark hazel eyes, Burr combined ambition with considerable political talent.[105] His father, Aaron Burr, Sr., had been the president of the College of New Jersey at Princeton. When his father died, Burr's maternal grandfather, the theologian, philosopher, and preacher Jonathan Edwards—America's greatest intellect in the first half of the eighteenth century—had succeeded him as president. Burr had entered the college at thirteen, and was thus a rough contemporary of Madison at Princeton despite being five years younger. He had been a field officer during the Revolutionary War, then set up as a lawyer in New York and entered politics.

Burr's insurgency against Clinton was potentially embarrassing for Madison. As Monroe wrote to Madison when informing him of the movement, "Some person of more advanced life and longer stand in public trust should be selected." Then people would know "what his principles really were." Monroe thought Burr would lose, and recommended telling New York Republicans to drop the idea. This might place them "in a disagreeable dilemma with Mr. Burr," but that could be "removed by the most soothing assurances of esteem and confidence on our parts, resting altogether on his youth etc."[106]

Ultimately Burr was dropped, and Clinton became the candidate. By a combination of Clinton's unpopularity, Hamilton's skill, and the general political ascendance of the Federalists, Adams won the vice presidential election handily. Clinton won New York, Virginia, North Carolina, and Georgia, receiving a total of 50 electoral votes. Adams won everything else, totaling 77.

Madison had founded a political party to take on Hamilton and his Federalists—and in their first major national test, his Republicans had lost. The congressional elections took place on a rolling basis starting in August 1792 and continuing into the autumn of 1793. In these the Republicans did slightly better, gaining some twenty-four seats, mostly new seats added as a result of the 1790 census. In the next Congress, Republicans would enjoy a very slight majority, estimated at 54 to 51, in the House of Representatives. Yet the initiative remained with Hamilton and the Treasury.

The two years Madison had spent arguing for a new party marked a critically important, indeed transformational, period in Madison's second political life. Madison still saw himself as driven by principled, constitutional commitments. But in furtherance of these objectives, he had become increasingly pragmatic and increasingly partisan. Still committed to the ideals of logic and the notion of a common good, he found himself writing rhetorical appeals to the agricultural class and denigrating industrial manufacture. His opponents were no longer reasonable people, but lovers of monarchy and enemies of the republic. The dream of political friendship and concord still existed in his mind. Yet in pursuit of it, he was now setting out to destroy his enemies using the tools of faction.

Madison would be the leader of the Republicans in the House. He and Jefferson were entering a long winter of opposition—one that would last the better part of a decade.

CHAPTER TEN

The President and His Party

...

THE ARGUMENT: *At Hamilton's urging, Washington proclaims neutrality in the war between France and England, ignoring the treaty of friendship between the United States and France. At Jefferson's urging, Madison attacks Washington's proclamation as potentially unconstitutional. The move reflects Madison's growing tendency to constitutionalize political disagreement by arguing that his opponents are not merely wrong but are violating the core principles of the republic.*

The unpopular Jay Treaty motivates Republicans nationwide—but puts Madison squarely in opposition to Washington. With Jefferson once again pressing him, Madison argues publicly that the treaty is unconstitutional because it makes commercial arrangements while bypassing the House of Representatives. An affronted Washington breaks with Madison forever.

ON DECEMBER 3, 1792, Citizen Louis Capet, formerly known as King Louis XVI, was brought to trial before the National Convention in Paris. Maximilien de Robespierre told the delegates that they were not judging an individual, who might be found innocent or guilty, but deciding the course of the Revolution. The former king could take no refuge in the new French Constitution, because he himself had subverted it. "With regret I pronounce this fatal truth," Robespierre concluded: "Louis must die so that the nation may live." On January 21, 1793, Louis was executed by guillotine in the Place de la Révolution. By February 1, France and England were at war.

Madison expressed no great concern about Louis's fate. In April 1793, the month after news of the execution had reached the United States, he wrote formally to the minister of the interior of the French Republic to accept the honorary French citizenship conferred on him by the National Assembly the previous summer.[1] Home in Virginia for congressional elections, he told Jefferson that "the mass of our citizens" felt sympathy "merely to the man and not the monarch." Nevertheless, Madison told Jefferson, most "plain men" had told him that "if [Louis] was a traitor, he ought to be punished as well as another man."[2]

On April 19, 1793, with news of the war confirmed, Washington held a cabinet meeting. France and the United States had signed a treaty of friendship in 1778 when France had come to America's aid in the Revolutionary War. To Madison and Jefferson, that treaty remained valid both legally and morally. Edmund Randolph, the attorney general, told the president that the treaty was still in effect.

Hamilton disagreed. France, he told Washington, had deposed its king and changed its form of government. The United States was therefore free under the law of nations to break the treaty of alliance. Hamilton cited Vattel's *The Law of Nations*. No copy of the book was at hand, and Randolph, taken by surprise, told Washington he would have to look up the passage to render judgment.[3]

Reporting to Madison, Jefferson was dismissive of the idea that "it should have been seriously proposed to declare our treaties with France void on the authority of an ill understood scrap in Vattel."[4] The passage was indeed ambiguous.[5] But Washington was prepared to accept Hamilton's interpretation. On April 22, 1793, three days after the cabinet meeting, Washington issued a brief proclamation that amounted to a declaration of neutrality—in effect, repudiating the treaty of friendship with France.[6]

To Jefferson, the Neutrality Proclamation could have only one meaning: Hamilton was now making foreign policy. Hamilton not only wanted the government of the United States to resemble that of Great Britain; he also favored alliance with that country. It was far better for Britain if the United States stayed neutral rather than adhering to its treaty with France.

Until now, the divisions between Madison and Jefferson's Republicans and Hamilton's Federalists had centered on domestic issues: the system of finance and the Constitution. Now they were transposed into the realm of foreign affairs. Hamilton and the Federalists were on the side of Britain. Madison, Jefferson, and the Republicans were on the side of France.

Jefferson hoped that America's revolutionary animosity toward England would be revived by the apparent need to choose sides between the adversaries. He applauded an article in a Boston newspaper in which "the old Tories have their names raked up again," considering it an indication "of the spirit which is rising."[7] He looked forward to the arrival of Edmond-Charles Genêt, the new revolutionary French ambassador, who had landed in Charleston on April 8 and was making his way slowly to Philadelphia. "His arrival," Jefferson predicted, "would furnish occasion for the people to testify their affections without respect to the cold caution of their government."[8] Madison hopefully agreed.[9]

Genêt's arrival in Philadelphia was accompanied by ceremony. Washington, concerned with preserving neutrality, did not arrange for a formal reception. Thirty prominent Republicans nevertheless greeted the French ambassador, and "a vast concourse of people attended them."[10] Genêt presented himself as the representative of a people in the closest amity with the United States. According to Jefferson, Genêt told the Americans, "We know that under present circumstances we have a right to call upon you. . . . But we do not desire it. We wish you to do nothing but what is for your own good, and we will do all in our power to promote it."[11]

Jefferson was rapturous. "It is impossible for anything to be more affectionate, more magnanimous than the purport of his mission," he wrote to Madison. "He offers everything and asks nothing."[12] Madison was thrilled to hear it. "The affection to France in her struggles for liberty," he wrote back, could "only be increased by a knowledge that she does not wish us to go to war."[13]

The enthusiasm for Genêt proved short-lived. In early June, Jefferson discovered that in Charleston, Genêt had fitted out four American ships and commissioned them as French privateers to attack British shipping. This had not been a secret in Charleston, where Genêt had been treated as a hero and entertained at a series of lavish parties. Yet Jefferson seems not to have known it.[14]

Genêt's commissioning of the privateers was a diplomatic disaster for the United States and for Jefferson as secretary of state. The privateers had seized several British ships on the open seas and brought them back to Charleston as prizes under the law of war. The use of American ships as French privateers, not to mention the taking of British ships, constituted a serious breach of the neutrality that Washington had announced. Pursuant to Washington's proclamation, U.S. citizens serving on the pri-

The President and His Party   375

vateers were arrested and prosecuted. Orders were sent to ports throughout the country prohibiting the fitting out of privateers.[15]

Once he reached Philadelphia, Genêt proved still more embarrassing
to Jefferson. He insisted on keeping his privateers in action and believed
that he could appeal to the American people's friendship with France
over the head of the president himself. In July, Jefferson wrote to Madison that "never in my opinion, was so calamitous an appointment made,
as that of" Genêt:

> Hotheaded, all imagination, no judgment, passionate, disrespectful
> and even indecent towards the president in written as well as verbal
> communications, talking of appeals from him to Congress, from them
> to the people, urging the most unreasonable and groundless
> propositions, and in the most dictatorial style etc. etc. etc.[16]

Jefferson's hope that Genêt would encourage popular support for a
French-American alliance had backfired. Genêt's behavior reflected the
emerging norms of the French Revolution—and showed how different
its tenor was from the American.[17]

Outflanked by Hamilton even on foreign policy, and embarrassed by
the advocate sent by his favored France, Jefferson wanted out of public
life. Madison urged him to stay in office for the good of the Republican
Party. "You must not make your final exit from public life till it will be
marked with justifying circumstances which all good citizens will respect,
and to which your friends can appeal," Madison urged him. "At the present crisis, what will the former think, what could the latter say?"[18]

Jefferson replied to Madison that he had spent twenty-four years in
"public service," and had served his "tour of duty." The debt he owed to
the people had been paid. Even his "enemies" admitted as much, Jefferson
pointed out. Since "the public then has no claim on me, and my friends
nothing to justify, the decision will rest on my feelings alone."[19]

From someone else's pen, these protestations might have seemed formulaic. But Jefferson really was exhausted and disillusioned by the rhythm
of constant battle against Hamilton and constant defeat at his hands.
"The motion of my blood no longer keeps time with the tumult of the
world," he wrote in an elegiac mode.[20]

These were the words of a man overwhelmed. Jefferson and Hamilton sat in cabinet meetings together and interacted face-to-face—even as Hamilton was attacking Jefferson's character in numerous anonymous newspaper essays. The experience of being so often in the company of an enemy who hated him and whom he hated—even in moments where friendship might have been expected to prevail—had drained Jefferson of the will to continue in office.

Washington, too, was exhausted, Jefferson told Madison. The president was "extremely affected by the attacks made and kept up on him in the public papers," attacks first on his domestic program and now his foreign policy that had been fomented by Jefferson and Madison. Washington's sensitivity was exquisite. "I think he feels those things more than any person I ever yet met with," Jefferson wrote. "I am sincerely sorry to see them."

Jefferson believed that, despite Washington's strong character, the "satellites and sycophants" around him had accustomed the president to such quasi-royal treatment that he could no longer bear criticism. "Naked he would have been sanctimoniously reverenced," Jefferson elegantly noted. "But enveloped in the rags of royalty, they can hardly be torn off without laceration."[21]

If Jefferson's feelings toward Washington's pain were sympathetic, Madison was becoming increasingly worried that Washington had succumbed to the influence of Hamilton. "I regret extremely the position into which the president has been thrown," Madison wrote to Jefferson. "The unpopular cause of Anglomany [that is, Anglomania] is openly laying claim to him." As a result, "his enemies . . . are playing off the most tremendous batteries on him."

Madison believed that Washington was partly to blame for his predicament. "The proclamation was in truth a most unfortunate error. It wounds the national honor, by seeming to disregard the stipulated duties to France." That was not all. The proclamation "wounds the popular feelings by a seeming indifference to the cause of liberty."[22]

A pattern had emerged in Madison's thinking: Policies advocated by Hamilton were not merely wrong; they were unconstitutional. Madison tried out for Jefferson a new objection to the Neutrality Proclamation: "It seems to violate the forms and spirit of the Constitution, by making the executive magistrate the organ of the disposition, the duty, and the interest of the nation in relation to war and peace."[23] Madison was saying that because the Constitution gave Congress the power to declare war, the

377 The President and His Party

president should not usurp that power by declaring neutrality. Like the Bank of the United States and the pro-industry subsidies that, according to Madison, went beyond the power of Congress, the declaration of neutrality exceeded the legitimate power of the president.

Although Madison may not have fully considered the consequences, one effect of his condemnation of the Neutrality Proclamation was that he himself was now committed to the view that George Washington had acted unconstitutionally. Holding such views—and expressing them—would drive a wedge between him and the sensitive Washington. A friend told Madison that "the president believes . . . that the Virginia interest, as it is called, designs to attack him, and that it gives him great uneasiness." The correspondent was cautious not to say that Washington specifically feared Madison. "However, this idea," he told Madison, "with the comments on his conduct in the papers . . . and the cunning insinuation . . . that the Republicans mean to intimidate him, correspond to enlist him in a party."[24] This was a direct warning to Madison: Criticizing the president too directly would make Washington into an open Federalist.

Enter the Lists

Given his disapproval of the Neutrality Proclamation as unwise and unconstitutional, Madison faced a dilemma. If he remained silent, the pro-British, Hamiltonian view would surely prevail. If he attacked the proclamation publicly, even anonymously, he would alienate Washington.

Until the beginning of July 1793, Madison said nothing. Hamilton, however, wrote a new, preemptive series of anonymous essays in the *Gazette of the United States* under the name "Pacificus." These were designed not only to convince the public that the Neutrality Proclamation was a good idea, but also to suggest to Washington that the Republicans—including Madison—were attacking him personally.[25]

In the essays, Hamilton offered a convincing argument for the president's power over foreign affairs. The Neutrality Proclamation related to the interaction between different governments. Unlike Congress, which was given only enumerated powers in the Constitution, the president possessed "the executive power"—meaning all executive power that was not explicitly denied him by the Constitution. Hamilton insisted, "This mode of construing the Constitution has indeed been recognized by Congress." Cleverly, he gave as his example "the power of removal from office" of cabinet officials—a power that Madison himself had argued the president could exercise without Congress.

Hamilton was showing skill in constitutional argument not inferior to Madison's. The president must still be able to act with respect to war and peace even when Congress had not, he pointed out. The executive was "charged with the execution of all laws, the law of nations as well as the municipal law"—and so must interpret treaties and act on the basis of his own interpretation.

Jefferson had no doubt that, given Hamilton's attack, Madison must strike back. He sent Madison the first three of Hamilton's essays with an exhortation. "Nobody answers him, and his doctrine will therefore be taken for confessed," Jefferson wrote. "For God sake, my dear sir, take up your pen, select the most striking heresies, and cut him to pieces in the face of the public. There is nobody else who can and will enter the lists with him."[26]

Madison tried to resist. He protested that, stuck in Virginia, he lacked "some material facts and many important lights" and so "the task would be in bad hands." He told Jefferson, "I am in hopes of finding that someone else has undertaken it."

Yet Madison could not refuse a direct request from Jefferson. "In the meantime I will feel my own pulse," he wrote, "and if nothing appears, may possibly try to supply the omission."[27] Madison's metaphor perfectly captured the dispositional difference between him and Jefferson. Jefferson had asked for a zealous warrior to "enter the lists." Madison responded with the equanimity of the man on the sidelines, calmly measuring his own heart rate. Four days later, Madison decided to accede to Jefferson despite the potential costs to his relationship with Washington.[28]

Madison's replies were published under the name "Helvidius." Helvidius Priscus was a Roman republican and Stoic philosopher who had addressed Emperor Vespasian by his private name rather than as "Caesar Augustus" and rejected the authority of his edicts. For his actions, Helvidius was exiled and then executed.[29] Madison's choice of the name emphasized an overreach in the federal executive power. The point would not be lost on Hamilton.

Unlike his previous essays, which Madison had composed swiftly and enthusiastically, the Helvidius essays came hard. "I have forced myself into the task of a reply," he wrote to Jefferson. "I can truly say I find it the most grating one I ever experienced." Even as he wrote, Madison dreaded the inevitable response from Hamilton. "One thing that particularly vexes me is that I foreknow from the prolixity and pertinacity of the writer, that the business will not be terminated by a single fire, and of course I must return to the charge in order to prevent a triumph without a victory."[30] Hamilton's quick pen and persistence, well known to Madison, made him a particularly detestable opponent.

Jefferson gave Madison the final notice of his resignation. "I informed the president by letter three days ago that I should resign the last day of September," he wrote in code. "Consequently I shall see you in the middle of October" in Virginia.[31]

Before leaving office, Jefferson made some effort to reconcile with Washington over the Neutrality Proclamation. It had become necessary for the United States formally to demand that Citizen Genêt be recalled. Jefferson wrote a letter to Gouverneur Morris, the U.S. ambassador to France, explaining to him the circumstances of the request. In the letter, which he showed Washington, Jefferson described the president's Neutrality Proclamation very carefully as having been an "expedient" measure "to remind our fellow citizens that we were in a state of peace with all the belligerent powers."

Explaining the course he had taken to Madison, Jefferson said that "this was the true sense of the proclamation."[32] The difference between a declaration and a proclamation of neutrality had constitutional overtones. To declare neutrality would be more akin to declaring war, the exclusive province of Congress.

Jefferson's conciliatory formulation made Madison's task all the more difficult. He had to criticize the Neutrality Proclamation without repudiating Jefferson's attempt to appease Washington. Jefferson made things harder still by writing to Madison that "it would place the Republicans in a very unfavorable point of view with the people to be cavilling about small points of propriety; and would betray a wish to find fault with the president."[33] It is a mark of Madison's commitment to Jefferson that he was not driven mad by this equivocation from the very same person who had, a month earlier, urged him to cut Hamilton to shreds.

Worst of all, the Neutrality Proclamation was politically popular. Genêt's outrageous behavior toward Washington had only hardened feelings against France. New York, Jefferson told Madison, had greeted Genêt with a cortège that "consisted only of boys and Negroes." The contrast with Genêt's arrival in the spring could not have been greater.

"Philadelphia, so enthusiastic for him, before his proceedings were known, is going over from him entirely." Thus, Jefferson advised that the "Republican Party" should "abandon Genêt entirely," embrace neutrality, and "avoid little cavils about who should declare it."[34]

As if to make Madison more nervous, at the same time that Jefferson was trying to guide him toward a moderate position on the declaration of neutrality, he told Madison to hurry up. "The president is extremely anxious to know your sentiments on the proclamation," Jefferson told him. "He has asked me several times." Jefferson had put Washington off: "I tell him you are so absorbed in farming that you write to me always about plows, rotations etc."[35] Madison had indeed included a few farming details in his letters to Jefferson, but this was a joke that Madison could not have found very funny.

Calamity

Madison sent his Helvidius essays to Jefferson, who passed them on to John Fenno's *Gazette of the United States*. Madison's earlier replies to Hamilton had been published in Freneau's *National Gazette*. Given the attacks on Madison and Jefferson for their association with Freneau, it must have seemed like a good time to publish somewhere else. It is unclear why Fenno, an associate of Hamilton's, agreed to publish the essays. Perhaps his goal was simply to sell newspapers—or maybe he thought Hamilton would get the better of the exchange.

Madison opened by saying that Hamilton's Pacificus essays seemed superficially plausible since they attempted to support Washington, "who enjoys the confidence and love of his country." In reality, however, the essays struck "at the vitals of [the] Constitution" and contradicted the "honor and true interest" of the United States.[36]

Madison then overstated Hamilton's position, claiming he had said that making wars and treaties were "by their nature" executive powers.[37] In contrast, Madison argued that only Congress had the power to declare war: foreign affairs must not and could not be the sole preserve of the president.

Madison went further by insisting that Hamilton was, as usual, trying to impose British monarchy on the United States, since the king had the prerogative to make war and treaties.[38] He quoted *Federalist* No. 75, where

Hamilton had written that the treaty-making power was "plainly" not part of the executive power alone, but rather belonged "properly neither to the legislative nor to the executive."[39] Unfortunately for Madison, only he and Hamilton knew for certain that Hamilton had written *Federalist* No. 75.

The theoretical nature of Madison's constitutional critique of Pacificus was particularly ill-timed. As Madison was ruminating about obscure details of the separation of powers, Hamilton was turning the Genêt affair into concrete political gain. The occasion was Genêt's self-destructive determination to engage national, Republican public opinion in favor of France. Federalists John Jay, now chief justice of the United States, and Senator Rufus King of New York leaked the story to the newspapers that Genêt had directly threatened to appeal to the people of the United States against the president's Neutrality Proclamation.

Genêt, in a glaring breach of protocol, then wrote directly to Washington—rather than to Jefferson—demanding that he declare the charge untrue. Jefferson wrote a letter to Genêt informing him that he should communicate through the secretary of state like any other ambassador. Genêt responded by sending the newspapers his letter as well as Jefferson's. As Jefferson put it to Madison, "Genêt has thrown down the gauntlet to the president . . . and is himself forcing [an] appeal to the people." Jefferson now believed that, "contrary to his professions" on arrival, Genêt had actually intended "to force us into the war."[40]

Hamilton turned Genêt's blunder against the Republicans. He encouraged a series of Federalist public meetings throughout the United States to pass resolutions condemning Genêt and supporting the Neutrality Proclamation. The goal of the highly popular meetings was to tar the Republican Party with the brush of treason for its association with France.

Madison visited Monroe to devise a strategy in response. They settled on drafting hopelessly defensive resolutions of their own that could be adopted by public meetings of a Republican cast. The resolutions praised Washington and reminded the public of the French alliance in the Revolutionary War. Rebutting the charge of treason, they alleged that an alliance with Britain would be "one great leading step towards assuming our government to the form and spirit of the British monarchy."[41]

The Republicans were trying desperately to distance themselves from

Genêt without falling into the arms of the British. The only tool they had left was to insist that the Federalists were enemies of republicanism who sought to turn the United States into a twin and ally of Britain. Madison asserted in a letter intended for publication that he was confident "what the sense of the people is":

> They are attached to the Constitution. They are attached to the president. They are attached to the French nation and Revolution. They are attached to peace as long as it can be honorably preserved. They are averse to monarchy. And to a political connection with that of Great Britain.[42]

Madison went on to ask, "Why then cannot the sense of the people be collected on these points, by the agency of temperate and respectable men who have the opportunity of meeting them"?[43] Why indeed—except that Madison was conveniently forgetting that the French ambassador had commissioned privateers to drag the United States into war; insulted George Washington, the father of the country; and all the while insisted that the American public approved of his course of action. Even in Virginia, Madison had trouble convincing public meetings to adopt the Republican resolutions.[44] Elsewhere in the country the results were worse.

Jefferson would be leaving office at a moment when the foreign policy of the United States had fallen into the hands of the Federalists. Madison described the situation to Jefferson as a "calamity." He persisted in believing that "the real sentiments of the people" were pro-French. But "the country is too much uninformed, and too inert to speak for itself; and the language of the towns which are generally directed by an adverse interest will insidiously inflame the evil."[45]

A further consequence of Jefferson's retirement was that the cabinet would now be Federalist controlled. The division had been between Hamilton and Henry Knox on one hand, and Jefferson and Edmund Randolph on the other. Yet in practice, Randolph's deep-seated tendency to equivocate meant that he was not always a reliable Republican. "He is the poorest chameleon I ever saw," Jefferson wrote to Madison, "having no color of his own, and reflecting that nearest him. When he is with me he is a Whig, with Hamilton he is a Tory, with the president he is what he thinks will please him."[46]

It might have seemed natural for Madison to fill Jefferson's spot in the cabinet. Jefferson told Madison that the president had said Madison "would be his first choice" except that Madison "had always expressed to him such a decision against public office that he could not expect he would undertake it."[47] This was a classically careful Washington formulation, politely telling Jefferson that his protégé Madison would be a worthy successor while implying that it would not come to pass. In any case, Madison would continue to serve in the House as, in effect, the leader of the loyal opposition.

Jefferson's days in Philadelphia ended in literal misery to go along with his political despair. Yellow fever hit the city. Even the cures were partisan, divided between a "Republican" cure of purges suggested by Dr. Benjamin Rush and a "Federalist" cure of cold baths advocated by Dr. Edward Stevens.[48] On September 8, 1793, Jefferson wrote to Madison* that "about 33 a day" were falling sick and that "it is the opinion of the physicians that there is no possibility of stopping it."[49]

Madison, ever cautious about catching disease, was worried for Jefferson. "I have long been uneasy for your health amidst the vapors of the Schuylkill," he wrote back. "The new and more alarming danger has made me particularly anxious that you were out of the sphere of it." He urged Jefferson to leave town "if the fever does not abate."[50]

Jefferson insisted that he would remain until the beginning of October because he had already said publicly that he would leave then, "and I do not like to exhibit the appearance of panic."[51] Four days later the bravado was gone. "The fever spreads faster," he wrote to Madison. "Deaths are now about 30 a day. It is in every square of the city. All flying who can."[52]

---

* Jefferson also reported to Madison the rumor that "Hamilton is ill with the fever." So extreme was Jefferson's dislike of Hamilton that he saw the threat of life-threatening illness as proof of Hamilton's bad character. "His family think him in danger, and he puts himself so by his excessive alarm," Jefferson wrote ungenerously. "He had been miserable several days before from a firm persuasion he should catch it." It was true that Hamilton, emotionally labile as ever, thought he was getting sick. Jefferson took the opportunity to be still more biting: "A man as timid as he is on the water, as timid on horseback, as timid in sickness, would be a phenomenon if the courage of which he has the reputation on military occasions were genuine." Jefferson, who had never seen a day's battle, wanted to deny the former Colonel Hamilton his reputation for bravery won during the American Revolution. Jefferson to Madison, September 8, 1793, *PJM*, 15:104. Later Jefferson had to admit that Hamilton really did have the fever, although he survived it.

So Rapid Was the Plague

Among those who fled Philadelphia was Dolley Payne Todd, a twenty-three-year-old recently wed mother of two small children. The older, John Payne Todd, had been born on leap day, February 29, 1792. The second son, William Temple Todd, had been born, equally auspiciously, on July 4, 1793.

Dolley came from a Virginia Quaker family that had owned slaves. In 1786, when she was eighteen, her father, John Payne, was among the first Virginia Quakers "who became doubtful and afterwards conscientiously scrupulous about . . . holding slaves as property," according to a memoir written later by Dolley's niece that reflected stories Dolley had told over the years. Other Virginians called Payne "a fanatic," so he moved to Philadelphia with his slaves—and freed them there.[53]

Dolley's father had come to Philadelphia with money and social connections. He sent his older son to Europe for education and travel. But, Dolley's niece later wrote, he denied his daughters "the acquirement of those graceful and ornamental accomplishments which are too generally considered the most important parts of female education." As a Quaker, Dolley was not taught music or dancing. Nevertheless their house was a gathering place for "gay Southerners" in Philadelphia. Dolley, who "grew in grace and beauty," had "numerous suitors" for her hand—all of whom she rejected.

John Payne found city life more expensive than he had expected, and when his son came back from Europe the two entered a partnership to sell starch. Their capital was in "revolutionary money," according to family tradition—and when it "suddenly depreciated in value, he failed and his family were reduced to poverty."[54] This vague formulation raises the possibility that Payne put the money from the sale of his Virginia lands into speculative instruments, perhaps as part of the general fervor for investment that had accompanied Hamilton's financial program. In any case, "unaccustomed to city life and the management of money matters," he lost everything.[55]

Depressed by his financial failure, Payne decided that Dolley should marry John Todd, "a young lawyer of promising talents also belonging to the Society of Friends." Todd "had long been a suitor of Dolley's," but she had "not inclined to relinquish her girlhood," at least not to Todd. Her father brought Dolley "to his bedside and told her how much happiness it would give his last moments to know that she was married." Dolley's niece later "heard her say, she did not wish to marry, it was a hard struggle, but she never for one instant thought of disobeying her father's wishes."[56] In November 1791 Dolley married Todd, bringing no dowry to the marriage. Her father died a year later.[57]

When the yellow fever hit in September 1793, John Todd took Dolley, her infant, and the one-and-a-half-year-old John Payne Todd, whom they called Payne, "on a litter" to Grays Ferry, on the Schuylkill River three miles away from the center of town.[58] He himself returned home to care for his own father, who had contracted the fever.

Dolley was beside herself with concern. "What a dread prospect," she wrote to her brother-in-law. "A revered father in the jaws of death, and a loved husband in perpetual danger.... I am almost distracted with distress and apprehension."[59] She asked her brother-in-law whether it was "too late" to get her husband and his father out of the city: "Can no interference of their earthly friends rescue them from the too general state?"[60]

It was indeed too late for John Todd's father and mother, both of whom succumbed. Todd went to see Dolley and their children at Grays Ferry, and she begged him not to go back to the center of the city. But Todd had to return to close his office and to care for another relation. When he came back from Philadelphia the next time, he was seriously ill.

Kept in a different room from Dolley to avoid infecting her, Todd was overcome with emotion. "The fever is in my veins!" he cried out to Dolley's mother, who was with him. "Let me behold her once more!" Dolley, "at the sound of his voice," ignored her mother's pleading that she not risk infection "but left her couch and throwing herself in his arms welcomed him affectionately as usual and would gladly have returned with him to Philadelphia." Her husband and her mother would not let her go. Todd went back to Philadelphia, reached the family's house, "and died in a few hours, so rapid was the plague."[61]

Dolley had been exposed—and she fell sick as well. Although she survived, her infant son William did not. "My poor dear little Dolley . . . the same day consigned her dear husband and her little babe to the silent grave," wrote Dolley's mother.[62] It was October 24, 1794. The yellow fever epidemic had made Dolley Payne Todd a widow and left her with one son, named for her own dead father.

Todd bequeathed her a small estate. Dolley quickly made a will of her own, leaving minor bequests to her brothers, aunt, and mother. The bulk would go to the education of her surviving son:

> As the education of my son is to him and to me the most interesting of all of the concerns, and far more important to his happiness and eminence in life than increase of his estate, I direct that no expense be spared to give him every advantage and improvement of which his talents may be susceptible.[63]

There was not enough money to support Payne. He would have to acquire a profession like his late father.

Sparkling Eyes

Meanwhile, Madison prepared to return to Philadelphia for the new congressional term that would begin in December. Washington briefly considered proposing that Congress meet somewhere else on account of the epidemic, and Madison wrote him a letter urging him to be careful of infringing on Congress's constitutional prerogative.[64] In the event, by the end of November the danger had passed and the city was up and running again,[65] rendering moot the question of the president's authority.[66]

The main business in Philadelphia would once again be foreign affairs. In June, the British government had issued the first in a series of "orders-in-council" that authorized the Royal Navy to capture and seize any ships trading with France or its colonies in the West Indies. In practice, this meant a direct threat to American ships engaged in that trade. Since Britain already excluded American ships from trading with its own West Indian colonies, this would amount to a stranglehold on U.S. trade with the Caribbean.

To Federalists, the answer was obvious: The United States needed a navy to protect its shipping from Britain and from Barbary corsairs, privateers who operated in the Mediterranean and eastern Atlantic.

Madison disagreed. Instead of building an expensive navy, which he believed to be incompatible with republicanism, Madison favored economic sanctions to help the United States to gain leverage. In a series of speeches in January 1794, he proposed seven resolutions that were intended to implement an aggressive trade policy against any nation with whom the United States did not have a commercial treaty or that itself blocked U.S. trade.[67]

The speeches were taken seriously. A fellow Republican said Madison had exhibited "elegance, accuracy, method and extensive information." He spoke for "two hours and a half during which time in a full House and thronged with spectators there was such perfect silence that you might almost have heard a pin fall." The overall effect was "eloquence which baffles everything I had ever heard and almost description."[68] Yet Madison lacked the political support to bring his resolutions to a vote, much less to get them passed. Importers had no interest in raising the cost of British goods in order to facilitate more American exports or shipping.

Abandoned by Jefferson and politically stymied, Madison then did something unexpected: He fell in love. Dolley Payne Todd had reentered Philadelphia society, and the suitors who had pursued her before her marriage had returned. "Gentlemen when they heard of her being in the street would station themselves in stores to see her pass. Everybody loved her; she had no vanity." Madison first saw Dolley this way, walking in Philadelphia. He was with Colonel Isaac Coles, a Virginia congressman (who was also, by coincidence, a cousin of Dolley's mother). Madison was "struck with her charms," which were considerable:

> Her height was 5 feet, 7 inches and three quarters, well proportioned, her features pleasing though not remarkable in form except her mouth which was beautiful in shape and expression—her hair was jet black and eyes blue, forming a contrast admired by many, her complexion was perfect, white as the driven snow.[69]

Madison sought assistance from his political ally and Princeton contemporary, Aaron Burr, then representing New York in the Senate. Burr knew Dolley—because Burr knew everybody.

Burr's self-appointed role in Philadelphia social life was to inject culture and taste into a city that, because of the influence of the Quaker elite, lacked both. He "did his best to counteract [Quaker] rules by presenting a box of colors with palette and drawing books to one, an English guitar with music to another, standard writings to a third and so on." These gifts to young women, violations of Quaker norms, were also expensive, "imported from England—their possession was doubly precious to those who could not afford their purchase." As Dolley recalled it, the gifts helped young Quaker women attain the accomplishments that would help them attract non-Quaker suitors, marry them, and escape the strictures of Quaker life. "In after years many of those young girls who married 'out of meeting' had cause to remember with gratitude the name of Aaron Burr!"[70]

Sometime in May, Dolley sent her sister Anna a note reading "Thou must come to me, Aaron Burr says that the great, little Madison has asked him to bring him to see me this evening."[71] The words "great" and "little" captured the greatness of Madison's political fame and the littleness of his personal stature. Dolley was some two inches taller than her new suitor. According to what Dolley later told her niece, "in his first interview, at her own house, she conquered the recluse bookworm Madison, 'who was considered an old bachelor.'" Madison had turned forty-three in March; Dolley would turn twenty-six in May.

According to a story recounted by Dolley's niece, the rumor of Dolley's conquest spread fast. Martha Washington, "impatient to know how true was the report," summoned Dolley to the president's residence and asked her bluntly if she was engaged to Madison.

The conscience-stricken widow hung her head and answered stammeringly, "No, madam." Mrs. Washington said, "If it is so, do not be ashamed to confess it, rather be proud, he will make thee a good husband, all the better for being so much older, we both advocate it."[72]

Any anecdote connected to the Washingtons runs the risk of having been invented after the fact.[73] Dolley left Philadelphia for a visit to Virginia at the end of May, shortly after she had met Madison, which would not have left much time for the rumor to spread and for Martha Washington to ask the question. Yet the story does capture the sense of Philadelphia as a very small place in which members of the government lived in close proximity to one another and knew each other's personal business.

It remained for Madison himself to convince Dolley that he was worthy. There were certainly competitors, and on June 1, 1794, Dolley's cousin Catharine Coles wrote to update her on some of them. One "Mr. Grove is in the pouts about you," she reported. Another unnamed suitor "round the corner is melancholy." A third, named Lawrence, "has made me his confidant, poor fellow. I fear he will not meet with success."

At length Coles got to the main event, namely Madison. "He told me I might say what I pleased to you about him," she commented mischievously. There followed an account of passionate love:

He thinks so much of you in the day that he has lost his tongue, at night he dreams of you and starts in his sleep a-calling on you to relieve his flame for he burns to such an excess that he will be shortly consumed and he hopes that your heart will be callous to every other swain but himself. [74]

These were not exactly Madison's words, but "he has consented to everything that I have wrote about him with sparkling eyes," Coles told Dolley. The humorous implication was that Madison, restrained as ever, had asked Coles to speak on his behalf. Considering Madison's inexperience with women and his lifelong difficulty with expressing passion, consenting to what Coles wrote counted as a genuine display of emotion.

Madison himself left Philadelphia for Virginia in the second week of June. By August he had proposed marriage. A fragment of a letter that he wrote to Dolley on August 18 suggests that she agreed. Madison said that a letter he had received from her was "precious." And, he wrote, "I hope you will never have another *deliberation*, on that subject. If the sentiments of my heart can guarantee those of yours, they assure me there can never be a cause for it."[75]

On September 16, 1794, James Madison and Dolley Payne Todd married at Harewood, a Virginia estate owned by George Steptoe Washington, a nephew of George Washington who was married to Dolley's younger sister Lucy. The minister was an Episcopal priest, Alexander Balmain. With this act, Dolley left the Society of Friends. "In the course of this day I give my hand to the man who of all others I most admire," she wrote to her close friend Eliza Collins Lee. "In this union I have everything that is soothing and grateful in prospect—and my little Payne will have a generous and tender protector."[76]

Dolley was not writing of love but of admiration and the calming prospect of life with Madison. To the letter, Dolley added a poignant postscript: "Evening. Dolley Madison! Alas!" It had been less than a year since the death of Dolley's husband John Todd and her son William. Dolley was making the pragmatic decision to marry the admirable and famous Madison. She allowed herself just a single word to mark the radical change her life had undergone in this short period of time.

Madison was even more understated in communicating the news of his marriage. On October 5, still at Harewood, he wrote a letter to Jefferson that began with arrangements to send deer owned by a neighbor;

went on to ask Jefferson for his advice on some architectural plans; and ended with a brief reference to his wedding two-and-a-half weeks earlier. "I have remained [at Harewood] since the 15th," he wrote, "the epoch at which I had the happiness to accomplish the alliance which I intimated to you I had been some time soliciting."[77]

Jefferson wrote back wishing "1000 respects to Mrs. Madison and joys perpetual to both."[78] Henry Lee wrote to Madison, "I hear with real joy that you have joined the happy circle and that too in the happiest manner." He offered "my most respectful congratulations" to Dolley, who "will soften I hope some of your political asperities."[79]

Lee's juxtaposition of Madison's marriage to his political troubles was insightful. Although Madison and Dolley returned to Philadelphia for the next session of the congressional term that would begin in November, Madison's determination to marry was connected to a desire to remove himself from politics and return to Virginia as Jefferson had done. He told Jefferson that he was considering retirement.[80]

Now it was Jefferson's turn to encourage Madison to stay in public life. "I do not see in the minds of those with whom I converse a greater affliction than the fear of your retirement," Jefferson wrote to Madison. "But this must not be, unless to a more splendid and more efficacious post."[81] Jefferson was telling Madison that he must remain in Congress unless he were to run for president. In the meantime, Madison would be even better placed to take up the position in Philadelphia of chief leader and advocate for the Republican Party. Jefferson had gone home. James Monroe had left the Senate to go to France as ambassador. The responsibility of opposition leadership in Philadelphia now fell to Madison alone.

Whiskey and Rebellion

Newly married, Madison and Dolley returned to Philadelphia to set up their household. By the time they arrived, an important change had taken place in the nature of the partisan debate between Republicans and Federalists. For the first time, the political differences between the two sides had contributed to an outbreak of violence.

The trouble had started three years earlier in rural Pennsylvania. Hamilton's tax on domestically distilled spirits—which Madison had voted for in a simpler, less partisan time—powerfully affected the people of the

Alleghenies. Along the Monongahela River, distilling rye whiskey was a way of life, and barrels of the liquor could be used as currency.

Since the summer of 1791 there had been more or less organized resistance to the whiskey tax. Individual tax collectors had been tarred and feathered. Meetings or "conventions" had formally declared the tax unlawful. Hamilton had from the start urged the use of force to collect the taxes. But Randolph, while attorney general, had not believed such measures were warranted, and Washington had decided not to send troops.[82]

Matters came to a head in the summer of 1794. The federal district attorney in Philadelphia sent subpoenas to sixty Monongahela distillers—and deputized a U.S. marshal to demand that they appear in court. The U.S. marshal was joined by the federal tax inspector for the region, General John Neville, himself a wealthy local distiller.

Their visit to deliver the subpoenas went awry, and the two men encountered resistance at a farm near Pittsburgh. On July 16, a group of thirty militiamen from the area of Mingo Creek surrounded Neville's home.

Neville, the tax inspector, then made a disastrous miscalculation. He fired on the men outside his house, killing one of them.[83] The next day, six hundred men appeared at the house, loosely led by James McFarlane, who had been a major during the Revolutionary War. Meanwhile, ten soldiers of the regular U.S. Army had come from Pittsburgh to assist Neville.

A firefight broke out. After an hour of shooting, McFarlane called for a cease-fire. He stepped out from under cover, and was shot to death. Enraged, the crowd burned Neville's house to the ground.[84]

After McFarlane's funeral, more groups of protesters began to coalesce. Would-be leaders urged violence. On August 1, seven thousand people gathered at Braddock's Field outside Pittsburgh.

A crowd this large could not have been made up of distillers alone. The citizens in the field had all the economic and social grievances of the West on their minds, from federal overreach to the government's apparent inability to protect them from Indian attacks. Some called for raids on the homes of rich people or on Pittsburgh itself. Others spoke of declaring western independence and allying themselves with Britain or Spain. One David Bradford, who had emerged as a leader, invoked the French Revolution and compared himself to Robespierre.*[85]

---

* He could not have known that, three days earlier, the revolutionary leader had gone to the guillotine, a victim of the Terror he had himself unleashed.

Hamilton was not a man to let a crisis go to waste. In a series of four anonymous essays in Philadelphia's *American Daily Advertiser*, he depicted "the existing insurrection" as a fundamental challenge to constitutional government. The protesters were telling the majority of the people that "the sovereignty shall not reside with you, but with us." This was faction: It "set up the will of the part against the will of the whole" and "the violence of a lawless combination against . . . sacred authority." Worse, it was "treason against society."

Hamilton left little doubt that what were called Democratic-Republican societies, essentially local branches of the Republican Party, were complicit in fomenting the treasonous rebellion. He pointed out that pro-rebel sympathizers were also opposed to the neutrality declaration. He argued that the Republican Party was leading the country into "civil war, the consummation of human evil."

Washington had been deeply affected by Shays's Rebellion eight years before. Now, with Hamilton urging him on, Washington determined to project force. He sent commissioners to meet with the leaders of the protesters, and simultaneously began to raise militia from Virginia, Pennsylvania, New Jersey, and Maryland. In a clever political move, Hamilton made sure that Henry Lee, then the Republican governor of Virginia, was appointed to lead the army.[86]

Most Republicans saw the suppression of the protesters as a Federalist project and opposed deploying the militia. But although Lee was a Republican, he had long wanted a military command that would bring him back to the fame he had achieved in the Revolutionary War.[87] His expedition of nearly thirteen thousand militia went ahead.

Lee told Madison that the lesson of rebellion was political unity: "Surely these things must influence our political leaders to harmonize more than they have lately done and to regard as a solemn truth that tolerable happiness to a nation had better be preserved than risked in pursuit of greater felicity."[88] The threat of populist disorder—coupled with the opportunity to serve in high command—was turning Lee rather abruptly into a Federalist.

Lee's contemporaries noticed the change. While Lee was away in Pennsylvania with the troops, the Republican-dominated Virginia assembly deposed him by declaring the governorship empty and electing a Republican substitute.[89] Lee had always taken politics personally. Now once again his "feelings [were] hurt beyond description," a friend told

Madison. Indeed, "in the course of wine after dinner" one evening while he was in the field, Lee offered a toast to Madison but then announced that Madison "had made frequent remarks reflecting upon his reputation as an individual."[90] The friendship between Lee and Madison was a casualty of the Whiskey Rebellion.

As had happened in Shays's Rebellion, the appearance of organized troops was enough for the protesters to melt away. "The western insurgents appear to have been brought either by reflection or fear to a perfect submission to the laws," Madison wrote to his father.[91] Ultimately, only two people were convicted of federal crimes in connection with the protest. Washington pardoned them, recognizing that it was best for the uprising not to have legal martyrs.

Ostensible Opposition

From the Federalist perspective, the government's response to the rebellion had been an unmitigated success. In his annual written address to Congress—what today would be the State of the Union—Washington told the story of how opposition to the excise had grown into rebellion. He explained accurately that "associations of men began to denounce threats against the officers employed" to collect the tax. Then he wrote: "From a belief, that by a more formal concert, their operation might be defeated, certain self-created societies assumed the tone of condemnation."[92] The "self-created societies" were the Democratic-Republican clubs. Echoing Alexander Hamilton, Washington was now blaming the Whiskey Rebellion on the Republican Party.

In the House, Federalists took Washington's lead and included a denunciation of the societies in the official reply to the president. Madison and the Republicans fought back. The societies were "innocent in the eye of the law," and therefore "could not be the object of censure to a legislative body," they claimed. It was, Madison argued, a question of "the liberty of speech and of the press." Attacking the societies would be a kind of bill of attainder, a particularized legislative condemnation prohibited by the Constitution. "Opinions are not the object of legislation," he intoned.[93]

The situation could hardly have been worse for the Republicans. Under Hamilton's influence, the president had joined the Federalist Party by openly condemning the Republicans in his address to Congress. Madison wrote to Jefferson that Hamilton was controlling Washington: "You will perceive his coloring in all the documents which have been published during his mentorship to the commander-in-chief."[94] In Madison's mind, Hamilton was now the mentor, Washington the pupil. Madison found himself defending the Republican Party against Washington's charge that it was responsible for an uprising.

At what should have been a moment of great triumph for him, Hamilton announced his intention to resign as secretary of the treasury effective January 31, 1795. His motives were not easy to discern. "We are here much at a loss to account for Hamilton's letter giving notice of his intention to resign," a friend wrote Madison from Virginia.[95]

It is possible that Hamilton was affected by a miscarriage suffered by his wife, Eliza.[96] Certainly his private letters at the time suggest that he felt depression rather than pleasure at his victory. His mind was "discontented and gloomy in the extreme," Hamilton wrote to Rufus King.[97] Madison, who could not imagine that Hamilton had any nonpolitical motivation, believed he intended to run for governor of New York against Republican Aaron Burr.[98]

The most probable explanation for Hamilton's resignation, however, is that he was broke, saddled with significant debts that he had accrued while secretary of the treasury.* Unlike Madison, who had always been able to rely on support from his father and stood to inherit Montpelier, Hamilton had emigrated from the West Indies with nothing and had spent most of his adult life in public office. He left the Treasury not to enter local politics but to set up a law practice in New York to support his family.[99]

In any case, Hamilton's departure was a godsend to the Republicans. Madison had lost battle after battle to Hamilton. But it was Hamilton, not he, who was leaving Philadelphia, leaving the administration, and therefore leaving George Washington. Henry Knox, the Federalist secretary of war, resigned as well. When the two were replaced, Washington's first cabinet would now have turned over almost completely. Edmund Randolph had replaced Jefferson as secretary of state. As attorney general

---

* Throughout Hamilton's term as secretary of the treasury and after, his Republican opponents suspected and insinuated that he must be making vast sums of money illicitly. For example, John Beckley reported to Madison the rumor that Hamilton had deposited £100,000 in a London bank while serving as secretary. John Beckley to Madison, May 25, 1795, *PJM*, 16:10. The rumors were false.

to replace Randolph, Washington had chosen the Philadelphian William Bradford—Madison's closest friend in the years after he left college and before he entered public life.* Now perhaps Madison could begin the process of winning Washington back to Virginia republicanism.

Treaty

It was not going to be easy. Washington had been criticized by the Democratic-Republican societies—and he was a man who found criticism almost unbearable. Given Washington's sentiments, it might have been wise for Madison to signal to the Democratic-Republican societies around the country that they should let the matter drop. Instead Madison encouraged public responses to Washington's allegations that the societies had contributed to the Whiskey Rebellion. In a letter to Jefferson, he referred to Washington's "attack" as having been "made on the essential and constitutional right of the citizen." As such, the blow "must be felt by every man who values liberty, whatever opinion he may have of the use or abuse of it by those institutions." He went on to tell Jefferson about responses that had been issued by societies in Baltimore, Newark, and Boston.[100]

While the hostility between the grassroots of Madison's party and the president continued to simmer, a negotiation was taking place in London that would be decisive for Madison's relationship with Washington. John Jay had been sent to negotiate a treaty with Britain that was supposed to confirm America's neutral position in the war, address trade, and improve the situation in which American ships did not have access to British ports.

Madison believed the time for negotiation was perfect. The revolutionary army of France, now organized into the greatest mass force the world had ever known, was winning. Jay had not sent any word of the treaty as of January 1795, but Madison explained to Jefferson that "it is expected here that he will accomplish much if not all he aims at." American leverage was at a maximum. "It will be scandalous, if we do not under present circumstances, get all that we have a right to demand."[101]

In fact, Jay had signed the treaty in November, but for reasons of his own did not send a copy of the document to the president until the spring.

* Bradford, appointed in January 1794, would die suddenly in August 1795.

The first rumors that Madison heard were worrisome. Robert R. Livingston of New York, a Republican who held the post of chancellor in the state and had previously been secretary of foreign affairs under the Continental Congress, wrote to Madison that, according to his sources, "Mr. Jay has sacrificed the essential interests of this country."[102] In private to Jefferson, Madison expressed his concerns: "I suspect that Jay has been betrayed by his anxiety to couple us with England, and to avoid returning with his finger in his mouth."[103]

On March 7, the treaty reached the president—who immediately ordered its contents kept secret. On March 26, Madison sent Monroe a summary of what the treaty was rumored to contain. Trade itself would become reciprocal, putting British and American vessels "on the same footing" in the ports of each. Smaller American vessels would be permitted to trade with the West Indies.[104]

The presentation of Jay's treaty to the Senate in June brought the conflict between Madison and Washington to a head. On June 8, 1795, the Senate met in a special secret session to read the treaty. The Senate printed thirty-one copies of the document, which they were supposed to keep secret among themselves. The treaty resolved outstanding reparations and promised repayment of pre-war debts; arranged disengagement along the western border; and created commissions to resolve boundary disputes. Most important and controversial, it also established most-favored-nation status for British trade to the United States—without extracting significant trade concessions from Britain.

Madison had returned home to Virginia with Dolley. He received an illicit copy of the treaty piecemeal in a series of four separate letters sent by South Carolina senator Pierce Butler, who commented that this "most important secret is much safer with you than in the hands of many to whom it is confided."[105] Butler expressed concern about whether the treaty was constitutional and asked Madison to send him back his opinion on it.

Before Madison could reply, the business was done. The Senate debate lasted just two weeks. On June 24, the Senate approved the entire treaty with the exception of part of a single article.[106] Butler's fourth letter, conveying the last portion of the treaty, also included news of the ratification. The process had been partisan, Butler told Madison: "Much artifice and maneuvering was practiced to keep the new recruits to their ranks."[107]

To Madison and other Republicans, the treaty was a disaster. The treaty "sacrifices every essential interest and prostrates the honor of our country," Robert R. Livingston wrote to Madison. "Our disgrace and humiliation . . . greatly exceeded my expectations."[108] Jay had conceded to Britain on every issue about which Republicans cared. The treaty promised Britain that it would be able to trade with the United States on terms as good as any other nation. Giving Britain most-favored-nation status meant that, as a matter of law, the possibility of discriminating against British products relative to other countries was closed permanently.

Yet Britain did not commit itself to allowing American products to enter Britain on the same terms or American ships to trade freely with British colonies. The U.S. concession was absolute and the gain was zero. When it came to the neutral rights of the United States to trade with France without British retaliation, Jay once again had gotten nothing. American ships trading with France or its colonies would remain lawful prizes to British warships.

Before, the United States could plausibly have told France that it could do nothing about Britain's threat to its shipping. Now, after the treaty, the arrangement looked like a formal decision to side with Britain rather than France in the war between the two. To Madison and his allies, this consequence was almost as bad as the concessions on trade policy. Madison believed Jay's treaty could be explained only by "the blindest partiality to the British nation and government and to the most vindictive sensations towards the French Republic."[109]

To Madison, the explanation was that John Jay and the Federalist Party were acting in the interests of the British government:

> Indeed, the treaty, from one end to the other, must be regarded as a demonstration that the party to which the envoy belongs . . . is a British party, systematically aiming at an exclusive connection with the British government.[110]

The Federalists would next choose to go to war against France, Madison predicted, and the Federalist victory in foreign policy would be complete.[111]

The Republicans needed a coordinated response. They found it in a series of public meetings to be held across the country denouncing the treaty. In Philadelphia, three hundred people ceremoniously burned a copy. In New York, one meeting on Wall Street actually turned violent when Hamilton, who approved of the treaty and may have given Jay the instructions in the first place, tried to address a hostile crowd of five hundred. As the audience became inflamed, heckling gave way to stone throwing. A rock hit Hamilton who, showing wit and grace, bowed and said, "If you use such knockdown arguments, I must retire."[112] To Jefferson, it seemed that the Jay Treaty provided an opportunity for Republicans to make up some of the ground they had lost to Federalists. He commented gleefully to Madison that the Republicans had "appealed to stones and clubs and beat [Hamilton] and his party off the ground."[113]

Crowds had even surrounded Washington's house in Philadelphia "huzzaing, demanding war against England, cursing Washington, and crying success to French patriots and virtuous Republicans," John Adams later recalled.[114] For the first time ever in Washington's entire career, he was squarely on the wrong side of public opinion.

Madison declined to tell Washington directly what he thought. The president "cannot, I am persuaded, be a stranger to my opinion on the merits of the treaty," he told Robert Livingston, who had written to Washington himself expressing opposition.[115] Madison must have hoped that Washington would change sides, abandon Hamilton and the treaty, and come over to Republicanism. Instead, Washington wrote to Hamilton for a detailed analysis of the treaty—by implication asking him to begin a public campaign to counteract Republican efforts.[116] Hamilton had left government, but he had not left politics, and he rose to the challenge.

In a new series of essays, this time writing as "Camillus," "Philo Camillus," and "Horatius," Hamilton mounted the defense. The Republicans were toadies of the French who would lead the United States into war with Britain, he argued. Britain had granted the United States concessions that no other country had ever received. The treaty would expand trade worldwide.

From Monticello, Jefferson watched Hamilton's energetic response in horrified admiration. "Hamilton is really a colossus to the anti-Republican Party," he wrote to Madison. "Without numbers, he is an host within himself." Unless the Republicans took immediate action, they would "give time to [Hamilton's] talents and indefatigableness," and could extricate the Federalists from their vulnerable position.[117]

Jefferson knew just one possible antidote to Hamilton's literary skill: Madison. "We have had only middling performances to oppose to him," he told Madison. "In truth, when he comes forward, there is nobody but yourself who can meet him." Hamilton and Madison were the ultimate gladiators of their two parties.

The problem was that by going into battle this time, Madison would have no choice but to alienate Washington permanently. On August 12, 1795, Washington had told his cabinet that he intended to sign Jay's treaty. Earlier, Washington had privately indicated that he might withhold his signature and try to force the British to withdraw their orders authorizing the targeting of American shipping with France. But on August 18, he signed.[118]

Given the nationwide debate over the treaty, Washington probably judged that delaying his signature would benefit the opponents of the treaty rather than its supporters. Another contributing factor may have been the shock Washington received at almost exactly the same time when British ambassador George Hammond presented him with a private, official letter written by French ambassador Joseph Fauchet.

The French ambassador's letter described Edmund Randolph, then secretary of state, as an unparalleled source of information about the inner workings of the government: "The precious confessions [*précieuses confessions*] of Mr. Randolph alone throw a satisfactory light upon everything that comes to pass."[119] Later in the dispatch, Fauchet referred to events that had taken place at the height of the Whiskey Rebellion, immediately after the seven-thousand-man protest at Braddock's Field. The cabinet was to meet to decide on whether troops should be sent. On the eve of the meeting, Fauchet reported, "Mr. Randolph came to see me with an air of great eagerness, and made me the overtures of which I have given you an account in my No. 6." The letter was referring to an earlier official dispatch, which was not included, and so the content of the "overtures" was not directly specified. The next sentence, however, was damning: "Thus with some thousands of dollars the republic could have decided on civil war or on peace!"[120]

When he saw the letter, Washington believed it meant that Randolph had asked the French ambassador for a bribe to influence the outcome of the cabinet meeting in which it would be decided whether to send an army to put down the Whiskey Rebellion. After consulting with treasury secretary Oliver Wolcott and secretary of war Timothy Pickering, Washington called Randolph to his office in the presence of the other two and grimly confronted him with the letter. Randolph fumbled and claimed he could not recall the details. The situation made it obvious that he was supposed to resign on the spot—so Randolph did.[121]

The effects of the episode on Washington's feelings toward the Republicans, including Madison, Randolph's friend, cannot be overstated. Randolph, trying to salvage his reputation, became a public enemy of Washington—and Washington believed that the Republican Randolph, a member of his cabinet for some six years, was a paid agent of the French government. For his part, Randolph told Madison that "among the objects, which the president and his party have in view, one is to destroy the Republican force in the United States. A conspiracy, more deeply laid and systematically pursued, has not yet occurred."[122] To Randolph, Washington was no longer an honest man who might be influenced by either Republicans or Federalists. "The president and his party" were a single Federalist unit, devoted to destroying the Republicans.[123]

The Congressional Power

In this atmosphere of worsening relations between Washington and the Republican Party, Madison set out to craft a political argument against the treaty that had now been approved by the Senate and signed by the president. Doing so would not be easy: The House of Representatives, Madison's branch of government, lacked any constitutional power over treaties. From Paris, Monroe wrote to him that "the eyes of the European world are turned upon your branch." Then he warned in cipher, "If you do not act with decision your reputation is gone and with it that of our country." Madison must choose between Washington and maintaining his own good reputation in France: "Delicacy for the character of others is ruin to your own."[124]

Monroe thought a constitutional amendment might be necessary to give the House the right to approve treaties. Alternatively, Monroe said, Madison might "get rid of the treaty in question." But how?

In a letter to Madison, Jefferson sketched out the bones of an argument that he might use. The treaty was an attempt by the Federalist Senate and president to stop the Republican House from regulating trade.[125] Thus, Jefferson concluded bluntly, "the whole commercial part of the treaty" was "unconstitutional."[126] Other Republicans also felt intuitively that there was something constitutionally wrong with what had happened. But Madison alone had the skill to explain how exactly the Constitution had been violated.

On March 10, 1795, Madison gave a long speech on the constitutional aspects of the treaty power. It was a remarkable performance: remarkable because in it, the leading author of the Constitution acknowledged that the document was significantly imprecise on the role of the House in treaty making. "It was to be regretted," Madison said, "that on the question of such magnitude as the present, there should be any apparent inconsistency or inexplicitness in the Constitution, that could leave room for different constructions." But that was exactly the situation. "As the case however has happened, all that could be done was to examine the different constructions with accuracy and fairness."[127]

Madison offered five different possible interpretations of the treaty power in relation to the president and Congress. Only the last two mattered. One of these, which Madison ascribed to the Federalists, was that the treaty power was "unlimited in its objects, and completely paramount in its authority."[128] The president could make a treaty on any subject he wanted, and if the Senate gave its consent by a two-thirds vote, the resulting treaty would become the law of the land. This view was closest to the explicit language of the Constitution, although Madison naturally did not say so.

The alternative was the emerging Republican view: that "the congressional power may be viewed as cooperative with the treaty power." This interpretation was more complex. Madison explained that, if the subject matter of a treaty fell within an area that the Constitution reserved to the power of Congress, then Congress—including the House of Representatives—could decide whether to pass laws that would implement the treaty. If Congress chose not to pass such laws, the treaty would not have any effect. In this sense, Congress had a role in implementing treaties. The president could sign them and the Senate could approve, but without action by the full Congress, the treaty would not matter.

The argument was clever. After all, Madison argued, the Constitution provided for "limitations and checks," and imposed substantive limits on what different branches could do. If the president could make a treaty on any subject into the law of the land, as the Constitution's text seemed to say, then the president could declare war without the House. He could create a standing army. Indeed, the president could circumvent the First

Amendment by making a treaty that limited free speech or established religion. These outrageous results showed that the treaty power must be limited.[129]

Madison was confident that his argument would be embraced by the House—at least in principle.[130] Unfortunately for Madison, his Republican colleagues did not appreciate the subtlety of his constitutional arguments. On March 24, the House passed a resolution demanding that Washington produce his instructions to Jay and the associated diplomatic correspondence. The demand implied that the House had direct authority over the treaty-making process.

On March 30, less than a week later, Washington sent a defiant reply to the House of Representatives. He would not provide the papers. "The nature of foreign negotiations requires caution, and their success must often depend on secrecy." Revealing the negotiations even after the fact "might have a pernicious influence on future negotiations, or produce immediate inconveniences, perhaps danger and mischief, in relation to other powers." In fact, the need for secrecy "was one cogent reason for vesting the power of making treaties in the president, with the advice and consent of the Senate." To give the House a right to the papers would "establish a dangerous precedent."[131]

Washington was indignant at the challenge to his authority. "I trust," he told Congress, "that no part of my conduct has ever indicated a disposition to withhold any information which the Constitution has enjoined upon the president as a duty to give." Wounded honor pushed Washington to insist that he knew his constitutional duties perfectly well: He had, after all, been at the Philadelphia convention.[132]

Breaking for the first time the promise of silence that the convention's attendees had followed at the time and afterward, Washington now disclosed that, in Philadelphia, "a proposition was made 'that no treaty should be binding on the United States which was not ratified by a law,' and that the proposition was explicitly rejected."[133] The convention had, in other words, expressly considered the possibility that the House would have to implement treaties through lawmaking—and had rejected that option.

To back up his assertion, Washington took the minutes of the Philadelphia convention, which had been entrusted to him for safekeeping, and sent them over to the State Department where they could be viewed publicly. If anyone looked, the records would reveal not only that the proposition had indeed been made and rejected—but also that Madison, like Washington, had voted against it.

Washington was revealing the proceedings of the convention in order to counteract Madison's interpretation of the Constitution. He was, he believed, demonstrating Madison to be a hypocrite. George Washington and James Madison were very close to a personal war.

Madison was upset about the president's harsh response. "The absolute refusal was as unexpected, as the tone and tenor of the message, are improper and indelicate," he wrote to Jefferson. Washington's argument was wrong in substance, Madison thought, and the president had been indelicate in revealing the proceedings of the Philadelphia convention.

Madison was convinced that Hamilton must be behind it. "If you do not at once perceive the drift of the appeal to the general convention and its journal," he went on, "recollect one of Camillus's last numbers."[134] Writing as Camillus, Hamilton had indeed argued that the Philadelphia convention meant to give the treaty power exclusively to the president and Senate. To Madison, "there is little doubt in my mind that the message came from New York."[135]

The Oracular Guide

On April 6, 1795, in response to Washington, Madison gave the first of the final two great speeches of his congressional career. He intended, Madison said, to maintain "the most respectful delicacy towards the other constituted authority," namely the president. Then he went on the attack. The president had "contested what appeared to him a clear and important right of the House." As for the president's reasons, "with all the respect he could feel for the executive," he could not regard them as "satisfactory or proper."[136] This was as close as Madison would come to condemning Washington publicly.

Turning to the House's power over treaties, Madison expressed "surprise" that Washington had appealed to "the proceedings in the general convention, as a clue to the meaning of the Constitution." The views of those who attended the convention "could never be regarded as the oracular guide in the expounding of the Constitution."[137]

The authority of the Constitution derived not from its authors, but from the people who ratified it:

As the instrument came from them, it was nothing more than the draft of a plan, nothing but a dead letter, until life and validity were breathed into it, by the voice of the people, speaking through the several state conventions.[138]

Madison's biblical metaphor of the dead letter being infused with life-spirit made the voice of the people into the voice of God. Madison had once considered the text of the Constitution so close to perfect that it did not need amendment. Now he was saying the public meaning of the Constitution mattered, not what the text had meant to the drafters. The reason for the change was that his own views at the Philadelphia convention arguably contradicted the interpretation of the Constitution that he was advancing.

In the congressional debate over the national bank, Madison had observed that the Philadelphia convention had rejected a motion to give Congress the power to grant corporate charters. Now, when the records of the convention went against him, he claimed evidence of the convention's proceedings should not matter. Washington had put Madison in an exceedingly awkward position.

Trying to change the subject, Madison turned to the state ratifying conventions to argue that "the treaty-making power was a limited power." The records were far from perfect, he warned. He preferred to focus on the proposed amendments that the state ratifying conventions had generated. He then listed numerous proposed amendments designed to limit the powers of the federal government, reasoning that those ratifying the Constitution could not possibly have believed that the treaty clause of the Constitution had "given to the president and senate, without any control lever from the House of Representatives, an absolute and unlimited power" to enact whatever laws they wished.[139]

Madison's point had merit. The Constitution could not have been ratified if the public had believed the president and Senate could circumvent Congress and adopt whatever laws they wanted through the means of adopting a treaty. But of course that was not what Washington was actually asserting. He was simply rejecting a novel doctrine whereby the House of Representatives would be able to exercise an effective veto over treaties.

Madison concluded his speech by saying that the House faced a choice. If Congress did not express formal opposition, "it would be inferred that the reasons in the [president's] message had changed the opinion of the House, and that their claims on those great points were relinquished." The House of Representatives must either stand up to the president or acknowledge that he was right and the House was wrong. "In either way, the meaning of the Constitution would be established, as far as depends on the vote of the House of Representatives."[140]

Despite his attempts to remain civil, Madison had acknowledged that he and the president were squarely at odds with respect to the meaning of the Constitution. Their alliance had been close, and the two men had been friends, albeit within the bounds of Washington's formality and Madison's deference. Madison had visited Mount Vernon many times. In tandem with Edmund Randolph, he had cajoled, urged, and ultimately convinced Washington to attend and chair the constitutional convention. He had advised Washington on essentially every aspect of congressional affairs. Now Madison and Washington were direct political opponents— and the world knew it.

One final step remained in the deterioration of Madison's friendship with Washington. On April 15, 1795, Madison gave his last important speech as a congressman. The topic was a resolution declaring that it was "expedient to pass the laws necessary for carrying into effect" the Jay Treaty. Madison began by attacking the treaty for conceding most-favored-nation status to Britain without getting anything in return. Britain would continue to take American ships and impress American seamen—and the United States appeared to acquiesce.[141]

Then Madison attacked the president. He might, he said, "be stepping on delicate ground," but he could not "think it improper to remark, that it was a known fact that the executive actually paused for some weeks after the concurrence of the Senate, before the treaty received a signature." Madison then surmised that Washington had delayed signing because he was hoping to convince the British government to revoke its orders allowing the seizure of American ships. He further suggested that Washington had signed in the end because he expected "that such a mark of confidence in the British government, would produce an abolition of the unlawful proceeding."[142]

Washington had been wrong—and by implication weak. The British order had not been revoked, and the seizures had not stopped. Madison concluded that had this been foreseen, "the treaty would not have been then signed."[143] Madison was charging that Washington had signed the

406 THE THREE LIVES OF JAMES MADISON

treaty in haste and in error, and should never have signed the treaty at all. Worse, Madison was suggesting that Washington himself must wish he had never signed the treaty in the first place.

On April 30, the treaty came to a vote, and the House divided 49 to 49. In a second vote, the law implementing the treaty passed by a vote of 51 to 48.

With Hamilton gone, Madison could no longer fulminate about the brilliance of his enemies.[144] He had to acknowledge the internal weakness of the Republicans. The Federalist policy of restoring close relations with Britain had been chosen over Madison's preference for trying to extract concessions from the former colonial master. Worse, Congress had followed the Federalists' vision by endorsing the unilateralism of a powerful executive wielding the treaty power. Madison had lost.

Calamity

There was one "consolation" to the defeat, Madison told Jefferson. It confirmed Madison's intention to resign from Congress and return to private life in Virginia. In this he would be imitating Jefferson, who had himself left Philadelphia and the government in the wake of repeated policy defeats at Hamilton's hands.

In New England, sentiment against the Republicans and in favor of the Jay Treaty was particularly strong. The merchant class of New England desperately feared that a war with its most important trade partner, Britain, would disrupt both exports and imports. "Such have been the exertions and influence of aristocracy, Anglicism, and mercantilism in that quarter, that Republicanism is perfectly overwhelmed," Madison told Jefferson.[145]

With the presidential election of 1796 a few months away, New England's staunch pro-treaty, pro-English policy boded ill for the Republicans. "It is generally understood that the president will retire," Madison wrote to Monroe in France. "Jefferson is the object on one side [and] Adams apparently on the other." The same "mercantile influence" that had depicted the Jay Treaty as a choice "between peace and war" could be expected to support Adams.[146] The "Republican cause" was "in a very crippled condition."[147]

The race would "probably turn on the vote of Pennsylvania," Madison predicted—"where many circumstances are at present unfavorable." As late as the end of September, with the election barely more than a month away, Madison told Monroe that although he had returned to Virginia, he had actively avoided seeing Jefferson so as "to present him no opportunity of protesting to his friend against being embarked in the contest."[148] Jefferson was not an active candidate for office. He was deemed so unwilling to enter public life that his closest friend and supporter was avoiding seeing him lest he deny that he was a candidate at all. Jefferson's "enemies are as indefatigable as they are malignant," Madison concluded glumly. "Whether he will get a majority of vote is uncertain. I am by no means sanguine."[149]

The Republicans' vice presidential candidate was Aaron Burr, selected for his New York and New England origins. Unlike Jefferson, Burr campaigned personally. "Burr has been out electioneering these six weeks in Connecticut, Vermont, Rhode Island, and Massachusetts," Madison's friend John Beckley told him. "But I doubt his efforts are more directed to himself than anybody else," Beckley added, with biting insight into Burr's character.[150] Burr, just forty years old, was campaigning for the future.

Hamilton, the most effective Federalist voice, attacked Jefferson harshly in a series of anonymous essays that were especially devastating on the subject of slavery. Hamilton ridiculed Jefferson both for his racist insistence on the biological inferiority of Africans and his simultaneous musings about the desirability of emancipation.[151] But Hamilton also strongly disliked the snobbish, prudish Adams, who had long disdained the "bastard" Hamilton for his Creole origins and sexual improprieties both real and imagined.[152]

This put Hamilton in a difficult position: He hated both presidential candidates, one for reasons of politics and the other personally. Rumor had it that Hamilton might come out of retirement and run for president himself. And if Hamilton could win Massachusetts, then Rhode Island, Vermont, Connecticut, New York, New Jersey, and Maryland "would all probably follow very unanimously."[153]

Hamilton had no such delusions—but he did develop a devious plan to weaken Adams without electing Jefferson. Adams's Federalist vice-presidential partner was Thomas Pinckney of South Carolina. In the electoral system as it then existed, each state's electors cast two votes. The person with the most votes would become president; the person with the second most votes would become vice president in the administration of

408 THE THREE LIVES OF JAMES MADISON

the candidate who defeated him. The system was a feature of a Constitution designed to combat faction, not accommodate party.[154]

In a partisan election, the electors were expected to vote for their preferred presidential and vice presidential candidates. A few votes could be held back to assure the right candidate won. Hamilton encouraged southern electors to cast their second ballots for Pinckney.[155] If enough did, Pinckney might end up as president despite the fact that he was not supposed to be the candidate of either party.

Hamilton's strategy almost worked. Adams got 71 electoral votes, Jefferson 68, and Pinckney 59. Burr got just 30, indicating that many southern Republican electors had voted for Jefferson and Pinckney, not the party ticket of Jefferson and Burr. Adams was furious with Hamilton, who had almost cost him the election and had thus weakened his presidency even before it began.

Although he had no intention of participating in cabinet meetings even if asked, Jefferson told Madison that he was perfectly content to serve as a passive vice president under his old associate.[156] Despite having just engaged in a partisan campaign, Jefferson was expressing a version of the ideology of nonpartisan political friendship embodied in Madison's constitutional design. "I can particularly have no feelings which would revolt in a secondary position to Mr. Adams," Jefferson wrote graciously. "I am his junior in life, was his junior in Congress, his junior in the diplomatic line, his junior lately in our civil government."[157]

If Jefferson, poised for a return to Philadelphia, seemed on the point of handing the republic over to the arch-Federalist John Adams, Madison seemed not to care.[158] He was trading places with Jefferson and going back to Virginia at precisely the moment when the Republican Party had been defeated nationwide. Madison did not even want to participate in Virginia politics. He wrote his father that his name should not be allowed to get onto the ballot for the Virginia assembly; his refusal was "sincere and inflexible," he said.[159]

The timing of his retirement also had strong personal appeal to Madison. Now that he was married, Madison could set himself up as the master of Montpelier. His father was ready to relinquish the position to his son and heir. Over the course of the year since his marriage, Madison had taken an increasingly central role in organizing the affairs of the plantation from afar. He had asked Monroe in Paris to buy good quality—but secondhand—French furniture, charging him as well to acquire anything that might be appropriate for "a young housekeeper." He even ordered a "chimney clock" if Monroe could procure it "within reasonable limits."[160]

Madison and Dolley left Philadelphia in March 1797. Madison had engaged in no serious congressional business at all since the Jay Treaty debacle. As far as Madison was concerned, his time in government had at long last come to an end. He was going home to assume for the first time the life of a Virginia gentleman farmer.

In the wake of the fight over the treaty, Washington did not repudiate Madison in the public way that he had repudiated Randolph. He did not believe Madison to be personally corrupt or in the pay of France. But Washington did believe that, in advancing the view that the House of Representatives might play a crucial role in implementing treaties, Madison had betrayed the Constitution.

In a deeper sense, Washington believed that Madison had betrayed him. Washington identified himself totally with the office he occupied. The job had been designed for him, and at the Philadelphia convention he had sat listening while the design was drawn. Washington had authorized the Jay Treaty. For Madison to declare that it went beyond his authority was tantamount to Madison accusing Washington himself of acting outside the bounds of his constitutional oath.

Washington's sense of honor meant that he could not forgive even the implication of such an accusation. The relationship between the two men was at an end. Madison would attend one more official dinner at the president's residence. But all personal contact between the two of them ceased. Madison was never invited to Mount Vernon again. In retirement, Washington never mentioned Madison's name.[161]

Partisan politics had done their work. Madison's friendship with Washington had been destroyed. Even with Washington, the greatest of Virginia gentlemen, it was impossible for Madison to sustain the republican ideal of maintaining friendship in the midst of political disagreement that had assumed constitutional dimensions. First Madison had defined Hamilton as his enemy and created a party to oppose him. Then Hamilton had conquered Washington. In the end, that meant Washington, too, had become an enemy. As leader of the domestic enemy, the Federalist Party, he had allied the United States with the foreign enemy, Great Britain. War with France could not be far away.

CHAPTER ELEVEN

In the Shade

...

THE ARGUMENT: *Madison, trying to enjoy married life in Virginia, is pulled back into politics by a series of crises. Thinking nationally, he writes a new political program for the Republicans in the form of a legislative report. The document—known as the "Principles of '98"—is a restatement of Madison's constitutional philosophy. The Republican Party, which long appeared to have been reactionary, now has an affirmative vision for the future.*

Republicanism as formulated by Madison triumphs in the election of 1800. Jefferson wins, after a messy fight in Congress occasioned by poor constitutional design and an accidental tie between Jefferson and vice-presidential candidate Aaron Burr. Madison's second public life, as a co-creator of partisanship, is at an end.

JAMES MADISON WAS FORTY-SIX YEARS OLD—and had held national or state political office for more than half that time. Now, in May 1797, he and Dolley left Philadelphia for Montpelier and private life. John Adams, newly elected president, did not believe the respite would last long. "It seems the mode of becoming great is to retire," he wrote to Abigail. "Madison I suppose after retirement of a few years is to become president or vice president. It is marvelous how political plants grow in the shade."[1]

At home in Montpelier, Madison designed and supervised the building of a forty-seven-foot-wide Palladian portico with four Doric columns—the plainest and therefore most republican of the classical orders. The pediment reached the forty-foot height of the house. An English visitor noted that the whole design "was executed by [the] proprietor without the assistance of an architect and of very ordinary materials" by means of "wooden molds in the shape of pillars filled with mortar and bricks." Madison also spoke to his guest of "someday laying out space for an English park, which he might render very beautiful from the easy graceful descent of his hills into the plains below."[2]

For Dolley, Virginia was not unfamiliar. She was returning to the state where she had grown up before moving with her family to Philadelphia. And although Dolley was moving into a house dominated by Madison's mother, Nelly Conway Madison, she brought her younger sister Anna Payne with her to Montpelier. Anna played music and loved to dance.[3] She would stay with Dolley until she herself married seven years later.

A persistent rumor, one Madison considered "pure fiction," had it that he would replace James Monroe as a special envoy to France.[4] There was some logic to the idea. Tensions with France had been building rapidly since the ratification of the Jay Treaty with Britain. Some three hundred U.S.-flagged ships had been taken as prizes by French privateers or naval vessels, mostly in the West Indies. After Monroe's recall, the French government had refused to accept the credentials of the new ambassador, Charles Cotesworth Pinckney of South Carolina.

Adams wanted to avoid war with France—but he also wanted to protect American shipping interests.[5] Jefferson proposed sending a special commission of three men: Madison, Pinckney, and Elbridge Gerry.[6] Madison was pro-French like Monroe, and so might be taken seriously or at least received by the French government.

When Adams floated Madison's name to his cabinet members, they reacted negatively. One, secretary of the treasury Alexander Wolcott, offered to resign.[7] They were staunch Federalists, and to them Madison was still the national leader of the Republican Party, even if he was out of Congress.[8] By June 1797, Jefferson confirmed that "nobody of Mr. Madison's way of thinking will be appointed."[9] Instead of Madison, Adams appointed the Virginia Federalist John Marshall alongside Pinckney and Gerry. The three left for France in July 1797.

A transformative new factor was shaping U.S. relations with France: the rise of Napoleon Bonaparte. The five-man Directoire that ruled France had sent Napoleon to Italy to get him out of Paris. There, he had won a series of stunning victories culminating in the subjugation of the Habsburg emperor of Austria in March 1797.[10]

On 18 Fructidor—September 4, 1797—troops loyal to Napoleon played a key role in the coup d'état that reestablished revolutionary government in France. Elections were annulled or canceled, leading opposition figures were exiled, and free speech was curtailed. Republicans, who tended to be both pro-French and pro–French Revolution, were optimistic. One wrote to Madison that, "having purged their country of priests, emigrants, and royalists," the members of the new Directoire "will probably feel friendly towards republics."[11] Jefferson welcomed Napoleon's "miraculous string of events" with enthusiasm because, he told Madison, Napoleon's "great" and "splendid" victories lessened the risk of American hostility to France.[12]

Jefferson's positive view of Napoleon's victories was shortsighted. Napoleon's influence did not portend a conciliatory policy toward the United States or anyone else. To the contrary, he was learning that anyone could be subjugated by the right kind of effective force. The United States was no exception.

Adams's handpicked delegation met a hostile reception in Paris. The new French foreign minister was the brilliant Charles-Maurice de Talleyrand-Périgord, an aristocratic bishop turned anticlerical revolutionary who had returned to France in 1796 after four years of exile in London and New York. While in the United States, Talleyrand had stayed with Aaron Burr and become close friends with Alexander Hamilton, whom he considered a great man.[13] Although he did not speak much English, Talleyrand had a strong understanding of American politics.

Talleyrand told the delegation that he would not receive them officially unless they offered some explanation for a pro-British speech that President Adams had given in May. Then, acting through intermediaries, Talleyrand let it be known to the delegates that the United States must also arrange a large loan to France and an enormous secret bribe of £50,000 to Talleyrand himself. Pinckney refused in the starkest terms: "No, no, not a sixpence!"[14]

Word that the visit was going badly filtered back across the Atlantic. "The unfavorable accounts as to our three plenipotentiaries got to Richmond while I was there," Madison wrote to Jefferson. "It seems to give extreme uneasiness to the warm and well-informed friends of Republicanism." A war with France would have the effect of "warping the public mind towards monarchy," he reminded Jefferson, who needed no reminding.[15]

Madison was hoping that disclosure of unsuccessful negotiations would tamp down war fervor, perhaps by revealing that the Adams administration had not tried very hard to avoid conflict. He considered

Adams "hot-headed" and "kindled into flame by every spark that lights on his passions." In comparison, Washington had been "cold, considerate and cautious." According to Madison, Adams, "a perfect Quixote as a statesman," was tilting against the windmill of France, "taking as much pains to get into war, as [Washington] took to keep out of it."[16] So horrified was Madison with Adams that he had forgotten his frustration with Washington.

In reality, Adams wanted to avoid open conflict with France, and when he received word of Talleyrand's bribery demand, he tried to keep the story quiet lest it produce a public outcry for war. On March 19, 1798, after repeated Republican insistence, Adams had no choice but to turn over his delegates' correspondence to Congress. The names of Talleyrand's intermediaries were replaced by the letters X, Y, and Z to preserve their anonymity in connection with the bribe.

What came to be called the "XYZ Affair" enraged a public already angry about French hostilities. Even Jefferson was shocked. The demand for the bribe had been "calculated to excite disgust and indignation in Americans generally," he told Madison. Jefferson believed that, rationally speaking, the letters on their own did not provide "one motive the more for our going to war." But he knew the political reality would be otherwise: "Such is their effect on the minds of wavering characters . . . that to wipe off the imputation of being French partisans, they will go over to the war-measures so furiously pushed by the other party."[17]

In the aftermath of the revelations, the Senate passed a bill to "purchase 12 vessels of from 14 to 22 guns, with which our frigates are to be employed as convoys and guarda costas [coast-guards]."[18] Jefferson hoped that war could be avoided, but expected that it could not. "In fact the question of war and peace depends now on the toss of cross and pile," he wrote Madison.[19] The coin toss that Jefferson had in mind was whether there would be an official declaration of war.

Even without a formal declaration, however, armed hostilities would become inevitable. "We see a new instance of the inefficacy of constitutional guards," Jefferson told Madison. "We had relied with great security on that provision which requires two thirds of the legislature to declare war. But this is completely eluded by majorities taking such measures as will be sure to produce war."[20]

Jefferson's carelessness was evident here: The Constitution allowed Congress to declare war by a simple majority. Nevertheless, the concern

414 THE THREE LIVES OF JAMES MADISON

was justified. John Adams never sought a declaration of war against France, and Congress never provided one. On July 7, 1798, however, Congress officially withdrew from the twenty-year-old treaties of alliance and amity with France.[21] Two days later, it authorized the seizure of all armed French ships that U.S. vessels might encounter on the high seas.

The resulting conflict between the United States and France was not war in the legal sense of the term—but it was war in effect. Conducted at sea, it featured continued French seizures of American merchant ships—and, eventually, retaliation by newly built frigates and armed revenue cutters.

Madison reviled the idea of undeclared war. "The Constitution supposes, what the history of all governments demonstrates, that the executive is the branch of power most interested in war, and most prone to it," he wrote to Jefferson. "It has accordingly with studied care, vested the question of war in the legislature: but the doctrines lately advanced strike at the root of all these provisions, and will deposit the peace of the country in that department which the Constitution distrusts as most ready without cause to renounce it."[22] A new name was needed for the constitutional anomaly of armed hostilities conducted by executive fiat without an official war declaration. The conflict between the United States and France would come to be called the Quasi-War, the Half-War, or, most pointedly, the Undeclared War.

Abominable and Degrading

The enthusiasm for war following the XYZ Affair put the Federalists in a powerful political position. This was the first war-craze since the Revolution, and it fueled xenophobic sentiment against not only the French but other foreigners from non-English-speaking countries. Consistent with their constitutional ideology, the Federalists took advantage of anti-immigrant feeling to strengthen the executive and weaken their Republican opponents. Jefferson reported to Madison that "one of the war-party, in a fit of unguarded passion declared some time ago they would pass a citizen bill, an alien bill, and a sedition bill."[23] The first of these extended the residency requirement for citizenship from five years to fourteen years. The alien bill allowed the president to deport or imprison unilaterally any foreigner whom he determined "dangerous to the peace and safety of the United States." The sedition bill was, Jefferson said, aimed at "the suppression of the Whig [i.e., Republican] presses" that were criticizing Adams and the rush to war.[24]

To Madison and Jefferson, these proposed bills represented crises. Jefferson told Madison he believed the citizenship bill was specifically directed at Albert Gallatin, a Swiss-born Republican of particular financial talent who was becoming a close associate of both men. Gallatin had immigrated to the United States in 1780, and in 1793 had been elected to the Senate from Pennsylvania. Federalists at the time claimed he had not satisfied the nine-year citizenship requirement for senators. Gallatin attempted to refute the claim, demonstrating that he had lived in the country for thirteen years and taken an oath of allegiance to the Commonwealth of Virginia in 1785. Nonetheless, the full Senate voted 14 to 12 to remove Gallatin from office. Gallatin was subsequently elected to the House, and had effectively become the Republican leader there since Madison's retirement. Jefferson thought that the Federalists "will endeavor to reach him by this bill."[25]

The loss of Gallatin from politics would be damaging to Republicans, but the sedition bill would be much more dangerous. While the Federalists controlled the presidency and Congress, the newspapers were Republicans' primary venue of opposition. In the best of circumstances, such newspapers relied on the unpredictable demand for subscriptions in order to survive. "If these papers fall," Jefferson told Madison, "Republicanism will be entirely browbeaten."[26] Madison agreed. "It is to be hoped," he wrote back to Jefferson, "that any arbitrary attacks on freedom of the press will find virtue enough remaining in the public mind to make them recoil on the wicked authors."[27]

Madison realized that public opinion, on which he had so much relied in forming the Republican Party, would not effectively check the Federalists at a time of enthusiasm for war. He mused to Jefferson that, because public opinion could be easily manipulated when it came to foreign relations, this was the area of government "most susceptible of abuse." The facts could be selectively "concealed or disclosed," their release timed to affect "particular views." Meanwhile, "the body of the people are less capable of judging and are more under the influence of prejudices, on that branch of their affairs, than any other."[28]

War enthusiasm, Madison believed, would enable the Federalists to restrict domestic freedom. "Perhaps it is a universal truth," he wrote to Jefferson, "that the loss of liberty at home is to be charged to provisions against danger real or pretended from abroad."[29] The observation was profound and far-reaching. Madison was identifying a phenomenon that would accompany every future foreign war but one: Threats from abroad would be used to justify infringement of civil liberties in the United States.

The First Amendment stated, "Congress shall make no law... abridging the freedom of speech, or of the press." The proposed sedition bill arguably infringed on this guarantee. Congress had never passed such legislation before. The presence of the external threat was a necessary condition for Congress's first major restriction on civil liberties in its history.

Adams used all the tools at his behest to strengthen the Federalist position. He issued a proclamation declaring May 9 "as a day of solemn humiliation, fasting and prayer." George Washington had declared days of Thanksgiving each year of his presidency. But Adams's day was something different, drawing on the New England custom of collective religious expression pegged specifically to immediate political events. The duty to pray was especially important "in seasons of difficulty and of danger," Adams's proclamation read. In the presence of "existing or threatening calamities, the just judgments of God against prevalent iniquity, are a loud call to repentance and reformation." Now was such a time.[30]

On May 7, 1798, Adams also published an open letter to a group of young Philadelphians in which he assured them that he only went to war out of necessity. To bring the point home, Adams told his version of the story of the American Revolution. "Before the birth of the oldest of you," he said condescendingly, "I was called to act with your fathers in concerting measures the most disagreeable and dangerous." His generation had acted, he insisted, "not from a desire of innovation, not from discontent with the government under which we were born and bred, but to preserve the honor of our country, and vindicate the immemorial liberties of our ancestors."[31] Adams was saying that the Revolution had not grown from any preference for republican government over monarchy. Independence had been nothing more than a necessity to insist on the rights of Americans as Englishmen.

Madison was disgusted. The speech was "the most abominable and degrading to fall from the lips of the first magistrate of an independent people," he wrote to Jefferson, "and particularly from a revolutionary patriot." Madison knew that Jefferson had a soft spot for Adams, but he also knew that Jefferson's commitment to republicanism was unstinting—and he was taking the opportunity to show Jefferson that Adams was a monarchist.[32]

Madison could not resist driving the point home to Jefferson. "Whether he always made this profession is best known to those ... who knew him in the year 1776," he said pointedly.[33] Either Adams had been a hypocrite republican then or he was a hypocrite monarchist now. Madison threw back at Jefferson the famous quip about Adams which Jefferson had once quoted to him. Benjamin Franklin had said that Adams was "always an honest man, often a wise one, but sometimes wholly out of his senses." The first two might still be true, Madison allowed. But Adams was by his conduct "verifying completely the last feature in the character drawn of him by Dr. Franklin."[34] To Madison, Adams had gone mad.

By July, the citizenship bill, two alien bills, and the sedition bill had passed.[35] The alien laws put foreigners at the absolute mercy of the executive. The Sedition Act, Jefferson told Madison, "among other enormities, undertakes to make printing certain matters criminal, though one of the amendments to the Constitution has so expressly taken religion, printing presses etc. out of their coercion." In Jefferson's opinion, the sedition bill "and the alien bill both are so palpably in the teeth of the Constitution as to show they mean to pay no respect to it."[36]

To Republicans, the passage of the Sedition Act was clear evidence of the Adams administration's "appetite for tyranny."[37] One circular letter deemed it "an open violation" of the First Amendment. But what should be done? The courts might declare the law unconstitutional. If not, the letter urged, "It behooves you and every citizen to endeavor, in the mode prescribed by the Constitution, to obtain its repeal."[38]

Deeply troubled by the Sedition Act, and urged by Madison to abandon his longtime respect for Adams, Jefferson decided to go further. To attack the law he considered unconstitutional, he would appeal directly to the states. He would undercut the federal law by outflanking the federal government.

Writing anonymously, Jefferson drafted nine resolutions that were adopted by the Kentucky state legislature.* The resolutions condemned the

---

* He may have intended them for the Virginia legislature, but Kentucky's met first. See "Editorial Note: The Kentucky Resolutions of 1798," January 1, 1798, to January 31, 1799, *PTJ*, 30:529–31.

Alien and Sedition Acts as unconstitutional. But they did much more than that. Jefferson's Kentucky Resolutions offered a new theory of the relationship between the state and the federal government under the Constitution.

The Constitution was a "compact" between "co-states," Jefferson asserted. Consequently, each of the parties to the compact had "an equal right to judge for itself" whether the Constitution had been violated, and how to redress the violation. According to this view, the federal government "was not made the exclusive or final judge of the extent of the powers delegated to itself."[39]

Jefferson was denying that Congress, the president, or the Supreme Court had the last word on the meaning of the Constitution. The states reserved the power to interpret it as well as adopt measures necessary to enforce their interpretations. Indeed, Jefferson insisted that the states were the *only* ultimate judges of what was constitutional, "they alone being parties to the compact, and solely authorized to judge in the last resort of the powers exercised under it." Congress was "not a party, but merely a creature of the compact." It was therefore subordinate to the "final judgment" of the states.[40]

The implications were stunning. In Jefferson's account, the Constitution had not been the act of "We the People of the United States." The states had created the Constitution and Jefferson renamed them "co-states" to emphasize their independence from one another and from the union. He was drawing on international law, according to which a compact among states—that is, a treaty—could be interpreted equally by each of the parties. The parties also reserved the authority to withdraw from the agreement. Jefferson was depicting the Constitution as nothing more than the treaty of a federation.

The consequence of this argument was that the states had the power to nullify federal laws. "Where powers are assumed which have not been delegated, a nullification of the act is the rightful remedy," Jefferson wrote.[41] He called on each of the "co-states" to "take measures of its own for providing that neither these acts, nor any others of the general government, not plainly and intentionally authorized by the Constitution, shall be exercised within their respective territories."[42] The sitting vice president of the United States was proposing that the state legislatures should take action to block federal law from being enforced.

Jefferson's response put Madison in a bind. Jefferson seemed to believe the radical doctrines he was espousing. More, he wanted the arguments in the Kentucky Resolutions to become the "principles" of the Republican Party and be used as a blueprint for its political strategy.

Yet Madison could not embrace Jefferson's arguments. Taken seriously, they amounted to a repudiation of the Constitution that was Madison's greatest achievement and had become the basis for all serious political debate in the United States. The Articles of Confederation might or might not have been a treaty of federation—the topic had been debated until the adoption of the Constitution had rendered it moot. But whatever the Constitution was, it had to be far more than a compact among "co-states."

As Madison had understood for himself and explained to anyone who would listen in the years before, during, and after the drafting and ratification of the Constitution, a mere federation could not survive the centrifugal forces that would pull it apart. Madison had designed a form of government that operated on the individual citizen, not on the states. This had been, he well knew, his most brilliant and original accomplishment. Jefferson proposed to reverse everything that made the Constitution unique.

Madison knew that when Jefferson was sufficiently riled up, he tended to extremes. So he chose not to respond directly to the draft that Jefferson sent him only after it had already been sent to Kentucky. Instead he wrote to Jefferson to ask him, rather gently, "Have you ever considered thoroughly the distinction between the power of the state, and that of the legislature, on questions relating to the federal pact?"[43] Reminding Jefferson that it had been state conventions, not the state legislature, that entered into the Constitution, was his way of hinting that the people, acting through their states, had created a Constitution—and that the state legislatures therefore did not have the power to nullify federal law.

Then Madison took a different tack. He drafted a much briefer set of resolutions of his own and submitted them through a friend to the Virginia assembly for adoption. Tellingly, Madison did not inform Jefferson that he was doing so.

Madison aimed to curtail Jefferson's radicalism—which, if not reined in, could damage the Republican Party and even the republic itself. Madison did not want to contradict Jefferson, who was not only his closest friend and closest political ally but was also in high dudgeon. He sought to minimize, not emphasize, the difference in their respective constitutional philosophies. The Virginia Resolutions were intended as a moderate alternative to Kentucky's radicalism.

Madison's Virginia Resolutions admitted that the Constitution was a compact that had conferred powers on the federal government—but not that the *states* had delegated their own powers to the federal government. Rather, Madison left room for the possibility that the *people* had delegated powers to the federal government directly. According to this subtle view, the states might be "parties" to the compact, but they were not the source of federal power.

The rest of the resolutions indicated that the states had "the right, and are in duty bound, to interpose" against the Alien and Sedition Acts.[44] The document called on other states to "concur." The states could undertake "necessary and proper measures" to cooperate with Virginia "in maintaining unimpaired the authorities, rights, liberties, reserved to the states respectively, or to the people."[45]

The right to "interpose" suggested by Madison was materially different from the right to nullify proposed by Jefferson. As far as the Virginia Resolutions were concerned, the job of the state legislature in the face of an unconstitutional federal law was to announce to the world that the law was unconstitutional—and no more.

When Jefferson saw a draft of the Virginia Resolutions, shown to him not by Madison but by their mutual friend Wilson Cary Nicholas, he was frustrated. Jefferson, who likely did not yet realize Madison was the author of the competing alternative, told Nicholas that instead of merely declaring the Alien and Sedition Acts unconstitutional, the states should declare that the laws "are, and were ab initio—null, void and of no force or effect."[46] The distinction was crucial. Declaring the laws to be "of no force or effect" implied that they should not be treated as law at all. Nicholas duly added Jefferson's proposed language, but it was excluded from the final resolution, which passed the Virginia legislature easily.

Jefferson had overplayed his hand. Seven different state legislatures officially rejected the Virginia and Kentucky resolutions, and three more issued condemnations. Instead of directing focus on the unconstitutionality of the Alien and Sedition Acts themselves, as Jefferson had intended, the responses all focused on the danger of one state, Kentucky, claiming the authority to nullify federal acts. For the Republicans, the loss was considerable. What should have been a chance to rally opposition to the Alien and Sedition Acts had instead led to national humiliation. If the

Republican cause was to be revived, Jefferson would have to elicit Madison's opinion rather than acting unilaterally.

Sedition and Reaction

Meanwhile, the Sedition Act went into effect, with dire results for Republicans. Congressman Matthew Lyon of Vermont, a Republican firebrand who the year before had gotten into a brawl with a Federalist opponent on the floor of the House of Representatives, had launched a newspaper whose name, *The Scourge of Aristocracy and Repository of Important Political Truth,* left no doubt of its sympathies.[47] In the paper, Lyon described John Adams as having "an unbounded thirst for ridiculous pomp, foolish adulation, and selfish avarice."[48] The published piece said nothing more than what most Republicans believed about Adams. Lyon was charged with sedition under the act, convicted, and sentenced to pay a $1,000 fine and serve four months in prison.

The Lyon conviction made it clear that Adams was using the Sedition Act to protect his reputation. Several thousand Vermonters submitted a petition to the president seeking waiver of Lyon's fine. According to Jefferson, Adams asked the person who brought in the petition whether Lyon himself had signed it. The answer was no: Lyon would not budge. Adams answered that "Penitence must precede pardon."[49] Adams was demanding an apology in exchange for exercising his constitutional power to pardon Lyon. Whether he knew it or not, Adams was essentially acknowledging that his motives were personal.

Madison wanted a vigorous Republican response. "I have been disappointed in seeing no step taken in relation to Lyon," he told Jefferson. Madison thought that Lyon, a member of Congress, must be constitutionally immune from the Sedition Act. "He is clearly within his privilege and it ought to be claimed for him," Madison explained.* Jefferson urged

---

* Madison did not specifically refer to the First Amendment. He may have been thinking of the speech and debate clause of the Constitution, which specifies that members of Congress "shall not be questioned" regarding "any speech or debate in either house." Or he may have had in mind the constitutional provision that congressmen "shall in all cases, except treason, felony, and breach of the peace, be privileged from arrest during their attendance at the session of their respective houses, and in going to and from the same." See Article I, Section 6. Lyon was not punished for speech made in the House but in a newspaper, and he was not attending a congressional session. But the four-month sentence would prevent him from attending Congress.

Madison to help the Republican cause and "publish your debates of the convention." Jefferson, who had not been at the convention, imagined that the debates would strengthen the argument for limited government. Madison might prefer not to publish confidential debates for personal reasons, Jefferson added, but there were "moral" reasons to do so. Anyway, he told Madison, "something is required from you as a set-off against the sin of your retirement."[50] The time was coming for Madison to take action.

Madison had no intention of publishing the constitutional debates, which would probably not have been helpful to the Republican cause. Moreover, Madison did not tell Jefferson that he himself had been on the side of broader national power at the convention.

Instead of following Jefferson's advice and focusing on the Constitution, Madison turned to foreign policy. He wrote two anonymous essays, which he sent to Jefferson to be published in the Philadelphia *Aurora General Advertiser*. They appeared in January and February of 1799.

The first of these, entitled "Foreign Influence," was an out-and-out attack on England. "Great Britain, above all other nations, ought to be dreaded and watched, as most likely to gain undue and pernicious ascendancy in our country," Madison wrote.[51] Britain's practical interest, he argued, was to suppress the growth of the potentially rivalrous American economy. Britain's ideological interest was "her *hatred and fear* of the *republican example* of our governments."[52] According to Madison, Britain feared the growth of republicanism worldwide, of which the French Revolution was the latest manifestation.[53] As an analysis of British political ideology, this account was not very convincing. The French Revolution was feared and detested in England for its radical Jacobinism and ensuing chaos, not its republicanism per se.

Pursuing this line of argument, Madison charged that Britain would try to subvert republicanism in America "by establishing a faction of its own in the country."[54] Madison then analyzed the stream of capital that traveled from England in "every shipment, every consignment, every commission," gathered in the "reservoirs" of "our seaport towns," and from thence "issue[d] a thousand streams to the inland towns, and country stores." As a result of this capital flow, "our country is penetrated to its remotest corners with the foreign poison."[55]

It could not be denied that the strongest interest group favoring good relations with Britain was the merchant class that depended on British capital and British credit. Federalists tended to be connected to manufacturing, commerce, and trade—and therefore had crucial reasons to favor Britain. Republicans, at least as Madison saw it,[56] were more likely to be involved in agriculture, whether in plantations such as Montpelier and Monticello or in the backcountry. They therefore had reason to oppose traders and capitalists, who were associated with Britain, and to favor France, Britain's natural enemy.*

In his second published essay, Madison turned to France and the formidable challenge of defending a continuing American alliance. The ancien régime had helped the United States against England. After the French Revolution, Madison had joined Jefferson in believing that France had become a natural ideological ally of the United States. But now, revolutionary France could no longer credibly be described as republican. The argument for ideological alliance with France was fading fast.

Rather than defending the Directoire, Madison sought to change the subject by deriving anti-Federalist lessons from its example. The Directoire was elected yet tyrannical, proof that electing officials (such as Adams) was no guarantee that they would act in the public interest. The Directoire was a powerful executive—again like Adams.[57] The argument fell flat. Adams had not come to power in a coup d'état. The Sedition Act, whatever its constitutionality, had been passed by Congress.

To Madison, the message for Americans was to avoid war, which not only destroyed lives, wasted treasure, and corrupted morals, but destroyed "the equilibrium of the departments of power." This was a typically Madisonian argument: War was hell—especially because it broke down the separation of powers. Even the mere threat of war could produce the same results: "An alarm is proclaimed—Troops are raised—Taxes are imposed—Officers military and civil are created." Then, even after "the danger is repelled or disappears," the standing army, the taxes, and the government offices ripe for political corruption would all persist.

Madison had restated the familiar, classically republican worry about

* In a final clever fillip, Madison impugned the press. Although it was meant to be the "guardian of public rights" and the "organ of necessary truths," the newspapers were, in fact, "tainted with partiality" and were pro-British. His explanation was that "the city papers are supported by advertisements." Those advertisements, in turn, "relate to articles of trade, and are furnished by merchants and traders." The press was subservient, in "prostration to advertising customers." Madison was ahead of his time in depicting editorial policy as dictated by advertisers' economic interests.

the rise of executive power in wartime. But he had not explained why the United States should allow attacks on its shipping without mounting a defense. And he had admitted that "when a state of war becomes absolutely and clearly necessary, all the citizens will submit with alacrity to the calamities inseparable from it."[58]

Actually, Adams, who had been forced into war by the XYZ Affair, wanted to bring the Quasi-War with France to a rapid close. Yet Madison could not acknowledge it. He told Jefferson that Adams's course of action leading to the war "displays a narrow understanding and a most malignant heart."[59] His personal view of Adams, never positive, had devolved into detestation.

Step Forward and Save the Country

On March 4, 1799, Madison's Virginia friend John Taylor of Caroline wrote to him that Patrick Henry had announced that he was coming out of retirement to run for the state assembly—this time as a Federalist. George Washington himself had recruited Henry, writing that he feared "the tranquility of the union, and of this state in particular, is hastening to an awful crisis."[60] Henry was telling everyone that Washington had "called on him to step forward and save his country."[61]

For the arch Anti-Federalist Henry to become a Federalist was astonishing to the point of being bizarre. He had, Taylor pointed out, rejected the Constitution as giving too much power to the federal government. Now he was joining the party that had extended that federal power so far that Madison had opposed it at every turn.[62] For the Federalists to embrace Henry was equally "laughable," Taylor wrote. "After the abuse formerly lavished upon that character, they now look up to [him] as the savior of his country."[63]

Taylor believed that Henry, encouraged by Washington, intended to use his position in the Virginia legislature to weaken support for Jefferson and thus block him from becoming president. "His apostasy is capable of a solution, only by considering it as the issue of a personal enmity to Mr. Jefferson and yourself," Taylor wrote. To achieve these goals, "he has sacrificed his principles to a party determined on your destruction."[64] Unless Madison entered the Virginia assembly, "there will be no member present capable of counterpoising Mr. Henry," Taylor continued. Even if Madison did not care about his own political future, if he could "discern a conspiracy" against his friend, would he "not step forward and save him?" Finally Taylor appealed to patriotism: "If you will not save yourself or your friend—yet save your country."[65]

The prospect of Henry coming back from the political grave was enough to convince Madison to reenter state politics.[66] Madison and one Captain James Barbour were the only candidates for the two seats, and they were elected without a poll being taken.[67]

Madison could now return to the assembly, yet the anticipated clash with Henry never materialized. Weakened by age, Henry could not withstand a trip he took to Charlotte County, Virginia, to make a campaign speech at the courthouse there in March 1799. In the speech, Henry apparently tried to square the circle, commenting that the Alien and Sedition Acts "were only the fruit of that Constitution the adoption of which he opposed."[68] If the report is accurate, Henry was suggesting that the suppression of free speech was part and parcel of the Constitution that Madison had advocated. The statement was a stinging rebuke to Madison, and evidence that Henry had not lost his ability to strike Madison at his most vulnerable points. But on June 6, 1799, before the assembly could meet, Henry died at the age of sixty-three.

Henry was gone and the personal threat to Jefferson eliminated—and Madison was back in politics. Jefferson hoped to visit Madison in Montpelier before leaving for Philadelphia. But Monroe advised him against it. According to Monroe, if Jefferson were known to have visited Madison, it would be made "a subject of some political slander, and perhaps of some political injury."[69] A visit between Jefferson, the expected Republican presidential candidate, and Madison, now an active Republican leader once again, could be made to look like a meeting for electioneering strategy, which was thought to be disreputable.

In reality, preparations for the election were already taking place. From Charleston, South Carolina, Charles Pinckney wrote to Madison that he must propose a bill in the Virginia assembly specifying that, in future presidential elections, "the electors of a president and vice president shall be elected by joint ballot." In the previous election, many states had split their presidential and vice presidential votes. "Mr. Adams carried his election by one vote from Virginia and North Carolina," Pinckney wrote, while Jefferson "had not one vote to the northward of Pennsylvania." Pinckney was anticipating another close election in which every vote would count. "Everything depends upon it," he warned Madison.[70]

Jefferson, too, was planning for the election. He wrote to Madison that henceforth, Republicans should give jobs only to Republicans and not to Federalists, however well qualified they might be. "It is advantage enough to [the] Feds to possess the exclusive patronage of the administration," he wrote. "So long as they go on the exclusive principle, we should do the same." In the past, he had thought Republicanism was incompatible with patronage. Now he had reversed course. "The Republicans should know that offices are to be given exclusively to their opponents by their friends no longer," Jefferson wrote.[71]

Jefferson also unveiled to Madison four national policies that he thought were necessary to win the election in light of "new circumstances." Jefferson numbered them:

1. Peace even with Great Britain.
2. A sincere cultivation of the union.
3. The disbanding of the army on principles of economy and safety.
4. Protestations against violations of the true principles of our Constitution, merely to save them, and prevent precedents and acquiescence . . . but nothing to be said or done in which shall look or lead to force, and give any pretext for keeping up the army.[72]

The election looming, Jefferson was trying to sum up the lessons of the past decade of Federalist ascension. Peace was popular, and so the Republicans should not be seen as the party of war toward Britain just because they wanted peace with France. Union was popular, too—the Kentucky Resolutions had overreached. Finally, Republicans must avoid making the mistake of the Whiskey Rebellion, in which they had allowed themselves to become associated with resistance that, in turn, justified the need for an army.

In 1796, Jefferson had been content to let Adams win the presidential election. This time he wanted to win. He told Madison that, in view of the upcoming elections, he expected their correspondence would be read by others. "From the commencement of the ensuing session," he told Madison, "I shall entrust the post offices with nothing confidential, persuaded that during the ensuing 12 months they will lend their inquisitorial aid to furnish matter for new slanders." Even writing in code would no longer be considered safe. "I shall send you as usual printed communi-

James Madison by Charles Willson Peale, 1792.
A man in his prime—poised for the surprise of his life.

Notes on the Bill of Rights by James Madison, June 8, 1789.
Madison was against the Bill of Rights before he wrote it. His
notes for his big speech to Congress introducing the draft.

Dolley Payne Madison by Gilbert Stuart, 1804. Dolley Madison as she looked when the Madisons moved to Washington. Because Jefferson was widowed, she was effectively First Lady for sixteen years.

Anna Payne Cutts by Gilbert Stuart, 1804. Dolley's sister
lived with the Madisons for years. Note the family
resemblance in the similar portraits.

James Monroe by Samuel F. B. Morse, 1819. Madison's close friend for more than thirty years—who twice ran against him for office and eventually succeeded him as president.

Edmund Randolph by Flavius Joseph Fisher. Madison's close friend and ally in planning the Philadelphia convention; governor of Virginia, first attorney general, second secretary of state. Randolph's fatal flaw was a tendency to equivocate.

Gouvenor Morris by James Sharpie, Jr., 1810. The Casanova of the framers, a key actor at the Philadelphia convention, and later ambassador to France.

William Paterson by C. Gregory Stapko. Madison's greatest headache in Philadelphia, author of the New Jersey plan that effectively forced the big states to compromise with the mid-Atlantic states and allow equal representation in the Senate regardless of population.

Alexander Hamilton by John Trumbull, 1806. Madison's close friend and ally, brilliant co-author of the *Federalist* papers, turned personal and political enemy and partisan opponent. Pansexual, passionate, and charismatic, moved by the will to power: the anti-Madison, ideal subject of a hip-hop musical.

Philip Freneau by Frederick Halpin. Madison's contemporary at Princeton, sometime "poet of the Revolution." Madison plucked him from obscurity to found and edit the *National Gazette,* a partisan Republican newspaper.

cations," Jefferson promised, "without saying anything confidential on them. You will of course understand the cause."[73]

The Report

The first order of business facing Madison when the Virginia assembly convened in December 1799, was an attack on Monroe, who had been nominated to be governor. A Federalist opponent demanded an investigation into Monroe's activities while ambassador to France. The demand was intended to dredge up Washington's decision to recall Monroe in the wake of the Jay Treaty. Washington, profoundly upset with the Republicans and sick of pro-French sentiment, had accused Monroe of neglecting his ambassadorial duties.* To make Monroe governor, Virginia Federalists now insisted, would, in effect, rebuke Washington for having recalled Monroe.[74]

The ploy, intended to embarrass the Republicans, struck a sore spot for Monroe, who had spent the better part of three years in a series of public newspaper imbroglios aggressively defending his conduct in France. Madison rose to champion his friend—and his party. He rejected the suggestion that electing Monroe would be tantamount to "a condemnation" of Washington. Ambassadors were "often" recalled "for reasons unconnected with their diplomatic character," Madison explained. Then he launched into a strong personal defense of Monroe. "Mr. Madison spoke highly of his private character as pure, and his public character as unimpeachable," reported the *Virginia Argus*. Far from being "injurious to the country," Monroe's mission to France had been "successful" in its "most delicate and important points."[75]

The audience in the Virginia assembly knew that they were seeing something memorable. James Madison, one of the greatest national politicians from Virginia, was defending his friend James Monroe, another great national figure. Madison's "appearance produced such a general rus-

---

* In fact, Monroe's performance as ambassador had been exemplary. The French government had been understandably infuriated by the Jay Treaty and the Washington administration's obvious preference for Britain. Monroe had labored to assure the French that the United States would in the long run retain common political and economic interests with France and that the French government should not provoke the United States. Without Monroe's close ties to France, U.S.-French relations might have broken down completely.

tling in the House that, for several minutes, we could not hear one word which he said," reported the *Argus*.[76] Virginia insiders knew how, a decade before, Monroe had opposed ratification of the Constitution and then run against Madison in a congressional district gerrymandered to keep Madison out of Congress. After the election, Madison had insisted to Jefferson that his friendship for Monroe was undiminished. Astonishingly, it was true.

With Monroe safely elected governor, Madison could turn to the most pressing political business for the Republican Party: crafting a formal legislative response to the seven states that had rejected the Kentucky and Virginia resolutions of 1798. His response, which would come to be called the Principles of '98, restated Madison's constitutional philosophy in the light of his continuing outrage over the Alien and Sedition Acts. Most immediately, the report functioned as the Republican platform for the national election of 1800—and it signaled that the Republican Party would not back away from a narrow construction of Congress's enumerated powers.

Madison condemned the Alien Act as unconstitutional. Foreigners from countries at peace with the United States were entitled to "sacred" rights of due process and habeas corpus, rights that the law frankly violated by giving the president absolute power to detain or deport aliens without a hearing.[77] He dismissed the idea that international law might justify the practice or that it was authorized through Congress's power to declare war.*

The Sedition Act roused Madison to an impressive and even magisterial attack. He insisted that Congress lacked the power to punish seditious libel. Supporters claimed authority derived from the common law. Relying on notes provided by Randolph, Madison argued that there was no unifying common law at the national level in the United States, and denied that the Constitution created any such thing by establishing the judiciary. Otherwise, Madison pointed out, Congress would have the authority to legislate on any matter covered by the common law, instead of being limited to its enumerated powers.[78]

---

* Madison also described the law as violating states' rights, because the Constitution authorized states to allow "the migration or importation of such persons as any of the states shall think proper to admit" until 1808. This clause, which Madison had objected to at the convention, was the one intended to allow the slave trade to continue until 1808. Madison avoided mentioning that this was the clause's purpose.

This brought Madison to the freedom of speech and the press. The people of the states had demanded the Bill of Rights. The First Amendment meant that the press was "wholly exempt from the power of Congress." Otherwise, "the amendment could neither be said to correspond with the desire expressed by a number of states, nor be calculated to extend the ground of public confidence in the government."

Madison's point was powerful. The Federalists claimed that the First Amendment prohibited only prior censorship, not punishment of seditious libel after it was published. "It would seem a mockery," Madison wrote, "that no law should be passed, preventing publications from being made, but that laws might be passed for punishing them in case they should be made."[79] If the Federalists were correct, this would imply that the people first created a limited, constitutional government without the power of regulating the press; then demanded a Bill of Rights to protect that liberty; then ratified a constitutional amendment that, in fact, gave Congress back the power to punish speech.[80]

In crescendo, Madison reached the most devastating part of his critique: The Sedition Act interfered with the people's electoral rights. The purpose of elections was to decide whether the government was performing well. If the government had behaved improperly, "it is natural and proper, that, according to the cause and the degree of their faults, they should be brought into contempt or disrepute, and incur the hatred of the people."[81]

Yet the Sedition Act expressly punished expressions of "contempt," "disrepute," and "hatred." It therefore interfered with "that information and communication among the people, which is indispensable to the just exercise of their electoral rights."[82] And because the law protected government officials but not candidates who were running for office, it would block the public from "free" elections based on equal information about all candidates.[83]

Madison was saying that free speech was necessary to produce "information and communication among the people," and that these, in turn, were necessary for elections to be meaningful. In drafting the Constitution, Madison had paid no attention at all to the phenomenon of free speech. His horror at the rise of Federalism had later pushed him to think about public opinion as the ultimate guarantor of liberty. Once public opinion mattered, it became clear that free speech would be necessary to keep public opinion informed. Madison's embrace of freedom of speech in the *Report of 1800* thus reflected the partisan politics of the 1790s—and it transformed the theory of republicanism.[84]

The report was also a victory of Madison's views over Jefferson's radicalism.* The Jefferson of 1798, frustrated by a decade of political defeats, had been looking to the states to protect Republicans from a Federalist Congress and president who violated the Bill of Rights. He had acted without consulting Madison—and the latter's subsequent efforts to moderate Jefferson's view had been too little, too late.

By 1800, Jefferson and Madison had decided that the only solution was to defeat the Federalists in a national election. To achieve that, the extremism of 1798 would best be forgotten. Jefferson would defer to Madison's moderation. Jefferson was now implicitly acknowledging that Madison had been right. More important, the two were now functioning as a political team, poised to lead a serious attempt to gain power for the Republican Party. Their alliance had never been closer. And the stakes of their joint efforts had never been higher.

The Prospect

Bishop James Madison, always a close reader of Madison's writings, sent a letter praising the report. "You have really swept the Augean stable," he wrote. "You have cleansed the Constitution from that filth which ambition, avarice, and ignorance was heaping up around it." Bishop Madison was, however, more focused on foreign policy than constitutional principles. In his mind, the great danger to the republic came from "forming navies and standing armies." It was therefore, he told his cousin, "necessary for you to proceed one step further." Madison should demonstrate, using the principles of Adam Smith in his *Wealth of Nations*, "that it would be fortunate for America, if she had not a single ship upon the ocean; at all events, not a single armed ship."[85]

---

* In the final paragraphs of the report, Madison returned to the theme that declaring the Alien and Sedition Acts unconstitutional in 1798 had been symbolic only. This statement repudiated Jefferson's attempt in the Kentucky Resolutions to insist that the states could interpose themselves to invalidate federal law. Then, rather than directly contradicting Jefferson, Madison had preferred to draft alternative resolutions that did not go as far. In the *Report of 1800*, intended as the Republican political program for the upcoming elections, Madison sought to ensure the victory of his moderate view over Jefferson's radicalism. This time, Madison knew, Jefferson would not contradict him.

The bishop told his practical cousin that if he would simply make this pacifist argument to the public, it "would probably I think, if not certainly, open the American mind," and "the great mass of the people" would suddenly be able "to see their real interests": The United States did not need a navy because it did not need shipping. Public opinion would then become "a Hercules" that would overawe the federal government and block a militaristic foreign policy.[86]

The two James Madisons were different people. But as was often the case, the ecclesiastical, academic cousin was taking the politician's theories to their logical conclusion. The Republican argument for limited government was, in its essence, also an argument against turning the United States into a naval and military power on the model of Britain. The United States must be a unique international actor. Republicans believed the United States must preserve itself from the temptation of turning into a far-flung empire.

The challenge now was to convince the public. In Congress, Republicans introduced a bill to repeal the laws passed in 1798–99 authorizing the growth of the army. The existing Congress rejected it.[87] The election of 1800 was the Republicans' opportunity to change public opinion—and the government.

The election season started early. In January, a group of Virginia legislators met "for the purpose of framing a Republican ticket" of presidential electors; the ticket was announced on March 7. Madison agreed to stand as a candidate for Congress.[88] If Jefferson was elected president, he would appoint Madison to the cabinet.

Jefferson was guardedly optimistic. "The Federalists begin to be very seriously alarmed about their election next fall," he wrote to Madison on March 4. The northern states would vote for Adams and the southern states for Jefferson. The outcome would depend on the mid-Atlantic states of Pennsylvania, New Jersey, and New York.[89] Jefferson believed that if he won Pennsylvania, he could win the election by adding either New Jersey or New York. If Jefferson lost New York, he would need to win both New Jersey and Pennsylvania, and so "the probabilities will be in favor of the Federalist victory."[90]

As Madison had warned in his report, Federalists used the Sedition Act to try to affect the election. The editor of *The Bee* in New London, Connecticut, had been sentenced to three months in prison and a $200 fine. In New York, a printer had been fined and jailed for a letter libeling

Hamilton. The editor of *The Vermont Gazette* was also fined and jailed.[91] In Pennsylvania, the journalist Thomas Cooper was sentenced to six months in prison and a $400 fine for libeling Adams.

Federalists also resorted to personal attacks on Jefferson, the first time this technique had been used in a presidential election. From Maryland, a Republican ally, lawyer and politician Gabriel Duvall, wrote Madison that the two main charges against Jefferson that could "materially affect his election are, the letter to Mazzei, and irreligion."[92] Duvall's letter wanted guidance from Madison, the Republican leader, on the right way to respond to such charges.

Jefferson's by now notorious letter to the Italian republican and former Virginia emissary to Europe Philip Mazzei, had been written in April 1796, before Jefferson had been elected vice president. In it, Jefferson had written to Mazzei, "It would give you a fever were I to name to you the apostates who have gone over to these heresies, men who were Samsons in the field and Solomons in the council, but who have had their heads shorn by the harlot England."[93] The American Samson was none other than George Washington, seduced and stripped of his powers by the British Delilah. Jefferson's typically over-the-top metaphor was read as an attack on Washington.

When the letter originally became public in 1797, Jefferson had told Madison, "It would be impossible for me to explain this publicly without bringing on a personal difference between Gen. Washington and myself, which nothing before the publication of this letter has ever done." Jefferson's solution had been to remain silent in reference to the letter, neither denying his authorship nor acknowledging it. Now Washington was dead, but Jefferson had to fear the other impact of the letter he had worried about initially: that it "would embroil" Jefferson "also with all those with whom his character is still popular, that is to say nine tenths of the people of the United States."[94] The nine-tenths figure was an understatement.

In the 1800 campaign, the Republicans followed Jefferson's own approach three years earlier: They simply ignored the letter. Madison's Maryland correspondent Duvall told him, "I have never yet understood that Mr. Jefferson acknowledged himself the author of that letter."[95] Madison told Duvall to keep quiet. Duvall got the message.

The charge of irreligion against Jefferson was not much easier to address. Jefferson was a confirmed Deist, who denied not only divine intervention in human affairs but also the divinity of Christ and the doctrine of original sin. A few years later, he would compile his own version of the Bible by using a scissors to cut out the passages he considered to have been actually spoken by Jesus. Pasting them together again, he produced what he called "the Philosophy of Jesus of Nazareth"—an edifying but much reduced version of the Gospels.[96]

Ultimately, despite these attacks on Jefferson, Adams was not popular or effective enough to stave off the Republican tide. In May, Madison received an excited letter from Republican ally John Dawson. "Dear Sir!" it began with an unusual exclamation mark. "The republic is safe. Our ticket has succeeded in the city of New York by a majority of about 400."[97] This was the work of Aaron Burr, the Republican vice-presidential candidate. His selection had undoubtedly garnered the New York City Republican vote for Jefferson, and with it the state. All that Republicans now needed to win, Madison told Monroe, was "a steady adherence to the principles and prudence" they had so far followed. It helped that the Federalist Party "is so industriously cooperating in its own destruction."[98]

The Federalists' self-destructive impulse came from an unlikely yet predictable source: Alexander Hamilton, who had first tried to interfere with Adams's election in 1796. Hamilton had once more decided to support a South Carolinian this time, Charles Cotesworth Pinckney, who was Adams's running mate. The strategy was, again, to convince a handful of Federalist electors not to vote for Adams but only for Pinckney. If Pinckney ended up with more votes than Adams as a result of the stratagem, he would be president, even though most of those who voted for him intended to elect him vice president. Hamilton went so far as to make a trip to New England in order to find other enemies of Adams to help achieve this end.[99]

Adams continued to detest Hamilton, and in a letter that he knew Hamilton might well see, he described him as a "bastard" who was "devoid of every moral principle."[100] Enraged, Hamilton attacked Adams head-on in the form of a circular letter aimed at potentially sympathetic Federalist electors. Adams lacked "sound judgment," Hamilton wrote, and could not maintain "a systematic plan of conduct." To this he added "the unfortunate foibles of a vanity without bounds, and jealousy capable of discoloring every object."[101] When the letter was leaked to the Republican press, Hamilton decided to publish it as a pamphlet. Monroe told Madison that the pamphlet was intended "to decry Adams, and throw the

British or anti-republican vote on Pinckney." It would do the Federalists "more harm than good," Monroe predicted cautiously.[102] In a letter to Jefferson, Bishop James Madison called Hamilton's attack "a thunderbolt" that made him "rejoice . . . that Republicanism is likely to be completely triumphant."[103]

In September, the Pennsylvania legislature was elected with a predominant Republican majority. A correspondent wrote to Madison that when the state legislature then chose electoral college delegates, "the immaculate Jefferson will be our next president." The writer exulted that "the genius of American liberty" would be "reanimated." He paused to note that the Sedition Act was still in effect and that the postmasters were "subservient to the views of the administration and my letters liable to interception." He would therefore hold back from expressing all his views: "My fears suppress the effusions of my pen."[104] The statement of fears may have been exaggerated for dramatic effect, but it reflected a genuine feeling of Republicans in the run-up to the presidential election. They expected to win; but in the light of the Sedition Act, they still wondered what tricks the Federalists might have held in reserve.

Dénouement

Meanwhile, news came from France that "Bonaparte has brought about another revolution."[105] On 18 Brumaire—November 9, 1799—Napoleon overthrew the Directoire and replaced it with a Consulate dominated by himself as first consul. Madison wrote to Jefferson, "A new scene is presented on the French theater, which leaves the dénouement more a problem than ever." He still expressed a vain "hope that monarchy may not be their object." But he had to acknowledge what he called "melancholy evidence" showing "that the destiny of the revolution is transferred from the civil to the military authority."[106] Events in France were an object "lesson" of "the danger of military usurpations or the intrigues between political and military leaders." History had never provided a "stronger" example— "nor to a country more in a situation to profit by it," namely the United States.[107]

Yet despite Madison's sense that the death of French republicanism held important lessons, American Republicans stood by their traditional pro-French policy. Republican John Dawson wrote to Madison that "however they may have violated the principles of their own constitution of republicanism, their government as regards foreign nations is more strong than ever." A strengthened Napoleon would continue the war against Britain and her allies—and so perhaps would ally with the United States, Dawson thought.[108] Madison wrote to Jefferson, "The posture of Europe, though dreadful to humanity in general, will I trust enforce the disposition of France to come to a proper adjustment with us."[109]

John Adams agreed, and was actively negotiating with France to end the Quasi-War. Envoys left the United States in late 1799, and by the spring of 1800 were negotiating with Talleyrand, who this time received them without demanding a bribe.[110] Ending the war would have helped Adams, but the rumors of the negotiations that reached the United States in the fall of 1800 incorrectly suggested that the talks had been suspended.[111] In fact, the commissioners in Paris signed a treaty ending the Quasi-War on September 30, 1800. Word would not get back to the United States until electors from all the states had been chosen.

As the election approached, Hamilton was not the only person thinking about the complex game of electors' vote casting. Aaron Burr wanted to assure that he would actually be elected vice president if Jefferson was elected president. In 1796, when John Adams had won, the Federalist vice-presidential candidate, Thomas Pinckney, had received fewer votes than Thomas Jefferson, the Republican presidential candidate.

Burr set out to prevent ticket splitting. Through his New York allies, he sent word to Madison to make sure that southern electors did not withhold their votes from him.[112] Madison agreed. He passed the message to Monroe, explaining that it was "important that all proper measures should emanate from Richmond for guarding against a division of the Republican votes, by which one of the Republican candidates may be lost."[113]

Monroe was prepared to assure that Republican electors would cast their votes for both Jefferson and Burr. But he also worried that if every single one of them did so, then Jefferson and Burr would tie. Under the Constitution, this would throw the election into the House of Representatives, where the result would be uncertain. Monroe sent an emissary to Madison to discuss privately how they should hold back at least a few votes from Burr. But the conversation never took place. Madison wrote to Monroe that the messenger has not as yet "touched on the subject to which" Monroe had alluded, and he had "not been led to start a conversation on it."[114] The messenger then left "without any allusion to ... the election."[115]

Madison told Monroe that he was confident that Jefferson would get all the Republican votes. "The worst therefore that could possibly happen would be a tie that would appeal to the House of Representatives." In that case, "the candidates would certainly I think be arranged properly, even on the recommendation of the secondary one."[116] Even if Jefferson and Burr tied, Burr would tell congressmen to vote for Jefferson and the matter would be settled easily.

On December 18, 1800, John Dawson wrote to Madison from the new city of Washington with disturbing news. No Republican had split his ticket. "There will be 73 for Jefferson, and the same number for Burr," throwing the election to the House of Representatives. The new House, in which Republicans would have the majority, would not convene until December 1801. The Congress that would sit until March was dominated by Federalists who would support Burr, "not from a wish to elect him, but to prevent a choice." The Constitution required a majority in the House. If the Federalists could prevent that, it would leave the country with no president.

"How are we to act?" Dawson asked Madison. "The Constitution appears to me defective—who is to be president? In short, what is to become of our government?"[117] Jefferson wrote to Madison that the situation "has produced great dismay and gloom on the Republican gentlemen here, and equal exultation in the Federalists."[118]

It was even possible that the Federalists might be able to choose a president of their own. They "openly declare they will prevent an election, and will name the president of the Senate pro tempore by what they say would only be a *stretch* of the Constitution," Jefferson told Madison. They might "pass a bill giving the appointment of Mr. Jay, appointed chief justice, or to Marshall as secretary of state."[119] Jefferson had a tentative plan in place for convincing some House Federalists to vote his way and avoid the result. Nevertheless "the month of February ... will present us storms of a new character," he predicted.[120]

Madison was horrified. "I can scarcely allow myself to believe that enough will not be found to frustrate the attempt to strangle the election of the people, and smuggle into the chief magistracy the creature of a faction," he wrote back to Jefferson. "It would seem that every individual member, with any standing or stake in society, or any portion of virtue or sober understanding must revolt at the tendency of such a maneuver."[121]

Yet despite these high-flown sentiments, Madison also realized that it was time to start preparing for contingencies. One option was "to acquiesce in a suspension or usurpation of executive authority to the meeting of Congress in December next." Suspending the presidency was a depressing and risky prospect. Madison preferred that Jefferson and Burr should issue "a joint proclamation or recommendation" calling the new Congress into session immediately in March instead of waiting until the next December. After all, Madison reasoned, one of the two men must be president. At least one of them must therefore have the authority to convene the legislature. "The intentions of the people would undoubtedly be pursued."[122]

Madison admitted that in constitutional terms, the process that he had in mind was "not strictly regular." But "the irregularity will be less in form than any other adequate to the emergency; and will lie in form only rather than substance." All other alternative "remedies proposed are substantial violations of the will of the people, of the scope of the Constitution, and of the public order and interest."[123]

Madison's constitutional pragmatism amounted to an admission that, as John Dawson had written to him a month before, the Constitution as drafted was defective. Madison still hoped that "all such questions will be precluded by proper decision of nine states in the House of Representatives."[124] But if necessary, Madison was prepared to break the form of the Constitution in order to save its substance.

Zealous Partisans

On February 11, 1801, Thomas Jefferson, the vice president of the United States sitting as president of the Senate, opened the certificates of election containing the ballots cast by the electors in the sixteen states. As expected, these gave Jefferson and Burr each 73 votes.[125]

In a stunning display of intransigence, the House of Representatives refused to give the election to Jefferson. The votes were by state delegation, and so a majority of each delegation had to vote for a candidate in order for that state to cast its ballot for the candidate. Eight states voted immediately for Jefferson—the seven states that were controlled by Republicans, plus Georgia, in which a Federalist congressman cast the deciding vote in Jefferson's favor. But Jefferson needed nine of the sixteen states to have a majority and become president.

Six Federalist-controlled states voted for Burr. They simply would not cast their votes for the hated Jefferson. Two states, Maryland and Vermont, split their internal congressional delegations evenly, and so cast no vote at all. The result was an 8–6–2 stalemate.

In the hopes of breaking the logjam, the House of Representatives voted again and again. As of 10 p.m. on February 11, the House had voted 17 times, each time yielding the same result. The next day, February 12, it voted 11 times more. "We voted 28 times," John Dawson reported to Madison. "I have not closed my eyes for 36 hours." Rumors abounded as to what the Federalists had in mind. "Some whisper that they mean to propose a legislative provision; others that the Senate on their meeting on the 4th of March will appoint a president pro tem. who will act as the president of the United States."[126] Six more House ballots over the next four days were also unsuccessful.

The Federalists had to decide: Would they continue the stalemate and take their chances with a constitutional crisis, or would they allow their archenemy Jefferson to be elected? Jefferson wrote to Madison that the Federalists had to consider "the certainty that a legislative usurpation would be resisted by arms." A related possibility, Jefferson told Madison, was "recourse to a convention to reorganize and amend the government."[127] A new constitutional convention was a Jeffersonian fantasy— and a Madisonian nightmare.

Into the stalemate came the figure—almost the specter—of Alexander Hamilton. Hamilton had managed to destroy his influence within the Federalist Party by his attack on Adams. But if there was one man Hamilton distrusted more than John Adams, it was Aaron Burr. "There is nothing in his favor," Hamilton had written to a friend in December. "He is bankrupt beyond redemption, except by the plunder of his country. If he can, he will certainly disturb our institutions to secure himself *permanent power* and with it *wealth*."[128] Burr, Hamilton asserted, had "no principle public or private."[129] It followed for Hamilton that Jefferson must be chosen over Burr as "the least of two evils."[130]

Hamilton and the Republicans had done deals years earlier over the tariff bill and the movement of the capital to the Potomac. Now Hamilton imagined that another deal with the Republicans was possible. He proposed "to obtain from Jefferson assurances on certain points," he told Gouverneur Morris. If Jefferson would promise "the maintenance of the present system, especially . . . the cardinal articles of public credit, a navy, neutrality," Hamilton would support him for the presidency.[131]

Publicly, Jefferson could never agree to such a deal. Privately, however, he told Samuel Smith of Maryland that he had no intention to eliminate the navy, reform the financial system, or fire Federalists in executive office. These assurances were communicated to Delaware Federalist James Bayard, who as the tiny state's sole congressman had cast the Delaware congressional vote for Burr on every ballot.[132] Bayard was a close correspondent of Hamilton's. Thus, while Hamilton did not exactly broker the deal, he certainly provided its outlines.

On the thirty-sixth ballot, cast February 17, 1801, Bayard cast a blank ballot, as did the Federalist congressmen from South Carolina. These two states therefore abstained instead of voting for Burr. In the two states whose delegations were evenly divided, Maryland and Vermont, the Federalist congressmen cast blank ballots, creating a majority within the delegations for Jefferson. The result was a 10–4–2 victory for Jefferson. The Republicans' greatest enemy had helped give the election of 1800 to Jefferson. The course for a Republican future was now set.

But John Adams would not go gently. "Mr. Adams embarrasses us," Jefferson wrote to Madison.[133] In his last two weeks in office, Adams and the Federalist Congress doubled the number of judicial circuits and appointed three new judges to each existing and newly created court, eighteen in all. The so-called midnight judges were partisan Federalists. All were immediately confirmed by the Federalist Senate, as was John Marshall, who became chief justice of the United States even while still serving as secretary of state. Adams also appointed forty-two justices of the peace to new positions, so many that Marshall and his State Department staff could not deliver commissions to all of them before Adams's presidency expired. Adams felt no compunction about exercising the full extent of his executive power until his very last moments in office.

To Madison, Adams's actions were troubling. "The conduct of Mr. Adams is not such as was to have been wished or perhaps expected," he wrote to Jefferson. The "perhaps" was his gentle way of reminding Jefferson that he had always been an Adams skeptic. "Instead of smoothing the path for his successor, he plays into the hands of those who are endeavoring to strew it with as many difficulties as possible." The difficulty was not simply political. Adams "does not manifest a very squeamish re-gard to the Constitution," Madison wrote proprietarily. He thought that some of Adams's appointments might actually be invalid.[134]

Notwithstanding Adams's last-minute efforts, the first partisan transi-tion under the constitutional system took place as scheduled. The infant republic of the United States of America had faced a constitutional crisis of serious dimensions. And despite Jefferson's speculations, no one, on either side of the battle, had seriously thought about trying to resolve it by force. Madison's constitutional machine was working.

BOOK III

WAR

...

CHAPTER TWELVE

Secretary of State

...

THE ARGUMENT: *Madison's third political life begins when he becomes secretary of state and Jefferson's closest confidant and adviser: a position close to co-president. The paradoxes of power that Madison must confront in this life begin with the deep contrast between republican constitutional theory and real-world power. In a global environment shaped by the conflict between Britain and France, Madison's overarching aim is to coerce the warring superpowers to treat the United States with respect—which in practice would mean allowing American ships to trade in the West Indies and Europe without seizing their goods and sailors.*

Madison's instinctive response—which determines the arc of his third political life—is to be faithful to the ideals of a new kind of republic that, unlike Old World empires, does not conquer by arms but by agreement and negotiation. He will exhaust every possible option before using force as a last resort. The international viability of the nation hangs in the balance.

ON MARCH 4, 1801, Jefferson was inaugurated, beginning his tenure by declaring, "We are all Republicans, we are all Federalists."[1] The message, superficially conciliatory, suggested that the era of partisanship was over. Yet partisanship could pass away in two ways: by mutual compromise or by the elimination of the views held by the other side. With Jefferson, Madison had brought the Republican Party into existence to defeat the Federalists entirely. That remained their goal—and the election of 1800 was the first major step toward accomplishing it.

Madison was not at the inauguration because his father, James Madison, Sr., had died a week before, at the age of almost seventy-eight. From home in Montpelier, Madison wrote to Jefferson of the "melancholy occurrence." His father had seemed to revive, then took a turn for the worse, "and yesterday morning rather suddenly, though very gently the flame of life went out."[2]

Characteristically private and restrained, Madison left no record of his grief. Following his lead, Jefferson, who nominated Madison to be secretary of state on March 5, simply offered "sincere condolences."[3] The South Carolinian Charles Pinckney, who had maintained a correspondence with Madison since the constitutional convention fourteen years earlier, commented in his usual tactless way that James Madison, Sr., should have lived to see his son secretary of state. Madison's father had "enjoyed" the benefit of Madison's accomplishments "more than most men," Pinckney wrote, and he was "only sorry that when we have triumphed and you are placed in a situation, so much calculated to give scope to your talents, this further enjoyment has been denied him."[4]

Madison did not reply. A few weeks before his fiftieth birthday, Madison was the master of Montpelier and the head of his family. He was starting a new phase in his political life at the same moment that he began a new era in his personal one.

For the first two months of Jefferson's presidency, Madison, who had been quickly confirmed by the Senate, stayed in Montpelier administering his father's complicated estate. The will was thirteen years old; two of his brothers had died since it had been written; and it did not cover all his father's property. "The will is also ambiguous in some important points," he explained to Jefferson, "and will raise a variety of questions for legal opinions if not controversies." Madison further had to contend with his father's handwritten alterations to the will, as well as "verbal intimations in his last moments of others." Madison concluded to Jefferson, "You will judge of the task devolved on me as extraordinary."[5]

There was a limit to how long Jefferson could wait for his friend—and to how long Madison could delay the responsibilities of office. On May 1, 1801, Dolley and James Madison arrived in Washington.

The capital was little more than a hastily constructed village of some three thousand people. It had 263 wood houses, mostly of poor condition, and 109 brick buildings.[6] There were no paved roads. As one foreign diplomat put it, Congress could have "acted much more wisely than by settling in the swamps."[7]

On arrival, the couple moved into the almost-new White House with Jefferson. There was no First Lady, and no prospect that there would be one so long as Jefferson was president.* Both Vice President Burr and Jefferson were widowers. Neither of Jefferson's daughters had accompanied him to Washington.[8] As the wife of the secretary of state, Dolley held the highest social rank of any woman in Washington.

Dolley had spent her formative teenage years in Philadelphia when it was the capital, enjoying a wide sphere of acquaintance for her age and stage of life. A decade later, in the comparatively parochial Washington, Dolley flourished. Captured in a contemporaneous portrait by Gilbert Stuart, she has dark, curled hair and lively deep-blue eyes. Sitting on a gilded chair, she wears a gold-fringed, Empire-cut dress with a plunging neckline and a gold necklace. Her cheeks are visibly rouged, and her lips have just a touch of light color complementing the gold.[9]

After a month in the White House, the Madisons took a house on Pennsylvania Avenue—the only well-maintained street—four blocks from Jefferson. They eventually moved into a new brick house at 1333 F Street, even closer to the White House and next door to William Thornton, the architect of the Capitol, and his wife, Anna Maria. The Madisons would remain in the same house for the next seven years.

Dolley from the start played a central role in Washington. Through it, her relationship with Madison was also transformed, as she became for the first time his full professional partner. She was hostess not only at the Madisons', but often at the White House, where she presided when Jefferson held mixed-sex dinners. At remote Montpelier, Madison had conducted politics mostly in writing. In the new capital, politics was conducted face-to-face, often through social contact. That was not Madison's natural inclination. It turned out to be Dolley's greatest skill.

Dolley's specialty was to downplay, minimize, and if possible resolve conflict. Dolley's dictated memoir said that "she felt that it was her duty to pour oil on the waters of discord, and draw malcontents into the fold of her husband."[10] The same memoir recorded that Dolley's disposition was so "harmonious" that when the "sound of her high heeled shoes" signaled her approach to a group of diners, "all ill feeling would be forgotten or suppressed and the topic changed."[11] Given Madison's association with the intense partisanship that had led the Republicans to power,

---

* Sally Hemings remained behind in Monticello, as did the small children they shared. Rumors of their relationship still had not reached the public. But her presence, to say nothing of children who resembled Jefferson, would have been awkward.

Dolley's emphasis on creating personal and political concord was especially advantageous—and her expressions of these goals were consciously chosen.

Augustus John Foster, secretary to the British ambassador Anthony Merry, wrote that Dolley "was so perfectly good tempered and good humored that she rendered her husband's house as far as depended on her agreeable to all parties."[12] Jefferson, on the other hand, irretrievably alienated Merry by publicly refusing to escort Mrs. Merry in to dinner at their first White House appearance, as protocol required. Instead Jefferson escorted Dolley, who tried to avert disaster by stepping back and telling him to "take Mrs. Merry."[13]

Moderating Jefferson's radical ideas and extreme behavior was usually Madison's job. Now it became Dolley's, particularly after Madison, out of a sense of duty, awkwardly imitated Jefferson and snubbed Elizabeth Merry as well. The Merrys demanded an apology. When none came, they boycotted the White House.

The Madisons' house became the only place the British ambassador could socialize with administration officials, which meant Dolley became the unofficial diplomat tasked with winning over Elizabeth and by extension, her husband. This she accomplished through charm and sheer force of character, despite her private dislike of Elizabeth Merry. Eventually Dolley could write that her relations with Mrs. Merry were "unusually intimate."[14] Dolley was using her distinct skills to achieve political objectives that Madison could not—objectives that fell within the sphere of their joint foreign-policy responsibilities.

Madison tried to learn from Dolley and convey warmth at the dinner table. He had always enjoyed close friendships with a few people. But cultivating strangers was a new challenge for him. As a member of a convention or a legislature, Madison's great strength lay in his ability to come up with original, compelling ideas. But as a secretary of state, he needed to forge relationships based on trust, not abstract principle. For this, the domestic sphere was all important—and Dolley was a crucial guide and teacher.

Under Dolley's tutelage, Madison developed what would become a lifelong habit of telling witty stories after dinner, the ideal venue for his particular brand of dry wit.[15] Merry's aide Foster, who had an opinion on every subject, judged that Jefferson was "more of a statesman, and a man of the world than Mr. Madison." But he thought that Madison "was better informed, and, moreover, a social, jovial and good humored companion full of anecdote."[16]

Foster described Madison as "a little man, with small features rather wizened when I saw him, but occasionally lit up with a good natured smile. He wore a black coat, stockings with shoes buckled, and had his hair powdered with a tail."[17] The description was confirmed by Edward Coles, a young cousin of Dolley's who said he "never knew [Madison] to wear any color other than black." Coles added that Madison's manner was "simple, modest, bland, and unostentatious" and that he "refrain[ed] from doing or saying anything to make himself conspicuous."[18]

The severe simplicity of Madison's appearance can be seen in the portrait Gilbert Stuart painted as a companion to the portrait of Dolley. Madison is in black with a white neck scarf, sitting in front of a red velvet curtain that looks like an artist's prop. In the background are some books in a bookshelf, well-thumbed symbols of scholarship. On top of the bookshelf are two fat volumes with a loose pile of papers thrown down on top of them. There are no classical columns or other references to the importance of Madison's position.

Madison's modest self-presentation was matched by the State Department, which was housed in a nondescript building to the left of the White House. There Madison "received foreign ministers in a very indifferent little room into which they were ushered by his clerk."[19] Republican manners eschewed pomp and ceremony, associating them with aristocracy, monarchy—and the military.

The Pasha

The job of secretary of state was a rude shock. Madison had designed a Constitution, founded a political party, and served with great distinction in Congress. By any measure, his political career had been among the most important in the early republic. Yet Madison's focus had been domestic, and he had no direct experience of foreign policy.

The first crisis arose almost immediately. The pasha of Tripoli, Yusuf Karamanli, demanded a tribute of some $225,000 to refrain from attacking U.S. shipping in the Mediterranean. This was business as usual for the rulers of the North African city-states of Tripoli, Tunis, and Algiers, known collectively as the Barbary powers. To protect their shipping, other countries either had to send a navy or pay the tribute. If they refused, the pasha—who was technically answerable to the Ottoman Empire but, in fact, operated independently—would declare war.

From Madrid, U.S. ambassador David Humphreys reported to Madison that Karamanli had "determined upon war against the United States and was sending his cruisers to sea accordingly." Humphreys explained to the new secretary of state that "to be at war with one of the Barbary powers subjects our commerce to nearly the same risk as to be at war with all of them." The moment that U.S. ships were known to be vulnerable, Barbary corsairs—Humphreys called them "pirates"—would attack.[20]

Humphreys recommended naval force. The United States, he reasoned, must choose between "the alternative of having a few frigates and light armed vessels in the Mediterranean, or of relinquishing our trade in it."[21] Sending the navy to the Mediterranean would also improve the position of the United States internationally, and "produce an almost incalculable effect in elevating our national character in the estimation of all Europe."

For a rising power such as the United States, Humphreys further argued, "national character and public opinion are far from being unimportant objects." He acknowledged that most "civilized nations" simply paid the Barbary bill and avoided conflict. But he urged the "manliness" of fighting back. Indeed, Humphreys claimed grandly, "You may rest assured that it would form, as it were, a new era in the naval history of mankind."[22]

The American who knew the Barbary States best agreed. James Leander Cathcart had been an eighteen-year-old sailor on the *Maria Boston*, an American-flagged merchant ship captured by Barbary privateers. He and the other sailors were taken captive, and he was sold as a slave in Algiers. Slavery in the Ottoman Empire was different from the American variety. Although they could be bought and sold, Ottoman slaves could advance to high positions. Cathcart rose to become a clerk and adviser to the dey of Algiers, in which role he eventually helped negotiate the 1796 treaty with the United States that allowed his freedom.

After two years back in the United States, Cathcart returned to Algiers to work for the U.S. consul, William Eaton. Cathcart wrote to Madison that "To conclude an honorable and advantageous peace is not sufficient." Rather, "we must do more, we must harass them until they become sensible of their inferiority, we must establish a national character in this river of thieves."[23]

Madison made no objection to the inflated rhetoric or ambitious military plans. Although republican theory should have made them skeptical of military adventures abroad, he and Jefferson wanted to begin the first Republican presidency by sending a signal that they were not to be taken lightly. On May 21, Madison issued a circular letter to American consuls in the Mediterranean announcing that the president had determined to send "a squadron of three frigates and a sloop of war" to confront the pasha of Tripoli. If the pasha had not, in fact, declared war, the squadron would simply make a tour of the Mediterranean and return home. Regardless, the expedition would "have the effect . . . of exhibiting to the Barbary powers a naval force from the United States."

Madison had spent a career in politics as a committed republican, opposed to maintaining or using regular army and navy forces. He could have advised Jefferson simply to pay the tribute sought by the pasha of Tripoli. Instead, after less than a month in office, Madison was sending U.S. naval forces into battle.[24]

By the end of July 1801, the small American fleet had blockaded Tripoli. On August 1, the schooner USS *Enterprise* engaged a vessel called the *Tripoli* off the Libyan coast. The Tripolitan ship was almost sunk, while the *Enterprise* emerged unscathed. The United States had won a symbolic victory—but the blockade proved ineffectual. Karamanli, the pasha of Tripoli, had no particular reason to concede, and every reason to continue authorizing attacks. Jefferson and Madison had drawn the United States into a low-level war—one that for the moment, at least, showed no reasonable prospect of success.

The Promises of White Folk

Jefferson and Madison were in daily proximity for the first time in years. Dolley's role in Jefferson's White House made the men into something like the family that Jefferson had imagined when he urged Madison to come live near Monticello. Federalist newspapers, observing the closeness, charged that Dolley had a sexual relationship with Jefferson, invoking the time the Madisons had spent living with Jefferson at the outset of his presidency.[25] The politically motivated allegation, intended to tarnish Dolley's virtue, Jefferson's morals, and Madison's masculinity, reflected the Federalists' reaction to Dolley's influence and to the extraordinarily collaborative nature of Jefferson's presidency. The men were so close, went the allegation, that they shared a wife between them.

With Republican political ideas ascendant, almost the only way to weaken Jefferson was to assassinate his character. Opponents, especially Congregationalist clerics in the Northeast, had long denounced Jefferson as an atheist. A new charge was now added: the accusation that Jefferson had fathered multiple children with Sally Hemings, his slave and the half sister of his deceased wife.

For the disclosure, Jefferson had no one to blame but himself—and his decision before the 1800 election to hire James Callender, a newspaper attack specialist, to write a pamphlet denouncing John Adams. Callender had characterized John Adams as a British toady; Adams, using the Sedition Act, had Callender convicted and jailed. While in prison in Richmond serving his sentence, Callender, with his nose for scandal, had learned of Jefferson's connection to Hemings.[26]

Callender's knowledge might not have been a threat to Jefferson, if only Jefferson had shown him loyalty. He pardoned Callender upon becoming president. But Jefferson failed to refund the $200 fine Callender had paid as part of his punishment. Jefferson ordered the U.S. marshal, a Federalist whom he had since replaced, to issue the refund. But the marshal would not repay the money he had collected while in office.

Callender was broke and betrayed—a dangerous combination. He wrote to Madison that Jefferson had given him "a solemn assurance that he 'would not lose one moment' in remitting" the fine—and then had done nothing. So momentous were his sacrifices on behalf of Republicanism, Callender believed, that "the story should have reached the heart of a millstone." Yet instead of compassion, he had been met with silence. "I might as well have addressed the letter to Lot's wife," Callender complained.

Callender then threatened Jefferson. "I am not the man," Callender warned, "who is either to be oppressed or plundered with impunity." Not content with seeking remittance of his $200 fine, Callender demanded from Madison that Jefferson give him the newly open position of postmaster of Richmond, Virginia.[27]

The situation had the makings of a disaster. Monroe, serving as governor of Virginia, wrote to Madison that Callender had visited him and seemed "so agitated that I requested of him to call again, hoping he might be more composed." Instead Callender had "returned in the evening in the same temper." Monroe unwisely told Callender that it was doubtful whether the president could order repayment. Monroe at first thought it might be best "to raise the amount by subscription and pay it to Callender" in the hopes of making him go away. But Monroe changed his mind, thinking that Callender would use that fact to embarrass "the government and its friends." Monroe warned Madison to be cautious: "Be assured that the president and yourself cannot be too circumspect in case he comes to Georgetown."[28]

Madison met with Callender at the end of May 1801 in what must have been an incredibly uncomfortable encounter: The cautious and prudent Madison, as restrained in his mores as in his politics, cannot have wanted to discuss his closest friend's sex life with a stranger. Callender was "implacable" toward Jefferson, Madison reported back to Monroe. Madison had to "bear the burden of receiving and repelling" Callender's claims. He hoped he had calmed Callender down, but noted that "it is impossible to reason concerning a man whose imaginations and passions have been so fermented."

To make matters worse, Callender was in love. Madison wrote to Monroe that his beloved was "young, beautiful in his eyes at least, and in a sphere above him." Callender wanted the postmaster job so he could afford to get married.[29]

Unsurprisingly, a plea that emphasized uncompromising hatred and ardent love failed to move Madison, who sent Callender "back in despair"—and Callender held it against him. Madison, Callender wrote later, "seemed to think that he had become a sort of semi-divinity, and that poor Callender was not worthy to become his footstool."[30] Callender promptly went to Rhodes's Hotel in Washington and got loudly and publicly drunk.[31]

Incredibly, the matter of Callender's $200 made its way around the cabinet, from Madison to treasury secretary Albert Gallatin, who cleverly established that the former U.S. Marshal still owed money to the Treasury, and was ultimately able to force him to repay Callender.[32] But as Monroe had predicted, Callender was not satisfied. He met with Madison again to demand the Richmond postmaster position. Madison put him off. Jefferson then unintentionally insulted Callender by offering him $50 to go away.

Callender was now enraged as well as financially desperate—and he turned his polemical talents against Jefferson. In September 1802, he published an account of Jefferson's relationship with Hemings in *The Recorder*. The opening line was memorable: "It is well known that the man, whom it delighteth the people to honor, keeps, and for many years has kept, as his concubine, one of his slaves. Her name is Sally." Callender was obliquely referring to the Book of Esther. Given that Jefferson had originally paid Callender to attack Adams, the book's central theme of turnabout could not have been more appropriate.[33]

The publication of the news that Jefferson and Sally Hemings had children together created a public, partisan national sex scandal not matched until the presidency of William Jefferson Clinton. Madison left no record of his reaction to the news. Neither he nor Jefferson ever publicly commented on the latter's relationship with Hemings.[34] Other Republicans consistently denied that Hemings's children were Jefferson's, and the facts were disputed for nearly two hundred years.

Nevertheless, Madison was closely connected to the Jefferson-Hemings relationship. Sometime later, on January 18, 1805, Sally gave birth to a son at Monticello. That son later told the story of his naming this way:

> As to myself, I was named Madison by the wife of James Madison,
> who was afterwards president of the United States. Mrs. Madison
> happened to be at Monticello at the time of my birth, and begged the
> privilege of naming me, promising my mother a fine present for the
> honor. She consented, and Mrs. Madison dubbed me by the name I
> now acknowledge, but like many promises of white folks to the slaves
> she never gave my mother anything.[35]

The son, James Madison Hemings, was known as Madison. A year later, Martha Jefferson Randolph, one of Jefferson's acknowledged daughters, gave birth herself at the White House. She named her son James Madison Randolph. The two boys, Jefferson's son and grandson, one born a slave and the other born free, bore through their lives the name Madison himself never passed on.

The Domain of France

The most significant issue Madison faced as secretary of state was the growing power of Napoleon and its consequences for Great Britain's ongoing confrontation with France. Since the French Revolution in 1789, the British had twice tried and failed to defeat the French Republic. In

February 1801, the two sides signed a peace that each expected to last only briefly. Napoleon had already begun conquering and consolidating a European empire. Britain would either have to accept his domination of the continent or fight again.

North America became part of Napoleon's emerging global strategy for fighting Britain. By the secret Third Treaty of San Ildefonso, Charles IV, the king of Spain, ceded the land west of the Mississippi River—known as the Louisiana Territory—to France. For Napoleon, acquiring the Louisiana Territory was part of a much bigger plan to develop the French empire in the Americas and reclaim the French colony of Saint-Domingue, the pearl of the Antilles, known today as Haiti.

Saint-Domingue was a vast expanse of sugar and coffee plantations, farmed through most of the eighteenth century by almost 500,000 enslaved Africans and populated also by more than 30,000 whites and another 27,000 free persons of color. It produced perhaps 40 percent of Europe's sugar and 60 percent of its coffee, providing enormous revenues for France.[36] Even by the standards of the century, slavery on Saint-Domingue was considered especially brutal. The combination of labor-intensive crops, tropical heat, and the constant threat of disease compounded the innate misery and humiliation of the slaves. Thousands died every year; thousands more were bought to take their places.

In 1791, inspired by French revolutionary ideals, slaves and free persons of color started an uprising. Among the leaders of this group was Toussaint Louverture. He introduced himself to the public in a famous, and famously concise, proclamation:

> Brothers and friends, I am Toussaint Louverture; perhaps my name
> has made itself known to you. I have undertaken vengeance. I want
> liberty and equality to reign in St. Domingue. I am working to make
> that happen. Unite yourselves to us, brothers, and fight with us for the
> same cause.[37]

In response, the French colonial commissioner had abolished slavery. This drew Toussaint to the French side, and for several years he governed the colony alongside a French commissioner. In principle, the colony was French. In practice, Toussaint maintained his own foreign policy. When Britain invaded the island as part of its war against postrevolutionary France, forces under Toussaint's control repelled them. During the

454 THE THREE LIVES OF JAMES MADISON

Quasi-War, Toussaint preserved trade with the United States, serving his own interests as well as those of the Adams administration.

Napoleon resolved to bring Saint-Domingue back under total French control as part of his plan for a North American empire. He prohibited Toussaint from invading the Spanish part of the island (today's Dominican Republic). Toussaint ignored him, conquered the whole island, and abolished slavery throughout. "He is certainly an extraordinary man," Madison's newly appointed representative reported from Saint-Domingue. "He commands everything in this island. . . . He appears to be adored by all the inhabitants of all colors; whether this proceeds from fear or love I cannot yet tell; but all speak of him as a just man."[38]

Napoleon, acting as first consul of France, sought to limit Toussaint's authority. He announced that henceforth all French colonies would be governed under a separate constitutional structure. This opened the possibility that slavery might be reintroduced in the colonies. In response, Toussaint appointed a constituent assembly that promulgated its own constitution on July 1, 1801. The document did not officially declare independence from France. But, in Madison's words, it would "proclaim in form, the independence of that island."[39] It also made Toussaint governor-general for life—Madison described the government as "a pure despotism"[40]—and abolished slavery forever. Toussaint was acting the role of a Napoleon. Napoleon did not intend to share the part.

Rumors that Napoleon had secretly acquired the Louisiana Territory began to reach Madison in the spring of 1801.[41] In May, Alexander Hamilton, perhaps hoping to create ties with the Jefferson administration after his indirect help in getting Jefferson elected by Congress, sent Madison a letter reporting that his sources had told him about the secret treaty. Madison wrote back briefly, politely, and a bit coldly explaining that "the cession of Louisiana by Spain to the French Republic . . . had been previously signified to his department from several sources, as an event believed to have taken place."[42] It was to be the last communication between the two men.

Madison himself was not so sure that a transfer of the Louisiana Territory to France would be bad for the United States. He wrote to his friend Wilson Cary Nicholas that "it may be inferred" that French "policy will take a shape fitted to the interests and conciliatory to the minds of the Western people."[43] In a letter to Monroe, a former ambassador to

France, Madison professed he was unsurprised that Napoleon had acquired the territory, and asked him for "any ideas [that] occur on it."[44]

Jefferson, however, thought French possession of Louisiana would be
a serious problem because of Napoleon's potential to block western trade
down the Mississippi.[45] Madison and Jefferson could avoid this, however,
by acquiring both West and East Florida, thus allowing access to the Gulf
of Mexico from the other side of the river. West Florida stretched from
the mouth of the Mississippi at New Orleans past Mobile and Pensacola
to the Apalachicola River near present-day Tallahassee. East Florida included the Florida peninsula.

In September 1801, Robert R. Livingston of New York was appointed
ambassador to France. Madison instructed him to try to buy both of the
Floridas, or "at least West Florida, through which several of our rivers,
particularly the important river Mobile, empty themselves into the sea."[46]
Madison did not know whether Spain had ceded the Floridas to France
in the same treaty that had ceded the Louisiana Territory. But if Spain
retained the rights to the territory, Livingston was to convince the French
to convince the Spanish to sell it to the United States. Madison notably
did not instruct Livingston to try to acquire the Louisiana Territory or
even New Orleans. Perhaps he simply did not expect that Napoleon
would agree.

Livingston landed in November. At the port of L'Orient in France, he
crossed a convoy of warships and troop transport vessels preparing to
leave for Saint-Domingue. Napoleon "evidently designs to leave no time
to Toussaint to fortify himself," Livingston correctly speculated.[47] He
subsequently ascertained that Napoleon intended to invade Saint-
Domingue with forty thousand French soldiers and considerable naval
power.[48] The timing was propitious. At almost that moment, France and
Britain signed the preliminary documents for the peace of Amiens. Each
side continued to prepare for war. But the lull made this the right opportunity for Napoleon to dispatch troops away from the European continent and to the West Indies.

Livingston reached Paris in December and was received by Napoleon
himself. The first consul's "deportment is easy, cheerful and dignified,"
Livingston reported. He made sure to tell Madison in code that "Everything here has a military appearance." This implied both that peace might
be short-lived and also that Napoleon's ambitions might not be satisfied

456 THE THREE LIVES OF JAMES MADISON

456 THE THREE LIVES OF JAMES MADISON

by the consulship. Livingston observed that Napoleon's administration was practically monarchic: "It has nothing that can be called republican in its form and still less in its administration."[49]

Meeting with Talleyrand, Livingston immediately raised the subject of Louisiana. Talleyrand at first tried to avoid the topic, "but when he found I pressed more closely he admitted that it had been a subject of conversation but that nothing had been concluded or even resolved on in that affair." Taking advantage of the opportunity, Livingston "left him with a hint that perhaps both France and Spain might find a mutual interest in ceding the Floridas to the United States."[50] The next day, having thought the matter over, Livingston concluded that "I am more and more confirmed . . . that Louisiana is a favorite object and that they will be unwilling to part with it on the conditions I mentioned."[51]

For months, nothing changed. At the end of February, Livingston wrote to Madison that although "every statesman here" considered the acquisition of Louisiana by France as a "great waste of men and money" that would "produce no possible advantage to the nation," there was no prospect of its being abandoned. "It is a scheme to which the First Consul is extremely attached and it must of course be supported."[52]

Great Liberality

On receiving Livingston's message, Madison wrote back that the time for action had come. He urged Livingston to tell Talleyrand that if Napoleon were to take over the territory, "it must have an instant and powerful effect in changing the relations between France and the United States."[53]

Madison directed Livingston to find out "the extent of the cession, particularly whether it includes the Floridas as well as New Orleans; and endeavor to ascertain the price at which these, if included in the cession, would be yielded to the United States." Madison gave no sense of how much he would pay, but hinted he was willing to go high: "Great liberality would doubtless be indulged by this government," he wrote. "The president wishes you to devote every attention to this object, and to be frequent and particular in your communications relating to it."[54]

Madison understated Jefferson's concerns. In a separate letter to Livingston, Jefferson declared that whoever owned New Orleans must be the "natural and habitual enemy" of the United States. If France ultimately took possession of New Orleans, "we must marry ourselves to the British fleet and the nation." In the past, France had been America's "natural friend." Now, it seemed, all that was about to change.[55]

The analysis was far-reaching, brilliant, and wildly overstated. Jefferson added that the subject had become politically pressing. "Every eye in the United States is now fixed on this affair of Louisiana," he wrote. "Perhaps nothing since the Revolutionary War has produced more uneasy sensations through the body of the nation."[56]

Taking up Madison's orders, Livingston tried to argue that it was not in France's best interests to possess the Louisiana Territory. In the summer of 1802, he wrote an essay to this effect, had it translated into French, and circulated some twenty copies among influential Parisians. Talleyrand was the true addressee, and he "promised to give it an attentive perusal," Livingston told Madison.[57]

After Talleyrand had read the essay, Livingston planned to make him a proposition to buy the two Floridas, "either with or without New Orleans." Livingston told Madison that New Orleans itself would not be very important if the United States acquired West Florida, which extended to the eastern bank of the Mississippi. Napoleon could thus keep the Louisiana Territory while selling West Florida, giving the United States unfettered access for goods from the Mississippi into the Gulf of Mexico. Livingston believed that "a much better passage may be formed on the east side of the river" than at the site of New Orleans.[58]

A few weeks later, on September 1, 1802, Livingston sent the bad news to Madison. "I have every reason to believe the Floridas are not included" in the secret treaty, he reported. Livingston had spoken to Talleyrand and "he told me frankly that every offer was premature, that the French government had determined to take possession first." Napoleon was preparing more arms and men to go to Saint-Domingue and Louisiana, and there was no brooking his will. "There never was a government in which less could be done by negotiation than here," Livingston explained. "There is no people, no legislature, no counselors," at least none that counted. "One man is everything—he seldom asks advice and never hears it unasked—his ministers are mere clerks and his legislature and counselors parade officers."[59]

Both Livingston's and Napoleon's advisers thought that building a North American empire was foolhardy. "Every reflecting man about him is against this wild expedition," Livingston wrote. But it did not matter because "no one dares to tell him so." Livingston hoped that the whole enterprise "will end in a relinquishment of the country and transfer of the capital [New Orleans] to the United States." War between France and England was coming. And the French possessions in the West Indies "call for much more than France can ever furnish."[60]

Saint-Domingue's call on French resources was indeed substantial. The forty-thousand-man force that Napoleon had initially sent to the island under his brother-in-law Charles Leclerc had met with early success.[61] Brutal fighting through the spring of 1802 brought Toussaint to the negotiating table. In May he obtained amnesty for himself and his senior officers, then submitted to house arrest.

But Napoleon, who planned to restore slavery on Saint-Domingue, was not about to let Toussaint remain on the island. Acting on Napoleon's orders, Leclerc's officer Jean Baptiste Brunet tricked Toussaint, seized him, and sent him to France. On arrival in July 1802, Toussaint was imprisoned in the castle of Fort de Joux, high in the Jura Mountains.

Toussaint's fall must have convinced Napoleon that his North American plans were proceeding apace. But in October 1802, with Toussaint imprisoned in the Jura, news reached Saint-Domingue that France had reestablished slavery in its colony of Guadalupe. Saint Domingue once again rose in rebellion against France, led by Jean-Jacques Dessalines, a onetime ally of Toussaint's who had only temporarily defected to the French.

Dessalines was saved from Toussaint's fate by the greatest yellow fever outbreak in human history.[62] The epidemic of 1802–3 would kill as many as fifty-five thousand Frenchmen and an unknown number of Saint-Domingueans. Wartime conditions, plentiful mosquitoes, and the concentration of previously unexposed French troops in crowded military camps and offshore ships created the perfect viral storm.[63] Only a few thousand troops survived the disaster, a catastrophe until then unparalleled in Napoleon's military career.

In November 1802, Leclerc himself succumbed to the disease. The tide had turned against the French, who surrendered to Dessalines a year later. Saint-Domingue, devastated by war, became an independent republic.

It took some time for word to reach France. As late as December 1802, Livingston did not think it would be possible to buy the Floridas. Talleyrand himself had said that "the first consul [is] *entêté* with this project," meaning that Napoleon, unaware of the Saint-Domingue disaster, was still obstinately committed to a North American empire.[64]

Madison and Jefferson decided that Livingston needed help. There was just one man whom they both trusted and who had extensive experience in France: James Monroe, who had been a well-liked ambassador before being ignominiously recalled by Washington eight years earlier. Monroe was appointed "minister extraordinary and plenipotentiary"— what today would be called a special envoy—for the express purpose of approaching the French government "on the subject of the Mississippi, and the territories eastward thereof." Monroe and Livingston were supposed to work together. Madison wrote to them officially in March 1803 that their object was to procure New Orleans and the Floridas.[65]

Livingston was less than thrilled. "I had established a confidence which will take some time for Mr. Monroe to inspire," he wrote to Madison.[66] Livingston did not want Monroe to take credit for whatever would happen when he arrived.

The Whole of Louisiana

On April 11, 1803, two days before Monroe reached Paris, Talleyrand met with Livingston and asked him quite suddenly "whether we wished to have the whole of Louisiana." Livingston was taken aback. He had predicted that eventually Napoleon would have to cede the entire territory. But he had no expectation that such an offer would be forthcoming immediately. Livingston "told him no, that our wishes extended only to New Orleans and the Floridas."[67]

Livingston was not being coy. He did not think the United States needed the Louisiana Territory as much as it did the Floridas. He wrote to Madison that "I would rather have confined our views to a smaller object." If he was ultimately able to purchase the Louisiana Territory, Livingston told Madison, he recommended that "it would be good policy to exchange the west bank of the Mississippi with Spain for the Floridas, reserving New Orleans."[68]

Talleyrand said that Napoleon wanted to sell the entire Louisiana Territory and asked Livingston to make him an offer. "He said that if they gave New Orleans the rest would be of little value," Livingston reported. Livingston replied that "it was a subject I had not thought of but I suppose we should not object to 20 millions" of francs provided that France paid claims pending against it by U.S. citizens for losses during the Quasi-War. Talleyrand answered almost as a matter of course "that this was too low," and asked Livingston to come back with a better offer the next day. Livingston told him that Monroe would be there in two days and that they would negotiate together. Livingston left the meeting optimistic and excited. "Perhaps however I am too sanguine in my expectations," he concluded. "We will not therefore dispose of the skin till we have killed the bear."[69]

Livingston would later insist that he had changed Napoleon's mind— but the yellow fever, and not Livingston's charm, was the deciding factor.* By April 1803, Napoleon had realized that Saint-Domingue was out of his grasp, and with it the prospect of a North American empire. Without Saint-Domingue, the Louisiana Territory was useless to him. What he needed was cash to prepare for his impending war with England.

From this point the negotiations went quickly. François Barbé-Marbois, Napoleon's minister of the treasury, offered the Louisiana Territory at the price of 100 million francs plus another 20 million to pay off French reparations to U.S. citizens. Livingston said the price was too high—but that "we would be ready to purchase provided the sum was reduced to reasonable limit."[70] Marbois countered with 60 million plus the 20 million in reparations.[71]

On May 13, 1803, Livingston and Monroe reported to Madison that they had signed a treaty to acquire the Louisiana Territory for 60 million francs and 20 million more for reparations to be paid to U.S. citizens.[72] Livingston and Monroe had been commissioned to purchase the Floridas, not the Louisiana Territory. Napoleon was offering the Louisiana Territory—and not the Floridas. They decided to go forward anyway. Purchasing the Louisiana Territory, "though not contemplated, is nevertheless a measure founded on the principles and justified by the policy of

* Livingston, eager to take credit for the Louisiana Purchase, continued to insist that Napoleon had reversed course because of his persuasive efforts. See Robert R. Livingston to Madison, May 12, 1803, *PJM SSS*, 4:590–94. No love was lost between Livingston and Monroe. The latter wrote to Madison, "The most difficult, vexatious and embarrassing part of my labor has been with my associate." Monroe to Madison, May 14, 1803, *PJM SSS*, 4:612. According to Monroe, although Livingston had "manifested an invariable zeal to promote the object of the cession, and to extend our rights on the Mississippi," it was not a coincidence that the deal had not been offered until Monroe's arrival. "My extraordinary mission was an act which speaks for itself," Monroe concluded. Ibid., 614. Later, Livingston leaked a self-serving memoir claiming credit for the deal, even altering dates to make it seem as though important aspects had occurred before Monroe's arrival. "The publication of the memorial is so improper," Madison told Monroe derisively, that it was hard to believe Livingston had actually approved it.

our instructions, provided it is thought a good bargain," Monroe later explained to Madison.[73]

The deal was stunning. The U.S. government had been prepared to pay 60 million francs for the Floridas, which included the eastern bank of the Mississippi near New Orleans. For the same price the United States was getting New Orleans itself—including "exclusive jurisdiction of the river"—and the entirety of the Louisiana Territory.

Make the Most of It

Excited by his success, Monroe proposed to Madison that he now travel to Spain "to endeavor to obtain the Floridas" as his original instructions and commission had proposed.[74] Before Monroe could leave, however, Livingston wrote an extraordinary letter to Madison explaining why such a trip might not be necessary. According to Livingston, the deal to purchase the Louisiana Territory already included at least some of the Floridas.

The basis for Livingston's idea was that the secret treaty between Spain and France had granted France all of the territory that had been known as the Louisiana Territory before 1763. That original Louisiana Territory, Livingston now claimed, had included the area that subsequently came to be known as the Floridas.[75] By this logic the United States could claim almost all of West Florida. Livingston was willing to stake his reputation on it: "I pledge myself that your right is good," he wrote confidently.[76]

Livingston told Madison that he had "insisted" while negotiating with Marbois "that this would be considered as within our purchase." Marbois, in response, "neither assented or denied." Instead he "said that all they received from Spain was intended to be conveyed to us." This refusal to answer should have told Livingston that France either had not acquired the Floridas or had no desire to sell them to the United States.

But Livingston interpreted it differently. After the deal was done, Livingston went back to Marbois seeking "a further explanation on the subject and to remind him of his having told me that Mobile was made a part of the cession." Marbois was once again coy. "He told me that he had no precise idea on the subject but that he knew it to be a historical fact and that on that only he formed his opinion."

Not to be deterred, Livingston went to see Talleyrand, demanding to know what France had gotten from Spain and what land it had intended to occupy when Napoleon originally planned to keep the Louisiana Territory. Talleyrand equivocated. Livingston asked Talleyrand how Spain "meant to give them possession." With as much wit as diplomacy, Talleyrand replied, "according to the words of the treaty."[77]

Livingston would not give up. "Then you mean that we shall construe it our own way?" he asked. Talleyrand's answer was again a masterpiece of subtlety. "I can give you no direction," said Napoleon's minister of foreign affairs. "You have made a noble bargain for yourselves and I suppose you will make the most of it."[78]

Livingston was offering Madison an aggressive, expansionist policy for the United States: take valuable territory without asking too many questions or worrying about justifications. His proposal rested on a tenuous legal theory. But it offered a convincing account of international power politics. "With this in your hand, East Florida will be of little moment and may be yours when you please," he advised. There would be no domestic opposition, he predicted. Jefferson should move soon, before Britain could claim the Floridas in the wake of a war with France: "At all events, proclaim your right and take possession."[79]

Less than a week earlier, Monroe had believed the Floridas still belonged to Spain. Now, taking account of Livingston's theory, Monroe convinced himself otherwise, and wrote to Madison that he was "inclined to believe the West Florida is comprised" in the purchase. "Indeed I think that the doctrine is too clear to admit of any doubt."[80] Nevertheless Monroe still proposed to go to Madrid—this time to negotiate for East Florida.[81]

Unauthorized

In Madrid, word of the Louisiana Purchase caused outrage. Ambassador Charles Pinckney reported that the Spanish court and its ministers were "surprised and chagrined" at the news. The reason for the surprise was specific: "The French in receiving it from Spain had promised never to part with it."

The Spanish flatly denied that the Floridas were included in the cession of Louisiana to France. Here they were on firm ground. The text of the treaty, disclosed to Pinckney, conferred the Louisiana Territory "with the same extent that it now has in the hands of Spain and that it had when France possessed it, and such as it ought to be according to the treaties subsequently concluded between Spain and other states." This language very clearly excluded both Floridas.

Meanwhile in Paris, Livingston and Monroe were growing nervous waiting for word from Madison. There was a very real danger that Napoleon would back out. Marbois went so far as to tell the Americans that if the United States failed to pay the full sum within three months after ratification, the treaty would be null and void.[82] Because he was Napoleon, the threat could not be taken as empty.[83]

When he received Monroe's letters reporting the initial French offer of the entirety of the Louisiana Territory, Madison wrote back with excitement that "the dawn of your negotiations has given much pleasure and much expectation." With uncharacteristic emotion he told Monroe that "we wait with anxiety your next dispatches." The "we" certainly referred to Madison and Jefferson, who knew they were on the brink of something historic. The possibility of purchasing "the country beyond the Mississippi was not contemplated in your powers," he told Monroe, only "because it was not deemed at this time within the pale of probability."[84]

In early July, Rufus King, returning from England, where he had been serving as ambassador, forwarded Madison letters from Livingston and Monroe describing the deal with France. Even before direct official notice from the two envoys arrived in the middle of the month, Jefferson foresaw a problem: "The Constitution has made no provision for our holding foreign territory, still less for incorporating foreign nations into our union," Jefferson put it.[85]

To Jefferson the obvious solution was to propose a constitutional amendment. He immediately wrote one, circulating it to his cabinet for comment. The draft amendment stated that Louisiana "is incorporated with the United States and made a part thereof." It then provided Congress with authority to act within the territory.

Madison did not like Jefferson's proposal. So he drafted an amendment of his own. Madison's began by stating that "Louisiana as ceded by France is made part of the United States." It went on to say that "Congress may make part of the United States other adjacent territories which have been justly acquired."[86] This formulation avoided expressly authorizing the acquisition of Louisiana, which would imply that a constitutional amendment was necessary to make the acquisition lawful. At the same time, it authorized Congress, without a further constitutional amendment, to make the Floridas part of the United States as well. The draft amendment also gave Congress the power to "sever from the United States territory not heretofore within the United States" so long as a majority of free men over twenty-one in the territory agreed.

The difficulty was that the cumbersome amendment process, as devised by Madison, would take time—and the treaty had to be concluded rapidly lest Napoleon change his mind. Jefferson's preferred approach was to accept that the executive had already "done an act beyond the Constitution" by the acquisition of the territory. In the light of the act, he would now request that Congress similarly act outside the Constitution and approve the deal. He intended to ask both houses—as Washington had refused to do regarding the Jay Treaty—"because both have important functions to exercise respecting" the treaty.[87] The Senate would have to give its consent to the treaty, and the House would have to initiate the bill providing funds to make the purchase.

Once the unconstitutional acquisition was accomplished, Congress could propose a constitutional amendment retrospectively validating all that had happened. To Jefferson, the lover of revolution, it was not a problem to acknowledge that the Constitution had been violated. The fundamental theory that government was always and only authorized to act on behalf of the people would supply the legitimacy that was lacking from constitutional authorization:

> It is the case of a guardian, investing the money of his ward in
> purchasing an important adjacent territory; and saying to him when
> of age, I did this for your good; I pretend to no right to bind you: you
> may disavow me, and I must get out of the scrape as I can: I thought
> it my duty to risk myself for you.

Power had not changed Jefferson's cavalier attitude toward governing institutions. His fine disregard had once led him to endorse resistance to the national government in the name of rights. With the executive branch under his control, Jefferson was now prepared to direct the national government to take bold action—even if it might be extra-constitutional.

Madison, opposed to Jefferson's constitutional disrespect when they were out of office, was equally opposed to Jefferson's proposed sleight-of-hand now that the Republicans wielded power. He rejected the idea of openly acknowledging that the Constitution would be violated both by the president's actions and by Congress's validation of them. Madison thought such an approach undercut the ideal of constitutional government. His amendment would not have acknowledged that either the president or Congress had done anything in violation of the Constitution.

Ultimately, Madison's position managed to influence Jefferson. By August 18, 1803, Jefferson was telling Madison that "the less we say about constitutional difficulties respecting Louisiana the better."[88] A week later, Jefferson proposed to Madison a different draft amendment. This new proposal began the same way as Madison's, by specifying that Louisiana would be "made a part of the United States." Like Madison's proposal, it provided for the eventual incorporation of Florida into the United States.[89]

In October, the Senate approved the treaty 24 to 7. On December 20, 1803, the Spanish formally ceded to the French at New Orleans, and the French, in turn, formally ceded the territory to the United States. The Floridas went unmentioned.

With the transfer accomplished, Jefferson let go of his plan for a constitutional amendment. Madison did nothing to raise the subject. As he had done repeatedly in the past, Madison had found a way to temper Jefferson's enthusiasms.

There was no Federalist opposition—because as a national political force, the Federalists were for the moment spent. The sole national figure who continued to press their cause was Chief Justice John Marshall, the Virginia cousin of Jefferson who had become a Federalist and served as Adams's secretary of state before being put on the Supreme Court at the end of Adams's presidency. Marshall, now the only Federalist to hold an important national office, creatively used the court as a platform to resist Republican dominance.

A centerpiece of Marshall's efforts was the case of *Marbury v. Madison,* which arose from his own failure as secretary of state to deliver commissions to all the justices of the peace whom Adams had nominated in the closing days of his administration. Madison had declined to deliver the commissions once he took Marshall's place as secretary. Could he be required to do so by the Supreme Court?

Marshall crafted a complicated opinion. First it said that William Marbury had a right to his commission, and that a right should have a remedy—a rhetorical rebuke to Madison and the Republicans. Then Marshall avoided direct confrontation with Madison by holding that, under the Constitution, the Supreme Court did not have authority to hear the case brought directly to it by Marbury, one of the justices of the peace who had not gotten his commission. The Judiciary Act purported to give the court jurisdiction. Marshall held that the Supreme Court could declare that law unconstitutional and treat it as null and void.

Madison could not object to the conclusion or the outcome. The case signaled, however, that life tenure on the Supreme Court might enable defeated political parties and their ideas to survive. Madison's Constitution had unexpected flexibilities in it. Creative constitutional actors could adapt them to their will. It would take 150 years, but the *Marbury* decision would eventually come to be understood as the foundation stone of judicial review—and an expression of Madison's own insight that there must be a national authority with the power and responsibility to curb states' abuses of minority rights.

Death or Liberty

The greatest and most successful slave uprising in the modern era had thrown the Louisiana Territory into the hands of the United States. Yet if Madison was at all conscious of the irony that Toussaint Louverture and the yellow fever had combined to spread American slavery, he did not show it. Among other things, white Virginians considered their own form of slavery starkly different from that practiced in the Caribbean.

Madison was keenly aware of the economic realities of slavery. "The expense of a Negro he estimated at $25 or $30 a year according to the situation," he told Augustus John Foster, the secretary to the British ambassador, who visited Montpelier. "And you can only calculate, on average, upon half the number of slaves being fit for service at any given time." As secretary of state, Madison "was under the necessity of trusting to his overseer a great deal." The overseer cost Madison £48 a year; after that, his next greatest expense was "clothing his Negroes."[90] After paying the overseer, clothing his slaves, "and deducting the expenses for repairs," he calculated that his profits from the main Montpelier property "did not exceed the overseer's pay."[91]

Foster observed that because Madison lived "at a distance from any town," the slaves were engaged in skilled labor, and "all articles that were wanted for farming or the use of the house were made on the spot." Foster saw "a forge, a turner shop, a carpenter, and wheelwright."[92] He noted that the enslaved people were, however, "unwilling to make their own clothes, and during the Revolutionary War, it was very difficult to get them to spin or card wool."[93] Although he noticed that "the slaves were not in control of their own housing arrangements as they would have liked to be," Foster came to the conclusion that Montpelier seemed like a village populated by "a happy thoughtless race of people under a kind master."[94]

Despite Foster's impressions, white Virginians lived with an ever-present fear of slave rebellion. Five years before his visit, Virginia had been rocked by an uprising led by a slave named Gabriel. Literate and trained as a smith, as his father had been, Gabriel belonged to Thomas Prosser, a prosperous landowner. Prosser profited by hiring Gabriel out as a skilled worker in Richmond and keeping a portion of his wages. Gabriel and other contemporary enslaved artisans also contracted with employers on their own. They worked alongside white artisans with whom they sometimes developed friendships and other social ties.[95]

Gabriel plotted his insurgency by focusing initially on town slaves and free people of color. He and his associates planned to march on Richmond with banners reading "Death or Liberty," a direct allusion to Patrick Henry's famous slogan. Gabriel directed his co-conspirators to spare the lives of whites who were actively against slavery or might be won over to their cause, including then-governor James Monroe.[96] The strategy suggested that Gabriel was influenced by Republican ideology, much in the way that Toussaint and the "black Jacobins" of the French Caribbean had been affected by French revolutionary ideas.

The plans for the insurrection were discovered before it could begin. The leaders were convicted and executed, while followers had their death sentences commuted. Gabriel initially escaped but was captured on board a schooner at Norfolk and returned to Richmond in irons, where he was later hanged.

Gabriel's uprising brought home the continuing contradiction of Republican government, which spoke of liberty and sometimes fantasized about abolition while preserving and entrenching slavery. Henry, the revolutionary hero, had been a slaveholder. Monroe, the Republican governor, owned slaves as well. Jefferson and Madison, the Republican leaders in national office, had just contracted to expand the nation's territory, and with it the geographical reach of slavery.

In the sphere of foreign relations, the fear of slave uprisings expressed itself in concern about a newly independent Haiti—and here Madison and Jefferson differed. Madison briefed Jefferson, telling him that "the blacks had lately been enabled by American supplies to advance against" the French in their ongoing war of independence.[97] In response to these gains, the French general enacted a decree condemning to death anyone found on board a ship going to or from a port occupied by the Haitian forces. This was an "atrocious proceeding," Madison said, which "transcends every former instance of barbarous misconduct towards neutrals."[98] Madison also found the attacks on American ships "highly irritating."[99] From a practical standpoint, Madison thought that "the French are likely to be driven out of the island,"[100] another reason not to side with France in relation to Haiti.

Yet Jefferson was hostile to an independent Haiti.[101] In November 1804, denouncing the threat to neutrality posed by his own citizens, he asked Congress to ban the Haiti trade.[102] John Armstrong, Jr., who had replaced Livingston as ambassador to France, reported to Madison that Jefferson's speech had been "well received by the emperor."[103] Jefferson's pro-French policy may have been shaped by his commitment to white racial superiority, which Madison did not share, and by his concerns about slave rebellion, which all Virginians did.[104]

A Dead Man

Burr hoped to become president; but he had made a fatal error. When he tied Jefferson in the electoral college in 1800, he had refused to repudiate House Federalists' efforts to make him president or otherwise stop Jefferson from taking office. As a result, Jefferson and Madison did not trust Burr. Monroe reported to Madison that Burr had told Henry Lee of Virginia "with apparent resentment that he had never been consulted or expected to be on a single point" while vice president.[105] Monroe added his own opinion of Burr. "I was always aware," he wrote to Madison prophetically, that "there would be much difficulty in the management of this man."[106]

Excluded from governing, Burr restricted his communication with Madison to occasional brief requests for patronage. Over time, it became clear to Burr that he would be dropped from the ticket in 1804. A New Yorker would still be needed for balance, and Jefferson settled on George Clinton, the state's Republican governor, as a replacement.

In search of political redemption, Burr decided to return to New York and run for the governorship that Clinton was leaving. Jeffersonian Republicans had made headway over Federalists in New York, but there was still a significant Federalist contingent. Seeking support, Burr made contact with extreme Federalists such as Timothy Pickering, Adams's former secretary of state. Pickering took seriously the idea that the New England states might secede from the union and form an alliance with Great Britain, thus freeing themselves from the yoke of Virginia's political dominance. He fantasized that Burr might be able to move New York into the Federalist camp and bring it into the regional New England alliance. Burr was prepared to feed the fantasy if it would help him get elected.[107]

The strongest charge that could be leveled against Burr was that he was a traitor to the Republican Party. Writing in the *American Citizen,* a New York newspaper, in January 1804, Republican editor James Cheetham quoted Hamilton as having "attributed to Burr one of the most atrocious and unprincipled of crimes." He noted that Burr had not challenged Hamilton to a duel in response. "Either he is guilty," wrote Cheetham, "or he is the most mean and despicable bastard in the universe."[108]

In the heat of the campaign, Burr let the slur pass. The *American Citizen* went on a rampage against him, claiming to have a list of "upwards of 20 women of ill fame with whom he has been connected." It also claimed to have a list of married women seduced by the widowed Burr. In April, Burr lost the election to the unobjectionable Republican Morgan Lewis.

Hamilton had helped block Burr from becoming president. Now Burr held him responsible for thwarting his comeback. Their political battle had deepened their mutual loathing. In June 1804, Burr saw a copy of a newspaper article attributing to Hamilton the statement that Burr was a dangerous man and should not be trusted with public office. The article also quoted a New York physician, Charles Cooper, as saying, "Really, sir, I could detail to you a still more despicable opinion which General Hamilton has expressed of Mr. Burr."[109] The exact nature of the "opinion" Hamilton expressed remains unknown. In any case, this time Burr challenged him to duel.[110]

Duels played a complicated role in the political culture of the early republic. The risk of death was always present—and it was precisely the danger that conferred the possibility of redeeming one's honor. Madison never came anywhere near one, and it is almost unthinkable that he would either have challenged or been challenged on the field of honor. But both Hamilton and Burr had very different dispositions from Madison.

On July 11, 1804, the Republican vice president of the United States faced the Federalist former secretary of the treasury on a stone ledge above the Hudson River at Weehawken, New Jersey. Burr, excluded from the Jefferson administration, was no longer an important Republican, and Hamilton had been out of government for years. Yet partisanship had shaped the confrontation between these political and now personal enemies—a sign of how politics could deepen ordinary animosity.

Before his duel with Burr, Hamilton told friends that he intended to fire in the air rather than try to hit Burr. Perhaps he thought that Burr would not shoot to kill, or perhaps he was creating a narrative should he be hit.

Both men fired. Hamilton's ball went over Burr's head. Burr's ball struck Hamilton just above his right hip. "I am a dead man," Hamilton declared. He died the next day, at home, having had the opportunity to say goodbye to his wife, children, and friends. Madison's greatest adversary was now gone from the political scene.

Madison never mentioned Hamilton's death in his correspondence with Jefferson—or with anyone else. The silence was surely intentional. The anti-republican Hamilton had died in a most un-republican way, pursuing honor through an archaic custom that appealed to the ideals of aristocracy. Madison could not mourn the death; nor could he bring himself to decry it.

With Hamilton's passing, the Federalist Party all but faded into the background. Despite Callender's shocking revelations about Sally Hemings and the scandal of the Hamilton-Burr duel, the Louisiana Purchase had made Jefferson so popular that his reelection was not seriously in doubt. In 1804, Jefferson and George Clinton ran against the rather ineffectual Charles Cotesworth Pinckney, who had been Adams's running mate in 1800. Jefferson won 162 electoral votes to Pinckney's 14. His 45.6 percent victory margin in the popular vote is to this day the highest ever in a contested two-party race.

The intense, familial bond between Madison and Jefferson, strengthened during Jefferson's first term, would continue into his second. But the luck that had blessed U.S. foreign relations in Jefferson's first four years in office would not continue for the next four. The war between Britain and France was heating up, and for the United States, the consequence was the threat to its shipping posed by British warships. Dealing with restrictions on U.S. trade would become almost the sole issue of Jefferson's second term. The challenge would put intense pressure on the Madison-Jefferson relationship—and squander nearly all the goodwill the Republicans had built with the American public.

CHAPTER THIRTEEN

Neutrality

...

THE ARGUMENT: *In his second term as secretary of state, Madison sets out to solve the key foreign policy challenge for a republican constitution: pressuring world powers such as Britain to respect the United States without resorting to war.*

He does so by inventing a republican theory of foreign affairs. Because wars will destroy republicanism, the United States must coerce foreign actors through economic sanctions. Drawing on his thinking from the 1780s, Madison proposes an embargo as the solution, intending to starve Britain's West Indian colonies. The embargo fails because it is too slow and Britain's economy too resilient.

Shifting from theorist to canny politician, Madison promises to lift the embargo in order to win the presidency and avert the disaster of a Federalist return to power. The ploy works, and Madison wins. But he has not yet given up on using economic sanctions to open trade. He just believes he needs to try different tools.

IN MAY 1804, Napoleon crowned himself emperor, and in August 1805, his armies swept into Austria. Hostilities between Britain and France began again in earnest, and Britain immediately seized twenty U.S. vessels in the English Channel and the North Sea.

The British based the seizure on a legal principle of their own devising known as the Rule of 1756. The rule asserted that Britain would not permit the ships of neutral countries to engage in trade during wartime that would have been prohibited to them in peacetime.[1]

The Rule of 1756 mattered because during peacetime, foreign ships, including U.S. ships, were barred by France from carrying cargo directly from French colonies to France. Like other colonial powers, France monopolized its own colonial trade for itself. In wartime, however, when its ships were vulnerable to the Royal Navy, France made an exception.

To carry goods between the French West Indies and France without breaking the Rule of 1756, U.S. ships usually made a stop in the United States along the way. By stopping, the American ships created the theoretical possibility that the goods on board might have been destined for the United States and not for France. The legal fiction was so common that it had a name: the "broken voyage."

From 1800 to 1805, Britain allowed the broken voyage and left U.S. ships alone. On June 22, 1805, however, a British court decided an admiralty case concerning a captured American merchant vessel called the *Essex*. In the decision, which would become notorious, the court held that interrupting a voyage did not make it legal. The effect of the decision was to authorize British ships to stop and search any American vessel bound for France or French-controlled Europe.

Monroe, serving as ambassador in London, went to see the British foreign secretary face-to-face to demand that the seized ships be restored to their rightful American owners. To his consternation, the official replied "that a neutral power had no right to a commerce, with the colonies of an enemy in time of war, which it had not in time of peace." This was precisely what the British court had said in the *Essex* decision. Monroe hotly disagreed, insisting that Britain had no right "to interfere with or control the commerce of a neutral power with the colonies of an enemy." The foreign secretary held firm: Britain would not "relax in the slightest degree."[2]

Meanwhile, back in Washington, Madison and Jefferson did not yet know of the British seizures. In fact, they were mulling over the possibility of "a provisional alliance with England." Spain had fallen under the "omnipotence of Bonaparte," Jefferson wrote, and would probably be hostile to American interests.[3] Unless the United States made overtures to Britain, it might find itself "off our guard and friendless."[4]

Driven by the goal of preserving neutrality, the key to his foreign policy strategy, Madison undertook to moderate Jefferson's sudden enthusiasm for a treaty with Britain. The role was a familiar one to him, and he knew how best to achieve it. He wrote to Jefferson that although "The conduct towards Great Britain is as delicate as it is important," the United States must not commit to Britain. The problem was, Madison explained gingerly, that alliance with Britain would pull the United States into the war, destroying neutrality.[5]

As usual, Madison's carefully calibrated intervention worked on Jefferson. "I think you have misconceived the nature of the treaty I thought we should propose to England," Jefferson wrote back a bit defensively. "I have no idea of committing ourselves immediately, or independently of our further will to the war." Jefferson now claimed he had intended only to agree with England that, "on the event of our being engaged in war with either France or Spain, during the present war in Europe," the United States would then "make common cause" with England. Jefferson thought Britain would agree to such a treaty because "the first wish of every Englishman's heart is to see us once more fighting by their sides against France." Alliance with the United States would be the most "popular" thing that the king and his ministers could do, Jefferson fantasized.[6]

As of late August 1805, then, Jefferson was ready to side with Britain in its war against Napoleon in order to cement control of the Louisiana Territory and acquire the Floridas. Madison, however, did not agree. He told Jefferson gently that there was no way to support Britain short of entering the war, putting the point more forcefully and bluntly than he had before: "If she is to be *bound*, we must be *so too*."[7] The United States could not ally itself with France and should not ally itself with England. Madison stood firmly for neutrality, the Republican (and republican) foreign policy as he had conceived it.

The exchange showed Madison's emerging double canniness as a politician. He by now possessed a virtuosic skill at restraining Jefferson's enthusiasms, including the president's sudden fervor for alliance with Britain. But Madison was also developing his political skill in foreign policy. Evaluating the interests of France and Britain alike, he sought to evade the trap of aligning the United States too closely with either side—no matter how tempting it might seem in the short term.

The Efficacy of an Embargo

The news that the British had seized American ships and reverted to the Rule of 1756 created a serious practical problem. The optimal American strategy, Madison still believed, was to stay out of the war and profit from trade. If the Royal Navy was interdicting American shipping, however, there would be no profit. Madison had already argued that war was not a good option. What, then, could the United States do to protect its merchant fleet?

On September 14, 1805, Madison wrote to Jefferson proposing that the United States use economic coercion. "The efficacy of an embargo . . . cannot be doubted," he wrote confidently.

> Indeed, if a commercial weapon can be properly shaped for the executive hand, it is more and more apparent to me that it can force all the nations having colonies in this quarter of the globe, to respect our rights.[8]

The key to leverage was the American supply of necessary goods—especially wheat, cotton, and wool—to both British and French colonies in the West Indies. Those colonies profitably grew sugarcane and coffee; but they did not produce the basic materials required to sustain their own export industries. Slaves had to be fed and clothed, as did their European masters. Without the American supply of such goods, Madison reasoned, the colonies would be unable to function.

This was an ingenious and ambitious idea. The United States was a commercial republic. It was not a military power. And according to republican principles, it must never become one. But the United States could pressure colonial powers such as Britain and France by cutting off supplies of U.S. goods to their West Indian colonies.

The term for one country's blocking the sale of its products to another was "embargo." Derived from Spanish, the word had originated to describe a ban or "arrest" on foreign ships entering or leaving a nation's ports. Its political use could be traced to ancient Athens.* But embargo had not been extensively tried as a tool of foreign policy in the modern period, and there was no substantial body of practice on which to base the experiment.[9]

The United States did have experience with a different form of economic sanctions: the boycott, in which one country refused to purchase goods exported by another. The American colonists had employed boy-

---

* In 432 BCE, Athens banned all merchants from the neighboring city of Megara from its own markets and those of the Delian League to which Athens belonged. That instance had not really succeeded—Megara appealed to Sparta, which used the embargo as part of its justification for starting the Peloponnesian War.

cotts as a means of coercion both before and during the Revolutionary War. Americans still believed, without any very decisive evidence, that their boycott had contributed to repeal of the Stamp Act and that British industry had suffered from American boycotts during the war itself.

Madison understood that simply boycotting British exports would not be sufficient to force Britain to leave American shipping unscathed. Britain had other markets for its goods, and a navy capable of protecting the ships that exported them. The viability of the embargo—and its foreign policy appeal—depended on the vulnerability of the West Indian colonies, the Achilles' heel of Britain's empire, as Madison saw it.

Republican though he might be, Madison now saw the interests of the United States in commercial terms. Through an embargo, he was prepared to sacrifice exports in the short term in order to protect U.S. shipping while maintaining neutrality.

Immoderate Grief

At the end of May 1805, Dolley began experiencing a "complaint near her knee." On June 4, she explained her condition to her sister Anna Payne Cutts: "I now write you from my bed to which I have been confined for 10 days with a sad knee—it became a painful tumor, and two doctors were called in, and the applications of caustic and so forth gives me hopes of getting well but heaven knows when as it promises to be tedious."[10] The treatment did not heal the tumor. Indeed, it may have made matters worse. "From a very slight tumor," the growth then "ulcerated into a very obstinate sore."[11]

At the end of July, Dolley was no better. The Madisons decided not to make their customary summer trip to Montpelier.[12] Instead they traveled to Philadelphia to seek treatment from Philip Syng Physick. Trained in London and Edinburgh, Physick established his medical reputation as a Republican physician of choice during the yellow fever epidemic of 1793 that killed Dolley's first husband and her baby. Appointed to a chair at the University of Pennsylvania,[13] Physick would come to be considered the father of American surgery.

Dolley managed the journey without too much discomfort. Although the season was thought "dangerous" because of the risk of yellow fever, Dolley told Anna that the trip was "a very pleasant one, as I was easier riding than any other position and my health and spirits revived every day that I rode." Her spirits ought to have been raised further by the physician's prognosis. "Dr. Physick has seen it, and says he will cure me in a month," she reported.[14]

Yet Dolley was overcome with fear and sadness. "Anna, if I was not afraid of death I could give way to most immoderate grief," she wrote to her sister. "I feel as if my heart was bursting." On the way to Philadelphia, the Madisons had "breakfasted at Grays," Dolley told Anna.[15] She did not need to explain that Grays Ferry was the spot just outside of Philadelphia on the Schuylkill River where she had been when her first husband died.

Now another husband was beside her in Philadelphia, and Dolley was desperately worried for his health as much as her own: "Fool that I am— here is my beloved husband sitting anxiously by me and who is my unremitting nurse." Dolley worried that she was putting her second husband into harm's way. "You know how delicate he is," she continued. "I tremble for him." While the couple had been traveling, "on the way one night he [was] taken very ill with his old bilious complaint. I thought all was over with me. I could not fly to him and aid him as I used to do—but Heaven in its mercy restored him next morning."[16] Dolley's extreme concern for Madison's passing indisposition hinted at the trauma she had gone through with her first husband twelve years before.

Physick's treatment of Dolley's knee went through several stages. First he "splintered it, that is fixed a bark nearly a yard long and with a bandage . . . [bound] it so tight that I cannot even lift it from the bed—not a step can I take."[17] Over the next three weeks, Physick "applied caustic three times to the wound." This was "a sad thing to feel," Dolley wrote, surely understating the pain of an acidic substance applied to an open wound. The goal was to avoid surgery as the caustic was said "to do everything that the knife could do." Meanwhile, Dolley was forced to stay in bed. "So tedious it is to heal that I am at times low spirited," she admitted.[18]

Dolley knew everyone in Philadelphia. "I have had the world to see me," she assured her sister.[19] But the experience of seeing "the world" in Philadelphia was not without its complications. Dolley had been officially excluded from the Society of Friends when she married the Episcopalian Madison. In Philadelphia, however, Quaker values were still the norm. Two Quaker women, Nancy Mifflin and Sally Lane, came to Dolley's bedside—and "remonstrated" with her for having too many guests. "On seeing so much company—they said that it was reported that half the city of Philadelphia had made me visits," Dolley told Anna.

Dolley did not enjoy being criticized while she was sick in bed. It reminded her of the experience of being a young single Quaker woman:

> This lecture made me recollect the times when *our Society* used to control me entirely and debar me from so many advantages and pleasures—and though so entirely [free] from their clutches, I really felt my ancient terror of them revive to disagreeable degree.[20]

The flashbacks of Philadelphia that Dolley experienced can only have increased with the outbreak of yellow fever. On August 20, the *Aurora General Advertiser* reported that "several cases" had appeared in southern Philadelphia, and that two people had died.[21] Some ten days later, Madison told Jefferson that "the fever is still limited but very deadly in its attacks. The present rainy weather is giving it more activity."[22] The rain must indeed have encouraged the mosquito population. At the same time, Madison told Jefferson that Dolley's progress had suffered a setback. "We hoped a few days ago that she would quickly be well," he wrote, "but a small operation which could not be avoided, will detain us yet a little longer."[23]

The Madisons were now trapped in Philadelphia by Dolley's bedridden condition—and the yellow fever was spreading. On September 9, Madison wrote to treasury secretary Albert Gallatin that "the fever has taken strong hold of Southwark, and cases begin to be sprinkled through a great part of the city."[24] By September 14, the Madisons had decided to leave the center of the city. They ended up at Grays Ferry again—exactly where Dolley had gone to escape the epidemic years ago.[25]

Dilemma

Meanwhile, Madison was wanted in Washington. Jefferson told him that he hoped to call a cabinet meeting on October 4 to consider the European war and its consequences for the United States.[26] But Dolley was not yet well enough to travel "without a manifest risk, the more to be avoided on the road, as she would be out of reach of the necessary aid," Madison wrote to Jefferson.[27] Madison took Dolley out riding in the hopes that she would be ready to travel, but the experiment was a failure. After the ride, Dolley experienced "sensations and appearances which threaten a renewal of her complaint."[28]

Madison was torn between Dolley, whom he had tended for three months, and Jefferson, who needed his secretary of state as confrontation with Britain became more probable. If the meeting could happen without him, Madison wrote hopefully, or if he could participate by letter, "I shall avail myself of your indulgence by remaining with my wife."[29] Jefferson explained that he could not hold a cabinet meeting without his secretary of state.[30] Yet Madison still could not bring himself to leave Dolley.[31]

The conflict between his love for Dolley and his concern for Jefferson was unique. But when he had to choose between his wife and his closest friend—who was also his president—Madison picked Dolley. He remained in Grays Ferry until the yellow fever epidemic receded and he was able to find Dolley a safe place to stay in Philadelphia. On October 23, almost two months after Jefferson had first summoned him, Madison finally left for Washington. He and Dolley would be apart for the next two months, the only significant separation in the entire course of their forty-two-year marriage.

While they were in different cities, Madison and Dolley wrote constant warm letters that reveal both the depth of their affection and their political alliance. The letters provide a window into the intimacy of the Madisons' relationship. The correspondence of John and Abigail Adams is voluminous, because the two were almost constantly apart during Adams's years in government, when Abigail preferred to stay in Quincy, Massachusetts. The correspondence between James Madison and Dolley Payne Madison is minimal, because the two preferred to be together.

Madison had just departed when Dolley wrote her first letter to him. "A few hours only have passed since you left me, my beloved," she wrote, "and I find nothing can relieve the oppression of my mind but speaking to you in this *only* way." The next day Dr. Physick talked about how wonderful Madison was, and Dolley found that his words, "like dewdrops on flowers, exhilarate as they fall!" She closed her letter poetically: "Adieu, my beloved, our hearts understand each other. In fond affection thine, Dolley P. Madison."[32]

Madison wrote to Dolley from the road, and she replied that she had dreamt of him with concern: "In my dreams last night, I saw you in your chamber, unable to move, from riding so far and so fast." She was gradually improving and hoped they would write to each other daily. "Farewell, until tomorrow, my best friend!" she wrote. "Think of thy wife! Who thinks and dreams of thee!"[33]

Madison wrote to Dolley from Washington that he was trying to get Dolley's son John Payne Todd, now thirteen years old, admitted to St. Mary's College in Baltimore, the best preparatory school near Washington. Madison, an Anglican educated among Presbyterians, had no qualms about sending Payne to a Catholic school, and he pulled strings to do it. His closing emphasized how powerfully he wanted Dolley back: "Let me know that I shall soon have you with me, which is most anxiously desired by your ever affectionate J. Madison."[34] For the emotionally restrained Madison, invoking anxiety, desire, and affection in the same sentence was virtually an outpouring of passion.

Madison and Dolley also engaged in some banter about Betsey Pemberton, a young woman of twenty-three who was acting as a companion to Dolley and sharing her bed in Madison's absence. Dolley told Madison that Betsey "puts on your hat to divert me, but I cannot look at her." Madison wrote back that he wished his "kisses" to be conveyed to "Miss P." "I wish I could give her more substantial ones than can be put on paper," Madison wrote in an uncharacteristic tone of flirtation. "She shall know the difference between them the moment she presents her sweet lips in Washington—after I set the example on those of another person whose name I flatter myself you will not find it difficult to guess."[35]

Madison was saying that he would kiss Dolley before he kissed Betsey, but both would get kissed on the lips. "With unalterable love I remain yours," Madison signed the letter.[36] Dolley wrote back that she hoped to travel soon to Washington. Betsey was "almost frantic with the prospect of seeing" her fiancé, Henry Waddell, Dolley wrote. But she also told Madison that Betsey "says she feels already your sweet kisses—what must somebody else do"?[37] Following Madison's lead, Dolley was triangulating her own excitement at seeing her husband through Betsey. Madison replied that he "rejoiced to hear that your knee remains perfectly healed." He concluded, "I can only add my best love to you, with a little smack for your fair friend, who has a sweet lip, though I fear a sour face for me."[38] In his final mention of Betsey Pemberton in their correspondence, Madison told Dolley to "give Miss P. a kiss for me and accept a thousand for yourself."[39]

Dolley returned to Washington at the end of November. As she was writing her last letters to Madison, Monroe was reporting from London with two pieces of news. Napoleon had won a great victory over the Austrians at Ulm, destroying "the structure of the Austrian army, consisting of 100,000 men." Total victory at Austerlitz would come in a few weeks' time. The other information was of "the naval victory which was obtained by Lord Nelson, who perished in the action, over the combined squadrons of France and Spain near Cadiz."[40]

The Battle of Trafalgar confirmed the structure of the war between Britain and France. The British would be supreme over the oceans. Napoleon would be master of the land, with "scarcely a ship at sea." Describing the situation, Monroe wrote to Madison that "as things now stand each of the parties forms a complete counterpoise to the other."[41] The consequences of this situation for the United States would be the central focus of Madison's thought for the next decade.

Gunboats

Madison's recommendation that Jefferson delay any approach to Britain had been sound advice. In October 1805, Monroe reported from London that Britain was impressing American merchant marine seamen into the Royal Navy and showing "no disposition" for "any restraint."[42] Some of these sailors were, in truth, deserters from the Royal Navy, according to a study commissioned by Albert Gallatin, secretary of the treasury.[43] From the U.S. perspective, however, impressment was a violation of sovereignty—and an excuse for the Royal Navy to continue stopping and searching American ships.

Monroe concluded that the systematic impressment was "probably an experiment" to see "what the United States will bear." If the Americans responded weakly, the British would "pursue the advantage gained to the greatest extent," stepping up impressment of seamen and "the prostration and pillage of our commerce through the war." If the United States wanted to be taken seriously, it must resist by force.[44]

By now Jefferson had come to realize that an attempt to make a deal with Britain would be futile. On November 22, 1805, he sent Madison a draft of his annual message to Congress, asking him for "a severe correction both as to style and matter."[45] The message came late in the congressional season, held up by the delay in Madison's return to Washington and the difficulty of determining British policy. It demonstrated that Jefferson had now accepted the reality of British hostility. "Since our last meeting," Jefferson told Congress, "the aspect of our foreign relations has considerably changed" as the result of British harassment of American shipping. Jefferson then turned to the Rule of 1756, denouncing it as unreasonable and suggesting measures be taken against it.[46]

Jefferson alluded to the possibility of war. "Some of these injuries may perhaps admit a peaceable remedy," he wrote. "But some of them are of a nature to be met by force only, and all of them may lead to it. I cannot, therefore, but recommend such preparations as circumstances call for."

Nevertheless, Jefferson's idea of war preparations was far from expansive. He proposed cannons and fortifications for port towns; and he called on Congress to organize the militia so that the United States could call upon its three hundred thousand able-bodied men between the ages of eighteen and twenty-six in case of war. But Jefferson did not ask Congress to augment the regular army.

Jefferson's naval proposals were if anything more modest. Of the six U.S. warships, five were now out of service and slated to be dismantled. USS *Constitution* was still in the Mediterranean, where it had served in the war against the Barbary States.[47] Jefferson made no request to restore the frigates to action, much less build new ones. Instead, he asked Congress only for "a competent number of gunboats." He did not say how many, only that "the number . . . must be considerable."[48]

Jefferson's interest in gunboats was closely connected to his distrust of major naval or military endeavors. Gunboats were small, single- or double-masted vessels designed to defend harbors and rivers but not go out to sea, much less fight British warships in the open ocean. Each one carried a single gun that fired twenty-four- or thirty-two-pound shot.[49] The *Constitution*, in comparison, was fitted with some sixty long guns. Gunboats were as republican as militia, or rather more so. They could not be repurposed for imperial adventures abroad.[50]

Madison proposed only minimal edits to Jefferson's draft,[51] an indication that he agreed with its basic thrust. What, then, were Jefferson and Madison doing in speaking belligerently while making no preparations for offensive war? The best answer is that they were trying to take Monroe's advice about projecting strength toward England while simultaneously adhering to their own republican principles, which strongly opposed aggressive war of any kind.[52] There was no immediate strategic reason to start building a navy, either. Britain ruled the seas. The United States could not realistically compete with the Royal Navy, which boasted some 950 vessels and had deployed 27 ships of the line at the Battle of Trafalgar alone. Whatever leverage the United States mustered must come from a different quarter.

New Men and New Maxims

In the new year of 1806, Congress began considering a non-importation bill, a boycott intended to pressure Britain to change its policies. From the start, the law reflected a compromise between pressuring Britain and preserving some of American importers' trade. The proposed boycott covered luxury goods, including anything made primarily of leather, silk, hemp, flax, tin, or brass; all forms of glass and silver; hats and ready-to-wear clothing; and expensive woolens such as stockings. But the bill exempted all inexpensive woolens, one of the most important British imports, as well as British coal, iron, and steel.

While the Non-Importation Act was being debated,* Madison took a highly unusual step, the result of his resolve to develop a new international law that served American interests in neutrality and free trade. He

---

* Around the same time, one Sidi Sulayman Mellimelli, an ambassador representing the Bey of Tunis, arrived in Washington with a retinue of eleven. Mellimelli, bearded, was dressed in scarlet and gold with a white turban; his group made a great impression in Washington on account of its "novel and singular appearance." William Plumer, *Memorandum of Proceedings in the United States Senate, 1803–1807* (New York, 1923), 359. According to Senator William Plumer's account—which may have been rumor—at Mellimelli's "application," the government provided "one or more women, with whom he spends a portion of the night." Irving Brant, in his six-volume biography of Madison, wrote that "Madison supplied the deficiency with 'Georgia a Greek,' and charged the cost to the State Department." Brant, *James Madison*, vol. 4, *Secretary of State, 1800–1809*, 306. Then Brant slyly quoted a letter written nearly six months later on an unrelated subject in which Madison told Jefferson that "it is not remiss to avoid narrowing too much the scope of the appropriations to foreign intercourse, which are terms of great latitude, and may be drawn on by very urgent and unforeseen occurrences." Madison to Jefferson, September 27, 1806; see James Morton Smith, *The Republic of Letters: The Correspondence Between Thomas Jefferson and James Madison 1776–1826* (New York: Norton, 1995), 1441. Brant never said that the phrase "appropriations to foreign intercourse" was intended as a joke by Madison. Subsequent biographers have retold and embellished this joke until it became Madison's, which sadly it was not. Dolley, however, did get a joke out of Mellimelli's visit. According to the story, recounted in Dolley's dictated memoir, as Mellimelli was leaving a party at the Madisons', he "caught a glimpse" of a large black woman servant who had brought coffee. Mellimelli "suddenly threw his arms around her and exclaimed that she was the only handsome woman in America." Cutts, *Queen of America*, 114.

published anonymously a work he had composed while Dolley was con-valescing, calling it *An Examination of the British Doctrine, Which Subjects to Capture a Neutral Trade, Not Open in Time of Peace.* Technically a pamphlet, the 204-page document was, in fact, a book on the history, evolution, and legal logic of British policies regarding neutral shipping. It was by far the longest piece of writing that Madison ever produced—and undoubtedly the dullest and worst written.

Teaching himself international law as he went, Madison wrote down essentially everything he knew. He adduced, quoted, and analyzed the most important international law writers of the sixteenth, seventeenth, eighteenth, and even early nineteenth centuries. He discussed every known European treaty touching on neutral trade. He reviewed in detail every relevant order issued by British authorities over more than a century, and every legal opinion produced by the Court of Admiralty over a similar period. It would be generous to speculate that Madison was so concerned for Dolley's health that his writing lacked focus or punch. But whatever the reason, the book never managed to carve out a sharp argument from the mass of legal material it presented.

A young Republican congressman named John Randolph put the criticism best. "A great deal is said about the laws of nations," Randolph commented in reference to the pamphlet. But this insistence on the law of nations was misplaced—because the law of nations was not really law at all. "What is national law but national power guided by national interest?" Randolph cogently asked his fellow congressmen. "You yourselves acknowledge and practice upon this principle where you can, where you dare—with the Indian tribes, for instance." The United States regularly distorted international law when it had made treaties with Native American tribes—and breached those treaties whenever it was felt to be in the national interest. Power, not law, Randolph declared, was the essence of foreign policy.[53]

Elected to Congress at the age of twenty-six, Randolph was an unusual figure. A lifelong bachelor, he wore boots and spurs in the House, even going so far as to affect a whip and hunting dogs there on occasion.[54] Randolph combined the pretensions of the aristocratic Virginia gentleman—he was a cousin of Jefferson's—with a radical commitment to the republican principles of 1798. A gripping public speaker, he could hold forth for hours without notes, overcome by near-manic states of inspired eloquence. The style and content flowed "from the impulse of the moment," he once explained. "When I do not feel strongly, I cannot speak to any purpose. These fits are independent of my volition."[55]

Randolph had chaired the Ways and Means Committee during Jefferson's first presidential term. But by 1805, Randolph had made enemies among Republicans as well as Federalists. He lost his leadership position within the party. Thus freed from loyalty, he turned on Madison, making him the chief object of his considerable hostility—and corresponding oratory.

In January 1806, Randolph acknowledged his break with the Republican Party. In a letter that he knew Jefferson would see, Randolph wrote that his cousin's administration "favors Federal principles, and, with the exception of a few great rival characters, Federal men. . . . The *old* Republican Party is already ruined, past redemption; new men and new maxims are the order of the day."[56] Randolph was emerging as Madison's most forceful and trenchant critic. For the rest of Madison's career, Randolph would play the role that Patrick Henry had in Madison's first political life: the brilliant strategic enemy whose rhetorical power exceeded Madison's and whose opposition was implacable and unrelenting.

Randolph did not have a clear affirmative answer of his own to what the United States ought to do about British trade restrictions. He was as contemptuous of war as a tool of foreign policy as he was of legal reasoning. But when it came to critique, Randolph was a master—and the *Examination* was a particularly juicy target. Treatises of international law were not going to change British policy. "If, sir, I were the foe (as I trust I am the friend to this nation)," Randolph declared, "I would exclaim, 'Oh that mine enemy would write a book!'"[57]

Randolph meant it literally. Madison was his political and therefore personal enemy, and Madison had written a book. That book was a bastard. "Some time ago, a book was laid on our tables," he told his colleagues. The book, "like some other bantlings, did not bear the name of its father." Even Madison's shallow anonymity, obviously necessary to the secretary of state for reasons of discretion, was fodder for Randolph's blistering attack.

Randolph also condemned the bill proposing non-importation as "milk-and-water . . . a dose of chicken-broth to be taken nine months hence."[58] The bill passed despite his objections, and Jefferson signed it in April 1806. The law as written allowed the president to put import restrictions into place if and when he judged it appropriate. Jefferson declined to implement the sanctions immediately, hoping to use the threat as a negotiating tool with Britain.

The man to do the negotiating would ordinarily have been Monroe, the ambassador in London. But while Congress was passing the Non-Importation Act, it simultaneously pressured Jefferson to send a different negotiator—ideally a Federalist who might be perceived as more conciliatory than the Republican Monroe and whose presence would suggest a new policy direction.[59] Jefferson and Madison agreed to send William Pinkney, a Maryland Federalist, to join Monroe in the negotiations.

Monroe had worried that such a thing might happen. In February 1806, before he knew about either the Non-Importation Act or Pinkney's appointment, he heard a rumor that the Federalist John Quincy Adams would be appointed "envoy extraordinary" to Britain in order to resolve the differences between the two countries. Monroe wanted desperately to avoid the appearance that he had been replaced or recalled, as he had been when he was Washington's ambassador to France. "I desire nothing but simple, strict justice," Monroe wrote to Madison. "I wish my conduct here to exist on its own ground, *and indeed everywhere*. That nothing be left to insinuation; for my enemies to misrepresent and my friends to explain."[60] By the time Madison received Monroe's letter, Pinkney had already been dispatched. Before official word could reach him, Monroe read the news of Pinkney's imminent arrival in the London newspapers.

Monroe felt deeply wronged, believing that Madison was treating him just as Washington had. He drafted a private letter to Jefferson in which he blamed Madison for the failure of his negotiations. No matter what course should be taken with respect to his appointment, he "expected as well by the claims of private friendship as from public considerations that I should receive early notice of it."[61]

Monroe did not immediately send the draft letter to Jefferson. But the ideas expressed in it reflected his conviction that his close friend Madison had betrayed him. "I was struck with astonishment and deeply affected by the reflection," he explained later, "as it was utterly impossible for me to trace the cause."[62]

John Randolph seized the opportunity to exploit a potential breach between Madison and Monroe. As Pinkney was being appointed, Randolph wrote to Monroe that he must return home to become the presidential standard-bearer of the true Republicans. Like Patrick Henry before him, Randolph had the instinct that Monroe's friendship for Madison could be turned to rivalry by the prospect of taking on Madison and defeating him.

Monroe responded to Randolph's first advance with a polite no. He was honored to be thought of as a candidate for president, Monroe told Randolph. But "the idea had better be relinquished." Madison took precedence, he explained. To challenge Madison would tear apart the Republican Party, "harrowing up their feelings and tearing up by the roots ancient friendships." Intraparty controversy might also open the door to a Federalist.[63]

Randolph wrote back to Monroe insisting that he reconsider. During Monroe's four years in Europe, Randolph claimed, Madison had changed, taking the country back to "the system of our predecessors." Although Madison might once have been a Republican, Randolph told Monroe, he was now effectively a Federalist.[64]

Monroe's interest had been piqued. This time, he did not completely resist the overture: "Circumstances have occurred during my service abroad," he replied to Randolph, "which were calculated to hurt my feelings and actually did hurt them." These circumstances—namely the appointment of Pinkney—"may produce a future change in the relation between . . . myself" and Madison. Monroe's sense of betrayal, combined with his unwavering ambition, made him vulnerable to Randolph's advances.

Sensibility and Sovereignty

Madison's diplomatic approach to Britain showed greater promise than the approach to France. Having given Monroe and William Pinkney some leverage in the form of the Non-Importation Act, Madison directed the envoys to emphasize two points in their negotiations in London.

First, Madison wanted Britain to stop impressing seamen. "So indispensable is some adequate provision," he told them officially, "that the president makes it a necessary preliminary" to ending the boycott.[65] Second, Britain must renounce the Rule of 1756. Madison recognized that "this may not be attainable" and he affirmed, realistically, that "too much ought not to be risked by an inflexible pursuit of an abstract right."[66] He therefore told the envoys that they could settle for a British guarantee to reinstate the legal fiction of the broken voyage to allow the American ships to bring goods unmolested to France.

Luck was with Monroe and Pinkney. In February 1806, William Pitt the Younger died in office. The extraordinary Pitt had become prime minister in 1783 at the age of twenty-four, and he had served in the role ever since, except for a three-year hiatus. He was replaced by Lord William Wyndham Grenville, who formed a coalition government.[67]

The change in British government afforded an opportunity for a softening of policy toward the United States. Grenville would not abandon the Rule of 1756 officially but was willing to reorganize the broken-voyage fiction. Whether or not the Non-Importation Act had been the cause, Monroe and Pinkney had gotten half of what Madison and Jefferson wanted.

Grenville would not agree, however, to stop impressing British sailors from American civilian ships. From the British perspective, disclaiming impressment was an open invitation for desertion, something the Royal Navy could ill afford, given that its sailors were paid little to do a dangerous job in poor conditions. The Grenville government offered Monroe and Pinkney a vague statement that Britain would exercise "caution" in impressing seamen.

Madison wrote to the envoys that Jefferson would not accept a treaty that offered "a formal adjustment" regarding trade but only "an informal understanding" regarding impressment. If Monroe and Pinkney could not get an agreement on impressment, an issue "so feelingly connected with the honor and sovereignty of the nation, as well as with its fair interests," they should leave with no treaty at all.[68] In lieu of a treaty, Jefferson proposed a gentlemen's agreement protecting American shipping—"a mutual understanding . . . that in practice each party will entirely conform to what may be thus informally settled." Britain would respect neutral trade and proceed more cautiously on impressment. Jefferson would stop the Non-Importation Act from going into effect, and would not have to pay the public price of a treaty that was silent on impressment.

By the time they got Madison's letter, Monroe and Pinkney had already signed the treaty. They knew an informal agreement would not satisfy the British and would be perceived as a failure of their mission.[69] Monroe and Pinkney were taking a calculated risk. Jefferson and Madison could reject the treaty or else accept its imperfection and submit it to the Senate. The envoys knew they had gotten the best deal that was realistically possible.

After thinking it over for almost two months, Jefferson decided to repudiate the agreement that Monroe and Pinkney had reached. Madison wrote to them on May 20, 1807, that although the president respected their efforts, he could not "reconcile" the failure to resolve the impressment issue "with his duty to our seafaring citizens, or with the sensibility or sovereignty of the nation."[70] Madison instructed the envoys to try to renegotiate. Jefferson's decision was fateful—and, in retrospect, badly mistaken.

The Chesapeake

While Monroe and Pinkney were negotiating, relative political calm had existed between the United States and Britain, notwithstanding the seizure of U.S. ships. Madison's pamphlet had been intended to stir up American sentiment. But two hundred pages of closely reasoned international law was hardly inflammatory.

That environment was about to change drastically. The original impetus was desertion from the Royal Navy, the issue that to the British lay behind the right of impressment. As it turned out, desertion and impressment had a symbolic power that went well beyond their practical effects.

In June 1807, several British warships were hovering off the coast of Norfolk, Virginia, reminders of British naval superiority. A few sailors from some of the ships managed to desert, either by swimming ashore or overpowering watchmen and stealing small boats. Rather than joining the merchant marine, as was common, at least four of this group assumed false names, joined the U.S. Navy, and shipped on USS *Chesapeake*, which was preparing to sail for the Mediterranean.[71]

Word reached Admiral Sir George Cranfield Berkeley, the commander of the Royal Navy's North American station at Halifax, Nova Scotia. Berkeley directed the captain of his flagship, HMS *Leopard*, to intercept the *Chesapeake* and get the men back. Ordinarily, British naval vessels boarded only American civilian vessels. Under the norms of maritime law, the warships of one sovereign state did not stop and search those of another neutral sovereign. To do otherwise could be construed as an act of war. Berkeley was changing the rules of the game.[72]

When the *Leopard* hailed the *Chesapeake* on June 22, 1807, no one on the American ship anticipated trouble, even though the *Leopard*'s gun-ports were open. The two ships drew beside each other, and the captain of the *Leopard* sent a lieutenant to the *Chesapeake* with a demand to search the ship for the deserters. The captain of the *Chesapeake,* Commodore James Barron, refused. The captain of the *Leopard* called out to the *Chesapeake* to comply.

The *Leopard* then fired on the *Chesapeake:* first a warning shot, then a full broadside from close range. After reloading, the *Leopard* fired again. The *Chesapeake,* taken completely by surprise, managed just a token, single shot in return. Three of the *Chesapeake*'s crew were killed and eighteen wounded. Barron, himself hit by a flying splinter, had no choice but to surrender. A boarding party from the *Leopard* rounded up the crew for inspection and took the four British deserters from the ship.[73]

From a naval perspective, the encounter between the *Leopard* and the *Chesapeake* was humiliating. Barron was court-martialed, found responsible for failing to foresee the attack, and suspended from the service for five years. His career was over.

From a national political perspective, the attack had a galvanizing effect. The public was outraged, infuriated, and united. National spirit, Madison wrote, "pervades the whole community [and] is abolishing the distinctions of party." The insult to "the sovereignty and flag of the nation, and the blood of citizens so wantonly and wickedly shed, demands, in the loudest tone, an honorable reparation."[74]

The *Chesapeake* attack gave Jefferson and Madison an opportunity. Jefferson issued a proclamation banning British armed ships from American waters and from landing at American ports; but this was a relatively minor response. Madison quickly dispatched a letter to Monroe in London with directions for how to conduct the conversation with the British government. His directive began with the declaration that "this enormity is not a subject for discussion." The United States would take the moral high ground.

Madison claimed in the letter that "the seamen taken from the *Chesapeake* had been ascertained to be native citizens of the United States." Madison added that "it is a fact also, affirmed by two of the men, with every appearance of truth, that they had been impressed from American vessels into the British frigate from which they escaped."[75] This was mostly true. Barron had, in fact, investigated the men's origins several months earlier, after receiving complaints from the British about sailors' desertions.* Three of the sailors, William Ware, Daniel Martin, and John Strachan, were native-born Americans.[76] The fourth man, Jenkin Ratford, was British—but had enlisted under an alias and was not identified by Barron during his initial investigation.

Madison directed Monroe to insist on "a formal disavowal of the deed, and restoration of the four seamen to the ship from which they were taken." But this was simply the prelude for a stronger demand: "As a security for the future, an entire abolition of impressment from vessels under the flag of the United States." Madison wanted to take advantage of the *Chesapeake* episode and get a promise to end impressment. Now, however, he believed the United States would not have to give anything in exchange.[77]

Madison anticipated that Britain might not agree. "Should reparation be refused," he told Monroe, then Monroe should hurry home—and he should arrange for the return of "all American vessels remaining in British ports; using for the purpose the mode least likely to awaken the attention of the British government."[78] Such a withdrawal meant preparation for war.[79]

The *Chesapeake* attack had not been an accident. Over the next few months, provocation followed provocation. The British squadron off Virginia continued to challenge American civilian ships, demonstrating what Madison called "a continued spirit of insolence and hostility." At one point, the squadron "actually blockaded" Norfolk "by forcibly obstructing all water communication with it."[80]

Meanwhile, in Halifax, Admiral Berkeley tried the captured sailors. Ratford, the British-born seaman, was convicted of desertion and hanged from the yardarm. The other three were sentenced to five hundred lashes each. One died during the whipping, and the other two chose to commit themselves to the Royal Navy rather than undergo the punishment.[81]

In London, the short-lived coalition government had fallen and been replaced by a more conservative one made up of former ministers of the late William Pitt. The notable accomplishment of the new Tory govern-

---

* Ware was from "Bruce's Mills, near Baltimore," according to Barron's report. He had actually served on the *Chesapeake* under Barron some years earlier before being impressed into the Royal Navy while serving as a merchant marine on the Bay of Biscay. Barron described Ware as "an Indian looking man." Daniel Martin was "a colored man" according to Barron, born free in Westport, Massachusetts. Strachan was "a white man" born on Maryland's eastern shore.

ment was the bombardment of Copenhagen, in which the Royal Navy shelled civilian neighborhoods of the city in order to pressure neutral Denmark to surrender its navy lest its ships fall into Napoleon's hands.[82]

George Canning, Britain's new foreign minister, would not allow the *Chesapeake* affair to force concessions on impressment. He was willing to acknowledge that Britain claimed no right to search warships for deserters, and expressed the intention to relieve Admiral Berkeley of his duty. He flatly refused, however, to make any change to British impressment policy.[83]

Complicating the problem was that Napoleon, struggling for ways to deal with British naval superiority, had adopted a trade policy with serious implications for American shipping. In the Berlin decree of November 1806 and the Milan decree of December 1807, Napoleon prohibited the importation of British goods anywhere that he controlled on the European continent. The goal of the so-called Continental System was to harm Britain's trading economy—and to retaliate against Britain's aim of monopolizing trade to France and her allies while simultaneously fighting Napoleon.

In response to the Berlin decree, Britain issued a new order-in-council—so called because the Privy Council enacted it on behalf of the Crown—expressly prohibiting neutral ships from trading between ports of the enemy. In November 1807, as Madison and Jefferson were learning of the rebuff to Monroe regarding the *Chesapeake,* the government announced yet another order, this one specifying that American vessels must stop in Britain and obtain permission before carrying any freight of any kind to the Continent. The order signaled that the new British government would not respect its predecessor's offer to allow American ships to carry produce to Europe so long as they stopped first in American ports.

The upshot was that American trade between the New World and Europe was now officially impossible. Britain would allow ships to reach Europe only if they first stopped in Britain. Napoleon would not allow any ship that had stopped in Britain to deliver any freight to continental Europe. Caught between the warring powers, neutral American ships would be able to trade only by fraud or stratagem. Madison's longtime hope that a neutral United States could profit from a war between France and England was looking very doubtful indeed.

Embargo

Faced with British intransigence and spurred by domestic outrage, Jefferson might have tried to rally public support for war with Britain. But his decision to use the *Chesapeake* incident to seek concessions over impressment put him in a complicated situation. He had to wait for a definitive answer from Britain. In the meantime, he had to avoid riling the public too much, lest it become unwilling to accept a possible compromise.

Over the summer, as Jefferson and Madison awaited London's response, Jefferson's private letters suggested that he considered war to be imminent. Yet speaking of war did not mean that Jefferson could realistically expect the United States to fight. Recourse to force looked just as improbable in December 1807 as it had two years earlier. The United States still had no offensive navy—and the *Chesapeake,* one of its original six frigates, had performed abysmally in its first hostile contact with a British ship. While it was true that Britain was occupied with its war against Napoleon, it was equally true that the Royal Navy had total control of the seas.

The solution was the one that Madison had suggested to Jefferson several years before: an embargo on all U.S. trade to the rest of the world, including French-controlled Europe, Britain, and Britain's West Indian colonies. Non-importation was unlikely to have a significant impact on Britain, since the United States was only one of several markets for British exports. The main key to success, in Madison's view, was the vulnerability of the West Indies. Without U.S. resources, he reasoned, the colonies would starve, and starve quickly.[84]

When news came from London that there would be no reparations for the *Chesapeake* incident, the Senate and House promptly passed an embargo bill by overwhelming margins. Unlike the Non-Importation Act, which had a clause specifying when its effects would come to an end, the embargo bill was written to last as long as necessary. On December 22, 1807, it became law.

Using embargo as a tool of international relations was extraordinarily radical. Its origins lay in an overlap between Madison's principled republican beliefs and his analysis of American power. Economic sanctions were meant to avoid creating a standing army or navy that could undermine republican constitutional government. Simultaneously, sanctions reflected the realistic assessment that the United States could affect the behavior of great powers only by economic means.

The embargo was also an enormous gamble. The Non-Importation Act was still in force. Embargoing all exports while severely limiting imports would reduce the American economy to a primitive state of self-reliance. The domestic costs were certain to be vast. If the United States suffered more from banning all exports than Britain suffered by losing America's raw materials, the embargo would fail.

The embargo therefore had to work quickly or it would not work at all. Albert Gallatin, secretary of the treasury, told the cabinet, "I prefer war to permanent embargo."[85] Gallatin did not want to expend resources on war, but he knew that an embargo was unsustainable for more than a short duration. Jefferson understood that the experiment was time limited. "I take it to be an universal opinion," he wrote to Madison, "that war will become preferable to a continuance of the embargo after a certain time."[86]

The embargo did fail to achieve its ultimate purpose. Napoleon had no objection to American pressure on the British. In April 1808, he issued the brilliantly perverse Bayonne decree. It stated that, since the U.S. embargo prohibited all American ships from trading with Europe, all American flagged ships in European ports must actually be British ships pretending to be American. They were therefore to be considered ships of Napoleon's enemy and could be seized.

The reaction in London was no better. Canning, the foreign minister, told William Pinkney that the embargo was a domestic U.S. law that had nothing to do with Britain or the king's "right of retaliation against his enemies."[87] Britain would make no more concessions because of the embargo than because of the Non-Importation Act or American outrage about the *Chesapeake*.

In the British West Indies, prices skyrocketed exactly as Madison had predicted. The price of a barrel of flour in Jamaica went from $7 before the embargo to a high of $40 by the fall of 1808. The British government responded by trying to find alternative sources of grain, and was able to get Jamaica about half the supply it would usually have received.[88] British imports of American cotton fell drastically, from a high of forty million pounds in 1807, when importers were frantically trying to get stocks to Europe in advance of any sanctions, to just twelve million pounds in 1808. The price of cotton spiked in London.[89]

The embargo thus had an impact. The problem was that the impact was not drastic enough to achieve the desired coercive effect quickly. The markets reeled but absorbed the price increases. The British colonies survived the temporary privation.

Similarly, Britain's export economy was more robust to external shocks than Madison had anticipated. Before the implementation of the Non-Importation Act, Americans purchased one-third of Britain's exports. As a result of non-importation, the American share declined to one-seventh.[90] But Britain's overall exports did not decline significantly, because Britain found new markets, specifically Spanish colonies in the New World.[91]

Meanwhile, in the United States, the consequences of the embargo were immediate and devastating. Patriotic sentiment could not restrain merchants from trying to sell their wares nor producers from wanting to get their goods to markets abroad. Tricks and strategies for avoiding the embargo proliferated.

The embargo did not prohibit American ships from carrying goods from port to port within the United States. The simplest way to evade the boycott was therefore to stock a ship and pretend to sail for another U.S. port, then put out to sea and head for the West Indies, British Canada, or Europe.

Adding to the embargo's problems, the federal government had no effective way to enforce it. Responsibility fell to the Department of the Treasury, which had customs houses in all U.S. ports, but no experience monitoring or blocking exports. In the summer of 1808, six months into the embargo, Gallatin told Jefferson that enforcement was not going well. To ensure that the embargo worked would require both a rule that no ship could leave port at all without advance permission, and "a little army" on the Canadian border to prevent smuggling. On top of that, Gallatin would need to be able to give his officers the authority to seize goods arbitrarily on the basis that they were intended for illegal export, without probable cause or warrant.[92]

Jefferson had no objections to such draconian measures. The only alternative to embargo was war, which would be even more coercive of American citizens. It therefore followed for him that whatever must be done to enforce the embargo should be done, and that Congress should pass laws enabling the executive to do it. Madison's policy of economic sanctions had led the Republicans to a policy of massive coercive authority over American citizens.

In principle, Madison had never objected to using force to make Americans obey the law. In his initial thoughts about constitutional reform, he had anticipated that whole states might refuse to comply with national trade policy, and imagined a national navy blockading them to compel obedience. He had later abandoned the idea as inferior to a federal government that operated directly on citizens. But economic sanctions could work only if strictly obeyed, and Madison was loath to abandon the government's right of enforcement.

For Jefferson, who had often encouraged resistance to overweening government, the contradiction was stronger. It was an irony of Jefferson's presidency that, in its last year, he found himself seeking greater and greater federal power over recalcitrant citizens. His republican gunboats were used not against invading British ships but to interdict smuggled exports.

The final important legislation of Jefferson's presidency, which he signed in January 1809, empowered the president to call out the militia to enforce the embargo. It also authorized federal officers to seize essentially any goods anywhere in the United States to avoid them being exported illegally. In order to get to sea, shipowners would have to post security bonds amounting to six times the value of the cargo.

These efforts were practically and politically unsustainable. Regionally specific, they hit the Federalist-leaning coast much harder than they did the mostly Republican interior. The Massachusetts legislature described the embargo as "a system of policy ruinous to their interests, and uncongenial to their enterprising spirit."[93] It condemned the enforcement act of January 1809 as "oppressive and unconstitutional, and not legally binding on the citizens of this state."[94] The embargo had turned the usual rules of federal power upside down. Virginia Republicans had maximized arbitrary central control. New England Federalists were insisting on individual liberties and asserting states' rights to resist what they deemed federal decrees.

We Ask for Talents

Monroe took Jefferson and Madison's rejection of the treaty personally. When he returned from England at the end of 1807, Jefferson tried to placate him by offering him the governorship of the Louisiana Territory. Monroe not only refused the job, he considered the offer an insult. He wrote to a friend that he was tempted to tell Jefferson "they must find another Sancho for his Barataria," a reference to the episode in *Don Quixote* in which Sancho Panza is made governor of a nonexistent island as a "reward" for his faithful service.[95]

Jefferson, likely acting on his own initiative, tried to stop a split between his two most important protégés. On February 18, 1808, shortly after Monroe's return, Jefferson wrote to Monroe urging him not to challenge Madison for the presidency. "I see with infinite grief a contest arising between yourself and another, who have been very dear to each other, and equally so to me," Jefferson wrote. The three men had been extremely close for almost thirty years.

Jefferson declared that he would be neutral between his two friends. "Independently of the dictates of public duty, which prescribes neutrality to me," he wrote, "my sincere friendship for you both will insure its sacred observance." Although he obviously favored Madison, Jefferson begged Monroe to salvage the relationship with Madison. He wished to enter retirement "carrying into it the affections of all my friends." Jefferson explained:

> I have ever viewed Mr. Madison and yourself as two principal pillars of my happiness. Were either to be withdrawn, I should consider it as among the greatest calamities which could assail my future peace of mind.[96]

Monroe did not take Jefferson's hint. To the contrary, he shared Jefferson's letter with associates and authorized them to say on the strength of its language "that Mr. Jefferson was not hostile" to his candidacy. This was a clever subversion of Jefferson's implicit message,[97] and a sign that Monroe wanted his challenge to Madison to be taken seriously.

Ultimately, Monroe allowed himself to become a presidential candidate, permitting Randolph to promote him. He did nothing officially himself; but in a document he never published, he also made it clear that if elected, he would serve.[98] As in the first few presidential elections, none of the other candidates actively campaigned. To allow yourself to be publicly supported was to run for office.

This was an eerie replay of the race between Madison and Monroe for the first Congress under the new Constitution. Then, Monroe had allowed Madison's enemy Patrick Henry to talk him into running against his friend. This time, Monroe let Madison's enemy John Randolph play the same role, once again challenging his closest friend and contemporary.

The reply of the mainstream Republicans was to strive for party unity. On January 23, 1808, a caucus of ninety-four Republicans in Congress gathered to nominate a single candidate. Eighty-three of them chose Madison. Three voted for Monroe, and three for George Clinton of New York, while five abstained.[99] This was the first time that the Republican caucus had acted as a nominating convention. The caucus announced expressly that it had "been induced to adopt this measure from the necessity of the case; [and] from a deep conviction of the importance of union to the Republicans throughout all parts of the United States."[100]

In Virginia, meetings of the state legislators held at almost the same time yielded a vote of 136 for Madison against 57 for Monroe.[101] This was a better result for Monroe than he achieved in Congress, but it was also far from a victory. From this point, Monroe would officially be an insurgent candidate.

Randolph did not give up. He responded to the party's endorsement of Madison by urging true-believing Republicans to vote for Monroe anyway. He signed and almost certainly also drafted an open letter of protest against the caucus that appeared in the *National Intelligencer* in March. It took the form of an all-out attack on Madison's character and accomplishments:

> We ask for energy, and we are told of his moderation. We ask for talents, and the reply is his unassuming merit. We ask what were his services in the cause of public liberty, and we are directed to the pages of the *Federalist*, written in conjunction with Alexander Hamilton and John Jay, in which the most extravagant of their doctrines are maintained and propagated. We ask for consistency as a Republican, standing forth to stem the torrent of oppression which once threatened to overwhelm the liberties of the country. We ask for that high and honorable sense of duty which would at all times turn with loathing and abhorrence from any compromise with fraud and speculation. We ask in vain.[102]

As usual, Randolph knew how to hit Madison at his most vulnerable points. Madison was indeed understated and moderate—with the result that he could be criticized for a lack of energy. By "talents" Randolph no doubt meant charisma, such as he himself possessed in ample quantities, but which Madison lacked.

By emphasizing Madison's onetime alliance with the arch-Federalist Hamilton, Randolph was charging that Madison had been transformed into a Federalist while serving as secretary of state. Federal powers enforcing the embargo already exceeded those that the Federalist administrations of Washington and Adams had used to collect tariffs and taxes. The charge was, therefore, not without some merit.

As for compromise, Randolph had identified one of the chief characteristics of Madison's political personality. He had compromised at the Philadelphia convention, over the Bill of Rights, and about the assumption of state debts. He had advised Jefferson to compromise over the need for a constitutional amendment to validate the Louisiana Purchase. To Randolph, such practicality was a vice. To Madison, it was an essential political virtue.

Madison needed a running mate from the Northeast, and George Clinton was the natural choice. Clinton himself hoped to be president, but because candidates did not declare themselves, Clinton was able to accept the vice-presidential nomination while simultaneously trying to defeat Madison. In various state caucuses, Clinton and Monroe supporters tried to keep their respective candidates alive.

The embargo was the central theme of the campaign. In effect, it had made foreign policy domestic. Madison's opponents charged that as secretary of state, he had pursued a policy of unmitigated hostility toward Britain, and that the embargo was an approved French tool to lead the United States into war. In contrast, Monroe was the moderate who had negotiated a treaty with England that would have led to peace, only to have Madison refuse to validate it.

Madison needed a political response. Facing his close friend in the most significant election of his life, he showed how far he had come as a skilled politician. Madison asked Jefferson to send Congress the entire correspondence among Madison, the British and French ambassadors to the United States, and the American emissaries abroad—including Monroe and Pinkney. These were then read out publicly in Congress over the course of six days. Madison was standing by his record—a record he had himself meticulously shaped in the knowledge that it might someday have to be made public.

The result was an enormous success for Madison. His letters were understood to suggest that the United States was insisting on the rights of neutrality and taking a strong stand against impressment—and that Britain had been completely intransigent. The record showed Madison as a hardliner. Monroe, the ambassador seeking a deal, appeared weak and soft. Public sentiment fell squarely behind Madison's toughness rather than Monroe's willingness to concede.[103]

That made the embargo itself the most serious threat to Madison's candidacy. By the time presidential electors were being selected in November and December, it was clear that the embargo had not moved the policies of either Britain or France. The opportunity for Madison's explanation came in Jefferson's final message to Congress for 1808. Madison drafted the speech, which was only logical given that the public would assume that Jefferson's policy reflected his own.

He opted for honesty. The embargo had been a "candid and liberal experiment," the president explained—and it had "failed." Because there had been "no other event . . . on which a suspension of the embargo by the executive was authorized," it remained in place for the moment. But the overwhelming and intended message was that the embargo would soon be lifted. In the text written by Madison, Jefferson told Congress that it would be up to its "wisdom . . . to decide on the course best adapted to such a state of things."[104]

This was a stunning political move. It showed a willingness to take a large, calculated risk with the presidency on the line. The embargo was hated, and Madison was to a great extent responsible for it. His answer was to lift it, acknowledging failure in the hope that the public would welcome the change rather than punish him for past error.[105]

Madison regretted his policy's failure. But by admitting it, he turned the necessity of ending the embargo into an electoral virtue. This was the height of the political sophistication that Madison had acquired over his long political career—and it came at just the right moment. A younger Madison might have tried to defend the embargo, based as it was on his own unchanged theory of how a republican foreign policy ought to operate. Running for president, Madison jettisoned it in an act of political jiujitsu that actually strengthened his candidacy.

To those who charged that the embargo was a plot to throw the United States into the arms of France and a war with Britain, its lifting was a devastating political counterblow. The only thing Madison's opponents could do was charge him with having dreamt up the embargo in the first place. But to do that involved asserting either that the United States should have gone straight to war or that it should have capitulated to British power. Neither alternative was politically plausible, much less popular. Madison had solved his political quandary by being candid about his failure and flexible about the future.

The gamble paid off. The public rewarded the decision to withdraw the embargo. Monroe got some Federalist votes in Virginia, but Madison won comfortably there; Monroe did not win any electors from any other state. Madison won twelve states to the Federalist Pinkney's five, carrying the electoral college 122 to 47.* Clinton got six presidential votes from New York, even while remaining Madison's vice-presidential running mate.

Congress moved to repeal the embargo as of March 4, 1809, Madison's inauguration day. The Republicans were under intense pressure to act quickly. In Massachusetts and Connecticut, the state legislatures in January adopted resolutions self-consciously modeled on the Virginia and Kentucky resolutions of 1798. They condemned executive enforcement of the embargo as unconstitutional and insisted on the states' right to interpose themselves. They also hinted darkly that "a perfect union" of the Federalist-voting New England states was necessary to resist federal usurpation.

The embargo had failed. But James Madison, its author, had acknowledged failure, endorsed repeal, and been elected president. He would come to office buoyed by an atmosphere of enthusiasm for the end of a policy he had himself initiated. The challenge he would face was captured by the reality of the embargo's collapse. The United States had chosen embargo over war. It would now have to contemplate the alternative.

---

* The Federalist states were New Hampshire, Massachusetts, Rhode Island, Connecticut, and Delaware.

CHAPTER FOURTEEN

President

...

THE ARGUMENT: *Madison enters the presidency focused on foreign affairs. Still committed to economic sanctions, he aims to play Britain and France against each other, giving each an incentive to lift trade prohibitions on U.S. shipping. Madison is trying to use a brilliant theoretical insight to achieve real-world results. Yet despite his belief that his ideas can bring order and balance, he struggles to assert the American place in the world.*

Eventually, despite Monroe's betrayal in running against him, Madison asks Monroe to become secretary of state. Madison needs a friend to share the burden of the presidency and a competent secretary of state. And because of his distinctive understanding of partisanship, Madison can tell himself that Monroe is not a true political enemy, but an ally who shares his underlying values. This overwhelming desire to avoid conflict—both within his own administration and in the creation of foreign policy—will be sorely tested.

ON MARCH 4, 1809, James Madison became the fourth president of the United States. The inauguration took place in the south wing of the Capitol, where the House met. The building, begun in 1793 on the basis of design by Madison's former Washington neighbor William Thornton, was still under construction.[1]

Madison approached the Capitol in a horse-drawn carriage. He asked Jefferson to ride with him, but the outgoing president declined, riding among the crowd on his own horse, without any servant or attendant. When they arrived at the Capitol, Madison went inside, and Jefferson "hitched his own horse to a post, and followed the multitude into the Hall of Representatives." Jefferson explained that he "wished not to divide with him the honors of the day—it pleased me better to see them all bestowed on him."² (In fact, Jefferson's show of republican self-effacement almost upstaged Madison.) The oath of office was administered by Chief Justice John Marshall, the last stalwart of Federalism left in the government. The galleries were full, and attempts to reserve seats for Washington's female elite were unsuccessful.

Madison began his inaugural address with an obvious fact: The war between Britain and Napoleon was affecting the United States, which had hoped to remain neutral. The problem lay with "the injustice and violence of the belligerent powers," England and France. "In their rage against each other," he declared, "principles of retaliation have been introduced equally contrary to universal reason and acknowledged law."³ Both countries, Madison maintained, were now violating neutral trade rights.

Nothing in Madison's speech suggested that he felt any personal fulfillment or accomplished ambition in becoming president—or that he thought his election stood for some greater national transformation, as Jefferson's had in 1800. Perhaps uniquely in the history of inaugural addresses, Madison told the assembled audience that he felt some "discouragement" in assuming the presidency. The emotion, he hastened to add, "sprung from my own inadequacy to [the] high duties" of office, not the challenges ahead.

Madison's assertion of inadequacy could be understood rhetorically. But Madison was a genuinely modest man. He knew that he lacked Jefferson's expressive flair or Washington's personal stature. He had not sought the presidency in fulfillment of the psychological drives that have powered so many into the office, for good or for ill. He had run because he believed he could successfully navigate the dangerous shoals of global war, charting a course that would force concessions while maintaining neutrality. His broader aim was to do for American foreign policy what he had done for domestic governance through the Constitution: design, create, and implement a model that would align republican liberty and the public interest.

To make this goal explicit, Madison explained why he would "not sink under the weight of this deep conviction" of his own shortcomings. Although he himself might be inadequate, his goals and his principles were not. "I find some support," he told the audience, "in a consciousness of the purposes and a confidence in the principles which I bring with me into this arduous service."⁴

Madison was taking the great, central lesson of his constitutional thinking and applying it to himself. He had designed the Constitution as a government of laws, not of men. With its checks and balances, the constitutional structure enabled it to transcend the ambitions of individuals and operate as a system that would act on behalf of the people. Thus understood, the key to successful government did not lie in the unique talents of any one person—not even the president.

Madison then summarized the political principles that had brought him to the presidency. In foreign affairs, the United States must "maintain sincere neutrality toward belligerent nations" and "foster a spirit of independence." It must "support the Constitution . . . in its limitations as in its authorities"; "respect the rights and authorities reserved to the states and to the people"; and preserve liberty of conscience and freedom of the press. As for defense, a standing army, which was a danger to liberty, must be kept "within the requisite limits," while "remembering that an armed and trained militia is the firmest bulwark of republics." The government should promote agriculture, manufactures, and commerce, as well as "the advancement of science." American Indians ("our aboriginal neighbors") ought to be saved "from the degradation and wretchedness of savage life" and brought to "a civilized state."[5]

Sincerely held though they might be, these principles could not resolve the dilemma of being caught between Britain and France. The Napoleonic Wars continued to follow their own relentless rhythm: The two sides had been fighting a brutal war on the Iberian Peninsula since 1807 and were on the brink of the War of the Fifth Coalition, which would be fought in Austria and Germany. Focused on each other, neither would permit American shipping.

War was not a viable option for a republic without a standing army. Yet the embargo, adopted as an alternative to war, had failed. Henry Lee,* who after his conversion to Federalism had become a harsh critic of the Jefferson administration, told Madison that he should not have mentioned neutrality at all in his inaugural address, and that "the less you connect your administration with the last, the better your chance to do good to your country."[6]

Promoting agriculture and domestic manufacture were desirable goals, of course. But although non-importation could potentially encourage do-

---

* Lee faced personal troubles. The next month, he would be jailed for debt and remain in confinement for a year until he could pay back his creditors.

mestic manufacture for domestic markets, economic sanctions were harmful to the export economy. And with respect to Native Americans, no peaceful means were readily available to improve border relations. White Americans wanted conquest for expansion, and Indian tribes wanted to keep the land on which they lived.

The Ball

After the inauguration, the Madisons went back to their own house on F Street for a reception intended for foreign ambassadors but in the event open to anyone who showed up.[7] "The street was full of carriages and people," wrote one firsthand witness, Margaret Bayard Smith, a biographer, novelist, essayist, and a close friend of Jefferson's. "We had to wait near half an hour before we could get in—the house was completely filled, parlors, entry, drawing room and bedroom." The president and First Lady stood by the drawing room trying to receive the overwhelming number of guests. Dolley "looked extremely beautiful, was dressed in a plain cambric dress with a very long train, plain round the neck without any handkerchief, and a beautiful bonnet of purple velvet and white satin with white plumes. She was all dignity, grace and affability."[8]

Following the reception, Madison and Dolley went to Long's Hotel near the Capitol for what would be the first inaugural ball ever held in the city. Jefferson arrived ahead of them, telling Smith a bit pointedly that it was the first ball he had attended in forty years.[9] Madison and Dolley entered to the sounds of a march composed specially for Madison. "She looked a queen," wrote Smith in a letter to a friend. "She had on a pale buff colored velvet, made plain, with a very long train, but not the least trimming, and a beautiful pearl necklace, earrings and bracelets."

Madison was inaugurated wearing a black suit made of American-manufactured cloth, a symbol of self-reliance. But Dolley felt no compunction to observe such restraint: "Her headdress was a turban of . . . velvet in white satin (from Paris) with two superb plumes, the bird of paradise feathers." Dolley was the first person to use the position of the president's wife to become an arbiter of fashion.[10]

Smith was also impressed by Dolley's conduct. "It would be absolutely impossible for anyone to behave with more perfect propriety," she wrote. "Unassuming dignity, sweetness, grace. It seems to me that such manners would disarm envy itself, and conciliate even enemies."

Dolley had been Madison's political partner for years now, and his presidency would showcase her diplomatic skills. Her behavior at the inaugural ball was a deliberate reinforcement of Madison's policy of conciliatory neutrality. "She was so equally gracious to both French and English, and so affable to all," Smith wrote. "She really, in manners and appearance, answered all my ideas of royalty."[11] Dolley's carefully calibrated equality was meant to contrast with the partiality for France that Jefferson had displayed in the early part of his presidency.

The ball itself was a huge success, at least if measured by the enthusiasm of the crowd and its eagerness to get close to the regal Dolley. "It was scarcely possible to elbow your way from one side to another," Smith reported. "Poor Mrs. Madison was almost pressed to death, for everyone crowded around her, those behind pressing on those before . . . to have a peep of her, and those who were so fortunate as to get near enough to speak to her were happy indeed." Quickly the hall exceeded its capacity and the atmosphere became close. "As the upper sashes of the windows could not be let down, the glass was broken, to ventilate the room, the air of which had become oppressive."[12]

Although he arrived early and left after two hours, Jefferson seemed to enjoy the proceedings. "I believe . . . that every demonstration of respect to Mr. Madison gave Mr. Jefferson more pleasure than if paid to himself," Smith wrote. "I do believe father never loved son more than he loves Mr. Madison."

Unlike Jefferson, Madison did not take particular pleasure in the ball—nor was he the center of attention. "Mr. Madison, on the contrary, seemed spiritless and exhausted," Smith noted. She told Madison with sympathy that she wished she had a chair to offer him so he could sit down. "'I wish so too,'" Madison replied, "with the most woebegone face, and looking as if he could scarcely stand." The managers of the ball asked Madison to stay for supper. He agreed, then turned to Smith and told her, "'but I would much rather be in bed.'"[13]

As the first First Lady to live in the White House—the "presidentess," in the terminology of the time—Dolley undertook the project of renovating the presidential residence. Abigail Adams had never occupied it, and Jefferson had been without a wife there. Dolley had been the de facto hostess during Jefferson's presidency, but over the next eight years, she would not only set the social tone for the unfinished capital; she would also permanently shape the role of First Lady.

Jefferson described the transformation of the White House in a letter to Joseph Dougherty, an occasional correspondent of his who had worked for John Adams while he was president. "If you were now at the president's house you would scarcely know it," Jefferson wrote. "The north front is become a wilderness of shrubbery and trees, there's wonderful changes in the house." Jefferson also made it clear that the impetus was Dolley's: "The president, or rather Mrs. Madison, has changed the office" to another room.

Jefferson ended with a cryptic comment that was almost certainly a further joke, if rather a cruel one.

> Mr. Barry is painting in the [president's] house, but Mrs. Madison cannot abide the smell of the paint: that may be on account of her pregnancy, but I think she will bring forth nothing more than dignity.[14]

Jefferson did not mean that Dolley was actually pregnant. She was forty-one, and she and Madison had never been close to having a child, so far as it is possible to determine. Having made light of Dolley's desire to move things around in the president's house, Jefferson was saying that Dolley's renovation project was in fact her "pregnancy"—one that would give birth to "dignity" rather than a child.

As president, the republican Jefferson had self-consciously worn the plainest corduroy suit and down-at-the-heel slippers even while receiving guests. He had caused diplomatic incidents by the casualness of the receptions he held for foreign diplomats. For him, the goal of improving the physical state of the White House was a subject of mild ridicule. Dolley had a different view. Her queenly garb and manner were intended to convey respect and seriousness. In her person and her official house, she would project dignity.

His Own Honor

The desire to manifest dignity resonated with the new foreign policy that Madison sought to establish for his new administration. As Jefferson's secretary of state, Madison had pushed his president to maintain strict neutrality between Britain and France, while trying to coerce both simultaneously with economic sanctions. The approach had failed. Madison hit upon the beginnings of a new strategy in the closing days of the Jefferson administration. It was still intended to maintain legal neutrality—but it aimed to do so by playing Britain and France against each other.

The Non-Intercourse Act of 1809, passed just a few days before Madison's inauguration, embodied the new, more refined approach. Now the United States would pressure Britain and France by threatening to trade exclusively with whichever of them agreed first. Instead of refusing to trade with both, the country would offer the advantage of its trade to one of the two sides, potentially helping its war effort.

As written, the law first ended the embargo, allowing American flagged ships to trade abroad. Then it specifically prohibited all trade with Britain and France—unless one of them would lift its edict against American shipping. If either Britain or France did so, the act authorized the president to restore shipping with that country.

The law's design had the hallmarks of Madison's foreign policy's beliefs. The theory of the Non-Intercourse Act was to use the conflict between Britain and France as a new form of leverage. As always, Madison was looking for a mechanism that a republican nation could use to achieve its goals absent a standing army or a meaningful navy.

Madison understood that the law was the product of compromise, unpopular even among the congressmen who enacted it. "No measure was ever adopted by so great a proportion of any public body," he wrote privately to William Pinkney in London, "which had a hearty concurrence of so small a one." What was more, Madison added, the act did not have much support nationally. It "seems to be as little satisfactory out of doors, as it was within," he wrote.[15]

Yet the act nearly worked. In January 1809, George Canning, the British foreign minister, had written to his country's ambassador to the United States, David Erskine, directing him to offer a withdrawal of the orders-in-council that authorized attacks on American shipping and to promise reparations for the attack on the *Chesapeake.* In return, the United States would have to make several concessions. Madison's government would have to trade with Britain and not France. It would have to accept that the Royal Navy would be allowed to seize American ships that did try to trade with France. And it would have to agree to acknowledge the Rule of 1756, so that U.S. ships could not carry products from the French West Indies to the French mainland using the legal fiction of the broken voyage.

Erskine got the instructions on April 7, 1809. He was struck by the fact that Madison had essentially intuited Canning's first condition. The Non-Importation Act specified that the United States would trade only with Britain, and not France, if the orders-in-council were lifted—exactly as Canning was offering. Erskine went optimistically to Madison's secretary of state, Robert Smith, to commence negotiations.

The undistinguished Smith was not Madison's first choice for the job. He had been secretary of the navy in the Jefferson administration. Because Jefferson did not believe in navies, the job was relatively insignificant, and Smith's talents were a match for it. For secretary of state, Madison wanted Albert Gallatin, the Swiss-born financial wizard who had been secretary of the treasury through the Jefferson administration.

But Samuel Smith of Maryland, a powerful senator and Robert's brother, blocked Gallatin's confirmation. Madison decided he had no choice but to keep Gallatin at Treasury, where he would not need to be reconfirmed, while accepting Robert Smith. He would act essentially as his own secretary of state, continuing the job he had done for eight years. During Smith's time in office, Madison, supremely free of ego, uncomplainingly ghostwrote many documents for his subordinate's signature.

When Erskine offered to remove the orders-in-council, Madison replied that while he would agree not to trade with France, he could not accept Canning's condition that the Royal Navy would enforce his promise. Erskine decided to gamble, and told Madison that he could drop that demand. Such risk-taking was not uncommon in international negotiations in the era before immediate communication. An emissary would go beyond his instructions when he believed that his supervisors would find the deal attractive. Sometimes the envoy's superiors would reject the deal, as Jefferson had repudiated the Monroe-Pinkney Treaty with Britain; but that gamble was part of the challenge of negotiation.

When it came to the Rule of 1756, Erskine went still further. Instead of telling Canning that the United States would relinquish "direct" trade between the French colonies and France, he reported simply that the United States would relinquish the trade. That was potentially misleading. But most likely, Erskine considered the whole question of the Rule of 1756 unimportant relative to the core issue, which was seizures of American ships. By this time in the war with Napoleon, the British had occupied much of the French West Indies. The question of trade between occupied French colonies and France was more symbolic than actual.

Before April was out, Madison signed an agreement with Erskine guaranteeing trade with Britain. Madison was triumphant. The embargo had failed, but his tweak through the Non-Intercourse Act had successfully anticipated British preference. This was more than a success of practical foreign policy. It was a confirmation of Madison's theory of economic coercion as a tool to achieve American goals.

Riding high, Madison directed Smith to include in his cover note to Erskine a strongly worded request for the punishment of Admiral Berkeley, who had ordered the attack on the *Chesapeake*. Smith's note read:

> I have it in express charge from the president to state that while he forbears to insist on the further punishment of the offending officer, he is not the less sensible of the justice and utility of such an example, nor the less persuaded that it would best comport with what is due from his Britannic Majesty to his own honor.[16]

To a modern ear, this sounds like a roundabout way of saying that the British ought to punish Admiral Berkeley as a matter of justice, good policy, and honor. In early nineteenth-century diplomatic terms, however, telling the king of England that it would be dishonorable not to do something about Berkeley was an extremely contentious statement. In a world where duels still existed, the culture of honor mattered.*

Madison surely understood that the wartime British government was unlikely to punish an admiral for being too aggressive. He had been writing diplomatic correspondence for eight years, and he also knew enough to realize that gratuitous language might give offense. To understand why he directed Smith to include this comment, therefore, it is necessary to recall that Madison owed his election as president in part to his decision to reveal the diplomatic correspondence surrounding the failed Monroe-Pinkney Treaty. Madison was creating a paper trail to show that he could be tough.†

---

* Later that year, the British foreign minister George Canning would fight a duel with Lord Castlereagh, another member of the cabinet, over a dispute in war planning. Canning lacked all dueling experience and was wounded in the thigh, but luckily for him did not die as Hamilton had. The conservative Portland government did, however, fall in the aftermath.

† Henry Adams in his *History of the United States of America During the Administrations of James Madison* was highly critical of the note. It showed one of Madison's "peculiarities,"

In the wake of his tentative agreement with Erskine, Madison made a calculated decision to announce that peace with Great Britain had finally come—before he received confirmation from the British government. On May 23, 1809, Madison sent a message to Congress making the agreement public and taking credit for the change in British policy. The British government, Madison claimed, had intuited the passage of the Non-Intercourse Act and directed Erskine to make a deal.

Madison then declared that trade with Britain would be reopened as of June 10, 1809.[17] It was not clear that the Non-Intercourse Act legally allowed him to act in anticipation of a future move by one of the other countries. But Madison did not want to wait several months for Britain to accept the deal and for news of the approval to travel back to the United States.[18]

To show that he was serious, in the same message Madison ordered the one hundred thousand–strong militia raised in 1808 to stand down.[19] Peace was at hand. In June, after the ban was lifted, some six hundred American ships set sail for Britain, packed with American goods that had been languishing during the embargo.[20] In July, Madison left Washington for Montpelier for his summer visit in a mood of exultation.

Folly

It was all too good to be true. Evidence that Erskine had misrepresented the British position began to reach Madison in June, when he learned that Britain had decreed a blockade on all the ports of Europe two months before.[21] Erskine scrambled to explain it away.[22] But by the end of July, the bad news reached Washington: The British government had repudiated Erskine's agreement and fired him. Not only would Britain continue to block U.S. trade from the French West Indies; it would also intercept and seize all U.S.-flagged ships bound for anywhere in Europe.

Gallatin wrote to Madison that the British must have decided that Napoleon needed U.S. shipping more than Britain did.[23] If Britain allowed American ships to trade, Napoleon would allow them, too—which

---

Adams argued, and "endangered the success of all his efforts." In Adams's assessment of Madison's words, "If he wished a reconciliation, they were worse than useless; but if he wished a quarrel, then he chose the right means." Adams, *History*, 1:69. Adams was neglecting the possibility that Madison's efforts were aimed at mollifying domestic U.S. opinion, which had been enraged by the attack on the *Chesapeake*.

would help his side in the war. Madison had hoped to play Britain and France against each other. Gallatin was telling him that Britain was never going to take the bait. "What course ought we then to pursue?" Gallatin asked. "This certainly is a most serious question." Neither he nor Madison had an answer.[24]

The president struggled to understand what had gone wrong. The British decision "surprises one in spite of all their examples of folly," he wrote back to Gallatin.[25] He added that his message to Erskine about punishing Admiral Berkeley might have scotched the deal. "I have a private letter of late date from London," he wrote, "which says it was whispered that the ministry were inclined to swallow the pill sent them; but that the king considered himself as insulted in what related to Berkeley, and positively refused his consent." Madison thought that "this is not impossible, and may assist in explaining the phenomenon."[26]

The central lesson that Madison took from the entire episode was that Britain could not be trusted to make a reasonable peace with the United States. Matters were not helped by the new ambassador the British government sent to replace the disgraced Erskine. Francis Jackson had a poor diplomatic reputation. On the eve of the bombardment of Copenhagen, he had been sent to Denmark to deliver the message that "there should be no neutrals."[27] Gallatin reported to Madison the rumor that at the time of Jackson's Copenhagen posting, even the prince regent (later King George IV) had said that Jackson "has undertaken a dishonorable mission."[28] Madison interpreted the decision to send Jackson as a hostile message. "The choice of such a man to heal the wound in our relations," he told Gallatin, "does not look well."[29]

Madison did not want to leave Montpelier for the capital in the heat of the summer. But the breakdown of his deal with Erskine left him no choice. "I find myself under the mortifying necessity of setting out tomorrow morning for Washington," he wrote Jefferson. Britain's "fraud and folly in her late conduct" required a meeting of the full cabinet.[30] He told Dolley that he would try to come back to Montpelier as soon as possible: "Everything around and within reminds me that you are absent, and makes me anxious to quit the solitude," he wrote to her.[31] At the cabinet meeting on August 9, 1809, Madison issued a proclamation reversing his earlier order to allow trade with Britain.[32] The humiliation of the failure was now complete.

Jefferson tried to soften the blow. He wrote to Madison that he had been right to hurry the reopening of trade with Britain before the agreement was ratified. "It proved to the whole world our desire of accommodation," Jefferson wrote, "and must have satisfied every candid Federalist on that head." Jefferson was implying that the door was now open for the Republicans to adopt a policy of explicit hostility toward Britain. Madison's eagerness to reach an accommodation with Britain would disprove the old charge that the Republicans were invariably pro-French. Now all that was required was for Napoleon to "have the wisdom to correct his injustice towards us." If that happened, Jefferson wrote, "I consider war with England as inevitable."[33] The letter reflected the changed relationship between the two old friends and allies now that Jefferson was removed from the executive decision-making process. Where once it had been Madison's role to reassure Jefferson when a policy failed, the retired Jefferson was trying to make Madison feel better after the latter's blunder.

Jefferson thought that Napoleon would now lift his ban on U.S. shipping. John Armstrong, the American ambassador to France, was similarly optimistic that Napoleon would be prepared to reach an understanding with Madison—so long as it would put the United States on a war footing with Britain. Between the United States and Britain there was a "political gulf, wide as the ocean that separates you" he wrote to Madison. "Between you and France nothing of the kind exists."[34] Armstrong hoped to meet Napoleon personally and arrange a reconciliation.[35]

Yet Napoleon, embattled as he was, showed little sign of softening. From London, ambassador William Pinkney expressed his skepticism. "I shall be greatly deceived if France relaxes at this time from her decrees against neutral rights," he wrote. "I should rather have expected additional rigor."[36] Pinkney was correct. Napoleon had no incentive to change his de facto policy of seizing those American vessels that managed to evade British capture and reach European ports. Indeed, in March 1810, Napoleon went so far as to formalize these seizures. He issued the Rambouillet decree, which retaliated for the Non-Intercourse Act by declaring that all American flagged ships that entered the ports of his empire would be seized and forfeited to the government. The decree was made retroactive, and some 150 American ships previously captured by France were now made the property of the emperor.[37]

Madison, treading cautiously, wrote to Secretary of State Smith that "reconciliation is our real object." In the hopes of changing British policy, Madison suggested delay. And he warned Smith that he should treat

514 THE THREE LIVES OF JAMES MADISON

Jackson formally but not warmly. "From the character of the man, and the temper of his superiors, anything beyond . . . politeness . . . is more likely to foster insolence than to excite liberality or goodwill."[38]

Madison soon ascertained that Jackson, in fact, had no authority to reach any arrangement with the United States. Worse, he was actively insolent and arrogant. Rather than engaging productively, Jackson told Robert Smith that he and Madison were personally responsible for the debacle of the failed agreement with Erskine. This amounted, Madison thought, to the "insinuation . . . that this government colluded with Mr. Erskine in violating his instructions."[39] Even the ineffectual Smith said he was "disposed, at present, to think it best to discontinue the correspondence with Jackson as unworthy of the attention of the government."[40] Madison had Smith inform Jackson that their conversations were at an end. Then he took the further step of instructing William Pinkney in London to request that the British government recall Jackson and send some better ambassador "with a different character."[41]

The repudiated agreement with Erskine and the appointment of the hostile Jackson marked a turning point in U.S.–British relations, in its own way more significant than the *Chesapeake* incident two years before. Madison was learning the subtleties of international diplomacy the hard way. Believing that Britain was open to an agreement had been a mistake. Although Madison was not yet prepared to admit it, and continued to insist on neutrality, the rebuff made war with Britain far more likely than it had been before.

The History of the Revocation

The Non-Intercourse Act had now definitively failed, as had the embargo before it. Madison had three options in the face of continued British and French seizures of U.S. shipping: acquiescence, war, or economic sanctions.

Acquiescence had both economic and strategic logic behind it. The bulk of federal revenue still came from customs. If the government was to balance its budget and retire its debt, as Republicans believed it should, the only solution was to reopen trade. Merchants and shippers would have to assume the risks of possible seizure. They were sophisticated economic actors and could hedge their bets, even if the insurance had become extraordinarily expensive.

Strategically, acquiescence would mean acknowledging that the United States lacked the influence necessary to affect the interests of the great European powers. If this was true, then Madison had been wrong for twenty-five years in thinking that economic sanctions provided new forms of leverage sufficient for a trading republic. To be sure, the failures of non-intercourse and embargo were powerful evidence for this position. Madison, however, was not prepared to give up his theory.

War represented the traditional option. Yet the problem with war was the same as it had been each time the Jefferson administration had contemplated it: The United States was woefully unprepared. It had almost no standing army. The navy remained essentially nonexistent. Even the militia had been disbanded.

Madison sought to make the war option at least somewhat more viable. In January 1810, he sent a message to Congress proposing legislation that would allow him to create a volunteer regular force of twenty thousand men. He proposed reenacting the law that authorized calling up and reorganizing one hundred thousand militia. Tentatively, the same message suggested that Congress might wish to put the ships of the existing navy, such as they were, back into service.[42]

In response to this request, Congress did nothing. Its inaction reflected national sentiment. Military preparations would be expensive—and nine years of Republican administration had convinced Congress that force was not going to be deployed in any case. Why spend money that the federal government did not have to raise a modestly sized army that it would not use?

This left Madison with the third option: economic sanctions. Madison's first proposal took the form of a bill introduced to Congress by Republican Nathaniel Macon of North Carolina. It would have allowed all American commerce, finally ending the self-inflicted harm of embargo and non-intercourse. If France or Britain continued to prohibit American shipping, then the United States would bar all British or French ships from bringing anything into American ports. The idea was plausible, but Macon's bill, drafted by Albert Gallatin, was too similar to the Non-Intercourse Act, and the Senate blocked it.

Madison then proposed a creative alternative, which came to be called Macon's Bill No. 2. This bill began by opening up all commerce with both Britain and France. Then it specified that if either Britain or France were to repeal its orders against American shipping, the other would have three months to do the same. If it did not, the United States would adopt non-intercourse with the country that had failed to follow in the footsteps of the other.

Macon's Bill No. 2 flipped the structure of past sanctions by using active trade, rather than passive non-trade, as a tool of leverage. In essence, the bill told Napoleon that the United States was going to reopen trade with Britain—while Britain, with her control of the seas, would continue to try to block American trade with Napoleon's Europe. Britain would be substantially helped in its war efforts by access to American raw materials. With far more to lose than Britain, Napoleon would have a tangible incentive to stop seizing American shipping. If he was prepared to stop, then the United States would not resume trade with Britain. Passed in May 1810, Macon's Bill No. 2 was a product of compromise, and Madison had no great confidence that it would succeed.

Three months later, Napoleon responded. On August 5, 1810, he had Jean-Baptiste de Nompère de Champagny, Duc de Cadore, send a letter to Secretary of State Smith announcing that the Berlin and Milan decrees barring U.S. shipping from the European continent "are revoked, and from 1 November, they will cease to be in force." He added a condition. The decrees would be lifted provided either that the British revoked their orders-in-council, or that the United States "shall cause their rights to be respected by the English" as provided for in Macon's Bill No. 2.[43]

The year before, when Madison had reached a deal with the British ambassador Erskine, he had publicized the arrangement and restarted shipping before waiting to see whether London would approve. With the letter of the Duc de Cadore expressing Napoleon's intent to revoke his decrees, Madison faced a parallel choice. He could act promptly under Macon's Bill No. 2 and start the process of discontinuing shipping with Britain, or he could wait until Napoleon actually revoked his decrees.

As he had done the last time, Madison opted for immediate action. Technically, the law authorized suspension of trade with the noncomplying country only after the first country to move had actually lifted its sanctions on American trade; and it assumed an unconditional lifting of sanctions against American shipping, while Napoleon had said he would end sanctions dependent on a condition. But Madison took precisely the same expansive approach as he had with Britain. On November 2, 1810, he issued a declaration: French seizures had ended, he announced. Britain would now have ninety days to revoke its orders-in-council. If it did not do so, trade with Britain would be suspended.

Madison thought Britain would probably revoke the orders.[44] He separately told Jefferson that he would be satisfied even if, having done so, Britain continued to blockade Europe in practice.[45] If that happened, Madison was confident that Congress would support him in defying Britain.

What emerges from Madison's account of the situation is that he believed the tactics embodied by Macon's Bill No. 2 had a better-than-even chance of success. He understood that there was some risk associated with the decision, but he wanted to use the French initiative to change the strategic balance. Referring to Napoleon's overture, Madison told Jefferson that "we hope from the step, the advantage at least of having but one contest on our hands at a time."[46] Perhaps now Madison could turn his attention to Britain.

Possession Should Be Taken

Madison had another reason to take the opening Napoleon was offering. He wanted Napoleon to bless his actions in West Florida.[47]

The impetus was the collapse of the Spanish Empire. On Dos de Mayo, 1808, crowds in Madrid had turned against Napoleon's forces and an uprising began that would become the six-year Peninsular War. Venezuela declared independence from Spain in April 1810, launching the career of Simón Bolívar, the Liberator. By the end of the summer, Peru, Colombia, Chile, and Mexico would all declare themselves free of Spanish authority.[48]

In West Florida, the scale of resistance to Spain was more modest—and considerably more cynical. As Spanish imperial rule broke down, different groups jockeyed to see who might be able to establish control. Although generally loyal to the Spanish crown, at least some English-speaking residents of the territory had flirted with the possibility of joining Aaron Burr's imagined western empire several years before.* They

---

* In May 1805, Burr had traveled from Pittsburgh to New Orleans, attempting to persuade the western states to secede and seize the Floridas. A year later, he was in the process of raising an army when he was captured and brought to Richmond to stand trial for treason. Before Burr could be tried, he fled to London.

now hit on the idea of declaring West Florida an independent republic, which would then make itself available for acquisition by the United States.

One direct approach to the United States came in the form of a letter to Madison sent by the self-styled General Samuel Fulton, a North Carolinian who had been an adventurer in the Kentucky and Tennessee territories before becoming commander of the Spanish militia in Baton Rouge. Fulton reminded Madison that in 1803, he had offered to quit Spanish employ and work for the United States. Madison had told him then "that nothing could be done at that moment nor until a new organization would take place." Consequently, Fulton explained, he had become a Spanish subject, had "organized the militia of the province," and was now "adjutant general and commandant of their cavalry." He boasted that he had been told by U.S. generals that they had never seen a militia "under better subordination."[49]

Fulton was a man of arms, not letters, and he put the position bluntly. "Seeing the unhappy situation of old Spain," he wrote, he had "but little hope that she can hold out much longer against the colossal power of Bonaparte." It followed that "should [Spain] fall we must of course change our masters here." If "the president and Congress judge right to take possession of this detached province," Fulton said, he would be very glad to serve. He was, he reminded Madison, "an ancient veteran"—probably of the Revolutionary War.[50]

On June 14, 1810, Madison met with William C. C. Claiborne, the governor of the Orleans Territory,* who then advised the judge of the territory, William Wykoff, to contact influential citizens of Baton Rouge and make certain that neither English nor French interference would affect the situation there. Almost simultaneously, Secretary of State Smith told a Georgia senator to find agents to go into both Florida territories to encourage sentiment in favor of the United States.

On July 25, a group of West Floridians who had been elected by their neighbors met for a convention at St. John's Plains. The delegates formally asked the Spanish representative in nearby Baton Rouge for permission to

---

* The land acquired in the Louisiana Purchase was divided administratively between the Orleans Territory, south of the 33rd parallel, and the Louisiana Territory north of it. (The 33rd parallel today marks the boundary between the states of Louisiana and Arkansas.) James Wilkinson was governor of the Louisiana Territory, Claiborne of the Orleans Territory to the south.

meet, thus connecting themselves to the Cortes, or proto-legislature, that had been formed in Spain as part of the rising against Napoleon.[51] But their choice of the convention form echoed the American revolutionary period and augured a plan to declare independence.

The delegates took their time, negotiating with the Spanish imperial official, then adjourning. In late September, using the pretext of the local Spanish official's desperate letters seeking assistance from his superiors, some members of the convention directed a local militia commander to seize the Spanish fort at Baton Rouge. A rump of the convention—ten of its fourteen members, all of them English-speaking—declared West Florida an independent republic on September 26.[52]

Madison understood that the self-declared government could, in principle, turn to Britain rather than the United States for protection. And he expressed concern that "from present appearances, our occupancy of West Florida would be resented by Spain, by England, and by France, and bring on, not a triangular, but a quadrangular contest."[53] But Madison also saw that this might be a unique opportunity to acquire West Florida without force.

A week later, on October 27, Madison promulgated a secret proclamation of his own. It began by reciting that the territory of West Florida, extending to the Perdido River, "has at all times, as is well-known, been considered and claimed by [the United States] as being within the colony of Louisiana conveyed by the . . . treaty." The French had not delivered the territory to the United States as promised. What was more, Madison concluded, if the United States failed to act, this "might be construed into a dereliction of their title, or an insensibility to the importance of the stake."[54]

Thus far the proclamation was almost apologetic. Madison was bending over backward to make it clear that the United States did not want to be seen as acting hostilely toward France. He even added that the status of West Florida "will not cease to be the subject of fair and friendly negotiation and adjustment" between the United States and France. This was an odd promise considering what was coming:

> Now be it known that I, James Madison, president of the United States of America, pursuant to these weighty and urgent considerations, have deemed it right and requisite, that possession should be taken of the said territory, in the name and behalf of the United States.[55]

West Florida would become part of the Orleans Territory governed by William Claiborne. Madison now politely "invited" the West Floridians to obey American control—and also "enjoined" or ordered them to do so. They were to "conduct themselves as peaceable citizens"—which meant they must obey without resistance.

The proclamation went on to make guarantees of liberty, property, and religious freedom. The West Floridians would certainly care about property, since their allegiance to Spain had traditionally been cemented by Spanish conferral of land grants. The reference to religion must have been intended to reassure Catholics that the largely Protestant United States would not interfere with their religious practices.

Avoiding controversy, Madison was careful never to assert that the seizure of the territory was legitimated by any act of the independent people of West Florida. A draft of the proclamation mentioned that the West Floridians had substituted "a self-created independent government" for Spanish rule; Madison struck it out.[56] Formally speaking, the U.S. claim rested on the Louisiana Purchase and nothing more.

While awaiting American action, the citizens of the self-declared Republic of West Florida drafted and adopted a constitution and hoisted a flag, a lone white star on a navy blue background. But when Claiborne's troops arrived at Baton Rouge on December 10, 1810, the West Floridians agreed to merge their republic into the United States.[57]

On December 5, Madison announced the existence of the secret proclamation in his annual message to Congress. He insisted on the "legality and necessity of the course pursued."[58] This legality depended on the highly doubtful claim that the Louisiana Purchase included both West and East Florida. Madison may have been concerned about possible British interference, as he told Jefferson and reiterated to Congress. But the seizure of West Florida* was an act of power politics. Madison took West Florida because he could. West Florida had been governed by the British, the French, and the Spanish over the course of more than a century. Now it would become American, and the transition marked the further expansion of the American empire.

For Madison, the seizure marked the emergence of a new, more assertive approach to politics. As a founding theorist he had relied on genius

---

* In practice this included the Baton Rouge district of West Florida but not the Mobile district, which remained under Spanish control.

and persuasion. As a political partisan he had used rhetoric and organization to muster votes. Even as secretary of state he had tried to use international law arguments to advance the American cause against Britain. Never before had he simply acted, in full knowledge that the legal justification for his actions was weak in the extreme. The presidency was gradually changing Madison. He was learning that sometimes, the only way to achieve his goals was to take decisive action.

The Emperor Would Comply

Madison's success in West Florida was not matched with regard to Britain. In the same annual message to Congress in which he announced the seizure of West Florida, Madison had to report the British response when told that the United States was threatening to cut off trade. The British had answered, Madison explained, "that the British system would be relinquished, as soon as the repeal of the French decrees should actually take effect."

Madison tried to make the best of this answer, but he failed to acknowledge the most serious problem raised by the British reply. Napoleon had said only that he *would* lift the Berlin and Milan decrees *if* Britain lifted the orders-in-council *or* the United States formally enforced its rights by cutting off trade with Britain. Britain was saying it was not going to lift its orders and let Napoleon restart trade. Napoleon had made the lifting of his decrees conditional on the British lifting the orders-in-council. Britain in response would make the lifting of the orders conditional on Napoleon lifting his decrees.

That left the initiative with Napoleon—and portended disaster. Napoleon now knew that if he actually lifted the decrees as he had promised, Britain would lift its orders-in-council, thereby facilitating trade between the United States and Britain.

If, however, Napoleon did *not* lift the Berlin and Milan decrees, the orders-in-council would remain in place, and the United States would thus be obligated to suspend trade with Britain. Eventually, the trade-related hostility might well lead to war. Such an eventuality could only help Napoleon, because it would put the United States on his side of the struggle against Britain.

Under the circumstances, Napoleon quite naturally did nothing. Madison had already started the ninety-day clock running against Britain, and he could not now back down without admitting that Napoleon's Berlin and Milan decrees had not actually been lifted. On February 2, 1811, when the ninety-day period ended, Madison officially suspended all trade with Britain.

Madison had been outfoxed by Napoleon. He could not admit it publicly. Privately, however, Madison told Robert Smith to call in the French ambassador, Louis-Charles-Barbé Sérurier, for a conversation. Madison wrote a script for Smith. The most important question in it was "Were the Berlin and Milan decrees revoked in full or in part on the first day of last November? Or have they any time posterior to that day been so revoked?"[59] The question revealed the difficulty of Madison's situation. Having publicly announced that the decrees had been revoked, he found himself weakly asking the French ambassador if that was, in fact, true.

Sérurier replied that "the emperor would fully comply with his engagements," but that he himself had left Paris before November 1 and so could not say what had happened after that.[60] The answer could only deepen Madison's concerns. It was empty of content, a sign that Sérurier had no power to reassure. Worse, it suggested that Napoleon might tweak the conditionality of his original revocation.

Madison was still learning international negotiation through painful trial and error. He had failed to make a deal with Britain. Now he had made the mistake of treating a promise from Napoleon as though it had already taken effect when it had not. The second error, like the first, had brought him closer to France and further from neutrality toward Britain. Slowly and gradually, against Madison's grand strategy and republican instincts, the United States was inching toward the possibility of war.

Unpleasant

Robert Smith did not think that the Berlin and Milan decrees had been lifted or that the administration should suspend trade with Britain as though they had been.[61] Over the course of months, he regularly told people outside the administration that he believed Napoleon had not really lifted the decrees.[62]

Most remarkably, Smith went so far as to tell the British chargé d'affaires, John Philip Morier, that in his opinion "those decrees were not repealed, and that before the rising of the present Congress the whole of [the] restrictive commercial system should be entirely done away."[63]

In a formal letter to Smith that Madison saw, Morier mentioned that Smith had "admitted that Great Britain had a right to complain."[64] Smith had been a poor secretary of state from the start, and had long allowed his disagreement with administration policies to be known. Now Madison had proof that Smith was actually making concessions to British diplomats that flatly contradicted his own policy directives.

The time had come for Madison to replace Smith. But removing him would not be easy. His brother Samuel was still a force in the Senate. Most recently, he had successfully blocked rechartering the Bank of the United States, whose original charter was set to expire on March 3, 1811. The congressional battle had pitted Samuel Smith against Albert Gallatin, whom Smith had prevented from becoming secretary of state.

In early March, after the bank's charter had lapsed, Gallatin wrote a letter to Madison submitting his resignation. The tone of the letter was bitter, and its warnings were dire. Gallatin's "personal situation" had "for some time been sufficiently unpleasant," he wrote. He had remained as secretary of the treasury only out of "a sense of public duty and attachment to yourself."

The problem, Gallatin strongly implied, was Secretary of State Smith. The administration needed "a perfect heartfelt cordiality amongst its members" to do its job. But "New subdivisions, and personal factions equally hostile to yourself and to the general welfare daily acquire additional strength." The consequences were "extensive and fatal," Gallatin asserted: Either he or Smith would have to go.[65] It is possible that Madison welcomed or even solicited Gallatin's threat to resign as a reason to fire Smith. But more likely, Gallatin simply decided it was time to force a decision.

Madison refused to do without Gallatin. Instead he waited for Smith to come to his office on ordinary business, and then fired him. He told Smith that he was interfering with the "harmony and unity" of the administration, not in cabinet meetings, but "in language and conduct out of doors, counteracting what had been understood within to be the course of the administration, and the interest of the public."

Madison hated confrontation. For him to present Smith with evidence of his personal disloyalty suggests the depth of his frustration. He did not consider Smith a political enemy, one whose views or actions threatened the republic. But by breaking with administration policy, Smith was not acting as a political friend should. The only solution was to remove him from office, restoring the balance and concord of the executive branch.

Smith resisted Madison's charge, insisting that he was "friendly personally" to Madison and had always acted "to the credit of [the] administration." Now that Smith had made the conversation personal, Madison reciprocated.[66] Since the men were friends, Madison echoed Smith, it had been hard to accept that Smith "should privately set himself against me in any respect." To make matters worse, there were people close to Smith whom Madison considered "among the best" of his "friends political and personal." Madison was referring to Jefferson. The thought of "distressing" those friends was "severely" painful, Madison said. The whole problem of what to do about Smith "had harassed" his "feelings in a degree equaled by no occurrence in my long political life."[67]

This talk of feelings underscored what Madison called "the awkwardness" of the situation. Smith demanded to know who had spoken against him. The president declined to say, but he did give Smith a list of his failings. He told Smith that he was troubled that in cabinet meetings Smith had claimed to support the Non-Intercourse Act as well as Macon's first and second bills, while opposing them outside the cabinet. Federalists "frequently quoted" Smith regarding private communications he received from American ambassadors abroad. Worst was "his conversation with Mr. Morier, in which he had expressed his disapprobation of the whole course of policy observed by the United States towards Great Britain."[68]

When Smith still would not relent, Madison told Smith to his face that he was incompetent. Smith's correspondence "was almost always so crude and inadequate" that Madison was "in the more important cases generally obliged to write them anew" himself, "under the disadvantage sometimes of retaining, through delicacy, some mixture of his draft."[69] Smith had not simply obliged Madison to do his job for him; he had actually made Madison's job harder since he had to work from Smith's "inadequate" drafts. Whatever "delicacy" had previously led Madison to protect Smith's feelings, it was gone now.

The conversation went on for some time. Finally, Smith threatened Madison with his political connections, who "would not desert him whatever course things might take." Madison replied by offering Smith the ambassadorship to Russia so that he could save face. Smith asked to consult other people about the offer, and Madison agreed, provided that Smith understood the job would begin on April 1, by which time he would have to end his tenure as secretary of state.[70]

Madison assumed that Smith would take the ambassadorship, and he wasted no time in lining up a successor. On March 20, the day after his conversation with Smith, Madison wrote to the man he intended to nominate, "intimating the near approach of a vacancy in the Department of State": James Monroe.[71]

Sincere Friendship

The choice was remarkable. Madison did not stand to gain any political ground by offering Monroe the job. Monroe had just been elected governor of Virginia, and would not have been a plausible candidate to run against the incumbent Madison again in 1812 from within the Republican Party. Madison's critic John Randolph would not suddenly soften toward Madison because he hired Monroe. To the contrary, Randolph turned against Monroe, who he believed had betrayed him by aligning himself with Madison.

But Madison needed an effective secretary of state immediately. His decision regarding the Berlin and Milan decrees had created a foreign policy crisis. He told Monroe he was "anxious to hear from you as soon as possible" about whether he would take the job. And he told Monroe that if he agreed, he wanted him to start immediately after the April 1 deadline that Madison had given Smith to submit his resignation. He closed the letter asking Monroe to "accept assurances of my great esteem and sincere friendship."[72]

For alongside the demands of office, Madison needed a friend. Since Jefferson had left for retirement in Monticello, Madison for the first time in his adult life lacked a close colleague with whom to discuss the political challenges of the moment. Jefferson, out of office, was also out of the political mix. Madison wanted Monroe as his secretary of state because he genuinely missed him—and because he saw a chance to restore the relationship that Monroe had broken by running for president against him.

Monroe, in Richmond, got Madison's letter and wrote back the next day, March 23, 1811. His response was measured. He began by telling Madison that the offer was a "proof of your confidence" that was "very gratifying to me, and will always be remembered with great satisfaction."

Monroe had felt repudiated by Madison before, and now could begin to feel vindicated. He went on to say that he had "every disposition to accept your invitation" and take the job. But first he wanted to clear the air.[73]

Monroe then laid out his differences with Madison on foreign affairs. He explained that his "views of policy towards the European powers" had not changed since his time as ambassador to Great Britain. Monroe had believed then and still believed that having failed to negotiate with France, the United States ought "to make an accommodation with England, the great maritime power, even on moderate terms, rather than hazard war, or any other alternative." Monroe wanted Madison to acknowledge his views as acceptable. "If you are disposed to accept my services under these circumstances, and with this explanation, I shall be ready to render them." He asked only that Madison send him a letter stating that "the present state of public affairs" required him to take the job. This, Monroe said, would allow him the political cover to quit the Virginia governorship.[74] It also meant that Monroe would receive a public, written affirmation of Madison's faith in him.

Madison wrote back that he saw "no serious obstacle" to working with Monroe. Ever since 1800, he told him, his overarching goal had been "avoiding war" with either Britain or France, remaining neutral while trading with both. If only one side would allow American trade, Madison would use that as leverage to make the other side do the same.

As for making "a cordial accommodation with Great Britain," Madison assured Monroe that he favored it and always had. There would be "differences of opinion" on how to get there, Madison admitted; but he and Monroe could disagree on tactics without undercutting "the necessary unity belonging to the executive department." Indeed, Madison went on, he did not believe that even the past failure of the Monroe-Pinkney Treaty would "necessarily" block renewed negotiation with Britain.

But Madison could not make a public statement that the crisis in foreign relations required Monroe's immediate appointment.[75] He could not afford to offend the powerful Smiths at such a politically sensitive moment.

An Insatiable Family

Madison had expected Robert Smith to submit his resignation and announce his acceptance of the ambassadorship to Russia by April 1. When nothing happened, Madison sent for Smith. He arrived with his resignation letter in hand, but now told Madison that he would not accept the ambassadorship because it had the "appearance of a mere expedient to get rid of him as secretary of state."[76]

Smith had changed his mind because of a rumor. He claimed that several congressmen had been told even before Madison had spoken to him that the president would offer him the Russian ambassadorship "with the view of putting Mr. Monroe in the Department of State."[77] Smith was deeply offended that he would be replaced so quickly. Madison's eagerness to get Monroe into the job had backfired.

A strange conversation followed in which Madison deepened his accusations against Smith in order to convince him to take the ambassadorship and avoid a public breach. He told Smith that the offer of the ambassadorship would stay open a little longer if Smith wanted the extra time. Smith flatly refused. Now Madison reiterated his reasons for dismissing Smith, all of which would be more than justifiable "not only to the public, if it should become necessary but even to the most partial of [Smith's] personal friends." Smith replied that he did not intend to create any scandal. Smith then "took his leave with cold formality, and I did not see him afterwards," Madison later recalled.[78]

Madison hoped that Jefferson could placate Smith.[79] But Jefferson wrote that there was nothing to be done about it. The Smiths were an "insatiable family," he told Madison, and would engage in "secret workings" against him. "They may sow discontent, but will neither benefit themselves nor injure you by it," Jefferson predicted. "The confidence of the public is too solid to be shaken by personal incidents."[80]

Soon after his second meeting with Madison, Smith completely changed his mind about not wanting publicity. He compiled a nineteen-page pamphlet, *Robert Smith's Address to the People of the United States,* and had it printed in Baltimore in June 1811. The purpose of the document was to embarrass Madison. Smith denounced Macon's Bill No. 2 as "unwise" and "humiliating."[81] He disparaged Madison's request to Congress of the previous January to reorganize the militia and recommission some gunboats as "halfway measures," a charge that was entirely accurate.[82]

But the most devastating aspect of the outgoing secretary of state's public attack was his insistence that the Berlin and Milan decrees had not, in fact, been repealed. Madison had told Congress in his proclamation that they were, but it was not so. The thrust of Smith's argument was that Madison had played into Napoleon's hands, opting for France over

Britain without any real evidence that France was truly friendly. According to Smith, he had advocated skepticism about the revocation of the decrees and urged firmness with respect to the seized property. Madison had rejected the advice and weakened the firmness.[83]

To be criticized so directly by the inept Smith was embarrassing to Madison. But the real trouble was that Smith's charge had bite: Madison had handled the Berlin and Milan decrees poorly. Privately, Madison claimed not to be disturbed by Smith's betrayal. "You asked me if we laughed over the Smith pamphlet," Dolley Madison wrote to her sister Anna. "Mr. M. did, but I did not—it was too impertinent to excite any other feeling in me than anger—he will be sick of his attempt when he reads all that will be replied to it."[84]

Whatever his casualness with Dolley, Madison had to respond. Unfortunately, Madison could not disclose what had transpired between him and Smith without revealing himself as the source, and Smith knew it. The best he was able to do was arrange a four-part "review" of Smith's *Address* in the *National Intelligencer*, probably written by Joel Barlow, whom Madison had chosen to go to France as ambassador. Madison knew the review was not enough. But his hands were tied.

Drawing the Sword

Surveying the British position, Madison thought that much turned on the madness of King George III. The prince regent, the future George IV, had "a conciliatory disposition" toward the United States, Madison believed. But the king, newly convalescent, was implacably opposed to the United States, which as far as he was concerned had rebelled against him personally. The conservative British cabinet inclined toward George III's position.[85]

Seeing no probability of a positive response from Britain, Madison believed he had little choice but to continue insisting, against the obvious facts, that the Berlin and Milan decrees had been revoked and that the British were therefore at fault for not lifting the orders-in-council. Writing to Richard Cutts, a Massachusetts Republican congressman who was married to Dolley's sister Anna, Madison said that "the decrees seem not to be in operation."[86] This was also the position taken by the *National Intelligencer*, which spoke on behalf of the administration.

Privately, Madison addressed the French ambassador Sérurier with "coldness."[87] Sérurier wrote to his superiors in Paris that the revocation of the decrees was now a "personal" issue for Madison.[88] This was an understatement. Madison had staked his entire foreign policy on the claim that the decrees had been revoked. He was not backing down, because both politically and strategically, he had no other choice.

When Madison departed for Montpelier in late July 1811, he had made neither public nor private comments that indicated a plan for war. To the contrary, he had brought Monroe into the cabinet with the promise of seeking reconciliation with Britain. Before leaving Washington, Madison issued a proclamation calling Congress to convene a special session on November 4, by which time Madison expected that there would be some news from Europe.

Over the course of the summer and fall, the impossibility of Madison's position became increasingly clear. Whatever Madison might insist publicly, the United States was not on friendly terms with France. Simultaneously, its relations with Britain were worse than ever. Madison had hoped to find a new mechanism of economic leverage against Britain, and had grasped at the supposed revocation of the Berlin and Milan decrees as a way to do that. This attempt now seemed to have failed, as had the embargo and non-intercourse before it. The ban on trade with England left the United States back where it had been before, with no obvious prospect for change.

With every avenue of economic sanctions apparently exhausted, all that remained to alter British policy was war. Ideally, Madison would not actually have to use force, just threaten it. To threaten credibly, however, Madison would need to motivate Congress to create a functional military—something it had been utterly unwilling to do when he last tried in January 1810.

A change in Congress's approach would require a change in public opinion. Madison might never be able to convince diehard Federalists that the United States should embark on hostilities with its chief trade partner. But he might be able to convince more moderate Federalists that war alone could end the series of economic sanctions that had proved so costly.

Some indication of this possibility could be seen in a letter from Henry Lee, who told Madison that true Federalists thought him "incapable of self-knowledge" when it came to Britain. The only thing that would convince them that Madison was not reflexively anti-British was "an actual settlement of past differences with the British government." The United

States and Britain were "the only two nations of the many in the world who understand the meaning of liberty." They were natural allies, according to Lee, and should be "united in the bonds of amity."

Yet at the same time, Lee believed that if reconciliation proved impossible, it would be better to have war than to continue "this state of semi-war." If there existed instrumental obstacles to peace, "they ought to be made known to the nation and we ought to be prepared for war." Uncertainty was worse than full-scale conflict. "A continuance in the present state of half-war, is of all others the most debasing to the national character and nearly as injurious as war itself to individual prosperity." He concluded by telling Madison to pick a side: "Take us out of the odious condition by restoration of amity, or by drawing the sword."[89]

The general public thought war was imminent. A petition from Republicans in the Illinois Territory, drafted in September, praised Madison for "steer[ing] clear of any alliance with either of the belligerent powers of the old world." But it also said that "at the same time we assure you of our firm support should you be obliged to seek by open war, the just and equal rights of a long injured nation." The petitioners said that they "prefer[red] war to an inglorious peace." And they were quick to add that they believed "British emissaries who are trading within our limits, are instigating the Indians to war with the United States."[90] At the frontier, it was understood that war with Britain could be used to justify seizing territory from Native Americans.

Madison did not anticipate a preemptive attack from the British side. In September he wrote to Secretary of War William Eustis that he was not "willing to presume a sudden or perfidious blow against our forts or towns." His interpretation of the news from Europe was that it did not "favor temerity in the existing cabinet of Great Britain." Furthermore, Augustus John Foster, the British ambassador appointed in 1811, had been relatively moderate in seeking an apology and reparations for an incident that had taken place in May when the frigate USS *President* fired on a much smaller British war sloop called *Little Belt*,* killing nine British sailors and wounding twenty-three.[91]

---

* *Little Belt* was sometimes also called *Lille Belt*, probably because the ship's original Danish name was *Lillebælt*. (She had been taken from Copenhagen by the British.) The episode was serious, because the American frigate was much larger and had many more guns than the British sloop. Both sides denied firing first.

Monroe did not want to reinforce the impression that war was inevitable. While Madison was still in Montpelier, Monroe wrote to Madison proposing that he cancel a planned visit to Jefferson, who was perceived as strongly pro-French and anti-British. Visiting him would be read as a step toward war.[92]

Madison, as ever, put friendship first and decided to go anyway. On the eve of his departure, Madison wrote to Gallatin to say he was prepared to meet any "amicable" disposition from the British side with warmth. His goal, he said, was to seek "a favorable and general adjustment of differences" between the countries.[93]

After seeing Jefferson, Madison wrote Dolley's brother-in-law Richard Cutts that "nothing has occurred latterly to vary the complexion of our foreign prospects." The British cabinet did not seem hostile, and he believed France was well on its way to returning seized American property. If one of these things changed, he implied, he would seek authorization from Congress for some kind of force. Madison was also optimistic that a renewed bout of illness suffered by King George III would empower British moderates. "From accounts of the latest date," he told Cutts, "it would seem that the *insane* sovereign of Great Britain cannot long be in the way of better councils."[94]

The Canadian Option

When the Madisons returned to Washington from Montpelier on October 1, 1811, they found what Dolley called "a sick and afflicted city." Pierre L'Enfant's original plan for the capital called for a canal running across its length. The canal was still unfinished, and Dolley blamed the stagnant water for causing "a bilious fever to prevail almost, through all its streets. Many died—and Congress convened, in some dread of contagion."[95]

The Congress that met despite the fear of disease featured some newly influential Republican figures who would become known as the war hawks. The most significant of these was thirty-four-year-old Henry Clay of Kentucky, who was elected Speaker of the House on his first day in Congress. Another prominent Republican was John C. Calhoun of South Carolina, just twenty-nine years of age, who had first been elected in 1810 and was now assigned by Clay to chair the House Foreign Relations Committee.

Dolley found the number of freshmen congressmen socially exhausting. "We have new members in abundance," she wrote to her friend Ruth Barlow, who had accompanied her husband, Joel Barlow, on his mission as ambassador to France. Dolley had to meet "their wives daughters etc. etc.," she explained. "I have never felt the entertainment of company oppressive until now—Oh! I wish I was in France with you for a little relaxation."[96]

Madison wanted to use his annual message to Congress to prepare the country for war if necessary. Albert Gallatin saw a draft and urged Madison to moderate it. A war, Gallatin warned, would be expensive and would have to be funded by debt. What was more, "the measures necessary to carry on the war must be unpopular and by producing a change of men may lead to a disgraceful peace, to absolute subservience hereafter to Great Britain, and even to substantial alterations in our institutions."[97]

Gallatin had further advice for Madison. "If war is certainly to ensue," Gallatin reasoned, "it is better, as soon as we are sufficiently ready, to make it at once, instead of announcing beforehand that determination and thereby enabling the enemy to strike at once, to sweep our commerce, to send a fleet and reinforcements on the coast and vicinity."[98] Gallatin's argument was sensible. It would be risky to declare war while the United States was completely unprepared to defend itself, much less go on the offensive. Although the Royal Navy was busy elsewhere, its fleet was so large that it could still cause major damage to American shipping and the U.S. coastline. Gallatin also told Madison to be careful in calibrating his threat: Madison needed to give Britain the political cover to accede while still being firm enough for Britain to back down.[99]

Taking Gallatin's advice to heart, Madison reframed his message so that it did not refer to a declaration of war. What Gallatin had called the "war paragraphs" in Madison's draft were now deliberately ambiguous. Britain had "brought home to the threshold of our territory" measures that "have the character, as well as the effect, of war on our lawful commerce." This was the only use of the word "war" anywhere in the document—and it was carefully hedged. The statement could be read to say that Britain was making war on the United States, which would justify a declaration of war in response. But it could also be read to say that Britain's actions were simply warlike. Britain had, after all, been seizing American commerce for more than five years without the United States' treating it as an act of war. Madison was trying to do what Gallatin had advised: threaten force without provoking a military response.

Madison emphasized that the situation was new. He told Congress that on his own initiative he had been "providing for the general security" by building up maritime defenses and by reconditioning "a portion of the gunboats . . . in particular harbors." Existing U.S. warships were cruising the coast, "with the addition of a frigate." None of this seemed very aggressive; and Madison made no specific request for more vessels.

When it came to land forces, Madison asked Congress to make "adequate provision" for "filling the ranks, and prolonging the enlistments of the regular troops." He requested a short-term "auxiliary force," without saying what size. He also asked for a "volunteer corps" of "patriotic" militia. And he reminded Congress of the importance of the "military seminaries," by which he meant West Point, founded in 1802 to train new Republican officers and counterbalance the Federalist-dominated officer corps.[100]

These requests hinted that Madison was contemplating a ground war of short duration. He did not yet reveal his strategy, but a close observer might have guessed that the target would be Canada. There was no other objective that the United States could achieve with a light land force that would put comparable pressure on Britain. The world's dominant navy could not be defeated on the high seas, and the British West Indies could be protected.

Canada, however, was a sparsely defended, large landmass that could be invaded and taken through superior numbers. If Britain were to lose Canada, it would lose its chief source of supplies for its colonies in the West Indies. Britain would then have to withdraw its orders-in-council and stop interfering with American shipping. It would also have to make whatever concessions the United States demanded in order to restore the viability of its own commodity-producing colonies.

The Prophet

In the same speech, Madison also indicated that a war against Britain would involve moving against its Native American allies. Specifically, Madison intended to confront the Wabash Confederation, which had come "under the influence and direction of a fanatic of the Shawanese tribe."

Madison was referring to the great Shawnee leader Tecumseh and his brother Tenskwatawa, known as "the Prophet." Beginning in 1805, Ten-

skwatawa had called on Native Americans to reject Europeanizing practices. He preached both individual ethical reform and a new direction for
the Indian nations more broadly. He urged his followers to give up alcohol and return to traditional clothing and culture, rejecting assimilationist
farming and even the use of guns instead of traditional weapons such as
the tomahawk and spear. Above all, Tenskwatawa called for an end to
land concessions being made to the United States.

Tecumseh became the political and military leader of a confederation
that arose in conjunction with his brother's cultural-religious revival. The
brothers agreed that the time for territorial concessions had ended. Tecumseh could see American expansion to the south, west, and northwest,
and concluded that the United States would never cease to grow if it could.
Native Americans should therefore ally themselves with a power that
would block American advances without trying to take away their lands.

From Tecumseh's perspective, alliance with Britain was the only plausible strategy to hold back the process of political, cultural, and literal
destruction of Native Americans. Before the American Revolution, the
British had been colonial expansionists on the North American continent. After the colonists became Americans, Britain's long-term geostra-
tegic interests favored containment of a growing United States. Because
the British could not spare troops for this purpose, the natural British
strategy was to use Native Americans and try to keep the United States
from spreading across the entirety of the continent.

Even as Madison was sending his message to Congress, a combined
militia and regular force under the command of William Henry Harrison, the governor of the Indiana Territory, approached Tecumseh's camp
at Prophetstown, where the Tippecanoe and Wabash rivers met. The
American force, one thousand strong, camped on November 6, 1811. Tecumseh was away recruiting more warriors, so Harrison arranged to meet
with Tenskwatawa the next day.

Badly outnumbered and without their military leader, the Prophet's
men took the initiative. Before dawn on November 7, a group of warriors
attacked Harrison's camp. Their first charge broke past American sen-
tries, inflicting substantial damage. A second charge caused still more
casualties. Eventually, however, the U.S. forces rallied, and after several
less-successful charges, the Indian force withdrew to Prophetstown.
Sixty-two of Harrison's men died either instantly or of their wounds, and

another 126 were injured. Thirty-six of Tenskwatawa's warriors died in the battle, a number that is known because the American soldiers scalped the bodies.

Back in Prophetstown, the Shawnees under Tenskwatawa made a calculated decision to withdraw. Even after suffering casualties, Harrison still had perhaps eight hundred able-bodied troops, and could easily destroy the town, which had women and children in it. Any commander of a mobile insurgent force would have done the same as the Prophet, and been happy with the results. Despite being outnumbered, the Shawnees had inflicted serious casualties. To sit and wait for a counterattack in force would have been folly.

The next day, November 8, Harrison sent an exploratory force to the town—and found it deserted. The troops confiscated beans and corn and burned Prophetstown. When Harrison wrote to Secretary of War Eustis describing what would come to be called the Battle of Tippecanoe, Eustis interpreted the report as news of a defeat. But over time, Harrison came to see the political value of declaring the Battle of Tippecanoe a victory and himself its eponymous hero. Tecumseh, for his part, now knew that the United States was prepared to use force against him. The necessity of an alliance with Britain was clearer than ever.

Energetic Measures

Although phrased carefully, Madison's message to Congress was widely interpreted as a definitive step away from economic sanctions and toward the threat of war. From Philadelphia a Republican reported "the raptures" that the speech had "almost universally diffused through the city." He claimed that "even many of the Federalists acknowledge it is high time that decisive and energetic measures should mark our future conduct to the belligerents."[101]

Henry Lee, who had urged Madison to choose between reconciliation and hostility, wrote that he could not "withhold the expression of my delight at the tone and manner of your message." With the highest compliment one American could give another, Lee told Madison that "it reminds us of Washington."[102]

From Cambridge, Massachusetts, Madison's old acquaintance Elbridge Gerry, who had become the Republican governor of the commonwealth the previous year, also sent praise. Madison's message, he wrote, "is clear, candid, firm and dignified, and cannot fail of convincing Great Britain, that your object is just, your demands are reasonable, and that you will support them at all events." Gerry assured Madison that his "resolution" would "unite the eastern part of the nation."[103]

Gerry was writing because he wanted Madison to appoint his son-in-law as the U.S. attorney for Massachusetts, so his optimism would have to be taken by Madison with a grain of salt. A month later, Gerry wrote again to Madison reporting on a conversation with John Adams, who had warned that if war led to full enforcement of a trade ban with Britain, the public would "overthrow the Republican governments of the New England states and make them completely Federal."[104] This was a more realistic assessment of New England politics than Gerry's own. But Federalist fears suggested that Madison's threat of war was being taken seriously.

Madison confided to Dolley that war was increasingly likely unless the British responded to his implicit threat by changing course. On December 22, 1811, in a letter to her sister, Dolley wrote, "I believe there will be war as M. sees no end to our perplexities without it." This was not enthusiasm for war but rather realism about British policy.[105]

Over the course of December, Republican-controlled state legislatures sent Madison formal messages declaring their support for force against Britain. The Pennsylvania General Assembly resolved "that when the submission, or resistance, to the unjust demands of the tyrant is the alternative, the latter only can be chosen by the freemen of America."[106] The South Carolina House of Representatives stated that commercial rights were the second most important aspect of independence after personal liberty, and that "without possessing them we sink into a more degraded state than that of colonies." Congress should "vindicate promptly, and at every hazard, our national honor."[107]

Perhaps most important, the South Carolinians told Madison, the economic sanctions were so unpopular that they were now politically impossible without a show of force. "From everything that has happened," the legislature concluded, "we believe it will be in vain to treat further on the subject of our differences, without accompanying our negotiations with acts."[108]

Despite these marks of encouragement from the states, Congress enacted no concrete measures of war preparation. In the wake of Madison's address to Congress, the House Foreign Relations Committee proposed to create a new force of ten thousand regular troops and a volunteer force of fifty thousand; it also recommended arming U.S.-flagged merchant ships, as Madison hoped.[109] Yet Congress did not act on any of these proposals.

Madison faced a tricky situation. He had begun to threaten force precisely because economic sanctions seemed to have failed. Yet despite the rising tide of anti-British sentiment, there was no immediate outrage or scandal that would motivate Congress and the American public to fight.

The Count

Seeking a way out of the quandary, Madison received what seemed like a political gift. In early January, Elbridge Gerry sent Madison a letter of introduction for Count Édouard de Crillon, "son of the celebrated duke who besieged Gibraltar, and was famous as a great military character." This Crillon had arrived in Boston "a day or two past" from England "in company with Capt. Henry, formerly of our army, you probably know, is also a great military character, and at every point, truly respectable." John Henry, an Irish-born immigrant, had served for a few years in the U.S. Army during the Quasi-War with France, and had lived in Vermont for the past decade. Gerry showed poor judgment in recommending him. In fact, Henry was unknown to Madison, was not a great military character, and was the opposite of respectable.

Crillon and John Henry duly proceeded to Washington, where they offered a proposition to Madison and Monroe. In 1809, Henry had acted as a kind of low-grade spy for the British governor of Canada, Sir James Craig, who wanted to know whether the New England states might secede from the union.[110] Craig was unimpressed by the quality of the intelligence Henry gathered and broke off the relationship. Henry then traveled to London in a failed attempt to get further employment or money from the British government.

On the ship back to Boston, Henry met the Count de Crillon, a figure out of Melville or Twain. Crillon was no count. He was an adventurer and confidence man named Paul-Émile Soubiron, the son of a goldsmith from the town of Lectoure in the French Pyrenees.[111] The count proposed to Henry that they take advantage of his letters to the governor of Canada by selling them to the Madison administration, which would welcome evidence of a British-paid spy meddling in U.S. politics. Henry would provide the letters, and Crillon would lend Henry an air of credibility by his aristocratic presence, a social advantage in provincial Washington. The two would share the proceeds of the sale and leave the country.

Madison bit. Crillon and Henry asked for the astounding sum of £25,000, or $125,000, for the letters. Monroe, acting for Madison, first accepted the offer, but then said he could offer no more than £10,000, which was all the money available in the president's secret emergency fund. When Henry seemed unwilling to compromise, Crillon said he would intervene, and Monroe "put the whole negotiation into his hands." Crillon told Henry to accept the £10,000 and that he would make up another £8000 by giving Henry a (nonexistent) estate that he owned in Spain.[112] Henry accepted the offer on February 7, 1812.[113]

In early March, Henry sailed for Europe. As soon as he was gone, Madison sent copies of his letters to Congress. The documents "prove," Madison claimed, that "a secret agent" of the British government "was employed in certain states . . . in fomenting disaffection to the constituted authorities of the nation." Henry, he asserted, had been involved "in intrigues with the disaffected, for the purpose of bringing about resistance to the laws, and eventually, in concert with a British force, of destroying the union."[114]

Madison hoped that publicizing the letters would drum up anger against Britain, motivate congressional support for war, and embarrass pro-British Federalists. In a note to Jefferson sending news of the letters, Madison told him that "this discovery, or rather formal proof of the co-operation between the eastern junto and the British cabinet will, it is to be hoped, not only prevent future evils from that source, but extract good out of the past."[115] Jefferson wrote back to Madison that he thought "the double treachery of Henry will do lasting good both here and in England" as it "prostrates" Federalists in the United States, and "will prove to the people of England . . . that the war is caused by the wrongs of their own nation."[116]

But the letters, although authentic enough,[117] were not especially shocking. There was a notable lack of specifics, and nothing to suggest that anyone in New England was actually planning secession, much less reunion with England. Releasing the letters failed to achieve the effect that Madison had hoped.

Madison's ploy enraged Federalists, who understood that Madison had been prepared to cast aspersions on the loyalty of New England Federalists in order to promote his war aims. In the spirit of the times, they arranged a boycott of the president's house. "The Federalists affronted to a man" ceased to attend Dolley's events, she wrote to her sister. "Not one (I mean of the two houses of Congress) will enter M's door since the communication of Henry to Congress."[118]

Congress—not withstanding the social boycott—was divided about the war. John Randolph and some of his followers were staunchly against it. A group called the "scarecrows" was prepared to threaten force but did not want to take steps that would commit the United States to fight. Last came the war hawks, including Clay and Calhoun. They, too, preferred not to fight if possible. But they were distinguished from the scarecrows by the perception that they were willing to back war measures if necessary. Madison's view was privately closer to Clay's and Calhoun's than to that of the scarecrows, but this was not entirely clear to Congress.

Randolph's argument was that a "war of conquest, war for the acquisition of territory and subjects," was fundamentally inconsistent with the ideals of republican self-government.[119] Republicanism rejected a standing army, and victory was not possible without one. He knew not how "gentlemen, calling themselves Republicans, could advocate such a war," Randolph thundered from the floor of the House. He reminded Republicans that they had opposed a standing army even under Washington, "who had given proof that he was above all human temptation."[120]

But perhaps Randolph's most devastating criticism related to the fundamental question of why the United States should go to war over mere commercial rights. The Non-Importation Act could simply be repealed, he pointed out. And, he asked his colleagues, "Will you plunge yourselves in war, because you have passed a foolish and ruinous law and are ashamed to repeal it!"[121]

Randolph mythologized himself and his followers, who had consistently opposed the Quasi-War with France in 1798 and now opposed war with England. They were "those firm and undeviating Republicans who then dared, and now dare, to cling to the ark of the Constitution, to defend it even at the expense of their fame, rather than surrender themselves to the wild projects of mad ambition!"[122] Madison, in contrast, was a traitor to the true constitutional faith.

The Orders Lifted

As March 1812 came to an end, Madison received news that the prince regent had been granted full power after George III's relapse into madness. But the softening of policy for which Madison had hoped had not come to pass. Instead, Prime Minister Spencer Perceval was expected to remain in office. As Madison summed it up to Jefferson, Perceval and his government "prefer war with us, to a repeal of their orders-in-council. We have nothing left therefore, but to make ready for it."[123]

On April 1, Madison sent Congress a message asking for immediate passage of a general embargo "on all vessels now in port or hereafter arriving, for the period of 60 days." This led Foster, the British ambassador, to ask Madison directly whether the embargo should be considered a war measure. "Oh! No, embargo is not war," Madison replied. The embargo would be in place for sixty days. At the end of that period, Congress would still be in session, and would be able to decide to renew it or not "according to circumstances."[124] Congress thought that even sixty days was too aggressive a schedule, and extended the embargo to ninety days.

War was almost averted. On May 10, 1812, Napoleon's new foreign minister, the Duc de Bassano, handed a document to Ambassador Barlow. The paper, dated April 28, 1811, was a copy of a formal declaration by Napoleon made at Saint-Cloud officially repealing the Berlin and Milan decrees, retroactive to November 1, 1810.[125] Barlow had been desperately seeking such a confirmation. A week earlier, on May 2, he had written to Madison explaining that his goal "all along" had been "to remove the cause of war with England" by getting Napoleon to state formally that the decrees were revoked. Yet "the object of this government being directly contrary," he had so far failed.[126] Now in response to Barlow's urging and a strong tone, Napoleon had changed his mind.*

* By backdating the Saint-Cloud decree to the previous April, Napoleon gave Madison what he had been seeking, but also simultaneously put him in an awkward political position. Napoleon was enabling Madison to prove, as he had been insisting all along, that the Berlin and Milan decrees were revoked. Yet at the same time, the decree as written purported to state that the decrees had been revoked in April 1811 on the basis of the Non-Intercourse Act passed by Congress against Britain on March 2, 1811. The embarrassing part for Madison was that he had pressed for the Non-Intercourse Act by arguing that the Berlin and Milan decrees had already been revoked when the Duc de Cadore told Ambassador Armstrong about it in 1810. As Madison put it when he saw the new Saint-Cloud declaration, the document depicted the Non-Intercourse Act as "the cause and itself as the

Barlow instantly understood that the new decree might enable the United States to avoid war by convincing the British to lift the orders-in-council. He sent a copy of the decree to Jonathan Russell, the U.S. ambassador to Britain. Receiving the letter, Russell passed it on to Lord Castlereagh, the British foreign secretary, on May 20.[127]

As Castlereagh received the note, the British government was in crisis. On May 11, as Prime Minister Spencer Perceval entered the lobby of the Parliament at Westminster, a man had approached him calmly, drawn a pistol, and shot him at point-blank range. Perceval died a few minutes later, the first (and still the only) British prime minister assassinated in office.[128]

The murder was not political. The killer was a British merchant who had spent five years in Russian prisons for debt and held the British government responsible for failing to get him out. Nevertheless, the assassination had political consequences. Perceval was replaced by Robert Jenkinson, 2nd Earl of Liverpool, who had been secretary of state for war in Perceval's government.

On June 23, 1812, the British government, relying on the rationale that Napoleon had at last repealed the Berlin and Milan decrees, finally lifted the orders-in-council. The underlying reasons were complex—but the decision had much to do with the success of Madison's economic sanctions and the threat of war during Britain's own economic crisis of 1810–11.

There had been extensive agitation against the orders-in-council by British merchants and manufacturers. A few months earlier, Henry Brougham (later Lord Brougham), a Scottish-born Whig elected in 1810, had charged in Parliament that the cabinet was "hurrying" Great Britain into "a war with America." Meanwhile "there was nothing to be seen in the manufacturing counties but misery—nothing to be heard but the cries of distress." An ally of Brougham's argued that the United States was becoming increasingly capable of producing its own manufactures. The northern states could take southern raw materials and not only supply U.S. needs but be able to export as well, threatening British market dominance.[129]

The main Tory argument against lifting the orders was that Napoleon

---

effect." Madison to Joel Barlow, August 11, 1812, *PJM PS,* 5:144. To Madison, the path of cause and effect ran in the other direction: The revocation of the Berlin and Milan decrees had caused him to adopt non-intercourse against Britain.

had not, in fact, lifted the Berlin and Milan decrees. With the Saint-Cloud decree in hand, that excuse was gone. The British government could now bow to domestic economic pressure. At the same time, Liverpool's government could avoid war with the United States, which did not serve British interests.

This should have been a moment of triumph for Madison. The combination of economic sanctions and the threat of force had, at long last, succeeded. Napoleon had reached the conclusion that he could end the ambiguity associated with his conditional repeal of the Berlin and Milan decrees, and had decided that it was time to respond to the strong tone Madison had communicated through Barlow. And just as Madison had long hoped, evidence of actual repeal had been enough to press the British to lift the orders-in-council.

But none of this mattered, because news of the Saint-Cloud decree would not arrive in Washington until the middle of July, and the British repeal would not be known until mid-August. Without evidence of change, Madison had little choice but to assume that Napoleon's intransigence continued and that the orders-in-council remained in place.

Logically the United States should go to war with France as well as England since neither country, to the best of Madison's knowledge, had capitulated. But as Madison reasoned, "to go to war against both, presents 1000 difficulties; above all that of shutting all the ports of the continent of Europe against her cruisers who can do little without the use of them." Nor would entering a "triangular war" convince the Federalists.[130]

Before making a final decision, Madison had a death in his own government. At the end of March, Dolley had written to her sister that "the vice president lies dangerously ill." While George Clinton failed, "electioneering for his office goes on beyond all description," Dolley noted.[131] On April 20, Clinton died after a month's illness.

There was no constitutional mechanism to replace a vice president, and because a presidential election loomed near, no one bothered to try. On May 18, the Republican congressional caucus gathered to nominate Madison for a second term. For vice president, sixty-four of the members voted for John Langdon, the Republican governor of New Hampshire. Sixteen voted for Elbridge Gerry, who had just been voted out of office as governor of Massachusetts. As John Adams had predicted, Massachusetts had turned Federalist as a result of the threat of war with Britain. News of the embargo had "arrived at Boston on the eve of our election, and was blazoned throughout the state with the utmost rapidity," Gerry reported to Madison.[132]

John Adams wrote to Madison urging him to find some use for Gerry. It was crucial to signal support for a politician who had been defeated on the basis of his association with Madison's war plans. "If he is not in some way or other supported, but suffered to sink," Adams wrote, "his principles and measures will be the dangerous, if not fatal discouragement in all this section of the union." Madison's relations with Adams had softened since Madison appointed the former president's son John Quincy Adams ambassador to Russia in 1809. Nonetheless, Madison ordinarily might not have been inclined to take the advice of a former Federalist president whom he had long disliked and distrusted.

But when Langdon declined the vice presidency, Madison was left with no choice. The Republican Party needed a vice presidential candidate from the North. Elbridge Gerry, who had made Madison's life difficult at the Philadelphia convention by refusing to endorse the draft constitution, became Madison's running mate by default.

The War Message

On June 1, 1812, Madison asked Congress to declare war. He was acutely aware of the criticism voiced by John Randolph and others that the United States should not go to war solely over the question of commerce. He knew that many in the Northeast did not favor war that would interfere with their British trade. And Madison wanted to avoid the suggestion that he was going to war simply because the economic sanctions he had long favored were a failure.

Madison needed a new account of why war was necessary. Producing an accessible, comprehensible explanation for the war was especially important because, although Madison was now advocating bold action, he had reached this conclusion only after years of exhausting every possibility of peace. His experience in founding the Republican Party had taught him the importance—and the skill—of crafting a narrative that could be understood and adopted by the public. As president, he had the stature to call for war. As politician, he had to build support.

His story began with impressment. At length, Madison described how "thousands of American citizens . . . have been torn from their country, and from everything dear to them," forced "to risk their lives in the battles of their oppressors, and to be the melancholy instruments of taking away those of their own brethren."

But that was not all. British cruisers were also "in the practice . . . of violating the rights and peace of our ports." They had "wantonly spilled American blood, within the sanctuary of our territorial jurisdiction." This was a reference to the *Chesapeake* incident five years before. Subsequent confrontations had spilled the blood of British, not American, sailors.

Having put impressment and harassment front and center, Madison now turned to commerce. "The great staples of our country have been cut off from their legitimate markets," he asserted. Britain had imposed blockades retroactively so as to capture shipping and hold on to it.

Only now did Madison come to the orders-in-council. The problem was difficult to state in publicly digestible terms. He reminded his audience that Britain had claimed the orders-in-council were intended as a war measure against Napoleon. Yet in practice, Britain licensed its own ships to trade with France. This proved that Britain objected to American commerce with Napoleon's Europe "not as supplying the wants of her enemies, which she herself supplies; but as interfering with the monopoly which she covets for her own commerce and navigation."[133] What was more, Madison added, Britain claimed to have a blockade on all of Europe even though the blockade existed only on paper. This contradicted the traditional British view that only an actual blockade counted as a war measure.[134]

Madison reminded his fellow Americans that he had sought peace. He recounted to Congress his 1809 agreement with British ambassador David Erskine, repudiated by the British government. Yet at the same time, he said, "a secret agent" of the British government had been engaged in intrigues aiming at "a subversion of our government." This reference to John Henry's mission on behalf of the governor of Canada was probably ill-chosen, as was the reference to the failed negotiations with Erskine. But Madison believed that he needed every argument he could muster. While he was at it, he claimed that attacks by Native Americans along the northwest frontier must be attributed to the influence of the British. He cited no evidence in support of this claim except unspecified past examples.[135]

Summing up, Madison beheld "on the side of Great Britain, a state of war against the United States; and on the side of the United States, a state of peace towards Great Britain." This was the strongest argument, stronger than any of the individual links in the chain that had led to it. Britain had systematically taken advantage of the weakness of the United States. That left the question of "whether the United States shall continue passive under these progressive usurpations, and these accumulating wrongs." Madison's answer was that the United States would oppose "force to force in defense of their national rights," and "commit a just cause into the hands of the Almighty disposer of events."[136]

Congress took up Madison's message the next day—and for the next seventeen days, in secret session, it debated the war that Madison had reluctantly sought. In the House, John Randolph sought to renew his arguments against a war of conquest. But Henry Clay and the war hawks of the younger generation did not believe that Republicanism prohibited a war that they considered necessary as a form of self-defense. The most Randolph could do was convince a substantial number of Republicans— nearly a quarter of those in the House—to abstain from voting in favor of the declaration.

The primary opposition to the war therefore came from Federalists. The vote in the House, taken June 4, was 79 to 49 in favor of war. The breakdown reflected not only party loyalty but also regionalism. The North was against the war; the South and West were for it. Because the South was more populous, and because African Americans were counted in the population, albeit at a rate of three-fifths of a person, the South was able to prevail.

Debate then turned to the Senate. Because population did not matter here, the vote was much closer. Ultimately the Senate approved the war resolution by a vote of 19 to 13. On June 18, 1812, Madison signed it.

The next day, wearing a hat with a cockade symbolizing war, the president visited "all the offices of the departments of war and navy," a "thing never known before" according to a member of his administration. He was sending a message of wartime resolve, and "stimulating everything in a manner worthy of a little commander in chief." The adjective "little" was meant fondly, not derisively—the way Dolley had meant it years before when she called him the "great, little Madison." Small in physical stature, Madison was rising to the occasion.[137]

The presidency had slowly transformed Madison's ideas and brought out a new aspect of his character. His fundamental aim in politics as in his life had always been to produce concord, harmony, and friendship. He had labored to avoid hostilities with Britain, exhausting every possible form of economic leverage to preserve peace.

Yet ultimately, the presidency had taught Madison that the world would not always conform to the rationality he so prized. Accepting this reality, Madison developed a new, bold form of resolve: the willingness to take decisive action in the face of serious risks. His goal of creating international concord had not changed. But in pursuit of that goal, he would now adopt the means of war.

CHAPTER FIFTEEN

War

...

THE ARGUMENT: *Almost as soon as the war has begun, Madison learns that Britain has lifted its ban on U.S. shipping. He faces a crucial decision: call off the war as unnecessary or fight it anyway. Madison chooses to fight on, but multiple attempts to invade Canada fail after state militia prove unreliable when used in attack.*

Meanwhile, Napoleon's disastrous defeat in Russia frees up resources for Britain to go on the offensive against the United States and blockade the Chesapeake. By June 1814, the war is no closer to being won than it was two years before—and the British now have troops ready to mount an assault on the United States.

FOR MADISON TO LEAD the United States into war demanded a fundamental change in the principles of a lifetime. The transformation had come gradually, through the repeated failures of his experiments with economic sanctions. With each rebuff from Britain and France, Madison had pragmatically adjusted his methods, seeking a way for the United States to gain leverage over global powers. Ultimately he had concluded that force was a necessary evil, overturning his belief that his constitutional republic must not and could not achieve its ends by fighting wars.

The declaration of war was the dramatic punctuation of this process of intellectual change—and it was a definitive moment in Madison's political life. Having reversed his nearly absolute republican commitment to peace, Madison was prepared to stake his presidency on the outcome of a war. It was the riskiest decision he had ever made. It was also the boldest.

Having opted for war, Madison did not act hastily or lightly. His military strategy, like all of his strategies, was carefully crafted. Madison, the first wartime commander in chief, took personal responsibility for it. His objective was to hit Britain at its weakest point and force concessions that would bring about peace quickly. The war plan called for a rapid invasion of Canada, to be undertaken before the British could send fresh ground troops from Europe or raise enough local Canadian militia to mount an effective defense.

Madison understood that it would have been ideal to overwhelm Canada with a single concentrated ground force, the technique pioneered by Napoleon. But he judged a focused attack to be practically unrealistic. In the time it would take to organize a large enough army, take Lower Canada, and bring the troops upriver to Upper Canada, Native Americans backed by the British could wreak havoc on U.S. settlements in the Northwest. A single concentrated attack "could not be attempted," Madison told Jefferson, "without sacrificing the western and northwest frontier, threated [sic] with an inundation of savages under the influence of the British establishment near Detroit."[1]

A further problem with launching a single attack was that Madison had to rely on the state militias. Settlers in Kentucky and Ohio were eager to conquer Upper Canada, and would provide "the requisite forces at once for that service." But these troops were "too distant from the other points" in Lower Canada.[2] The army to march on Montreal would have to come from New England and New York.

Madison therefore organized two separate forces for the invasion. One, an army under the direction of Brigadier General William Hull, the governor of the Michigan territory, would form at Detroit and invade Upper Canada. Hull had fought in the American Revolution, and had quickly been promoted through the ranks. He had turned down the command when Secretary of War Eustis first offered it to him, but eventually accepted.

The other army, led by Major General Henry Dearborn, would organize in New York State, cross into Canada at the Niagara Peninsula, and attack Montreal. As a young man, Henry Dearborn had served in the Revolutionary War from Bunker Hill to Valley Forge to Yorktown. Although he had been Jefferson's secretary of war, Dearborn had no direct experience of command as a general officer. Madison's choices were limited. The United States had not been in a major land conflict for twenty-five years. Few generals were left from the Revolutionary War who were young enough to lead again.

Hull entered Canada on July 12, 1812, with a force of 1,200 Ohio militia and 300 regular army troops.[3] The invasion went badly from the start.

Five days after it began, a mixed British–Native American force arriving by canoe took Fort Michilimackinac on Mackinac Island from the Americans. This put a British force behind Hull. Ahead of him was the British encampment at Fort Malden. The commander of that fort captured a schooner that Hull had sent to Detroit, which carried, among other things, his plans for the attack.

Meanwhile, Hull was now hemmed in. Because there had been as yet no attack on Lower Canada, British forces from Niagara were free to come and reinforce Fort Malden.[4]

Hull retreated to Detroit. Sensing the American's indecision, Major General Isaac Brock, the British commander of Upper Canada, left York, the provincial capital (now Toronto), and led 50 regulars and 250 Canadian militia to reinforce Fort Malden. There Brock met Tecumseh, who had brought several hundred of his own warriors and was now joined by Wyandot and local Mackinac Indians. Together Brock and Tecumseh advanced on Detroit, exaggerating their strength by dressing militia in the uniforms of regular troops, making loud war whoops, and lighting individual campfires rather than large collective ones.

The ruse worked. Hull panicked. Fearing the slaughter of civilians inside Fort Detroit, he surrendered his entire army to Tecumseh and Brock on August 16, 1812. The war was barely two months old, and the planned invasion of Canada was floundering. Inaccurate reports came to Madison of "a battle, in which 500 of the brave Ohio volunteers were left on the ground to the scalping knife of the savage."[5] The president interrupted a trip to Montpelier with Dolley to rush back to Washington.[6] As it turned out, the truth was more embarrassing—and more worrisome. Hull had given up without firing a shot.

The surrender shocked the public and bruised morale.[7] "Do you not tremble with resentment, at this treacherous act?" Dolley wrote to her cousin.[8] Monroe described "the astonishment and mortification which this most extraordinary event has produced here [in Washington], and indeed everywhere."[9] Hull's conduct, he thought, had been "weak, indecisive, and pusillanimous."[10] From Ohio, a correspondent wrote that Hull would have been "hunted and shot like a mad dog" if he had not been captured.[11]

With the presidential election of 1812 about to take place, the "disaster" of Detroit had the potential to be politically damaging. "I fear that the failure of Hull will produce much injury to the Republican Party and cause," Monroe wrote to Madison. Secretary of War Eustis was devastated. "I have never seen a man more profoundly oppressed by misfortune than he really is," Monroe told Madison. Paul Hamilton, the secretary of the navy, went to Monroe "and intimated a fear that there was danger of [Eustis's] mind being affected."[12]

Meanwhile, Brock took what troops he had from Detroit and went east to reinforce Niagara. There, in October, Brock and some 2,000 British and Indian troops confronted a detachment of regular army troops and 3,500 New York militia under the command of New York landowner and politician Stephen Van Rensselaer. The battle was joined on October 11, when the U.S. regulars and several hundred militia crossed the river and tried to take Queenston Heights, just above Niagara Falls.

Rallying volunteer Canadian militia from York, Brock swung into battle wearing his red regular army uniform and, according to legend, a scarf given to him by Tecumseh. Brock was killed almost instantly, and the battle seemed poised to go to the Americans. The regular U.S. troops and some militia were on the high ground. The moment had come for the rest of the New York militia to cross the river into Canada and secure the heights before British volunteers could arrive.

Van Rensselaer, a Federalist recruited in the hopes of creating bipartisan support for the war, gave the order. But at the crucial moment, his militia balked. Less than one-third of Van Rensselaer's 3,500 men crossed the river. The others, most of whom had never seen a battle, refused to go. The result was an American collapse. British major general Roger Hale Sheaffe, Brock's second-in-command, arrived with reinforcements and attacked Queenston Heights in concert with Chippewa forces. In the battle that followed, the Americans lost perhaps one hundred dead. Nine hundred and fifty-five soldiers and militia surrendered to Sheaffe.

Dearborn, who had not been on the battlefield, wrote to Madison to describe with understatement "the unfortunate event at Niagara." He blamed Van Rensselaer for attacking too soon rather than waiting to gather a larger force with artillery. The problem had not been too few troops, but too few troops willing to fight. That did not matter to Van Rensselaer, who asked to be relieved of his command.

In his letter to Madison, Dearborn defended the war's bad start. "I have not been insensible of the difficulties and embarrassments that we must unavoidably encounter at the commencement of a war, especially an offensive war," Dearborn wrote. "But we shall ultimately overcome all difficulties and show the world that although we make a clumsy beginning, we are nevertheless capable of prosecuting a war with vigor and effect." To these brave words Dearborn added a republican excuse calculated to appeal to Madison: "Perhaps it is best, all things considered, that we should find it difficult to commence war. We might otherwise be too ready to engage in wars."[13] The philosophical lecture might have been more appreciated if it had not come from a general who had just let down his commander in chief.

Following on the surrender at Detroit, the defeat at Queenston Heights made it obvious that the war was not going to end quickly. "The surrender of one army after another, is extremely distressing to the people of this country," wrote an anonymous correspondent from Virginia in a letter to Madison. The problem, the correspondent believed, was that the ground force used to attack Canada was simply not big enough. "For God's sake let us have no more defeats and surrenders. Call out a sufficient force at once, and let Canada be overrun at any rate this winter."[14]

But raising a sufficiently large army turned out to be a formidable and frustrating challenge. In theory, the Constitution gave Congress the authority to create a fighting force without depending entirely on the whim of the states. Yet now the New England states frankly refused to provide militia—and they offered a constitutional justification for their refusal: Congress could provide for the raising of regular troops. But the state militias could not be conscripted to take the United States into an offensive war without the states' permission.

"The people of this state view the war as unnecessary," declared the Connecticut General Assembly. Under the Constitution, the federal government had "the power to call forth the militia to execute the laws, to suppress insurrection, and repel invasion," the Connecticut legislature acknowledged. Otherwise, "to the states respectively is reserved the entire control of the militia, except in the cases specified." It followed from "that important provision of the Constitution" that the Connecticut legislature could refuse to comply.[15]

Madison was outraged by the states' refusal to deploy their militias, which he saw as a direct contradiction of basic constitutional logic. In his message to Congress in November, Madison called the states' argument "a novel and unfortunate exposition of the provisions of the Constitution relating to the militia." To Madison, it was "obvious, that if the authority of the United States, to call into service and command the militia, for the public defense, can be thus frustrated, even in a state of declared war," then the United States was "not one nation."[16]

Beyond the problem of national unity, Madison was troubled by the inevitable effect of denying Congress the capacity to use the militia for offensive war. The result would be a need for "large and permanent military establishments," he argued. Such a standing army was "forbidden by the principles of our free government," he claimed. The militia was "meant to be a constitutional bulwark" against precisely the danger of a standing army.

In November, Dearborn himself went north in the hopes of leading New York militia alongside regular troops in a fresh invasion attempt. As he began to march toward Canada, the New York militia refused to cross the border—and Dearborn was forced to turn around. Recognizing the failure, Dearborn advised Madison that in the future the United States could not rely on militia and therefore must not "attempt more than the strength of our regular force would be fully competent to." Almost as an afterthought, Dearborn offered his resignation. Madison did not accept it. He had not yet given up hope that militia could be used to fight the war. But he was beginning to recognize that the federal government might not be able to rely on militia as he had expected.

No Armistice

As the failures on the Canadian border multiplied, Madison had to confront fateful decisions. Britain's orders-in-council had been revoked the day before the United States declared war. In the middle of August, word reached Madison of a British offer of an immediate armistice "to suspend hostilities both at sea and on land."[17] Madison now knew that the combination of economic sanctions, the threat of hostilities, and Napoleon's highly questionable revocation of the Berlin and Milan decrees had together achieved the foreign policy goal he had sought for the better part of a decade. Britain had conceded even before the fighting had begun. Should Madison therefore call off the war?

The idea was not far-fetched. The Connecticut legislature advised as much: "The revocation of the Orders in Council, it is hoped, will be met by a sincere spirit of conciliation on the part of our administration, and speedily restore to our nation the blessings of a solid and honorable peace."[18] Had Madison known of the revocation before Congress declared war, he likely would have claimed victory and declined to press forward. And if he had sought a declaration of war nonetheless, Congress almost certainly would not have agreed.

Madison considered pulling back from the brink—but not for long. By going to war, he had already redefined his presidency, along with the entire Republican position on foreign affairs. Accepting the armistice would have signaled weakness. What was more, Madison still thought the United States had the strategic advantage. There simply were not enough British troops in Canada to defend against an effective invasion or to counterattack the United States.

Another factor was public sentiment, which inevitably had been stirred up with the declaration of war. That such sentiment could be difficult to control had become clear over the summer in Baltimore, where pro-war Republicans had rioted, targeting a pro-Federalist, antiwar newspaper.* Madison understood that such displays of public enthusiasm could actually backfire, weakening the war effort. Yet the Baltimore riots were evidence that the war was popular, at least among Republicans. Reversing its course almost before it had gotten started might have generated frustrated anger at Madison and his administration.

Even after the initial failure to invade Canada became clear, Madison's position did not change. He told the British in no uncertain terms that the repeal of the orders-in-council would not suffice to end the war unless Britain immediately "stop[ped] impressments from American ships" and discharged any American seamen already impressed.

Yet whatever its place in the political rhetoric of declaring war, impressment had not been the issue that drove the hostilities. The British had been impressing sailors at least since the outbreak of Britain's wars with France. Trade, not impressment, was the cause of the War of 1812.

---

* After the declaration of war in June, a mob had methodically demolished the building that housed the paper. A month later, in late July, the newspaper was published again, and again the mob gathered. This time a group of Federalists that included Henry Lee holed up in a house and fired into the mob, killing two of its members. Baltimore authorities moved the Federalists to a jail, allegedly for their protection. The Republican mob overran the jail, attacking the Federalists. Lee was badly beaten, suffering injuries that left him disabled the rest of his life. Another Federalist, like Lee a former Revolutionary War general, was killed outright.

Like Jefferson before him, Madison was using impressment as an excuse not to reconcile with Britain.

Madison's decision to continue the war made sense only in the light of his belief that the United States could win it, notwithstanding the early setbacks. He also surely believed that the strategic position of the United States would improve as a result of the war. If Britain was prepared to revoke the orders-in-council at the mere threat of hostilities, then logically, more could be extracted by using force. Britain was still embroiled in its war with Napoleon, and would not be able to spare ground troops. Given these circumstances, it made sense for the United States to proceed, and so gain a strategic advantage over the country that had been repressing its trade in various ways since the Revolution. Having owned the decision to go to war in the first place, Madison now owned the decision to stay at war even in the face of the British armistice offer.

Madison's resolve to continue fighting was aided by a public relations victory that counterbalanced the fall of Detroit and the general ineffectiveness of the Canadian campaign: the victory of USS *Constitution* over HMS *Guerriere.* No neutral observer would have expected the Eastern Seaboard to be a site of American victories over the Royal Navy. The United States had six frigates, none carrying more than forty-eight guns. Globally, the British had more than three hundred comparable frigates, and dozens of much larger and more powerful ships of the line. Even with a relatively small fleet off the coast of North America, Britain appeared to enjoy naval superiority.

On August 19, 1812, the *Constitution,* commanded by Captain Isaac Hull—nephew to the disgraced General Hull—encountered a slightly smaller British ship, the *Guerriere,* some six hundred miles east of Boston. The captain of the *Guerriere,* eager to test an American ship in battle, and perhaps disrespectful of the *Constitution*'s capacity, pursued. A pitched gun battle followed. The two ships became entangled, and when the *Guerriere* lost her mainmast, Hull's *Constitution* won. Hull tried to tow the *Guerriere* into Boston as a prize, but she was too badly damaged and had to be scuttled. The *Constitution* returned to Boston carrying the surviving crew of the British ship. In a twist of fate, Hull arrived just around the time the news came that his uncle had surrendered the fort at Detroit.[19] The younger Hull was hailed as an immediate national hero, much as his uncle became an instant scapegoat.

Election

There was some poetic justice for Madison that his only good war news came from a ship named for his greatest creation. But the victory of the *Constitution* had another benefit. Madison could use it to tell Americans that this was a war about the oceans—and about national independence on them. Addressing Congress, he made the best of it, not only praising Hull "for the victory actually achieved" but adding that the effective use of force at sea "proved that more could have been done, in a contest requiring more."[20] The ultimate reason for the war, Madison claimed, was sovereignty at sea. Not to have declared war "would have acknowledged on the element, which forms three fourths of the globe we inhabit, and where all independent nations have equal and common rights, the American people were not an independent people, but colonists and vassals."[21] The victory of the *Constitution* over the *Guerriere* had to be made into a symbol of America's willingness and capacity to fight, because on land, things were going badly.

Six months into the conflict, Madison now chose to redefine the War of 1812 as a second war of independence. This was an enormously important step. Notably, Madison had not mentioned national independence when addressing Congress in June. Actual hostilities had clarified Madison's thinking about the overarching purpose of the struggle. And he knew that independence and sovereignty were much stronger and more popular justifications than trade and impressment.

Madison's recasting of the War of 1812 came just in time for the presidential election, which took place over the month of November. The Federalist Party, which had not held the presidency in twelve years, remained weak at the national level. Only two Federalists could plausibly be nominated and get elected.

One was Rufus King, the New York senator who had been the Federalist vice-presidential candidate in the unsuccessful elections of 1808 and 1812. King had been an active participant in the Philadelphia convention and then ambassador to the Court of St. James's. Born in Massachusetts, he could expect support from New England Federalists. King also wanted the nomination.

The other nationally known Federalist was Chief Justice John Marshall, who from the Supreme Court had kept up a steady stream of subtle and not-so-subtle blows against Republican political hegemony. Following the practice of the time, Marshall also wrote anonymous newspaper articles emphasizing and restating the arguments he made in his judicial opinions. The fact that Marshall was chief justice posed no constitutional barrier to his nomination. Although he was a Virginian who would probably not be able to take Virginia from Madison, he would certainly do well in the northern states where the war was unpopular.

But the death of vice president George Clinton had an unexpected effect on the Federalists' choice. After Clinton died, the New York Republicans shifted their allegiance to his nephew, DeWitt Clinton, who had served briefly in the U.S. Senate and was now simultaneously the mayor of New York City and lieutenant governor of New York State. Dolley, with her alert political antennae, had sensed the younger Clinton's presidential ambitions as early as December 1811, when he visited Washington and she was said to have asked pointedly "what that fellow wanted here."[22] Dolley was worried about Madison's reelection, expressing her concerns to her sister Lucy Payne Washington, who wrote back reassuringly that "you despair too soon about our ticket."[23]

Dolley's instincts had been correct. After boycotting the national Republican caucus that nominated Madison, the New York Republicans nominated Clinton for president. No Federalist could win the presidency without New York's electoral votes. Rufus King might be able to beat Madison in New York; but he would not be able to beat DeWitt Clinton. The Virginian Marshall certainly could not beat Clinton in New York. The Federalists therefore decided to make the Republican Clinton their own de facto national candidate. This, they reasoned, was their best chance to defeat Madison. "DeWitt and the Smiths and I know not who all, intend to break us down," Dolley wrote to her niece.[24]

In keeping with the practice of the time, as well as his personal preference, Madison did not campaign. In fact, he barely acknowledged the election, so focused was he on the war. Perhaps this reflected his confidence that the public would not vote him out of office when he had just begun to fight. It may also have been a consequence of the fact that the candidate opposing him came from the same political party. Madison treated the election of 1812 as a nonevent.

Whatever the reason, the decision was unwise. Clinton turned out to be a strong candidate. Running across party lines, he needed the votes of southern Republicans, who were mostly in favor of the war. He also needed the votes of northern Federalists, who were overwhelmingly against it. His answer was to straddle the regional divide, both supporting and opposing the war depending on his audience.

He almost pulled it off. Despite the contradictions in his policies, or perhaps because of them, Clinton won the entire Northeast except for Vermont. He won his home state of New York, and his support ran as far south as New Jersey and Delaware. In an election that lasted from late October until early December, Clinton got a total of 89 electoral votes and 47.6 percent of the popular vote.

Madison won the South, plus Pennsylvania and Vermont, for a total of 128 electoral votes and 50.4 percent of the popular vote.[25] Pennsylvania determined his victory. Without its support, he would have lost to Clinton.

The election revealed the depth of the national divide. As a wartime candidate, Madison received fewer electoral votes and less of the popular vote than he had received in 1808. The Northeast, relying on trade and vulnerable to attack from the sea, did not want war with Britain. The South and the West each stood to benefit from wartime expansionism, and they supported Madison and the war. The United States was far from unified—and the war was just getting under way.

Attract More Troops

In the aftermath of Hull's surrender at Detroit, Monroe saw an opportunity. Politically, it was necessary to create distance between Hull and the administration, and Monroe wrote to Madison suggesting that Hull be charged with dereliction of duty before a military tribunal. "Tenderness is due to him," Monroe said carefully, "but having lost the army, he is responsible."[26]

Monroe also wanted to advance his own career. He offered to take a leave of absence from his duties as secretary of state, assume military command, and try to reconquer Detroit. He told Madison he hoped "to serve the active part of the campaign, then return to my station here" in Washington.[27]

Madison replied to Monroe's repeated suggestions[28] with classic understatement, saying that "the experiment might even have an injurious recoil" on the administration if things went badly. Careful not to offend the sensitive Monroe, Madison added that it would be difficult to give Monroe the high military rank he wanted.[29]

Instead Madison named William Henry Harrison to lead an expedition against Detroit. Harrison, the Indiana Territory governor who had claimed victory in the Battle of Tippecanoe, "would certainly attract more troops" than any other choice, Madison told Monroe.[30] It was a mark of the difficulties faced by the administration that the president had to tell his secretary of state not to resign to go to war. And it was a mark of the war effort's weakness that the commander in chief had to consider which general's personality and background would be more likely to generate an army for him to command.

Harrison did indeed have some success raising volunteers in Kentucky, where settlers accustomed to fighting Native Americans were prepared to sign up for limited, seasonal terms of service. By early October, Madison was confident that Harrison would raise between 800 and 1,200 troops,[31] and he bragged about Harrison's force of Kentucky and Ohio volunteers in his November address to Congress.[32]

In January, approaching Detroit with caution, Harrison sent Brigadier General James Winchester, a Tennessee planter who had also been a contender for the western command, to set up an outpost on the Maumee River. Winchester made camp near the site of modern Perrysburg, Ohio, roughly seventy miles south of Detroit. On arrival, Winchester was approached by settlers from Frenchtown, some forty miles north in the direction of Detroit, who begged him to protect them from Native American attacks. On his own authority, Winchester sent a detachment to Frenchtown, and on January 18, 1813, they entered Frenchtown and drove away a small British garrison. Winchester then made camp there.

Harrison later claimed that he had objected to the advance northward because it would divide his forces. Yet Harrison did not order Winchester to retreat. The Frenchtown settlers were friendly to the United States and were vulnerable. What was more, Harrison "had also been informed, that the supplies to be procured there were considerable." And Harrison felt he should show "respect" for Winchester, "an officer of high rank and experience."[33]

Observing Winchester's advance, British colonel Henry Procter, who had entered Detroit with Isaac Brock and was now in command there after Brock's heroic death, decided to go on the offensive. On January 22, he attacked Frenchtown with 1,300 regular British soldiers, Canadian militia, and Native Americans. Winchester was ill-prepared, and when it looked as though his force would be overrun, he allowed his army to surrender. Nine hundred and one of his 934 men were either killed or captured. Winchester himself got away.

Procter had no intention of holding Frenchtown. Withdrawing back toward Detroit, he left behind between thirty and sixty wounded prisoners under the guard of his Native American allies. After he was gone, the Native Americans killed the prisoners. The episode came to be called the River Raisin Massacre, for the river that ran beside Frenchtown.[34]

By the time Madison was inaugurated as president on March 4, 1813, his planned attack on Canada was on hold and victory seemed further off than it had nine months before when the war began. He kept his inaugural address short. First he reminded the public that the war must be understood as a second war of independence for the status of seas and sailors: "On the issue of the war," he declared, "are staked our national sovereignty on the high seas, and the security of an important class of citizens, whose occupations give the proper value to those of every other class." He condemned the British for allying themselves with Native Americans who committed massacres like the one at River Raisin. The British did not, "it is true, take into their own hands the hatchet and the knife devoted to indiscriminate massacres; but they have let loose the savages armed with these cruel instruments."[35]

Madison understood that a reiteration of the war's purposes and an attack on British honor would not on their own convince critics of the war effort. He therefore closed by arguing that the British had refused terms that would have ended the war, and that the United States would inevitably win. The nation's "military resources," he insisted, "are amply sufficient to bring the war to an honorable issue." The American population was "more than half that of the British Isles," he claimed. The economy was strong, and "a general prosperity is visible in the public countenance."[36]

Madison told his audience that "the patriotism, the good sense, and the manly spirit" of American citizens promised "cheerfulness" in bearing "the common burden." In essence, Madison was trying to convince the public to support the war by telling them that they did, in fact, support it. He finished by promising that American victories on the sea would soon be matched by victories on land. Nothing was needed to assure such victories "but the discipline and habits which are in daily progress."[37] He believed that success lay within reach; but by now he also realized the tremendous difficulty of grasping it.

Nothing like a System of Defense

Madison's faith in the eventual and inevitable success of a Canadian invasion depended on the continuation of Britain's struggle against Napoleon. On June 24, 1812, six days after Madison had declared war on Britain, Napoleon had crossed the Neman River into Russia with his Grande Armée of 680,000 soldiers. The invasion was the direct result of the strategic logic of domination. Without subduing Russia, Napoleon could not force Britain to seek peace—and he thrived on high-risk initiative.

Famously, the Russians fell back, burning their own fields as they went so that Napoleon's troops would not be able to live off the land. On September 14, Napoleon entered a deserted Moscow. A month later, his army began to starve. As Napoleon retreated to Smolensk and then Vilnius, his situation became increasingly dire.

By the time the Grande Armée left Russian territory in December 1812, only twenty-seven thousand able-bodied troops remained. Napoleon fled ahead of them to Paris. Prussia and Austria defected from Napoleon's side and entered a new coalition with Britain. The tide of the Napoleonic Wars had turned.

Madison's ambassador to France, Joel Barlow, followed Napoleon into Russia. From Paris, Ruth Barlow kept Dolley abreast of her husband's travels. "I wrote you in my last that my husband was on his way to Wilna [Vilnius], sent for by the emperor," she wrote on November 25, 1812. Barlow was an excellent and intrepid traveler, but Ruth noted that "the roads from Berlin to Wilna are generally bad, and not very safe."[38] The situation in the east was far worse than she imagined. Napoleon was already on the run when Barlow reached Vilnius. In brutal, subzero temperatures, Barlow turned back and tried to head west. Napoleon overtook him, passing without pause in his race for Paris and safety. Barlow died of pneumonia in Zarnowiec, near Cracow, on December 26—a victim of his own dogged pursuit of Napoleon.

By March 10, 1813, Madison began to receive news of Napoleon's Russian overreach. He sent Jefferson a New York newspaper including an account of what he called "the catastrophe of the French army." Madison was still hopeful, insisting that the report "is doubtless much exaggerated," although he acknowledged that "there is no doubt that the losses are beyond example." He reasoned, not implausibly, that Napoleon had conquered so much territory in Europe that "it will not be surprising, if with the terrors of his name, he should surmount his difficulties."[39]

Nonetheless, Madison realized that the dynamics of his war were about to change. If Britain went on the offensive, the consequences could be serious, and he took steps accordingly. In the same letter reporting Napoleon's disaster, he told Jefferson that Russia had offered to mediate peace between the United States and Britain. Madison, who considered the development a sign of Russian sympathy, intended to agree to the offer.[40] Having previously rejected the British offer of an armistice, Madison wrote in April to Monroe that he was open to the possibility of a cease-fire during the Russian mediation, so as to spare the "effusion of blood."[41]

The East Coast in particular was vulnerable to naval attack. St. George Tucker, professor of law at the College of William and Mary, reported from Williamsburg a rumor that "the enemy's predatory excursions are likely to be extended up the rivers, unless checked by some efficient means."[42] Madison took the danger seriously. "The southern states, particularly Virginia, seem to be marked out for the little vengeance of the British cabinet," he wrote back to Tucker.[43]

As a British fleet approached, it became conceivable that Madison himself could be in danger. He received a detailed warning to this effect from Jonathan Dayton, a New Jersey politician who had been the youngest member of the Philadelphia convention twenty-five years earlier and had subsequently found his career tainted after he lent money to Aaron Burr on the eve of his conspiracy. Dayton told Madison that he had heard some Englishmen in New York discussing a plan for a "bold attempt . . . to seize your person and papers, and convey you to the fleet" in the Atlantic. Dayton speculated that the kidnapping attempt could be accomplished by sending a boat disguised as a cotton-carrying coaster, with "40 or 50 seamen and marines to be concealed in the hold" up the Chesapeake to Georgetown. The force could abduct Madison and take him downriver to a waiting British ship.[44]

By the middle of April 1813, the prospect of attack was no longer theoretical. A small British fleet under the command of Admiral George Cockburn had actually entered the Chesapeake Bay. Cockburn steered clear of Baltimore, but he looted and burned the port of Frenchtown, Maryland, and fired on Havre de Grace. He then sailed across the bay, burning Georgetown and Fredericktown on Maryland's Eastern Shore, effectively blockading the Chesapeake.[45]

Monroe wrote to Madison expressing his "anxiety for the situation of the inhabitants on the . . . shores, of the bay, and rivers emptying into it, as well as of the principal towns" of Maryland. The problem was simple: "At present there is nothing like a system of defense organized for the general protection of these places against this [British] squadron." There was no "concerted plan of communication," and hence no warning of when the British would appear. There was "no preparation" made until "the danger is at hand, and then, everything is hurry and confusion." There was no remedy for the blockade.[46]

From Connecticut, Madison received a report that a seventy-four-gun ship of the line and two frigates were "under the lee of Block Island" some "12 or 15 miles northeast of Montauk." From this position the ships could effectively blockade nearly all of Connecticut's commerce.[47] Connecticut shippers were either obtaining licenses from the British or else accepting payment from them when their stocks were confiscated. "It certainly, sir, must be seen," wrote Madison's correspondent, that "if the shameful traffic is permitted, our enemy can be supplied under shadow of our own laws, with as much facility as though the country was in their own power."[48] The lesson was clear. If the British could spare enough ships to expand the blockade up and down the coast, they could achieve something very like a total victory.

A Severe and Tedious Attack

Madison's reaction to the threat was to harden his attitude toward Britain and double down on continuing the war. In November 1813, a visiting Scottish editor, Francis Jeffrey, who had a long conversation with the president, noted that he was downright confrontational. Madison blamed British "obstinacy and insolence" for starting the conflict and criticized attacks on "defenseless villages." He denigrated the way the British had communicated the possibility of a negotiated settlement through the same admiral who was directing the blockade of the coast, an approach Madison called "unprecedented" and said he could not take seriously. The visitor was "surprised at this sort of challenge . . . thrown out by a sovereign to a private individual in his drawing room."[49] The pugnacious tone reflected Madison's frustration; Jeffrey, the only British subject at hand, was the recipient of a rare outburst of emotion.

The prospect of a substantial British fleet advancing on the East Coast also gave Madison a strategic reason to refocus on attacking Canada. In January, Madison had appointed a new secretary of war, John Armstrong, a former New York senator and Jefferson's ambassador to France. Armstrong recognized that he could not get enough troops to cross the Niagara and take Montreal. He therefore directed Henry Dearborn to raise an army in upstate New York and proceed to attack Kingston, Ontario. From Kingston, Dearborn was to advance to York.

But Dearborn decided against attacking the well-defended Kingston. Instead, in conjunction with Commodore Isaac Chauncey, commander of U.S. vessels on the Great Lakes, Dearborn planned to raid York from the water. On April 27, 1813, Chauncey landed an army of 1,700 on the outskirts of York under the command of Brigadier General Zebulon Pike. The city was defended by 800 men under Major General Roger Hale Sheaffe. After many of Sheaffe's Canadian militia fled the battle, the remaining regular troops withdrew into the city, and Sheaffe ordered the York powder magazine to be blown up rather than allow it to be captured. The invaders did not anticipate the explosion, which killed or wounded two hundred of them. Pike was hit by debris and died shortly after his victory was accomplished.[50]

Shocked by the explosion and the death of their commanding officer, the Americans went on a rampage in the capital of Upper Canada. They burned and looted public buildings and private dwellings alike. Pro-American residents of York joined in the melee, targeting local enemies who favored British rule.

Madison was quick to take credit for the victory, and did not acknowledge the undisciplined aftermath. Addressing Congress in May, he asserted that "the attack and capture of York is . . . a presage of future and greater victories."[51] In the short term, the victory at York had a positive public relations effect.[52] Militarily, the benefits of the campaign were less pronounced. The Americans captured a single British ship and a few naval stores intended for British ships on Lake Erie. York had no fundamental strategic value to the United States. On May 8, Dearborn abandoned the city, bringing his troops back where they had started in anticipation of a further attack on Fort George.

Taking steps to open negotiations with Britain through the mediation of Russia, Madison decided to name Gallatin and James Bayard, a Federalist senator from Delaware, to join John Quincy Adams in conducting the talks. Madison trusted Gallatin completely. Bayard was a good political choice because he had voted against the war, but had shown support once the war was declared.

Gallatin and Bayard embarked for St. Petersburg in May, before Madison submitted their nominations for Senate confirmation. Perhaps he judged that confirmation would be more likely once the emissaries were already on their way. If so, he was mistaken. Gallatin had always been unpopular in the Senate, which now attacked him through a nonbinding resolution that announced he could not serve simultaneously as secretary of the treasury and as an envoy to the peace negotiations. This delayed his confirmation, a defeat for Madison.

Madison was losing what little influence he had over the Senate—even when his goal was to end the increasingly unpopular war. Virginia congressman John Wayles Eppes, a Republican ally who had been married to Jefferson's daughter,[53] told Madison that he had made a political mistake by nominating Gallatin. "Many of your best friends and among that number myself regret the appointment," Eppes said. It would be "a public calamity" to lose Gallatin from Treasury—and Gallatin would have to resign under existing law if he was out of the office for more than six months.[54]

The political challenge to the Gallatin appointment brought home the way the war had reintroduced partisan division to national politics. For Madison, who generally abhorred personalized conflict, it was bad enough that the Senate was hostile to his secretary of the treasury, and by extension to himself. Worse was that the Republican-Federalist split, which Jefferson's victory in 1800 seemed to have ended, had now returned—and Madison himself was partially responsible. The decision to go to war had raised the stakes of political conflict enormously. The war's poor progress further reduced the possibility of national unity. Now, emboldened by regional opposition to the war, the Federalists were making their first serious comeback in thirteen years.

Faced with difficult war circumstances and divisive political opposition, Madison fell seriously ill. On June 14, 1813, Dolley told vice president Elbridge Gerry that Madison "was sick in his chamber and could not meet his friend that day." Dolley attributed the illness to Madison being "worried by the opposition given to his nomination of Mr. Gallatin, and his apprehension for the fate of his foreign negotiations."[55]

On June 16, Madison was supposed to meet a Senate committee at eleven a.m. But he did not appear. The next day, June 17, Madison again wrote to Wells that he was "too much indisposed to see the committee this morning," but hoped to meet them the next day.[56] By now Madison was very sick with a condition he called bilious fever, and which may possibly have been malaria—or more likely a bout of the migraine to which he was sometimes subject.[57] Rumors began to spread that Madison was near death. John Adams was told that Madison "lives by laudanum and could not hold out four months."[58]

Madison had reached the low point of his presidency—indeed of his life. The war on which he had bet the future of the country was a year old and could show few measurable gains. The world's strongest navy was blockading larger and larger portions of the coast. Regional division was fueling partisan politics that hamstrung him in Congress. And he was confined to his room by an illness that seemed to symbolize his apparent political incapacitation.

Toward the end of June, however, Madison rallied. By July 7, the newspapers were writing that he had recovered.[59] Elbridge Gerry's son, who met Madison for the first time that day, noted in his journal that the president "bears the marks of age, and of a very strong mind."[60]

Madison's physical comeback did not mean the end of the political obstacles he faced. On July 19, 1813, the Senate rejected Gallatin's nomination as envoy to the peace talks by a vote of 18 to 17. On July 20, Madison proposed a new embargo bill more extensive than any of the bills enacted before the war. His logic was straightforward: The United States could not continue supporting the very enemy who was blockading its ports.

As a last resort, Madison was prepared to use all means to support his proposed war measure—including religion, which he had always tried to keep out of politics. On July 23, he drafted a proclamation announcing a national day of "public humiliation and prayer" in response to "times of public calamity." Attentive as ever to the concerns of religious liberty, Madison took pains in the proclamation not to overstep his public role, merely "recommend[ing] to all, who shall be piously disposed" to assemble "in their respective religious congregations" on the second Thursday in September to thank God for his blessings and ask forgiveness for America's sins.[61]

Madison's list of blessings and prayers was much more specific. He suggested, for example, thanking God for efforts "to extend and establish the arts and manufactures."[62] He also asked the public to pray to God to "inspire all citizens with the love of their country," so as to create "those fraternal affections and that mutual confidence, which . . . make us safe at home and respected abroad."[63] This was a plea to the divine for public confidence in his war policy.

Most overt, Madison made a direct comparison between the current war and the War of Independence. Just as God had been "graciously pleased" to "raise" Americans

> to the station of an independent and sovereign people; so he would now be pleased, in like manner, to bestow his blessing on our arms in resisting hostile and persevering efforts of the same power, to degrade us on the ocean.[64]

Madison was invoking his most important and powerful justification for the war, the same one he had first expressed to Congress the previous autumn. And this time, he was asking God to accomplish it.

The Senate was unmoved by Madison's eloquence—or by any prayers he elicited. It rejected his proposed embargo bill on July 28. Combined with the defeat of Gallatin's nomination to the mediation, the defeat of such a necessary war measure signaled that Madison's presidency was in trouble.

To recover the political initiative Madison had to regain the military initiative. The East Coast was largely undefended. That left only one way to win the war: the conquest of Canada.

We Have Met the Enemy

To avoid repeating the failure of the initial ground invasion, Madison sought to gain a naval advantage on the Great Lakes before trying again. Indeed, Madison had told Congress in late May that "the augmentation of our naval force . . . is in progress. On the lakes our superiority is near at hand."[65]

Privately, Madison had turned the corner, and was confident of success this time. On August 30, Dolley wrote to her close friend Hannah Galla-tin, who was in Europe with her husband, describing the president's defiant state of mind. "Mr. Madison says," Dolley wrote, "that though his enemies *imagine* they have prevailed *in a degree* against him, their machinations will treble his friends." Dolley predicted that eventual victory would "show him to the world as he really is, one of the best, as well as the greatest men."[66]

The key battle for control of the Great Lakes would take place on September 10, 1813. In the most dramatic naval engagement in American history to that time, Oliver Hazard Perry brought his flagship, USS *Lawrence*, into battle with the British fleet on Lake Erie. The *Lawrence* was named for Captain James Lawrence, who in June 1813 had been killed after losing a battle between his frigate, the *Chesapeake*, and a larger British frigate, HMS *Shannon*. Lawrence's dying words had been, "Don't give up the ship." Perry had the words sewn onto a battle flag and hoisted over the *Lawrence*.

The encounter with the British began badly for Perry, who nearly joined Lawrence in the pantheon of fallen captains. Subjected to a withering barrage for two and a half hours, the *Lawrence* was disabled and most of her crew injured. Perry now gave up the ship, and, bringing his battle flag with him, rowed to a surviving vessel, USS *Niagara*, where he assumed command. Risking everything on a single maneuver, Perry raised his flag and sailed the *Niagara* directly through the line of British ships, firing broadside from both port and starboard. The desperate technique worked, and Perry won the day. Perry sent news of his dramatic victory to Harrison in a message that began, "We have met the enemy, and he is ours."

Secretary of the navy William Jones told Madison the good news on September 21. Madison was thrilled by "the brilliant achievement of Perry."[67] Madison urged Jones to award a captain's commission to "the hero of Lake Erie," provided it could be done "consistently with rules not to be violated."[68] Perry's victory was the most important of the war, and Madison wanted to bring attention to it.

The opportunity now arose for victories on the ground to back up the one on Lake Erie. Madison had managed to rid himself of the ineffectual Henry Dearborn in July, relieving him of his command after getting reports that Dearborn was unwell.[69] Dearborn at first refused to accept the dismissal, insisting that "an officer of my grade" should not be removed from command except because of "the most obvious, unequivocal and outrageous misconduct."[70] Madison had good political reason to let

Dearborn save face.[71] A House committee had proposed to start an inquiry into "the causes which have led to the multiplied failures . . . on our western and northwestern frontier."[72] The last thing Madison wanted was for Dearborn to criticize Madison if called to testify. He offered Dearborn a command defending New York City. Dearborn accepted,[73] and Madison was finally free of Dearborn's military mediocrity.

Command of the invasion of Canada now shifted to William Henry Harrison. He would lead a combined army of militia from Ohio, Kentucky, Tennessee, Georgia, and New York. Monroe told Madison that Harrison's army was meant to be "so much superior to that of the enemy, as to leave no doubt of his success, especially after the command of the lake is secured."[74]

Seizing the advantage created by Perry's victory, Harrison moved on Detroit, only to find that British colonel Henry Procter had retreated in anticipation of his arrival. Tecumseh had forcefully urged Procter to stay and fight: "We must compare our father's conduct to a fat animal that carries its tail upon its back," Tecumseh reportedly said, "but when affrighted, it drops it between its legs and runs off."[75]

Tecumseh and his warriors accompanied Procter on his retreat from Detroit because they had no better option. Harrison chased Procter and caught him on the afternoon of October 4, 1813, at Moraviantown on the Thames River, some eighteen miles from Fort Malden outside Detroit. Harrison's forces outnumbered Procter's more than two to one. When the battle was joined the next morning, the Kentucky volunteers immediately broke the British lines. Procter fled the field with 250 of his men. The rest of the British regulars and militia surrendered.[76]

Tecumseh and his warriors stood and fought alone. They were charged by militia cavalry led by Richard Mentor Johnson, a Kentucky congressman who had joined the war effort and raised his own 1,000-man brigade. The Native American force repelled the charge from the middle of a swamp. Johnson received five separate wounds. In the fighting, someone, perhaps Johnson, struck Tecumseh with a bullet, felling him. With Tecumseh dead, his force retreated. Harrison's army celebrated by looting the pacifist Christian settlement at Moraviantown and burning it to the ground.

Tecumseh was the greatest Native American general ever to face the United States. For Johnson, the claim to have killed him became the defining element of his public reputation and a subsequent career that peaked as vice president to Martin Van Buren. Although the battle gave the United States control over the frontier around Detroit, Tecumseh's death was a far more important result. In his absence, the British lost the capacity to ally with an organized Native American force in the Northwest. Native Americans lost far more: the author of their alliance with an empire that wanted to contain American expansion westward. On receiving the news, Madison called it an "important success." He was confident that "the impression made . . . on the savages is what was to be expected; and will favor much the sequel of our operations on the Canada side of the war."[77]

Almost simultaneously, Madison heard that Commodore Isaac Chauncey had finally managed to find and fight the enemy on Lake Ontario, capturing four schooners and three hundred prisoners.[78] In Madison's estimation, this meant that the British must have withdrawn from the lake. From their base at Sackets Harbor, New York, on the eastern end of Lake Ontario, the American forces could now "cut off communication between the upper and lower portions of Canada." This would effectively place Ontario under American control, and it raised the possibility of an American assault on Montreal and Quebec City downriver.[79]

From Sackets Harbor, Secretary of War Armstrong reported to Madison that the British had fallen back on Kingston, just across the mouth of the St. Lawrence River that led to Montreal. Armstrong contemplated the British force at Kingston and what was left of the British fleet on Lake Ontario. He reported to Madison that "I have no doubt but that they will risk their fleet, to destroy our army." In Armstrong's view, "whether we succeed against Kingston or Montreal, the fleet must perish."[80]

Madison had believed that Harrison's victory at the Battle of the Thames and Chauncey's victory on Lake Ontario meant that the conquest of Canada was almost accomplished. Armstrong was making it clear that he did not agree. Harrison had not captured Procter, who was still trying to gather more troops. The British fleet on Lake Ontario was not completely eliminated. And winter was coming.

Armstrong decided to send his eight thousand troops from Sackets Harbor down the St. Lawrence River in small boats toward Montreal. They would rendezvous with an army of four thousand men that was supposed to come north from Plattsburgh, New York, under the command of Major General Wade Hampton, and make the assault on Montreal together.

Because Armstrong was the secretary of war, he could not lead the troops into battle. Instead the force out of Sackets Harbor was put under the command of General James Wilkinson—a highly problematic figure who had been for many years secretly in the pay of Spain and had taken part in Aaron Burr's conspiracy, preserving his career only by turning on Burr at the crucial moment. So limited was the pool of experienced generals that Wilkinson was still one of the highest-ranking officers in the entire U.S. Army.

The St. Lawrence campaign quickly became a debacle. Hampton moved first, heading north from Plattsburgh by boat and reaching Four Corners, New York, where his army stopped to wait for Wilkinson on the Chateauguay River. When Wilkinson did not appear, Hampton, concerned about dwindling supplies, decided to advance. At the Canadian frontier, the New York militia abandoned him, as they had done the previous year to Dearborn. Hampton's force was now 2,600 instead of 4,000.

The British responded by sending militia to block Hampton at a crossing of the Chateauguay. On October 25, Hampton sent 1,000 of his men to flank the British defense and take the ford. After they had gone, he received a letter from Armstrong telling him that Wilkinson had been put in charge of the Sackets Harbor troops, and instructing him to build quarters for 10,000 men to spend the winter.

Hampton interpreted Armstrong's letter to mean that Wilkinson would not be coming anytime soon. The whole plan of attack on Montreal was now in jeopardy. Hampton might have withdrawn immediately— except that he had just sent 1,000 of his men into battle. Instead he sent a letter of resignation to Armstrong, and sat down to see what would happen.

The detachment of Hampton's men encountered the British position on the Chateauguay River on October 26. In the battle that followed, 23 Americans were killed, with another 62 wounded or missing in action, and 16 captured. Hampton concluded that he could not take the objective. More important, he had already decided not to advance. He therefore retreated to Plattsburgh, where he had begun. The Battle of the Chateauguay was an ignominious failure.

Wilkinson did no better. After a long delay, he left Sackets Harbor and headed down the St. Lawrence River with his 8,000 men. When the British sent 900 men to chase them, Wilkinson deployed a reargaurd of 2,500 troops. The two sides met at Crysler's Farm on November 11, where the British repelled four American attacks.

Wilkinson's initial impulse was to continue toward Montreal. But the day after the battle, he received word from Hampton informing him of his decision to withdraw rather than wait for Wilkinson's army. The move ended Madison's hopes of conquering Lower Canada and winning the war before winter.

Wilkinson had survived treason and treachery. But this display of military incompetence was the final blow to his reputation and career. Armstrong held him responsible for the failure and relieved him of his command.

The crowning disaster of the St. Lawrence campaign followed almost immediately. After Wilkinson had decamped from Sackets Harbor, Armstrong ordered William Henry Harrison to take his troops from Fort George, where they had gone after the Battle of the Thames, and defend Sackets Harbor. This, in turn, left Fort George vulnerable.

Brigadier General George McClure, the American commander of Fort George, begged for New York militia to defend the Niagara frontier. But before reinforcements could arrive, McClure abandoned the fort in a panic, burning the adjacent Canadian town of Newark in his retreat.[81] A combined British and Native American force led by Procter, who had escaped from Harrison at the Thames, responded by taking Fort Niagara. Then the British retaliated by burning Buffalo, Lewiston, and other small settlements along the Niagara frontier. From Albany, a correspondent told Madison that "the panic which these events have spread in the inhabitants . . . is so great that they are abandoning their possessions and retiring to the interior."[82]

Slow in Its Movements

Madison had been achingly close to victory—and missed it. Although he left no direct record of his private thoughts, he must have been disappointed after his optimism at the start of the campaign. Dolley alluded to the glum state of affairs in the White House in a letter to Jefferson's daughter Martha. "It would be weak in me to tell and tiresome to you, to hear our *particular occupation* in this Great City," she wrote.[83] Once again,

Madison was now on the political defensive, preoccupied with finding a way to end the war. Dolley even reported a rumor that Federalists in Congress were going to impeach Madison on the charge of being too much under the influence of France.[84]

In his annual message to Congress, delivered in December 1813, Madison tried to accentuate the positive. "It would have been highly satisfactory" to report that the British had accepted the Russian offer of mediation, he said. But he had not heard anything from his delegation to St. Petersburg, and so the United States must continue to fight for its rights.

Madison then trumpeted Perry's victory on Lake Erie and Chauncey's on Lake Ontario. He praised Harrison's strategy and Johnson's leadership, and passed over the humiliation of the St. Lawrence campaign in a single sentence. "The prospect" of taking Montreal and Quebec City, "at one time so favorable, was not realized."[85]

In the conclusion to his message, Madison argued that the benefits of the war outweighed its costs. Although it had interrupted international commerce, the war had "cherished and multiplied our manufactures," functioning as a subsidy to domestic industrialization.[86] He also offered a constitutional excuse for the war's slowness: "Our free government, like other free governments, though slow in its early movements, acquires, in its progress, a force proportioned to its freedom." At the same time, he called on Congress to revise the militia laws. This amounted to an admission that the militia, that "great bulwark of defense and security for free states," was failing to function and had escaped national control.

Monroe blamed John Armstrong, the secretary of war, for the poor state of affairs. Reportedly Armstrong had told members of Congress that "the militia could not be relied on," a damaging acknowledgment of weakness.[87] Monroe summed up Armstrong's defects: "Indolent except for improper purposes, he is incapable of that combination and activity, which the times require."

The verdict was not surprising. "My advice to you therefore is to remove him at once," Monroe counseled.[88] "If continued in office," Armstrong "will ruin not you and the administration only, but the whole Republican Party and cause."[89] The concern for the party read as concern for Monroe's own future. He was the most probable next Republican presidential candidate, unless the war should succeed and Armstrong emerge as its hero.

Madison did not reply to Monroe. Possibly he believed that Monroe, who had sought an active role in command, was motivated by jealousy of Armstrong's importance in the war effort. If Armstrong were fired, Monroe was the only option to replace him—and Madison needed Monroe to continue as secretary of state. Madison left Armstrong in his job. Perhaps Madison made no attempt to replace Armstrong for the simple reason that he had no better option.

As 1813 came to an end, Madison faced the possibility that his entire war strategy had failed. From the outset, Madison had believed the conquest of Canada would assure British surrender. Yet two efforts had now been repulsed. In theory, the summer of 1814 offered a third chance. But Napoleon's disastrous Russian campaign meant that Britain might be able to send British regular forces to invade the Eastern Seaboard. If a serious attack came from that quarter, the United States was poorly positioned to defend against it.

Madison was, therefore, profoundly relieved when, in late December, word reached him that the British foreign secretary Lord Castlereagh had written to Monroe proposing direct peace negotiations. Castlereagh's offer had come before he had learned of the failure of the St. Lawrence campaign. The offer was a response to news of American dominance on Lake Erie and Lake Ontario.

Madison instructed Monroe to reply immediately, accepting the offer of direct negotiations to take place in Gothenburg, Sweden. Madison now wanted the war over, and was willing to consider any possible means to end it.

The Defense of a Wilderness

By late spring, Madison had decided not to renew the attack on Montreal or Quebec. Although the British had abandoned the attempt to defend most of Upper Canada, protecting only the territory to the east of Fort Erie, they had strengthened their defenses at Kingston on Lake Ontario.[90] Secretary of the Navy Jones wrote to Madison in late May arguing that it would be folly to use the navy in "the defense of a wilderness, while our Atlantic frontier—our flourishing cities, towns and villages, cultivated farms, rising manufactories, public works and edifices; are deprived of the services and protection of this valuable body of men."[91]

The British ground forces in Canada had sent Madison word through captured American general William Winder that they were interested in an armistice.[92] Madison was happy to consider the offer. But he acknowledged that the commander of the Royal Navy in Halifax would likely think different, and so the United States would have to brace for further attacks along the Eastern Seaboard. "The aggregate intelligence from Europe," Madison told Monroe, "warn us to be prepared for the worst measures of the enemy and to their worst forms."[93]

On June 7, 1814, Madison's cabinet met and decided to try to regain the offensive by attacking the upper Great Lakes.[94] Without opposition, the cabinet advised sending "4 or 5 vessels, and 800, or 1000 troops" to take a British depot that was believed to exist near Lake Huron, with a view to retaking Michilimackinac, at the upper tip of the Michigan peninsula.

With only Monroe expressing concern about the risk, the cabinet also decided that, if Chauncey could gain control of Lake Ontario, the United States could then once more take the capital of Upper Canada at York. The cabinet also decided to build armed barges at Sackets Harbor to harass communications along the St. Lawrence, and to "make demonstrations towards Montreal, as a diversion of the enemy from operations westward."[95] Madison's notes of the meeting made no mention of any discussion of further defense of the Eastern Seaboard—or of Washington.

As the summer of 1814 began, then, Madison, ever rational, understood the strategic situation of the war in terms of Britain's conflicting interests. On the one hand, as the result of victories over Napoleon, Britain would now have more troops available for an invasion of the United States. On the other, Britain still had an economic interest in making peace.[96]

Some offensive action was necessary, and Madison had not wholly given up on trying to invade Canada a third time. But chastened by previous failures, he no longer viewed that objective as inevitably successful. For the most part, he understood that the United States could do little but wait—for a British offensive or a British peace initiative, whichever was coming.

CHAPTER SIXTEEN

Failure and Redemption

...

THE ARGUMENT: *Battle-hardened British veterans of the Peninsular War against Napoleon march on an undefended Washington. At the brief battle of Bladensburg, Madison watches as hastily organized militia flee the field. The city is sacked.*

Madison shows leadership in returning quickly to the capital and restoring government. The embarrassment of the temporary loss of the city is mitigated by the successful defense of Baltimore and Plattsburgh.

The failure of the British assaults leads the British prime minister to ask the Duke of Wellington to take command of the war effort. Wellington advises that victory is impossible without naval control of the Great Lakes, and recommends a peace treaty. A deal is struck at Ghent.

Remarkably, Madison emerges from the war as a hero. He leaves his presidency with the country entering a nonpartisan era of good feelings, his constitutional design triumphant.

TWO YEARS INTO THE WAR, Madison did not expect the British naval harassment to escalate into full-scale invasion or an attempt to take Washington. The Revolutionary War had demonstrated that the British Army could not hope to hold populated territory within the United States. The capital, whose location had been fixed by political compromise, had no inherent strategic value.

Madison's view was based on his typically calm, dispassionate judgment. So far, the British had fought the war according to highly rational principles. Their professional officers had conducted a model defense, working alongside Canadian militia and Native Americans. The atrocities and pillaging that had taken place had been mostly on the U.S. side.

It was in the British interest to end the war, as the British peace initiative showed.

Others, however, took the danger of invasion seriously. James Barbour, the governor of Virginia, wrote to Madison in June 1814 that one of the "possible consequences" of "the revolution which has recently occurred in Europe" was that Great Britain could "strike any part of our Atlantic frontier with impunity. She can penetrate deep into our interior and the capital itself must fall, without some preliminary preparation."[1]

Madison wrote back to Barbour observing hopefully that Britain might "be restrained" from invasion because of "an estimate of her interest in making peace." Nevertheless, Madison told Barbour, "it is incumbent on us . . . to be prepared as well as we can, to meet the augmented force which may invade us." The preparations, Madison went on, had two components: regular troops and militia. Regular forces would be "applied in a way, deemed most conducive to the public safety." The clear implication was that Barbour, a state governor, would have nothing to do with the deployment of federal troops.

The state militia was the second component of defense. Should it be called up immediately in anticipation of a possible attack? Madison's answer was no. He had "no information either as to the amount, or the particular destination of forces that may be sent against us." Given that, he reasoned, "an immediate call of militia into service" would be a mistake because it "would waste a resource on which eventually everything may depend." Calling the militia too soon would also "rapidly exhaust our pecuniary means." The solution was to wait and see where the attack might come.[2]

Madison was right that deploying militia would be costly, but as Barbour had intimated, it was not hard to guess what Britain's targets of invasion might be. British forces had been harassing the Chesapeake watershed since the war began. The capital at Washington was important symbolically, and the port of Baltimore was important strategically. Madison's cabinet should have brought this point to his attention if he did not see it himself. But the cabinet's combination of internal divisions and (except for Monroe) mediocrity distracted it from playing the advisory role Madison needed.

Madison remained focused on negotiating a peace with Britain, to the apparent exclusion of all else. In an extended cabinet meeting on June 23 and 24, 1814, the secretaries of war and navy, John Armstrong and William Jones, both said they would accept a peace treaty "silent on the subject of impressment." Monroe was willing take a treaty in which the British would disclaim impressment "limited to a certain period." George Campbell, who had replaced Albert Gallatin as secretary of the treasury, agreed.* Only attorney general Richard Rush objected to a treaty that would defer impressment and commerce "to a separate negotiation."[3]

Three days later, on June 27, Madison called the cabinet together once again. This time he shared a letter from Gallatin and James Bayard, part of the delegation sent to negotiate with Britain. The letter argued that the British government would not renounce impressment, while the British public would enthusiastically support a renewed assault on the United States.[4] Shaken, Monroe and Campbell now agreed that they would accept a treaty, even one that did not mention impressment.[5] The cabinet was desperate for peace.

Defense

On July 1, 1814, the cabinet finally took up the question of defending Washington. The members tallied the available troops, which came to about three thousand regular army forces and a theoretical force of ten thousand militia "to be designated and held in readiness."[6] The next day, Madison directed Armstrong, the secretary of war, to "digest and report to the president, corresponding precautionary means of defense." The idea was to defend the Atlantic ports using militia who would be called up by "the governors of the several states," a plan similar to the one that had been adopted at the cabinet meeting for Washington and Baltimore.[7]

Privately, however, the cabinet was divided on the seriousness of the threat of invasion. George Campbell, the new secretary of the treasury, told Monroe that he believed "no danger whatever existed" because "Great Britain would send very few men here."[8] Monroe thought otherwise. "It would be safest to act on the presumption, that the dangers which are possible, will occur," he wrote at the time. Monroe suggested calling Congress into special session "for the purpose of providing more

* Gallatin had finally been confirmed by the Senate, this time as a delegate to negotiate with Britain.

ample funds, preventing exportation of specie from the country, establishing a national bank, and doing everything that will give energy to the government and success to the war." The effect of these actions would be to strengthen the federal government by rallying "the passions of the people" in this moment of insecurity.[9]

Madison adopted a middle position between Campbell and Monroe, writing to Elbridge Gerry that it was "impossible to divine the course" that the British cabinet would choose. Britain's "sober interests" called for ending the war; but the "passions of the moment" might call for an invasion. If Britain attacked, Madison expected, "we can see nothing before us but another combat, *pro aris et focis*"—a war to defend the very homes and hearths of the American people.[10]

Despite his awareness of the stakes, Madison did not order further steps in defense of the Chesapeake. Instead he turned to his secretary of war, with whom he was becoming increasingly frustrated.

Armstrong had consolidated regiments without telling the president. He had approved medical regulations that required a presidential signature—and Madison had first learned of them in the newspaper. Most significant, Armstrong had issued "instructions to military commanders relating to important plans and operations" without informing Madison at all.[11]

On August 13, 1814, Madison wrote Armstrong a scathing letter in which he found it necessary "to make some remarks on the relations in which the head of the department stands to the president, and to lay down some rules for conducting the business of the department."[12] Madison was reminding Armstrong—fully two years into the conflict—that the secretary of war had to submit important military decisions for the president's review. Knowing what needed advance approval would "be facilitated by the confidence between the executive and the head of the department."[13] But that confidence was lacking.

In a tone of rebuke, Madison then laid out ten numbered rules for Armstrong to follow in the future, each one specifying what orders must be reviewed by the president before being issued. He added that "of course" communications containing military intelligence should be sent to him "immediately." It should not have been necessary to spell out these rules, Madison implied. The only reason not to fire the secretary of war was the possibility of imminent British attack on Washington.

Washington Is Their Object

The British could take either or both of two river routes to Washington. The direct route was the Potomac, which could be followed upriver past Alexandria and branched into two forks just below the spot where the capital had been built. The alternative was the Patuxent River, which could be followed north until the soldiers would have to march west to Washington, crossing the eastern branch of the Potomac (now called the Anacostia River) at Bladensburg, Maryland. The Potomac route was speedier; the Patuxent, stealthier.

On August 18, 1814, five days after Madison's letter of reprimand to his secretary of war, barges carrying nearly 4,500 British troops entered the Patuxent River and began to row upstream. Many of them were British regulars, veterans of the Peninsular War in Spain; others were marines. All were experienced and well trained. The next day, August 19, they were at Benedict, Maryland, thirty-eight miles overland from Washington. Despite the short distances, it was not easy for Madison to gain intelligence on the British movements, because no effective means of communicating had been established. At the crack of dawn on August 20, Monroe rode out to Benedict to do his own reconnaissance.

He arrived at eight in the morning, and at one o'clock p.m. wrote to Madison that the enemy had landed. He had seen the British boats from afar, "but being at the distance of 3 miles, and having no glass, we could not count them." The British were, he believed, "still debarking their troops," but he could not obtain "any satisfactory information" of their number. "The general idea also is that Washington is their object, but of this I can form no opinion at this time," Monroe wrote. The nearby cities of Georgetown and Alexandria, both on the Potomac, also were potential targets. Nonetheless, a last-minute defense should be mounted.[14]

The defense of Washington was under the command of Brigadier General William Winder, whose six thousand men were almost entirely local militia rapidly called into service over the previous two months. As late as Saturday evening, August 20, Winder did not know where the enemy was. Returning from the eastern branch of the Potomac below Washington, he told Madison, he had passed "a dragoon coming express from Col. Monroe." The messenger told him that "he had no letter for me but that he bore one for you"—Monroe's early afternoon message.

Because it was addressed to Madison, not Winder, the commanding general did not read it, but he did beg the president for "any intelligence communicated to you which may be useful for me to know."[15]

The president passed on Monroe's information to Winder as soon as he got it. He wrote back to Monroe the next morning, August 21, that more calls for militia were under way, "and we hope they will be prompt." American troops "in general will be raw, though numerous," he wrote. He advised that "the true course will be to pelt the enemy from the start, with light troops, taking advantage of grounds and positions for artillery, and throwing in all sorts of obstructions in the routes."[16] This was good tactical advice—provided the enemy could be found and the militia organized to meet them.

Still in search of the British, Monroe set off on the morning of August 21 to ride the main road from Benedict to Washington. Having gone twelve miles from Benedict, he found "that no troops have passed in this direction." Monroe sent a message to Madison concluding, correctly, that instead of heading directly for Washington, the British were continuing north along the Patuxent River, where they would confront a small flotilla of U.S. boats at Pig Point—just twenty-four miles from the capital.[17] Monroe told Madison that he would head in that direction via the hamlet of Nottingham and report back. He still "had no means of forming a correct estimate" of the British troop strength.[18] The president of the United States was facing an invasion of the capital—and his only reliable source of intelligence was his secretary of state, acting as a scout.

As Monroe arrived in Nottingham that evening, the small guard of Americans at the town's entrance suddenly saw the British troops advancing on the settlement. "We observed it, at the precise moment when our retreat was still practicable," Monroe wrote to Madison at eleven o'clock that night. "I left, as the enemy entered," he reported.[19]

Monroe assessed the British force as "between 800 and 1000 men in the barges," but he did not know how many were on foot. Monroe also reported that there was a separate convoy of men and barges on the Potomac River to the east. "The movement in the two rivers is doubtless combined," he surmised. Without any useful intelligence, he could not rule out the possibility of a two-pronged attack. Still, Monroe ended his late-night communication hopefully. "The difficulty" was to find and engage the enemy, but "if they can be checked, we must destroy them, and we surely can check them."[20]

At five o'clock in the morning on August 22, Madison wrote back to Monroe. Ascribing his own characteristic prudence to the British generals, Madison expressed surprise that the enemy "should venture on an enterprise to this distance from the shipping," especially if the British were "without cavalry." Nevertheless, Madison acknowledged that the enemy "may however count on the effect of boldness and celerity on his side, and the want of precaution on ours."[21]

Madison's extreme calm reflected his measured disposition and his penchant for weighing risks in the light of experience. To this point in the war, Madison and his generals had behaved with the utmost caution. Their British counterparts, shorthanded and on the defensive, had been similarly careful to avoid any major confrontation, given superior American numbers. But the attack up the Patuxent was unlike anything Madison had seen before. The daring maneuver was being led by Major General Robert Ross, who had risen from lieutenant colonel over six years of service in the brutal and bloody Peninsular War. Wounded leading his troops into fire just six months earlier at the Battle of Orthez, Ross had earned the respect of his veteran army. And he knew that no American force would compare to the French enemy the British had defeated on the Iberian Peninsula.

At ten o'clock that morning, Madison wrote to Monroe surveying the situation as he understood it. "I fear not much can be done more than has been done, to strengthen the hands of Gen. Winder," he wrote. "As fast as succours [that is, reinforcements] arrive here they will be hastened on" to the defenses. "But the crisis I presume will be of such a short duration, that but few even from the neighboring country will be on the ground before it is over."[22] Faced with an impending invasion of the capital and his own potential capture, Madison remained as cool and logical as ever.

As Madison was writing, the British were marching to Upper Marlboro, sixteen miles from the capital. "Our troops were on the march to meet them," Monroe reported to Madison, "but in too small a body to engage."[23] At Pig Point, the small American flotilla was overmatched. The American sailors burned their boats and withdrew. Before sending his letter to Madison on the evening of August 22, Monroe added a postscript: "Monday 9 o'clock," he wrote. "You had better remove the records."[24]

Stronger than Had Been Reported

On the morning of August 22, Madison rode out from Washington to meet General Winder and his troops. Madison had no experience of battle but did not shrink from confronting it.

Dolley described the scene of his departure in a letter she wrote the next day to her sister Lucy and may later have edited. Madison "inquired anxiously whether I had courage, or firmness to remain in the president's house until his return, on the morrow, or succeeding day." Dolley replied bravely "that I had no fear but for him and the success of our army." Madison then "left me, beseeching me to take care of myself, and of the cabinet papers, public and private."[25]

Madison spent the night with the troops on the eastern branch of the Potomac. By the next day, Tuesday, August 23, 1814, Madison was still trying to get a sense of the British strength—and to calculate what their next move would be. "The reports as to the enemy have varied every hour," he wrote to Dolley. "The last and probably truest information is that they are not very strong, and are without cavalry and artillery, and of course that they are not in a condition to strike in Washington." Madison explained calmly that "you will not see me this morning" if there was an attack, but that "I hope I shall be with you in the course of" the day, "perhaps later in the evening." He signed himself, "Your devoted husband."[26]

As the day progressed, Madison, still collected, reevaluated the probability of an attack. He sent a second note to Dolley, written hastily in pencil. This time he told her "that the enemy seemed stronger than had been reported and it might happen that they would reach the city, with the intention to destroy it." He therefore urged her to "be ready at a moment's warning to enter my carriage and leave the city."

Dolley made sure she was ready. She "pressed as many cabinet papers into trunks as to fill one carriage," and she told her sister that "Our private property must be sacrificed, as it is impossible to procure wagons for its transportation." The First Lady could not get wagons because every conveyance in Washington was now in use by the residents fleeing the anticipated arrival of British troops. "My friends and acquaintances are all gone," Dolley wrote.[27]

The capital was approaching a full panic. Yet Dolley, having prepared for a hasty departure, settled down bravely to wait for Madison. "I am determined not to go myself until I see Mr. Madison safe, and he can accompany me," she wrote to Lucy. She was concerned for Madison's safety not so much from the British as from angry residents of Washington. "I hear of much hostility towards him," she told her sister. "Disaffection stalks around us." A company of one hundred men "who were stationed as a guard in the enclosure" near the president's house had abandoned their posts.[28]

On the morning of Wednesday, August 24, Madison received an express note that General Winder had sent to Secretary of War Armstrong asking for "the speediest counsel." Passing the note along to Armstrong, Madison went to Winder's headquarters. He was soon joined by Monroe; William Jones, secretary of the navy; and Richard Rush, the attorney general. Winder told Madison that they had received "certain intelligence that the enemy" was headed for Bladensburg. With the agreement of the cabinet, Monroe left immediately to coordinate a defense. An hour passed. Winder "was at the moment setting off to hurry on the troops to Bladensburg," Madison later recalled, when George Campbell, the secretary of the treasury, arrived, followed by Armstrong.[29]

Someone, probably Madison, asked Armstrong "whether he had any arrangement or advice to offer in the emergency." Armstrong, incredibly, said he had nothing to recommend. Then he made the unhelpful observation "that as the battle would be between militia and regular troops, the former would be beaten."[30]

As the men left the house to mount their horses, Campbell, speaking indirectly, said to Madison "that he was grieved to see the great reserve of the secretary of war . . . who was taking no part on so critical an occasion." Campbell then explained that Armstrong was holding his tongue because "the means of defending the district had been committed to Gen. Winder," and, in a clear reference to Madison's letter in August, he did not want "to intrude his opinions without the approbation of the president."

Madison was astonished. The capital was in jeopardy, and Armstrong was sulking.[31] It is a mark of Madison's self-control that, with an enemy army minutes away, he took the time to address his petulant secretary of war and coax him into participating in the defense. The president turned his horse to Armstrong, and "expressed to him my concern and surprise, at the reserve he showed at the present crisis." He told Armstrong that he hoped the "paper of instructions"—Madison's letter—did not "restrain him in any respect from the exercise of functions belonging to his office."

Madison ordered Armstrong to "proceed to Bladensburg, and give any aid to Gen. Winder that he could." If "any difficulty on the score of authority should arise, which was not likely, I should be near at hand to remove it." Armstrong, apparently satisfied, said he would go to Bladensburg "and be of any service to Gen. Winder he could."[32]

Madison went immediately to the marine barracks to see Jones, the secretary of the navy, and then set out for Bladensburg. His plan was to bring the whole cabinet together there, meet with Winder, and figure out what to do. Madison was riding into the battle, not away from it.

Attorney General Rush at his side, Madison rode to Bladensburg, only to discover that "Winder was not there and that the enemy were entering it." Narrowly avoiding the British, Madison found Monroe, Winder, and Armstrong. He told Armstrong that this was his chance to give Winder advice. As Madison later recalled, "the unruliness of my horse prevented me from joining in the short conversation that took place" between Armstrong and Winder. "When it was over," Madison asked Armstrong whether he had made any recommendations. He said that he had not.[33]

A Lack of Spirit

Before Winder and Monroe had arrived at Bladensburg, a major general of Maryland militia named Tobias Stansbury had placed his forces there in a defensive posture on the western side of the eastern branch of the Potomac. This was already a mistake: Stansbury had commanded Lowndes Hill, a much better location on the eastern side of the river, but had withdrawn overnight after learning of Winder's retreat. With no time to dig a fortification of his own, Stansbury took advantage of an existing earthwork, which provided some protection. But it had been dug for larger artillery than he had, thus restricting his guns' field of fire. Stansbury deployed his ragtag, hastily called-out militia to the south of the earthwork. In principle they were supposed to defend the artillery. In practice, they were too far away for the job, and exposed to British fire.

When Winder and Monroe arrived on the morning of August 24, they each tried to improve the tactical situation by moving militia units to different places than Stansbury had done. The amateurism of the entire effort cannot be overstated. Until 1812, Winder had been a lawyer. Monroe had not served a military function in thirty years, and as secretary of state, he was not in the chain of command.

The Americans had some six thousand men in the field. But those in the front lines did not realize that a militia raised in the District of Columbia had arrived and was gathered a mile behind them, nor did they realize that a small corps of sailors and marines under Joshua Barney had also arrived in reinforcement.

Back in Washington, Dolley had spent the morning "since sunrise . . . turning my spyglass in every direction and watching with unwearied anxiety, hoping to discern the approach of my dear husband and his friends." At noon, she noted, "alas, I can descry only groups of military wandering in all directions, as if there was a lack of arms, or of spirit to fight for their own firesides!"[34] The disorder Dolley observed reflected the fact that there was no fallback plan to protect the city. The entire American defense was concentrated at Bladensburg.

The Battle of Bladensburg began at one in the afternoon, with Madison as commander in chief present and watching. Wave after wave of disciplined British soldiers crossed the river in the face of considerable fire. Although the advancing troops took casualties—a total of 64 dead and 185 wounded—they had soon broken the first two American lines.

Stunned by the advance, and frightened by Congreve rockets that the British were firing, the militia fled. Barney's corps of sailors and marines alone held their ground. But when they, too, were abandoned by supporting militia, they were overrun.

By four o'clock, the battle was over. The Americans had lost only a few dead, perhaps 21, and another 50 wounded. The smallness of the losses demonstrated the completeness of the American flight. Nothing more stood between the British and Washington. Madison stayed until "it became manifest that the battle was lost." Then he and Rush "fell down into the road leading to the city and returned to it."[35]

At three o'clock in the afternoon, Dolley was still in Washington. "Will you believe it, my sister?" she wrote to Lucy. "We have had a battle or skirmish near Bladensburg, and I am still here within sound of the cannon!" Madison had sent "two messengers covered with dust" telling Dolley to flee; but still she waited.[36] She told her family later that "she seemed to have lived a life-time while waiting . . . for the return of her husband." Her "fear that he would be taken prisoner amounted to agony!"[37]

According to an account written later by Paul Jennings, born into slavery at Montpelier in 1799 and now, at the age of fifteen, working at the president's house, "Mrs. Madison ordered dinner to be ready at three, as usual."[38] Jennings "set the table myself, and brought up the ale, cider, and wine, and placed them in the coolers, as all the cabinet and several military gentlemen and strangers were expected."[39]

"At just about three," Jennings recalled, "as Sukey, the house servant, was lolling out of a chamber window," another messenger from the battle arrived. This was James Smith, "a free colored man who had accompanied Mr. Madison to Bladensburg." Smith "galloped up to the house, waving his hat, and cried out, 'Clear out, clear out! Gen. Armstrong has ordered a retreat!'"[40]

Jennings remembered that "all then was confusion." Dolley "ordered her carriage, and passing through the dining room, caught up what silver she could crowd into her old-fashioned reticule, and then jumped into the chariot with her servant girl, Sukey, and Daniel Carroll, who took charge of them."[41]

Dolley described a similar course of events. She managed to get a wagon and "filled it with the plate and most valuable portable articles belonging to the house," she reported. Dolley intended to send the valuables to the Bank of Maryland. "Whether it will reach its destination . . . or fall into the hands of British soldiery, events must determine," she explained.[42]

Dolley also ordered the Gilbert Stuart portrait of Washington removed for safekeeping. Charles Carroll, a friend of hers (whom Jennings remembered as Daniel Carroll) arrived "to hasten my departure," she told Lucy, narrating in the present tense: Carroll "is in very bad humor with me because I insist on waiting until the large picture of Gen. Washington is secure, and it requires to be unscrewed from the wall." Eventually "this process was found to be too tedious for these perilous moments," she wrote. "I have ordered the frame to be broken, and the canvas taken out." Once this was done, the "precious portrait" was "placed in the hands of two gentlemen of New York, for safe keeping."[43]

Dolley left the city not only to escape a conquering army, but to avoid being trapped in a traffic jam of fleeing militia. "And now, dear sister, I must leave this house," she wrote, "or the retreating army will make me a prisoner in it, by filling up the road I am directed to take."[44] Her intended destination was Charles Carroll's house, Bellevue, in Georgetown. The sense of confusion was captured in a brief letter to Dolley sent by Anna Payne Cutts. "My Sister," Anna wrote, "Tell me for God's sake where you are and what [you are] going to do . . . we can hear nothing but what is horrible here—I know not who to send this to—and will say but little."[45]

Thomas Jefferson by Rembrandt
Peale, 1800. The first Republican
president—Madison's closest
friend in the world.

James Madison by
Gilbert Stuart, circa
1805–1807. The
scholar-statesman
with his books.

First Consul Bonaparte by Antoine-Jean Gros, 1802. Napoleon on the cusp of empire. His career would shape Madison's—and the world.

Born a slave, Toussaint Louverture led Haiti to freedom in history's most successful slave uprising and became governor and ruler of a nation. His confrontation with Napoleon ultimately brought the Louisiana territory into Madison and Jefferson's reach.

Margaret Bayard Smith by Charles Bird King, circa 1829. Journalist, social critic, novelist, intimate of presidential households. She left an extraordinary running account of the Madisons' partnership in their presidential milieu.

SMITHSONIAN INSTITUTE

Aaron Burr, attributed to Gilbert Stuart, circa 1793. The man who introduced Madison to Dolley; served as Jefferson's one-term vice president; tried to create a new Western breakaway republic; and killed Hamilton in a duel.

COLLECTION OF THE NEW JERSEY HISTORICAL SOCIETY/WIKIMEDIA COMMONS

Albert Gallatin by Gilbert Stuart, circa 1803. Swiss immigrant; financial genius; Republican leader; Madison's secretary of treasury and peace negotiator.

John Randolph by John Wesley Jarvis, 1811. Madison's scourge and congressional critic, a radical believer in the old Republican values. The Virginian Randolph wore boots and spurs on the House floor and affected a whip and dogs.

A letter from James Madison to Dolley, August 27, 1814. Madison and Dolley rarely chose to be apart in almost forty-two years of marriage. The few times they were, they wrote to each other multiple times a day.

LIBRARY OF CONGRESS

Capture and burning of Washington by the British, 1814. The low point of the War of 1812 and Madison's presidency, from which he rebounded remarkably quickly.

LIBRARY OF CONGRESS

Tenskwatawa by George Catlin, 1830. Brother of Tecumseh and known as the Prophet, he started and led a pan-tribal movement to reclaim Native American traditions, cultures, and religious beliefs.

Tecumseh by Benson John Lossing (from a pencil sketch by Pierre Le Dru), circa 1808. The greatest Native American general, and the last Indian leader with a credible strategy and chance to contain U.S. expansion. A British ally against Madison in the War of 1812.

John Armstrong by Rembrandt Peale, 1808. Madison's incompetent secretary of war, fired after the burning of Washington.

Paul Jennings, 1840s? and certainly before 1874. Born a slave at Montpelier, he served the Madisons in the White House and Montpelier. He later bought his freedom from Dolley and published an invaluable memoir describing the fall of Washington and Madison's death.

Dolley Madison and Anna Payne by Matthew B. Brady, circa 1848.
Dolley lived into the era of the daguerreotype. With her niece and
companion Annie Payne Cutts. Dolley's sister Mary Cutts wrote two
versions of a memoir of Dolley's life that relied heavily on family
traditions that seem likely to have come from Dolley's lips directly.

Madison reached the White House not long after Dolley had left. He found it deserted. As the French ambassador Sérurier reported to Talleyrand, the fleeing militia were flooding the town "in the greatest confusion." Madison tried to stem the flow, with "a firmness and constancy worthy of better success." Sérurier, who lived a few hundred feet from the president's house, had a clear view of the events from his front door. According to Sérurier, Madison "coolly mounted his horse, accompanied by some friends," and rode for the Little Falls bridge that would take him to Virginia.[46]

The British were expected at any moment. In Bladensburg, Ross gave his victorious and exhausted troops two hours' rest on the battlefield and marched for Washington at six o'clock. "In the meantime," Jennings later wrote, "a rabble, taking advantage of the confusion, ran all over the White House, and stole lots of silver and whatever they could lay their hands on."[47] In the lull between the flight of the U.S. government and the arrival of the British troops, the city was ungoverned.

By eight o'clock in the evening, the British had camped a quarter mile from the Capitol. Ross and a few of his officers rode into town, and someone fired at them from the northeast corner of Capitol Square. Ross's horse was shot from under him. He responded by ordering his soldiers to burn the house from which the shots had come.[48] Around nine o'clock, Ross ordered a detachment of his men to set fire to the Capitol itself. Ross was sending a clear message: The United States was now facing an adversary capable of winning the war, not just defending Canada.

According to Paul Jennings, who had left the president's house with Dolley and did not witness the events himself, "when the British did arrive" at the house, they found the meal set for Madison and his cabinet earlier in the afternoon. "They ate up the very dinner, and drank the wine, etc. that I had prepared for the president's party," Jennings wrote.[49] Admiral George Cockburn, who had led the harassment of the Chesapeake Bay for the past eighteen months, was present with Ross. According to legend, Cockburn himself offered an ironic toast to "Jemmy's health" as his officers drank.[50]

At eleven o'clock that night, Sérurier reported to Talleyrand in his dispatch, a British "colonel, preceded by torches, was seen to take the direction of the White House." Ross gathered all the Madisons' furniture into one room, the better to fuel the blaze. Shortly thereafter, the torches were used on the White House, which went up in flames. With the Capitol and the president's house on fire, the British then torched the War and Treasury departments.

The burning of Washington was temporarily paused by a thunderstorm. The next morning, Ross ordered the fires restarted. His troops began a methodical effort to destroy every government building. Exercising military restraint—and in the process demonstrating that the plan was intentional and coordinated—the British did not loot or burn private property.

At nine o'clock on August 25, 1814, some twenty-four hours after its arrival, the British Army marched out of Washington back toward Bladensburg. Ross had accomplished his objective. Washington could no longer function as the seat of government. Beyond that, holding the city had no strategic value, and there was no reason to remain. It was now time to return to the ships and prepare for the next step—which would logically be an attack on Baltimore.

Ross's troops marched all night, rested briefly, and marched again. Before dark on August 26 they were back to their barges at Upper Marlboro.

Hide Our Heads

On the night of the twenty-fourth, Dolley slept at the house of a Mrs. Love, "two or 3 miles over the river." In the morning, Dolley left Mrs. Love's, then "called in" at another house, and went upstairs.

Her anonymous hostess reflected the frustration of the citizens of Washington. "The lady of the house learning who she was, became furious," Jennings remembered Sukey, Dolley's enslaved servant, telling him. She "screamed out . . . 'Miss Madison, is that you, come down and go out, your husband has got mine out fighting, and damn you, you shan't stay in my house; so get out!'"[51] With little alternative, Dolley left.

On August 25, Dolley's safety at the front of his mind, Madison headed for Wiley's Tavern, some sixteen miles from the city, where he and Dolley were briefly reunited.[52] At the tavern, Madison heard rumors that the British were coming to capture him. At midnight, he fled, planning to cross the Potomac near Great Falls and join Winder at Montgomery, Maryland. The storms, however, had made the Potomac impassable in the dark. Charles Jared Ingersoll, a Republican congressman, recalled that

Madison and a few others sheltered for the night in "a hovel in the woods."[53]

The next day, August 26, Madison reached Montgomery at six in the evening, only to find that Winder and Monroe had already left, marching with the army in the direction of Baltimore. Madison then went to Brookeville, Maryland, ten miles away.

The next morning, August 27, Madison received word from Monroe "that the enemy were on their way to Marlboro, and recommending that we all repair to the city as soon as possible."[54] Madison wrote to his secretaries of war and navy—he could not know exactly where they were—directing them to come back to Washington.[55]

At the same time, Madison wrote to Dolley ("my Dearest") telling her of his plans to "set out" for Washington "immediately," and asking her to do the same. The president's house was no more. "I know not where we are in the first instance to hide our heads," Madison wrote to Dolley, "but shall look for a place on my arrival."[56]

Conditions in Washington were dangerous. Although the British troops had by and large followed orders that prohibited them from looting private property,[57] Washingtonians had begun stealing from one another even before the British arrived; they continued after the British had gone.[58] Mayor James H. Blake had fled the city in advance of the British arrival, and did not return until the twenty-sixth, the day after the British marched out. In the interim, there was no legal authority in the city.[59]

The power vacuum fed fears of slave revolt. On returning, Blake had called a public meeting at McKeown's Hotel on Pennsylvania Avenue to try to create order and prevent a slave uprising.[60] As Madison was planning to come back, Blake wrote to him that he had been "up all night patrolling the streets and guarding public and private property—collecting arms and ammunition." The nighttime patrols and the gathering of weapons were intended to establish the safety of the city against the people who served its white residents.

When Madison got back to Washington at five o'clock on August 27, he found a city that had been sacked, devastated by fire, and disordered almost to the point of anarchy. Nor was the attack fully over. As Madison arrived, Fort Washington on the Potomac, the only substantial fortification near the city, was under bombardment. This time the assault came not from Ross, but from the secondary force that the British had sent up the Potomac as a diversion. Contradicting his earlier letter, Madison now warned Dolley against returning because she might have to flee again, which "would have a disagreeable effect."[61]

Fort Washington did fall—and in embarrassing fashion. The fort was oriented toward the river and was vulnerable from the rear. Consequently, the commander had earlier been ordered by Winder to destroy the fortification if it was on the point of being overrun by Ross's ground forces. After Ross's army had gone, the commander blew it up anyway and retreated, rather than face bombardment.[62]

Fortunately for Madison, the British ships attacking from the Potomac had no intention of occupying the city, which was of no greater use to them than to Ross. The government buildings had already been burned. Yet the ships' presence represented the continuing threat of bombardment. Alexandria was the first settlement in the line of fire.

The Alexandria town council, acting on its own, wasted no time. Negotiating directly with the British, the council offered all the ships in the Alexandria harbor, as well as naval stores and merchandise, if the British would agree not to burn the town. The offer was accepted, and the British gained an extra 21 vessels, more than 15,000 pounds of flour, 800 hogsheads of tobacco, and 150 bales of cotton.[63]

Georgetown was equally undefended, and its citizens "were preparing to follow the example" of Alexandria, Monroe noted. That was not all. The citizens of Washington "were preparing to send a deputation to the British commander, for the purpose of capitulating," Monroe recorded. Winder had brought the army to Baltimore, where Ross could be expected to attack next, and no militia remained at the capital. "Never was there a time," Monroe wrote, "when greater promptitude, decision, and energy, were necessary."[64]

Madison rose to the occasion. He ordered Monroe to take command of Washington and provide for its defense. Told about the plan to send a delegation to surrender to the British, Madison "forbade the measure." The citizens objected that their situation "was deplorable." The residents feared "their houses might be burnt down" if they did not formally surrender to the second British force. Monroe told them "that he had been charged by the president with authority to take measures for the defense of the city. . . . If any delegation moved toward the enemy, it should be repelled by the bayonet."

Acting at Madison's behest, Monroe deployed artillery on both sides of the Potomac.[65] Madison was reasserting authority—his own and that of the U.S. government. The defeat had panicked the residents of the capital. But it had not shaken Madison, who now set about righting the ship of state.

A Short Distance Before Me

On the evening of August 29, while the British ships were still on the Potomac, Madison went to see Armstrong at his lodgings. The failed defense of the capital had determined the fate of the secretary of war. Madison was direct. He told Armstrong that in Washington, "violent prejudices were known to exist against the administration" for failing to protect the city. The anger was "particularly against" Madison and Armstrong "as head of the War Department," Madison said. Such militia as remained were especially enraged with Armstrong. Indeed, Madison told Armstrong that he had "within a few hours received a message from the commanding general of the militia informing" him "that every officer would tear off his epaulets, if General Armstrong was to have anything to do with them."[66]

Madison made it clear that he intended to replace Armstrong. The troops were willing to deal with Monroe, he explained, "who was very acceptable to them." The only "question was, what was best to be done. Any convulsion at so critical a moment could not but have the worst consequences."

Armstrong responded with some asperity. He was "aware of the excitement" against him, he said, which had been created by "intrigues." The "excitement was founded on the most palpable falsehoods," he insisted. He could not remain in Washington while Monroe exercised the functions of secretary of war. He offered to resign if "it was thought best," or alternatively he could "retire from the scene, by setting out immediately on a visit" to his family in New York. Madison advised Armstrong not to resign, since it would reflect badly on Armstrong and Madison alike. The president instead recommended withdrawal to New York, which "would avoid the existing embarrassment."[67]

With the question of what to do apparently settled, Armstrong went back to defending himself. Madison listened to Armstrong's bluster and outrage before calmly suggesting that if someone had to take the fall, it should be Armstrong. "I could not in candor say," Madison told him, "that all that ought to have been done had been done and in proper time."[68]

Madison's slow burn of frustration was accelerating. He now blamed Armstrong for the defeat. The secretary of war "had never appeared to enter into a just view either of the danger of the city . . . or of the consequences of its falling into the hands of the enemy," Madison intoned. Armstrong "had never himself proposed or suggested a single precaution or arrangement for its safety." Rather, "everything done on that subject [had] been brought forward by myself." Indeed, Madison claimed that the difference of opinion between them had led Madison to "a reduction of my arrangements to the minimum," to avoid being disobeyed.[69] This was a damning admission: Madison, the president, had lessened his own efforts to protect the capital because he doubted whether his secretary of war would execute his orders.

·Madison was certainly right that Armstrong had not lifted a finger to prepare the defense of Washington. At the same time, Madison was trying to deflect responsibility for the disaster. He was, after all, commander in chief. The failures of his secretary of war were his failures, too. The burning of the capital had made Madison realize—finally—that he could not both lead effectively and simultaneously keep the peace with an incompetent and recalcitrant subordinate.

It was characteristic of Madison that, having expressed his pent-up frustration, he immediately sought reconciliation. Madison told Armstrong "that it was not agreeable thus to speak." He had chosen Armstrong "from a respect to his talents, and the confidence that he would exert them for the public good." He reminded the secretary of war that he had "always treated him with friendliness and confidence." And Madison suggested that he would prefer not to fire Armstrong officially. "There was but a short distance" for Madison to go before the end of his "public career," the president observed. "My great wish, next to leaving my country in a state of peace and prosperity," he insisted, "was to have preserved harmony and avoid changes."[70]

Republican concord—symbolized by harmony within his administration—was always Madison's objective, even in this moment of extreme strain. Armstrong appeared to accept his guidance. Madison thought that they "parted as usual in a friendly manner."

Considering that Madison had relieved Armstrong and blamed him for the most visible military disaster in the nation's nearly forty-year history, this was wishful thinking. The next morning, Armstrong sent Madison word that he intended "to proceed immediately to visit his family" in New York, as Madison had suggested. But as soon as Armstrong reached Baltimore the next week, he sent Madison his resignation.[71] A public battle over responsibility for the fall of Washington was about to begin.

The Latest Disaster

Dolley made it back to Washington on August 28, 1814, where Madison found her at her sister Anna's house. With the ruins of the White House "still smoking," the two had to decide where to stay. At first they set up a temporary presidential residence at Anna's on F Street. Then they moved to Octagon House at Eighteenth Street and New York Avenue, just a couple of blocks from the White House. The home, which still stands, was owned by a Federalist, Colonel John Tayloe III, and, appropriately enough, designed by William Thornton, architect of the burned Capitol. The Madisons would spend a year there—and would never reoccupy the White House, which was not rebuilt until after Madison's presidency came to an end.[72]

Any personal relief that Madison felt on seeing Dolley home safe had to be made secondary to responding publicly to the national disaster. From Philadelphia, to which news of the burning of the city had traveled fast, Madison's old ally Tench Coxe reported that a prominent citizen had told him that "the catastrophe has arrived." The critic had not spared Madison, asserting that "the capture of our metropolis . . . ought to have been prevented and that he 'hoped to see the government brought to the block.'" Outraged and defensive, Coxe said, "I did not consider it as a catastrophe at all." He claimed that the British had used "a covert movement, by a back river." In any case, "the intrinsic value of Washington was politically little."[73]

This sort of denial was unlikely to succeed. Richard Rush, the attorney general, sent Monroe a draft document intended to get ahead of the story. "We should be prompt to tell of the act ourselves and in our own way, without holding back as if from shame," Rush recommended.[74] Rush emphasized that the British had acted "by a sudden incursion" and come with superior numbers. "Their possession of [the city] was but for a few hours," Rush wanted to say. Yet in that short time the British had, "against the usages of civilized warfare," destroyed public archives, "wantonly overturning monuments of taste and the arts that were nowise connected with military" purposes. Rush wanted to use the British depredations to appeal to public patriotism and raise morale.[75]

An alternative narrative was proposed by Secretary of the Navy William Jones. In a memorandum to Madison, Jones began by stating that the success of the attack was "strictly in the nature of surprise and cannot again happen." The public would soon recover "if it is seen that within ten days after a ruffian foe effected a destruction of the capital, all the functions of government are exercised with order, convenience, and tranquility on the same spot." Americans would be impressed by the rapid restoration of government, and the British enemy would "thus be robbed of the fruit of his enterprise and will have acquired nothing but the shame of his vandalism."[76]

Jones was offering excellent advice, which he followed with several pages of detailed recommendations. Congress should meet in the Patent and Post Office building, which the British had not burned. With great specificity, Jones laid out plans for defending the city going forward. "A plain, simple, cheap, and efficient work is all that is required" in the short term, he advised.[77]

Madison decided to issue a presidential proclamation in a tone of moral outrage as suggested by Rush, not Jones. At this low moment of the war, leadership required passion, not practicality. The burning of Washington, he declared, was unjustified under "the principles of humanity, and the rules of civilized warfare." The British were giving "the existing war the character of extended devastation and barbarism, at the very moment of negotiations for peace."[78] And Madison rejected British charges that the U.S. Army had committed "wanton destruction" in Upper Canada that justified retaliation, including the burning of York.

Poignantly, Madison received a reassuring note from Jefferson, who could not "withhold the expression of" his "sympathies." Jefferson alone understood that as president, "all you can do is to order, [and] the execution must depend on others, and failures be imputable to them alone." Jefferson was talking about Armstrong. Kindly—and doubtfully— Jefferson said, "Had General Washington himself been now at the head of our affairs, the same event would probably have happened." Jefferson closed his letter by offering to sell his collection of "9 or 10,000 volumes" of books to the Library of Congress to replace what had been lost when the British burned the Capitol.[79] For Madison, who had to bear the shame of the sack of Washington alone, the tenderness of Jefferson's letter was a reminder that his closest friend would not abandon him.

Baltimore

For Madison, the immediate challenge was now the defense of Baltimore, an essential harbor strategically located in the very middle of the country.

If the British could overcome the fort, break through the militia, and take the third largest city in the United States, there was nothing to stop them from repeating the exercise up and down the coast. During the Revolutionary War, only French intervention had protected the United States from Britain's superior naval power. This time there would be no assistance from France or anywhere else.

In theory, Brigadier General William Winder should have led the defense of Baltimore. But the inhabitants of the city, having observed Winder's failure at Bladensburg, wanted no part of him. A committee of Baltimore citizens, acting on its own authority, gave the defense of the city to Senator Samuel Smith, the brother of the former secretary of state and a longtime adversary of Madison's.

Monroe and Madison treated General Winder's subordination as a fait accompli—and Winder ended up commanding a small unit in Baltimore under the direction of Smith, the senator turned militia general. Monroe, who had assumed command of Washington, wrote to Madison that he was willing to give it up to Winder, to make up for Winder's repudiation by the Baltimore committee.[80] But Monroe did not really want to cede control, and knew Madison would not ask him to do so.[81]

The fight for Baltimore began on the night of September 11, 1814, as Admiral Cockburn landed General Ross's force of 4,700 men on the outskirts of the city. The battle was joined the next afternoon, September 12. Smith's defenses outside Baltimore were better than those Winder had managed to mount at Bladensburg. Ross led his troops from the front, and was killed by a rifle bullet in the chest. One of his lieutenants followed with a charge against the American center. Some of the militia fled, and the center retreated back to a position in front of the city's primary line of defense. But it held there. Twenty-four Americans were killed and 139 wounded. Fifty more were taken prisoner. The British suffered 345 fatalities. The assault was paused, and the British decided to try from the sea.[82]

The bombardment of Fort McHenry, famously witnessed from a British ship on the harbor by Francis Scott Key, began on the morning of September 13 and continued for nearly twenty-four hours. Unlike Fort Washington, Fort McHenry did not surrender its colors. The British made a final attempt at an amphibious assault on the night of the fourteenth. When that, too, failed, the British withdrew. Baltimore had been successfully defended by a combination of federal and militia troops and a soundly constructed fortification, steadfastly maintained.

The British gave up on the Chesapeake campaign.[83] Ross, the general who had masterminded it, was dead. Baltimore was the only prize worth having, and the British had failed to get it. In a message to Congress on September 20, Madison could brag that Baltimore had been successfully defended "by militia volunteers aided by a small body of regulars and seamen" and that the burning of Washington had "interrupted for a moment only the ordinary public business at the seat of government."[84]

Madison also benefited from another significant U.S. victory. On September 11, 1814, the United States had defeated the British in a dramatic naval engagement. The Battle of Plattsburgh, as it came to be known, marked a serious attempt by Sir George Prévost, the British commander in chief in North America, to launch offensive operations from the North. Prévost led an army of 11,000 men, many of them Peninsular War veterans, down the western side of Lake Champlain to take Plattsburgh, New York. They were met by 3,500 hastily gathered Vermont and New York militia, concentrated in three newly built forts.

In a naval battle on the lake, three U.S. warships, a sloop, and ten gunboats defeated a British flotilla of four warships and twelve gunboats. Over five days of fighting, Prévost's force suffered some two thousand casualties. Ultimately Prévost judged that, even if he could take Plattsburgh by land, he could not maintain his supply lines without control of the water—and he withdrew. The rebuffed invasion would turn out to have determinative significance.

The war remained unpopular with many, and Madison's leadership was now rebounding from the disaster at Washington. Yet addressing Congress less than a month after the Capitol had been burned, Madison could not help but acknowledge that "our enemy is powerful in men, and money; on the land, and on the water." The British enemy was "aiming, with his undivided force, a deadly blow at our growing prosperity, perhaps at our national existence." This was the first time Madison had ever said publicly that Britain might intend to reverse the effects of the Revolutionary War. In the past, Madison had called the War of 1812 a second war of independence in the sense that it aimed to achieve true American sovereignty on the seas. After the burning of Washington, Madison could plausibly suggest that American independence itself was at stake.

Monroe, his eyes on the future, wanted to be secretary of war. "The Department of War ought to be immediately filled," he wrote to Madison. "I think also, that I ought to take charge of it."[85] Madison agreed with alacrity, naming Monroe secretary of war within two days of receiving his letter. Monroe would be secretary of state and secretary of war at once, holding both positions until the spring of 1815.

Madison's hope still rested on reaching a negotiated peace with the British. The talks were going slowly. Madison told Jefferson about reports he had received from his negotiators in Ghent, sent roughly two months before. The British wanted to exclude American ships from fishing in parts of the Atlantic, and sought cession of a substantial part of Maine. They also wanted the United States to demilitarize the Great Lakes, while allowing British forces there. The commissioners had been "in perfect harmony of opinion on the arrogance of such demands," Madison recounted. He predicted that his representatives would leave Ghent without a treaty. "Nothing can prevent it," he told Jefferson, "but a sudden change in the British cabinet not likely to happen."[86]

Had Madison possessed up-to-date information about the negotiations, he would not have been any more optimistic. As Madison was writing to Jefferson, Dolley's son John Payne Todd was reporting from Ghent, where he had accompanied the U.S. negotiators to learn diplomacy. "The progress made in the negotiation would be seen to be not great; it has been conducted in a manner extremely dilatory," Todd told Madison. The British commissioners repeatedly went back to their superiors before replying to any American initiative, suggesting that they lacked authority. Todd feared, however, that they were acting "from an intention to procrastinate the negotiation in order to give time to expeditions against the United States to act."[87] The United States hoped for a peace treaty; the British still thought they could win.

Secret Treason

In New England, public condemnation of the war continued to grow. In mid-October 1814, the Massachusetts legislature voted to call the other New England states to participate in a convention in Hartford, Connecticut. The purposes of the convention were stated carefully. It would make proposals for the collective self-defense of the northeastern states, and it would suggest new constitutional amendments of common interest.

The idea of a convention was a provocation to the federal government, to Madison personally, and to the Republican Party. Massachusetts was not formally advocating secession or a separate peace with Britain. But wartime conditions coupled with the geographical restriction of the convention strongly suggested that a regionalist solution to the war was possible.[88] In the Northeast, opposition to the war was so strong that the public might be prepared to accept the end of the union in exchange for an end to the war and its economic costs.

Connecticut's legislature responded promptly, issuing a statement attacking the war as Madison's creation and nominating seven delegates to join the twelve who would come from Massachusetts. Rhode Island's legislature agreed to send four delegates—four more than it had sent to the constitutional convention in Philadelphia in 1787. The Vermont legislature refused to send delegates, but one Vermont county sent a delegate of its own. New Hampshire's legislature was not in session, but two New Hampshire counties sent delegates.

The Hartford convention was scheduled to meet on December 15, 1814. Its meetings would take place in secret. As Madison had reason to recall from the Philadelphia convention, secret proceedings allowed plentiful leeway for a convention to take a direction very different from the one proposed by the state legislatures that called it in the first place.

An extreme interpretation of the proposed Hartford convention came to Madison from Mathew Carey, an Irish-born newspaperman and printer who lived in Philadelphia. For several years, Carey had been writing letters to Madison warning of the potential dangers of Federalist opposition. Now he told Madison that "a conspiracy of the most treasonable kind has been maturing for years, whose object is the destruction of our form of government." He predicted that Federalist efforts would lead to "all the horrors of civil war, anarchy, and probably terminate in despotism, after the ruin of as fair a form of government as ever the mind of man conceived." And he expressed frustration with the way Madison seemed to "regard the whole with calm and philosophical tranquility, although every day brought the catastrophe nearer."[89]

Carey may have been overstating the threat, but he was certainly correct about Madison's attitude of "calm and philosophical tranquility." Madison was the first president to lead the United States into a declared war. Adams before him had signed the Sedition Act during the Quasi-War with France and used it to prosecute critics. Yet Madison showed no inclination whatever to punish antiwar beliefs or sentiments. Faced with a secret convention that might lead to secession, Madison took no steps to block it from happening.[90]

It is essentially impossible to imagine any subsequent wartime president—all of whom, without exception, engaged in at least some attempts to suppress opposition—allowing the Hartford convention to go forward. Madison's approach reflected his refusal to panic in the face of political challenge. It also resulted from his authorship of the First Amendment and his opposition to the Sedition Act as violating that amendment's guarantee of free speech. Madison would not violate the principles of liberty to save liberty itself.

Writing to Virginia governor-elect Wilson Cary Nicholas, Madison acknowledged that "the conduct of the eastern states" was "the source of our greatest difficulties in carrying on the war." Madison blamed antiwar opinion in New England on the region's traditional ruling class. "Their object is power," he wrote. "If they could obtain it by menaces, their efforts would stop there. These failing, they are ready to go to every length for which they can train their followers."[91]

Despite this frank assessment, Madison would not accept the theory that the Hartford convention could lead to secession. It was simply too unrealistic when seen from the standpoint of power-hungry New England leaders. "Without foreign cooperation," he reasoned, "revolt and separation will hardly be risked." If they attempted "so profligate an experiment," the leaders would have to confront the unpredictable effects on the rest of the public. As a result, "the best may be hoped, but the worst ought to be kept in view."[92]

The analysis was vintage Madison. He had no illusions about his opponents' motivations. Yet he attributed rationality to their efforts. He thus reached the conclusion that they could not be as dangerous as others believed. "In the meantime," Madison concluded, "the course to be taken by the government is full of delicacy and perplexity." This, too, was a characteristic assessment of Madison's own objectives. Where others would have acted aggressively, he preferred delicacy. And where others saw simplicity, he recognized that complex circumstances required deep thought.

Madison waited until early January to react to the convention. On January 9, 1815, he told Monroe that it would make sense to organize a volunteer "force in the East to repel the enemy, and put rebellion down."[93] The next evening, Monroe met with Brigadier General Robert Swartwout and sent him to Springfield, Massachusetts, "for the purpose of gaining correct intelligence of the real designs and intended movements of the Hartford convention."[94] Separately, Madison sent Colonel Thomas Jesup to Connecticut to keep watch over the Hartford convention, authorizing him to use New York militia to quell any attempt at rebellion.[95]

Ultimately, Madison's cautious assessment proved prescient. The convention did call for a collective self-defense arrangement to be created among New England states and paid for by taxes raised within those states. This was a challenge to the federal authority to provide for the common defense.

The convention's final resolution was its most pointed. If "peace should not be concluded and the defense of these states should be neglected, as it has been since the commencement of the war," the delegates declared, then another convention should be held in Boston the following June. The delegates to that convention should be invested "with such powers and instructions as the exigency of a crisis so momentous may require." The threat of a further convention echoed the resolutions of the abortive Annapolis convention of 1786, where Hamilton had saved the day by proposing a further convention to be held next year in Philadelphia.[96] The implication was that, if the war did not end soon, the New England states would discuss secession or a separate peace.

Yet the convention did not openly call for the breakup of the union. Its wait-and-see attitude reflected confidence that dissatisfaction would only continue to grow. No simple solution was available to Madison except for the one proposed by the Hartford convention itself: to bring the war to an end.

Madison had every reason to want the war over. As usual, his feelings were expressed best by Dolley. At the end of December, Dolley wrote optimistically to Hannah Gallatin, whose husband was negotiating with the British at Ghent, "I *will yet* hope we may have no more war." But Dolley was also, like Madison, genuinely unsure about the course of events. "If we do" have more war, she continued "alas—alas we are not *making* ready, as we ought to do. Congress trifle away the most precious of *their days*—days that ought to be devoted to the defense of their *divided* country." The division of which Dolley spoke had indeed reached its maximum point. And she did not exaggerate when she described Congress's inaction. Like Madison, Congress was waiting to see if the negotiations in Ghent could succeed.

Ghent

Fortunately for Madison, the talks did succeed. On December 24, 1814, the American delegation of Gallatin, John Quincy Adams, James Bayard, and House Speaker Henry Clay reached agreement with their British counterparts. The Treaty of Ghent restored the status quo that existed before the war. It made no mention of impressment, nor of the orders-in-council, which had been repealed just as war was being declared. The treaty provided for the restoration of land, property, and prisoners. All remaining disputes would be submitted to a commission that would be created for the purpose. Both sides promised to make peace with any Indian tribes with whom they had been at war. The two sides also agreed on a nonbinding provision that condemned the slave trade as "irreconcilable with the principles of humanity and justice" and called for both sides to use their "best endeavours" to bring about "its entire abolition."

The Americans had strong reasons to welcome the treaty. Madison's original war aim had been to reverse British restrictions on U.S. shipping from the Caribbean to the European continent. The end of the Napoleonic Wars meant that such restrictions would be over. Impressment of sailors had become an important rhetorical and symbolic goal to justify a war that was based on economic interest. Peace in Europe meant that impressment, too, would now become a thing of the past.

The burning of Washington had shown that the United States was vulnerable to costly counterattack. Repeated efforts had shown that the United States could not conquer Canada. On the Great Lakes, the U.S. Navy had failed to achieve complete naval dominance, and Royal Navy ships remained on Lake Ontario. Now that Britain could spare troops and ships, the initiative had shifted.

The British decision to sign the treaty was more complicated. By the fall of 1814, the British public had no desire to keep fighting. But the key factor was the Battle of Plattsburgh. When news of Prévost's retreat had reached England in October, Lord Liverpool, the prime minister, decided to appoint the Duke of Wellington, victor in the Peninsular War, commander of North American forces. Wellington replied that he had "no objection to going to America," but he warned Liverpool that Prévost had been right to retreat from Plattsburgh. Without control of the Great Lakes, Wellington wrote, "it is impossible, according to my notion, to maintain an army in such a situation as to keep the enemy out of the whole frontier, much less to make a conquest."[97] If named as commander, he would be going to America "to sign a peace which might as well be signed now."[98]

Wellington advised Liverpool to negotiate a return to the status quo before the war, because, strictly speaking, the British had made few gains. Even if Britain "had territory, as I hope you soon will have New Orleans," Wellington recommended negotiating for Louisiana separately.[99] The analysis had a decisive influence on Lord Liverpool. The greatest British general of the age was telling the prime minister to sign a treaty. Within six weeks of Wellington's letter, the deal at Ghent had been reached and the treaty signed. When the Battle of Waterloo happened the following June, Wellington would be there—not invading New York from Canada.

New Orleans

Madison did not know that the Duke of Wellington had saved him. Neither the British nor the American forces even knew the war was—at least on paper—over. Instead Madison watched with trepidation as plans for the British invasion of New Orleans advanced. The United States had no significant naval defense there. The citizens of the Louisiana Territory had become Americans only recently, and their loyalties were unlikely to be deeply felt. This, after all, was where Burr had hoped to create a separate nation just a decade earlier. And if the British took New Orleans, they could shut down all shipments coming down the Mississippi—including produce from western states necessary to sustain the rest of the country.

From New Orleans, William Claiborne, the presidentially appointed governor of the territory, explained to Madison that the situation was serious. If the British "should contemplate a serious invasion of the state (and this seems to be the general opinion), the country must fall, if it be left to her own resources."[100] The British were "intriguing with our Negroes," Claiborne reported. Worse, the British had "even made overtures of friendship, to the pirates and smugglers of Barataria," led by the freebooters Jean and Pierre Lafitte. Claiborne hoped for military aid, and told Madison that he had also written letters to the governors of Kentucky and Tennessee "to urge them to hasten on reinforcements."[101]

The mastermind of the British invasion was Admiral Alexander Cochrane, who had conducted the attack on Washington alongside Major General Robert Ross. On November 26, 1814, Cochrane set sail from British-owned Jamaica to Louisiana. Word of the supposedly secret mission leaked, and Cochrane on arrival discovered that his intentions were "publicly known."

The city's salvation, if any was forthcoming, depended on Andrew Jackson and his three thousand volunteers, then at Pensacola with hopes of invading West Florida.* When news of the impending attack reached Jackson, he marched his army two hundred miles along the Gulf Coast to New Orleans, racing against Cochrane's approach from the sea. By the time Cochrane and part of his force arrived, Jackson was waiting.

On December 23 and 24, Jackson's volunteers attacked the British at the Villeré plantation east of the city, where they were encamped. The British line held,[102] but the strength of the assault convinced Cochrane to wait for the rest of his troops before attacking New Orleans. This gave Jackson more time to strengthen the defenses of the city.

The rest of the British force under Sir Edward Pakenham, Wellington's brother-in-law, arrived on Christmas Day. On January 8, 1815, Pakenham arrayed 8,000 troops for a nighttime assault on the now-fortified city. Jackson responded with artillery, muskets, and rifle fire, some of it

---

* Jackson's presence at Pensacola was a story in itself. Throughout the War of 1812, Jackson had fought a series of bloody battles—and massacres—that formed part of the Creek War, which pitted rival Creek factions against each other. Jackson eventually exacted a punishing treaty that dispossessed not only his Creek enemies but his erstwhile Creek allies. After that, Monroe had repeatedly warned Jackson not to cross the Perdido River and invade West Florida. Meanwhile, the British established a base at Spanish-owned Pensacola, and in September 1814 attempted an unsuccessful amphibious assault on Mobile, which Wilkinson had held since April 1813. Jackson now had an excuse to ignore Monroe's orders, and on November 7, 1814, he took Pensacola with only a few shots fired, blocking the British from using it as a base to attack the Eastern Gulf Coast to New Orleans.

from 2,250 Kentucky volunteers who had arrived only a few days before. In the ensuing battle, the British lost nearly 300 dead, including Pakenham; 1,262 wounded; and some 500 prisoners. The Americans lost 6 killed and 7 wounded. The lopsided numbers were like something out of medieval myth—an American Agincourt.

Madison was no more aware of the victory in New Orleans than of the Treaty of Ghent. On January 14, still awaiting news of "the fate of New Orleans," Dolley wrote to her friend Hannah Gallatin that "our anxieties cannot be expressed."[103] A week later, George Ticknor, a young Boston-born lawyer who would become one of the great American literary scholars of the nineteenth century, had dinner with the Madisons and twenty guests at the White House. He had brought a letter of introduction from John Adams, and was seated between Madison and Dolley. Ticknor recorded that, before dinner, "a servant came in and whispered to Mr. Madison, who went out." As Madison left, "it was mentioned about the room that the southern mail had arrived, and a rather unseemly anxiety was expressed about the fate of New Orleans, of whose imminent danger we heard last night." Madison "soon returned, with added gravity, and said that there was no news! Silence ensued. No man seemed to know what to say at such a crisis, and, I suppose, from the fear of saying what might not be acceptable, said nothing at all."[104]

Despite his concern about events in New Orleans, Madison maintained his composure. At dinner, he was "more free and open" than Ticknor had expected, "starting subjects of conversation and making remarks that sometimes savored of humor and levity."[105] At the decisive moment in the war, Madison was as calm and controlled as ever, demonstrating his leadership skills on an intimate scale.

A Most Happy Point of Time

On February 4, Madison received the best news of the war. "I send you letters from General Jackson which give an account of a victory truly glorious," Monroe wrote to him. It had taken nearly a month for Jackson's letters of January 9 to reach Washington. Madison sent back praise for Jackson's defense of the city as well as his "personal energy and distinguished gallantry in the field." He was pleased by the fact that despite predictions to the contrary, New Orleanians had shown loyalty to the

United States—and that volunteer militia from Tennessee and Kentucky had actually shown up to fight.[106]

On February 11, 1815, a messenger arrived in New York carrying a copy of the Treaty of Ghent. In two days, news of the peace had reached Washington. On the evening of February 14, Monroe got the text of the treaty from a messenger and put it into Madison's hands. According to Dolley's niece's memoir, Madison had been quiet and "desponding" as he waited for news from Ghent. When he finally received and read the treaty, "a glow of contentment gradually overspread his countenance and the shade of disquietude passed away." Madison's reaction to the end of the war was not "rejoicing" but relief and contentment in the knowledge that the United States had survived—and had therefore prevailed.[107]

Among Madison's household, the response was more joyful. Dolley's cousin Sally Coles went to the stairs calling out "Peace! Peace!" recalled Paul Jennings. Wine was served "liberally" to the servants. Jennings played the "President's March" on his violin. John Susé, the White House doorman who had helped Jennings remove the Gilbert Stuart portrait of Washington, stayed drunk for two days.[108]

Friends and cabinet members gathered the next day to congratulate the president in person. Dolley, "the most conspicuous object" present, was the focus. Margaret Bayard Smith noted the "radiance of joy" on her face, which sent the message "that all uncertainty was at an end, and the government of the country had in very truth 'passed from gloom to glory.'"[109]

Richard Rush wrote to Madison bluntly that the news had come "at a most happy point of time for our interests and our fame." The victory at New Orleans created the impression that the British had given up on their efforts to invade the United States, and that this had ended the war. In a certain way, this interpretation was true. The treaty had been signed before the Battle of New Orleans. But Wellington had advised peace because the defense of Baltimore and the Battle of Plattsburgh had shown the near impossibility of a successful invasion.

Rush told Madison: "Your anxious moments, sir, will now be fewer; your labors abridged; your friends, more than ever, gratified; an unmanly opposition more than ever confounded; the nation, in your day, advanced anew in prosperity and glory." The enthusiasm was more than formulaic. As Rush saw it, peace would also bring substantial domestic political gains. Republican "friends" would be able to claim victory. Federalists who had opposed the war and hinted at a separate New England confederacy would now be discredited. With the orders-in-council gone and peace restored, the nation could pursue economic growth.[110]

Madison replied to Rush with quiet satisfaction. "The terms of peace will I hope be satisfactory to our country," he said. "With the events of the war, they cannot fail to command the respect of every other."[111]

Here in a nutshell was Madison's interpretation of the war. Because the conflict had ended with the repulsing of British invasion, the United States must now "command the respect" of every country on earth. Its independence and sovereignty were confirmed on sea and on land. The nation had withstood attack by the power that had defeated Napoleon. That alone made it reasonable to accept the status quo antebellum as the basis of peace.

A Peculiarly Welcome Peace

In sending the peace treaty to Congress, Madison offered a public statement of how he wanted the War of 1812 to be remembered. "I congratulate you, and our constituents," he told Congress, "upon an event which is highly honorable to the nation, and terminates, with peculiar felicity, a campaign signalized by the most brilliant successes." The peace was honorable insofar as it did not require the United States to cede any territory.

There was indeed a "peculiar felicity" that the war had ended when it did—at a moment when Madison had not expected it to end, and when the coincidental timing of the Battle of New Orleans made the public feel that the war had ended on a note of triumph. In reality, there had been only three "brilliant successes" in the two and a half years of fighting: the victory of the *Constitution* over the *Guerriere;* Perry's success on Lake Erie; and Jackson's triumph at New Orleans.

In his statement Madison characterized the "late war" as "reluctantly declared by Congress," but "a necessary resort, to assert the rights and independence of the nation."[112] Madison also claimed that the war's "success" could be attributed to the "wisdom" of Congress, "the patriotism" of the American people, "the public spirit of the militia," and the "valor of the military and naval forces of the country."[113] In fact, Congress had refused to give Madison the troops he needed. Most of the public had refused any sacrifice and avoided military service. The militia had frequently fled the field. The regular army had performed doubtfully at best. The navy deserved some of the credit for American survival, but had not defended the Eastern Seaboard successfully. And even on the Great Lakes, it had never managed to achieve the genuine control that would have allowed for the easy conquest of Canada.

Had the United States lost the war, Madison would have shouldered the burden alone. In victory, however, he was taking pains to spread the credit equally across the various participants in the war effort. He had learned the political lesson that success has a thousand fathers.

Madison added optimistically that a review of the American conduct of the war could be accomplished "without reproach." He then wisely changed the subject to the "gallant men, whose achievements . . . so essentially contributed to the honor of the American name, and to the restoration of peace." The nation must give its heroes "approbation and applause," since these were "at once, the reward, and the incentive, to great actions."

The rapid movement from reviewing the war to praising the veterans was especially clever. Madison understood that the entire war could be assessed and found wanting, from the decision to declare it through the failure to conquer Canada or defend the capital. Delicately but firmly, Madison meant to imply that a congressional inquiry into the causes of the failure would be unpatriotic—because it would amount to criticism of those who fought the war. Here Madison set an influential precedent for subsequent American unwillingness to shine harsh light on wars that produced mixed results—a precedent whose echoes could be felt as late as the wars in Vietnam, Iraq, and Afghanistan.

Now Madison turned to policy suggestions. He urged Congress to maintain a regular army, expand the navy, improve harbor defenses, and provide for the training of militia as well as the education of regular officers. "Experience has taught us," Madison said, that the "pacific dispositions of the American people" and "their political institutions" would not exempt the United States from the need to fight wars. "A certain degree of preparation" was "indispensable to avert disaster" and would also give "the best security for the continuance of peace." The recommendations were altogether logical in the light of the experience of the previous decade.

What was striking was how much Madison's message to Congress differed from his earlier conception of government. As secretary of state and then president, Madison had pioneered the idea of economic sanctions as a republican substitute for force. He had based his approach on the idea that the United States was a new kind of country that would achieve its goals without fighting. He had believed, and still believed, that the political institutions he had done so much to create were also pacific, designed to promote peace by making it especially difficult and therefore unappealing to wage war.

Now, having learned the lessons of armed conflict, Madison was offering a coda to his form of republicanism. He was not adopting Hamilton's vision of the United States as a global naval power, or imagining a standing army designed for conquest. Instead he was proposing that the country maintain regular military forces capable of self-defense and incremental territorial expansion. And it would be Madison's strategic vision, not Hamilton's, that prevailed. It called for a modestly sized armed force capable of assuring the U.S. place in the world relative to great powers—and acquiring frontier territory through modestly sized border wars. It was followed by Madison's successors through the Mexican-American War and up to Southern secession and the Civil War.[114]

Madison also told Congress that it should consider "the means to preserve and promote the manufactures which have sprung into existence, and attained an unparalleled maturity, throughout the United States during the period of the European wars." It was noteworthy that Madison, who had founded the Republican Party on a platform opposed to the promotion of manufacturing, was now arguing that Congress should seek "guardianship" of the growing industry.

The reasons for Madison's development were once more based on experience. At the Philadelphia convention and in the *Federalist*, he had argued for a mixed economy with both agricultural and manufacturing components. His move to an aggressively agrarian stance had been a product of political necessity as he opposed Hamilton's Federalist Party, coupled with a sense that northeastern manufacturing interests were prepared to subvert the interests of the agricultural South.

Now, with European trade about to expand, Madison was eager to take credit for the growth of domestic manufacturing that had resulted in part from his own policies of economic sanctions. The end of economic sanctions would leave American industry vulnerable to external competition. Madison did not want to squander the advantages that had been gained as the unintentional result of his now-abandoned approach.

Writing three-quarters of a century later, Henry Adams, the grandson of John Quincy Adams, would interpret Madison's postwar policies as the adoption of the Federalist program associated with his great-grandfather John Adams. This influential reading of Madison's position overstated the case. Madison's proposed military would not be a full Federalist force ready for aggressive warfare. And Madison had never fully embraced Jefferson's strong agrarianism, except as a matter of political rhetoric.

Notwithstanding his republican beliefs, Madison had gambled his political legacy on war. And he had triumphed—despite failing to achieve his original goals. The key to his success was changing the meaning of the war as it was fought, depicting it as a second war of independence to establish national sovereignty on the seas. Reframing the narrative transformed the result into a victory, even though the United States had won no new territory from Britain.

Madison's presidential legacy was now assured. He had striven to avoid war, and his economic sanctions proved in retrospect that he had embraced force only when it was unavoidable. He had shown decisiveness in choosing to fight, and had doubled down on his bet by refusing the initial British armistice offer. He had protected civil liberties, even in the face of potential treason and secession. And in the process he had cemented the dominance of the Republican Party, which aspired—according to Madison's constitutional vision—to end partisanship altogether.

Legacy

...

ON MARCH 21, 1815, the war over and the peace assured, Madison and Dolley left for the quiet of Montpelier. Almost two years remained in Madison's presidency. But there was every reason to expect that they would be uneventful compared with the previous thirty-five years he had spent in almost continuous public service.

His goal during this period was to establish policy principles that would put the United States on a firm footing for the foreseeable future. That legacy would embody Madison's constitutional vision. It would unify the disparate accomplishments of the three phases of his career into a single, integrated arc.

In May, at Montpelier, Madison received the shocking news that Napoleon had escaped from Elba and would again lead a French army into the field. Yet despite the danger that renewed European war might bring back trade sanctions and restore impressment, Madison remained calm. If war came, he told Alexander Dallas, "our great objects will be to save our peace and our rights."[1]

Unlike Hamilton, Madison did not see the United States as a future global superpower. He understood America's role in world affairs more modestly. Madison believed that a republic should focus on trade, not domination—and take advantage of struggles between the major global actors.[2]

In his annual message to Congress delivered in December 1815, Madison gave concrete policy form to more of the themes that would make up his legacy. The regular army had been reduced to a peacetime level of ten thousand men.[3] Madison described this as a compromise. Strictly speaking, it left the nation with a standing army, a violation of Madison's prewar republican ideology. But the war had taught that militia were not enough. Some regular standing force was needed for a nation that had to confront great powers.

A moderately sized standing force saved money and preserved republicanism from the danger of military subversion—without leaving the nation wholly unprepared in case of future conflict. This was Madison's military legacy. It reflected a constitutional design that did not prohibit a standing army, combined with a republican concern not to let the army become so powerful that it could threaten liberty.

Turning to the economy, Madison called for limited tariffs to encourage industry. Free trade was ideal as a matter of "theory," he told Congress. That had always been his belief, relying on Adam Smith. But "exceptions to the general rule" were appropriate to nurse emerging manufacturing industries.[4] At every stage of his career, Madison had emphasized possible exceptions to absolutely unfettered exchange. His legacy on trade was to pursue the goal of open access through the use of tools fitted to specific political and economic circumstances. Whatever its desirability in theory, free trade was not always desirable in practice.

The national bank had played an important part in shaping the U.S. economy, and Madison now said he was open to a bill to recharter it. The previous January, he had explained to Congress that his old objections to the bank had been removed "by repeated recognitions, under various circumstances, of the validity of such an institution, in acts of the legislature, executive, and judicial branches of government."[5] All three branches of government, backed by "the general will of the nation," had now for many years treated the bank as constitutional.[6] Therefore, the bank now *was* constitutional.

This was proof that Madison's legacy included recognition that the Constitution could evolve—and that its framers' original intention did not always control its meaning. He had opposed Hamilton's proposed national bank as unconstitutional, relying on his own knowledge and belief that the document produced in Philadelphia did not authorize Congress to charter a bank. But he had come to accept that the bank became constitutional after Congress and the president adopted it anyway and it functioned for twenty years. When a bill to charter the second national bank came before him, Madison signed it, no longer deeming an amendment necessary.[7]

Madison proposed one congressional initiative that, he said, did require an amendment, and which demonstrated his commitment to a strict interpretation of the Constitution. New canals and roads would bring the disparate parts of the country closer together, which would have economic benefits as well as a desirable "political effect." Congress was best placed to undertake national infrastructure projects that spanned multiple states: an infrastructure needed national legislation. Yet Madison's enduring constitutional vision did not allow him to ignore the limits on Congress's enumerated powers.

When an infrastructure bill did come before Madison, he vetoed it—despite the fact that it had been passed by his own party. The construction of roads and canals, he explained, was not an enumerated power of Congress. It could only conceivably be authorized under the Congress's power to raise taxes "to provide for the common defense and general welfare." Hamilton had relied on this language to justify both the national bank and subsidies for manufacturing.

Madison's rejection of Hamilton's broad interpretation of the general welfare clause had resulted in the creation of the Republican Party. It was no exaggeration to say that the debate over the clause's meaning had defined Madison's second political life. Now, at the end of the third period of his career, Madison once more insisted that a broad interpretation of the welfare clause "would have the effect of giving to Congress a general power of legislation instead of the defined and limited one hitherto understood to belong to them." The only solution was for the public to exercise "the same wisdom and virtue . . . which established the Constitution in its actual form" and pass an amendment.

Madison saved the veto for the last day of his presidency. The timing showed that he viewed his entire career as a coherent whole, devoted to the shaping and realization of a consistent constitutional vision. The veto itself was a rebuttal of Hamilton's reading of the Constitution, and therefore Madison's last victory in the battle that had given birth to American partisanship. By making the final public act of his presidency one of constitutional limitation, Madison was also gesturing back to his first political life as founding constitutional genius. Insisting that he understood the true meaning of the Constitution reminded the nation that he had done more than anyone else to create it.

The Anniversary of the Constitution

Today a president gives his last State of the Union address a year before leaving office. But Madison's final message to Congress was delivered in December 1816, just a few months before the end of his term. He used it to focus attention on the Constitution—and on its connections to the rest of his career.

Madison congratulated the American people on having "reached in safety and success their fortieth year as an independent nation." But the anniversary of independence was less important for Madison than the twenty-fifth anniversary of the Constitution, which he treated as a significant milestone.

"For nearly an entire generation," Madison told Congress, the people "have had experience of the present Constitution, the offspring of their undisturbed deliberations and other free choice." In its generational life-span, Madison argued, the Constitution had been shown

> to bear the trials of adverse as well as prosperous circumstances, to contain in its combination of the federate and elective principles a reconcilement of public strength with individual liberty, of national power for the defense of national rights with a security against wars of injustice, of ambition, and other vainglory in the fundamental provision which subjects all questions of war to the will of the nation itself, which is to pay its costs and feel its calamities.[8]

Madison was offering an overarching assessment of the success of the Constitution he had imagined, designed, and implemented. And with an eye to his presidential legacy, he was focusing on the Constitution's ability to function under the "adverse" conditions of war.

Liberty was Madison's highest political value. Even in wartime, it was more important than winning quickly or decisively. Republicans, including Madison, had always feared that wartime government would turn into despotism. Adams and the Federalists had sharply curtailed the freedom of speech during the undeclared Quasi-War, evidence that the danger was real and that infringements on liberty could happen in the United States, notwithstanding the text of the Constitution.

Madison wanted to demonstrate that the Constitution could preserve freedom no matter what challenges it faced. Now that the United States had survived, Madison could point proudly to the fact that he and his government had maintained liberty in wartime. Free speech and free assembly had been extended even to those New Englanders who hated the war so much that they contemplated a separate peace with Britain and the dissolution of the union—and convened the Hartford Convention to consider both. To have upheld First Amendment protections in the face of such a challenge was not simply a vindication of Madison's presidency, but of the Constitution itself.

Constitutional freedom was the central core of Madison's legacy. It brought together the three eras of his political life. In the first phase, he had designed the Constitution to preserve liberty. In the second, he had created the Republican Party to defend constitutional liberty against subversion by the Federalists. Now he was pointing out that constitutional liberty had endured even during the war he prosecuted in the third. And it had extended even to Federalists on the verge of subverting the Constitution once again.

The constitutional structure also created a balance that prevented the public from pursuing unjust wars of "ambition" or "vainglory," like those of Napoleon. Here Madison alluded to the fact that he had tried for a decade to keep the United States out of war, and had chosen force only when he could see no other option. This argument also had the benefit of making the existence of ongoing opposition to the war into a constitutional virtue.

The War of 1812 had been fought by a country with geographical boundaries substantially greater than the thirteen original colonies. Madison told Congress that the Constitution, "so dear to us all," had shown that it could function in an "expanding" nation that would grow further still. This was an invocation of Madison's lifelong commitment to expanding the territory of the United States.

Madison was referring to the legacy of his grand theory that a larger, extended republic would preserve liberty better than a small, factious republic. The theory had always been difficult to demonstrate. Now Madison was claiming that, after a quarter century, his theory had been proven correct. The United States itself was getting bigger—and liberty was better preserved than ever before.

Reaching the climax of the last major public address of his presidency, Madison delivered a moving tribute to the Constitution and its values. The American people were, he said, devoted "to true liberty and to the Constitution." The "great principles" of the Constitution included "a government which watches over the purity of elections, freedom of speech and of the press, [and] the trial by jury." The Constitution prohibited "encroachments and compacts between religion and the state"—the very issue that brought Madison into the public eye for the first time as a young man. It protected "the maxims of public faith," the payment of government debts, and "the security of persons and property."[9]

Finally, Madison addressed the role of the Constitution in global affairs. Government under the Constitution, he claimed, would avoid "intrusions on the internal repose of other nations" and do justice to all other countries while requiring justice from them. Under the Constitution, the government would refine its internal laws to become consistent with "the precepts of an enlightened age and the sentiments of a virtuous people." It would, by "appeals to reason" and by example, "infuse" international law with a "spirit" of peace. Madison's ideal government would, "in a word," fulfill "the most noble of all ambitions—that of promoting peace on earth and goodwill to man."[10]

Madison had always kept his religious beliefs to himself. Now he was placing the Constitution in the role of secular savior. Madison truly believed that the Constitution would produce domestic tranquility and friendship, then spread those same values of peace globally, creating a world of free peoples coexisting peacefully and ruling themselves under their own free constitutions. No greater or more ambitious legacy could be imagined.

Acquired More Glory

In the eyes of his contemporaries, Madison's retirement was glorious. Riding the coattails of Madison's popularity, Monroe won the presidency with more than 68 percent of the popular vote. He defeated New York Federalist Rufus King in sixteen of nineteen states. Madison's friend of nearly forty years had twice tried and failed to defeat him in elections. By following Madison rather than trying to supplant him, Monroe was finally getting his turn to lead.

Madison and Dolley left Washington within a month of Monroe's inauguration, traveling by steamboat down the Potomac to meet their carriage and proceed to Montpelier. A companion on the journey later recalled that Madison "during the voyage was as playful as a child; talked and jested with everybody on board," bringing to mind "a schoolboy on a long vacation."[11]

Madison had reason to be joyful. Monroe's victory marked the definitive end of Hamilton's Federalist Party and the birth of what would soon be dubbed the Era of Good Feelings. This period of single-party government corresponded almost precisely to Madison's original ideal of republican concord under the Constitution. Madison's constitutional vision was ascendant.

And Madison was the first—and perhaps only—president to leave office under such favorable conditions. Adams had been voted out after a single term. Jefferson had retired in the wake of the failure of Madison's embargo. Washington had been lionized on his retirement, but more for his prior role in leading the Revolutionary War—and for the fact of the retirement itself—than for his actual accomplishments as president.

Adams wrote to Jefferson that he pitied Madison in his post-presidential years because he did not have children. Children "cost us grief, anxiety, often vexation, and sometimes humiliation," wrote Adams, whose older son had died an alcoholic and whose younger son would become president. But it is "cheering to have them hovering about us," Adams observed, "and I verily believe they have contributed largely to keep us alive." Madison had his books, but "books cannot always expel ennui," the equally bookish Adams believed.

Nevertheless, alongside the pity he expressed for "Brother Madison's" childlessness, Adams added an assessment of Madison's presidency that sounded almost jealous. "Notwithstanding a thousand faults and blunders," Adams told Jefferson, "his administration has acquired more glory, and established more union, than all his three predecessors, Washington, Adams, and Jefferson, put together."[12]

One former president writing to another, comparing all four presidencies, concluded that Madison's had been by far the most successful—even more so than the revered Washington's. This was the judgment of the age, and Madison was well aware of it.

Atonement: The Legacy of Slavery

The Montpelier to which Madison returned had undergone substantial change since the days of his father. It was now designed to function as the setting for a long, peaceful retirement in which Madison could receive visitors from a grateful nation and beyond. In that capacity, it was supposed to stand for a vision of republican tranquility—the one Madison had designed for the United States itself.

To that end, during his brief hiatus from national politics in the Adams administration, Madison had added a portico to the front of the building.

At the outset of his presidency, he had built two wings, bringing the style into parallel with both the White House and Jefferson's Monticello. He had begun to plant a substantial, French-style garden, and now developed it further. As designed, Madison's garden did not emphasize shrubbery, but rather drew the viewer's eye to the forest in which Montpelier was set.[13] To the right of the house was a newly built classical temple with a statue of liberty on the top of it.

Seen from our perspective, the plantation at Montpelier stands as a reminder of Madison's lifelong reliance on slave labor—and the efforts he made to grapple with the problem of slavery writ large. What is especially relevant to Madison's racial legacy is that he, too, was clearly thinking about the same topic.

In the middle of his lawn, less than fifty yards behind the house, Madison built several model homes for the slaves who worked in and around the house. The original slave quarters had been hidden from view by brick walls, as they were at Mount Vernon and Monticello, to avoid the visual juxtaposition with ornamental gardens. Madison, taking a different path, now knocked down the old slave quarters to build the new ones, which were wood framed with proper floors, fireplaces, and glass windows.[14]

Madison intended the homes to justify the institution of slavery, at least as practiced in Montpelier. Enlightened British landowners had been building model villages for their estate workers for two decades. Madison was following their example. Through it, he was also suggesting a highly tendentious analogy between his slaves and the free workingmen of Britain. Most of Madison's one hundred slaves still lived in cabins near the fields where they worked—cabins not nearly as attractive or well built as the slave quarters by the house.[15] But Madison evidently wanted visitors from around the world, who would come to him as they had to Washington and Jefferson, to see that his slaves were treated well.

This attitude toward slavery is an important, and troubling, part of Madison's legacy. Unlike Jefferson, he did not regard people of African descent as inherently inferior—nor did he have sexual or romantic connections to his slaves.[16] He was willing to recognize that slaves' aspiration to freedom was a human right. Yet he believed that slavery as he practiced it was morally permissible, and even something to be admired.

To make matters more complicated, Madison favored emancipation in theory—and in retirement, he took the time to think through the problem and make a proposal in connection with it. His opportunity arose in the spring of 1819, when an abolitionist Philadelphia Quaker named Robert J. Evans wrote to him soliciting his views for "the weight" which Madison's opinions "must necessarily have with his fellow citizens."[17]

Madison wrote back within a few days of receiving the letter, a rapid turnaround that showed he had already been thinking deeply about the question and was waiting for a chance to express his ideas. He understood just how significant the question of slavery would be to his legacy, and the threat it posed to the glory of his accomplishments at every stage of his life.

Slavery had, after all, cast its shadow over Madison's entire existence. He had been born at Montpelier, where his own grandfather was believed to have been killed by enslaved Africans. His Constitution set an end date for the slave trade, but preserved slavery and fixed the three-fifths compromise. His Republican Party had relied on southern support, and compared to northeastern Federalism, it had been a bulwark of pro-slavery sentiment. His presidency had not featured any notable progress toward emancipation. Now Madison had returned to spend the rest of his days among slaves on the same plantation where his life had begun.

Conscious that he was writing for the ages, the ex-president and slaveholder began with a general overview. Slavery was an "evil" that was both "deep-rooted" and "widespread." The emancipation of slaves, Madison wrote, therefore: "Ought to be 1. Gradual. 2. Equitable and satisfactory to the individuals immediately concerned. 3. Consistent with the existing and durable prejudices of the nation."[18]

Almost thirty-five years had passed since Madison had written a private memorandum for William Thornton expressing his support for the idea, then new, that freed blacks should be resettled in Africa. He had written to Thornton that whites and freed blacks would not be able to live in harmony on the North American continent because of white prejudice.[19] Now Madison wrote that if freed blacks were denied "equal rights political or social," they inevitably would be "dissatisfied with their condition as a change only from one to another species of oppression." He predicted that whites would fear blacks' "vindictive recollections" for past wrongs done to them. The result would be "reciprocal antipathies doubling the danger."[20]

Expecting that freed blacks would remain oppressed, and believing that it was impracticable to separate communities of free blacks from whites, Madison returned to the idea of colonization and repatriation, recently introduced to the United States by the American Colonization Society.[21] Writing to Evans, he endorsed the society's plan to purchase land in Liberia and settle freed blacks there. "The experiment," he wrote, "merits encouragement from all who regard slavery as an evil, who wish to see it diminished and abolished by peaceable and just means; and who have themselves no better mode to propose."

Indeed, Madison thought that the society's colonization plan, which applied only to "blacks already free, or who may be gratuitously emancipated" by enlightened masters, did not go far enough.[22] He proposed for "the plan to be extended to the great mass of blacks" by purchasing their freedom. Madison estimated "the number of slaves to be 1,500,000, and their price to average $400." It would therefore cost roughly $600 million to buy all the slaves in the United States with the consent of their owners and send them to Africa.

Voluntary contributions would never raise enough money to pay the masters, Madison reasoned. This was a job for the federal government, provided its powers were suitably augmented. "The object to be attained, as an object of humanity, appeals alike to all," he wrote. "It is the nation which is to reap the benefit. The nation therefore ought to bear the burden." The sum of $600 million seemed enormous, but Madison had a plan in mind. By "providential blessing," the United States had "a resource commensurate to this great object": the "vacant territory" of the American continent.

According to Madison's idea, the United States should raise the money to buy slaves' freedom by selling two hundred million acres at three dollars an acre, or alternatively three hundred million acres at two dollars an acre. By putting the land into private hands, the United States would be "planting one desert with a free and civilized people," white Americans. At the same time, it would be "giving freedom to another people, and filling with them another desert," namely Africa.

Madison understood that the American continent would be "vacant" only by the displacement of American Indians—a process in which he had played a role through the War of 1812 and the defeat of Tecumseh. But he tried to make a rhetorical virtue of the fact that he wanted to compensate the descendants of enslaved Africans by selling land taken from the first Americans. "If in any instances, wrong has been done by our forefathers to people of one color, by dispossessing them of their soil,"

620 THE THREE LIVES OF JAMES MADISON

Madison wrote, "what better atonement is now in our power than that of making what is rightfully acquired a source of justice and of blessings to a people of another color?"*

Evans hoped to make Madison's view public. But in the final line of his letter, Madison asked that he not attribute it to him. His reticence about public ascription was noteworthy—and not to Madison's credit. Fourteen years later, at the age of eighty-two, Madison became the president of the American Colonization Society, a symbolic role he held to the end of his life. Yet even then, there was clearly a difference to Madison between publicly endorsing the society's goal of sending free blacks to Liberia, and his own far more ambitious scheme to end slavery through compensated emancipation and resettlement.

Ultimately, Madison was willing to call for abolition in private correspondence, but not to deviate in public from the orthodoxy of his class. He owned his slaves throughout his retirement, and found himself unable to convince a number of them to accept emigration in exchange for their freedom. At the same time, he continued to insist that colonization was the only permanent solution to the problem of slavery, clinging to that belief even as it became clear that the solution was unrealistic and unworkable.[23]

In 1829, when Virginia was revising its state constitution, Madison, then seventy-eight, attended the convention and made a single speech—on the topic of how slaves should be counted for purposes of taxation. Madison began by reminding his audience of the danger of the tyranny of the majority. In this case, the majority was white non-slaveholding Virginians who might do "injustice" to the minority of slaveholders by raising taxes on slaves. Then he argued for borrowing the three-fifths compromise from the federal Constitution and using it as the measure for taxing slaves as property.[24]

Yet despite taking this distinctly pro-slavery stance, Madison in the course of the speech offered the argument that enslaved persons should be conceived as humans, not property. "It is due to justice," he said,

---

* Blaming the "wrong" of taking the continent on "our forefathers" drew attention away from Madison's own legacy in dispossessing Native Americans, including the Creeks. Yet the mention of "atonement" from earlier "wrongs" did perhaps imply that expropriation of the continent was a kind of sin.

due to humanity: due to truth; to the sympathies of our nature: in fine, to our character as a people, both abroad and at home, that they should be considered, as much as possible, in the light of human beings; and not as mere property. As such they are acted upon by our laws; and have an interest in our laws. They may be considered as making a part, though a degraded part of the families to which they belong.[25]

The ambivalence of the speech perfectly encapsulates Madison's life-long contradictory views of the enslaved people on whose labor he depended. On the one hand, slaves were "human beings" with "an interest in our laws." On the other hand, humanity extended only "as much as possible" to slaves. They were to be considered property, even if not "mere property." They were family members, but their status was nonetheless a "degraded" one.

Toward the end of his life, Madison was urged by the abolitionist Edward Coles, a cousin of Dolley's, to emancipate his slaves.[26] After struggling with Dolley's financial needs and the possible danger of formally freeing the slaves only at her death, Madison chose to leave Dolley the title to the enslaved persons, including in his official will only the stipulation that the slaves not be sold except by their own consent "or in the case of their misbehavior." According to a family tradition, Madison left separate written instructions to Dolley to emancipate his slaves when she died.[27] If this message in fact existed, Dolley was unable or unwilling to fulfill it.[28]

Notes

Madison could not have engaged in a posthumous act of emancipation even had he wanted to, because Dolley could not afford it. As president, Madison had not had time to focus on running Montpelier, and when he returned, he had to borrow money to live.[29] Meanwhile, Virginia crop yields were changing. Uninterrupted planting of tobacco had exhausted the soil, and Madison managed just one successful tobacco crop and one successful wheat crop in the nineteen years of his retirement.[30]

Madison took a serious interest in farming. He gave an address to the Agricultural Society of nearby Albemarle County that reflected wide reading and was republished locally and nationally.[31] In it he applied a version of his constitutional reasoning to the problem of agriculture: Nature produced challenges and imposed some constraints. But human reason and will could be used to address those challenges. Contra Malthus, the population could be expanded, like the republic.[32]

Improved farming helped stabilize Montpelier's finances. But it was not enough to create a financial legacy, because Madison also had to spend significant sums on Dolley's son John Payne Todd. While taking part in the Ghent negotiations, Payne had lived like a young European aristocrat, and he came home owing at least $8,000, much of it borrowed using Madison's name and spent on gambling.[33]

Madison paid the debts. It set a bad precedent. For the rest of Madison's life, Payne would contract debt, often from gambling, then turn to his mother and Madison to pay it off, occasionally waiting in debtors' prison until the money reached his creditors. Madison tried to hide the worst of it from Dolley. In 1836, Madison told Dolley's brother that she knew about $20,000 he had spent paying off Payne's debts, and that he had spent another $20,000 without her knowledge[34]—a total of roughly $800,000 in today's value.

As a consequence, beyond the hundred enslaved Africans and Montpelier itself, Madison had just one asset that he could leave to Dolley to support her after his death: his papers, particularly his notes of the Philadelphia convention, which had remained private.[35] Madison understood that the Constitution would be his most significant legacy. With time on his hands and his eye on posterity, Madison revised the notes twice, once as he began to copy his original manuscript, and again in the 1830s. He also edited notes he had taken of the proceedings of the old, pre-Constitution Congress. By preparing his notes for publication, Madison was consciously participating in the creation of his own historical record while helping to provide for Dolley.

Over his lengthy retirement, Madison also took pains to get the original versions of letters he had sent over the years from descendants of the original recipients.[36] Effectively, Madison was editing his own papers, a vast corpus of thousands of documents. In doing so he was keenly aware not only of the historical importance of his actions and thoughts during his public career, but of the value of the record for future generations of Americans.

Madison believed that the full set of papers he had edited, when published in three volumes, would earn $100,000 or more for Dolley.[37] As it turned out, this estimate was too optimistic. Congress eventually agreed to acquire the three volumes for $30,000; it later paid $25,000 for a second group of papers.[38] Dolley's economic situation would remain unstable even after the sale.

Madison's notes are a historical record of the first importance. Although other notes of the convention exist, none are so complete. As he intended, Madison's version of the creation of the Constitution became the standard narrative of the event.

It is highly unusual for a major historical actor to be the major historical chronicler of the events in which he participated. Only Julius Caesar's two great war histories come close—and they are overshadowed by his death, which as told by others became a parable of republican resistance to autocracy. Madison, in contrast, narrated the triumph of republicanism through debate, conversation, negotiation, and consent. In his telling, he is no more than first among equals, as indeed he was in Philadelphia. His tool is reason—the epitome of republican aspiration. And if Madison subtly exaggerated the reasoned character of the debates and the articulate qualities of the delegates, himself included, that exaggeration reflected not egotism, but his own profound belief in the capacity of measured discourse to produce a government that would protect liberty.

A Change of Mind

As the regional divide over slavery became increasingly contentious, threatening the long-term prospect of national unity, the constitutional order itself began to seem vulnerable. States' rights were no longer a bulwark against federal power, but potentially a mechanism for secession and systemic collapse. Madison sensed the dangers of disunion. "It cannot be denied," he wrote in a letter in 1836, that "our country presents phenomena of an ill omen." But Madison was as hopeful as ever that a time would come when "the public mind may be calm and cool enough for that resort."[39]

As he told his fellow Virginians in his last public speech, to the state's constitutional convention, the union of the states was itself "in the eyes of the world a wonder: the harmonious establishment of a common government over them all, a miracle." He believed the union would survive—by human compromise, not divine intervention. "I cannot but flatter myself, that, without a miracle, we shall be able to arrange all our difficulties," he went on. "I never have despaired. Notwithstanding all the threatening appearances we have passed through, I have now more than a hope, a consoling confidence that we shall at last find that our labors have not been in vain."[40]

Madison's intellectual capacities never deserted him. In 1830, Jared Sparks, editor of *The North American Review* and future president of Harvard, visited Montpelier. He noted in his journal that "the intellect and memory of Mr. Madison appear to retain all their pristine vigor." Over five days, Madison told Sparks dozens of stories of the Revolution, the Philadelphia convention, and his presidency. "He is peculiarly interesting in conversation," wrote Sparks, "cheerful, gay, and full of anecdote." Madison remained a skillful raconteur: "never a prosing talker, but sprightly, varied, fertile in his topics, and felicitous in his description and illustration."[41]

In the last six months of his life, he could no longer walk. "But his mind was bright," recalled Paul Jennings, the slave who stayed closest to him. "With his numerous visitors he talked with as much animation and strength of voice as I ever heard him in his best days."[42] Dolley's family memoir recorded that he was "in the full possession of all his noble faculties," and that his "mental powers never dimmed, though his body was cramped by disease."[43]

Madison became increasingly ill toward the end of June 1836. Only a few days remained until July 4, the sixtieth anniversary of independence. Jefferson and Adams had both died exactly ten years before on that same symbolic date. The doctors thought that they could keep Madison, the last surviving member of the constitutional convention, alive long enough to make it to the anniversary. But Madison refused to be "unnecessarily stimulated" in order to be kept alive until July 4.[44]

Jennings was present to the end. Sukey, a slave who had been with Madison and Dolley in the White House and at Montpelier, brought Madison breakfast on June 28, 1836. Madison could not swallow it, Jennings remembered.

Madison's niece, Nelly Willis, was in the room. "What is the matter, Uncle James?" she asked.

"Nothing more than a change of mind, my dear," Madison replied.

With that, "his head instantly dropped, and he ceased breathing as quietly as the snuff of a candle goes out."[45]

Madison had always been a creature of mind. That his death would be merely a change in that sphere perfectly captured his life and beliefs.

The Father of the Constitution

Madison was called "the father of the Constitution" as early as 1829, after an election in which both presidential candidates claimed to be his followers.[46] In American historical memory, Madison's legacy as constitution maker, the work of his first political life, would come to overshadow his legacy as a political partisan and as a statesman and president who led the nation through its first declared war.

The reasons are not hard to see. The Constitution endured, while the first Republican Party passed away. The War of 1812, experienced as a victory for a new republic seeking independence and survival, paled compared with the traumas of the Civil War and the epochal victories of the world wars. A nation that had replaced Britain as a global superpower had little reason to remember a war fought to a draw against its former colonial master.

And if the Constitution was the rallying cry of union, Madison was its defining voice. In a long eulogy that was also the first Madison biography, John Quincy Adams biblically contrasted the "still small voice" of Madison's Constitution with "the whirlwind, the earthquake, and the fire" of revolution, war, and civil dissension. It was "the voice that stills the raging of the waves and the tumults of the people—that spoke the words of peace—of harmony—of union." Those who sought that voice, Adams concluded, should "'to the last syllable of recorded time,' fix your eyes upon the memory, and listen with your ears to the life of James Madison."[47]

The title "father of the Constitution" properly placed Madison alongside Washington, the father of his country. Jefferson never earned a parallel accolade, but his tombstone described him as "author of the declaration of American independence." The men's accomplishments were markedly different, as were their characters. Washington had won a great military victory and declined a crown. He managed the difficult first presidency with sufficient gravitas to cement his unmatched place in the hearts of his countrymen. Jefferson's great "genius," to use Madison's word, was his preternatural ability to express memorably the philosophical truths on which the nation was built. His political career was driven by his enthusiasm for those ideals, which underlay both his successes and failures.

Madison was something else. If Washington inspired by his presence and example, and Jefferson by his words, Madison inspired through his creation, the Constitution. He left a legacy composed of enduring ideas and institutions, not battles or aphorisms or personal drama. His historical importance lies in having designed our most fundamental political structures and our most lasting categories of political thought. Although Washington and Jefferson are more famous, the United States is Madisonian much more than it is Washingtonian or Jeffersonian.

The relation between friends and enemies lay at the very center of Madison's political ideas—and his life. In the first of his political lives, he exercised his own genius to imagine the Constitution as a model of political friendship running in parallel to his own highly valued personal friendships, including the one with Jefferson. He crafted the Constitution to enable reasonable people to participate in a common enterprise while still disagreeing. His design was intended to minimize the effect of faction, thereby keeping partisan politics at bay.

The legacy of this optimistic, even utopian constitutional ideal can be seen in the continuing American aspiration to nonpartisanship. More than the citizens of almost any other democracy, Americans to this day say they oppose political parties and want their politicians to transcend party loyalty. This is a distinctly Madisonian vision of political concord, shaped and sustained by constitutional institutions that are supposed to create checks and balances on their own.

Yet Madison is simultaneously also responsible for initiating one of the characteristic features of partisanship in the United States, namely the charge that political enemies are not just wrong on policy, but are subverting the Constitution itself. In this sense, Madison is not only a father of nonpartisanship, but of political partisanship as well. He reached this position in the course of his second political life, defined by his struggles with Hamilton, the founder who can most justly be considered his nemesis.

It was Hamilton who taught Madison that his idealistic, nonpartisan constitutional design would not inevitably succeed. Having been Madison's closest political friend during ratification, Hamilton betrayed both Madison and the Constitution itself—at least by Madison's lights. His efforts to create a financial infrastructure that would ally the federal government with the interests of the bond markets seemed to Madison to subvert the very foundations of republican government, giving power to capitalists instead of the people. That made Hamilton into Madison's enemy by virtue of being, Madison came to believe, an enemy of the Constitution.

To defeat a political enemy required a political party. By joining Jefferson to form the Republican Party and beat the Federalists, Madison had to give up his nonpartisan ideals—at least until victory could be assured. Operating as a Republican partisan, Madison did not simply criticize Federalist policies. He depicted Hamilton and the Federalists as Anglophile monarchists committed to the overthrow of the Constitution itself.

Today, when U.S. politicians of all stripes denounce one another in bitter partisan struggle, they follow this model, whether consciously or not. Partisan opponents are accused of wanting to roll back the protections of the Bill of Rights. A president from another party is accused of wanting to expand executive power to the point of monarchy. An opposition Congress is charged with blocking constitutional government from proceeding according to its rules. All these arguments have their origins in Madison's constitutional condemnation of the Federalists.[48]

Abroad, Madison's legacy includes the American effort—not always achieved—to preserve its republican character while operating as a world power. This was the defining theme of Madison's third political life as statesman and president. Deeply committed to American neutrality, Madison initiated the use of economic sanctions as a substitute for military force. In the process, he learned that sanctions have limits. He was the first American president to enter office deeply opposed to the use of military force and then lead the country into war. He was not the last.

More important, Madison's global legacy includes the eventual spread of constitutional government throughout much of the world. Madison did not invent the word "constitution" or the idea of a form of government that could be defined in a document. But he invented and theorized the modern ideal of an expanded, federal constitution that combines local self-government with an overarching national order. And he both shaped and defended the idea that such constitutional governments are designed to protect the liberty of the individual and of minorities.

Today that model of liberty-protecting constitutional government exists, modified by time and experience, through the Americas, in Europe, in Asia, and in Africa. It is the most influential American idea in global political history. It may be the most important political idea of the modern era.

With its defects and remedies, its flaws and fixes, constitutional government remains the best option the world has known for enabling disparate people to live together in political harmony. It is Madison's legacy—and ours.

Acknowledgments

...

I BEGAN THIS PROJECT knowing it would be the longest and most challenging I had ever undertaken, and it was. I would like to thank especially those who read or commented on the entire manuscript in its varied and evolving forms: Jack Rakove, the master of Madison scholars; my former research assistant and student, now professional colleague, Jill Goldenziel, who has also read in manuscript and improved all my earlier books; my once-and-always teachers Sanford Levinson and Elizabeth Hyde; Mika Kasuga, who edited and line-edited the book at Random House; Scott Kominers; Medha Gargeya; Nathaniel Orbach; and Isaac Gelbfish. My experiences teaching alongside Joseph Koerner shaped my thinking about friends and enemies in the constitutional sphere, and my many discussions of Madison and Jefferson with Margaret Koerner powerfully influenced my thinking about their characters and relationship. For sustained, challenging, supportive conversations about Madison and his world at crucial junctures of my thinking I am very grateful to Annette Gordon-Reed, Eric Nelson, Bernard Bailyn, Andrew Wylie, and Arielle Davidoff. For excellent research assistance I would like to thank Mark Jia, Carly Anderson, Melissa Proctor, Menachem Butler, Sylvanus Polky, Clément Turjman, Matthew King, and Shmuel Weiss.

The historians, archivists, and educators at James Madison's Montpelier and the Robert H. Smith Center for the Constitution opened their hearts and their database to me, for which I am grateful. It has been a pleasure to meet and learn from such dedicated scholars who share a sense of commitment to the honest and faithful chronicling of Madison's life and legacy.

The staff of the Harvard Law School Library has been locating and retrieving hard-to-find sources for me almost every day for more than six years. Special thanks are due to George Taoultsides of the library who compiled the bibliography to reflect the mass of material that I have tried to digest.

Shannon Whalen-Lipko manages every aspect of my professional life so skillfully and seamlessly that I can dive into the eighteenth and nineteenth centuries while knowing she has the twenty-first covered. I could not have written the book—or managed my other duties—without her execution and management skills.

My children, Jaemin and Mina, have put up with Madison for half of their lives, and I have benefited enormously from their patience, interest, and engagement. Jaemin and I still don't agree on whether Madison was morally obliged to back out of the War of 1812 after the armistice offer, and maybe we never will. Mina, an expert on Hamiltoniana, has been generous in tolerating my writing about the other side, and kind about my pain at the depiction of Madison in her favorite musical.

I would like to thank Jenny for teaching me so much about what it means to be close.

Notes

...

The Papers of James Madison are cited as follows:

> PJM   *The Papers of James Madison,* ed. William T. Hutchinson and William M. E. Rachal (Chicago: University of Chicago Press, 1962–); (taken over by Charlottesville: University of Virginia Press).
>
> PJM SSS   *The Papers of James Madison, Secretary of State Series,* ed. Robert J. Brugger (Charlottesville: University of Virginia Press, 1986–).
>
> PJM PS   *The Papers of James Madison, Presidential Series,* ed. Robert A. Rutland (Charlottesville: University of Virginia Press, 1984–).
>
> PJM RS   *The Papers of James Madison, Retirement Series,* ed. David B. Mattern (Charlottesville: University of Virginia Press, 2009–).
>
> PJM DE   *The Papers of James Madison, Digital Edition,* ed. J.C.A. Stagg (Charlottesville: University of Virginia Press, 2010–).

EPIGRAPH

1. William W. Story, ed., *Life and Letters of Joseph Story* (Boston: C. C. Little and J. Brown, 1851), 2:420.

CHAPTER ONE | FRIENDSHIPS

1. On education and the making of gentlemen out of "middling" sorts, see Gordon S. Wood, *Empire of Liberty: A History of the Early Republic, 1789–1815* (New York: Oxford University Press, 2009), 22–27.
2. Rebecca Catlett Conway Moore, in her will dated November 6, 1759, left six slaves to her son William Moore (Madison's mother's half brother) and to Madison "to be equally divided between them." Madison came into this inheritance on his eighteenth birthday, March 16, 1769. For her will, see Will Book: 1, King George County Court House, Virginia. The database compiled by historians and archivists at James Madison's Montpelier, generously shared with the author, gives the document number as MRD-S 36323. We know that Sawney and Billey, also mentioned in the will, went to Madison rather than Moore. The other slaves mentioned are Phil, Ben, Sarah, and Judith. See also Jane Moore (Gray) Hagan, "The Family of John Moore of Caroline and King George Counties," *Virginia Magazine of History and Biography* 52 (1944):

62–67. Sawney is sometimes said to have been born around 1737. See, e.g., Douglas B. Chambers, *Murder at Montpelier: Igbo Africans in Virginia* (Jackson: University Press of Mississippi, 2005), 153–56. Yet it seems more likely that he was closer in age to Madison, based on an 1829 description (and valuation) that estimated Sawney "at 78 years of age" in the estate of Nelly Conway Madison, Madison's mother. See MRD-S 24469. I have not been able to determine why Sawney is listed in Nelly's estate when he was willed to Madison directly by Nelly's mother in her 1759 will.

On August 10, 1769, Sawney was still with Madison, who wrote that day to his tutor Thomas Martin that Sawney "tells me that your mother and brothers are determined to accompany you to Virginia" and told Martin (who was in New Jersey) to give Sawney the change from a payment Madison had sent him. See Madison to Thomas Martin, August 10, 1769, *PJM*, 1:43. Ralph Ketcham, *James Madison: A Biography* (Charlottesville: University of Virginia Press, 1971), 28, estimates that by then Madison had been in Princeton for approximately two weeks; see also *PJM*, 1:44n.7. For a similar assessment see Irving Brant, *James Madison*, vol. 1, *The Virginia Revolutionist: 1751–1780* (Indianapolis: Bobbs-Merrill, 1941), 83. This is volume one of Brant's six-volume work; I cite his books on Madison with volume number as well as subtitle. See also Michael D. Dickens, "Threads of Influence: James Madison and the 'Old Nassovians'" (unpublished manuscript, 2016), 35 and n.47. Dickens notes that Madison's family owned more slaves than any other family sending a student to Princeton at the time. Ibid., 53.

3. On male friendship in the period, including at Princeton in particular, see Caleb Crain, *American Sympathy: Men, Friendship, and Literature in the New Nation* (New Haven, Conn.: Yale University Press, 2001); and Richard Godbeer, *The Overflowing of Friendship: Love Between Men and the Creation of the American Republic* (Baltimore: Johns Hopkins University Press, 2009). On the broader question of friendship and politics in the early republic, see Joanne Freeman, *Affairs of Honor: National Politics in the New Republic* (New Haven, Conn.: Yale University Press, 2002).

4. Ross was one of the signers of a letter dated May 20, 1769, from a large group of Princeton students to Rachel Wilson of Kendal, a Quaker preacher, inviting her to speak at the college. If he was already at Princeton in May 1769, he was likely a member of the class that arrived in 1768. See *Bulletin of Friends' Historical Society of Philadelphia* 8, no. 25 (November 1917).

5. Madison's later account of the two young men's efforts to accomplish their plan of study is described in "James Madison's Autobiography," ed. Douglass Adair, *The William and Mary Quarterly* 3 (1945): 197.

6. Richard A. Harrison, *Princetonians, 1769–1775: A Biographical Dictionary* (Princeton, N.J.: Princeton University Press, 1980), 165.

7. *PJM*, 1:61–65. The literal reference is, of course, to castration, but the context suggests a completed sexual act. Madison is sometimes said to have founded the Whig Society. See, e.g., Michael Signer, *Becoming Madison: The Extraordinary Origins of the Least Likely Founding Father* (New York: Public Affairs, 2015), 45. But if the Whig Society was founded on June 14, 1769, as the successor society's history states, that was before Madison arrived at Princeton. See "History," *The American Whig-Cliosophic Society* (blog), https://whigclio.princeton.edu/about/history/.

8. Of Moses Allen, Madison wrote, "The lecherous rascal there will find / A place just suited to his mind / May whore and pimp and drink and swear / Nor more the garb of Christians wear." Allen went on to become a minister and a chaplain in Georgia's

revolutionary army, and died trying to escape from a British prison ship. *PJM*, 1:67n.12.

9. See John Quincy Adams, *An Eulogy on the Life and Character of James Madison, Fourth President of the United States; Delivered at the Request of the Mayor, Aldermen, and Common Council of the City of Boston, September 27, 1836* (Boston: John H. Eastburn, 1836), 10. Adams took it seriously. For Jefferson's attitude, see Ketcham, *James Madison*, 35.

10. April C. Armstrong, "A Brief History of the Architecture of Nassau Hall," *Mudd Manuscript Library Blog*, June 17, 2005, https://blogs.princeton.edu/mudd/2015/06/a-brief-history-of-the-architecture-of-nassau-hall/.

11. John Witherspoon, *Lectures on Moral Philosophy* (Princeton, N.J.: Princeton University Press, 1912; repr., 2012).

12. Ibid. On Witherspoon's intellectual biography and influence, see Jerry H. Morrison, *John Witherspoon and the Founding of the American Republic* (South Bend, Ind.: University of Notre Dame Press, 2005); see also Dickens, "Threads of Influence," 40–50. On the reading list, see Dennis F. Thompson, "The Education of a Founding Father: The Reading List for John Witherspoon's Course in Political Theory, as Taken by James Madison," *Political Theory* 4 (1976): 523–29.

13. Ketcham, *James Madison*, 23.

14. Madison to James Madison, Sr., July 23, 1770, *PJM*, 1:50.

15. Madison to William Bradford, April 28, 1773, *PJM*, 1:83.

16. See *Virginia Newspaper Project*, Library of Virginia, http://www.lva.virginia.gov/public/vnp/.

17. Madison to Bradford, April 28, 1773, *PJM*, 1:83.

18. Madison to James Madison, Sr., August 12, 1773, *PJM*, 1:92.

19. Cf. E. Digby Baltzell, *Puritan Boston and Quaker Philadelphia* (New Brunswick, N.J.: Transaction Publishers, 1996).

20. Madison to Bradford, December 1, 1773, *PJM*, 1:101.

21. Later Madison recalled that his reading in Virginia "mingled miscellaneous subjects with the studies intended to qualify him for the Bar" but acknowledged that he formed "no absolute determination" actually to practice law. Adair, "James Madison's Autobiography," 198; see also "James Madison, Autobiographical Notes, Dec. 1830," *Founders Early Access*, University of Virginia Press, http://rotunda.upress.virginia.edu/founders/default.xqy?keys=FOEA-print-02-02-02-2230; and Madison's autobiographical sketch sent to James Kirke Paulding, January 1832, quoted in *PJM*, 1:70. On reading law not as a profession but as a "desirable attribute of a man of learning," see Wood, *Empire of Liberty*, 23.

22. Madison to Bradford, December 1, 1773, *PJM*, 1:101.

23. Ibid.

24. Madison to Bradford, January 24, 1774, *PJM*, 1:105. A famous analogous explanation of the Revolution can be found in Edmund Burke's speech "Conciliation with the Colonies," delivered in Parliament on March 22, 1775. Burke said:

> All Protestantism, even the most cold and passive, is a sort of dissent. But the religion most prevalent in our northern colonies is a refinement on the principle of resistance; it is the dissidence of dissent, and the Protestantism of the Protestant religion. This religion, under a variety of denominations agreeing in nothing but in the communion of the spirit of liberty, is predominant in

most of the northern provinces; where the Church of England, notwithstanding its legal rights, is in reality no more than a sort of private sect, not composing most probably the tenth of the people.

Famously, Burke explained southern resistance—despite the prevalence of the Church of England there—as a result of slavery:

> In Virginia and the Carolinas they have a vast multitude of slaves. Where this is the case in any part of the world, those who are free, are by far the most proud and jealous of their freedom. Freedom is to them not only an enjoyment, but a kind of rank and privilege.

"Speech of Edmund Burke, Esq., On Moving His Resolutions for Conciliation with the Colonies," March 22, 1775, in *Edmund Burke: Pre-Revolutionary Writings*, ed. Ian Harris (Cambridge: Cambridge University Press, 1993), 223–24. For a deep analysis of the speech, see Eric Nelson, "What Kind of Book Is the *Ideological Origins?*" in a forthcoming volume in honor of the fiftieth anniversary of Bernard Bailyn's *Ideological Origins of the American Revolution* (Cambridge, Mass.: Harvard University Press, 1967). Of course, when Madison was writing, revolutionary sentiment in Virginia was nascent at best. That tends to undercut both his theory of northern resistance and Burke's theory of southern resistance.

25. Baptists and Quakers who did not want to support the minister chosen by the majority could, albeit sometimes with difficulty, obtain official certificates that allowed them to opt out of paying those taxes.

26. Madison to Bradford, January 24, 1774, *PJM*, 1:105.

27. See, e.g., Kenneth Fincham and Peter Lake, "The Ecclesiastical Policy of King James I," *Journal of British Studies* 24 (1985): 169–207.

28. Was Madison right? Perhaps the recognition of religious difference helped spur some New Englanders to oppose British rule. Yet it is also true that within years, Virginia, too, would rise in rebellion, despite its tradition of an established church. The classic view to this effect remains that of Alan Heimert, *Religion and the American Mind: From the Great Awakening to the American Revolution* (Cambridge, Mass.: Harvard University Press, 1966), who associates the religious revivals of the Great Awakening with the growth of a national spirit and the pre-stirrings of independence. What is most important about Madison's idea is that it shows his powerful rejection of an established church, and his willingness to blame an apparent lack of anti-British patriotism on its effects.

29. Madison to Bradford, January 24, 1774, *PJM*, 1:106.

30. Ibid.

31. Ibid.

32. Ibid.

33. Interestingly, Witherspoon did not particularly focus on religious liberty in his writings. His course of lectures on moral philosophy, recorded almost verbatim by students, never mentions the issue at all, even as Witherspoon touches upon the duties of religion and the importance of civil freedoms. Witherspoon, *Lectures on Moral Philosophy*, 45–52 (duties of man to God), 56–58 (alienable and unalienable natural rights). Witherspoon's lone published reference to religious liberty appears in 1776, in a famous sermon he gave in Princeton in support of independence. Even there, Witherspoon restricts himself to commenting that "there is not a single instance in

history in which civil liberty was lost, and religious liberty preserved entire. If therefore we yield up our temporal property, we at the same time deliver the conscience into bondage." John Witherspoon, *The Dominion of Providence over the Passions of Men* (Philadelphia: R. Aitken, 1776). This falls short of a full-throated defense.

34. The Westminster Confession of Faith of 1646, written by an "assembly of divines" at Westminster dominated by Presbyterians, was officially embraced by the Scottish Presbyterians and remained their creed thereafter. Its twentieth chapter, entitled "Of Christian Liberty, and Liberty of Conscience," held that "God alone is Lord of the conscience, and has left it free from the doctrines and commandments of men." See *The Westminster Confession of Faith*, Center for Reformed Theology and Apologetics, www.reformed.org/documents/wcf_with_proofs/index.html?body=/documents/wcf _with_proofs/ch_XX.html.

35. Madison to Bradford, April 1, 1774, *PJM*, 1:112–13.

36. Ibid.

37. Ibid.

38. Madison to Bradford, January 24, 1774, *PJM*, 1:105.

39. On James Madison, Sr.'s investment in the Loyal Company, see Ketcham, *James Madison*, 12; for Jefferson, see Anthony F. C. Wallace, *Jefferson and the Indians: The Tragic Fate of the First Americans* (Cambridge, Mass.: Harvard University Press, 1999), 9, 21–49. Other Virginians had received land grants in recompense for fighting.

40. On Logan, the sources are complex, but the best information seems to come from Moravian missionary John Heckwelder, who spent significant time among Shawnees and others in the Ohio country. See Randolph C. Downes, "Dunmore's War: An Interpretation," *Mississippi Valley Review* 21, no. 3 (1934): 312 and n.5. See also Wallace, *Jefferson and the Indians*, 5.

41. Dunmore's delegate was the physician John Connolly. On the affair, see Jack M. Sosin, "The British Indian Department and Dunmore's War," *Virginia Magazine of History and Biography* 74, no. 1 (January 1966): 44; Downes, "Dunmore's War," 322.

42. Ibid.

43. Madison to Bradford, July 1, 1774, *PJM*, 1:114.

44. Madison to Bradford, August 23, 1774, *PJM*, 1:120.

45. See James Corbett David, *Dunmore's New World: The Extraordinary Life of a Royal Governor in Revolutionary America—with Jacobites, Counterfeiters, Land Schemes, Shipwrecks, Scalping, Indian Politics, Runaway Slaves, and Two Illegal Royal Weddings* (Charlottesville: University of Virginia Press, 2013), 56–93. See also Downes, "Dunmore's War," 312–13.

46. The exact origin of the message and how it was delivered are not known. It may have been spoken by Logan, or reported and translated by Logan's brother-in-law John Gibson, whose wife and unborn child had been murdered at Yellow Creek. For an argument that it cannot have been spoken by Logan, see Thomas McElwain, "'Then I Thought I Must Kill Too': Logan's Lament: A 'Mingo' Perspective," in *Native American Speakers of the Eastern Woodlands: Selected Speeches and Critical Analyses*, ed. Barbara Alice Mann (Westport, Conn.: Greenwood Press, 2001), 108–21. McElwain applies a linguistic analysis, arguing that terms used in the English text do not correspond to vocabulary or concepts present in Iroquoian language. (He also argues, inter alia, that Tahgahjute, or Logan, was of Oneida rather than Cayuga parentage, ibid., 111.) The argument is convincing, but of course it still leaves the possibility that

Logan spoke some version of this text in English, or that Logan's brother-in-law, John Gibson, spoke it in English as a nonliteral translation or version of ideas expressed previously by Logan. Doubtless the English text draws consciously on the deliberately archaic style of the King James Bible; it would not have represented literal speech even in the late eighteenth century for a native English speaker.

47. Madison to Bradford, January 20, 1775, *PJM*, 1:136.
48. Ibid.
49. Bradford to Madison, [March 3–6?], 1775, *PJM*, 1:138; and see note 10 after Madison to Bradford, January 20, 1775, *PJM*, 1:137–38.
50. Thomas Jefferson, *Notes on the State of Virginia*, ed. Frank Shuffelton (New York: Penguin Books, 1999), 67–68.
51. Madison to Bradford, July 1, 1774, *PJM*, 1:115.
52. Bradford to Madison, August 1, 1774, *PJM*, 1:118.
53. Madison to Bradford, July 1, 1774, *PJM*, 1:115.
54. Madison to Bradford, August 23, 1774, *PJM*, 1:120.
55. On the term "concord," its origins in Aristotelian thought, and its reception by Francis Hutcheson and then by Adam Smith in his *Theory of Moral Sentiments*, see Istvan Hont, *Politics in Commercial Society: Jean-Jacques Rousseau and Adam Smith* (Cambridge, Mass.: Harvard University Press, 2015), 5–13.
56. Madison to Bradford, August 23, 1774, *PJM*, 1:120. ("The enjoyment of your company in Philadelphia has so revived and increased my pristine affection for you, that I found great pleasure in that token of your affectionate kindness.") Madison had visited Philadelphia in May 1774.
57. Ibid. ("I assure you I heartily repent of undertaking my journey to the North when I did. If I had it to perform now, the opportunity of attending the Congress would be an infinite addition to the pleasures of it. I cannot help congratulating you on your happy situation in that respect.")
58. Ibid.
59. Bradford to Madison, October 17, 1774, *PJM*, 1:125.
60. Bradford to Madison, January 4, 1775, *PJM*, 1:131.
61. Madison to Bradford, November 26, 1774, *PJM*, 1:129.
62. Ibid.
63. Madison to Bradford, January 20, 1775, *PJM*, 1:135.
64. Ibid.
65. Madison to Bradford, November 26, 1774, *PJM*, 1:129.
66. Madison to Bradford, June 19, 1775, *PJM*, 1:153.
67. Ibid.
68. Adair, "James Madison's Autobiography," 199.
69. Madison to Joseph Delaplaine, September 1716, *Founders Early Access*, University of Virginia Press, http://rotunda.upress.virginia.edu/founders/default.xqy?keys=FOEA -search-1-1&expandNote=on#match1. The document, an autobiographical sketch, describes itself as a "Memorandum sent Sepr. [*sic*] 1816, to Mr. Delaplaine, at his request," and appears to be a kind of rough draft of his autobiography.
70. Lynne Cheney has argued that Madison indeed suffered from temporal lobe epilepsy. Lynne Cheney, *James Madison: A Life Reconsidered* (New York: Viking, 2014), 4, 6, 18, 88, 328. In 1941, influenced by psychoanalytic theory, Irving Brant thought that Madison experienced hysterical seizures that mimicked epilepsy. Brant, *James Madison*, vol. 1, *The Virginia Revolutionist*, 106–7. Both approaches reflect the au-

thors' cultural context more than the limited evidence. On no other occasion did Madison ever refer to epilepsy or seizures. Migraines match this description as well as the other "bilious attacks" he suffered occasionally throughout his life.

71. See Gordon S. Wood, *The Creation of the American Republic, 1776–1787* (New York: W. W. Norton, 1972), 312 and more generally 306–43.

72. Thomas Jefferson, "Autobiography: 1743–1790," *The Avalon Project,* Yale Law School, http://avalon.law.yale.edu/19th_century/jeffauto.asp.

73. Thomas S. Kidd, *Patrick Henry: First Among Patriots* (New York: Basic Books, 2011), 24–25 and 25n.35.

74. Ibid.

75. David, *Dunmore's New World,* 94; Kidd, *Patrick Henry,* 102.

76. "Address to Capt. Patrick Henry and the Gentlemen Independents of Hanover," May 9, 1775, *PJM,* 1:146.

77. Madison to Bradford, June 19, 1775, *PJM,* 1:153.

78. See Chambers, *Murder at Montpelier;* and Ann L. Miller, *The Short Life and Strange Death of Ambrose Madison* (Piedmont, Va.: Orange County Historical Society, 2001), 25–31. Chambers argues for an Igboan *obeah* (conjure) context for the poisoning and sees the murder as the "charter" event for Montpelier. Both books provide context for the alleged murder through other poisoning and murder trials in the region. Miller, 70, argues that the trials were not "show trials" produced by "panic or blind racism," given that some defendants were acquitted and not all who were convicted were executed.

79. Madison to Bradford, July 28, 1775, *PJM,* 1:161.

80. *PJM,* 1:173.

81. *PJM,* 1:174.

82. Colonial charters, including those of Pennsylvania, Rhode Island, and Delaware, protected religious conscience. But these were royal grants, not documents of self-government, and their guarantees did not go as far.

CHAPTER TWO | RISE

1. See, e.g., Dennis J. Pogue, *Founding Spirits: George Washington and the Beginnings of the American Whiskey Industry* (Buena Vista, Va.: Harbour Books, 2011).

2. On treating potential voters, see John Gilman Kolp, *Gentlemen and Freeholders: Electoral Politics in Colonial Virginia* (Baltimore: Johns Hopkins University Press, 1998), 28–32. Kolp revises the discussion in Edmund Morgan, *Inventing the People: The Rise of Popular Sovereignty in England and America* (New York: W. W. Norton, 1988).

3. Madison's account was written much later. *PJM,* 1:193.

4. Ibid.

5. Ibid.

6. David Armitage, *The Declaration of Independence: A Global History* (Cambridge, Mass.: Harvard University Press, 2007).

7. Ketcham, *James Madison,* 85 and 683n.27 (citing Richard Henry Lee to Jefferson, October 5, 1778). For that letter, see *The Papers of Thomas Jefferson,* ed. Julian P. Boyd (Princeton, N.J.: Princeton University Press, 1950), 2:214–16. Hereinafter cited as *PTJ.*

8. Ketcham, *James Madison,* 85.

9. Philip Mazzei to Madison, June 13, 1779, *PJM*, 1:285–86.

10. *PJM*, 1:287n.3.

11. The capture was accomplished by George Rogers Clark, who had gone to primary school with Madison and then become a military leader in Kentucky. Clark had initially taken Fort Vincennes from the British with 175 volunteer Virginia militia and help from French-speaking settlers. Hamilton retook the fort with 500 men, including both Indians and Europeans. Clark struck back. In the freezing temperatures of February 1779, he marched 270 American and French-speaking militia 150 miles across the "drowned lands" of the Wabash floodplain and conquered Vincennes once more. The prize of his logistical accomplishment was General Hamilton, whom he handed over to Jefferson. See Wallace, *Jefferson and the Indians,* 65 et seq.; and see Patrick Henry in Council to Virginia Delegates in Congress, November 14, 1778, *PJM* 1:260–62 (describing Clark's progress with "one hundred & seventy or eighty men").

12. Wallace, *Jefferson and the Indians,* 65 and 349n.32. There were almost certainly atrocities on both sides. See ibid., 60–71.

13. "Order of Virginia Council of State Placing Henry Hamilton and Others in Irons," *PJM*, 1:288–89.

14. Ibid., 290–91.

15. Andrew Burstein and Nancy Isenberg, *Madison and Jefferson* (New York: Random House, 2010), 70–71.

16. "Election to Virginia House of Delegates Voided," May 27, 1778, *PJM*, 1:242.

17. David Hume, "Of Money," in *Political Essays,* ed. Knud Haakonssen (Cambridge: Cambridge University Press, 1994), 116–17.

18. Ibid., 138.

19. "Money," [September 1779–March 1780], *PJM*, 1:303. Madison's exact formulation was to ask if profit from British foreign trade were raised to 400 percent, "would not their home market, in case of such a fall of prices, be so exhausted by exportation—and in case of such a rise of prices, be so overstocked with foreign commodities, as immediately to restore the general equilibrium?"

20. *PJM*, 1:304.

21. Ibid., 306.

22. Ibid., 309.

23. The essay would be published in the *National Gazette* more than a decade later, December 19 and 22, 1791. In his own autobiography, Madison explained that he had written it "to prepare himself" for service in Congress during "an unavoidable detention," presumably the cold winter of 1779–80. *PJM*, 1:310n.1.

24. Madison to James Madison, Sr., March 20, 1780, *PJM*, 2:1.

25. Madison to Jefferson, May 6, 1780, *PJM*, 2:20.

26. Madison to Jefferson, March 27, 1780, *PJM*, 2:6.

27. Ibid.

28. Brant, *James Madison,* vol. 2, *The Nationalist: 1780–1787,* 14 and 422n.5 (quoting Anne-César, Chevalier de La Luzerne).

29. The tradition was initiated by Brant, *James Madison,* vol. 2, *The Nationalist;* and see especially Lance Banning, *The Sacred Fire of Liberty: James Madison and the Founding of the Federal Republic* (Ithaca, N.Y.: Cornell University Press, 1995); Jack Rakove, *Original Meanings: Politics and Ideas in the Making of the Constitution* (New York: Knopf, 1996), 37–38.

30. Banning, *Sacred Fire*, 18.

31. Willard Sterne Randall, *Benedict Arnold: Patriot and Traitor* (New York: William Morrow, 1990), 582–83; Alan Taylor, *The Internal Enemy: Slavery and War in Virginia, 1772–1832* (New York: Norton, 2013), 27.

32. Madison to Edmund Pendleton, January 3, 1781, *PJM*, 2:297.

33. George Nicholas made the motion. Kidd, *Patrick Henry*, 159.

34. Rev. James Madison to Madison, January 18, 1781, *PJM*, 2:293.

35. Madison to Jefferson, April 3, 1781, *PJM*, 3:46.

36. Madison to Jefferson, April 3, 1781, *PJM*, 3:47, and see 48n.19. Madison had signed himself "Your friend and servant" once before, Madison to Jefferson, June 6, 1780, *PJM*, 2:39.

37. Madison to Jefferson, April 16, 1781, *PJM*, 3:71–72.

38. Ibid.

39. Ibid.

40. Madison to Jefferson, November 18, 1781, *PJM*, 3:308.

41. Madison to Edmund Randolph, September 30, 1782, *PJM*, 5:170.

42. Ibid.

43. See *PJM*, 3:175n.16. In 1830, Madison claimed his opposition was based on the thought that Congress under the Articles of Confederation lacked the authority to incorporate; but in the absence of contemporaneous evidence, it is difficult to know if Madison was retrojecting later constitutional concerns about the bank into that earlier debate.

44. "Notes on Debates," February 20, 1783, *PJM*, 6:265–66.

45. Hamilton laid out the argument for the bank to Morris in a letter just after Morris became superintendent of finance. See Alexander Hamilton to Robert Morris, April 30, 1781, *Papers of Alexander Hamilton*, ed. Harold C. Syrett (New York: Columbia University Press, 1961), 2:604–35. Hereinafter cited as *PAH*.

46. "Notes on Debates," February 21, 1783, *PJM*, 6:271–72.

47. *PJM*, 6:275n.6. The note refers to an earlier use of the phrase in the same speech.

48. Thus, according to a classic British definition of 1733–34, "by constitution we mean . . . that assemblage of laws, institutions and customs, derived from certain fixed principles of reason, directed to certain fixed objects of public good, that compose the general system, according to which the community hath agreed to be governed." Henry Bolingbroke, "A Dissertation upon Parties," in *Bolingbroke: Political Writings*, ed. David Armitage (Cambridge: Cambridge University Press, 1997), 88.

49. "Report on Address to the States by Congress," [April 25] 1783, *PJM*, 6:496–97.

50. Adams, *Eulogy on the Life and Character of James Madison*, 15.

51. Brant, *James Madison*, vol. 2, *The Nationalist*, 31 (quoting Martha Dangerfield Bland to Frances Bland Tucker, March 20, 1781).

52. Brant, *James Madison*, vol. 2, *The Nationalist*, 33.

53. Edmund Randolph to Madison, September 20, 1782, *PJM*, 5:150–51.

54. Madison to Edmund Randolph, September 30, 1782, *PJM*, 5:170.

55. Ketcham, *James Madison*, 109.

56. Jefferson to Madison, April 14, 1783, *PJM*, 6:459.

57. Ibid.

58. Madison to Jefferson, April 22, 1783, *PJM*, 6:481.

59. Jefferson to Madison, May 7, 1783, *PJM*, 7:25.

60. Both miniatures survive in the collection of the Library of Congress. For Kitty

Floyd's portrait, see the catalog at www.loc.gov/item/95522342/. For Madison's, including the braided lock of hair, see www.loc.gov/item/95522332/ and www.loc.gov/pictures/item/95522406/.

61. On locks of hair incorporated in eighteenth-century miniatures, see Hanneke Grootenboer, "Treasuring the Gaze: Eye Miniature Portraits and the Intimacy of Vision," *The Art Bulletin* 88, no. 3 (2006): 496–507. On the symbolic meaning, see J. Hurl-Eamon, "Love Tokens: Objects as Memory for Plebeian Women in Early Modern England," *Early Modern Women* 6 (2011): 181–86, "When given as a love token, hair or an article of clothing symbolically placed the giver in the power of the recipient. Though not a sign of formal betrothal, such love tokens actually transcended the practical economic level of marital promises and represented a larger avowal of complete emotional attachment and surrender."

62. Madison to Edmund Randolph, June 3, 1783, *PJM*, 7:108.

63. Madison to Edmund Randolph, July 28, 1783, *PJM*, 7:257.

64. Madison to Jefferson, August 11, 1783, *PJM*, 7:268.

65. Ibid.

66. The reference to New Jersey is a bit unclear—perhaps Kitty had remained behind in New Brunswick and not gone to Long Island, or perhaps Madison had expected her back there. For the suggestion that Kitty remained the entire time in New Brunswick, see *PJM*, 7:270n.3.

67. "An —— agst —— is in general an impediment of —— to them. —— character will —— &c. —— which every —— the —— of being demanded of them. Toward the capricious[?] —— for a profession of indifference at what has happened, I —— do not —— forward and have faith in a day of some more propitious turn of fortune." Madison to Jefferson, August 11, 1783, *PJM*, 7:268. Interpretation is in the eye of the beholder, but it seems probable that Madison was adopting a philosophical tone. The "profession of indifference" in context does not seem to be a description of what Kitty had said to him, but what he was saying to Jefferson: that he would take the philosopher's attitude of indifference at his bad luck, and would himself look forward "and have faith" that he would have better luck in the future—"some more propitious turn of fortune." In any case, it is difficult to read into these fragments any major expression of despair on Madison's part.

68. Jefferson to Madison, August 31, 1783, *PJM*, 7:298.

69. Ibid.

70. For an account of triangulation, see Eve Kosofsky Sedgwick, *Between Men: English Literature and Male Homosocial Desire* (New York: Columbia University Press, 1985).

71. Madison to James Madison, Sr., September 8, 1783, *PJM*, 7:304 (by September 8, Madison had heard that his mother was somewhat better); Madison to Jefferson, September 20, 1783, *PJM*, 7:353 (referring to "solicitude of a tender and infirm parent" as a reason to return to Virginia).

72. Mary Lucile "CC" Proctor, ed., "After-Dinner Anecdotes of James Madison: Excerpt from Jared Sparks' Journal for 1829–31," *The Virginia Magazine of History and Biography* 60, no. 2 (April 1952), 264.

73. Madison to Edmund Randolph, August 30, 1783, *PJM*, 7:296.

74. Madison to Jefferson, September 20, 1783, *PJM*, 7:354.

75. It was difficult to imagine putting the capital in a state unsympathetic to the establishment of Congress as a meaningful national authority. Pennsylvania took until late September 1783 to enact its agreement to the authority of Congress to raise

revenue through tariffs and taxes, as well as its agreement to change the method of apportioning commonly shared financial burdens. *PJM,* 7:295n.8.

76. *PJM,* 7:295n.9.

77. Madison to Edmund Randolph, August 30, 1783, *PJM,* 7:296.

78. Ibid.

79. "Pennsylvania, An Act for the Gradual Abolition of Slavery, 1780," *The Avalon Project,* Yale Law School, http://avalon.law.yale.edu/18th_century/pennst01.asp.

80. Somerset v. Stewart, 98 Eng. Rep. 510 (K.B. 1772).

81. Madison to James Madison, Sr., September 8, 1783, *PJM,* 7:304.

82. Ibid.

83. It seems probable that he died in 1795. Madison wrote a letter to his father saying he could tell "Old Anthony and Betty that their son Billey is no more." This Billey died on a voyage to New Orleans when he became sick, took medicine, and "tumbled in a fainty fit overboard and never rose." Madison to James Madison, Sr., December 27, 1795, *PJM,* 16:174. See also materials compiled on Billey in the Montpelier Database, Notes N-50396. It is also possible, however, that the Billey mentioned in the letter was not the same person.

84. Madison to James Madison, Sr., September 8, 1783, *PJM,* 7:304.

85. Jefferson to Madison, December 11, 1783, *PJM,* 7:406.

86. Madison to Jefferson, December 10, 1783, *PJM,* 7:401.

87. Ibid. See also Mary Sarah Bilder, "James Madison, Law Student and Demi-Lawyer," *Law and History Review* 28, no. 2 (2010): 390–449. Madison wrote to Randolph that he was still reading. "I am however far from being determined ever to make professional use of it." Madison to Edmund Randolph, July 26, 1785, *PJM,* 8:328.

88. Madison to Jefferson, December 10, 1783, *PJM,* 7:401 and n.4.

89. Jefferson to Madison, June 17, 1783, *PJM,* 7:156–57.

90. Madison to Jefferson, December 10, 1783, *PJM,* 7:401.

91. Madison to Jefferson, February 11, 1784, *PJM,* 7:418.

92. Madison to Edmund Randolph, March 10, 1784, *PJM,* 8:3.

93. Ibid.

94. *PJM,* 7:416–17. On Vattel's influence, see Thomas Lee, "Making Sense of the Eleventh Amendment: International Law and State Sovereignty," *Northwestern University Law Review* 96 (2002): 1027, 1061–67. Vattel's treatise was influential not least because it was available in French rather than Latin.

95. Madison noted that Article V of the Articles of Confederation referred to "treason, felony, or breach of the peace" in the different context of protecting members from being detained on their way to and from Congress. This might mean that a breach of the peace was different from a high misdemeanor. Madison to Edmund Randolph, March 10, 1784, *PJM,* 8:3–4.

96. Madison to Edmund Randolph, March 10, 1784, *PJM,* 8:4.

97. Ibid.

98. Ibid.

99. Ibid.

100. Ibid.

101. Jefferson to Madison, February 20, 1784, *PJM,* 7:427.

102. Madison to Jefferson, March 16, 1784, *PJM,* 7:11.

103. Ibid.

104. Jefferson to Madison, February 20, 1784, *PJM,* 7:427.

105. Ibid., 427–28.
106. Ibid.
107. Madison to Jefferson, March 16, 1784, *PJM*, 7:12–13.
108. See Annette Gordon-Reed and Peter S. Onuf, *"Most Blessed of the Patriarchs": Thomas Jefferson and the Empire of the Imagination* (New York: W. W. Norton, 2016).
109. See Noah Feldman, *Divided by God: America's Church-State Problem—and What We Should Do About It* (New York: Farrar, Straus and Giroux, 2004), 34 and n.40. For the full text of the law, see Robert S. Alley, ed., *James Madison on Religious Liberty* (Buffalo: Prometheus Books, 1985), 52.
110. Ibid.
111. Madison to Jefferson, July 3, 1784, *PJM*, 8:93–94.
112. Ibid.
113. Jefferson to Madison, December 8, 1784, *PJM*, 8:178.
114. Patrick Henry to Madison, April 17, 1784, *PJM*, 8:18.
115. Ibid.
116. Madison to Jefferson, July 3, 1784, *PJM*, 8:93.
117. "Madison's Notes for Debates on the General Assessment Bill," December 23–24, 1784, *PJM*, 8:198.
118. On Henry's desire to restore virtue, see Kidd, *Patrick Henry*, 167.
119. Madison to Jefferson, January 9, 1785, *PJM*, 8:229. For the text of the resolution, see Ragosta, *Wellspring of Liberty*, 109 (citing *Journal of the House of Delegates*, November 11, 1784).
120. For Madison's gloss, see Madison to Jefferson, January 9, 1785, *PJM*, 8:229.
121. *PJM*, 8:196.
122. *PJM*, 8:197.
123. Ibid., 199.
124. Madison to Monroe, December 24, 1784, *PJM*, 8:200.
125. Madison to Monroe, November 27, 1784, *PJM*, 8:157–58. ("Mr. Henry the father of the scheme is gone up to his seat [i.e., elected governor] for his family and will no more sit in the House of Delegates, a circumstance very inauspicious to his offspring.")
126. Madison to Monroe, April 12, 1785, *PJM*, 8:261.
127. Ibid.
128. Madison to Jefferson, April 27, 1785, *PJM*, 8:268.
129. Madison to Jefferson, August 20, 1785, *PJM*, 8:345.
130. "Memorial and Remonstrance Against Religious Assessments," ca. June 20, 1785, *PJM*, 8:299.
131. Ibid.
132. Ibid.
133. Any attempt to legislate in connection with religion implied either that the government had the authority to decide on religious truth or else that religion might be subordinated to the goals of government; both were false, and the latter was "an unhallowed perversion of the means of salvation."
134. Ibid.
135. In the run-up to independence, Madison had theorized to William Bradford that the lack of revolutionary fervor in Virginia could be explained by the established church having created an atmosphere of servile acquiescence. The fact that Virginia

had, eventually, become a hotbed of revolutionary spirit had not caused him to give up the argument.

136. "Memorial and Remonstrance," *PJM*, 8:302.

137. "Memorial and Remonstrance," *PJM*, 8:300.

138. Madison wrote to Monroe that the "people of the middle and back counties, particularly the latter," considered the law "an alarming usurpation of their fundamental rights" and would disobey it, even if the legislature "should give it the form" of law. Madison added, "I own the bill appears to me to warrant this language of the people." Madison to Monroe, June 21, 1785, 8:306.

139. He told his friends that his document had been solicited by an opponent of the bill, Colonel George Nicholas of Albemarle County, where Jefferson lived, and that the choice of anonymity was his own. Madison to Edmund Randolph, July 26, 1785, *PJM*, 8:328.

140. George Mason served as the intermediary, telling Washington that he was not at liberty to mention the name of the author. See Stuart Leibiger, *Founding Friendship: George Washington, James Madison, and the Creation of the American Republic* (Charlottesville: University of Virginia Press, 1999), 49.

141. Ragosta, *Wellspring of Liberty*, 131; *PJM*, 8:298.

142. Madison to Jefferson, August 20, 1785, *PJM*, 8:345.

143. Ragosta, *Wellspring of Liberty*, 132.

144. Madison to Jefferson, January 22, 76, *PJM*, 8:474.

CHAPTER THREE | CRISIS

1. Madison to Jefferson, September 7, 1784, *PJM*, 8:113.

2. Madison to Jefferson, October 17, 1784, *PJM*, 8:120.

3. Fort Stanwix had been the site of the original treaty between the Six Nations and Britain that nominally ceded the land south of the Ohio River to Virginia.

4. Madison to Jefferson, September 7, 1784, *PJM*, 8:113.

5. Madison to Jefferson, September 15, 1784, *PJM*, 8:115.

6. Madison to Jefferson, September 7, 1784, *PJM*, 8:114.

7. It is unclear whether Lafayette favored some form of abolition or simply hoped to convince slaveholders to manumit their slaves voluntarily. This issue was live in Virginia, where in the autumn 1785 legislative session, several petitions were put forward calling for the repeal of a law that allowed for such private, voluntary manumissions. Madison told Jefferson that these bills "were not thrown under the table [i.e., tabled] but were treated with all the indignity short of it," and a bill to that effect "was thrown out on the first reading by considerable majority." Madison to Jefferson, January 22, 1786, *PJM*, 8:477.

8. Madison to Jefferson, January 22, 1786, *PJM*, 8:477.

9. Similarly, Madison, reporting on a later Virginia legislative session to George Washington, told him that several petitions for the gradual abolition of slavery were rejected "without dissent but not without an avowed patronage of its principle by sundry respectable members." Madison to Washington, November 11, 1785, *PJM*, 8:403–4.

10. Madison to Edmund Randolph, July 26, 1785, *PJM*, 8:328.

11. Madison to Jefferson, August 12, 1786, *PJM,* 9:97. See also Brant, *James Madison,* vol. 2, *The Nationalist,* 339 and 456n.21.

12. On Monroe see Harry Ammon, *James Monroe: The Quest for National Identity* (New York: McGraw-Hill, 1971); and Harlow Giles Unger, *The Last Founding Father: James Monroe and the Nation's Call to Greatness* (Philadelphia: Da Capo Press, 2009). On his relationship with Madison, see Chris DeRose, *Founding Rivals: Madison vs. Monroe, the Bill of Rights, and the Election That Saved a Nation* (Washington, D.C.: Regnery, 2011).

13. Conversion is not an exact science. A louis d'or was equal to 24 livres, so 4,000 golden louis would have been 96,000 livres. A livre's buying power in the 1780s before the French Revolution was roughly $3.

14. Madison to Jefferson, August 12, 1786, *PJM,* 9: 97–98.

15. Jefferson to Madison, December 16, 1786, *PJM,* 9:212–13.

16. Ketcham, *James Madison,* 146–47.

17. Jefferson to Madison, December 8, 1784, *PJM,* 8:179.

18. Ibid.

19. Madison to Jefferson, April 27, 1785, *PJM,* 8:270.

20. Ibid., 266.

21. Madison to Monroe, August 7, 1785, *PJM,* 8:333. On his reading of *The Wealth of Nations,* see Madison to Jefferson, April 27, 1785, *PJM,* 8:266.

22. Ibid., 334.

23. Madison to Monroe, August 7, 1785, *PJM,* 8:334.

24. Ibid., 333.

25. Ibid.

26. Madison to Monroe, January 22, 1786, *PJM,* 8:483.

27. Ibid.

28. Edmund Randolph to Madison, March 1, 1786, *PJM,* 8:495.

29. Madison to Monroe, March 14, 1786, *PJM,* 8:498.

30. Ibid.

31. Madison to Monroe, March 19, 1786, *PJM,* 8:505. Madison quotes Monroe's letter of February 16, 1786, which is not extant.

32. Ibid.

33. Ibid.

34. Madison to Jefferson, March 18, 1786, *PJM,* 8:501.

35. "Notes on Ancient and Modern Confederacies," April–June[?], 1786, *PJM,* 9:5–6.

36. Ibid., 17.

37. Ibid., 20–21.

38. Madison to Jefferson, August 12, 1786, *PJM,* 9:94–95; James Madison to Ambrose Madison, August 7, 1786, *PJM,* 9:89.

39. Monroe to Madison, September 3, 1786, *PJM,* 9:113–14.

40. Madison to Jefferson, August 12, 1786, *PJM,* 9:93. For Jefferson's famous description, see Jefferson, *Notes on the State of Virginia,* 21. Jefferson published the *Notes* in Paris in 1785 in a private printing, but he wrote it earlier, in 1781–82. It is probable that Madison had read it when he wrote the letter, but he did not directly allude to Jefferson's naturalist description or theorizing about how the geological features were formed. I am grateful to Elizabeth Hyde for pointing out to me that Madison was referring to the same spot about which Jefferson had written.

41. Madison to Jefferson, August 12, 1786, *PJM,* 9:93.

42. Ibid., 96.

43. Reardon, *Edmund Randolph,* 84.

44. Writing to Monroe from Annapolis, Madison mentioned that two commissioners were present from New York without bothering even to mention Hamilton by name. Madison to Monroe, September 11, 1786, *PJM,* 9:121.

45. See, for example, Hamilton to John Laurens, April 1779, *PAH,* 2:34–38; Hamilton to John Laurens, September 11, 1779, *PAH,* 2:165–69; September 16, 1780, *PAH,* 2:431–32.

46. Alexander Hamilton to Elizabeth Hamilton, September 8, 1786, *PAH,* 3:684; and see Ron Chernow, *Alexander Hamilton* (New York: Penguin, 2004), 222–23.

47. On Jay's friendship with Hamilton, see Chernow, *Alexander Hamilton,* 204. (Hamilton and his wife "stood high on the 'supper and dinner list' compiled by Sarah and John Jay when they settled at 8 Broadway after returning from France in 1784.")

48. Proctor, "After-Dinner Anecdotes of James Madison," 257.

49. Chernow, *Alexander Hamilton,* 222.

50. Ibid., 139, 157, 171, and 183.

51. Madison to Noah Webster, October 12, 1804, *PJM SS,* 8:161; Brant, *James Madison,* vol. 2, *The Nationalist,* 386. See also *PAH,* 3:686–90.

52. John T. Morse, *Life of Alexander Hamilton* (Cambridge, Mass.: John Wilton and Son, 1876), 1:167. Morse gives no source for the story, which has been repeated as true by several recent sources, including Chernow, *Alexander Hamilton,* 223–24, and Garry Wills, *Explaining America: The Federalist* (New York: Penguin Books, 2001), 12.

53. "Proceedings of Commissioners to Remedy Defects of the Federal Government: 1786," September 11, 1786, *The Avalon Project,* Yale Law School, http://avalon.law.yale.edu/18th_century/annapoli.asp.

54. Ibid.

55. Ibid.

56. "Outline for Speech Opposing Paper Money," ca. November 1, 1786, *PJM,* 9:156–57; "Notes for Speech Opposing Paper Money," ca. November 1, 1786, *PJM,* 9:158–59.

57. Madison to Monroe, October 5, 1786, *PJM,* 9:141.

58. Ibid.

59. Ibid.

60. Henry Lee to Madison, October 19, 1786, *PJM,* 9:144.

61. Ibid.

62. Eric Nelson, *The Greek Tradition in Republican Thought* (Cambridge: Cambridge University Press, 2004).

63. Henry Lee to Madison, October 25, 1786, *PJM,* 9:145.

64. General Henry Knox, Washington's number two through most of the Revolutionary War, reported that the protesters' "creed" was "that the property of the United States, has been protected from confiscation of Britain by the joint exertions of all, and therefore ought to be the common property of all." George Washington to Madison, November 5, 1786, *PJM,* 9:161.

65. Ibid.

66. Ibid.

67. Madison to George Washington, November 8, 1786, *PJM,* 9:166.

68. Madison to Washington, December 7, 1786, *PJM,* 9:199.

69. Ibid.

70. Madison to Washington, December 24, 1786, *PJM,* 9:224.

71. Leonard L. Richards, *Shays's Rebellion: The American Revolution's Final Battle* (Philadelphia: University of Pennsylvania Press, 2002), 19–35.

72. Madison to George Muter, January 7, 1787, *PJM*, 9:230.

73. On January 9, he also reported the rumor that the rebels had "opened a communication with the Viceroy of Canada." Madison to Edmund Pendleton, January 9, 1787, *PJM*, 9:245.

74. Madison to George Muter, January 7, 1787, *PJM*, 9:230.

75. Jefferson to Madison, January 30, 1787, *PJM*, 9:247.

76. Ibid., 248.

77. Ibid.

78. Ibid. Jefferson's light tone should not suggest he did not take his own view seriously. Referring to the potential treaty with Spain, he told Madison that if Americans to the west of the Alleghenies chose to form their own country, nothing could be done about it. Jefferson also insisted for the record (and somewhat contrary to fact) that he had no personal financial stake: "I never had any interest westward of the Allegheny, and I never will have any."

79. Indeed, as late as February 18, 1787, Madison wrote to Edmund Randolph that the resolution had still not been acted upon. By now, Massachusetts delegates wanted to delay raising troops pending the success "of their state measures, some of which are likely to be pretty vigorous." Madison to Edmund Randolph, February 18, 1787, *PJM*, 9:272. See also Madison's notes on the debate in Congress, February 19, 1787, *PJM*, 9:276–77.

80. Thus in Congress on February 19, 1787, Madison made the point that Congress appeared not to possess express authority under the "tenor of the Confederation" to interfere "in the internal controversies of a state." "Notes on Debates," *PJM*, 9:277. In context he was agreeing with Massachusetts delegates that plans to raise troops should now be temporarily suspended; in practice he was certainly trying to lay the political ground for augmented federal power.

81. Madison to Washington, March 18, 1787, *PJM*, 9:315. See also Madison to Edmund Randolph, March 11, 1787, *PJM*, 9:307 (reporting the restoration of calm but adding "there is reason to apprehend that everything is not yet right in Massachusetts and that the discontents are rather silenced than subdued").

82. Jefferson to Madison, December 20, 1787, *PJM*, 10:338.

83. Madison to Eliza House Trist, February 10, 1787, *PJM*, 9:259.

84. Madison to Edmund Randolph, February 18, 1787, *PJM*, 9:271–72.

85. Ibid.

86. Ibid.

87. Ibid.

88. Madison to Jefferson, February 15, 1787, *PJM*, 9:269.

89. Madison to Washington, February 21, 1787, *PJM*, 9:286.

90. Ibid.

91. "Notes on Debates," February 21, 1787, *PJM*, 9:291–92.

92. Ibid., 291.

93. Madison to Washington, February 21, 1787, *PJM*, 9:286.

94. Madison to Edmund Randolph, February 25, 1787, *PJM*, 9:299.

95. Edmund Randolph to Madison, March 7, 1787, *PJM*, 9:303 and 304n.1.

96. Ibid.

97. Edmund Randolph to Madison, March 1, 1787, *PJM*, 9:301.

98. Edmund Randolph to Washington, March 11, 1787, *The Papers of George Washington: Confederation Series,* ed. W. W. Abbot (Charlottesville: University of Virginia Press, 1997), 5:83–84.

99. Washington to Edmund Randolph, March 28, 1787, *Papers of George Washington: Confederation Series,* 5:112–14.

100. Edmund Randolph to Washington, April 2, 1787, *Papers of George Washington: Confederation Series,* 5:121–22.

101. Madison to Edmund Randolph, March 25, 1787, *PJM,* 9:331.

102. Edmund Randolph to Madison, March 1, 1787, *PJM,* 9:301.

103. Ibid., 319–20.

104. "Notes on Debates," March 13, 1787, *PJM,* 9:309.

105. Ibid.

106. Ibid., 310.

107. Ibid., 310–11.

108. Ten days later, Madison returned to meet with Don Diego de Gardoqui, this time accompanied by the other members of the Virginia congressional delegation. This meeting went slightly better, with Madison presenting his arguments in a more coherent fashion. Gardoqui made essentially the same set of replies. Madison noted to himself that "the futility of many of [Gardoqui's] arguments and answers, satisfied the [Virginia] delegates that they could not appear convincing to himself, and that he was of course pursuing rather the ideas of his court than his own." "Notes on Debates," March 29, 1787, *PJM,* 9:339.

109. Madison to Jefferson, March 19, 1787, *PJM,* 9:319.

110. Madison to Jefferson, March 19, 1787, *PJM,* 9:320–21.

111. "Notes on Debates," Wednesday, March 21, 1787, *PJM,* 9:326–27.

112. Ibid., 327.

113. Ibid.

114. Virginia Delegates to Edmund Randolph, March 19, 1787, *PJM,* 9:324–25.

115. Edmund Randolph to Madison, March 27, 1787, *PJM,* 9:335.

116. Ibid.

117. Washington to Madison, March 31, 1787, *PJM,* 9:342.

118. Ibid.

119. Ibid.

120. Ibid.

121. Madison to Jefferson, March 19, 1787, *PJM,* 9:318.

122. Madison to Edmund Randolph, April 15, 1787, *PJM,* 9:378.

123. Ibid.

124. "Vices of the Political System of the United States," April 1787, *PJM,* 9:348.

125. Ibid., 351.

126. Ibid.

127. Ibid., 352.

128. Ibid.

129. Ibid., 348–50.

130. Ibid., 350.

131. Ibid., 350–51.

132. Ibid., 353.

133. Ibid., 354.

134. Ibid., 355.

135. Ancient writers had noticed that republics were susceptible to the taking of property by the property-less majority, and this idea had been received by early modern republican thinkers. See Nelson, *Greek Tradition in Republican Thought*. But Madison formulated his analysis as a general rule about the nature of a majority and the threat to majoritarianism, not simply as a concrete concern about property rights.

136. Ibid., 355.

137. Ibid.

138. Ibid., 156.

139. Mary Sarah Bilder, *Madison's Hand: Revising the Constitutional Convention* (Cambridge, Mass.: Harvard University Press, 2015), 45, writes that "the extended discussion of the eleventh vice may have been added at a later time to the manuscript" and that it "cannot yet be definitively shown to predate the Convention." Although Bilder never states her thesis explicitly, she seems to believe that Madison's theory of enlargement emerged at the convention and was then retrojected by him knowingly into his earlier writings and into his convention speeches. See 309n.13: "An alternative chronology may prove to be the extended eleventh Vice (written most likely during the Convention or at its immediate conclusion), the October 24 [1787] letter [to Jefferson], Federalist 10, and the rewritten June 6 [1787] speech [which Bilder speculates may have been written as late as 1789]."

     This must be the basis for Bilder writing that she "hope[s] to persuade that Madison was not the intellectual father of the Constitution." Ibid., 7. Here I think Bilder goes substantially too far. She cannot deny that Madison had read Hume; and both the idea of enlargement and the idea of a national negative can be traced in their infant form to Hume's essay, discussed in the next note. There is no reason to think Madison would have initially adopted only the negative without enlargement, since the negative makes sense only if exercised by officials of an enlarged national government. It follows that Madison adopted both. As I shall argue, Madison maintained both elements until after the convention, when the negative had been rejected. He then grudgingly gave up the negative—as in his letter of October 24, 1787, where he argues for it even after having lost—while keeping enlargement. In *Federalist* No. 10, he jettisoned the negative entirely and made enlargement the crux of his argument, a move with serious logical difficulties, as I shall also show.

     The evidence for what Bilder calls the "conventional chronology"—that is, Madison's own—begins with the fact that he had no reason to retrospectively brag about the national negative given that it was rejected by the convention. Beyond this basic problem with Bilder's challenge to Madison's account of the development of his thought, Bilder herself acknowledges that by April 1787, before the convention, Madison had circulated an outline of the proposed system, which featured the negative. Ibid., 44–45. What is more, Bilder cites a letter from Virginia congressman William Grayson, dated April 16, 1787. In the letter, Grayson reports having spoken in New York with "some of the gentlemen of the convention" who were "for going a great way" with respect to "reform." Grayson wrote, "Some of them are for placing Congress in loco of the King of G.B.—; besides their present powers—; for giving them a perpetual duty on imports & exports. Figure to yourself how the States will relish the idea of a negative on their laws &c &c &c." William Grayson to William Short, April 16, 1787, "Letters of the Delegates to Congress," 24:226–27.

     This letter shows with clarity that the idea of a national veto was in circulation before the convention, almost certainly among Virginia delegates who were in touch with Grayson. The origin of the veto idea was surely Madison; and as we shall see in this chapter, he used the metaphor of the British king's negative power in describing his idea to Edmund Randolph. The overwhelmingly likely conclusion is that Madison developed the negative and enlargement ideas during the period in which he was writing the essay on vices.

140. At the end of his essay "The Idea of a Perfect Commonwealth," Hume wrote:

> We will conclude this subject, with observing the falsehood of the common opinion, that no large state, such as France or Great Britain, could ever be modelled into a commonwealth, but that such a form of government can only take place in a city or small territory. The contrary seems probable. Though it is more difficult to form a republican government in an extensive country than in a city; there is more facility, once when it is formed, of preserving it steady and uniform, without tumult and faction. . . . In a large government, which is modelled with masterly skill, there is compass and room enough to refine the democracy, from the lower people, who may be admitted into the first elections or first concoction of the commonwealth, to the higher magistrates, who direct all the movements. At the same time, the parts are so distant and remote, that it is very difficult, either by intrigue, prejudice, or passion, to hurry them into any measures against the public interest. —David Hume, *Political Essays*, ed. Knud Haakonssen (Cambridge: Cambridge University Press, 1994), 232.

Hume's influence on Madison was first noticed by Douglass Adair in his 1943 doctoral dissertation and then published in two influential essays, "The Tenth Federalist Revisited," *The William and Mary Quarterly* 8 (1951): 48–67; and "'That Politics May Be Reduced to a Science': David Hume, James Madison, and the Tenth Federalist," *Huntington Library Quarterly* 20 (1957): 343. The essays and others are collected in Douglass Adair, *Fame and the Founding Fathers: Essays* (Indianapolis: Liberty Fund, 1998). The dissertation was subsequently published as Douglass Adair, *The Intellectual Origins of Jeffersonian Democracy: Republicanism, the Class Struggle, and the Virtuous Farmer* (Lanham, Md.: Lexington Books, 2000). For the argument that Hume's influence on Madison went even further, see Mark G. Spencer, "Hume and Madison on Faction," *The William and Mary Quarterly* 59 (2002): 869–96. For the view that Hume's influence has been overstated, see Mark G. Spencer, *David Hume and Eighteenth-Century America* (Rochester, NY: University of Rochester Press, 2005), 159–87.

It is important to note that Hume did not define the effect or goal of the larger commonwealth as the protection of minorities. And as Edmund Morgan has pointed out, Hume's radically decentralized proposed commonwealth was utterly different from the national government that Madison proposed. Edmund S. Morgan, "Safety in Numbers: Madison, Hume, and the Tenth 'Federalist,'" *Huntington Library Quarterly* 49 (1986): 95–112. Madison's proposed national veto did resemble a proposal included in Hume's essay, however.

141. "Vices of the Political System of the United States," *PJM*, 9:357.
142. Ibid.
143. Ibid.
144. Ibid.
145. Ibid.
146. For a famous and influential discussion of this idea of the "filtration of talent," see

Gordon Wood, *The Creation of the American Republic, 1776–1787* (New York: W. W. Norton, 1972), 506–18. See also Wood, *Empire of Liberty,* 33–34.

147. Ibid.
148. Ibid. Hume's perfect commonwealth also included a veto power by a supervising senate. But Hume's senate had no other legislative power, and indeed in his commonwealth all legislative power was local. See Morgan, "Safety in Numbers," 101–2.
149. Madison to Jefferson, March 19, 1787, *PJM,* 9:318.
150. Ibid.
151. Ibid., 318–19.
152. Madison to Edmund Randolph, April 8, 1787, *PJM,* 9:369.
153. Ibid.
154. Ibid.
155. Ibid.
156. Ibid.
157. Ibid.
158. Ibid., 371.
159. Ibid.
160. Madison to Washington, April 16, 1787, *PJM,* 9:384.
161. Ibid.
162. Ibid.
163. Ibid., 385.

CHAPTER FOUR | PHILADELPHIA

1. In the intervening four years he had kept in touch with both House and her widowed daughter, Eliza House Trist. The previous summer, after the Annapolis convention, he had spent several weeks in Philadelphia, which led his friend Henry Lee to speculate that Madison was "in full gallop to the blessed yoke of marriage." But there is no evidence of any romantic interest on Madison's part in the intense run-up to the Philadelphia convention. His long friendship with Trist seems to have been entirely platonic. Henry Lee to James Madison, October 19, 1786, *PJM,* 9:144. For discussion, see Bilder, *Madison's Hand,* 39–40, 279n.11, and 280n.18.
2. Judges John Blair and George Wythe moved in first, then James McClurg, a physician and professor of medicine.
3. The house, whose address was later changed to 524–30 Market Street, would become Washington's residence when he was president and then that of John Adams, and would be called President's House. On the escort, see Ketcham, *James Madison,* 192. Washington had told Madison that he could not attend the convention without insulting the Society of the Cincinnati, an influential group of Revolutionary officers whose presidency he intended to resign. In the event, he solved the problem by reaching Philadelphia six days after the Cincinnati had met. Then, without attending the meeting, he accepted the presidency of the society that he had previously said he would not take. See Washington to Randolph, April 9, 1787, *Papers of George Washington,* Confederation Series, 5:135–36.
4. See "Madison's Preface" in James Madison, *Notes of Debates in the Federal Convention of 1787,* ed. Adrienne Koch (Athens: Ohio University Press, 1966), 17. Hereinafter cited as Madison's *Debates.*

The publication history of the *Notes* is complex; see Bilder, *Madison's Hand,* 237–38. The edition I have cited here is the only widely available, single-volume paperback version of Madison's *Notes*. It reprints the text edited by C. C. Tansill and published by the Government Printing Office in 1927. Tansill, in turn, used James Madison, *The Debates in the Federal Convention of 1787 Which Framed the Constitution of the United States of America,* ed. Gaillard Hunt and James Brown Scott (New York: Oxford University Press, 1920; Buffalo, N.Y.: Prometheus Books, 1987); the original is two volumes but was republished as one volume by Prometheus. I have thus essentially used the Hunt and Scott text, checking it against Bilder's editorial comments. Also available is Max Farrand's four-volume *The Records of the Federal Convention of 1787* (New Haven, Conn.: Yale University Press, 1966), which according to Bilder pays less attention to Madison's own edits. I cite Farrand for notes other than Madison's.

5. Bilder, *Madison's Hand,* passim.

6. Ibid., 14.

7. Bilder has argued that Madison's first concern was to produce a legislative diary-like account to share with Jefferson, who was in France. The statement of the historical importance of the notes came when Madison was describing the historical value of what he had produced, and hoping Congress would purchase his record. Bilder, *Madison's Hand,* 19. That said, Bilder does not argue that the statements about the historical importance of the stakes of the convention were later interjections into Madison's notes.

8. June 26, 1787, Madison's *Debates,* 195.

9. June 26, 1787, Madison's *Debates,* 196; and see Max Farrand, *The Framing of the Constitution of the United States* (New Haven, Conn.: Yale University Press, 1913), 61–62.

10. Proctor, "After-Dinner Anecdotes of James Madison," 257.

11. Farrand, *Framing of the Constitution,* 38–39.

12. Ibid., 37.

13. May 30, 1787, Madison's *Debates,* 34.

14. May 29, 1787, Madison's *Debates,* 35.

15. Benedict De Spinoza, *Theological Political Treatise,* ed. Jonathan Israel (Cambridge: Cambridge University Press, 2007), 228; Seymour Feldman, ed., *Ethics: With the Treatise on the Emendation of the Intellect and Selected Letters,* trans. Samuel Shirley, 2nd ed. (Indianapolis: Hackett, 1992), 102 (preface to part 3).

16. Its pronunciation could have been French, but Abigail Adams, who often wrote names phonetically, spelled the name "Governeer," so Americans likely pronounced it that way. See Richard Brookhiser, *Gentleman Revolutionary: Gouverneur Morris, the Rake Who Wrote the Constitution* (New York: Free Press, 2003), xiii and 223n.2.

17. Brookhiser, *Gentleman Revolutionary,* 10 (arm); 61 (leg).

18. On Morris and sexuality, see Thomas A. Foster, *Sex and the Founding Fathers: The American Quest for a Relatable Past* (Philadelphia: Temple University Press, 2014), 143–44; Thomas Foster, "Reconsidering Libertines and Early Modern Heterosexuality: Sex and American Founder Gouverneur Morris," *Journal of the History of Sexuality* 22, no. 1 (2013): 65–84.

19. May 29, 1787, Madison's *Debates,* 35.

20. This was Robert Yates. Cf. "Notes of Major William Pierce on the Federal Convention of 1787," *American Historical Review* 3 (January 1898): 310–34, 327. ("Some of his Enemies say he is an anti-federal Man, but I discovered no such disposition in him.")

21. May 30, 1787, Madison's *Debates,* 38.

22. May 30, 1787, Madison's *Debates*, 37. This was George Read, considered a good lawyer and an amiable fellow but an unimpressive speaker. "His powers of oratory are fatiguing and tiresome to the last degree," wrote William Pierce. "His voice is feeble, and his articulation so bad that few can have patience to attend to him." "Notes of Major William Pierce," 330.

23. May 30, 1787, Madison's *Debates*, 37.

24. May 31, 1787, Madison's *Debates*, 39.

25. May 31, 1787, Madison's *Debates*, 40.

26. Cf. "Notes of Major William Pierce," 329.

27. John K. Alexander, "The Fort Wilson Incident of 1779: A Case Study of the Revolutionary Crowd," *The William and Mary Quarterly* (October 1974): 589–612.

28. May 31, 1787, Madison's *Debates*, 40.

29. May 31, 1787, Madison's *Debates*, 42.

30. May 31, 1787, Madison's *Debates*, 43.

31. May 31, 1787, Madison's *Debates*, 44.

32. May 31, 1787, Madison's *Debates*, 44.

33. May 31, 1787, Madison's *Debates*, 45.

34. June 1, 1787, Madison's *Debates*, 47.

35. June 1, 1787, Madison's *Debates*, 45.

36. Eric Nelson, *The Royalist Revolution: Monarchy and the American Founding* (Cambridge, Mass.: Harvard University Press, 2014). Others who expressed similar views at the time probably deployed them only rhetorically, in the hopes of bolstering the case for revolution without seeming too disloyal. See John Phillip Reid, *The Ancient Constitution and the Origins of Anglo-American Liberty* (Dekalb: Northern Illinois University Press, 2004). Wilson, however, seems to have meant the argument sincerely, or at the very least, he convinced himself that his arguments in favor of a powerful monarch made inherent sense.

37. June 1, 1787, Madison's *Debates*, 45.

38. Still, Pierce thought Rutledge was "too rapid in his public speaking to be denominated an agreeable Orator." "Notes of Major William Pierce," 333.

39. He then took the position that he favored a single executive, who would "feel the greatest responsibility and administer the public affairs best"; but he did not favor giving that person "the power of war and peace." This was an answer to his fellow South Carolinian Pinckney, who had said that possessing the war power would make the executive an elected monarch. June 1, 1787, Madison's *Debates*, 46.

40. "Notes of Major William Pierce," 326.

41. June 1, 1787, Madison's *Debates*, 46.

42. Ibid.

43. Ibid.

44. June 1, 1787, Madison's *Debates*, 47.

45. Bilder, *Madison's Hand*, 68, notes that according to Rufus King, Madison said that "the best plan will be a single executive of long duration"; and that Madison omitted this statement from his own notes.

46. Ibid.

47. June 1, 1787, Madison's *Debates*, 48.

48. Ibid.

49. June 2, 1787, Madison's *Debates*, 58.

50. June 2, 1787, Madison's *Debates*, 56–57.

51. On June 7, 1787, Dickinson would restate his position with the metaphor that compared "the proposed national system to the solar system, in which the states were the planets, and ought to be left to move freely in their proper orbits." Wilson "wished he said to extinguish these planets." Madison's *Debates,* 84. Wilson replied cleverly that while he did not wish to extinguish the planets, "neither did he on the other hand, believe that they would warm or enlighten the sun." June 7, 1787, Madison's *Debates,* 85.

52. June 2, 1787, Madison's *Debates,* 56.

53. Bilder, *Madison's Hand,* 70–73. At 73, Bilder argues that "the June 6 speech was likely composed after the Convention" and inserted in the notes later. For reasons having to do with the development of Madison's ideas, I am skeptical of Bilder's most general claim, roughly that Madison did not treat enlargement as the solution to the problems of the republic before the convention. As I argue, Madison always saw enlargement—an idea partly derived from Hume—as crucial to achieve his "desideratum." But he considered the veto as the technology for making the enlargement scheme work. After the convention, while writing *Federalist* No. 10, he reluctantly gave up the veto—while preserving enlargement. See chapter 5. If Bilder were correct, Madison would hardly have emphasized the veto in his record of the convention.

54. William Pierce's notes read:

> Mr. Maddison [*sic*] in a very able and ingenious speech, ran through the whole scheme of the government—pointed out all the beauties and defects of ancient republics; compared their situation with ours wherever it appeared to bear any analogy, and proved that the only way to make a government answer all the end of its institution was to collect the wisdom of its several parts in aid of each other whenever it was necessary. Hence the propriety of incorporating the judicial with the executive in the revision of the laws. He was of opinion that joining the judges with supreme executive magistrate would be strictly proper, and would by no means interfere with that independence so much to be approved and distinguished in the several departments. "Notes of Major William Pierce," 323.

> Rufus King's notes for June 4, 1787, read:

> Madison—The judiciary ought to be introduced in the business of legislation—they will protect their department, and united with the executive make its negatives more strong. There is weight in the objections to this measure—but a check on the legislature is necessary, experience proves it to be so, and teaches us that what has been thought a calumny on a republican government is nevertheless true. In all countries are diversity of interests, the rich and the poor, the Dr. and Cr., the followers of different demagogues, the diversity of religious sects—the effects of these divisions in ancient governments are well known, and the like causes will now produce like effects. We must therefore introduce in our system provisions against the measures of an interested majority—a check is not only necessary to protect the executive power, but the minority in the legislature. The independence of the executive, having the eyes of all upon him will make him an impartial judge—add the judiciary, and you greatly increase his respectability.

> Farrand, *Records of the Federal Convention,* 1:108.

55. June 6, 1787, Madison's *Debates*.
56. June 6, 1787, Madison's *Debates*, 76.
57. Ibid.
58. June 6, 1787, Madison's *Debates*, 77.
59. Ibid.
60. Bilder, *Madison's Hand*, 199, writes that the reference to slavery "only tenuously related to the speech" and argues that it is evidence that the speech was written by Madison in March 1790, when Congress was debating slavery. In fact, however, the slavery example perfectly exemplified the danger of majority oppression of a minority. It is also unclear why Madison would have retrojected this argument into a reconstructed 1787 convention speech in 1790, given that he continued then to warn Quakers against pressing abolitionist arguments on Congress.
61. June 6, 1787, Madison's *Debates*, 77.
62. Ibid.
63. Ibid. Rufus King's notes for June 6, 1787, also record that Madison argued that "the election may safely be made by the people if you enlarge the sphere of election." Farrand, *Records of the Federal Convention*, 1:143.
64. Farrand, *Records of the Federal Convention*, 1:146–47. Farrand writes that Hamilton's notes are undated but "seem to refer to Madison's speeches of [June 6]." Ibid., 146n.13. If contemporaneous, Hamilton's responses would strongly suggest that Madison indeed made the argument about interests in his June 6 speech. Bilder, *Madison's Hand*, 288n.8, downplays the significance of Hamilton's responses, writing that "Hamilton may have understood Madison better than other notetakers—or the note could reflect discussion outside the convention." See also Bilder, *Madison's Hand*, 308–9 and 9n.13.
65. Farrand, *Records of the Federal Convention*, 1:146.
66. Pierce noted "the propriety of incorporating the Judicial with the Executive in the revision of the Laws"; King noted Madison suggesting that "the judiciary ought to be introduced in the business of Legislation—they will protect their department, and united with the Executive make its negatives more strong."
67. Bilder, *Madison's Hand*, 71–72, repeatedly says Madison was proposing a "Council of revision." He was certainly proposing a national negative, but he did not use this phrase according to any of the notetakers, himself included, and the composition and location of the negative were not so clear.
68. June 8, 1787, Madison's *Debates*, 88.
69. Ibid.
70. June 7, 1787, Madison's *Debates*, 84–85. See Bilder, *Madison's Hand*, 75, for Dickinson's allegation that Madison wanted to abolish the states (and destroy the planets)—a criticism that Madison muted in his own notes. See also ibid., 77.
71. June 8, 1787, Madison's *Debates*, 89.
72. Ibid., 91.
73. Ibid., 89–90.
74. Ibid., 91. This was Gunning Bedford, speaking on June 8, 1787.
75. A hint of it could have been seen the day before in the vote for the state legislatures to elect the Senate, but even Madison had been prepared to accept this proposal so long as it did not imply equal representation in the Senate.
76. "Notes of Major William Pierce," 328.
77. June 9, 1787, Madison's *Debates*, 95.

78. Ibid., 97.
79. June 11, 1787, Madison's *Debates*, 99.
80. Proctor, "After-Dinner Anecdotes of James Madison," 260. Madison also recorded his role in his contemporaneous legislative diary. See Bilder, *Madison's Hand*, 30.
81. June 11, 1787, Madison's *Debates*, 99.
82. June 13, 1787, Madison's *Debates*, 117.
83. According to William Pierce, "He is very happy in the choice of time and manner of engaging in a debate and never speaks but when he understands his subject well." "Notes of Major William Pierce," 328.
84. June 15, 1787, Madison's *Debates*, 119.
85. June 15, 1787, Madison's *Debates*, 121.
86. June 15, 1787, Madison's *Debates*, 120.
87. Madison's *Debates*, 118n. The statement appears in the printed editions of Madison's notes, but its provenance is uncertain.
88. June 16, 1787, Madison's *Debates*, 121.
89. Ibid., 122.
90. June 12, 1787, Madison's *Debates*, 106.
91. June 12, 1787, Madison's *Debates*, 107.
92. Ibid.
93. Ibid., 111.
94. June 16, 1787, Madison's *Debates*, 122.
95. Ibid., 123.
96. Ibid.
97. Ibid., 127.
98. Ibid., 128.
99. Ibid., 129.
100. Ibid., 134.
101. Ibid.
102. Ibid., 135.
103. Ibid.
104. Ibid., 136.
105. Ibid.
106. Ibid., 137.
107. Ibid.
108. It was recorded by Judge Robert Yates of New York, who also took notes that day. Madison did not include it in his notes, but may have acknowledged it indirectly in a note to his own papers. Farrand, *Records of the Federal Convention*, 1:293n.9.
109. Ibid., 1:301.
110. June 19, 1787, Madison's *Debates*, 140–41.
111. Madison was not quite arguing that the Articles of Confederation had, in fact, been a treaty. To do so would have required taking the position that the states were individually sovereign, and Madison had no reason to go this far. Later that day, Luther Martin of Maryland would actually argue that the states had become separate sovereigns after the Declaration of Independence. James Wilson would counter that the states had never become independent sovereigns and that the Declaration had constituted them as the United States of America the very instant they were no longer part of the British Empire. Madison made neither claim. All Madison aimed for was to refute Paterson's suggestion that the convention could not break the principle of

equal suffrage embodied in the Articles. To achieve that, it was enough to say that if the Articles were a treaty, the treaty could be considered without force.

112. June 26, 1787, Madison's *Debates*, 193.

113. Ibid., 194.

114. Ibid., 195.

115. June 28, 1787, Madison's *Debates*, 206.

116. Farrand, *Records of the Federal Convention*, 1:459.

117. June 28, 1787, Madison's *Debates*, 209.

118. Ibid.

119. Ibid.

120. Ibid., 210–11.

121. In a letter he wrote three years later, a few weeks before his death, he repeated his doubts about the divinity of Jesus Christ even as he affirmed his belief in a God who governed by providence. Benjamin Franklin to Ezra Stiles, March 9, 1790, *The Papers of Benjamin Franklin*, American Philosophical Society and Yale University, http://franklinpapers.org/franklin/framedVolumes.jsp?vol=45&page=113.

122. June 29, 1787, Madison's *Debates*, 211.

123. "Notes of Major William Pierce," 326.

124. June 29, 1787, Madison's *Debates*, 219.

125. Ibid., 213–14.

126. Ibid., 214. This was what had happened in Europe, where "armies kept up under the pretext of defending" the public had, in fact, "enslaved the people." By contrast, if there were no "alarms of external danger," it was unlikely that the "system of absolute power" that could be found in Europe would be accepted by the public.

127. Ibid., 216.

128. Ibid.

129. Ibid.

130. June 30, 1787, Madison's *Debates*, 224.

131. Ibid., 227. James Wilson proposed a less accommodating compromise. The Senate could be apportioned on the basis of one vote per 100,000 citizens, with states falling below that minimum nevertheless allowed a single senator. This was, he said, a "temporary concession to the small states" until their population should rise. Madison, recalcitrant, said he would agree with Wilson provided the Senate was not made subject to the states by having its members elected by legislatures. This would have required going backward from a point the convention had already agreed upon. In effect, then, Madison was not really prepared to accept even Wilson's mild compromise.

132. July 2, 1787, Madison's *Debates*, 232.

133. Ibid., 236.

134. Farrand, *Records of the Federal Convention*, 1:522–23.

135. A mid-nineteenth-century source speaks of the "Reformed Calvinistic Church." B. F. Morris, *The Christian Life and Character of the Civil Institutions of the United States* (Philadelphia: George W. Childs, 1864), 253–54. This was almost certainly the building identified as the "Dutch Calvinist Church" in George Heap's engraving of the city's skyline, available at http://teachingamericanhistory.org/convention/map/.

136. "William Rogers," *Penn Biographies*, University Records and Archives Center, University of Pennsylvania, www.archives.upenn.edu/people/1700s/rogers_william .html. On July 4, 1779, eight years earlier, Rogers, serving with the Continental army in a campaign against the Six Iroquois Nations, had preached a sermon to the troops

in the field on the text of Psalms 32:10, "But he that trusteth in the Lord, mercy shall encompass him about." See "Journal of Rev. William Rogers, D. D.," in *Journals of the Military Expedition of Major General John Sullivan Against the Six Nations of Indians in 1779 with Records of Centennial Celebrations,* ed. Frederick Cook (Auburn, N.Y.: Knapp, Peck and Thompson Printers, 1887), 250, www.usgwarchives.net/pa/1pa/1picts/sullivan/rogers.html.

137. See Morris, *Christian Life and Character,* 253–54; see also David Barton, *The Myth of Separation: What Is the Correct Relationship Between Church and State?* (Aledo, Tex.: Wallbuilders Press, 1992), 107–11.

138. July 5, 1787, Madison's *Debates,* 239.

139. Ibid., 240.

140. Ibid.

141. Ibid., 241.

142. Ibid.

143. Ibid.

144. Ibid., 242.

145. Ibid., 243.

146. Ibid.

147. General Charles Cotesworth Pinckney and Pierce Butler; July 11, 1787, Madison's *Debates,* 268.

148. Such as Elbridge Gerry and Nathaniel Gorham of Massachusetts.

149. July 12, 1787, Madison's *Debates,* 278.

150. Ibid., 279.

151. Ibid.

152. Ibid., 281.

153. July 13, 1787, Madison's *Debates,* 285.

154. Ibid., 286.

155. Ibid., 287.

156. July 14, 1787, Madison's *Debates,* 289.

157. Ibid., 293–95.

158. Ibid., 295.

159. July 16, 1787, Madison's *Debates,* 299.

160. Ibid., 300–1.

161. Ibid., 300.

CHAPTER FIVE | **COMPROMISE**

1. July 17, 1787, Madison's *Debates,* 304.

2. July 17, 1787, Madison's *Debates,* 305.

3. Ibid.

4. July 17, 1787, Madison's *Debates,* 312.

5. July 19, 1787, Madison's *Debates,* 326.

6. July 21, 1787, Madison's *Debates,* 336.

7. July 21, 1787, Madison's *Debates,* 340.

8. July 21, 1787, Madison's *Debates,* 341.

9. July 21, 1787, Madison's *Debates,* 343–46.

10. July 25, 1787, Madison's *Debates,* 364.

11. July 25, 1787, Madison's *Debates*, 363–66.

12. July 25, 1787, Madison's *Debates*, 368.

13. July 26, 1787, Madison's *Debates*, 375.

14. On August 7, Madison argued that, at least in principle, "viewing the subject in its merits alone, the freeholders of the Country would be the safest depositories of Republican liberty," and only those owning property would be permitted to vote. A careful reading shows that Madison was worried about the exercise of suffrage by people with no property at all, not by the commercial or manufacturing classes. "In future times," he predicted, "a great majority of the people will not only be without landed, but any other sort of, property. These will either combine under the influence of their common situation; in which case, the rights of property and the public liberty, will not be secure in their hands: or which is more probable, they will become the tools of opulence and ambition, in which case there will be equal danger on another side." August 7, 1787, Madison's *Debates*, 403–4. The statement therefore was consistent with Madison's political economy.

15. Madison to Jefferson, July 18, 1787, *PJM*, 10:105.

16. Madison to James Madison, Sr., July 28, 1787, *PJM*, 10:118.

17. Ibid.

18. At the time, Madison put an advertisement in *The Virginia Gazette* at his father's request offering a $10 reward for the capture of "a Mulatto slave, named Anthony," and $20 for bringing Anthony back to Montpelier. *PJM*, 9:155n.1.

19. Madison to James Madison, Sr., July 28, 1787, *PJM*, 10:118.

20. Ibid.

21. Ibid.

22. August 6, 1787, Madison's *Debates*, 390.

23. Max M. Mintz, *Gouverneur Morris and the American Revolution* (Norman: University of Oklahoma Press, 1970), 76; and see Brookhiser, *Gentleman Revolutionary*, 34 and 225n.8.

24. August 8, 1787, Madison's *Debates*, 411.

25. Ibid.

26. Ibid.

27. Ibid.

28. Ibid.

29. Ibid., 411–12.

30. Morris's proposal failed by a vote of 10 to 1, with only New Jersey voting for it. Ibid.

31. August 8, 1787, Madison's *Debates*, 414.

32. August 13, 1787, Madison's *Debates*, 438.

33. Ibid., 437–39.

34. August 13, 1787, Madison's *Debates*, 445.

35. August 15, 1787, Madison's *Debates*, 461.

36. Ibid., 462.

37. Delaware's vote reflected Dickinson's agreement with Mercer "as to the power of the judges to set aside the law. He thought no such power ought to exist." Ibid., 463.

38. August 16, 1787, Madison's *Debates*, 467.

39. August 21, 1787, Madison's *Debates*, 500.

40. Ibid., 501.

41. Ibid., 501–2.

42. Ibid., 502.

43. Ibid., 502–3.
44. August 22, 1787, Madison's *Debates,* 503.
45. Ibid.
46. Ibid., 504.
47. Ibid.
48. Ibid.
49. Ibid., 505.
50. Ibid., 507.
51. Ibid., 508.
52. August 24, 1787, Madison's *Debates,* 522.
53. August 25, 1787, Madison's *Debates,* 530.
54. Ibid., 532.
55. Ibid.
56. August 13, 1787, Madison's *Debates,* 448.
57. August 31, 1787, Madison's *Debates,* 567.
58. Ibid.
59. September 10, 1787, Madison's *Debates,* 612.
60. Ibid.
61. See Reardon, *Edmund Randolph,* 127 and 411n.15 (citing Madison to Jefferson, December 9, 1787). In that letter (*PJM,* 10:312), Madison says that "the Governor," namely Randolph, and Mason "do not object to the substance of the government but contend for a few additional guards in favor of the rights of the states and of the people."
62. September 12, 1787, Madison's *Debates,* Koch 630.
63. Ibid.
64. September 13, 1787, Madison's *Debates,* 632–33. The formulation was changed, although the principle remained in place.
65. September 13, 1787, Madison's *Debates,* 632.
66. September 13, 1787, Madison's *Debates,* 633.
67. Ibid.
68. September 15, 1787, Madison's *Debates,* 649.
69. Ibid.
70. September 15, 1787, Madison's *Debates,* 651.
71. Ibid.
72. Ibid.
73. September 15, 1787, Madison's Debates, 652.
74. Ibid.
75. September 15, 1787, Madison's *Debates,* 653.
76. Ibid.
77. September 15, 1787, Madison's *Debates,* 653–54.
78. September 15, 1787, Madison's *Debates,* 655.
79. Ibid.
80. September 15, 1787, Madison's *Debates,* 656.
81. Ibid.
82. Ibid.
83. Ibid.
84. September 15, 1787, Madison's *Debates,* 657–58.
85. September 15, 1787, Madison's *Debates,* 658.
86. September 15, 1787, Madison's *Debates,* 659.

87. Ibid.
88. See Eric Slauter, *The State as a Work of Art: The Cultural Origins of the Constitution* (Chicago: University of Chicago Press, 2009), 1–5.
89. "Papers of Dr. James McHenry on the Federal Convention of 1787," *American Historical Review* 11 (April 1906): 618.
90. That term was applied to the states, which were guaranteed a republican form of government.
91. Madison to Jefferson, October 24, 1787, *PJM*, 10:206.
92. Madison to Jefferson, October 24, 1787, *PJM*, 10:208.
93. Madison to Jefferson, October 24, 1787, *PJM*, 10:209. Bilder thinks that this letter may have preceded the speech Madison inserted in his convention notes for June 6; see Bilder, *Madison's Hand*, chapter 4. This letter shows that the idea of the negative, which had been crucial to his views at the convention, remained in his mind even after it had been rejected definitively.
94. He therefore rejected the view that in the British Empire, Parliament must necessarily be sovereign because someone must be. At the same time, he suggested, as he had at the convention, that the royal prerogative to veto laws passed within the empire was necessary to preserve "the unity of the system."
95. Madison to Jefferson, October 24, 1787, *PJM*, 10:210.
96. Ibid., 211.
97. Ibid.
98. Ibid., 212.
99. Ibid.
100. Ibid., 214.
101. Ibid.
102. Ibid.
103. Ibid.
104. Ibid.
105. Ibid., 215.
106. Ibid.
107. Ibid.
108. Pauline Maier, *Ratification: The People Debate the Constitution, 1787–1788* (New York: Simon and Schuster, 2010), 53–54.
109. Ibid., 82.
110. On the practice of using such names, see Godbeer, *Overflowing of Friendship*, 18; Crain, *American Sympathy*, 28.
111. Madison to Washington, October 18, 1787, *PJM*, 10:197.
112. Madison to Edmund Randolph, October 21, 1787, *PJM*, 10:199.
113. Ibid.
114. Livy 2.7 (trans. B. O. Foster).
115. *Federalist* No. 1, *The Federalist Papers*, ed. Clinton Rossiter (New York: Mentor, 1961), 35. Hereinafter referred to as "Rossiter."
116. Ibid.
117. *Federalist* No. 2, Rossiter, 39.
118. *Federalist* No. 3, Rossiter, 43.
119. Chernow, *Alexander Hamilton*, 240.
120. He did not ask Aaron Burr. See ibid.
121. Cf. Hont, *Politics in Commercial Society*, 7–13.

122. Chernow, *Alexander Hamilton*, 240.

123. *Federalist* No. 10, Rossiter, 76.

124. Ibid.

125. *Federalist* No. 10, Rossiter, 79–80.

126. Ibid., 80–81.

127. Ibid., 83.

128. Ibid.

129. Ibid., 84.

130. Bilder, *Madison's Hand*, speculates that Madison did not write the relevant section of the essay considering enlargement and the negative on vices at the same time as he wrote the rest of his vices essay, but added it later. But her tentative chronology cannot account for why Madison emphasized the negative in the vices essay and at the convention; gave it a last whirl in his letter to Jefferson; then abandoned it in *Federalist* No. 10. The evolution of his thought reflects the defeat of the negative at the convention.

131. Tench Coxe to Madison, August 18, 1787, *PJM*, 10:152, and n.1.

132. Madison to Coxe, October 1, 1787, *PJM*, 10:183; see also Madison to Coxe, October 26, 1787, *PJM*, 10:222–23.

133. Coxe to Madison, September 27, 1787, *PJM*, 10:175.

134. Madison to Washington, September 30, 1787, *PJM*, 10:179–80.

135. Washington to Madison, October 10, 1787, *PJM*, 10:189–90.

136. Madison to Washington, October 14, 1787, *PJM*, 10:195.

137. Coxe to Madison, October 21, 1787, *PJM*, 10:201.

138. Ibid.

139. Archibald Stuart to Madison, November 2, 1787, *PJM*, 10:234.

140. Edmund Randolph to Madison, ca. October 29, 1787, *PJM*, 10:229–30.

141. Ibid.

142. Rev. James Madison to Madison, October 1, 1787, *PJM*, 10:183–84.

143. Ibid.

144. James McClurg to Madison, October 31, 1787, *PJM*, 10:233.

145. Washington to Madison, November 5, 1787, *PJM*, 10:242.

146. Larry D. Kramer, "Madison's Audience," *Harvard Law Review* 112 (1999): 611–79.

147. Archibald Stuart to Madison, November 2, 1787, *PJM*, 10:234.

148. Madison to Ambrose Madison, November 8, 1787, *PJM*, 10:244.

149. John Dawson to Madison, November 10, 1787, *PJM*, 10:248.

150. Ibid.

151. Madison to Washington, November 18, 1787, *PJM*, 10:253–54 and n.3. Madison added to Washington that "a fourth may possibly bear a part." This was William Duer, who did, in fact, draft several essays that were not ultimately included in the series.

152. *Federalist* No. 14, Rossiter, 101.

153. Ibid., 101–2.

154. Ibid., 103–4.

155. Ibid., 104.

156. Ibid., 105.

157. Madison to Edmund Randolph, December 2, 1787, *PJM*, 10:290.

158. Madison to Washington, December 20, 1787, *PJM*, 10:334.

159. Lawrence Taliaferro to Madison, December 16, 1787, *PJM*, 10:329.

160. Madison to Jefferson, December 9, 1787, *PJM*, 10:311.

161. Ibid. Madison's assessment from New York was paralleled by that of his friend Henry Lee, who also described three similar parties. Lee described Patrick Henry's party as "opposed to any system, was it even sent from heaven which tends to confirm the union of the states." Henry Lee to Madison, ca. December 20, 1787, *PJM*, 10:339. It is conceivable that this undated letter, docketed by Madison as "December 1787," had actually reached Madison before he wrote to Jefferson on December 9.

162. Madison to Jefferson, December 9, 1787, *PJM*, 10:312.

163. Ibid.

164. Madison to Archibald Stuart, December, 14, 1787, *PJM*, 10:326.

165. Jefferson to Madison, December 20, 1787, *PJM*, 10:336.

166. Ibid.

167. Ibid.

168. Jefferson to Madison, December 20, 1787, *PJM*, 10:337.

169. Jefferson had two quirky "smaller objections": the possibility that facts as well as law could be appealed to the Supreme Court, and "the binding of all persons legislative, executive and judiciary by oath to maintain that Constitution." Jefferson to Madison, December 20, 1787, *PJM*, 10:337. The former was a lawyer's concern. Jefferson and Madison had corresponded at great length about the design of the judiciary in Virginia, including the question of appeals, and Jefferson quite reasonably thought that appellate courts should not revisit factual matters decided by lower courts or by juries. The latter, an objection to the oath in support of the Constitution, was more remarkable. It was not that Jefferson believed the oath should be to the United States, say, rather than the Constitution. It was, rather, that Jefferson, like Madison, disliked oath taking by public officials altogether, considering it unnecessary at best and promoting superstition at worst.

170. Ibid.

171. Joseph Jones to Madison, December 18, 1787, *PJM*, 10:330.

172. Madison to Jefferson, December 20, 1787, *PJM*, 10:331. See also Maier, *Ratification*, 120, 122.

173. Maier, *Ratification*, 122–23.

174. Ibid., 137.

175. Madison to Edmund Randolph, January 10, 1788, *PJM*, 10:356.

176. Henry Lee to Madison, ca. December 20, 1787, *PJM*, 10:339.

177. Ibid.

178. Madison to Edmund Randolph, January 10, 1788, *PJM*, 10:355.

179. Ibid.

180. Ibid., 354.

181. Ibid.

182. Ibid., 356.

CHAPTER SIX | RATIFICATION

1. *Federalist* No. 37.

2. Ibid.

3. Ibid.

4. Ibid.

5. Ibid.

6. Plutarch, *Lives,* I.29.

7. Rufus King to Madison, January 16, 1788, *PJM,* 10:376. Eventually Gerry would get into a near fight with Francis Dana, the delegate who had defeated him, on the floor of the convention.

8. Madison to Randolph, January 20, 1788, *PJM,* 10:398; substance matched in letter to Washington of the same date.

9. Madison to King, January 23, 1788, *PJM,* 10:409.

10. Archibald Stuart to Madison, January 14, 1788, *PJM,* 10:374. Stuart also thought that "the anti-constitutional fever which raged here some time ago begins to abate and I am not without hopes that many patients will be restored to their senses." Ibid.

11. Tench Coxe to Madison, January 16, 1788, *PJM,* 10:375.

12. *Federalist* No. 42.

13. *Federalist* No. 43.

14. *Federalist* No. 43.

15. *Federalist* No. 44.

16. Ibid.

17. Ibid.

18. *Federalist* No. 46.

19. *Federalist* No. 48.

20. Ibid.

21. *Federalist* No. 49.

22. Ibid.

23. Ibid.

24. Ibid.

25. *Federalist* No. 51.

26. Ibid.

27. Ibid.

28. Ibid.

29. Ibid.

30. Ibid.

31. Ibid.

32. King to Madison, January 23, 1788, *PJM,* 10:411.

33. Nathaniel Gorham to Madison, January 27, 1788, *PJM,* 10:436; Maier, *Ratification,* 192–93.

34. King to Madison, January 27, 1788, *PJM,* 10:436–37.

35. Madison to Randolph, January 20, 1788, *PJM,* 10:398; Madison to Washington, January 20, 1788, *PJM,* 10:399.

36. Madison to Washington, January 20, 1788, *PJM,* 10:399; substance matched in letter to Randolph of the same date.

37. Coxe to Madison, January 27, 1788, *PJM,* 10:435.

38. Maier, *Ratification,* 194–96.

39. King to Madison, January 30, 1788, *PJM,* 10:445.

40. Maier, *Ratification,* 192.

41. King to Madison, February 3, 1788, *PJM,* 10:465.

42. King to Madison, February 6, 1788, *PJM,* 10:475.

43. Ibid.

44. Madison to Washington, February 15, 1788, *PJM,* 10:510. Four days later, Madison wrote to Jefferson that "it is generally understood that an adoption is a matter of certainty" for New Hampshire. Madison to Jefferson, February 19, 1788, *PJM,* 10:519.
45. Madison to Edmund Pendleton, March 3, 1788, *PJM,* 10:554.
46. Ibid.
47. Washington to Madison, February 5, 1788, *PJM,* 10:469.
48. *Federalist* No. 54.
49. Ibid.
50. Ibid.
51. Ibid.
52. Ibid.
53. Ibid.
54. *Federalist* No. 55.
55. Ibid.
56. Ibid.
57. Madison to Eliza House Trist, March 25, 1788, *PJM,* 11:5.
58. Ibid.
59. George Nicholas to Madison, April 5, 1788, *PJM,* 11:8.
60. Ibid., 9.
61. Ibid.
62. Ibid.
63. Ibid., 10.
64. Madison to George Nicholas, April 8, 1788, *PJM,* 11:12.
65. Madison to Washington, April 10, 1788, *PJM,* 11:20.
66. Ibid.
67. Madison to George Nicholas, April 8, 1788, *PJM,* 11:13.
68. Cyrus Griffin to Madison, May 5, 1780, *PJM,* 11:38.
69. Alexander Hamilton to Madison, April 3, 1788, *PJM,* 11:7.
70. Hamilton to Madison, May 11, 1788, *PJM,* 11:41 and n.1. Their continued correspondence was known to their allies. Rufus King, writing from New York to update Madison on post-ratification elections in Massachusetts and Connecticut, commented that "your correspondence with Hamilton and others here, will furnish you with the prospects in this state." King to Madison, May 25, 1788, *PJM,* 11:58.
71. Hamilton to Madison, May 19, 1788, *PJM,* 11:53–54.
72. Ibid., 54.
73. Hamilton to Madison, April 3, 1788, *PJM,* 11:7.
74. Hamilton to Madison, May 11, 1788, *PJM,* 11:41.
75. Hamilton to Madison, May 19, 1788, *PJM,* 11:54.
76. Madison to Washington, June 4, 1788, *PJM,* 11:77.
77. Ibid. Madison wrote that his side approved of Mason's proposal "contrary to his [Mason's] expectations."
78. *The Documentary History of the Ratification of the Constitution: Ratification of the Constitution by the States,* vol. 8–10: *Virginia* (Madison: State Historical Society of Wisconsin, 1990), June 4, 1788, 9:929.
79. Ibid.
80. Ibid.
81. Ibid., 931.
82. Ibid., 934.

83. Ibid., 931–36.
84. Ibid., 933.
85. Madison to Washington, June 4, 1788, *PJM*, 11:77.
86. *Documentary History of the Ratification of the Constitution*, June 4, 1788, 9:937.
87. Madison to Washington, June 4, 1788, *PJM*, 11:77.
88. *Documentary History of the Ratification of the Constitution*, June 5, 1788, 9:949.
89. Ibid., 950.
90. Ibid., 952.
91. Ibid.
92. Ibid., 954.
93. Ibid., 959–60.
94. Maier, *Ratification*, 275 (citing "News from Virginia," *Massachusetts Centinel*, June 25, 1788, *Documentary History of the Ratification of the Constitution*, 10:1684.
95. Ibid., 968.
96. Ibid.
97. Bilder, *Madison's Hand*, 73, argues that the speech in the records of the convention was written later by Madison and then introduced into the record.
98. *Documentary History of the Ratification of the Constitution*, June 6, 1788, 9:989.
99. Ibid.
100. Ibid.
101. Ibid., 990.
102. Ibid.
103. Madison was not, of course, arguing that majorities were always bad. Indeed, he condemned Henry for what he considered "a glaring inconsistency" between Henry's complaint that the proposed constitution was too difficult to amend and Henry's condemnation of the right of nine states to adopt a constitution. The charge of inconsistency was unfair: Henry could plausibly criticize the proposed constitution for being insufficiently democratic while challenging the Philadelphia convention's right to break the Articles of Confederation's principle of unanimity. But in the course of making the charge, Madison himself criticized the way the Articles required the consent of all the states to do anything substantive: "Could any thing in theory be more perniciously improvident and injudicious than this submission of the will of the majority to the most trifling minority?" he asked. Madison was being no less inconsistent than Henry. He rejected the minority veto over the majority in Congress, while simultaneously wanting to limit the capacity of the majority in the state legislatures. *Documentary History of the Ratification of the Constitution*, June 6, 1788, 8:991.
104. Ibid., 9:993.
105. Ibid., 994.
106. Ibid., 996.
107. *Documentary History of the Ratification of the Constitution*, June 7, 1788, 9:1010.
108. Bilder, *Madison's Hand*, 77, says that Madison later edited this speech in the records of the convention to erase two points, one on state judges following state law, and the other on the futility of distinguishing state from federal authority.
109. *Documentary History of the Ratification of the Constitution*, June 7, 1788, 9:1010, 1033.
110. Ibid., 1034.
111. Ibid., 1035.
112. In the medical parlance of the time, a bilious attack meant a combination of headache, abdominal pain, and constipation.

113. Madison to Hamilton, June 9, 1788, *PJM*, 11:101.
114. Madison to King, June 9, 1788, *PJM*, 11:102.
115. Ibid.
116. Madison to Coxe, June 11, 1788, *PJM*, 11:102.
117. *Documentary History of the Ratification of the Constitution,* June 11, 1788, 9:1144.
118. Ibid., 1148.
119. Ibid., 1148–50.
120. Ibid.
121. Ibid., 1169.
122. *Documentary History of the Ratification of the Constitution,* June 10, 1788, 9:1115.
123. *Documentary History of the Ratification of the Constitution,* June 11, 1788, 9:1152.
124. Madison to John Blair Smith, June 12, 1788, *PJM*, 11:120.
125. Ibid.
126. Ibid.
127. *Documentary History of the Ratification of the Constitution,* June 12, 1788, 10:1210.
128. Ibid., 1213.
129. Ibid.
130. *Documentary History of the Ratification of the Constitution,* June 12, 1788, 10:1223.
131. Ibid.
132. Ibid.
133. Madison to John Blair Smith, June 12, 1788, *PJM*, 11:120.
134. Madison to George Washington, June 13, 1788, *PJM*, 11:134.
135. Hamilton to Madison, June 8, 1788, *PJM*, 11:99–100.
136. Madison to Hamilton, June 16, 1788, *PJM*, 11:144.
137. *Documentary History of the Ratification of the Constitution,* June 16, 1788, 10:1302.
138. Ibid., 1303.
139. *Documentary History of the Ratification of the Constitution,* June 17, 1788, 10:1338.
140. Ibid., 1338–39.
141. Ibid., 1339.
142. Ibid.
143. Madison to Washington, June 18, 1788, *PJM*, 11:153.
144. Madison to Coxe, June 18, 1788, *PJM*, 11:151.
145. *Documentary History of the Ratification of the Constitution,* June 17, 1788, 10:1365–69.
146. Madison to Hamilton, June 20, 1788, *PJM*, 11:157.
147. *Documentary History of the Ratification of the Constitution,* June 20, 1788, 10:1412–19.
148. Ibid., 1418.
149. Ibid., 1417.
150. *Documentary History of the Ratification of the Constitution,* June 24, 1788, 10:1474.
151. Ibid., 1476.
152. Ibid.
153. Ibid., 1481.
154. Ibid.
155. Ibid., 1498–99.
156. Ibid., 1499.
157. Ibid., 1500.
158. Ibid., 1504.
159. Ibid., 1501.
160. Ibid., 1506.

161. Ibid.
162. Ibid.
163. Maier, *Ratification*, 313.
164. Madison to Hamilton, June 27, 1780, *PJM*, 11:182.

CHAPTER SEVEN | THE BILL OF RIGHTS

1. Quoted in George Lee Turberville to Madison, October 29, 1788, *PJM*, 11:323. Edmund Randolph supported the call for a convention, which in a way brought him full circle to the view he held at the end of the Philadelphia convention. Edmund Randolph to Madison, August 13, 1788, *PJM*, 11:231.
2. George Lee Turberville to Madison, October 27, 1788, *PJM*, 11:319.
3. George Lee Turberville to Madison, October 29, 1788, *PJM*, 11:323.
4. Washington to Madison, June 23, 1788, *PJM*, 11:170.
5. Madison to James Madison, Sr., July 1, 1788, *PJM*, 11:185 ("John is so well as to be able to travel"); Madison to James Madison, Sr., July 27, 1788, *PJM*, 11:208. ("John continues to be sick and is in very low plight indeed. Although he walks about, I think his thorough recovery extremely doubtful.")
6. Madison to James Madison, Sr., July 27, 1788, *PJM*, 11:208.
7. Madison to Washington, August 24, 1788, *PJM*, 11:241.
8. Edmund Randolph to Madison, November 5, 1788, *PJM*, 11:335–36.
9. Edmund Randolph to Madison, November 10, 1788, *PJM*, 11:338–39.
10. Ibid.
11. Edward Carrington to Madison, November 9, 1788, *PJM*, 11:336.
12. Edmund Randolph to Madison, November 10, 1788, *PJM*, 11:339.
13. George Lee Turberville to Madison, November 10, 1788, *PJM*, 11:340.
14. Ibid.
15. George Lee Turberville to Madison, November 13, 1780, *PJM*, 11:343–44.
16. Ibid.
17. Madison to Edmund Randolph, November 2, 1788, *PJM*, 11:329.
18. Rev. James Madison to Madison, November 22, 1788, *PJM*, 11:359.
19. Edward Carrington to Madison, December 2, 1788, *PJM*, 11:378. Madison did not receive the letter until he was already home in Orange County. See Madison to Randolph, March 1, 1789, *PJM*, 11:453.
20. Alexander White to Madison, December 4, 1780, *PJM*, 11:380.
21. Madison to Edmund Randolph, November 23, 1788, *PJM*, 11:363.
22. Madison to Jefferson, December 8, 1788, *PJM*, 11:384.
23. Madison to Monroe, November 5, 1788, *PJM*, 11:333.
24. Burgess Ball to Madison, December 8, 1788, *PJM*, 11:385.
25. Ibid.
26. Joseph Jones to Madison, April 5, 1789, *PJM*, 12:48.
27. Burgess Ball to Madison, December 8, 1788, *PJM*, 11:386.
28. George Lee Turberville to Madison, December 12, 1788, *PJM*, 11:393.
29. Andrew Shepherd to Madison, December 14, 1788, *PJM*, 11:396.
30. Madison to James Madison, Sr., December 18, 1788, *PJM*, 11:400 (stating that he had arrived in Alexandria "this morning").
31. Hardin Burnley to Madison, December 16, 1788, *PJM*, 11:398–99.

32. George Nicholas to Madison, January 2, 1789, *PJM*, 11:406.

33. Benjamin Johnson to Madison, November 19, 1789, *PJM*, 11:424.

34. Cf. *Federalist* No. 37.

35. George Nicholas to Madison, January 2, 1789, *PJM*, 11:406.

36. Ibid.

37. Madison to George Eve, January 2, 1789, *PJM*, 11:404.

38. Ibid.

39. Ibid., 405.

40. Benjamin Johnson to Madison, January 12, 1789, *PJM*, 11:414.

41. Madison to Thomas Mann Randolph, January 13, 1789, *PJM*, 11:416.

42. Ibid.

43. Ibid.

44. For this account see Brant, *James Madison*, vol. 3, *Father of the Constitution: 1787–1800*, 242–43 and 489n.24, quoting Hunt, *Madison*, 165; see also Ketcham, *James Madison*, 277 and 695n.17, citing Henry Stephens Randall, *The Life of Thomas Jefferson* (New York: Derby and Jackson, 1858), 3:255 (giving date of the Trist memorandum as December 3, 1827).

45. *PJM*, 11:439n.2.

46. For vote totals from *The Virginia Herald*, February 12, 1789, see *PJM*, 11:438–39n.1.

47. Washington to Madison, February 16, 1789, *PJM*, 11:446.

48. See John Leland to Madison, February 15, 1789, *PJM*, 11:442–43. Leland, the influential Baptist leader, wrote modestly, "If my undertaking in the cause conduced nothing else towards it, it certainly gave Mr. Madison one vote."

49. Edward Carrington to Madison, February 16, 1789, *PJM*, 11:445. Four days later, Carrington wrote again to Madison asking him to help find him a job in the new government. Carrington to Madison, February 20, 1789, *PJM*, 11:449.

50. Madison to Edmund Randolph, March 1, 1789, *PJM*, 11:453.

51. Madison to Jefferson, March 29, 1789, *PJM*, 12:37.

52. Whether he succeeded is debatable. On the one hand, the two men continued a courteous correspondence. Monroe to Madison, April 26, 1789, *PJM*, 12:113 (referring to a lost letter from Madison); Madison to Monroe, May 13, 1789, *PJM*, 12:159; Monroe to Madison, June 15, 1789, *PJM*, 12:219. On July 19, 1789, Monroe wrote to Madison suggesting that they complete their purchase together of land in the Mohawk Valley of New York. They subsequently did so; hence, they were still business partners. *PJM*, 12:297 and n.1. Madison also asked Hamilton to forward a letter to Philip Schuyler inquiring about the character of the seller. Madison to Hamilton, October 5, 1789, *PJM*, 12:428 and 428.n.

53. For the departure, see *PJM*, 11:443n.1. For the arrival, see Madison to James Madison, Sr., March 24, 1789, *PJM*, 11:450. Madison reached Baltimore on March 4, Philadelphia on the seventh.

54. For example, in his letter of March 8, 1789, Madison warned Washington of a plan to establish a Spanish colony on the far side of the Mississippi that would welcome American settlers. He concluded: "All these circumstances point out the conduct which the new government ought to pursue with regard to the western country and Spain." *PJM*, 12:6.

55. Madison to Washington, March 5, 1789, *PJM*, 12:3; Madison to Washington, March 8, 1789, *PJM*, 12:5. For Madison's arrival, see Madison to Washington, March 19, 1789, *PJM*, 12:22.

56. Rev. James Madison to Madison, March 1, 1789, *PJM*, 11:454.

57. Madison to Edmund Randolph, March 1, 1789, *PJM*, 11:453.

58. Madison to Tench Coxe, February 16, 1789, *PJM*, 11:443.

59. Madison to Jefferson, October 17, 1788, *PJM*, 11:296.

60. Ibid.

61. Jefferson to Madison, July 29, 1789, *PJM*, 12:315.

62. "Speech of April 8, 1789," *PJM*, 12:65.

63. "Speech of April 9, 1789," *PJM*, 12:69.

64. Fisher Ames to George Minot, May 3, 1789, *Works of Fisher Ames* (Boston: T. B. Wait, 1809), 1:569; see also Wood, *Empire of Liberty*, 61–62.

65. Ibid. Ames also said Madison was "a man of sense, reading, address, and integrity"—but "Frenchified in his politics." See also Wood, *Empire of Liberty*, 61–62, for references to Ames's letter as well as an assessment of Madison's preparation as the source of his influence.

66. "Speech of April 9, 1789," *PJM*, 12:71.

67. Ibid., 72.

68. "Speech of April 25, 1789," *PJM*, 12:110.

69. "Speech of May 4, 1789," *PJM*, 12:127.

70. Ibid., 129.

71. Ibid., 123.

72. "Address of the House of Representatives to the President, May 5, 1789," *PJM*, 12:132–33.

73. Madison to Jefferson, May 23, 1789, *PJM*, 12:182.

74. *PJM*, 12:154.

75. Madison to Jefferson, May 23, 1789, *PJM*, 12:182.

76. Jefferson to Madison, July 29, 1789, *PJM*, 12:315.

77. Madison to Jefferson, May 23, 1789, *PJM*, 12:182.

78. "Speech of May 11, 1789," *PJM*, 12:155.

79. Ibid.

80. On the debate, see Rakove, *Original Meanings*, 347–50.

81. "Speech of May 19, 1789," *PJM*, 12:170–71.

82. "Speech of June 16, 1789," *PJM*, 12:226.

83. Ibid., 229.

84. "Removal Power of the President," June 17, 1789, *PJM*, 12:232.

85. Ibid., 238.

86. Ibid., 232.

87. Madison to Edmund Randolph, May 31, 1789, *PJM*, 12:190.

88. On North Carolina, see, e.g., Benjamin Hawkins to Madison, June 1, 1789, *PJM*, 12:192.

89. "First Speech of June 8, 1789," *PJM*, 12:196.

90. "Second Speech of June 8, 1789," *PJM*, 12:198.

91. Ibid., 199.

92. Ibid., 200.

93. Ibid., 207.

94. Ibid., 207–8.

95. Ibid., 201.

96. Ibid.

97. Ibid., 201.

98. Ibid.
99. Ibid., 201–2.
100. Ibid., 202.
101. Ibid., 209.
102. Ibid., 203.
103. Ibid.
104. Ibid., 204–5.
105. Ibid., 206.
106. Ibid., 201–12.
107. Ibid., 206–7.
108. He did not say whether the "independent tribunals" he had in mind were the state courts, bound to enforce the Constitution; the Supreme Court; or the federal courts, which were as yet uncreated. Presumably his argument encompassed all of the above. Madison's claim that the courts would be "an impenetrable bulwark against every assumption of power in the legislative or executive" was especially tricky. Less than ten days later, in discussing the removal power, Madison would tell congressional colleagues that the courts had no special authority in determining the separation of powers as between the executive and the legislature.

 Technically, this statement was not inconsistent with his insistence that the judiciary would stand against usurpation of power by the other branches. The judiciary could take a special interest in protecting individual liberties while remaining neutral with respect to conflict between the two other branches of government. Yet there was a certain tension between the heroic picture of future judicial activism in favor of rights and the modest picture of judicial restraint in the face of interbranch conflict. Madison had not fully thought through the question of judicial activism. His argument was original and potentially far-reaching—but it was not yet developed.
109. Ibid., 207.
110. Ibid., 202.
111. Tench Coxe to Madison, June 18, 1789, *PJM*, 12:239.
112. Pacificus, *The Daily Advertiser*, August 14, 1789, *PJM*, 12:335.
113. "Speech of August 13, 1789," *PJM*, 12:333.
114. "Speech of August 15, 1789," *PJM*, 12:340.
115. "Speech of August 15, 1789," *PJM*, 12:341–42.
116. Madison to Richard Peters, August 19, 1789, *PJM*, 12:347.
117. "Speech of August 17, 1789," *PJM*, 12:344 and see note there.
118. Madison to Edmund Pendleton, August 21, 1789, *PJM*, 12:348.
119. Madison to Alexander Y., August 24, 1789, *PJM*, 12:352.
120. Wood, *Empire of Liberty*, 69–70, writes: "There is no question that it was Madison's personal prestige and his dogged persistence that saw the amendments through the Congress . . . when all is said and done the remaining ten amendments— immortalized as the Bill of Rights—were Madison's."
121. *PJM*, 12:60.
122. Ibid., 61.
123. "Speech of September 3, 1789," *PJM*, 12:370.
124. Ibid., 371.
125. "Speech of September 4, 1789," *PJM*, 12:374.
126. "Speech of September 21, 1789," *PJM*, 12:416.
127. Madison to Edmund Pendleton, September 23, 1789, *PJM*, 12:419.

128. "Speech of September 26, 1789," *PJM*, 12:422.
129. To Henry Lee, he wrote that compromise might nevertheless be inevitable. Madison to Henry Lee, October 4, 1789, *PJM*, 12:425–26.
130. Edmund Randolph to Madison, July 19, 1789, *PJM*, 12:299.
131. Ibid.
132. For the letter and this inference see Reardon, *Edmund Randolph*, 178–79 and 423n.35.
133. Hamilton to Madison, October 12, 1789, *PJM*, 12:435.
134. Madison to Hamilton, November 19, 1789, *PJM*, 12:450.
135. Ibid.
136. Jefferson to Madison, July 29, 1789, *PJM*, 12:315.
137. Jefferson to Madison, August 28, 1789, *PJM*, 12:361.
138. Ibid., 362; and see Adam Lebovitz, "Franklin Redivivus: The Radical Constitution, 1791–1799" (unpublished manuscript).
139. Jefferson to Madison, August 28, 1789, *PJM*, 12:362.
140. Ibid., 363.
141. Madison to Jefferson, November 1, 1789, *PJM*, 12:439.
142. Stephen Braidwood, *Black Poor and White Philanthropists: London's Blacks and the Foundation of the Sierra Leone Settlement 1786–91* (Liverpool: Liverpool University Press, 1994), 63–128.
143. "Memorandum on an African Colony for Freed Slaves," October 20, 1789, *PJM*, 12:437.
144. Ibid.
145. Ibid., 438.
146. Ibid.
147. Ibid.

CHAPTER EIGHT | DEBTS

1. Madison to Washington, December 5, 1789, *PJM*, 12:459.
2. Ibid.
3. Edward Carrington to Madison, December 20, 1789, *PJM*, 12:464.
4. Madison to Washington, January 4, 1790, *PJM*, 12:466.
5. Madison to Washington, January 4, 1790, *PJM*, 12:467 and n.2.
6. Ibid.; and see Madison to James Madison, Sr., January 21, 1790, *PJM*, 13:1; and Madison to Jefferson, January 24, 1790, *PJM*, 13:3. The letters to his father and Jefferson also both mention that the treatment for the dysentery left him with "piles," another unpleasantness of which the late eighteenth century felt less embarrassed than our own.
7. Hamilton to Madison, January 20, 1790, *PJM*, 13:1.
8. Jefferson to Madison, January 9, 1790, *PJM*, 12:469; Madison to Jefferson, February 4, 1790, *PJM*, 13:18.
9. Jefferson to Madison, September 6, 1789, *PJM*, 12:382.
10. Ibid.
11. Ibid., 383.
12. Ibid., 385.
13. Ibid.
14. Ibid., 386.

15. As if to prove he was in earnest, Jefferson added the suggestion that copyrights and patents should be protected "for 19 instead of 14 years" as had been proposed. The choice of nineteen would familiarize Americans with the term of years corresponding to a Jeffersonian generation. Ibid., 386–87.

16. Madison to Jefferson, February 4, 1790, *PJM,* 13:22.

17. Ibid.

18. Ibid.

19. Ibid.

20. Ibid.

21. Ibid.

22. Ibid., 24.

23. Thus Hume on the theorists of consent:

> But would these reasoners look abroad into the world, they would meet with nothing that, in the least, corresponds to their ideas, or can warrant so refined and philosophical a system. On the contrary, we find, everywhere, princes who claim their subjects as their property, and assert their independent right of sovereignty, from conquest or succession. . . . Were you to preach, in most parts of the world, that political connexions are founded altogether on voluntary consent or a mutual promise, the magistrate would soon imprison you, as seditious, for loosening the ties of obedience; if your friends did not before shut you up as delirious, for advancing such absurdities. David Hume, "Of the Original Contract, in *Political Essays,* 188–89.

And on tacit consent:

> Such an implied consent can only have place, where a man imagines, that the matter depends on his choice. But where he thinks (as all mankind do who were born under established governments) that by his birth he owes allegiance to a certain prince or certain government; it would be absurd to infer consent or choice, which he expressly, in this case, renounces and disclaims. Ibid., 193.

24. Madison to Jefferson, February 4, 1790, *PJM,* 13:24.

25. Hume, "Of the Original Contract," 19–97.

26. Madison to Jefferson, February 4, 1790, *PJM,* 13:24.

27. Ibid., 25.

28. Alexander Hamilton, *Report on Public Credit,* January 9, 1790, *PAH,* 6:65–110; and see Chernow, *Alexander Hamilton,* 297–98.

29. *Report on Public Credit,* 70.

30. Ibid., 72.

31. Ibid., 106.

32. Ibid., 71.

33. Benjamin Rush to Madison, February 27, 1790, *PJM,* 13:68.

34. Ibid.

35. Henry Lee to Madison, March 4, 1790, *PJM,* 13:88–89.

36. Benjamin Rush to Madison, March 10, 1790, *PJM,* 13:97.

37. Ibid.

38. Hamilton, *Report on Public Credit,* 73, 77.

39. See, e.g., "Speech of February 11, 1790," *PJM,* 13:36–37.

40. Ibid., 37.
41. Ibid., 38.
42. According to Edmund Randolph, in Fredericksburg, "perhaps three-fourths were in favor of the partition between original and actual holders." Edmund Randolph to Madison, March 2, 1790, *PJM,* 13:79. But in more commercial Georgetown and Alexandria, Randolph reported, "your discrimination has, as it is said, few advocates." Edmund Randolph to Madison, March 6, 1790, *PJM,* 13:92.
43. Madison to Benjamin Rush, March 8, 1790, *PJM,* 13:94.
44. Hamilton, *Report on Public Credit,* 79–80.
45. Ibid.
46. Ibid.
47. "Speech of March 1, 1790," *PJM,* 13:72. In fact, Virginia had not paid off most of its debts. See Rakove, *James Madison and the Creation of the American Republic,* 3d ed. (New York: Pearson, 2006), 106.
48. "Speech of March 2, 1790," *PJM,* 13:80–82. This put Madison in the awkward position of both arguing that the government should spend more money to make whole the states that had paid their debts, and insisting that Congress was under no obligation to assume state debts at all and therefore should act circumspectly.
49. *PJM,* 13:99.
50. Madison to Edward Carrington, March 14, 1790, *PJM,* 14:05; Madison to Edmund Randolph, March 14, 1790, *PJM,* 13:106 (using identical language "very doubtful").
51. Madison to Edmund Randolph, March 21, 1790, *PJM,* 13:110.
52. *PJM,* 13:153.
53. "Speech of April 22, 1790," *PJM,* 13:164.
54. Ibid., 167.
55. Ibid., 167–68.
56. Ibid., 168.
57. Stephen wrote to Madison after hearing a (false, at the time) rumor of Hamilton's death: "We had a report here that the secretary of the treasury was killed in a duel, and were all in mourning." Adam Stephen to Madison, April 25, 1790, *PJM,* 13:176. Hamilton had indeed narrowly averted a duel that arose out of the assumption debate. See Chernow, *Alexander Hamilton,* 308–9.
58. Adam Stephen to Madison, March 3, 1790, *PJM,* 13:83. Introducing his couplet, Stephen wrote:

> Reflecting on the feeble attempts of the different states to establish a revenue, and observing them repealing or altering the laws every session, and giving so great advantage to sheriff or collector to prey upon the poor, makes me in some measure up like Hamilton and Mr. Pope did to the immortal Newton.... The report has already advanced the credit of the nation, and it is the general wish of the people in my circle that it may be adopted.

> The parallel to Madison's own concerns about state legislatures and their unjust actions is worth noting.

59. "Speech of February 11, 1790," *PJM,* 13:32; "Speech of February 12, 1790," *PJM,* 13:39.
60. Madison to Edmund Randolph, March 21, 1790, *PJM,* 13:110.
61. Madison to Benjamin Rush, March 20, 1790, *PJM,* 13:109.
62. Madison to Tench Coxe, March 28, 1790, *PJM,* 13:128.
63. Tench Coxe to James, March 31, 1790, *PJM,* 13:132.

64. Ibid., 132.
65. John Parrish to Madison, May 28, 1790, *PJM*, 13:232. See also Madison's speech of February 11, 1790, *PJM*, 13:33, where Madison said that if "foreigners take the advantage of liberty afforded them by the American trade, to employ our shipping in the slave trade between Africa and the West Indies, when they are restrained from employing their own by restrictive laws of their nation," it would be possible for Congress to act: "If this is the case, is there any person of humanity that would not wish to prevent them?" The true answer to that rhetorical question, of course, was yes. The slave trade was good business, especially in Rhode Island.
66. John Parrish to Madison, May 28, 1790, *PJM*, 13:232.
67. Ibid.
68. Ibid.
69. Madison to John Parrish, June 6, 1790, *PJM*, 13:240.
70. Edward Carrington to Madison, April 7, 1790, *PJM*, 13:142.
71. George Lee Turberville to Madison, April 7, 1790, *PJM*, 13:143.
72. Ibid.
73. Benjamin Rush to Madison, April 10, 1790, *PJM*, 13:146.
74. Henry Lee to Madison, April 3, 1790, *PJM*, 13:136.
75. Robert E. Lee was not born until 1807.
76. Madison to Henry Lee, April 13, 1790, *PJM*, 13:147.
77. Henry Lee to Madison, April 3, 1790, *PJM*, 13:137.
78. Madison to Henry Lee, April 13, 1790, *PJM*, 148.
79. Madison to James Madison, Sr., June 13, 1790, *PJM*, 13:241–42. Madison instructed his father to plant the rice first "in a flower pot of rich earth, and then shift the contents of the pot into the ground so as not to disturb the roots. A few of the grains may be tried at once in the garden in a strong soil."
80. Ibid., 242.
81. Josiah Parker[?] to Madison[?], undated, *PJM*, 13:246.
82. Cf. Chernow, *Alexander Hamilton*, 327–28, who writes that there was already "an emerging consensus" on linkage before the meeting.
83. *PTJ*, 17:205
84. Ibid., 17:206.
85. Ibid., 206.
86. Ibid.
87. As Madison explained in an address to Congress, there was no way for Congress truly to guarantee that this would not happen: "But what more can we do than pass a law for the purpose? It is not in our power to guard against the repeal. Our acts are not like those of the Medes and Persians, unalterable. A repeal is a thing against which no provision can be made." "Speech of July 6, 1790," *PJM*, 13:264. Here Madison was accomplishing two opposite tasks: insisting that "the plighted faith of the government," as he put it, would ensure that the government transferred to the Potomac; and giving the Pennsylvanians a sliver of hope that Congress could change its mind, thereby raising the value of the option they were contemplating.

Even some supporters of the Potomac site feared that Congress would change its mind. George Nicholas wrote to Madison disapprovingly from Kentucky that "the eastern members must have now given up all expectations of ever again getting [the capital] to the north of Philadelphia; will they not naturally therefore support that place and if they do will the Pennsylvanians regard their contract with the southern members?" Nicholas believed only a presidential veto of an eventual repeal bill would be effective. George Nicholas to Madison, December 31, 1790, *PJM,* 13:338.

88. *PTJ,* 17:206–7.

89. Ibid., 207.

90. Madison to Monroe, July 4, 1790, *PJM,* 13:261–62.

91. Ibid., 262.

92. Three weeks later, writing to Monroe about the impending passage of the assumption, Madison claimed that he still opposed it even though "in its present form it will very little affect the interest of Virginia in either way." He had not "overcome" his other objections, he wrote, and he had even stated some of them publicly. "At the same time," Madison said, "I cannot deny that the crisis demands the spirit of accommodation to a certain extent. If the measure should be adopted, I shall wish it to be considered as an unavoidable evil, and possibly not the worst side of the dilemma." Madison to Monroe, July 24 or 25, 1790, *PJM,* 13:282–83.

It is noteworthy that Madison was preserving cover for himself in a letter to Monroe that certainly was less than fully honest. It was true, of course, that Madison considered "a spirit of accommodation" appropriate—but he had actually acquiesced in the "unavoidable evil" of assumption. He similarly wrote to his father that those who voted for the assumption "did so on the supposition that it was a lesser evil than to risk the effect of rejection on the states which insisted on the measure." He pointed out that "I could not bring myself to concur with them," but concluded that he considered it "now incumbent on us all to make the best of what is done." After all, "in a pecuniary light, the assumption is no longer of much consequence to Virginia, the sum allotted to her being about her proportion of the whole. . . . She will consequently pay no more to the general treasury than she now pays to the state treasury." Madison to James Madison, Sr., July 31, 1790, *PJM,* 13:284.

93. Madison to Washington, July 21, 1788, *PJM,* 11:190. The description of the Constitution as "a machine that would go of itself" is however much later, used first in 1888 by James Russell Lowell, "The Place of the Independent in Politics," *Literary and Political Addresses* (Boston: Houghton and Mifflin, 1904), 252.

94. Madison to James Madison, Sr., August 14, 1790, *PJM,* 13:292.

95. Ibid., 293.

96. Mason's given reasons related mostly to the easy navigability of the river up to Georgetown but not beyond. The river was narrow, he said, which made the location safe from big ships. The location was also defensible by land, "as derived from the high and commanding hills around it." Jefferson to Washington, September 17, 1790, *PJM,* 13:297–98. Jefferson wrote the memo in the first person plural; the other member of the "we" was Madison.

97. Jefferson to Madison, September 20, 1790, *PJM,* 13:299.

98. Jefferson to Madison, September 23, 1790, *PJM,* 13:299. The saga of the horse did not end there. After Jefferson sent a servant to pick it up from Madison and brought the horse home, the horse took sick and died. Madison did not want Jefferson to pay him for it, reasoning that "from the symptoms mentioned it can scarcely be doubted that the malady must have been friendly of that which proved fatal." He proposed an independent arbitrator to decide who should bear the loss of the horse. In the end, Jefferson insisted on paying anyway. Madison to Jefferson, January 11, 1791, *PJM,* 13:352 and n.1.

99. "Instructions for the Montpelier Overseer and Laborers," November 8, 1790, *PJM,* 13:302.

100. Ibid., 303; see also 304, where the same instruction is given to Lewis Collins.
101. *PJM*, 13:315.
102. Ibid., 13:316.
103. Ibid., 13:322.
104. "Speech of December 16, 1790," *PJM*, 13:323.
105. "Speech of December 22, 1790," *PJM*, 13:328.
106. Ibid., 329.
107. "Speech of December 23, 1790," *PJM*, 13:330.
108. "Speech of December 24, 1790," *PJM*, 13:333.
109. The bill was held over to the next congressional term, and Madison was asked by Virginia Quaker Robert Pleasants to renew his proposed exemption. Pleasants to Madison, June 6, 1791, *PJM*, 14:30; Pleasants to Madison, August 8, 1791, *PJM*, 14:70. He agreed to do so, but bluntly refused to introduce another bill that would have called for the abolition of slavery. Virginia Quakers had themselves only recently reached the definitive conclusion that being a member of the Society of Friends was incompatible with slaveholding. Madison told Pleasants frankly that his constituents who had elected him were slaveholders with an interest in continuing the practice, and that he therefore could not and would not sponsor an abolition bill. He also warned him that pressing the issue would produce backlash: In Virginia, the assembly might pass a law actually outlawing the practice of freeing one's own slaves. Madison to Pleasants, October 30, 1791, *PJM*, 14:91–92.
110. "Speech of January 6, 1791," *PJM*, 13:349.
111. Hamilton, *Report on the Further Provision Necessary for Establishing Public Credit (Report on a National Bank)*, December 13, 1790, *PAH*, 7:305.
112. Ibid., 307.
113. Madison to Edmund Pendleton, January 2, 1791, *PJM*, 13:344. The letter also contains an important discussion of the meaning of the clause of the Constitution making treaties the supreme law of the land. Responding to Pendleton's query whether a provision of the proposed debt-resolution treaty with Great Britain operated automatically or required subsequent legislation to implement, Madison wrote:

    As treaties are declared to be the supreme *law* of the land, I should suppose that the *words* of the *treaty* are to be taken for the *words* of law, unless the stipulation be expressly or necessarily executory, which does not in this instance appear to be the case. Ibid., 342.

    What is noteworthy about this simple formulation is that it is exactly the opposite of the rule adopted by the Supreme Court of the United States in Medellín v. Texas, 552 U.S. 491 (2008), according to which treaties do not become the supreme law of the land without subsequent legislation unless they expressly state that they are intended to become so.
114. Madison to James Madison, Sr., January 23, 1791, *PJM*, 13:358.
115. "Notes on Banks," February 1, 1791, *PJM*, 13:364–65. Madison was relying on Adam Anderson, *Historical and Chronological Deduction of the Origin of Commerce from the Earliest Accounts to the Present Time, Containing a History of the Great Commercial Interests of the British Empire* (London, 1764), for Machiavelli's view; *PJM*, 13:367n.4.
116. "Notes on Banks," February 1, 1791, *PJM*, 13:366.
117. Anderson, *Origin of Commerce.*
118. "Notes on Banks," *PJM*, 13:366.

119. Ibid.
120. "Notes on the Bank of England," *PJM*, 13:367–68.
121. "Speech of February 2, 1791," *PJM*, 13:373.
122. Ibid.
123. Ibid. In his notes, Madison had observed that the Bank of Amsterdam had survived a run in 1672, paying off all its depositors. But the Bank of Amsterdam was, he believed, designed for the convenience of merchants, not to shore up the government—and its obligations therefore probably did not exceed its deposits, as those of the Bank of the United States would. "Notes on Banks," *PJM*, 13:366.
124. Ibid., 373–74. Madison also argued that the bank would give "an undue preference to the holders of a particular denomination of the public debt, and to those at and within reach of the seat of government. If the subscriptions should be rapid, the distant holders of paper would be excluded altogether." His point was that the bank's stockholders would be located in the financial centers, and this would give them an advantage over bondholders spread across the country.
125. Ibid., 374.
126. Ibid.
127. Ibid.
128. Ibid., 375. In passing, Madison devoted a long paragraph to refuting the "novel doctrine" that the phrase "general welfare" gave Congress a "general power" to do whatever was needed so long as it does not interfere with the powers of the states. In response, Madison said that a national bank would, in fact, interfere with state governments. More important, "Interference with the power of the state was no constitutional criterion of the power of Congress." If Congress did not have a power, it could not exercise it. If it did have a power, Congress could exercise it "although it should interfere with the laws, or even the constitution of the states." Finally, if Congress could incorporate a bank on the theory that this did not interfere with states, then Congress could incorporate any company it wished—or even religious societies. "Congress might even establish religious teachers in every parish, and pay them out of the Treasury of the United States, leaving other teachers unmolested in their functions." Ibid., 375–76. This was an odd argument indeed in the light of the establishment clause, which Madison seems momentarily to have forgotten.
129. Ibid., 377.
130. Ibid., 378.
131. Ibid., 381.
132. *PJM*, 13:388n.6.
133. *PJM*, 13:396n.1.
134. Madison told the story to Jared Sparks in 1830. Proctor, "After-Dinner Anecdotes of James Madison," 257.
135. "Opinion on the Bank," February 23, 1791, *PAH*, 7:98; see also Chernow, *Alexander Hamilton*, 354. Wood, *Empire of Liberty*, 145, says Hamilton worked on the opinion for a week.
136. Madison to Ambrose Madison, March 2, 1790, *PJM*, 13:402.
137. Jefferson to James Madison, March 13, 1791, *PJM*, 13:404 and n.2.
138. Madison to Jefferson, March 13, 1791, *PJM*, 13:405.
139. Ibid., 405–6.
140. Madison to Ambrose Madison, March 2, 1790, *PJM*, 13:402.
141. "Notes on Hudson Valley Lodgings," post–April 24, 1791, *PJM*, 14:14.

142. Monroe to Madison, February 28, 1791, *PJM*, 13:401.

143. Madison to Monroe, April 12, 1791, *PJM*, 14:5.

144. Madison to Jefferson, May 1, 1791, *PJM*, 14:15.

145. Ibid.

146. Ibid.

147. Jefferson to Madison, July 21, 1791, *PJM*, 14:49–50.

148. Ibid., 50.

149. Madison wrote back to Jefferson that there was a possibility Freneau would accept—and that if he did, "in the conduct and title of the paper, it will be altogether his own." Madison to Jefferson, July 24, 1791, *PJM*, 14:52. Freneau promised a decisive answer by the end of July. Philip Freneau to Madison, July 25, 1791, *PJM*, 14:57.

150. Madison to Joseph Jones; Mann Page, Jr.; and Charles Simms, post–August 23, 1791, *PJM*, 14:71, 72, 73.

151. Madison to Jefferson, May 1, 1791, *PJM*, 14:16.

152. Jefferson to Madison, May 9, 1791, *PJM*, 14:19.

153. For a lengthy report of a conversation between Beckwith and Madison, in which Beckwith's unofficial status was the primary topic, see "Memorandum by Madison to Jefferson," April 18, 1791, *PJM*, 14:7–9. The meeting seems to have been the first occasion on which Madison acted as an unofficial diplomat on behalf of Jefferson, who could not meet with Beckwith given the latter's unofficial status.

154. Madison to Jefferson, May 12, 1791, *PJM*, 14:22.

155. Ibid., 23.

156. Jefferson to Madison, May 9, 1791, *PJM*, 14:18.

157. The discourses were published between April 1790 and 1791 in the *National Gazette*. They were later collected and published, still technically anonymously but with a hint at their authorship, as *Discourses on Davila: A Series of Papers, on Political History* (Boston: Russell and Cutler, 1805).

158. See Nicholas Westbrook, "Prince Taylor," in *African American National Biography*, ed. Henry Louis Gates, Jr., and Evelyn Brooks Higginbotham (New York: Oxford University Press, 2008), 516; and Annette Gordon-Reed, *The Hemingses of Monticello: An American Family* (New York: W. W. Norton, 2008), 466–67.

159. Ibid.

160. "Notes on Lake Country Tour," May 31–June 7, 1791, *PJM*, 14:27.

161. Madison to Jefferson, June 27, 1791, *PJM*, 14:37.

162. Madison to Jefferson, June 23, 1791, *PJM*, 14:36.

163. Madison to Jefferson, July 10, 1791, *PJM*, 14:43.

164. Ibid., 36. When Madison later realized that John Quincy Adams was the author, he commented that "there is more of method also in the arguments, and much less of clumsiness and heaviness in the style, than characterize [Adams's] writings." Madison to Jefferson, July 13, 1791, *PJM*, 14:46. Madison persisted in believing that "the partisans of Mr. Adams's heresies [even in the eastern states] are perfectly insignificant in point of number—that particularly in Boston he is become distinguished for his unpopularity." Ibid.

165. Jefferson to Madison, June 28, 1791, *PJM*, 14:38.

166. Jefferson did not make matters better by pushing for Paine to be appointed postmaster general. Jefferson to Madison, July 10, 1791, *PJM*, 13:44. Madison unwisely endorsed the undertaking, writing to Jefferson that "I wish you success with all my

heart and your efforts for Paine. Besides the advantage to him which he deserves, an appointment for him, at this moment would do public good in various ways." Madison to Jefferson, July 13, 1791, *PJM*, 14:47. What Madison meant was that if George Washington appeared to endorse Paine by making him postmaster general, it would lessen the criticism of Jefferson for endorsing Paine's pamphlet. But, of course, for precisely this reason, Washington was not going to appoint Paine to anything; Jefferson was therefore keeping the issue alive when he should have been trying to kill it. On July 21, Jefferson acknowledged to Madison that Paine would not be appointed. Jefferson to Madison, July 21, 1791, *PJM*, 14:50.

167. Federal Reserve Bank of Philadelphia, *The First Bank of the United States: A Chapter in the History of Central Banking* (2009), 4, 6.

168. Jefferson to Madison, July 6, 1791, *PJM*, 14:41–42.

169. Madison to Jefferson, July 10, 1791, *PJM*, 14:43.

170. Ibid.

171. Madison to Jefferson, July 13, 1791, *PJM*, 14:47.

172. Jefferson to Madison, July 10, 1791, *PJM*, 14:44.

173. Madison to Jefferson, August 8, 1791, *PJM*, 14:69.

174. Ibid.

175. Madison to Jefferson, July 10, 1791, *PJM*, 14:43.

176. Henry Lee to Madison, August 24, 1791, *PJM*, 14:73–74.

177. Ibid.

178. Chernow, *Alexander Hamilton*, 360.

179. Congress had created the commission and named what Madison called the "commissioners for purchasing in the public debt." For his view that this method of legislative appointment was perfectly constitutional, see his speech of December 7, 1791, *PJM*, 14:143.

180. Federal Reserve Bank of Philadelphia, *First Bank of the United States*, 6–7.

181. Madison to Jefferson, July 24, 1791, *PJM*, 14:53.

182. Ibid.

183. Jefferson to Madison, July 27, 1791, *PJM*, 14:58.

184. Madison to Jefferson, July 31, 1791, *PJM*, 14:61.

185. Jefferson to Madison, August 18, 1791, *PJM*, 14:71.

186. Washington to Madison, October 27, 1791, *PJM*, 14:87–88. The address of the house is at *PJM*, 14:86–87. Henry Lee wrote to Madison criticizing the opening paragraph of the address, which rather formulaically recited that the happiness of the country flowed from heaven but also to a "degree" from "the Constitution and laws of the United States." Lee rejected that the government had nothing to do with it: "We owe our prosperity such as it is . . . to our own native vigor as a people and to a continuation of peace, not to the wisdom or care of government." Henry Lee to Madison, January 8, 1792, *PJM*, 14:23.

Madison replied that, writing as part of a committee, he had used the word "degree" as an intentional qualifier. But he also insisted that "the United States though enjoying less prosperity than is usually represented, owe their prosperity in a degree, though by no means in the extravagant degree pretended by interested sycophants, to the establishment and influence of the general government." The system under the Constitution was not perfect, but it was "better in many respects than it would have been under the old system." In particular, the Constitution limited "certain abuses of state legislation" and it encouraged "uniformity and stability" through "the regulations of commerce, in place of the fickle and interfering laws of the states." Madison to Henry Lee, January 21, 1792, *PJM*, 14:193.

CHAPTER NINE | ENEMIES

1. "Population and Emigration," November 19, 1791, published November 21, 71, *PJM*, 14:121.
2. "Consolidation," December 3, 1791, published December 5, 1791, *PJM*, 14:138.
3. Edmund Pendleton to Madison, December 9, 1791, *PJM*, 14:145. Pendleton told Madison that the arguments had focused on international law: "Grotius, Pufendorf, Vattel and others were worried in the service." Ibid.
4. William Madison to Madison, December 3, 1791, *PJM*, 14:137.
5. Ibid.
6. Madison wrote:

> I am at a loss what to say as to brother William's adventuring into public life. The prospect of service to his country does not appear to me to call for much personal sacrifice. Nor can the honor, the profit or the pleasure of the undertaking, be any object. At the same time if his inclination is on that side, and his private affairs will admit, I would not be understood to discountenance the measure. I recommend it to him however not to make an attempt without a tolerable certainty of success, and by no means to run into the error of courting it by the usual practices. If he wishes to establish himself in the good will of the County, the only durable as well as honorable plan will be to establish a character that merits it. Madison to Ambrose Madison, October 11, 1787, *PJM*, 10:191–92.

> On Madison's relationship to William, see Stuart L. Butler, "James Madison's Brother Willey," White House Historical Association, www.whitehousehistory.org/james-madisons-brother-willey.

7. Madison to William Madison, December 13, 1791, *PJM*, 14:149.
8. Ibid.
9. See Patrick Henry to Madison, April 17, 1784, *PJM*, 8:18.
10. Madison to William Madison, December 13, 1791, *PJM*, 14:149.
11. "Public Opinion," December 19, 1791, *PJM*, 14:170.
12. "Notes for Essays," *PJM*, 14:158.
13. "Public Opinion," December 19, 1791, *PJM*, 14:170.
14. Ibid.
15. "Government," January 2, 1792, *PJM*, 14:179.
16. He repeated the same argument in an essay published January 19, urging that public opinion, the source of "stability of all governments and security of all rights," must demand that the government adhere to the Constitution. "Every citizen" must keep an eye out for "invasion of the dearest rights," and every citizen must be prepared "to avenge the unhallowed deed." "Charters," January 18, 1792, published January 19, 1792, *PJM*, 14:192.
17. *Report on Manufactures*, December 1791–January 1792, *PAH*, 10:303.
18. Madison to Henry Lee, January 1, 1792, *PJM*, 14:180.

19. Henry Lee to Madison, January 8, 1792, *PJM*, 14:184.

20. Madison to Henry Lee, January 21, 1792, *PJM*, 14:193.

21. Ibid., 193–94.

22. Madison to Edmund Pendleton, January 21, 1792, *PJM*, 14:195.

23. "Speech of February 6, 1792," *PJM*, 14:221–24.

24. "Parties," published January 23, 1792, *PJM*, 14:197–98.

25. Nelson, *Greek Tradition in the Republican Thought.*

26. "British Government," January 28, 1792, published January 30, 1792, *PJM*, 14:202.

27. Henry Lee to Madison, January 29, 1792, *PJM*, 14:204.

28. Ibid.

29. "Government of the United States," February 4, 1792, published February 6, 1792, *PJM*, 14:218.

30. Ibid.

31. Ibid.

32. "Speech of February 6, 1792," *PJM*, 14:222. Technically the topic was not the report on manufactures but a bill encouraging cod fisheries. Nevertheless, Madison used it as an opportunity to preview his views on the unconstitutionality of subsidies. As he later wrote to Edmund Pendleton, "The constitutional doctrine . . . advanced in the report has been anticipated on another occasion, by its zealous friends; and I was drawn into a few hasty animadversions." Madison to Edmund Pendleton, February 21, 1792, *PJM*, 14:235.

33. According to these enemies, Madison argued, Congress had the power to do anything it wanted, including encroaching on the states' jurisdiction. Congress

    > may take the care of religion into their own hands; they may establish teachers in every state, county, and parish and pay them out of the public treasury; they may take into their own hands the education of children, establishing in like manner schools throughout the union; they may assume provision for the poor; they may undertake the regulation of all roads other than post-roads; in short everything, from the highest object of state legislation, down to the most minute object of police, would be thrown under the power of Congress. Ibid., 223.

    The parade of horribles could have come straight from the Anti-Federalist Patrick Henry's warnings against the ratification of the Constitution. If the enemies of the true form of government were to succeed, there would be no state government left at all. The federal behemoth would swallow everything from education to roads to the details of everyday governance.

34. "Republican Distribution of Citizens," published March 3, 1792, *PJM*, 14:244.

35. The two had been linked conceptually and rhetorically at least since 1587, when John Howes wrote that "Bedlem and Bridewell are nere kinsemen in condicion." R. H. Tawney and Eileen Power, eds., *Tudor Economic Documents* (London: Longwell, 1924), 3:443.

36. "Republican Distribution of Citizens," *PJM*, 14:246.

37. Ibid.

38. "Fashion," March 20, 1792, published March 22, 1792, *PJM*, 14:257–58.

39. Ibid., 258.

40. Ibid.

41. "Property," March 27, 1792, published March 29, 1792, *PJM*, 14:267.

42. Ibid.
43. Ibid.
44. Madison to Edmund Pendleton, March 25, 1792, *PJM*, 14:263.
45. Ibid.
46. Madison to Henry Lee, March 28, 1782, *PJM*, 14:27.
47. "The Union: Who Are Its Real Friends," March 31, 1792, published April 2, 1792, *PJM*, 14:274.
48. Ibid.
49. Ibid.
50. Ibid.
51. Ibid.
52. Ibid.
53. Ibid.
54. Ibid., 274–75.
55. Ibid., 275.
56. Joseph Jones to Madison, April 6, 1792, *PJM*, 14:280.
57. Madison to Henry Lee, April 15, 1792, *PJM*, 14:288.
58. Edmund Pendleton to Madison, April 28, 1792, *PJM*, 14:294–95.
59. "Memorandum on a Discussion of the President's Retirement," May 5, 1792, *PJM*, 14:299–300.
60. Ibid., 300.
61. Ibid., 301.
62. Ibid.
63. Ibid.
64. Ibid., 302.
65. Ibid.
66. Ibid.
67. Ibid.
68. Ibid., 302–3.
69. Ibid., 303.
70. Ibid., 303.
71. Ibid., 303, 304.
72. Washington to Madison, May 20, 1792, *PJM*, 14:310–11.
73. Ibid., 311.
74. Ibid., 312.
75. Ibid., 310.
76. Madison to Washington, June 20, 1792, *PJM*, 14:321.
77. Ibid., 323.
78. Jefferson to Madison, June 29, 1792, *PJM*, 14:333.
79. Nancy Rosenblum, *On the Side of Angels: An Appreciation of Parties and Partisanship* (Princeton, N.J.: Princeton University Press, 2010).
80. John Beckley to Madison, August 1, 1792, *PJM*, 14:345–46.
81. John Beckley to Madison, September 2, 1792, *PJM*, 14:356.
82. Jefferson to Madison, June 29, 1792, *PJM*, 14:333.
83. *Gazette of the United States*, August 11, 1792, *PJM*, 14:350n.6.
84. John Beckley to Madison, September 2, 1792, *PJM*, 14:356.
85. Madison to Edmund Randolph, September 13, 1792, *PJM*, 14:364 and 365n.1.
86. Ibid., 365.

87. Ibid.
88. Ibid., 365.
89. *PJM*, 14:368. See also Monroe to Madison, September 18, 1792, *PJM*, 14:367.
90. *PJM*, 14:369.
91. *Dunlap's American Daily Advertiser*, October 20, 1792, *PJM*, 14:387, 388.
92. Ibid., 389–91.
93. "A Candid State of Parties," September 22, 1792, published September 26, 1792, *PJM*, 14:370.
94. Ibid.
95. Ibid., 371.
96. Ibid.
97. On the Whiskey Rebellion, see Thomas P. Slaughter, *The Whiskey Rebellion: Frontier Epilogue to the American Revolution* (Oxford: Oxford University Press, 1986).
98. "Candid State of Parties," *PJM*, 14:371.
99. Ibid.
100. Ibid., 372.
101. Ibid., 371.
102. Ibid., 371–72.
103. Ibid., 372.
104. Ibid.
105. David O. Stewart, *American Emperor: Aaron Burr's Challenge to Jefferson's America* (New York: Simon and Schuster, 2011), 14–15.
106. Monroe to Madison, October 9, 1792, *PJM*, 14:378–79.

CHAPTER TEN | THE PRESIDENT AND HIS PARTY

1. Madison to the minister of the interior of the French Republic, April 1793, *PJM*, 15:4.
2. Madison to Jefferson, April 12, 1793, *PJM*, 15:7.
3. *PJM*, 15:11n.2. Jefferson became increasingly frustrated with Randolph, whose vote he needed in the cabinet to counteract Hamilton and Henry Knox. "Everything, my dear sir, now hangs on the opinion of a single person," he wrote to Madison, "and that the most indecisive one I ever had to do business with. He always contrived to agree in principle with one, but in conclusion with the other." Jefferson to Madison, May 13, 1793, *PJM*, 15:16.
4. Jefferson to Madison, April 28, 1793, *PJM*, 15:10.
5. On one hand, Vattel wrote, "If the nation had deposed her king in form," it "would be interfering in the government of the nation, and doing her an injury" to intervene. This suggested that ordinarily the treaty should remain in place because what happened in the internal governance of a treaty partner was its own business. Yet, on the other hand, Vattel went on to say, "If this change renders the alliance useless, dangerous, or disagreeable" to the country that had entered a treaty, it was "at liberty to renounce it." The country wishing to withdraw could assert that it "would not have entered into an alliance with that nation, had she been under her present form of government." Emmerich de Vattel, *The Law of Nations; Or, Principles of the Law of Nature, Applied to the Conduct and Affairs of Nations and Sovereigns,* trans. Joseph Chitty (Philadelphia: T. and H. W. Johnson, 1863), 212, bk. 2, para. 197. Madison wrote back to Jefferson that, although he had no copy of Vattel with him in Virginia

and no copy of the French-American treaty, either, he found the "attempts to shuffle off the treaty altogether by quibbling on Vattel . . . contemptible for the meanness and folly of it." Madison to Jefferson, May 8, 1793, *PJM,* 15:13.

6. George Washington, "Neutrality Proclamation, 22 April 1793," *Founders Online,* National Archives, http://founders.archives.gov/documents/Washington/05-12-02-0371.

7. Jefferson to Madison, May 5, 1793, *PJM,* 15:12 and nn.4–5.

8. Jefferson to Madison, April 28, 1793, *PJM,* 15:10.

9. Madison to Jefferson, May 27, 1793, *PJM,* 15:22.

10. Jefferson to Madison, May 19, 1793, *PJM,* 15:19.

11. Ibid.

12. Ibid.

13. Madison to Jefferson, May 29, 1793, *PJM,* 15:23.

14. Jefferson to Madison, June 2, 1793, *PJM,* 15:24.

15. Ibid.

16. Jefferson to Madison, July 7, 1793, *PJM,* 15:43.

17. Ibid.

18. Madison to Jefferson, May 27, 1793, *PJM,* 15:22.

19. Jefferson to Madison, June 9, 1793, *PJM,* 15:26.

20. Ibid., 26–27.

21. Ibid.

22. Madison to Jefferson, June 19, 1793, *PJM,* 15:33.

23. Ibid.

24. John Taylor to Madison, June 20, 1793, *PJM,* 15:36.

25. Pacificus, No. 1, *Gazette of the United States,* July 29, 1793, *PAH,* 15:33–34.

26. Jefferson to Madison, July 7, 1793, *PJM,* 15:43.

27. Madison to Jefferson, July 18, 1793, *PJM,* 15:44–45.

28. Madison to Jefferson, July 22, 1793, *PJM,* 15:47.

29. Tacitus, *Histories,* 4.5–9; Suetonius, *Life of Vespasian,* 15; Dio Cassius 65.12.2. See also Sam Wilkinson, *Republicanism During the Early Roman Empire* (London: Bloomsbury Academic, 2012), 73.

30. Madison to Jefferson, July 30, 1793, *PJM,* 15:48.

31. Jefferson to Madison, August 3, 1793, *PJM,* 15:30.

32. Jefferson to Madison, August 11, 1793, *PJM,* 15:55.

33. Ibid., 56.

34. Ibid., 57.

35. Ibid., 58.

36. Helvidius No. 1, August 24, 1793, published August 26, 1793, *PJM,* 15:66.

37. Ibid., 67–68, quoting Hamilton, Pacificus No. 1.

38. Ibid., 72.

39. Ibid., 73.

40. Jefferson to Madison, August 25, 1793, *PJM,* 15:74.

41. "Resolutions on Franco-American Relations," August 27, 1793, *PJM,* 15:79–80.

42. Madison to Archibald Stuart, September 1, 1793, *PJM,* 15:88.

43. Ibid.

44. *PJM,* 15:78.

45. Madison to Jefferson, September 2, 1793, *PJM,* 15:93.

46. Jefferson to Madison, August 11, 1793, *PJM,* 15:57–58.

47. *PJM*, 15:95.
48. See *PJM*, 15:325n.1. Hamilton actually published a letter praising Stevens's treatment on September 11, 1793.
49. Jefferson to Madison, September 8, 1793, *PJM*, 15:104.
50. Madison to Jefferson, September 16, 1793, *PJM*, 15:112–13.
51. Ibid.
52. Jefferson to Madison, September 12, 1793, *PJM*, 15:106.
53. Mary Estelle Elizabeth Cutts, *The Queen of America: Mary Cutts's Life of Dolley Madison*, ed. Catherine Allgor (Charlottesville: University of Virginia Press, 2012), 90. The memoir has a complex production history. Many passages reflect what must have been oral traditions from Dolley. Some sound as if they might have been dictated directly, which would be possible if Cutts kept notes.
54. Ibid., 91.
55. Ibid.
56. Ibid., 92.
57. Ibid., 27.
58. Ibid., 93.
59. Dolley Payne Todd to James Todd, October 4, 1793, 9 p.m., *The Selected Letters of Dolley Payne Madison*, ed. David B. Mattern and Holly C. Shulman (Charlottesville: University of Virginia Press, 2003), 24. Hereinafter cited as *Letters of DPM*.
60. Ibid., 24–25.
61. Cutts, *Queen of America*, 93.
62. Mary Payne to Margaret Hervey, October 24, 1793, quoted in Ketcham, *James Madison*, 378 and 703n.11; see also Catherine Allgor, *A Perfect Union* (New York: Henry Holt, 2006), 25.
63. "Will of Dolley Payne Todd," May 13, 1794, *Letters of DPM*, 27.
64. Madison to Washington, October 24, 1793, *PJM*, 15:129–30.
65. John Beckley to Madison, November 20, 1793, *PJM*, 15:141.
66. Jefferson to Madison, November 2, 1793, *PJM*, 15:133; Jefferson to Madison, November 9, 1793, *PJM*, 15:135.
67. "Speech of January 3, 1794," *PJM*, 15:167–70.
68. William Lyman to Samuel Henshaw, January 17, 1794, quoted in *PJM*, 15:148–49.
69. Cutts, *Queen of America*, 94–95.
70. Ibid., 96.
71. Ibid., 95.
72. Ibid., 96.
73. Certainly the word "thee" came from the recounting by the Quaker-raised Dolley, not from Martha Washington.
74. Catharine Coles to Dolley Payne Todd, June 1, 1794, *PJM*, 15:342; see also the same letter in *Letters of DPM*, 27–28.
75. Madison to Dolley Payne Todd, August 18, 1794, *PJM*, 15:351.
76. Dolley Payne Todd to Eliza Collins Lee, September 16, 1794, *PJM*, 15:357.
77. Madison to Jefferson, October 5, 1794, *PJM*, 15:359–60.
78. Jefferson to Madison, October 30, 1794, *PJM*, 15:366.
79. Henry Lee to Madison, October 23, 1794, *PJM*, 15:359.
80. Jefferson shared the thought with Madison's cousin Rev. James Madison. Rt. Rev. James Madison to Madison, November 12, 1794, *PJM*, 15:374.

81. Jefferson to Madison, December 28, 1794, *PJM*, 15:428.

82. Richard H. Kohn, "The Washington Administration's Decision to Crush the Whiskey Rebellion," *The Journal of American History* 59, no. 3 (1972): 570.

83. William Hogeland, *The Whiskey Rebellion: George Washington, Alexander Hamilton, and the Frontier Rebels Who Challenged America's Newfound Sovereignty* (New York: Simon and Schuster, 2006), 154.

84. Ibid.

85. Ibid., 163.

86. Hamilton to Henry Lee, August 25, 1794, *PAH*, 17:142–43. Hamilton wrote "in place of the secretary at war, who is absent." See also Hamilton to Henry Lee, August 25, 1794, *PAH*, 17:143–45. It appears from the letter that Hamilton was actively coordinating and planning a military response.

87. He had lobbied Madison to get himself named to command the ill-fated federal force that Washington had sent to fight the Miami confederacy after St. Clair's defeat in 1791, but Madison had been unable to procure the position for him because Lee was too junior. See letters back and forth from 1791 to 1792.

88. Henry Lee to Madison, September 23, 1794, *PJM*, 15:359.

89. *PJM*, 15:359n.1.

90. William Branch Giles to Madison, April 12, 1795, *PJM*, 15:509.

91. Madison to James Madison, Sr., November 10, 1794, *PJM*, 15:372.

92. Ibid.

93. Madison to Jefferson, November 16, 1794, *PJM*, 15:379. Madison believed that Hamilton's goal was to use the Whiskey Rebellion to justify the creation of "a standing army to enforce the laws," yet held out hope that Washington would not himself agree.

94. Ibid.

95. Joseph Jones to Madison, December 5, 1794, *PJM*, 15:409.

96. This is the suggestion of Chernow, *Alexander Hamilton*, 478–79.

97. Alexander Hamilton to Rufus King, February 21, 1795, *PAH*, 18:278; see also Chernow, *Alexander Hamilton*, 481.

98. Madison to Monroe, December 4, 1794, *PJM*, 15:408.

99. Joseph Jones to Madison, December 26, 1794, *PJM*, 15:424. ("Hamilton told Henry Lee, in the western counties while they were lately there on the expedition that he must retire and go to the bar where he could make his £2000 per annum whereas since in office he has spent what he had before—about £3000, except a lot and house and that if he was now to die his family must depend on the grandfather for support—this account differs widely from common report.")

100. Madison to Jefferson, December 21, 1794, *PJM*, 15:419.

101. Madison to Jefferson, January 11, 1794, *PJM*, 15:441.

102. Robert R. Livingston to Madison, January 30, 1795, *PJM*, 15:460.

103. Madison to Jefferson, February 15, 1795, *PJM*, 15:473.

104. Madison to Monroe, March 26, 1795, *PJM*, 15:496–97.

105. Pierce Butler to Madison, June 12, 1795, *PJM*, 16:15 and 16n.2.

106. This limited the size of American ships trading with the British West Indies and barred any American ships from carrying a variety of colonial products anywhere other than the United States.

107. Pierce Butler to Madison, June 26, 1795, *PJM*, 15:24.

108. Robert R. Livingston to Madison, July 6, 1795, *PJM*, 16:34.

109. Madison to Robert Livingston, August 10, 1795, *PJM,* 16:47.
110. Ibid.
111. The result of the treaty, Livingston fretted, would be that France would "push us to choose between a war with her or Britain." Robert R. Livingston to Madison, July 6, 1795, *PJM,* 16:34.
112. Chernow, *Alexander Hamilton,* 490.
113. Jefferson to Madison, August 3, 1795, *PJM,* 15:43.
114. John Adams to William Cunningham, Jr., October 15, 1808, *A Review of the Correspondence Between the Hon. John Adams, Late President of the United States, and the Late Wm. Cunningham, Esq., Beginning in 1803, and Ending in 1812* (Salem, Mass.: Cushing and Appleton, 1824), 36. See also Joseph Ellis, *Founding Brothers: The Revolutionary Generation* (New York: Vintage Books, 2002), 137; Chernow, *Alexander Hamilton,* 487. (Both misquote "huzzaing" as "buzzing.")
115. Madison to Robert R. Livingston, August 10, 1795, *PJM,* 16:48.
116. Washington to Alexander Hamilton, August 31, 1795, *PAH,* 19:205–6.
117. Jefferson to Madison, September 21, 1795, *PJM,* 16:88.
118. Reardon, *Edmund Randolph,* 309–10.
119. Ibid., 324.
120. Ibid., 327.
121. Ibid., 311–12.
122. Edmund Randolph to Madison, November 1, 1795, *PJM,* 16:117.
123. Monroe, too, felt alienated from Washington by the story. "To read a dispatch of the French minister handed by the British was not right," he wrote to Madison. "But to be the dupe of that trick was worse let the merit of the poor victim be what it may." Monroe to Madison, November 8, 1795, *PJM,* 16:124.
124. Monroe to Madison, October 29, 1795, *PJM,* 16:115.
125. Jefferson to Madison, September 21, 1795, *PJM,* 16:88.
126. Jefferson to Madison, November 26, 1795, *PJM,* 16:134. Jefferson was describing John Marshall's view, expressed in the Virginia legislature, "that the whole commercial part of the treaty (and he might have added the whole unconstitutional part of it) rests in the power of the House of Representatives ... and as the articles which stipulate what requires the consent of the three branches of the legislature must be referred to the House of Representatives for their concurrence, so they, being free agents, may approve or reject them, either by a vote declaring that, or by refusing to pass acts."
127. "Speech of March 10, 1796," *PJM,* 16:256.
128. Ibid., 256.
129. Ibid., 260–61.
130. Madison to Jefferson, March 13, 1796, *PJM,* 16:264.
131. George Washington, "Washington's Response to a Congressional Request for Documents, 30 March 1796," *The Washington Papers,* University of Virginia, http://gwpapers.virginia.edu/documents/washingtons-response-to-a-congressional-request-for-documents-30-march-1796/; Washington, "Message to the House Regarding Documents Relative to the Jay Treaty, March 30, 1796," *The Avalon Project,* Yale Law School, http://avalon.law.yale.edu/18th_century/gw003.asp.
132. Ibid.
133. Ibid.
134. Madison to Jefferson, April 4, 1796, *PJM,* 16:286, 287n.3.

135. Ibid., 286, 287n.4.
136. "Speech of April 6, 1796," *PJM,* 16:292.
137. Ibid., 295.
138. Ibid., 296.
139. Ibid., 296–99.
140. Ibid., 301.
141. "Speech of April 15, 1796," *PJM,* 16:314–24.
142. Ibid., 324.
143. Ibid.
144. Madison to Jefferson, May 1, 1796, *PJM,* 16:343.
145. Madison to Jefferson, May 9, 1796, *PJM,* 16:352.
146. Madison to Monroe, May 14, 1796, *PJM,* 16:357–58.
147. Madison to Jefferson, May 22, 1796, *PJM,* 16:364.
148. Madison to Monroe, September 29, 1796, *PJM,* 16:403.
149. Ibid.
150. John Beckley to Madison, October 15, 1796, *PJM,* 16:409.
151. Chernow, *Alexander Hamilton,* 512–13. Chernow proposes that one of the essays alludes obliquely to Jefferson's relationship with Sally Hemings, which would become a national issue in later elections. For a Republican view of Hamilton's attacks, see John Beckley to Madison, October 15, 1796, *PJM,* 16:409.
152. Chernow, *Alexander Hamilton,* 521–25.
153. John Beckley to Madison, June 20, 1796, *PJM,* 16:373.
154. I owe this point to Alex Star.
155. Chernow, *Alexander Hamilton,* 514.
156. Jefferson to Madison, January 22, 1797, *PJM,* 16:473. ("I cannot have a wish to see the scenes of '93 revived as to myself, and to descend daily into the arena like a gladiator to suffer martyrdom in every conflict.")
157. Jefferson to Madison, January 1, 1797, *PJM,* 16:440 and 441n.2. Madison conveyed the contents of the letter to Benjamin Rush to pass on to Adams, but he advised Jefferson against actually sending the letter in a detailed analysis that included the following astute observation: "You know the temper of Mr. Adams better than I do: but I have always conceived it to be rather a ticklish one." Madison also suggested that he and Jefferson must share a view of "the beauty and policy of cultivating Mr. Adams's favorable dispositions, and giving a fair start to his executive career." Madison to Jefferson, January 15, 1797, *PJM,* 16:456.
158. Madison to Jefferson, January 8, 1797, *PJM,* 16:447.
159. Madison to James Madison, Sr., March 12, 1797, *PJM,* 16:500.
160. Madison to Monroe, May 14, 1796, *PJM,* 16:358.
161. Leibiger, *Founding Friendship,* 216, 220.

CHAPTER ELEVEN | IN THE SHADE

1. John Adams to Abigail Adams, January 14, 1797, *Papers of John Adams,* ed. L. H. Butterfield (Cambridge, Mass.: Harvard University Press, 1973) 11:496; see also *PJM,* 17:xix.
2. Margaret Bailey Tinkcom, "Caviar Along the Potomac: Sir Augustus John Foster's 'Notes on the United States,' 1804–1812," *The William and Mary Quarterly,* 3rd ser., 8,

no. 1, *James Madison, 1751–1836: Bicentennial Number* (January 1951), 96–98. Foster visited in 1804. He noted that "a pleasure ground . . . would in fact be very expensive, and all hands are absolutely wanted for the Plantation."

3. See Cutts, *Queen of America*, 105–6.

4. Madison to Jefferson, January 22, 1797, *PJM*, 16:471.

5. As one of Madison's correspondents put it, "Our merchants have ruled the executive—throughout this business." Henry Tazewell to Madison, June 4, 1797, *PJM*, 17:18.

6. Stanley Elkins and Eric McKitrick, *The Age of Federalism: The Early American Republic, 1788–1800* (Oxford: Oxford University Press, 1993), 542 and 865n.45.

7. Ibid., 542–43.

8. Hamilton, who like Adams did not want war with France, privately favored the idea of sending Madison. But Hamilton and Adams had almost no relationship after Hamilton had tried to block Adams from the presidency, and so there was no possibility for them to coordinate their efforts. In any case, Hamilton, himself out of Philadelphia politics, seems not to have appreciated fully the depth of opposition to Madison from Federalists who had remained in government. Ibid., 544–45.

9. Jefferson to Madison, June 1, 1797, *PJM*, 17:10.

10. For the American understanding, see Henry Tazewell to Madison, June 4, 1797, *PJM*, 17:17.

11. John Dawson to Madison, December 10, 1797, *PJM*, 17:58.

12. Jefferson to Madison, June 15, 1797, *PJM*, 17:24.

13. See Chernow, *Alexander Hamilton*, 466.

14. Mabel L. Webber, "The Thomas Pinckney Family of South Carolina," *The South Carolina Historical and Genealogical Magazine* 39, no. 1 (1938): 23.

15. Madison to Jefferson, January 21, 1798, *PJM*, 17:69.

16. Madison to Jefferson, February 18, 1798, *PJM*, 17:82.

17. Ibid.

18. Jefferson to Madison, March 29, 1798, *PJM*, 17:102.

19. Ibid.

20. Jefferson to Madison, March 21, 1798, *PJM*, 17:99.

21. "Statute 2, Ch. LXVII," *A Century of Lawmaking for a New Nation: U.S. Congressional Documents and Debates, 1774–1875,* Library of Congress, http://memory.loc.gov/cgi-bin/ampage?collId=llsl&fileName=001/llsl001.db&recNum=701.

22. Madison to Jefferson, April 2, 1798, *PJM*, 17:104.

23. Jefferson to Madison, April 26, 1798, *PJM*, 17:120.

24. Ibid., 121.

25. Jefferson to Madison, April 26, 1798, *PJM*, 17:120.

26. Ibid.

27. Madison to Jefferson, May 5, 1798, *PJM*, 17:126.

28. Madison to Jefferson, May 13, 1798, *PJM*, 17:130.

29. Ibid.

30. John Adams, "Proclamation Proclaiming a Fast-Day, 23 March 1798," *Founders Online,* National Archives, http://founders.archives.gov/documents/Adams/99-02-02-2386.

31. John Adams, "From John Adams to PA., Young Men of Philadelphia, 7 May 1798," *Founders Online,* National Archives, http://founders.archives.gov/documents/Adams/99-02-02-2450.

32. Madison to Jefferson, May 20, 1798, *PJM*, 17:134. Madison told Jefferson that the speech clarified Adams's remarks to Madison "that there was not a single principle the same in the American and French revolutions." The conclusion was clear, Madison said. "The abolition of royalty was it seems not one of his revolutionary principles."

33. Ibid.

34. Madison to Jefferson, June 10, 1798, *PJM*, 17:150.

35. Jefferson to Madison, May 24, 1798, *PJM*, 17:136.

36. Jefferson to Madison, June 7, 1798, *PJM*, 17:143.

37. Henry Tazewell to Madison, July 12, 1798, *PJM*, 17:163.

38. Circular Letter from John Dawson, July 19, 1798, *PJM*, 17:165.

39. Jefferson to Madison, November 17, 1798, *PJM*, 17:175.

40. Ibid., 179.

41. Ibid.

42. Ibid., 181.

43. Madison to Jefferson, December 29, 1798, *PJM*, 17:191. Ratification by convention, not legislature, had been a preoccupation of Madison's since well before Philadelphia. See infra.

44. "Virginia Resolutions," December 21, 1798, *PJM*, 17:189.

45. Ibid., 190.

46. Jefferson to Wilson Carey Nicholas, November 29, 1798, *PTJ*, 30:590; and see *PJM*, 17:187.

47. David McCullough, *John Adams* (New York: Touchstone, 2001), 494. Insulted by Roger Griswold of Connecticut, Lyon spat in Griswold's face. Griswold hit him with a cane, Lyon took tongs or a poker from the fireplace, and the two men fought until separated.

48. *PJM*, 17:174. See also J. Fairfax McLaughlin, *Matthew Lyon, the Hampden of Congress: A Biography* (New York: Wynkoop Hallenbeck Crawford, 1900).

49. Jefferson to Madison, January 3, 1799, *PJM*, 17:193.

50. Jefferson to Madison, January 16, 1799, *PJM*, 17:210.

51. "Foreign Influence," January 23, 1799, *PJM*, 17:215.

52. Ibid., 216.

53. Ibid.

54. Ibid.

55. Ibid., 218–19.

56. Wood, *Empire of Liberty*, argues throughout (e.g., 217–35) that much Republican support, especially in the Northeast, came from the "middling" class of small merchants and entrepreneurs. This emphasis on a class analysis of Republicanism requires Wood to argue that Madison and Jefferson were unable to appreciate or were unaware of this source of support—since they identified the party with agriculture, not commerce or manufacture. It also demands an explanation of why this rising class, which Wood considers to have been enabled by Hamilton's financial reforms, eschewed Federalism.

57. Ibid., 240.

58. Ibid., 241.

59. Madison to Jefferson, February 8, 1799, *PJM*, 17:229.

60. George Washington to Patrick Henry, January 15, 1799, quoted in *PJM*, 17:246. See also Kidd, *Patrick Henry*, 239–40.

61. John Taylor to Madison, March 4, 1799, *PJM*, 17:245.
62. Kidd, *Patrick Henry*, 236–43, argues that "by the late 1790s, Henry had turned his attention away from the threat of the national government to the assault on traditional virtue and religion associated with the French Revolution." Ibid., 243. This cannot account for his willingness to reenter politics on the side of the party that had adopted the Alien and Sedition Acts.
63. Ibid., 245.
64. Ibid.
65. Ibid., 246.
66. The letter is lost but Taylor referred to it in a letter of his own. *PJM*, 17:246n.1 and 247.
67. *PJM*, 17:249n.1.
68. Kidd, *Patrick Henry*, 241.
69. Jefferson to Madison, November 22, 1799, *PJM*, 17:277.
70. Charles Pinckney to Madison, September 30, 1799, *PJM*, 17:272.
71. Jefferson to Madison, November 26, 1799, *PJM*, 17:280.
72. Ibid.
73. Jefferson to Madison, November 22, 1799, *PJM*, 17:277.
74. *PJM*, 17:286.
75. Ibid., 287.
76. *PJM*, 17:286.
77. Ibid., 318–19.
78. Ibid., 331–32. The final version of the report adopted by the Virginia assembly amended Madison's language to provide that there might be certain "particular parts of the common law" that "may have sanction from the Constitution, so far as they are necessarily comprehended in the technical phrases, which express the powers delegated to the government." See Madison to Jefferson, January 12, 1800, *PJM*, 17:354–55 and n.1. Madison's objection to the language is unwarranted, but here his lack of legal experience was a factor. The law of admiralty, for example, and other aspects of the law of nations, could enter federal law only through the common law—and the Constitution clearly contemplated jurisdiction over such matters by the federal courts. For a further amendment, see Madison to Jefferson, January 18, 1800, *PJM*, 17:357.
79. Madison to Jefferson, January 18, 1800, *PJM*, 17:336.
80. Ibid. Madison explained why it was a mistake to reason from English law to the U.S. Constitution. Unlike Congress with its enumerated powers, Parliament was "unlimited in its power." The rights of Englishmen established by Magna Carta and the English Bill of Rights were therefore "not reared against the Parliament, but against the royal prerogative." Rather than guaranteed rights, they were "merely legislative precautions, against executive usurpations." For this reason, Parliament could not restrict itself from regulating speech. It could only prohibit "previous restraint by licensers appointed by the king." In contrast, in the United States, the First Amendment was a protection against Congress. For it to mean anything, the First Amendment "must be an exemption, not only from the previous inspection of licensers, but from the subsequent penalty of laws."
81. Ibid., 342.
82. Ibid., 343.
83. Ibid., 344–45.
84. Madison was also saying that in a republic, it was appropriate for the public to feel

contempt and hatred for a bad government. The political culture of the late eighteenth century had assumed a degree of polite deference to one's betters. The partisan battles of the 1790s had convinced Madison that traditional deference was no longer appropriate, at least as it might be directed to a bad, anti-republican government. For Madison to embrace contempt and hatred as natural and appropriate political sentiments reflected the degree to which political culture had changed in the previous decade.

85. Rt. Rev. James Madison to Madison, January 9, 1800, *PJM,* 17:353.
86. Ibid., 353.
87. Stevens Thomson Mason to Madison, January 16, 1800, *PJM,* 17:356 and n.1.
88. *PJM,* 17:361n.1.
89. Jefferson to Madison, March 4, 1800, *PJM,* 17:369.
90. Ibid.
91. Stevens Thomson Mason to Madison, April 23, 1800, *PJM,* 17:382 and nn.1–3.
92. Gabriel Duvall to Madison, April 28, 1800, *PJM,* 17:384. Duvall was later named a justice of the Supreme Court by Jefferson—becoming, according to David P. Currie, "The Most Insignificant Justice: A Preliminary Inquiry," *University of Chicago Law Review* 50, no. 2 (Spring 1983): 466. But see Frank H. Easterbrook, "The Most Insignificant Justice: Further Evidence," ibid., 481.
93. Jefferson to Philip Mazzei, April 24, 1796, *PTJ,* 29:82.
94. Jefferson to Madison, August 3, 1797, *PJM,* 17:35–36.
95. Gabriel Duvall to Madison, April 28, 1800, *PJM,* 17:384.
96. See Thomas Jefferson, *The Jefferson Bible: The Life and Morals of Jesus of Nazareth,* ed. Harry R. Rubenstein, Barbara Clark Smith, and conservation by Janice Stagnito Ellis (Washington, D.C.: Smithsonian Books, 2011). On his religious views, see Edwin Gaustad, *Sworn on the Altar of God: A Religious Biography of Thomas Jefferson* (Grand Rapids, Mich.: William B. Eerdmans, 1996).
97. John Dawson to Madison, May 4, 1800, *PJM,* 17:386.
98. Madison to Monroe, May 23, 1800, *PJM,* 17:390.
99. Chernow, *Alexander Hamilton,* 616–18.
100. John Adams to James McHenry, May 31, 1800, *PAH,* 24:557. McHenry had been Adams's secretary of war, and was close to Hamilton. See Wood, *Empire of Liberty,* 273–74.
101. "Letter of Alexander Hamilton, Concerning the Public Conduct and Character of John Adams, Esq. President of the United States," *PAH,* 25:86–234; see also Elkins and McKitrick, *Age of Federalism,* 738.
102. Monroe to Madison, November 3, 1800, *PJM,* 17:430.
103. Bishop James Madison to Jefferson, November 1, 1800, *PTJ,* 32:238–39. Elkins and McKitrick, *Age of Federalism,* 739, attribute the letter to Madison, an attribution repeated in Chernow, *Alexander Hamilton,* 622 and 772n.2. The "thunderbolt" and the rejoicing would be highly unusual coming from Madison, who did indicate in a letter to Jefferson that he had read the pamphlet closely. See Madison to Jefferson, January 10, 1801, *PJM,* 17:454.
104. John G. Jackson to Madison, September 25, 1800, *PJM,* 17:414.
105. John Dawson to Madison, February 1, 1800, *PJM,* 17:362.
106. Madison to Jefferson, February 14, 1800, *PJM,* 17:363.
107. Ibid., 364.
108. John Dawson to Madison, February 23, 1800, *PJM,* 17:366.
109. Madison to Jefferson, April 20, 1800, *PJM,* 17:380.

110. Jefferson to Madison, April 4, 1800, *PJM,* 17:378.
111. Monroe to Madison, October 8, 1800, *PJM,* 17:420.
112. David Gelston to Madison, October 8, 1800, *PJM,* 17:418–19n.1; David Gelston to Madison, November 21, 1800, *PJM,* 17:438.
113. Madison to Monroe, October 21, 1800, *PJM,* 17:426.
114. Madison to Monroe, November 10, 1800, *PJM,* 17:434.
115. Madison to Monroe, November 10, 1800, *PJM,* 17:435.
116. Ibid.
117. John Dawson to Madison, December 18, 1800, *PJM,* 17:443.
118. Jefferson to Madison, December 19, 1800, *PJM,* 17:444.
119. Jefferson to Madison, December 26, 1800, *PJM,* 17:448.
120. Jefferson to Madison, December 19, 1800, *PJM,* 17:444.
121. Madison to Jefferson, January 10, 1801, *PJM,* 17:453.
122. Ibid.
123. Ibid.
124. Ibid.
125. Under the Constitution, each certificate was supposed to include a "list of all the persons voted for, and of the number of votes for each." Georgia's certificate contained a list, but it did not specify that Jefferson and Burr were the candidates "voted for." If the Georgia ballot had been discounted, then neither Jefferson nor Burr would have had a majority of the ballots cast. The election would have been sent to the House of Representatives not between the two of them, but between the top five vote getters. Jefferson, emphasizing substance over form, simply ignored the irregularity. He knew perfectly well how Georgia had voted, as did everyone else. With the tie vote, the election turned the next day to the House of Representatives. On the episode, see Bruce Ackerman and David Fontana, "How Jefferson Counted Himself In," *The Atlantic,* March 1, 2004.
126. John Dawson to Madison, February 12, 1801, *PJM,* 17:464–65.
127. Jefferson to Madison, February 18, 1801, *PJM,* 17:467.
128. Alexander Hamilton to Oliver Wolcott, Jr., December 16, 1800, *PAH,* 25:257; see Chernow, *Alexander Hamilton,* 632 and 773n.7.
129. Alexander Hamilton to Gouverneur Morris, December 24, 1800, *PAH,* 25:272.
130. Alexander Hamilton to Gouverneur Morris, December 26, 1800, *PAH,* 25:275; see Wood, *Empire of Liberty,* 284.
131. Alexander Hamilton to Gouverneur Morris, December 24, 1800, *PAH,* 25:272; see also Chernow, *Alexander Hamilton,* 636 and 773n.29.
132. Chernow, *Alexander Hamilton,* 639.
133. Ibid.
134. Madison to Jefferson, February 28, 1801, *PJM,* 17:475. Madison believed some appointments might be "null"—not, as Jefferson thought, because they were made after Adams had lost the presidency, but because some of Adams's appointments were to offices that had not yet been vacated.

CHAPTER TWELVE | SECRETARY OF STATE

1. Monroe wrote to Madison that "Mr. Jefferson's address . . . avows principles which are perfectly sound, and commands the unqualified approbation of the Republicans,

while it conciliates the opposite party." Monroe to Madison, March 11, 1801, *PJM SSS,* 1:11.

2. Madison to Jefferson, February 28, 1801, *PJM,* 17:475.
3. Jefferson to Madison, March 12, 1801, *PJM SSS,* 1:12.
4. Charles Pinckney to Madison, March 16, 1801, *PJM SSS,* 1:22.
5. Madison to Jefferson, March 7, 1801, *PJM SSS,* 1:6.
6. *Letters of DPM,* 40.
7. Tinkcom, "Caviar Along the Potomac," 73, 77.
8. Gordon-Reed, *Hemingses of Monticello,* 563.
9. Reproductions make Dolley's eyes look brown or black, but contemporaneous reports say her eyes were blue.
10. Cutts, *Queen of America,* 111.
11. Ibid., 115–16.
12. Tinkcom, "Caviar Along the Potomac," 106. Less charitably, Foster wrote that Dolley achieved her mastery as a hostess despite being "an uncultivated mind and fond of gossiping." He commented that she "must have been a very handsome woman," a backhanded compliment if there ever was one. Foster also reported that "during the time when Congress sat at Philadelphia [Madison] fell in love with Mrs. Todd who presided at the boardinghouse where he lived and married her." He was confusing Madison's friendship with Eliza House Trist, but Dolley's mother had also briefly kept a boardinghouse in Philadelphia, so the class-based snub hit home.
13. Cutts, *Queen of America,* 138; see also Allgor, *Perfect Union,* 85.
14. Allgor, *Perfect Union,* 98–99.
15. For a collection, see Mary Lucile "CC" Proctor, "After-Dinner Anecdotes of James Madison: Excerpt from Jared Sparks' Journal for 1829–31," *The Virginia Magazine of History and Biography* 60, no. 2 (April 1952): 255–65.
16. Ibid.
17. Tinkcom, "Caviar Along the Potomac," 106.
18. Coles, quoted in *James Madison: A Biography in His Own Words,* ed. Merrill D. Peterson (New York: Newsweek, 1974), 250–51.
19. Ibid., 74.
20. David Humphreys to Madison, April 14, 1801, *PJM SSS,* 1:92.
21. Ibid.
22. Ibid.
23. James Leander Cathcart to Madison, July 2, 1801, *PJM SSS,* 1:370–71.
24. The American consul in Tunis, William Eaton, recommended to Madison that the United States attempt to win the war by trick. His idea was to capture the Tripolitan commodore, "a British renegade—Mourad Rais, alias, Peter Lisle." The proposed method was to "let our ships of war approach all Barbary corsairs under English colors till they are distinguishable," then change flags once they had gotten up close. Once Lisle was "secured, a strategem may be used to decoy the Bashaw [pasha] into an American frigate and thus end the war." William Eaton to Madison, May 25, 1801, *PJM SSS,* 1:227. In fact, false flags were used by the *Tripoli* in the encounter of August 1, 1801.
25. Allgor, *Perfect Union,* 95.
26. Callender's facts were approximate, rather than precise, but they were accurate enough to suggest that he got them from people close to the Jefferson household. Gordon-Reed, *Hemingses of Monticello,* 554–61.

27. Ibid., 118.

28. Monroe to Madison, May 23, 1801, *PJM SSS*, 1:223.

29. Madison to Monroe, June 1, 1801, *PJM SSS*, 1:244–45.

30. Michael Durey, *"With the Hammer of Truth": James Thomson Callender and America's Early National Heroes* (Charlottesville: University of Virginia Press, 1990), 147.

31. Ibid.

32. Albert Gallatin to Madison, May 29, 1801, *PJM SSS*, 1:236 and 237n.4.

33. See Gordon-Reed, *Hemingses of Monticello*, 554; and cf. Esther 6:6–11 for the man "whom the king delighteth to honor."

34. On Jefferson's reactions see Gordon-Reed, *Hemingses of Monticello*, 583–85.

35. *The Memoirs of Madison Hemings* (1873), available at *Frontline*, PBS, www.pbs.org/wgbh/pages/frontline/shows/jefferson/cron/1873march.html. Gordon-Reed shows that Dolley was not at Monticello on the date of Madison's birth, but suggests that events must have occurred in September 1804, when Dolley and Madison were, in fact, at Monticello and Sally "was in her sixth month of pregnancy." Gordon-Reed, *Hemingses of Monticello*, 589.

36. Stephan Palmié and Francisco A. Scarano, eds., *The Caribbean: A History of the Region and Its Peoples* (Chicago: University of Chicago Press, 2013), 219, 226.

37. Madison Smartt Bell, *Toussaint Louverture: A Biography* (New York: Pantheon, 2007), 104.

38. Tobias Lear to Madison, July 20, 1801, *PJM SSS*, 1:445.

39. Madison to Wilson Cary Nicholas, July 10, 1801, *PJM SSS*, 1:394.

40. Madison to Robert R. Livingston, July 11, 1801, *PJM SSS*, 1:402.

41. David Humphreys to Madison, March 23, 1801, *PJM SSS*, 1:36.

42. Madison to Alexander Hamilton, May 26, 1801, *PJM SSS*, 1:228–29.

43. Madison to Wilson Cary Nicholas, July 10, 1801, *PJM SSS*, 1:394.

44. Madison to Monroe, June 1, 1801, *PJM SSS*, 1:245.

45. Madison to Charles Pinckney, June 9, 1801, *PJM SSS*, 1:275.

46. Madison to Robert R. Livingston, September 28, 1801, *PJM SSS*, 2:145.

47. Robert R. Livingston to Madison, November 12, 1801, *PJM SSS*, 2:237.

48. Robert R. Livingston to Madison, November 22, 1801, *PJM SSS*, 2:265.

49. Robert R. Livingston to Madison, December 31, 1801, *PJM SSS*, 1:359.

50. Robert R. Livingston to Madison, December 10, 1801, *PJM SSS*, 2:304.

51. Robert R. Livingston to Madison, December 12, 1801, *PJM SSS*, 2:309. The letter refers to "what I wrote you yesterday." The comment was imprecise insofar as "it" should have referred to the Floridas rather than Louisiana; but perhaps Livingston was already thinking of them jointly.

52. Robert R. Livingston to Madison, February 26, 1802, *PJM SSS*, 2:493.

53. Madison to Robert R. Livingston, May 1, 1802, *PJM SSS*, 3:175–76.

54. Ibid., 176.

55. Jefferson to Robert R. Livingston, April 18, 1802, *PTJ*, 37:264.

56. Ibid.

57. Robert R. Livingston to Madison, August 10, 1802, *PJM SSS*, 3:468.

58. Ibid.

59. Robert R. Livingston to Madison, September 1, 1802, *PJM SSS*, 3:536.

60. Ibid.

61. Estimates of total numbers of French troops sent to the island range from 60,000 to 82,000. See John S. Marr and John T. Cathey, "The 1802 Saint-Domingue Yellow

Fever Epidemic and the Louisiana Purchase," *Journal of Public Health Management Practice* 19, no. 1 (2013): 77–82, 78.

62. Marr and Cathey, "The 1802 Saint-Domingue Yellow Fever Epidemic," 77.

63. Ibid., 79.

64. Robert R. Livingston to Madison, December 20, 1802, *PJM SSS*, 4:204.

65. Madison to Robert R. Livingston and Monroe, March 2, 1803, *PJM SSS*, 4:364.

66. Robert R. Livingston to Madison, March 3, 1803, *PJM SSS*, 4:385.

67. Robert R. Livingston to Madison, April 11, 1803, *PJM SSS*, 4:500.

68. Ibid.

69. Ibid., 501.

70. Robert R. Livingston to Madison, April 13, 1803, *PJM SSS*, 4:513.

71. Ibid., and see Monroe to Madison, April 15, 1803, *PJM SSS*, 4:521–22.

72. Robert R. Livingston and Monroe to Madison, May 13, 1803, *PJM SSS*, 4:601–6.

73. Monroe to Madison, May 18, 1803, *PJM SSS*, 5:13.

74. Monroe to Madison, May 18, 1803, *PJM SSS*, 5:12–13.

75. Robert R. Livingston to Madison, May 20, 1803, *PJM SSS*, 5:19.

76. Ibid., 19.

77. Ibid.

78. Ibid.

79. Ibid., 20.

80. Monroe to Madison, June 7, 1803, *PJM SSS*, 5:72.

81. Monroe to Madison, May 23, 1803, *PJM SSS*, 5:25.

82. *PJM SSS*, 5:71n.2.

83. Robert R. Livingston and Monroe to Madison, May 7, 1803, *PJM SSS*, 5:67.

84. Madison to Monroe, June 25, 1803, *PJM SSS*, 5:117.

85. Jefferson to John C. Breckenridge, August 12, 1803, *PTJ*, 41:186.

86. Proposed constitutional amendment, *PJM SSS*, 5:156.

87. Jefferson to John C. Breckenridge, August 12, 1803, *PTJ*, 41:186. When Madison was editing the draft legislation for Jefferson, he noted that it was important to "avoid, what the theory of our Constitution does not seem to admit, the influence of deliberations and anticipations of the House of Representatives on a treaty depending in the Senate." "Memorandum to Thomas Jefferson," October 1, 1803, *PJM SSS*, 5:480. This view, strikingly different from the one that Madison held with respect to the Jay Treaty when he was in the House of Representatives, probably reflects a different perspective taken by a sitting secretary of state relative to a member of the House.

88. Jefferson to Madison, August 18, 1803, *PJM SSS*, 5:323.

89. Jefferson's proposed amendment also included a remarkable provision unmentioned by Madison: All the territory north of the Arkansas River should be put aside for "Indians in exchange for equivalent portions of land occupied by them." The northern part of the Louisiana Territory would remain solely Indian territory unless changed by constitutional amendment. Jefferson to Madison, August 24, 1803, *PJM SSS*, 5:340–41.

90. Tinkcom, "Caviar Along the Potomac," 97.

91. Ibid.

92. Ibid., 98.

93. Ibid. This narrative presumably came directly from Madison. During the Revolutionary War, when British cloth had been boycotted, the Madisons had apparently wanted their slaves to provide for their needs by preparing wool for cloth making. The general implication was that the slaves had some capacity to resist their master's desires.

94. Ibid., 98. Foster considered himself less racist than many of his contemporaries. When Jefferson at Monticello gave Foster his "opinions in regard to the mental qualities of the Negro race," Foster noted that Jefferson's opinions "were certainly not favorable for he considered them to be as far inferior to the rest of mankind as the mule is to the horse." Foster thought Jefferson was wrong. "The black race is, however, as susceptible of refined civilization, and as capable to the full of profiting by the advantages of education as any other of any shade whatever," he wrote in his notes. This "must be admitted, in contradiction to Mr. Jefferson's prejudices." Ibid.

95. On Gabriel, his rebellion, the context, and its social meaning, see Douglas R. Egerton, *Gabriel's Rebellion: The Virginia Slave Conspiracies of 1800 and 1802* (Chapel Hill: University of North Carolina Press, 1993); James Sidbury, *Ploughshares into Swords: Race, Rebellion and Identity in Gabriel's Virginia* (Cambridge: Cambridge University Press, 1997); *Gabriel's Conspiracy: A Documentary History*, ed. Philip J. Schwartz (Charlottesville: University of Virginia Press, 2012).

96. Egerton, *Gabriel's Rebellion*, 50–51.

97. Ibid.

98. Madison to Jefferson, April 1, 1805, *PJM SSS*, 9:97.

99. Madison to Robert R. Livingston, March 31, 1804, *PJM SSS*, 6:643, 644.

100. Madison to Jefferson, April 5, 1805, *PJM SSS*, 9:217.

101. *PJM SSS*, 7:328n.6. In August, the British ambassador to the United States, Anthony Merry, complained to Madison about American ships bringing "contraband" goods such as arms to the West Indies in violation of U.S. neutrality. See Anthony Merry to Madison, August 31, 1804, *PJM SSS*, 7:662.

102. Thomas Jefferson, "Fourth Annual Address to Congress, November 4, 1804," *The Avalon Project*, Yale Law School, http://avalon.law.yale.edu/19th_century/jeffmes4.asp.

103. John Armstrong to Madison, every 14, 18 to 5, *PJM SSS*, 9:40.

104. Cf. Egerton, *Gabriel's Rebellion*, 170–72, relying in part on Michael Zuckerman, *Almost Chosen People: Oblique Biographies in the American Grain* (Berkeley: University of California Press, 1993), 210–18.

105. The text reads "favd. the views." Monroe to Madison, May 23, 1801, *PJM SSS*, 1:223. In context, this cannot mean "favored"—Lee was telling Burr he should have stood aside, not that he could have defeated Jefferson.

106. Ibid.

107. Ketcham, *James Madison*, 434; Henry Adams, *History of the United States of America During the First Administration of Thomas Jefferson* (New York: Antiquarian Press, 1962), 2:160–91.

108. Chernow, *Alexander Hamilton*, 673.

109. Ibid., 681.

110. Ibid., 683. Probably the allegation was that Burr was politically traitorous. The charge may have had a sexual side; yet Hamilton himself had been blackmailed over an adulterous affair, and it seems unlikely that he would have taken this tack in criticizing Burr.

CHAPTER THIRTEEN | NEUTRALITY

1. Lester H. Woolsey, "Early Cases on the Doctrine of Continuous Voyages," *American Journal of International Law* 4, no. 4 (October 1910): 823, 833–34.

2. Monroe to Madison, August 20, 1805, *PJM SSS,* 10:231.

3. Jefferson to Madison, August 7, 1805, *PJM SSS,* 10:183.

4. Ibid., 220.

5. Madison to Jefferson, August 20, 1805, *PJM SSS,* 10:230.

6. Ibid.

7. Ibid., 276.

8. Madison to Jefferson, September 14, 1805, *PJM SSS,* 10:322.

9. In 1794, when Britain had captured some 250 U.S. ships in the West Indies shortly after the outbreak of war with revolutionary France, Congress had voted two thirty-day embargoes on all ships then in American harbors. Madison had supported the plan in Congress, arguing that "the readiest expedient for stopping [Britain's] career of depredation of those parts of our trade which thwart her plans, will be to make her feel for those which she cannot do without." Madison to Horatio Gates, March 24, 1794, *PJM,* 15:287. Whether that brief episode of non-exportation had worked was uncertain. Congress had come close at the time to passing a general prohibition on all trade with England. A tie-breaking vote in the Senate by vice president John Adams had blocked the legislation, and the negotiation of the Jay Treaty had eased tensions with Britain. The episode served chiefly to introduce the germ of the embargo idea into U.S. politics.

10. Dolley Payne Madison to Anna Payne Cutts, June 4, 1805, *Letters of DPM,* 61.

11. Madison to Monroe, September 24, 1805, *PJM SSS,* 10:366.

12. Allgor, *Perfect Union,* 108.

13. Physick's name sounded as though it had been invented as an advertisement for himself, but, in fact, he had been born in Philadelphia to a father who bore the same name and was not a physician. See "Philip Syng Physick (1768–1837)," *Penn Biographies,* University of Pennsylvania University Archives and Records, www.archives .upenn.edu/people/1700s/physick_philip_syng.html.

14. Dolley Payne Madison to Anna Payne Cutts, July 29, 1805, *Letters of DPM,* 62.

15. Ibid.

16. Ibid.

17. Dolley Payne Madison to Anna Payne Cutts, July 31, 1805, *Letters of DPM,* 63.

18. Dolley Payne Madison to Anna Payne Cutts, August 19, 1805, *Letters of DPM,* 64.

19. Dolley Payne Madison to Anna Payne Cutts, July 31, 1805, *Letters of DPM,* 63.

20. Dolley Payne Madison to Anna Payne Cutts, August 19, 1805, *Letters of DPM,* 65.

21. Madison to Jefferson, August 20, 1805, *PJM SSS,* 10:230 and n.6.

22. Madison to Jefferson, September 1, 1805, *PJM SSS,* 10:277.

23. Ibid.

24. Madison to Albert Gallatin, September 9, 1805, *PJM SSS,* 10:310. In the same letter, Madison reported neutrally to Gallatin that he had received word from the U.S. consul in Algiers informing him that "the Bacris and Busnachs with all the other principal Jews in Algiers had been massacred by the rabble who wish to get an Arab administration in place of the Turkish." Ibid., 311. Naftali Busnach, adviser to the Bey of Algiers, had indeed been assassinated and a massacre of Jews had followed on the "Black Sabbath" of Saturday, June 29, 1805. A contemporary elegy written by an anonymous author in Algerian Arabic recorded forty-two dead. H. Z. (J. W.) Hirschberg, *A History of the Jews in North Africa,* ed. Eliezer Bashan and Robert Attal (Leiden, Netherlands: E. J. Brill, 1981), 2:38.

25. Madison to Jefferson, September 14, 1805, *PJM SSS,* 10:323.

26. Jefferson to Madison, September 18, 1805, *PJM SSS*, 10:353.

27. Madison to Jefferson, September 30, 1805, *PJM SSS*, 10:387.

28. Madison to Jefferson, October 5, 1805, *PJM SSS*, 10:411.

29. Ibid.

30. Jefferson to Madison, October 11, 1805, *PJM SSS*, 10:421.

31. Madison to Jefferson, October 20, 1805, *PJM SSS*, 10:454.

32. Dolley Payne Madison to Madison, October 23, 1805, *PJM SSS*, 10:462–63.

33. Dolley Payne Madison to Madison, October 26, 1805, *PJM SSS*, 10:469–70.

34. Madison to Dolley Payne Madison, October 28, 1805, *PJM SSS*, 10:472. Madison asked Bishop John Carroll, the first American Catholic bishop and the founder of Georgetown University, to go on his behalf to see Bishop Louis-Guillaume-Valentin Dubourg, who had just founded the school. At first Dubourg said admission was quite "impossible," there being about twenty on the list for admission, whom he could not accommodate." Carroll urged a "claim" . . . which, "though perhaps an unfounded one, but of which I made use." He told Dubourg "that Mrs. Madison had bespoken a place a year ago, and perhaps more." Dubourg took the hint and immediately said "that such being the case, he would certainly make a proper provision." John Carroll to Madison, October 29, 1805, *PJM SSS*, 10:478–79.

35. Madison to Dolley Payne Madison, October 31, 1805, *PJM SSS*, 10:484.

36. Ibid.

37. Dolley Payne Madison to Madison, November 2, 1805, *PJM SSS*, 10:494.

38. Madison to Dolley Payne Madison, November 11 or 18, 1805, *PJM SSS*, 10:521.

39. Madison to Dolley Payne Madison, November 15, 1805, *PJM SSS*, 10:540.

40. Monroe to Madison, November 11, 1805, *PJM SSS*, 10:522.

41. Monroe to Madison, December 11, 1805, *PJM SSS*, 10:654.

42. Monroe to Madison, October 18, 1805, *PJM SSS*, 10:444.

43. Charles Patrick Neimeyer, *War in the Chesapeake: The British Campaigns to Control the Bay, 1813–14* (Annapolis, Md.: Naval Institute Press, 2015), 22.

44. Ibid., 445–46.

45. Jefferson to Madison, November 22, 1805, *PJM SSS*, 10:571.

46. Jefferson, "Fifth Annual Message to Congress," December 3, 1805, in *Founders Early Access*, http://founders.archives.gov/documents/Jefferson/99-01-02-2746.

47. Ian W. Toll, *Six Frigates: The Epic History of the Founding of the U.S. Navy* (New York: W. W. Norton, 2006), 280.

48. Jefferson, "Fifth Annual Message to Congress," December 3, 1805.

49. Toll, *Six Frigates*, 284–85.

50. Ibid., 285–86.

51. Madison to Jefferson, November 24, 1805, *PJM SSS*, 10:578.

52. To be sure, Monroe himself, who was more hawkish than either Madison or Jefferson, nevertheless recommended only to "put our country, by invigorating the militia system and increasing the naval force, in a better state of defense." Monroe to Madison, December 23, 1805, *PJM SSS*, 10:683. The republican ideology, combined with the realistic limits on America's offensive capacities, constrained Monroe, too.

53. John Randolph, "Speech on Mr. Gregg's Motion," March 5, 1806, in Russell Kirk, *John Randolph of Roanoke: A Study in American Politics with Selected Speeches and Letters* (Indianapolis: Liberty Fund, 1997), 345.

54. David Johnson, *John Randolph of Roanoke* (Baton Rouge: Louisiana State University Press, 2012), 56.

55. Ibid., 131.

56. Ibid., 103–4 and 274n.98, quoting John Randolph to George Hay, January 3, 1806.

57. Ibid., 340.

58. Bradford Perkins, *The Creation of a Republican Empire, 1776–1865* (Cambridge: Cambridge University Press, 1993), 123.

59. Adams, *History of the United States of America During the First Administration of Thomas Jefferson,* 3:399–400; Unger, *Last Founding Father,* 187.

60. Ibid., 401.

61. Unfinished draft of a letter from Monroe to Jefferson, June 1, 1807, *Writings of James Monroe,* 5:5.

62. Monroe to Jefferson, March 22, 1808, *Writings of James Monroe,* 5:31.

63. Ibid., 467.

64. John Randolph to Monroe, September 16, 1806, *Writings of James Monroe,* 4:487. See also Ketcham, *James Madison,* 438 and 708n.50; Allgor, *Perfect Union,* 151.

65. Madison to Monroe and William Pinkney, May 17, 1806, *Writings of James Madison,* 7:377–78.

66. Ibid., 380.

67. Known as the "Ministry of All the Talents."

68. Madison to Monroe and William Pinkney, February 3, 1807, *Writings of James Madison,* 7:396.

69. Perkins, *Creation of a Republican Empire,* 124.

70. Madison to Monroe and William Pinkney, May 20, 1807, *Writings of James Madison,* 7:418–19.

71. Toll, *Six Frigates,* 292.

72. Ibid., 292–94.

73. Ibid., 296–98.

74. Madison to Monroe, July 6, 1807, *Writings of James Madison,* 7:455.

75. Ibid., 7:454–55.

76. "Commodore Barron's Inquiry into the Presence of Deserters Aboard the Chesapeake," April 7, 1807, *Prelude to the War of 1812,* Mariner's Museum, https://www.marinersmuseum.org/sites/micro/usnavy/08/08e.htm.

77. Madison to Monroe, July 6, 1807, *Writings of James Madison,* 7:456.

78. Ibid., 458.

79. Ibid., 460.

80. Madison to Monroe, July 17, 1807, *Writings of James Madison,* 7:463.

81. Madison to Monroe, October 21, 1807, *Writings of James Madison,* 7:467.

82. Toll, *Six Frigates,* 304.

83. Ibid., 305–6.

84. See below.

85. Bradford Perkins, "Embargo: Alternative to War," in *Essays on the Early Republic, 1789–1815,* ed. Leonard W. Levy and Carl Siracusa (Hinsdale, Ill.: Dryden Press, 1974), 322, first published in Bradford Perkins, *Prologue to War: England and the United States, 1805–1812* (Berkeley: University of California Press, 1968). Perkins takes the view, originally expressed by Richard Hofstadter, that Jefferson hoped to "refrigerate" war sentiment for the summer and reawaken it in December, but by then public support for the war had dwindled. To my mind, this reflects closely (though no doubt unconsciously) Franklin Delano Roosevelt's gradual process of winning over American public opinion to enter World War II, with the *Chesapeake* incident

standing in for Pearl Harbor. It was never going to be realistic for Jefferson to go to war, and in my view he did not intend to do so.

86. Jefferson to Madison, March 11, 1808, *Founders Online,* National Archives, https://founders.archives.gov/?q=%20Author%3A%22Jefferson%2C%20Thomas%22%20Period%3A%22Jefferson%20Presidency%22&s=1111311111&sa=&r=351&sr=madison%20james. See also Francis D. Cogliano, *Emperor of Liberty: Thomas Jefferson's Foreign Policy* (New Haven, Conn.: Yale University Press, 2014), 239.

87. Ibid., 129.

88. Ibid.

89. Perkins, "Embargo," 329.

90. Ibid., 330.

91. Ibid.

92. Ibid., 327–28.

93. Herman Vandenburg Ames, *State Documents on Federal Relations* (Philadelphia: University of Pennsylvania, 1900), 5:31, https://archive.org/stream/cu31924092685415#page/n33/mode/2up.

94. Ibid., 35.

95. Unger, *Last Founding Father,* 192.

96. Ibid.

97. Brant, *James Madison,* vol. 4, *Secretary of State: 1800–1809,* 429–30.

98. Ibid., 429.

99. Ibid., 426.

100. Ibid.

101. Ibid., 425.

102. "Address to the People of the United States," *National Intelligencer,* March 7, 1808. For the text see, e.g., Adams, *History of the United States of America During the First Administration of Thomas Jefferson,* 4:227.

103. Brant, *James Madison,* vol. 4, *Secretary of State,* 445–47.

104. Thomas Jefferson, "Eighth Annual Message to Congress," November 8, 1808, *The Avalon Project,* Yale Law School, http://avalon.law.yale.edu/19th_century/jeffmes8.asp.

105. Wood, *Empire of Liberty,* 657, writes that Jefferson and Madison "were opposed to the repeal of the embargo." Yet regret at its failure, which Wood shows for Jefferson at 658n.105, is not the same as opposition to repeal once failure was evident and repeal inevitable.

CHAPTER FOURTEEN | PRESIDENT

1. On the collapse of September 19, 1808, see Benjamin Henry Latrobe to Madison, September 8, 1809, *PJM PS,* 1:362.

2. Margaret Bayard Smith, *The First Forty Years of Washington Society: Portrayed by the Family Letters of Mrs. Samuel Harrison Smith (Margaret Bayard) from the Collection of Her Grandson, J. Henley Smith* (New York: Charles Scribner's Sons, 1906), 410.

3. "First Inaugural Address," March 4, 1809, *PJM PS,* 1:15–16.

4. Ibid., 16.

5. Ibid., 16–17.

6. Henry Lee to Madison, March 5, 1809, *PJM PS,* 1:20.

7. See Smith, *First Forty Years*, 411–12.

8. Margaret Bayard Smith to Susan B. Smith, March 4, 1809, in Smith, *First Forty Years*, 58.

9. See Smith, *First Forty Years*, 412.

10. Martha Washington wore good silk dresses, but the sophistication of Parisian fashion had not reached the United States in her era. Abigail Adams had rarely presented herself at the seat of government, and never dressed in such finery.

11. Margaret Bayard Smith to Susan B. Smith, March 4, 1809, in Smith, *First Forty Years*, 62.

12. Ibid., 61.

13. Ibid., 63.

14. Ibid., 200.

15. Madison to William Pinkney, March 17, 1809, *PJM PS*, 1:56.

16. *PJM PS*, 1:204 (citing *American State Papers: Documents, Legislative and Executive, of the Congress of the United States* [38 vols.; Washington, 1832–61], *Foreign Relations*, 3:296.

17. "Message to Congress," May 23, 1809, *PJM PS*, 1:200.

18. Madison to Jefferson, August 16, 1809, *PJM PS*, 1:327.

19. Ibid., 201.

20. Ketcham, *James Madison*, 494.

21. Britain was going beyond the normal practice recognized by international law, in which a blockade meant that actual ships blocked an actual harbor. Its order was declaring a formal or legal blockade, which purported to justify stopping all neutral ships headed to Europe, regardless of any actual blockade on continental ports. This was the opposite of the conciliation that Erskine had promised. Madison wrote to Jefferson that "the puzzle created by the order of April struck everyone." Madison to Jefferson, June 20, 1809, *PJM PS*, 1:261.

22. According to Erskine, the British had not expected his negotiations to succeed, and had therefore adopted strong measures in anticipation that they would fail. "This explanation seems as extraordinary as the alternatives it shows," Madison wrote drily to Jefferson. If the British government "means to be trickish, it will frustrate the proposed negotiation," he worried. Ibid., 261–62.

23. Albert Gallatin to Madison, July 24, 1809, *PJM PS*, 1:300.

24. Ibid.

25. Perhaps, Madison speculated, British policy was intended to give an advantage to London-based "smugglers in sugar and coffee" who were breaking the British blockade to send supplies to Europe. If this were so, it would be "an outrage in all decency [such as] was never before heard of, even on the shores of Africa" where the Barbary States engaged in their own form of naval blackmail. Madison to Albert Gallatin, July 28, 1809, *PJM PS*, 1:309.

26. Ibid.

27. Caesar Rodney to Madison, September 6, 1809, *PJM PS*, 1:358.

28. Albert Gallatin to Madison, July 4, 1809, *PJM PS*, 1:300–1.

29. Madison to Albert Gallatin, July 30, 1809, *PJM PS*, 1:312.

30. Madison to Jefferson, August 3, 1809, *PJM PS*, 1:317.

31. Madison to Dolley Payne Madison, August 7, 1809, *PJM PS*, 1:319; see also Madison to Dolley Payne Madison, August 9, 1809, *PJM PS*, 1:320.

32. "Presidential Proclamation," August 9, 1809, *PJM PS*, 1:320–21.

33. Jefferson to Madison, August 17, 1809, *PJM PS,* 1:331.
34. John Armstrong to Madison, September 18, 1809, *PJM PS,* 1:383.
35. John Armstrong to Madison, August 20, 1809, *PJM PS,* 1:337.
36. William Pinkney to Madison, August 19, 1809, *PJM PS,* 1:336.
37. *Lectures on the Growth and Development of the United States,* ed. Edwin Wiley (New York: American Educational Alliance, 1916), 5:237.
38. Madison to Robert Smith, September 15, 1809, *PJM PS,* 1:378.
39. Madison to William Pinkney, October 23, 1809, *PJM PS,* 2:28.
40. Madison to Jefferson, November 6, 1809, *PJM PS,* 1:55.
41. *PJM PS,* 2:67 and n.1.
42. "Message to Congress," January 3, 1810, *PJM PS,* 2:158.
43. *PJM PS,* 2:463n.1. On its face, Napoleon's condition should have caused no difficulty. Under the terms of Macon's Bill No. 2, one of the two eventualities that Napoleon specified was guaranteed to occur. Either Britain would suspend its orders-in-council and leave American trade unmolested—which Napoleon now claimed was fine with him—or else the United States would adopt total non-intercourse with Britain. Obviously Napoleon expected the latter to occur rather than the former; but from the U.S. perspective, either alternative was better than nothing.
44. Madison to John Armstrong, October 29, 1810, *PJM PS,* 2:598.
45. Madison to Jefferson, October 19, 1810, *PJM PS,* 2:585.
46. Ibid.
47. Madison to John Armstrong, October 29, 1810, *PJM PS,* 2:598. "If France is wise she will neither dislike it herself, nor promote resentment of it in any other quarter. She ought in fact, if guided by prudence and good information, to patronize at once, a general separation of South America from old Spain. This event is already decided, and the sole question with France is whether it is to take place under her auspices, or those of Great Britain."
48. Andrew McMichael, *Atlantic Loyalties: Americans in Spanish West Florida, 1785–1810* (Athens: University of Georgia Press, 2008), 160.
49. Samuel Fulton to Madison, April 20, 1810, *PJM PS,* 2:320.
50. Ibid. He claimed also that he had met Madison in Philadelphia in 1795, at which time Madison had offered him "friendship and service" that he would now "reclaim."
51. McMichael, *Atlantic Loyalties,* 159.
52. Ibid., 164–66. See also *PJM PS,* 2:315–16.
53. Madison to Jefferson, October 19, 1810, *PJM PS,* 2:585.
54. "Presidential Proclamation," October 27, 1810, *PJM PS,* 2:595.
55. Ibid.
56. *PJM PS,* 2:596n.2.
57. McMichael, *Atlantic Loyalties,* 170–71.
58. "Annual Message to Congress," December 5, 1810, *PJM PS,* 3:51.
59. Draft of Robert Smith to Louis-Charles-Barbé Sérurier, February 20, 1811, *PJM PS,* 3:174.
60. *PJM PS,* 3:175n.1.
61. This according to a report by Joseph Gales, Jr., in his diary. See *PJM PS,* 3:145n.3.
62. John Wayles Eppes to Jefferson, January 31, 1811, *PJM PS,* 3:143.
63. Brant, *James Madison,* vol. 5, *The President: 1809–1812,* 273 and 509n.13.
64. Ibid.
65. Albert Gallatin to Madison, March 7, 1811, *PJM PS,* 3:208.

66. Ibid., 256.
67. Ibid.
68. Ibid., 257.
69. Ibid., 258.
70. Ibid., 260–61.
71. Madison to Monroe, March 20, 1811, *PJM PS,* 3:226.
72. Ibid., 226.
73. Monroe to Madison, March 23, 1811, *PJM PS,* 3:229–30.
74. Ibid., 230.
75. Ibid., 236.
76. "Memorandum on Robert Smith," April 11, 1811, *PJM PS,* 3:261.
77. *Robert Smith's Address to the People of the United States* (s.n., 1811), 2.
78. "Memorandum on Robert Smith," April 11, 1811, *PJM PS,* 262–63.
79. Madison to Jefferson, April 1, 1811, *PJM PS,* 3:239.
80. Jefferson to Madison, April 7, 1811, *PJM PS,* 3:250.
81. *Robert Smith's Address to the People of the United States,* 4.
82. Ibid., 5.
83. Ibid., 6–14.
84. Dolley Payne Madison to Anna Payne Cutts, July 15, 1811, *Letters of DPM,* 148.
85. Madison to Jefferson, July 8, 1811, *PJM PS,* 3:373.
86. Ibid., 388–89.
87. *PJM PS,* 3:389n.2.
88. Ibid.
89. Henry Lee to Madison, August 19, 1811, *PJM PS,* 3:424.
90. "From the Inhabitants of St. Clair County, Illinois Territory," September 6, 1811, *PJM PS,* 3:446–47.
91. Madison to William Eustis, September 8, 1811, *PJM PS,* 3:452.
92. Monroe to Madison, September 13, 1811, *PJM PS,* 3:458.
93. Madison to Albert Gallatin, September 14, 1811, *PJM PS,* 3:460.
94. Madison to Richard Cutts, September 30, 1811, *PJM PS,* 3:473.
95. Dolley Payne Madison to Ruth Barlow, November 15, 1811, *Letters of DPM,* 150. Mosquitoes bred in the canal may indeed have been responsible for whatever disease spread.
96. Ibid., 151.
97. Ibid.
98. Ibid., 536.
99. Ibid.
100. Theodore J. Crackel, "The Military Academy in the Context of Jeffersonian Reform," in *Thomas Jefferson's Military Academy: Founding West Point,* ed. Robert M. S. McDonald (Charlottesville: University of Virginia Press, 2004), 111.
101. Francis Bailey to Madison, November 6, 1811, *PJM PS,* 4:7.
102. Henry Lee to Madison, November 8, 1811, *PJM PS,* 4:10.
103. Elbridge Gerry to Madison, November 17, 1811, *PJM PS,* 4:23.
104. Elbridge Gerry to Madison, December 12, 1811, *PJM PS,* 4:64.
105. Dolley Payne Madison to Anna Payne Cutts, December 22, 1811, *Letters of DPM,* 154.
106. "Resolutions of the General Assembly of Pennsylvania," December 20, 1811. *PJM PS,* 4:80–81.
107. "Address of the House of Representatives of South Carolina," *PJM PS,* 4:85.

108. Ibid., 86.
109. "Report of House Select Committee on Foreign Relations," November 29, 1811. See *PJM PS*, 4:109n.3.
110. F. Murray Greenwood, "John Henry," *Dictionary of Canadian Biography*, www .biographi.ca/en/bio.php?BioId=38087.
111. In a delightful, and no doubt largely fictional, memoir of his travels and frauds, Soubiron/Crillon later wrote that Henry told him that he had been "about to succeed in dividing the five states of the North—in separating them from the American union—when the affair of the *Chesapeake*" foiled his plans. In Soubiron's telling, Henry did not admit that he had been rejected by the British. Rather, he claimed to be ready to turn on his former masters because he had visited his native Ireland "and seen her destruction; our palaces turned into prisons, our mansions into barracks, and our best citizens loaded with chains of despotism." Henry Adams, "Count Edward de Crillon," *American Historical Review* 1 (1895): 54, 58 (reproducing and translating original document).
112. Ibid., 63. No such estate existed, of course.
113. No one knows how the money was divided, although in a later letter to Henry, Crillon/Soubiron spoke of having "obtain[ed] the result which brought you $50,000." In the same letter, Soubiron also said that he expected to be paid 84,000 francs by the American ambassador Joel Barlow on his arrival in Paris—although this never happened because he was arrested upon arrival in France. Ibid., 68. It appears that the primary way Soubiron profited was by accepting a gift of $1,000 from Henry and requesting a loan of $6,000, for which he provided worthless securities as collateral. Greenwood, "John Henry."
114. "To Congress," March 9, 1812, *PJM PS*, 4:235.
115. Madison to Jefferson, March 9, 1812, *PJM PS*, 4:237. Madison's secretary of the navy wrote to his former attorney general Caesar Rodney that the disclosure "must give rise" to the question of war notwithstanding "the indecisions of Congress." *PJM PS*, 4:236n.3.
116. Jefferson to Madison, March 26, 1812, *PJM PS*, 4:263.
117. Greenwood, "John Henry."
118. Dolley Payne Madison to Anna Cutts Madison, March 20, 1812, *Letters of DPM*, 157. The boycott ended by March 27, when Dolley reported that so many Republicans had come to the president's house that the Federalists had "changed their tack . . . such a rallying of our party has alarmed them into a return."
119. John Randolph, "Speech Against War with England," December 10, 1811, reprinted in Kirk, *John Randolph of Roanoke*, 365.
120. Ibid., 357.
121. Ibid., 367.
122. Ibid., 358.
123. Madison to Jefferson, April 3, 1812, *PJM PS*, 3:287 and 288n.2.
124. *PJM PS*, 4:280n.1.
125. Joel Barlow to Madison, May 12, 1812, *PJM PS*, 4:379 and 380n.5.
126. Barlow to Madison, May 2, 1812, *PJM PS*, 4:359–60.
127. Monroe to Madison, July 12, 1813, *PJM PS*, 6:420–21.
128. David C. Hanrahan, "The Assassination of the Prime Minister, Spencer Perceval," *The Public Domain Review*, http://publicdomainreview.org/2012/05/08/the-assassination -of-the-prime-minister-spencer-perceval/.

129. Alexander Baring, in *Hansard Parliamentary Debates*, 1st ser., vol. 21 (1812), March 3, 1127–28.

130. Madison to Jefferson, May 25, 1812, *PJM PS*, 4:415.

131. Dolley Payne Madison to Anna Cutts Madison, March 27, 1812, *Letters of DPM*, 158.

132. Elbridge Gerry to Madison, May 19, 1812, *PJM PS*, 4:398 and n.1.

133. "To Congress," June 1, 1812, *PJM PS*, 4:434.

134. Ibid., 435–36.

135. Ibid., 436.

136. Ibid., 437.

137. Richard Rush to Benjamin Rush, June 20, 1812. The passage was first used by Henry Adams in his *History*, 6:229 and n.2. Rush's reference to Madison's "little round hat and huge cockade" was likewise not intended derisively, nor did Adams present it as though it were. Yet contemporary writers often treat the image that way, possibly under the unconscious influence of Michael Dukakis's tank-helmet debacle in his run for the presidency in 1988. See, e.g., Wood, *Empire of Liberty*, 660 ("the war seemed as ludicrous as the diminutive commander-in-chief with his oversized cockade").

CHAPTER FIFTEEN | WAR

1. Madison to Jefferson, August 17, 1812, *PJM PS*, 5:165.

2. Ibid.

3. "Two hundred members of the Ohio militia refused to cross over into Canada, claiming they were a defensive force only and could not fight outside the United States." Wood, *Empire of Liberty*, 677.

4. Albert Gallatin to James Madison, August 13, 1812, *PJM PS*, 5:152.

5. Thomas Acheson to Madison, August 25, 1812, *PJM PS*, 5:192.

6. Dolley Payne Madison to Edward Coles, August 31, 1812, *Letters of DPM*, 172. The couple had reached Dumfries, Virginia, about a third of the way home, when Madison had to turn back.

7. David S. Heidler and Jeannie T. Heidler, "Detroit, Surrender of," in *Encyclopedia of the War of 1812*, ed. David S. Heidler and Jeannie T. Heidler (Santa Barbara, Calif.: ABC-CLIO, 1997), 153–54.

8. Dolley Payne Madison to Edward Coles, August 31, 1812, *Letters of DPM*, 172.

9. Monroe to Henry Dearborn, August 28, 1812, *Writings of James Monroe*, 2:218.

10. Monroe to Jefferson, August 31, 1812, *Writings of James Monroe*, 2:220.

11. Brant, *James Madison*, vol. 6, *Commander in Chief: 1812 to 1836*, 75 and 542n.9 (quoting John Graham to Monroe, August 28, 1812).

12. Monroe to Madison, September 2, 1812, *PJM PS*, 5:253.

13. Henry Dearborn to Madison, October 24, 1812, *PJM PS*, 5:411.

14. Unidentified correspondent to Madison, October 28, 1812, *PJM PS*, 5:416.

15. "Declaration of the Connecticut General Assembly," August 25, 1812, *PJM PS*, 5:195–96.

16. "Annual Message to Congress," November 4, 1812, *PJM PS*, 5:429.

17. Madison to Jefferson, August 17, 1812, *PJM PS*, 5:166.

18. "Declaration of the Connecticut General Assembly," August 25, 1812, *PJM PS*, 5:196.

19. Mark Lardas, Constitution *vs.* Guerriere: *Frigates During the War of 1812* (Oxford: Osprey Publishing, 2009), 48.

20. "Annual Message to Congress," November 4, 1812, *PJM PS*, 5:429–30.
21. Ibid., 433.
22. See Allgor, *Perfect Union*, 277 and 455n.46, citing "Letters of Abijah Bigelow, Member of Congress, to His Wife, 1810–1815," *American Antiquarian Society Proceedings* 40 (1930): 322.
23. Lucy Payne Washington to Dolley Madison, date unknown, *Letters of DPM*, 146–47 and n.5. The editors give July 1811 as a speculative date, which would put the letter a year before the election. Allgor quotes the letter in the context of the 1812 election; see *Perfect Union*, 277.
24. Dolley Payne Madison to Anna Cutts Madison, March 20, 1812, *Letters of DPM*, 157.
25. Rufus King accounted for the rest of the votes and did not come close to winning any state.
26. Monroe to Madison, September 2, 1812, *PJM PS*, 5:252–53. Madison accepted the suggestion. Hull was court-martialed, convicted, and sentenced to death. Madison commuted the sentence.
27. Monroe to Madison, September 2, 1812, *PJM PS*, 5:253.
28. Monroe to Madison, September 4, 1812, *PJM PS*, 5:265.
29. Madison to Monroe, September 5, 1812, *PJM PS*, 5:270.
30. Ibid.
31. Madison to William Plumer, October 6, 1812, *PJM PS*, 5:369.
32. "Annual Message to Congress," November 4, 1812, *PJM PS*, 5:428.
33. William Henry Harrison to Monroe, January 26, 1813, *PJM PS*, 5:626.
34. Philip P. Mason, ed., *After Tippecanoe: Some Aspects of the War of 1812* (East Lansing: Michigan State University Press, 2011), 90.
35. "Second Inaugural Address," March 4, 1813, *PJM PS*, 6:85–86.
36. Ibid.
37. Ibid., 87.
38. Ruth Barlow to Dolley Payne Madison, November 25, 1812, *PJM PS*, 5:471–72.
39. Madison to Jefferson, March 10, 1813, *PJM PS*, 6:100.
40. Ibid., 100–1.
41. Madison to Monroe, April 1, 1813, *PJM PS*, 6:170.
42. St. George Tucker to Madison, March 19, 1813, *PJM PS*, 6:135.
43. Madison to St. George Tucker, March 19, 1813, *PJM PS*, 6:135. Tucker also suggested to Madison that he might wish "to establish a communication by means of telegraphs," and offered to send Madison a model of a French telegraph that he had himself built almost twenty years earlier. St. George Tucker to Madison, March 19, 1813, *PJM PS*, 6:135. Madison considered the suggestion intriguing: "The subject of telegraphs being critically interesting," he wrote, "the model of yours will be thankfully received." Madison to St. George Tucker, March 19, 1813, *PJM PS*, 6:135. Tucker sent the model. See St. George Tucker to Madison, March 26, 1813, *PJM PS*, 6:155. But Madison, who lacked the resources to assemble an army to invade Canada, had no time or money to focus on the still uncertain technology of telegraphy.
44. Jonathan Dayton to Madison, April 9, 1813, *PJM PS*, 6:184–85.
45. Heidler and Heidler, "George Cockburn," in *Encyclopedia of the War of 1812*, 115–16.
46. Monroe to Madison, April 13, 1813, *PJM PS*, 6:192–93.
47. Cushing Eells to Madison, May 17, 1813, *PJM PS*, 6:320.
48. Ibid.
49. "Francis Jeffrey's Account of a Conversation with Madison," November 18, 1813, *PJM*

PS, 7:46–47. Jeffrey, later a law lord, was one of the founders of the *Edinburgh Review* and its first official editor.

50. Richard V. Barbuto, "Battle of York," in *Encyclopedia of the War of 1812,* 568–69.

51. "To Congress," May 25, 1813, *PJM PS,* 6:340–41.

52. It also made Dearborn look better than he had previously. "I congratulate you, on Dearborn's brilliant debut at York," wrote John Adams. Adams to Madison, May 14, 1813, *PJM PS,* 6:305.

53. After Mary ("Maria") Jefferson Eppes's death in childbirth, Eppes seems to have followed Jefferson's model in taking an enslaved woman called Betsy Hemmings as his unacknowledged partner, having several children with her. See Gordon-Reed, *Hemingses of Monticello,* 51.

54. John Wayles Eppes to Madison, June 29, 1813, *PJM PS,* 6:400–1.

55. Gerry reported the conversation to his wife, Ann Gerry, on June 15, 1813. See *PJM PS,* 6:393n.1.

56. Madison to William Hill Wells, June 17, 1813, *PJM PS,* 6:393.

57. Madison was treated by an infusion of Peruvian bark that contained quinine. Brant, *James Madison,* vol. 6, *Commander in Chief,* 188. From this, Cheney, *James Madison,* 390–91, concludes the disease was malaria and that the quinine in the bark cured it. But it may have been some other ailment entirely that went away eventually independent of the treatment.

58. Ibid.

59. *PJM PS,* 6:393n.1; Brant, *James Madison,* vol. 6, *Commander in Chief,* 184–88.

60. *The Diary of Elbridge Gerry, Jr.,* ed. Annette Townsend (New York: Brentano's, 1927), 178. Gerry Jr. said Madison was "reclining on a setee [*sic*] or couch" propped up by pillows and was still "pale and wan."

61. "Presidential Proclamation," July 23, 1813, *PJM PS,* 6:458.

62. Ibid.

63. Ibid., 459.

64. Ibid.

65. Madison to Congress, May 25, 1813, *PJM PS,* 6:340.

66. Dolley Payne Madison to Hannah Gallatin, August 30, 1813, *Letters of DPM,* 181.

67. Madison to William Jones, September 23, 1813, *PJM PS,* 6:651.

68. Ibid.

69. Henry Dearborn to Madison, July 24, 1813, *PJM PS,* 6:461 and n.1.

70. Henry Dearborn to Madison, August 17, 1813, *PJM PS,* 6:535.

71. Madison to Henry Dearborn, August 8, 1813, *PJM PS,* 6:503.

72. Ibid., 504n.1.

73. Ibid.; Henry Dearborn to Madison, October 21, 1813, *PJM PS,* 6:706.

74. Monroe to Madison, August 17, 1813, *PJM PS,* 6:537.

75. The original source of the quote is War of 1812 participant and novelist John Richardson in *Richardson's War of 1812* (Toronto: Historical Publishing, 1902), 206.

76. John Sugden, *Tecumseh's Last Stand* (Norman: University of Oklahoma Press, 1990), 213.

77. Madison to William Jones, October 18, 1813, *PJM PS,* 6:702.

78. Madison to William Jones, October 15, 1813, *PJM PS,* 6:697.

79. Ibid.

80. John Armstrong to Madison, October 20, 1813, *PJM PS,* 6:705.

81. The commander, McClure, claimed he had been ordered to do so by Secretary of War Armstrong. Armstrong defended himself by claiming that he had authorized the burning of Newark "only in case it should be necessary to the defense of Fort George. In that case the measure would be justifiable." *PJM PS*, 7:145n.1.

82. Daniel D. Tompkins to Madison, January 3, 1814, *PJM PS*, 7:167.

83. Dolley Payne Madison to Martha Jefferson Randolph, January 9, 1814, *Letters of DPM*, 182.

84. Ibid.

85. "Annual Message to Congress," December 7, 1813, *PJM PS*, 7:83.

86. Ibid., 88.

87. Monroe to Madison, December 27, 1815, *PJM PS*, 7:139.

88. Ibid., 140.

89. Ibid.

90. John Armstrong to Madison, May 1, 1814, *PJM PS*, 7:448.

91. William Jones to Madison, May 25, 1814, *PJM PS*, 7:521–22.

92. Winder was involved in a complicated and embarrassing episode that occupied a good deal of Madison's attention during the spring of 1814. He had been captured by British forces at the Battle of Stoney Creek the previous June, and held as a prisoner of war. The circumstances of his detention were themselves complicated. In October 1812, when the war was new, Britain had filed treason charges against twenty-three British-born U.S. soldiers who had been taken prisoner at the Battle of Queenston Heights. The men were shipped to England for trial. In retaliation, the United States singled out twenty-three British prisoners of war and identified them as hostages who would be executed should anything happen to the American soldiers set to be tried for treason in England.

    In an escalating cycle, the British then identified forty-six American prisoners of war as hostages; the United States then increased its number of British hostages. *PJM PS*, 7:xxiv. Winder, detained in Quebec, went to Sir George Prévost, the British commander, and asked to be paroled to Washington to resolve the situation by asking Madison to change his policy. Prévost sent Winder to Washington carrying a message of a possible armistice along the Canadian border. Madison authorized Winder to negotiate a prisoner exchange; he also authorized him to negotiate an armistice on the condition that it apply to the East Coast, not just the Canadian border.

    Prévost was not prepared to negotiate an armistice that would remove Britain's advantageous position along the Atlantic coast. But he did tell Winder that he would agree to a partial prisoner exchange—while holding on to the twenty-three British-born American soldiers who were facing trial in Britain. Winder brought the message to Madison in April. Madison and Monroe could not accept the terms of the proposed convention or agreement, because it refused to offer any compromise on the basic question of the American soldiers who were being charged with treason. But because Prévost had already begun to release his hostages, Madison reciprocated by releasing the hostages held by the United States.

93. Madison to Monroe, May 21, 1814, *PJM PS*, 7:508.

94. See letters from Madison to John Armstrong, William Jones, and Monroe, June 3, 1814, *PJM PS*, 7:534–36.

95. "Memorandum on Cabinet Meeting," June 7, 1814, *PJM PS*, 7:545.

96. Madison to James Barbour, June 16, 1814, *PJM PS*, 7:561.

CHAPTER SIXTEEN | FAILURE AND REDEMPTION

1. James Barbour to Madison, June 13, 1814, *PJM PS*, 7:555–56.
2. Madison to Barbour, June 16, 1814, *PJM PS*, 7:561–62.
3. "Memorandum on Cabinet Meeting," June 23 and 24, 1814, *PJM PS*, 7:584.
4. *PJM PS*, 7:591n.1.
5. "Memorandum on Cabinet Meeting," June 27, 1814, *PJM PS*, 7:591.
6. "Memorandum on the Defense of the City of Washington," July 1, 1814, *PJM PS*, 8:2.
7. Madison to John Armstrong, July 2, 1814, *PJM PS*, 8:5.
8. Monroe to ———, July 3, 1814, *The Writings of James Monroe*, ed. Stanislaus Murray Hamilton (New York: G. P Putnam's Sons, 1901), 5:285.
9. Ibid., 286.
10. Madison to Elbridge Gerry, July 5, 1814, *PJM PS*, 8:9.
11. Madison to Armstrong, May 24, 1814, *PJM PS*, 7:513.
12. Madison to John Armstrong, August 13, 1814, *PJM PS*, 8:98.
13. Ibid., 99.
14. Monroe to Madison, August 20, 1814 (1 p.m.), *PJM PS*, 8:119–20.
15. William H. Winder to Madison, August 20, 1814 (Saturday evening), *PJM PS*, 8:123.
16. Madison to Monroe, August 21, 1814 (8 a.m.), *PJM PS*, 8:128.
17. Monroe to Madison, August 21, 1814, *PJM PS*, 8:129.
18. Ibid.
19. Monroe to Madison, August 21, 1814 (11 p.m.), *PJM PS*, 8:130.
20. Ibid.
21. Madison to Monroe, August 22, 1814 (5 a.m.), *PJM PS*, 8:131.
22. Madison to Monroe, August 22, 1814 (10 a.m.), *PJM PS*, 8:132.
23. Monroe to Madison, August 22, 1814, *PJM PS*, 8:133.
24. Ibid.
25. Dolley Payne Madison to Lucy Payne Washington Todd, August 23, 1814, *Letters of DPM*, 193.
26. James Madison to Dolley Payne Madison, August 23, 1814, *PJM PS*, 8:134.
27. Dolley Payne Madison to Lucy Payne Washington Todd, August 23, 1814, *Letters of DPM*, 193.
28. Ibid.
29. "Memorandum of Conversations with John Armstrong," August 24, 1814, *PJM PS*, 8:134. The editors of Madison's papers suggest that the notes were not made before Armstrong resigned on September 4, 1814. They also suggest that Madison probably "copied them during his retirement years; they were also emended in his hand." Ibid., 136n.1.
30. "Memorandum of Conversations with John Armstrong," August 24, 1814, *PJM PS*, 8:134.
31. Ibid.
32. Ibid.
33. Ibid.
34. Dolley Payne Madison to Lucy Payne Washington Todd, August 23, 1814, *Letters of DPM*, 193.
35. "Memorandum of Conversations with John Armstrong," August 24, 1814, *PJM PS*, 8:135.

36. Dolley Payne Madison to Lucy Payne Washington Todd, August 23, 1814, *Letters of DPM,* 193.

37. Cutts, *Queen of America,* 124–25.

38. Paul Jennings, "A Colored Man's Reminiscences of James Madison," published in Elizabeth Dowling Taylor, *A Slave in the White House: Paul Jennings and the Madisons* (New York: Palgrave MacMillan, 2012), 231.

39. Ibid.

40. Ibid., 231–32.

41. Ibid., 232.

42. Dolley Payne Madison to Lucy Payne Washington Todd, August 23, 1814, *Letters of DPM,* 193.

43. Ibid., 194. The portrait was taken down from the wall by John Susé, "a Frenchman, then door-keeper," and a slave named "Magraw, the president's gardener," Jennings recalled. Jennings, "Colored Man's Reminiscences," 232.

44. Ibid., 194.

45. Anna Cutts to Dolley Payne Madison, ca. August 23, 1814, *Letters of DPM,* 194.

46. Sérurier to Talleyrand, August 27, 1814, quoted and translated by Henry Adams, *History of the United States in the Administrations of James Madison,* 2:146.

47. Jennings, "Colored Man's Reminiscences," 232.

48. Adams, *History of the United States in the Administrations of James Madison,* 144–45.

49. Jennings, "Colored Man's Reminiscences," 234.

50. Anthony S. Pitch, *The Burning of Washington: The British Invasion of 1814* (Annapolis, Md.: Bluejacket Books, 1998), 118; Ketcham, *James Madison,* 210 and 721n.8.

51. Jennings, "Colored Man's Reminiscences," 233.

52. *PJM PS,* 8:140.

53. Ibid.; Charles Jared Ingersoll, *Historical Sketch of the Second War Between the United States of America, and Great Britain* (Philadelphia: Lea and Blanchard, 1849).

54. Madison to William Jones, August 27, 1814 (10 a.m.), *PJM PS,* 8:143.

55. Madison to John Armstrong, August 27, 1814 (10 a.m.), *PJM PS,* 8:143.

56. Madison to Dolley Payne Madison, August 27, 1814 (10 a.m.), *PJM PS,* 8:144.

57. Pitch, *Burning of Washington,* 99, 135–37.

58. Jennings, "Colored Man's Reminiscences," 232.

59. Madison's old acquaintance and neighbor William Thornton, the architect of the Capitol, who was serving as the first superintendent of the U.S. Patent Office, had tried on his own recognizance to do something. Raised and educated in Britain, Thornton found it natural to communicate with British officers. He had convinced them not to burn the patent office when they had torched other public buildings, and had tried without notable success to discourage private looting. A medical doctor, Thornton had also visited the British wounded, whom Ross had left behind in his haste to return to his ships. The officer in charge of the wounded was concerned that any British soldiers who remained in the city after the departure of Ross's army might be shot. Thornton suggested that Americans patrolling the city at night might bring British soldiers with them on joint operations to avoid any gunfights with British stragglers. *PJM PS,* 145n.1. Blake resented Thornton's actions, which highlighted his own failure to remain in the city. The two exchanged angry letters in the newspapers, with Blake accusing Thornton of treating with the enemy and Thornton hinting at Blake's dereliction of duty. Ibid.

60. *PJM PS*, 8:145n.1.
61. Madison to Dolley Payne Madison, August 28, 1814, *PJM PS*, 8:146.
62. *PJM PS*, 8:152n.2.
63. Ibid.
64. "James Monroe's Draft Memoranda on the Events of 20–24 August 1814," *PJM PS*, 8:150–51.
65. Ibid., 151–52.
66. "Memorandum of a Conversation with John Armstrong," August 29, 1814, *PJM PS*, 8:153.
67. Ibid.
68. Ibid.
69. Ibid., 155.
70. Ibid.
71. John Armstrong to Madison, September 4, 1814, *PJM PS*, 8:178.
72. Cutts, *Queen of America*, 125–26.
73. Tench Coxe to Madison, August 30, 1814, *PJM PS*, 8:156–57.
74. Richard Rush to Monroe, August 28, 1814, *PJM PS*, 8:147.
75. Ibid., 148.
76. William Jones to Madison, September 1, 1814, *PJM PS*, 8:162.
77. Ibid., 164.
78. "Presidential Proclamation," September 1, 1814, *PJM PS*, 8:167.
79. Jefferson to Madison, September 24, 1814, *PJM PS*, 8:246–47.
80. Monroe to Madison, August 31, 1814, *PJM PS*, 8:161 and n.1.
81. Monroe to Madison, September 7, 1814, *PJM PS*, 8:189–90.
82. Who won the militia assault is therefore a matter of interpretation. See, e.g., Wood, *Empire of Liberty*, 691, who says that the British "defeated" the militia. But the city did not fall, which suggests that the defense was therefore successful.
83. Although it took some time to be certain of it. On September 19, Monroe, acting as secretary of war, ordered Smith to release 2,641 federal troops from Baltimore to defend Washington. Aware of the order, the citizens' committee of vigilance and safety, the same group of Baltimore citizens that had chosen Smith, sent a delegation to Madison asking for federal funds to reimburse the expenditures that had been made in defense of the city as well as the cost of future defense.
84. "Annual Message to Congress," September 20, 1814, *PJM PS*, 8:225.
85. Monroe to Madison, September 25, 1814, *PJM PS*, 8:244–45.
86. Madison to Jefferson, October 10, 1814, *PJM PS*, 8:297–98.
87. John Payne Todd to Madison, October 9, 1814, *PJM PS*, 8:294.
88. Richard Buel, Jr., *America on the Brink: How the Political Struggle over the War of 1812 Almost Destroyed the Young Republic* (New York: Palgrave Macmillan, 2005), 189–218.
89. Mathew Carey to Madison, October 30, 1814, *PJM PS*, 8:340.
90. See Reginald C. Stuart, *Civil-Military Relations During the War of 1812* (Santa Barbara, Calif.: ABC-CLIO, 2009), 104–10.
91. Madison to Wilson Cary Nicolas, November 26, 1814, *PJM PS*, 8:401.
92. Ibid., 401–2.
93. Monroe to Madison, January 10, 1815, *PJM PS*, 8:501. ("I have seen Generals Swartwout and Porter, the first last night and both this morning. They express the ideas which prevailed last night with you of organizing by volunteer and other laws a force in the East to repel the enemy and put rebellion down."

94. *PJM PS*, 8:501n.1.

95. *PJM PS*, 8:387n.1; and see generally James Banner, *To the Hartford Convention: The Federalists and the Origins of Party Politics in Massachusetts* (New York: Alfred A. Knopf, 1970).

96. Ibid.

97. Wellington to Liverpool, November 9, 1814, *The Dispatches of Field Marshal the Duke of Wellington, K.G. During His Various Campaigns in India, Denmark, Portugal, Spain, the Low Countries, and France: From 1799 to 1818*, ed. John Gurwood (London: John Murray, 1834–39), 9:425–26. See also John R. Grodzinski, "The Duke of Wellington, the Peninsular War, and the War of 1812, Part II: Reinforcements, Views of the War and Command in North America," *The War of 1812 Magazine* 6 (April 2007).

98. Ibid.

99. Ibid.

100. William C. C. Claiborne to Madison, September 22, 1814, *PJM PS*, 8:235.

101. Ibid.

102. Heidler and Heidler, "Battle of New Orleans," in *Encyclopedia of the War of 1812*, 380.

103. Dolley Payne Madison to Hannah Gallatin, January 14, 1815, *Letters of DPM*, 197.

104. "George Ticknor's Account of a Dinner at the President's House," January 21, 1815, *PJM PS*, 8:519–20.

105. Madison "pretty distinctly intimated to me his own regard for the Unitarian doctrines," Ticknor wrote. After dinner, Ticknor was alone with Madison and Dolley, and "Mr. M. gave amusing stories of early religious persecutions in Virginia." Dolley, for her part, "entered into a defense and panegyric of the Quakers, to whose sect, you know, she once belonged." Ibid., 520–21. In what might have been intended as a broad hint to Ticknor to keep the dinner conversation private, Madison also mentioned Francis Jeffrey, the editor of the *Edinburgh Review*, who had dined with Madison the previous year and then spoken negatively of Madison to friends in Boston. Jeffrey's name, when mentioned by Madison, "seemed to strike him with a sudden silence," Ticknor noted. Ticknor got the point. He "was careful in my replies, and did not suffer him to know that I had ever seen Jeffrey or his journal." Ibid., 520.

106. Monroe to Madison, February 3, 1815, *PJM PS*, 8:554 and n.2. Madison also issued a presidential proclamation officially pardoning the Barataria freebooters led by the Lafitte brothers for any federal crimes they might have committed in the past. The Lafittes and their followers had chosen the right side in the battle of New Orleans, rejecting British advances and joining Jackson after being promised a pardon in return. See William C. Davis, *The Pirates Laffite: The Treacherous World of the Corsairs of the Gulf* (Orlando, Fla.: Harcourt, 2005).

107. Cutts, *Queen of America*, 132.

108. Jennings, "Colored Man's Reminiscences," 234. The march was probably "President Madison's March," composed by Alexander Reinagle, or perhaps a different march of the same name by Peter Waddel. For an 1809 facsimile of the sheet music for the latter, see the *Frances G. Spencer Collection of American Popular Sheet Music*, Baylor University, http://contentdm.baylor.edu/cdm/ref/collection/fa-spnc/id/22780.

109. Quoted in Ingersoll, *Historical Sketch of the Second War*, 2:64–65. For the attribution to Smith, which is surely correct, see Hugh Howard, *Mr. and Mrs. Madison's War: America's First Couple and the Second War of Independence* (New York: Bloomsbury Press, 2012), 291 & 337n.41.

110. Richard Rush to Madison, February 15, 1815, *PJM PS*, 8:579.

111. Madison to Richard Rush, February 15, 1815, *PJM PS*, 8:579.
112. "To Congress," February 18, 1815, *PJM PS*, 8:599.
113. Ibid., 600.
114. See Samuel J. Watson. *Peacekeepers and Conquerors: The Army Officer Corps on the American Frontier, 1821–1846* (Lawrence: University Press of Kansas, 2013). The modestly sized antebellum army protected the Canadian border, fought and expelled Native Americans, and undertook the Mexican-American War. The antebellum navy patrolled the African coast to fight the slave trade and remained small until Congress began to build steam-powered warships in the 1850s.

CONCLUSION | LEGACY

1. Madison to Alexander Dallas, May 4, 1815, *The American Founding Era*, University of Virginia Press, http://rotunda.upress.virginia.edu/founders/default.xqy?keys=FGEA -chron-1810-1815-05-04-8; also cited in Ketcham, *James Madison*, 600 and 723n.41.
2. Thus, when in August came news of Wellington's decisive victory over Napoleon at Waterloo, Madison again reacted coolly, evaluating the new balance of power in Europe. Madison to Monroe, August 10, 1815 ("If there be an end of Bonaparte, the maritime jealousy of the continent must be a bridle on the maritime ambition of Great Britain"), *The American Founding Era*, University of Virginia Press, http://rotunda .upress.virginia.edu/founders/default.xqy?keys=FGEA-chron-1810-1815-08-10-9. Madison received definitive news of Waterloo on August 20, writing to Richard Rush that "the same comments probably occur to all of us." Madison to Richard Rush, August 20, 1815, *The American Founding Era*, University of Virginia Press, http://rotunda .upress.virginia.edu/founders/default.xqy?keys=FGEA-chron-1810-1815-08-20-4.

    Reacting to a report that Napoleon's brother Joseph Bonaparte planned to visit him at Montpelier "incognito," Madison took steps to bar the approach. "Whatever sympathy may be due to fallen fortunes," he wrote to Alexander Dallas, "there is no claim of merit in that family on the American nation; nor any reason why its government should be embarrassed in any way on their account." Madison to Alexander Dallas, September 15, 1815, *The American Founding Era*, University of Virginia Press, http://rotunda.upress.virginia.edu/founders/default.xqy?keys=FGEA-chron-1810 -1815-09-15-4; and see Ketcham, *James Madison*, 601 and 723n.42.
3. Reginald C. Stuart, *Civil-Military Relations During the War of 1812* (Santa Barbara, Calif.: ABC-CLIO, 2009), 126–27.
4. "Seventh Annual Message to Congress," December 5, 1815, *Writings of James Madison*, 8:341.
5. "To the Senate," January 30, 1815, *PJM PS*, 8:541.
6. Ibid.
7. Madison also proposed a national university, which he apparently now believed could be lawfully chartered even though it was unmentioned in the Constitution.
8. Madison, Message to Congress, December 3, 1816, Founders Online Early Access, available at https://founders.archives.gov/?q=Project%3A%22Madison%20Papers%22 %20Author%3A%22Madison%2C%20James%22%20Period%3A%22Madison%20 Presidency%22&s=1511311111&r=1183.
9. Ibid.
10. Ibid.

11. Ralph Ketcham, "An Unpublished Sketch of James Madison by James K. Paulding," *Virginia Magazine of History and Biography* 67 (1959): 432, 435.

12. John Adams to Jefferson, February 2, 1817, *The Adams-Jefferson Letters,* ed. Lester J. Capon (1959; republished 1971), 1:507–8.

13. Andrea Wulf, *Founding Gardeners: The Revolutionary Generation, Nature, and the Shaping of the American Nation* (New York: Alfred A. Knopf, 2011), 195–96.

14. Ibid., 197–98.

15. Ibid.

16. The African-American Kearse family preserves the tradition that they are descended from James Madison and an enslaved woman named Coreen. According to a website maintained by Dr. Bettye Kearse, the "family credo" is: "Always remember—you're a Madison. You come from African slaves and a president." See The Other Madisons (blog), www.bettyekearse.com/the-other-madisons/. The Montpelier Documentary Record of Slave Names does not include any enslaved person with the name Coreen or a similar name. That, of course, is not dispositive. More suggestive is that Madison and Dolley had no children, despite the fact that Dolley had just recently had two children when they married. This makes it seem probable that Madison was unable to reproduce. DNA testing might be possible even without a confirmed direct James Madison descendant if technology permits extraction from the lock of hair of Madison's enclosed in his miniature portrait at the Library of Congress. The Kearse family could also very well be descended from other members of the Madison family.

17. Robert J. Evans to Madison, June 3, 1819, *PJM RS,* 1:464–65.

18. Madison to Robert J. Evans, June 15, 1819, *PJM RS,* 1:468.

19. "Memorandum on an African Colony for Freed Slaves," October 20, 1789, *PJM,* 12:437.

20. Madison to Robert J. Evans, June 15, 1819, *PJM RS,* 1:469.

21. Madison had not attended the society's inaugural meeting in Washington on December 21, 1816. But James Monroe, the president-elect, was there, as were Madison allies such as Henry Clay and enemies, including John Randolph. See Early Lee Fox, *The American Colonization Society 1817–1840* (Baltimore: Johns Hopkins University Press, 1919).

22. Madison to Robert J. Evans, June 15, 1819, *PJM RS,* 1:469.

23. See Drew McCoy, *The Last of the Fathers: James Madison and the Republican Legacy* (Cambridge: Cambridge University Press, 1989), 307–8.

24. "Speech in Virginia Convention, December 2, 1829," *Founders Early Access,* University of Virginia, http://rotunda.upress.virginia.edu/founders/default.xqy?keys=FOEA -print-02-02-02-1924.

25. Ibid.

26. Edward Coles to Madison, January 8, 1832, *Founders Online,* National Archives, http://founders.archives.gov/documents/Madison/99-02-02-2506. See also Kurt E. Eichtle and Bruce G. Carveth, *Crusade Against Slavery: Edward Coles, Pioneer of Freedom* (Carbondale: Southern Illinois University Press, 2011), 157–66.

27. Edward Coles to Nelly C. Willis, December 10, 1855, box 2, folder 18, Edward Coles Papers, MS C0037, Princeton University Library; the Montpelier archive number is MRD-S 27873. Thanks to Lydia Neuroth for help in locating the exchange of letters. Coles offered several proofs. He reported that Henry Clay had told him that "Mrs. Madison mentioned to him that her husband expected her to free his slaves at her death." And he asked Nelly Willis, Dolley's niece, whether it was true as he had heard from William Taylor that Willis had told him that Robert Taylor, who helped

Madison with his will, reported that Madison decided not to free the slaves in his will but commented that "Mrs. Madison knew his wishes and views and would carry them into effect at her death." In reply, Nelly Willis's son wrote back to Coles denying the story. But he added that according to Willis, "It was generally believed at the time that they were left to Mrs. Madison with the understanding that she would emancipate them at her death." Then he added a story told by Nelly Willis: On Madison's death, she was present when Dolley took two sealed papers from his desk: his will and another "to be opened only by my wife." According to Willis, "This last paper of which nothing more was ever heard was thought to have contained written directions on the subject of the slaves." John Willis to Edward Coles, December 19, 1855; same Princeton box; MRD-S 27875.

28. At her death she had just five remaining slaves, having sold all the others for cash. Eichtle and Carveth, *Crusade Against Slavery*, 164–65.

29. Madison to Jefferson, February 24, 1826, *Founders Online*, National Archives, https://founders.archives.gov/documents/Jefferson/98-01-02-5934; and see Wulf, *Founding Gardeners*, 203.

30. Wulf, *Founding Gardeners*, 203.

31. "Address to the Agricultural Society of Albemarle," May 12, 1818, *PJM RS*, 1:263. The theme was the importance of applying reason and logic to the improvement of agriculture. Madison ranged widely, from comparisons with "the state of agriculture in China and Japan"; to the introduction of agriculture "among the Peruvians"; to an excursus on whether North American Indians had possessed agricultural knowledge and then lost it or whether they had never had sophisticated agriculture at all. He discussed the range and number of plant and animal species. He even offered an early argument against human "destruction, not only of individuals, but of entire species."

32. Ibid., 267.

33. Ketcham, *James Madison*, 601.

34. Ibid.

35. Some elements of the convention had become known when Washington made public the official journal of the convention as part of his constitutional dispute with Madison over the treaty-making power.

36. Proctor, "After-Dinner Anecdotes of James Madison," 264.

37. *Letters of DPM*, 317.

38. Ibid., 319, 322.

39. Madison to unknown correspondent, March 1836, *Writings of James Madison*, 9:610.

40. "Speech in Virginia Convention," December 2, 1829, *Founders Early Access*, University of Virginia, http://rotunda.upress.virginia.edu/founders/default.xqy?keys=FOEA-print-02-02-02-1924.

41. Proctor, "After-Dinner Anecdotes of James Madison," 264.

42. Jennings, "Colored Man's Reminiscences," 236.

43. Cutts, *Queen of America*, 177.

44. Ibid.

45. Ibid.

46. The earliest reference I have found is *Niles' National Register*, January 3, 1829, 35:297 ("Madison, who may be called the father of the Constitution.")

47. Adams, *Eulogy on the Life and Character of James Madison*, 87; and see 1 Kings 19:11–13.

48. It is worth noting that Hamilton did not reciprocate this technique—perhaps because Madison's vision of limited government did not allow it.

Bibliography

...

Abbot, W. W., ed. *Papers of George Washington, Confederation Series.* Charlottesville: University of Virginia Press, 1997.

Adair, Douglass. *Fame and the Founding Fathers: Essays.* Indianapolis: Liberty Fund, 1998.

———. "James Madison's Autobiography." *The William and Mary Quarterly* 2, no. 2 (1945): 191–209.

———. "The Tenth Federalist Revisited." *The William and Mary Quarterly* 8, no. 1 (1951): 48–67.

Adams, Henry. "Count Edward de Crillon." *American Historical Review* 1, no. 1 (1895): 51–69.

———. *History of the United States of America During the First Administration of Thomas Jefferson.* New York: Antiquarian Press, 1962.

Adams, John. *The Works of John Adams. Notes by Charles Francis Adams.* 10 vols. Boston: Little, Brown, 1851.

Adams, John Quincy. *An Eulogy on the Life and Character of James Madison, Fourth President of the United States; Delivered at the Request of the Mayor, Aldermen, and Common Council of the City of Boston, September 27, 1836.* Boston: John H. Eastburn, City Printer, 1836.

Alexander, John K. "The Fort Wilson Incident of 1779: A Case Study of the Revolutionary Crowd." *The William and Mary Quarterly* 31, no. 4 (October 1974): 589–612.

Allgor, Catherine. "Margaret Bayard Smith's 1809 Journey to Monticello and Montpelier: The Politics of Performance in the Early Republic." *Early American Studies* 10, no. 1 (2012): 30–68.

———. *A Perfect Union: Dolley Madison and the Creation of the American Nation.* New York: Henry Holt, 2006.

The American Whig-Cliosophic Society (blog). Available at https://whigclio.princeton.edu/about/history/.

Ames, Fisher. *Works of Fisher Ames.* Boston: T. B. Wait, 1809.

Ames, Herman Vendenburg. *State Documents on Foreign Relations.* (1900). Available at https://archive.org/details/cu31924092685415.

Ammon, Harry. *James Monroe: The Quest for National Identity.* New York: McGraw-Hill, 1971.

Anderson, Adam. *Historical and Chronological Deduction of the Origin of Commerce from the Earliest Accounts to the Present Time, Containing a History of the Great Commercial Interests of the British Empire.* 1762.

Annals of Congress. Washington, D.C.: Joint Committee on the Subject of the Public Printing, 1862. Available at http://lcweb2.loc.gov/ammem/amlaw/lwac.html.

Armitage, David. *The Declaration of Independence: A Global History.* Cambridge, Mass.: Harvard University Press, 2007.

Armstrong, April C. "A Brief History of the Architecture of Nassau Hall." *Mudd Manuscript Library Blog.* Available at https://blogs.princeton.edu/mudd/2015/06/a-brief -history-of-the-architecture-of-nassau-hall/.

The Avalon Project. Yale Law School, Lillian Goldman Law Library. Available at http:// avalon.law.yale.edu/.

Backus, Isaac. *A History of New England, with Particular Reference to the Baptists.* New York: Arno Press, 1969.

Bailey, Jeremy D. *James Madison and Constitutional Imperfection.* Cambridge: Cambridge University Press, 2015.

Bailyn, Bernard. *The Ideological Origins of the American Revolution.* Cambridge, Mass.: Harvard University Press, 1967.

Ball, Terence, and J.G.A. Pocock, eds. *Conceptual Change and the Constitution.* Lawrence: University Press of Kansas, 1988.

Baltzell, E. Digby. *Puritan Boston and Quaker Philadelphia.* New Brunswick, N.J.: Transaction Publishers, 1996.

Banner, James. *To the Hartford Convention: The Federalists and the Origins of Party Politics in Massachusetts.* New York: Alfred A. Knopf, 1970.

Banning, Lance. *The Jeffersonian Persuasion: Evolution of a Party Ideology.* Ithaca, N.Y.: Cornell University Press, 1978.

———. *The Sacred Fire of Liberty: James Madison and the Founding of the Federal Republic.* Ithaca, N.Y.: Cornell University Press, 1995.

Barlow, Joel. *A Review of Robert Smith's Address to the People of the United States: Originally Published in the "National Intelligencer."* Philadelphia: Printed by John Binns, 1811.

Beard, Charles A. *An Economic Interpretation of the Constitution of the United States.* New York: Macmillan, 1913.

Bell, Madison Smartt. *Toussaint Louverture: A Biography.* New York: Pantheon, 2007.

Bemis, Samuel Flagg, and Grace Gardner Griffin. *Guide to the Diplomatic History of the United States, 1775–1921.* Washington, D.C.: Government Printing Office, 1935.

Berens v. Rucker. 1 W. Black. 314 (1761).

Berkin, Carol. *The Bill of Rights: The Fight to Secure America's Liberties.* New York: Simon and Schuster, 2015.

Bilder, Mary Sarah. "James Madison, Law Student and Demi-Lawyer." *Law and History Review* 28, no. 2 (2010): 389–449.

———. *Madison's Hand: Revising the Constitutional Convention.* Cambridge, Mass.: Harvard University Press, 2015.

Billias, George Athan. *Elbridge Gerry: Founding Father and Republican Statesman.* New York: McGraw-Hill, 1976.

Bolingbroke, Henry. "A Dissertation Upon Parties." In *Bolingbroke: Political Writings.* Edited by David Armitage. Cambridge: Cambridge University Press, 1997.

Bolton, Theodore. "The Life Portraits of James Madison." *The William and Mary Quarterly* 8, no. 1 (1951): 25–47.

Borneman, Walter R. *1812: The War That Forged a Nation.* New York: HarperCollins, 2004.

Bowman, Albert Hall. *The Struggle for Neutrality: Franco-American Diplomacy During the Federalist Era.* Knoxville: University of Tennessee Press, 1974.

Boyd, Julian P., et al., eds. *The Papers of Thomas Jefferson.* 34 vols. Princeton, N.J.: Princeton University Press, 1950–.

Brant, Irving. *James Madison.* Vol. 1, *The Virginia Revolutionist: 1751–1780.* Indianapolis: Bobbs-Merrill, 1941.

———. *James Madison.* Vol. 2, *The Nationalist: 1780–1787.* Indianapolis: Bobbs-Merrill, 1948.

———. *James Madison.* Vol. 3, *Father of the Constitution: 1787–1800.* Indianapolis: Bobbs-Merrill, 1950.

———. *James Madison.* Vol. 4, *Secretary of State, 1800–1809.* Indianapolis: Bobbs-Merrill, 1953.

———. *James Madison.* Vol. 5, *The President: 1809–1812.* Indianapolis: Bobbs-Merrill, 1956.

———. *James Madison.* Vol. 6, *Commander in Chief: 1812–1836.* Indianapolis: Bobbs-Merrill, 1961.

Broadwater, Jeff. *James Madison: A Son of Virginia and a Founder of the Nation.* Chapel Hill: University of North Carolina Press, 2012.

Brown, Christopher Leslie. *Arming Slaves: From Classical Times to the Modern Age.* New Haven, Conn.: Yale University Press, 2006.

Brugger, Robert J., et al., eds. *The Papers of James Madison: Secretary of State Series.* 10 vols. Charlottesville: University of Virginia Press, 1986–2014.

Buckley, Thomas E. *Church and State in Revolutionary Virginia, 1776–1787.* Charlottesville: University of Virginia Press, 1977.

Buel, Jr., Richard. *America on the Brink: How the Political Struggle over the War of 1812 Almost Destroyed the Young Republic.* New York: St. Martin's Press, 2005.

Bulletin of Friends' Historical Society of Philadelphia 8, no. 25 (November 1917).

Burke, Edmund. *Edmund Burke: Pre-Revolutionary Writings.* Edited by Ian Harris. Cambridge: Cambridge University Press, 1993.

Burlamaqui, J. J. *The Principles of Natural and Politic Law.* Columbus, Ohio: Joseph H. Riley, 1859.

Burr, Nelson Rollin. *The Story of the Diocese of Connecticut: A New Branch of the Vine.* Hartford, Conn.: Church Missions Publishing, 1962.

Burstein, Andrew, and Nancy Isenberg. *Madison and Jefferson.* New York: Random House, 2013.

Callender, James Thomson. *The History of the United States for 1796; Including a Variety of Interesting Particulars Relative to the Federal Government Previous to That Period.* Philadelphia: Snowden and McCorkle, 1797.

———. *The Prospect Before Us.* Richmond, Va.: M. Jones, et al., 1800.

Capon, Lester J., ed. *The Adams-Jefferson Letters: The Complete Correspondence Between Thomas Jefferson and Abigail and John Adams.* 2 vols. Chapel Hill: University of North Carolina Press, 1959.

Carlyle, Thomas. *The French Revolution.* 1837.

Cathcart, J. L. *The Captives.* Compiled by J. B. Hewkirk. La Porte, Ind.: Herald Print, 1902.

Chacon, Richard J., and David H. Dye. "Introduction to Human Trophy Taking: An Ancient and Widespread Practice." In *The Taking and Displaying of Human Body Parts as Trophies by Amerindians,* edited by Richard J. Chacon and David H. Dye, 21–22. New York: Springer, 2007.

Chambers, Douglas B. *Murder at Montpelier: Igbo Africans in Virginia.* Jackson: University Press of Mississippi, 2005.

Chase, Philander, et al., eds. *Papers of George Washington: Confederation Series.* Charlottesville: University of Virginia Press, 1992.

Cheney, Lynne. *James Madison: A Life Reconsidered.* New York: Viking, 2014.

Chernow, Ron. *Alexander Hamilton.* New York: Penguin, 2004.

Cogliano, Francis D. *Emperor of Liberty: Thomas Jefferson's Foreign Policy.* New Haven, Conn.: Yale University Press, 2014.

Coit, Margaret L. *John C. Calhoun: American Patriot.* Boston: Houghton Mifflin, 1950.

"Commodore Barron's Inquiry into the Presence of Deserters Aboard the Chesapeake," April 7, 1807. Available at https://www.marinersmuseum.org/sites/micro/usnavy/08/08e.htm.

Cook, Frederick, ed. *Journals of the Military Expedition of Major General John Sullivan Against the Six Nations of Indians in 1779 with Records of Centennial Celebrations.* Auburn, N.Y.: Knapp, Peck and Thompson, 1887. Available at www.usgwarchives.net/pa/1pa/1picts/sullivan/rogers.html.

Cornell, Saul. *The Other Founders: Anti-Federalism and the Dissenting Tradition in America, 1788–1828.* Chapel Hill: University of North Carolina Press, 1999.

Crackel, Theodore J. "The Military Academy in the Context of Jeffersonian Reform." In *Thomas Jefferson's Military Academy: Founding West Point,* edited by Robert M. S. McDonald. Charlottesville: University of Virginia Press, 2004.

Crain, Caleb. *American Sympathy: Men, Friendship, and Literature in the New Nation.* New Haven, Conn.: Yale University Press, 2001.

Currie, David P. "The Most Insignificant Justice: A Preliminary Inquiry." *University of Chicago Law Review* 50 (1983): 466–80.

Cutts, Mary Estelle Elizabeth. *The Queen of America: Mary Cutts's Life of Dolley Madison.* Edited by Catherine Allgor. Charlottesville: University of Virginia Press, 2012.

Dangerfield, George. *The Awakening of American Nationalism, 1815–1828.* New York: Harper and Row, 1965.

David, James Corbett. *Dunmore's New World: The Extraordinary Life of a Royal Governor in Revolutionary America—with Jacobites, Counterfeiters, Land Schemes, Shipwrecks, Scalping, Indian Politics, Runaway Slaves, and Two Illegal Royal Weddings.* Charlottesville: University of Virginia Press, 2013.

Davis, William C. *The Pirates Laffite: The Treacherous World of the Corsairs of the Gulf.* Orlando, Fla.: Harcourt, 2005.

DeRose, Chris. *Founding Rivals: Madison vs. Monroe, the Bill of Rights, and the Election That Saved a Nation.* Washington, D.C.: Regnery, 2011.

Dickens, Michael D. "Threads of Influence: James Madison and the 'Old Nassovians.'" Unpublished manuscript, 2016.

Diggins, John Patrick. *John Adams.* The American Presidents Series. New York: Times Books, 2003.

Downes, Randolph C. "Dunmore's War: An Interpretation." *Mississippi Valley Review* 21, no. 3 (1934): 311–30.

Dudley, William S., ed. *The Naval War of 1812: A Documentary History.* Washington, D.C.: Naval Historical Center, Department of the Navy, 1985.

Durey, Michael. *"With the Hammer of Truth": James Thomson Callender and America's Early National Heroes.* Charlottesville: University of Virginia Press, 1990.

Easterbrook, Frank H. "The Most Insignificant Justice: Further Evidence." *University of Chicago Law Review* 50 (1983): 481–503.

Eckenrode, H. J. *Separation of Church and State in Virginia: A Study in the Development of the Revolution.* Richmond, Va.: Davis Bottom, 1910.

Edmunds, R. David. *Tecumseh and the Quest for Indian Leadership*. New York: Pearson Longman, 2007.

Egerton, Douglas R. *Gabriel's Rebellion: The Virginia Slave Conspiracies of 1800 and 1802*. Chapel Hill: University of North Carolina Press, 1993.

Eichtle, Kurt E., and Bruce G. Carveth. *Crusade Against Slavery: Edward Coles, Pioneer of Freedom*. Carbondale: Southern Illinois University Press, 2011.

Elkins, Stanley, and Eric McKitrick. *The Age of Federalism*. New York: Oxford University Press, 1993.

Elliott, Charles Burke. "The Doctrine of Continuous Voyages." *American Journal of International Law* 1, no. 1 (1907): 61–104.

Ellis, Joseph J. "Founding Brothers." Review of *The Republic of Letters: The Correspondence Between Thomas Jefferson and James Madison, 1776–1826*, edited by James Morton Smith. *The New Republic*, January 30, 1995.

———. *Founding Brothers: The Revolutionary Generation*. New York: Alfred A. Knopf, 2000.

———. *The Quartet: Orchestrating the Second American Revolution, 1783–1789*. New York: Alfred A. Knopf, 2015.

English, William Hayden. *Conquest of the Country Northwest of the River Ohio, 1778–1783 and Life of General George Rogers Clark*. Indianapolis: Bowen-Merrill Company, 1896.

Farrand, Max. *The Framing of the Constitution of the United States*. New Haven, Conn.: Yale University Press, 1913.

———, ed. *The Records of the Federal Convention of 1787*. 4 vols. New Haven, Conn.: Yale University Press, 1966.

Feldman, Noah. *Divided by God: America's Church-State Problem—and What We Should Do About It*. New York: Farrar, Straus and Giroux, 2005.

Feldman, Stephen M. *Free Expression and Democracy in America*. Chicago: University of Chicago Press, 2008.

Ferguson, Adam. *Institutes of Moral Philosophy*. 1773.

Ferguson, E. James, ed. *Selected Writings of Albert Gallatin*. Indianapolis: Bobbs-Merrill, 1967.

Fincham, Kenneth, and Peter Lake. "The Ecclesiastical Policy of King James I." *Journal of British Studies* 24 (1985): 169–207.

Finkelman, Paul, ed. *Slavery and the Founders: Race and Liberty in the Age of Jefferson*, 2nd ed. New York: M. E. Sharpe, 2001.

———, ed. *Encyclopedia of the New American Nation: The Emergence of the United States, 1754–1829*. Detroit: Charles Scribner's Sons, 2006.

Fischer, David Hackett. *Albion's Seed: Four British Folkways in America*. New York: Oxford University Press, 1989.

Foster, Augustus John. *Jeffersonian America: Notes on the United States of America, Collected in the Years 1805–6–7 and 11–12*. Edited by Richard Beale Davis. San Marino, Calif.: Huntington Library, 1954.

Founders Early Access. National Archives and University of Virginia Press. Available at https://founders.archives.gov/about/EarlyAccess.

Founders Online. National Archives and University of Virginia Press. Available at https://founders.archives.gov/.

Fox, Early Lee. *The American Colonization Society 1817–1840*. Baltimore: Johns Hopkins University Press, 1919.

Franklin, Benjamin. *The Papers of Benjamin Franklin.* American Philosophical Society and Yale University. Available at http://franklinpapers.org/franklin/framedVolumes .jsp?vol=45&page=113.

Frary, I. T. *They Built the Capitol.* Richmond, Va.: Garrett and Massie, 1940.

Freeman, Joanne. *Affairs of Honor: National Politics in the New Republic.* New Haven, Conn.: Yale University Press, 2002.

Fritz, Jean. *The Great Little Madison.* New York: Penguin, 1989.

"Fulton-L Archives." *RootsWeb.* Available at http://archiver.rootsweb.ancestry.com/th/ read/FULTON/2001–09/1001204244.

Furstenberg, Francois. "The Significance of the Trans-Appalachian Frontier in Atlantic History." *American Historical Review* 113, no. 3 (2008): 647–77.

Gaustad, Edwin. *Sworn on the Altar of God: A Religious Biography of Thomas Jefferson.* Grand Rapids, Mich.: William B. Eerdmans, 1996.

Gay, Sydney Howard. *James Madison.* American Statesmen Series. Boston: Houghton, Mifflin, 1898.

Gerry, Elbridge, Jr. *The Diary of Elbridge Gerry, Jr.* Edited by Annette Townsend. New York: Brentano's, 1927.

Gerson, Noel B. *Mr. Madison's War: 1812, the Second War for Independence.* New York: Julian Messner, 1966.

Godbeer, Richard. *The Overflowing of Friendship: Love Between Men and the Creation of the American Republic.* Baltimore: Johns Hopkins University Press, 2009.

Gordon-Reed, Annette. *The Hemingses of Monticello: An American Family.* New York: W. W. Norton, 2008.

———, and Peter S. Onuf. *"Most Blessed of the Patriarchs:" Thomas Jefferson and the Empire of the Imagination.* New York: Liveright Publishing, 2016.

Graves, Donald E. "Why the White House Was Burned: An Investigation into the British Destruction of Public Buildings at Washington in August 1814." *The Journal of Military History* 76, no. 4 (October 2012): 1095–127.

Greenwood, F. Murray. "John Henry." *Dictionary of Canadian Biography.* Available at www.biographi.ca/en/bio.php?BioId=38087.

Grodzinski, John R. "The Duke of Wellington, the Peninsular War and the War of 1812, Part II: Reinforcements, Views of the War and Command in North America." *The War of 1812 Magazine,* April 2007. Available at www.napoleon-series.org/military/Warof1812/2007/ Issue6/c_Wellington1.html.

Grootenboer, H. "Treasuring the Gaze: Eye Miniature Portraits and the Intimacy of Vision." *The Art Bulletin* 88, no. 3 (2006): 496–507.

Gross, Robert A. Review of *Shays's Rebellion: The American Revolution's Final Battle,* by Leonard L. Richards. *The New England Quarterly* 76, no. 1 (March 2003): 126–30.

Gutzman, Kevin R. C. *James Madison and the Making of America.* New York: St. Martin's Griffin, 2012.

Hagan, Jane Moore (Gray). "The Family of John Moore of Caroline and King George Counties." *Virginia Magazine of History and Biography* 52, no. 1 (1944): 62–67.

Haggard, Robert F. "The Politics of Friendship: Du Pont, Jefferson, Madison, and the Physiocratic Dream for the New World." *Proceedings of the American Philosophical Society* 153, no. 4 (2009): 419–40.

Hamilton, Alexander, James Madison, and John Jay. *The Federalist Papers.* Edited by Clinton Rossiter. New York: Mentor Books, 1961.

Hanrahan, David C. "The Assassination of the Prime Minister, Spencer Perceval." *The*

Public Domain Review. Available at http://publicdomainreview.org/2012/05/08/the
-assassination-of-the-prime-minister-spencer-perceval/.

Harrison, Richard A. *Princetonians, 1769–1775: A Biographical Dictionary.* Princeton, N.J.:
Princeton University Press, 1980.

Heidler, David S., and Jeanne T. Heidler, eds. *Encyclopedia of the War of 1812.* Santa Barbara, Calif.: ABC-CLIO, 1997.

Heimert, Alan. *Religion and the American Mind: From the Great Awakening to the American
Revolution.* Cambridge, Mass.: Harvard University Press, 1966.

Hickey, Donald R. *The War of 1812: A Forgotten Conflict.* Urbana: University of Illinois
Press, 2012.

Hirschberg, H. Z. *A History of the Jews in North Africa.* 2 vols. Edited by Eliezer Bashan
and Robert Attal. Leiden, Netherlands: E. J. Brill, 1974–81.

Hitsman, J. Mackay, and Donald Graves. *The Incredible War of 1812.* Toronto: Robin Brass
Studios, 1999.

Hogeland, William. *The Whiskey Rebellion: George Washington, Alexander Hamilton, and
the Frontier Rebels Who Challenged America's Newfound Sovereignty.* New York: Simon
and Schuster, 2006.

Hont, Istvan. *Politics in Commercial Society: Jean-Jacques Rousseau and Adam Smith.* Cambridge. Mass.: Harvard University Press, 2015.

Horn, James, Jan Ellen Lewis, and Peter S. Onuf. *The Revolution of 1800: Democracy, Race,
and the New Republic.* Charlottesville: University of Virginia Press, 2002.

Howard, Hugh. *Mr. and Mrs. Madison's War: America's First Couple and the Second War of
Independence.* New York: Bloomsbury, 2012.

Hume, David. *Political Essays.* Edited by Knud Haakonssen. Cambridge: Cambridge University Press, 1994.

Hunt, Gaillard. *The Life of James Madison.* New York: Doubleday, 1902.

———, and James Brown Scott, eds. *James Madison: The Debates in the Federal Convention
of 1787 Which Framed the Constitution of the United States of America.* New York: Oxford
University Press, 1920.

Hurl-Eamon, Jennine. "Love Tokens: Objects as Memory for Plebian Women in Early
Modern England." *Early Modern Women: An Interdisciplinary Journal* 6 (2011): 181–86.

Hutchinson, William T., and William M. E. Rachal, eds. *The Papers of James Madison.*
Chicago: University of Chicago Press, 1962–.

Ingersoll, Charles Jared. *Historical Sketch of the Second War Between the United States of
America, and Great Britain.* Philadelphia: Lea and Blanchard, 1849.

Iredell, James. Charge to the Grand Jury, in Case of *Fries.* 9 Fed. Cas. 829, no. 5, 126
C.C.D.Pa. 1799.

Jackson, Andrew. "Andrew Jackson to Thomas Pinckney March 28, 1814." *The Daily National Intelligencer,* April 18, 1814.

Jefferson, Thomas. *The Jefferson Bible: The Life and Morals of Jesus of Nazareth.* Edited by
Harry R. Rubenstein, Barbara Clark Smith, and Janice Stagnito Ellis. Washington,
D.C.: Smithsonian Books, 2011.

———. "Memoir, Correspondence, and Miscellanies, from the Papers of Thomas Jefferson." Edited by Thomas Jefferson Randolph. Boston: Gray and Bowen, 1830. Available
at www.gutenberg.org/files/16784/16784-h/16784-h.htm#link2H_4_0064.

———. "Notes on the State of Virginia." Library of Congress. Available at www.loc.gov/
resource/lhbcb.04902.

Jennings, Paul. "A Colored Man's Reminiscences of James Madison." In Elizabeth Dowling Taylor, *A Slave in the White House: Paul Jennings and the Madisons.* New York: Palgrave MacMillan, 2012.

Johnson, David. *John Randolph of Roanoke.* Baton Rouge: Louisiana State University Press, 2012.

Kauffman, Bill. *Forgotten Founder, Drunken Prophet: The Life of Luther Martin.* Wilmington, Del.: ISI Books, 2008.

Kenyon, Cecelia M. *The Antifederalists.* Indianapolis: Bobbs-Merrill, 1966.

Kerry, Paul E., and Matthew S. Holland. *Benjamin Franklin's Intellectual World.* Madison, N.J.: Fairleigh Dickinson University Press, 2012.

Kester, Scott J. *The Haunted Philosophe: James Madison, Republicanism, and Slavery.* Lanham, Md.: Lexington Books, 2008.

Ketcham, Ralph. *James Madison: A Biography.* Charlottesville: University of Virginia Press, 1971.

———. *The Madisons at Montpelier.* Charlottesville: University of Virginia Press, 2009.

———. "Review Essay: The Papers of James Madison." *Journal of the Early Republic* 33, no. 4 (2013): 763–69.

———. "An Unpublished Sketch of James Madison by James K. Paulding." *Virginia Magazine of History and Biography* 67, no. 4 (1959): 432–37.

Kidd, Thomas S. *Patrick Henry: First Among Patriots.* New York: Basic Books, 2011.

Kiernan, Denise, and Joseph D'Agnese. *Signing Their Rights Away: The Fame and Misfortune of the Men Who Signed the United States Constitution.* Philadelphia: Quirk Books, 2011.

Kirk, Russell. *John Randolph of Roanoke: A Study in American Politics, with Selected Speeches and Letters.* Indianapolis: Liberty Press, 1978.

Klarman, Michael J. *The Framers' Coup: The Making of the United States Constitution.* New York: Oxford University Press, 2016.

Kohn, Richard H. "The Washington Administration's Decision to Crush the Whiskey Rebellion." *The Journal of American History* 59, no. 3 (1972): 567–84.

Kolp, John Gilman. *Gentlemen and Freeholders: Electoral Politics in Colonial Virginia.* Baltimore: Johns Hopkins University Press, 1998.

Kramer, Larry D. "Madison's Audience." *Harvard Law Review* 112, no. 3 (1998–99): 611–79.

Lardas, Mark. *Constitution vs Guerriere: Frigates During the War of 1812.* Oxford: Osprey Publishing, 2009.

Latimer, Jon. *1812: War with America.* Cambridge, Mass.: Harvard University Press, 2007.

Leibiger, Stuart Eric. *Founding Friendship: George Washington, James Madison and the Creation of the American Republic.* Charlottesville: University of Virginia Press, 1999.

———. "Founding Friendship: Washington, Madison, and the Creation of the American Republic." *History Today* 51, no. 7 (2001): 21–27.

Leichtle, Kurt E., and Bruce G. Carveth. *Crusade Against Slavery: Edward Coles, Pioneer of Freedom.* Carbondale: Southern Illinois University Press, 2011.

Levy, Leonard W. "On the Origins of the Free Press Clause." *UCLA Law Review* 32 (1984–85): 177–218.

———. *Origins of the Bill of Rights.* New Haven, Conn.: Yale University Press, 1999.

Looney, J. Jefferson, ed. *Papers of Thomas Jefferson: Retirement Series.* 12 vols. Princeton, N.J.: Princeton University Press, 2004–.

Madison, Dolley. *The Selected Letters of Dolley Payne Madison.* Edited by David B. Mattern and Holly C. Shulman. Charlottesville: University of Virginia Press, 2003.

Madison, James. *An Examination of the British Doctrine, Which Subjects to Capture a Neutral Trade, Not Open in Time of Peace.* 1806.

———. *Notes of Debates in the Federal Convention of 1787.* Edited by Adrienne Koch. Athens: Ohio University Press, 1966.

———. *The Writings of James Madison.* Edited by Gaillard Hunt. 9 vols. New York: G. P. Putnam's Sons, 1900–1910.

Maier, Pauline. *Ratification: The People Debate the Constitution, 1787–1788.* New York: Simon and Schuster, 2010.

"Map of Historic Philadelphia in the late 18th Century." TeachingAmericanHistory.org. Available at http://teachingamericanhistory.org/convention/map/.

Marr, John S., and John T. Cathey. "The 1802 Saint-Domingue Yellow Fever Epidemic and the Louisiana Purchase." *Journal of Public Health Management Practice* 19, no. 1 (2013): 77–82.

Mason, Philip P., ed. *After Tippecanoe: Some Aspects of the War of 1812.* East Lansing: Michigan State University Press, 1963.

Mattern, David B., ed. *The Papers of James Madison: Retirement Series.* Charlottesville: University of Virginia Press, 2013.

McCoy, Drew R. *The Last of the Fathers: James Madison and the Republican Legacy.* Cambridge: Cambridge University Press, 1989.

McCullough, David. *John Adams.* New York: Simon and Schuster, 2001.

McDonald, Forrest. *Novus Ordo Seclorum: The Intellectual Origins of the Constitution.* Lawrence: University Press of Kansas, 1985.

McElwain, Thomas. "'Then I Thought I Must Kill Too': Logan's Lament: A 'Mingo' Perspective." In *Native American Speakers of the Eastern Woodlands: Selected Speeches and Critical Analyses.* Edited by Barbara Alice Mann. Westport, Conn.: Greenwood Press, 2001.

McGuire, Robert A. *To Form a More Perfect Union: A New Economic Interpretation of the United States Constitution.* New York: Oxford University Press, 2003.

McLaughlin, J. Fairfax. *Matthew Lyon, the Hampden of Congress: A Biography.* New York: Wynkoop Hallenbeck Crawford, 1900.

McMichael, Andrew. *Atlantic Loyalties: Americans in Spanish West Florida, 1785–1810.* Athens: University of Georgia Press, 2008.

———. "The Kemper 'Rebellion': Filibustering and Resident Anglo American Loyalty in Spanish West Florida." *Louisiana History: The Journal of the Louisiana Historical Association* 43, no. 2 (2002): 133–65.

"The Memoirs of Madison Hemings, 1873." *Frontline.* PBS. Available at www.pbs.org/wgbh/pages/frontline/shows/jefferson/cron/1873march.html.

Miller, Ann L. *The Short Life and Strange Death of Ambrose Madison.* Orange, Va.: Orange County Historical Society, 2001.

Miller, John C. *Crisis in Freedom: The Alien and Sedition Acts.* Boston: Little, Brown, 1951.

Mintz, Max M. *Gouverneur Morris and the American Revolution.* Norman: University of Oklahoma Press, 1970.

Monroe, James. *The Writings of James Monroe.* Edited by Stanislaus Murray Hamilton. 7 vols. New York: G. P. Putnam's Sons, 1900.

Morgan, Edmund S. *Inventing the People: The Rise of Popular Sovereignty in England and America.* New York: W. W. Norton, 1988.

———. "Safety in Numbers: Madison, Hume, and the Tenth 'Federalist.'" *Huntington Library Quarterly* 49, no. 2 (1986): 95–112.

Morison, Samuel Eliot. "Our Most Unpopular War." *Proceedings of the Massachusetts Historical Society* 80 (January 1968): 38–54, 166.

Morris, B. F. *The Christian Life and Character of the Civil Institutions of the United States.* Philadelphia: George W. Childs, 1864.

Morrison, Jerry H. *John Witherspoon and the Founding of the American Republic.* South Bend, Ind.: University of Notre Dame Press, 2005.

Morse, John T. *Life of Alexander Hamilton.* Cambridge, Mass.: John Wilton and Son, 1876.

Neimeyer, Charles Patrick. *War in the Chesapeake: The British Campaigns to Control the Bay, 1813–14* (Annapolis, Md.: Naval Institute Press, 2015), 22.

Nelson, Eric. *The Greek Tradition in Republican Thought.* Cambridge: Cambridge University Press, 2004.

———. "What Kind of Book Is the *Ideological Origins?*" In forthcoming volume in honor of the fiftieth anniversary of Bernard Bailyn's *Ideological Origins of the American Revolution.* Cambridge, Mass.: Harvard University Press, 2017.

Newman, Paul Douglas. *Fries's Rebellion: The Enduring Struggle for the American Revolution.* Philadelphia: University of Pennsylvania Press, 2004.

Oakes, James. "Was Madison More Radical Than Jefferson?" *Journal of the Early Republic* 15, no. 4 (1995): 649–55.

Odo, William. "Destined for Defeat: An Analysis of the St. Clair Expedition of 1791." *Northwest Ohio Quarterly* 65, no. 2 (1993): 68–93.

Orieux, Jean. *Talleyrand: The Art of Survival.* New York: Alfred A. Knopf, 1974.

Osborne, Jeff. "Constituting American Masculinity." *American Studies* 49, no. 3/4 (2008): 111–32.

The Other Madisons Blog (blog). Available at www.bettyekearse.com/the-other-madisons/.

Palmié, Stephan, and Francisco A. Scarano, eds. *The Caribbean: A History of the Region and Its Peoples.* Chicago: University of Chicago Press, 2013.

"Papers of Dr. James McHenry on the Federal Convention of 1787." *American Historical Review* 11, no. 3 (1906): 595–624.

Penn Biographies. University of Pennsylvania University Archives and Records. Available at www.archives.upenn.edu/people/bioa.html.

Perkins, Bradford. *The Cambridge History of American Foreign Relations.* Cambridge: Cambridge University Press, 1993.

———. *The Creation of a Republican Empire, 1776–1865.* Cambridge: Cambridge University Press, 1993.

———. "Embargo: Alternative to War." In *Essays on the Early Republic, 1789–1815,* edited by Leonard W. Levy and Carl Siracuse. Hinsdale, Ill.: Dryden Press, 1974.

Peterson, Merrill D., ed. *The Founding Fathers, James Madison: A Biography in His Own Words.* New York: Newsweek, 1974.

Pickering, Timothy. *A Review of the Correspondence Between the Hon. John Adams, Late President of the United States, and the Late Wm. Cunningham, Esq., Beginning in 1803, and Ending in 1812.* Salem, Mass.: Cushing and Appleton, 1824.

Pitch, Anthony S. *The Burning of Washington: The British Invasion of 1814.* Annapolis, Md.: Bluejacket Books, 1998.

Pocock, J.G.A. *The Machiavellian Moment: Florentine Political Thought and the Atlantic Republican Tradition.* Princeton, N.J.: Princeton University Press, 1975.

Pogue, Dennis J. *Founding Spirits: George Washington and the Beginnings of the American Whiskey Industry.* Buena Vista, Va.: Harbour Books, 2011.

Poling, Jim, Sr. *Tecumseh: Shooting Star, Crouching Panther.* Toronto: Dundurn Press, 2009.

Powell, H. Jefferson. *A Community Built on Words: The Constitution in History and Politics.* Chicago: University of Chicago Press, 2002.

Proctor, Mary Lucile "CC," ed. "After-Dinner Anecdotes of James Madison: Excerpt from Jared Sparks' Journal for 1829–31." *The Virginia Magazine of History and Biography* 60, no. 2 (April 1952): 255–65.

Ragosta, John. *Wellspring of Liberty: How Virginia's Religious Dissenters Helped Win the American Revolution and Secured Religious Liberty.* New York: Oxford University Press, 2010.

Rakove, Jack N. *James Madison and the Creation of the American Republic.* New York: Pearson, 2007.

———. *Original Meanings: Politics and Ideas in the Making of the Constitution.* New York: Alfred A. Knopf, 1996.

"Rambouillet Decree." *Casebook: The War of 1812.* English translation available at http://casebook.thewarof1812.info/Official_documents_files/RambouilletDecree/text.html.

Randall, Henry S. *The Life of Thomas Jefferson.* New York: Derby and Jackson, 1858.

Randall, Willard S. *Benedict Arnold: Patriot and Traitor.* New York: William Morrow, 1990.

Reardon, John J. *Edmund Randolph: A Biography.* New York: Macmillan, 1974.

Remini, Robert V. *Andrew Jackson and the Course of American Empire, 1767–1821.* New York: Harper and Row, 1977.

———. *The Battle of New Orleans.* New York: Viking, 1999.

———. *Daniel Webster: The Man and His Time.* New York: W. W. Norton, 1997.

Richards, Leonard L. *Shays's Rebellion: The American Revolution's Final Battle.* Philadelphia: University of Pennsylvania Press, 2002.

Rosen, Deborah A. *Border Law: The First Seminole War and American Nationhood.* Cambridge, Mass.: Harvard University Press, 2015.

Rosen, Gary. *American Compact: James Madison and the Problem of Founding.* Lawrence: University Press of Kansas, 1999.

Rosenblum, Nancy. *On the Side of Angels: An Appreciation of Parties and Partisanship.* Princeton, N.J.: Princeton University Press, 2010.

Rutland, Robert Allen. *James Madison: The Founding Father.* New York: Macmillan, 1987.

Rutland, Robert A., et al., eds. *The Papers of James Madison: Presidential Series.* 8 vols. Charlottesville: University of Virginia Press, 1984–2015.

Schwarz, Michael. "The Great Divergence Reconsidered: Hamilton, Madison, and U.S.-British Relations, 1783–89." *Journal of the Early Republic* 27, no. 3 (Fall 2007): 407–36.

Schwarz, Philip J., ed. *Gabriel's Conspiracy: A Documentary History.* Charlottesville: University of Virginia Press, 2012.

Scott, James Brown. *James Madison, Notes on Debate in the Federal Convention of 1787 and Their Relation to a More Perfect Society of Nations.* Union, N.J.: Lawbook Exchange, 2001.

Sedgwick, Eve Kosofsky. *Between Men: English Literature and Male Homosocial Desire.* New York: Columbia University Press, 1985.

Selden, John. *Table-Talk.* Edited by Edward Arber. London, 1869.

Sheehan, Collen A. "Madison v. Hamilton: The Battle Over Republicanism and the Role of Public Opinion." *The American Political Science Review* 98, no. 3 (2004): 405–24.

Sheldon, Garrett Ward. *The Political Philosophy of James Madison.* Baltimore: Johns Hopkins University Press, 2001.

———, and Daniel L. Dreisbach. *Religion and Political Culture in Jefferson's Virginia.* Lanham, Md.: Rowman and Littlefield, 2000.

Signer, Michael. *Becoming Madison: The Extraordinary Origins of the Least Likely Founding Father.* New York: PublicAffairs, 2015.

Slaughter, Thomas P. *The Whiskey Rebellion: Frontier Epilogue to the American Revolution.* New York: Oxford University Press, 1986.

Slauter, Eric. *The State as a Work of Art: The Cultural Origins of the Constitution.* Chicago: University of Chicago Press, 2009.

Smith, James Morton. *The Republic of Letters: The Correspondence Between Thomas Jefferson and James Madison 1776–1826.* New York: W. W. Norton, 1995.

Smith, Margaret Bayard. *The First Forty Years of Washington Society: Portrayed by the Family Letters of Mrs. Samuel Harrison Smith (Margaret Bayard) from the Collection of Her Grandson, J. Henley Smith.* New York: Charles Scribner's Sons, 1906.

Sofka, James. "American Neutral Rights Reappraised: Identity or Interest in the Foreign Policy of the Early Republic." *Review of International Studies* 26, no. 4 (2000): 599–622.

Somerset v. Stewart. 98 Eng. Rep. 510 (K.B. 1772).

Sosin, Jack M. "The British Indian Department and Dunmore's War." *Virginia Magazine of History and Biography* 74, no. 1 (1966): 35–50.

Spalding, Matthew, and Patrick J. Garrity. *A Sacred Union of Citizens: George Washington's Farewell Address and the American Character.* Lanham, Md.: Rowman and Littlefield, 1996.

Spencer, Mark G. *David Hume and Eighteenth-Century America.* Rochester, N.Y.: University of Rochester Press, 2005.

———. "Hume and Madison on Faction." *The William and Mary Quarterly* 59, no. 4 (2002): 869–96.

Stagg, J.C.A. *Mr. Madison's War: Politics, Diplomacy, and Warfare in the Early American Republic, 1783–1830.* Princeton, N.J.: Princeton University Press, 1983.

"Statute 2, Ch. LXVII." *A Century of Lawmaking for a New Nation: U.S. Congressional Documents and Debates, 1774—1875.* Library of Congress. Available at http://memory.loc.gov/cgi-bin/ampage?collId=llsl&fileName=001/llsl001.db&recNum=701.

Stewart, David O. *American Emperor: Aaron Burr's Challenge to Jefferson's America.* New York: Simon and Schuster, 2011.

———. *Madison's Gift: Five Partnerships That Built America.* New York: Simon and Schuster, 2015.

———. *The Summer of 1787.* New York: Simon and Schuster, 2007.

Stourzh, Gerald. *Alexander Hamilton and the Idea of Republican Government.* Stanford, Calif.: Stanford University Press, 1970.

Stuart, Reginald C. *Civil-Military Relations During the War of 1812.* Santa Barbara, Calif.: ABC-CLIO, 2009.

Sturgis, Amy H. *Tecumseh: A Biography.* Westport, Conn.: Greenwood Press, 2008.

Sugden, John. *Tecumseh's Last Stand.* Norman: University of Oklahoma Press, 1990.

Syrett, Harold C., ed. *Papers of Alexander Hamilton.* New York: Columbia University Press, 1961–.

Szatmary, David P. *Shays' Rebellion: The Making of an Agrarian Insurrection.* Amherst: University of Massachusetts Press, 1980.

Tawney, R. H., and Eileen Power, eds. *Tudor Economic Documents.* London: Longwell, 1924.

Taylor, Alan. *The Internal Enemy: Slavery and War in Virginia, 1772–1832.* New York: W. W. Norton, 2013.

Taylor, Elizabeth Downing. *A Slave in the White House: Paul Jennings and the Madisons.* New York: Palgrave Macmillan, 2012.

Thomas, George. *The Founders and the Idea of a National University.* Cambridge: Cambridge University Press, 2015.

Thompson, Bradley C. *John Adams and the Spirit of Liberty.* Lawrence: University Press of Kansas, 1998.

Thompson, Dennis F. "Bibliography: The Education of a Founding Father. The Reading List for John Witherspoon's Course in Political Theory." *Political Theory* 4, no. 4 (1976): 523–29.

Tinkcom, Margaret Bailey. "Caviar Along the Potomac: Sir Augustus John Foster's 'Notes on the United States,' 1804–1812." *The William and Mary Quarterly* 8, no. 1 (1951): 1751–836.

Toll, Ian W. *Six Frigates: The Epic History of the Founding of the U.S. Navy.* New York: W. W. Norton, 2006.

Tucker, Spencer C. *The Jeffersonian Gunboat Navy.* Columbia: University of South Carolina Press, 1993.

Unger, Harlow Giles. *The Last Founding Father: James Monroe and a Nation's Call to Greatness.* Cambridge, Mass.: Da Capo Press, 2009.

Vattel, Emer de. *The Law of Nations; Or, Principles of the Law of Nature, Applied to the Conduct and Affairs of Nations and Sovereigns.* Translated by Joseph Chitty. Philadelphia: T. and H. W. Johnson, 1863.

Vile, John R., William D. Pederson, and Frank J. Williams, eds. *James Madison: Philosopher, Founder, and Statesman.* Athens: Ohio University Press, 2008.

Virginia Newspaper Project of the Library of Virginia. Available at www.lva.virginia.gov/public/vnp/.

Wallace, Anthony F. C. *Jefferson and the Indians: The Tragic Fate of the First Americans.* Cambridge, Mass.: Harvard University Press, 1999.

Washington, George. *The Papers of George Washington.* University of Virginia. Available at http://gwpapers.virginia.edu/documents/washingtons-sixth-annual-message-to-congress/.

Watson, Samuel J. *Peacekeepers and Conquerors: The Army Officer Corps on the American Frontier, 1821–1846.* Lawrence: University Press of Kansas, 2013.

Webber, Mabel L. "The Thomas Pinckney Family of South Carolina." *The South Carolina Historical and Genealogical Magazine* 39, no. 1 (1938): 23.

The Westminster Confession of Faith of 1646. Center for Reformed Theology and Apologetics. Available at www.reformed.org/documents/wcf_with_proofs/index.html?body=/documents/wcf_with_proofs/ch_XX.html.

White, Richard. *The Middle Ground: Indians, Empires, and Republics in the Great Lakes Regions, 1650–1815.* Cambridge: Cambridge University Press, 1991.

Wiley, Edwin, ed. *Lectures on the Growth and Development of the United States.* New York: American Educational Alliance, 1916.

Wilkerson, Sam. *Republicanism During the Early Roman Empire.* London: Continuum, 2001.

Wilkins, Lee. "Madison and Jefferson: The Making of a Friendship." *Political Psychology* 12, no. 4 (1991): 593–608.

Wills, Garry. *James Madison.* The American Presidents Series. New York: Henry Holt, 2002.

Wilson, James. *The Works of James Wilson*. Edited by Robert Green McCloskey. Cambridge, Mass.: Harvard University Press, 1967.

Witherspoon, John. *The Dominion of Providence over the Passions of Men: A Sermon Preached at Princeton on the 17th of May, 1776*. Philadelphia: R Aitken, 1776.

———. *Lectures on Moral Philosophy*. Edited by Varnum Lansing Collins. Princeton, N.J.: Princeton University Press, 1912.

Wood, Gordon S. *The Creation of the American Republic, 1776–1787*. New York: W. W. Norton, 1972.

———. *Empire of Liberty: A History of the Early Republic, 1789–1815*. New York: Oxford University Press, 2009.

———. "Is There a 'James Madison Problem'? In *Liberty and American Experience in the Eighteenth Century*, edited by David Womersley. Indianapolis: Liberty Fund, 2006.

Woolsey, Lester H. "Early Cases on the Doctrine of Continuous Voyages." *American Journal of International Law* 4, no. 4 (October 1910): 823–47.

Wright, Esmond. "A Civil Correspondence." *History Today* 46, no. 7 (1996): 56–58.

Wulf, Andrea. *Founding Gardeners: The Revolutionary Generation, Nature, and the Shaping of the American Nation*. New York: Alfred A. Knopf, 2011.

Yarborough, Minnie Clare. *The Reminiscences of William C. Preston*. Chapel Hill: University of North Carolina Press, 1933.

Young, Edward. *The Complaint; or, Night Thoughts on Life, Death, and Mortality (A Poem)*. London, 1743.

Zuckerman, Michael. *Almost Chosen People: Oblique Biographies in the American Grain*. Berkeley: University of California Press, 1993.

Index

...

and Count de Crillon, "letters" from, 537–38, 705*n*.115, 705*nn*.111–13

distrust of British, 512, 514

and economic sanctions as alternative to military force, xv, xvii, 502, 507, 514–15, 529, 536–37, 541–42, 547, 552, 608, 609, 627

failed negotiations with Erskine, 509–11, 511–12, 544, 702*nn*.21–22

failed negotiations with Jackson, 513–14

firing of Robert Smith, 523–25, 526–28

goals of, 503–4, 510, 526, 531, 546

hat with cockade of, 545, 706*n*.137

illness during War of 1812, 564–65, 708*n*.57

inaugural addresses, 502–5, 559–60

inaugural ball, 506

influences for peace with Britain and, 526, 529–30, 532

influences for war with Britain and, 535, 536

insult of king of England, 510, 512

learning curve of, 514, 520–21, 522, 545–47, 608

legacy of, 609, 610–21

and Macon's Bill No. 2, 515–17, 527, 703*n*.43

and Monroe as secretary of state, 525–26

national infrastructure, request for, 612

need for "tough" public image, 510

and Non-Intercourse Act, 508, 510, 511, 513, 514, 524, 540–41

policy of neutrality, 229–30, 503, 504, 507–8, 514, 526, 627

political principles of, 504, 599, 610–12, 612–15

strategic vision for military, 608, 614, 714*n*.114

war decision and message, 542, 543–46, 547

and war preparation, 529, 536–37, 545, 706*n*.137

see also War of 1812

Madison, James, as House Representative (1789–1797), 626–27

and abolition of slave trade, avoidance of bill for, 300–302, 676*n*.109

as author of addresses for Washington and House, 262–63, 312

and bill of rights, 263, 267–71, 271–74, 274–77

and British threat to American shipping, 386–87, 472–73, 474, 482, 487–88, 508, 509, 698*n*.9

and British vessels, taxation of, 259, 261–62

and Cabinet, dealings with, 279–83

campaign for, 247–56, 310

and Compromise of 1790, 305–10

and conscientious objectors, support for, 313–14, 676*n*.109

and Constitution, interpretation of, 265–67, 319–20

dispute with Hamilton and Washington over Jay Treaty, 396, 398, 400–402, 405–6, 687*n*.126

dispute with Hamilton over "benefits" of public debt, 286, 293–94

dispute with Hamilton over federal assumption of state debt, 297–300, 305–10, 673*n*.48

dispute with Hamilton over national bank, 314–23

dispute with Hamilton over Neutrality Proclamation, 372, 373–82

dispute with Hamilton over payments to debt holders, 294–96, 673*n*.42

orders-in-council (*cont.*):
   and public debate in Britain on,
      541–42
   repeal of, 541, 542, 554, 601, 606
   and threat of war, 533, 540, 541,
      542
Origin of Commerce (Anderson), 317
Orleans Territory, 518, 520
Ottoman Empire, 86, 448

pacifism, 269, 313–14, 431
Paine, Thomas, 326–27, 329–30, 361,
      678*n*.166
Pakenham, Sir Edward, 603–4
paper currency vs. hard currency, 80,
      314–15, 318, 331–32, 677*n*.124
"parchment (paper) barriers," 206, 272,
      274
Parrish, John, Jr., 301–2
"Parties" essay (Madison), 345–48
partisanship
   and JM's path from nonpartisan to
      Republican, xiv, xv–xvi, xvii, 256,
      263, 326, 337, 345–48, 357, 360, 363,
      367–69, 626–27
   and JM's view of enemies as
      subversive, xiv, 18, 248, 286, 337,
      344–45, 349, 350–51, 356, 372,
      376–77, 626–27, 681*n*.33, 716*n*.47
   see also newspapers, partisan; political
      parties
"passions," JM's two uses of, 215
Patent and Post Office building, 594,
      711*n*.59
Paterson, William, 126, 129, 130, 131–32,
      133, 138, 146, 655*n*.83
Patuxent River, 579, 580, 581
Payne, Anna (Cutts), 388, 411, 476–78,
      528
Payne, John, 384–85
Peale, Charles Willson, 46,
      639–40*nn*.60–61
Peloponnesian War, 475
Pemberton, Betsey, 480

Pendleton, Edmund, 213, 276, 279, 316,
      339, 354, 676*n*.113, 680*n*.3, 681*n*.32
Peninsular War, 517, 579, 581, 596, 602
pen names, use of, 177–78, 274, 377, 378,
      398
Pennsylvania, 128, 138, 141, 195, 202, 406
   and location of capital, 277, 279, 305,
      307, 310, 674*n*.87
   and ratification of constitution, 195,
      202
   and Whiskey Rebellion, 390–94
Pennsylvania General Assembly, 536
Pennsylvania Journal, The, 16
Pensacola, 455, 603
Perceval, Spencer, 539, 541
Perry, Oliver Hazard, 567, 568, 572, 606
Peru, 517
Philadelphia, Pa.:
   as financial center, 330
   as temporary capital, 277, 305, 307,
      310
   and yellow fever, 383, 385–86
Philadelphia convention, 598, 608
   and agreement of silence, 172, 402,
      622, 716*n*.34
   and basic draft of constitution, 128
   bill of rights, need for, 151, 165–66
   checks and balances, plans for, 137,
      154, 159–60
   Committee of Detail at, 155, 156, 157,
      159, 161
   compromise at, 140–41, 143–44,
      145–50, 163–64, 172, 656*n*.131
   constitution, signing of, 166–70, 171
   discussion concerning Congress,
      112–15, 137, 153–54, 159–61
   discussion of amendments, 128, 165,
      166–67, 659*n*.61
   discussion of equal representation in
      Senate, 119, 125–26, 143
   discussion of executive, 115–18, 152,
      153, 154–55, 160
   discussion of judiciary, 152–53, 160
   discussion of national negative (veto
      power), 123–25, 131, 151–52, 152–53